W9-CMP-744

WEST GEORGIA REGIONAL LIBRARY SYSTEM

Donated To:
West Ga. Reg. Library
By:
Maurice K. Townsend, Pres.
West Georgia College

THE LIBRARY OF
SOUTHERN CIVILIZATION

THE LIBRARY OF
SOUTHERN CIVILIZATION

Lewis P. Simpson, Editor

Twelve Years a Slave, by Solomon Northup
Edited by Sue Eakin and Joseph Logsdon

Bricks Without Straw, by Albion Tourgée
Edited by Otto H. Olsen

Still Rebels, Still Yankees and Other Essays,
by Donald Davidson

Brokenburn: The Journal of Kate Stone, 1861–1868
Edited by John Q. Anderson

The Great South, by Edward King
Edited by W. Magruder Drake and Robert R. Jones

Lanterns on the Levee: Recollections of a Planter's Son,
by William Alexander Percy

The Diary of Edmund Ruffin
Edited by William Kauffman Scarborough

THE DIARY OF
EDMUND RUFFIN

Edmund Ruffin, from a portrait in the governor's office, Richmond

COURTESY OF VIRGINIA STATE LIBRARY

THE DIARY OF
EDMUND RUFFIN

❦

VOLUME II
THE YEARS OF HOPE
April, 1861–June, 1863

EDITED, WITH AN INTRODUCTION
AND NOTES, BY
WILLIAM KAUFFMAN SCARBOROUGH

Louisiana State University Press
Baton Rouge
1976

ISBN 0–8071–0183–4
Library of Congress Catalog Card Number 75–165069
Copyright © 1976 by Louisiana State University Press
All rights reserved
Manufactured in the United States of America
Set in VIP Caledonia
Designed by Jules B. McKee

"Rather than submit to Yankee domination . . . it would be better for all to be killed in battle. If we are to be held as subject provinces, I would prefer that our despotic ruler & master should be any power of Europe, even Russia or Spain, rather than the Northern States."

Edmund Ruffin, April 30, 1862—Following the fall of
New Orleans

296330 WEST GEORGIA REGIONAL LIBRARY SYSTEM

Contents

Illustrations

Edmund Ruffin, from a portrait painted for the Virginia Agricultural
Society and now hanging in the private office of the governor of
Virginia. Courtesy of Virginia State Library   Frontispiece

Facing Page

Marlbourne, Hanover County, Virginia, 1936. Courtesy of Virginia
State Library   334

Ruffin family group, *circa* 1850–55. Courtesy of Mr. and Mrs. Sterling P. Anderson, Jr., of Upper Marlbourne, Virginia   335

Maps

Page

Introduction

For those like Edmund Ruffin, who had long nurtured the dream of southern independence, the first two years of the Civil War brought alternating moods of hope and despair. The exuberant optimism engendered by the bloodless occupation of Fort Sumter and the rout of Union forces at First Manassas soon gave way to doubt and frustration as Federal armies pressed slowly, but inexorably, into the southern heartland, while, at the same time, the ever-tightening northern blockade produced severe shortages and spiraling prices on the home front. Still, until the fateful week in July, 1863, when news of the simultaneous disasters at Gettysburg and Vicksburg reverberated across the Confederacy, the dream endured. In this, the second of what is now projected as a three-volume edition of the Ruffin diary, the stalwart Virginian chronicles events from the aftermath of Fort Sumter to the eve of Gettysburg during what, for him, perhaps can best be labeled "the years of hope."

I

Although his mobility was increasingly limited by the ravages of time, Ruffin was admirably situated to provide a perceptive daily commentary on events and personalities of the Civil War period. Dividing most of his time between his sons' plantations— Beechwood on the James River and Marlbourne, located just northeast of Richmond on the Pamunkey River—and residing for several extended periods in Richmond, the diarist was constantly in an area exposed to Federal incursions during successive campaigns against the Confederate capital. Moreover, despite his physical infirmities, the aging Ruffin was sufficiently active to indulge his propensity to "go where the action was." Thus, he participated in the Bull Run campaign, enduring the hardships of a private soldier for three weeks and climaxing his service with an artillery shot nearly as memorable and much more effective than that which he had directed against Sumter three months before. His eyewitness account of the agony and suffering of those left on the Manassas battlefield is matched only by his description of the like spectacle as he rode gingerly over the ground at Seven Pines with cannonballs and shells still whistling over his head. On other occasions the intrepid old Virginian inspected Confederate installations at Fort Macon, North Carolina, and along the Potomac; viewed the C.S.S. *Virginia* in dry dock at Norfolk following her dramatic encounter with the U.S.S. *Monitor*; and spied upon General George B. McClellan's camp at Harrison's Landing, directly across the James from Beechwood.

Perhaps the highlight of this second volume is the diarist's vivid account of the tribulations inflicted upon the civilian population during McClellan's ill-fated Peninsular campaign against Richmond in the spring and summer of 1862. As the Yankee horde advanced slowly up the peninsula, supposedly loyal and trusted Negroes began to desert in droves to the invaders, thus manifesting to Ruffin and other astonished slaveholders their inherent dissatisfaction with the station in life assigned to them under the "peculiar institution." The whites, too, soon took flight, although their course was directed away from the enemy rather than toward him. In mid-May, Marlbourne was evacuated by all members of the household except Mrs. Robert E. Lee and her two grown daughters, who, having taken temporary refuge there, remained behind and soon found themselves within the enemy's lines in the midst of a sea of rebellious blacks. But, incredibly, they were not molested, and two weeks later, with his family still in that precarious and isolated position, General Lee was elevated to the command of what would soon be designated the Army of Northern Virginia. In late June, as McClellan prepared for his final thrust against Richmond and with Union gunboats in command of the James below Drewry's Bluff, Beechwood was also abandoned. In a moving passage, which Clement Eaton has called an "elegy on the passing of the Old South,"[1] the disconsolate Ruffin took leave of his deserted old homestead and fled first to Ruthven and later, as Federal units landed on the south bank of the James, to Petersburg. After a brief occupation, in which Beechwood was used as a Union command post, the enemy retired, and the diarist returned to view and recount in graphic detail the wanton destruction inflicted upon his former property by the vengeful Yankees.

[1] Clement Eaton, *A History of the Old South: The Emergence of a Reluctant Nation* (3rd ed.; New York: Macmillan Publishing Company, 1975), 3.

Introduction

Fascinating as are these first-hand accounts, the principal utility of the wartime diary inheres in the author's commentary upon issues and actors in that fractricidal conflict. Following the precedent established in the prewar portion of the journal, he provides candid portraits of numerous civil and military figures. Readily predictable are his assessments of the rival presidents. He considered Lincoln to be mediocre in intellect and ability and, in the context of the wartime situation, a tyrant and dictator almost without precedent in modern times. Blinded by his virulent hatred of all Yankees, he characterized the northern chief executive, variously, as "a low & vulgar blackguard," "a clown & mountebank," a "despicable wretch," and "a low minded & narrow minded man." Displaying more detachment in his appraisal of Davis, Ruffin thought him the best man for the job at the outset but gradually grew disenchanted, criticizing him for appointing many incompetents to office, for his lenient attitude toward both northern spies and southern deserters, and for his failure to retaliate for alleged Union outrages against persons and property in occupied portions of the South. Such softness on the part of the Confederate president, he attributed to Davis' recent religious conversion. No Confederate military leader—not even Lee, whom he initially feared was "too much of a red-tapist to be an effective commander in the field"—stood as high in Ruffin's estimation as his fellow Virginian, Stonewall Jackson. As the diarist explained on one occasion, "he not only performs more important work in less time than any other commander, but he tells of his performances in fewer words." When Jackson was mortally wounded at Chancellorsville, Ruffin termed his death "a great calamity" for the Confederacy and wrote a moving eulogy in which he lauded the fallen hero for his military proficiency, his unselfish devotion to duty, his modesty, and his devout Christian character.

Despite his personal lack of military training or experience, Ruffin's comments on wartime strategy are remarkable for their perception and insight. Thus, he recognized very early the threat posed by Union naval superiority, which enabled the North not only to blockade the southern coast but also to seize coastal cities and control the western rivers. Although he was a Virginian, he understood full well the importance of the West and became increasingly apprehensive about Confederate prospects in that theater. So depressed was he by the fall of New Orleans in April, 1862, that he was compelled to admit for the first time "the *possibility* of the sub-

[xv]

jugation of the southern states." Frustrated by the apparent inability of southern generals to capitalize on decisive tactical victories, he repeatedly urged a more aggressive prosecution of the war. Like many of his fellow countrymen, he could not understand the failure of Confederate authorities to follow up the victory at First Manassas by invading the North—"carrying the war into Africa," as he phrased it. Evoking the memory of Francis Marion, the "Swamp Fox" of the Revolution, he urged that guerrilla tactics be employed in the southern hinterland and advocated retaliatory raids into northern border states by mobile strike forces commanded by such dashing leaders as John Hunt Morgan and Nathan Bedford Forrest. "I wish to put the cost & the sacrifices of war on the enemy's territory," he asserted, "& to make them feel the horrors of war." Perhaps such tactics would not have altered the result, but, especially in light of our recent experiences on the Asiatic mainland, one wonders whether a more offensive posture might not have proved more efficacious for the Confederacy.

In retrospect, it seems likely that the ultimate fate of the Confederacy was determined largely by the attitude of the major European neutrals. Accordingly, the diarist's analyses of the prospects for European intervention are particularly illuminating. At the outset of the war Ruffin, like most Southerners, displayed great faith in the power of "King Cotton" to force intervention, at least to the extent of raising the blockade. The *Trent* affair, which he termed the greatest "insult . . . offered to the British government in the last century," reinforced his conviction that England would intercede in behalf of the Confederacy. But he was soon sobered by the Lincoln Administration's capitulation, remarking bitterly that "such an act of abject humiliation has not been paralleled by any civilized nation in the last century." Thereafter, he became increasingly pessimistic, concluding that Britain actually stood to benefit from a continuation of the conflict and that she would seriously consider intervention only in the unlikely contingency that a total northern victory seemed imminent.

However, influenced by reports in the northern and European press, Ruffin's hopes for foreign assistance rose again in the fall of 1862. Indeed, that possibility together with Democratic successes in the autumn elections induced in him the belief "that negotiations for peace will be on foot before the winter is over." But, as a consequence of Lee's repulse at Antietam and the ensuing Preliminary

Introduction

Emancipation Proclamation, the British ministry declined to act, and from December, 1862, through February, 1863, the diarist's hopes rested with Napolean III. Even after Secretary of State William H. Seward officially rejected a French offer of mediation, Ruffin clung to the vain hope that France would intervene alone. Only after the outbreak of an insurrection in Russian Poland which distracted the French Emporer's attention from American affairs did Ruffin reluctantly conclude that the Confederacy could no longer look to Europe for any succor. If she were to survive, she would have to rely exclusively upon her own resources and her own devices.

As the fortunes of the South deteriorated, Ruffin became increasingly embittered against her northern adversaries. Already a pronounced Yankeephobe when the war began, his animosity approached maniacal proportions as the invading armies took their toll of lives and property. Utterly convinced of the moral rectitude of the southern cause, he castigated the North for waging an aggressive, unjust, and immoral war. But, philosophical arguments aside, it was the plunder of property that seemed most to incense him. As early as June, 1861, he began to complain of "outrages of murder, & destruction of private property" perpetrated by enemy troops near Hampton, Virginia. Thereafter, with each new encroachment upon Confederate territory, his vitriolic pen reached new heights of denunciation. Thus, as a massive Union naval expedition steamed out of Hampton Roads in late October, 1861, en route to Port Royal, South Carolina, he charged that "it conveys an army of robbers, house-burners, wanton destroyers of property . . . slave-stealers & inciters of negro insurrection, ravishers & murderers." The following summer, stung by a series of reverses in the western theater, he renewed his attack, comparing the Yankees to "pirates, who rob & murder, without scruple or limit, unoffending persons, merely to obtain possession of their property." The struggle with the North, he raged, was the "most iniquitous & unjust of modern wars." The ultimate humiliation for Ruffin came two months later when the Federals seized Beechwood, causing damage estimated by the former proprietor at not less than $150,000. Clearly, the diarist was not the only one infected with feelings of hatred and vengeance.

Nor was Ruffin's ire directed solely against the Yankees. The mass desertions of slaves during the Civil War finally brought home to southern whites the painful truth that those smiling black faces did not necessarily reflect deep-seated contentment with the system.

For many, including Ruffin, it was a shattering realization. When the Ruffin slaves began absconding *en masse* to the enemy in the wake of McClellan's march up the peninsula, the stunned diarist could only express astonishment at "the delusion of the negroes." Even Jem Sykes, the trusted black foreman at Marlbourne, had joined in the general uprising on that estate. Ruffin castigated his former chattels for their ingratitude and denounced the Yankees for misleading the Negroes and encouraging such flights with false promises. In reprisal for the conduct of their runaway relatives, slaves from disloyal families were sold, and the remaining servants were removed to a more secure site. Some months later, as the blue tide began to recede from the peninsula, most of the runaways returned. But the master-slave relationship would never again be quite the same. As he approached Marlbourne for the first time following the restoration of the owners' authority, the diarist admitted that "it is to me very painful to meet my former slaves to whom I was attached by ties of affection on their part (as I believed) as well as on mine, under such changed circumstances." For their part, the slaves, having "seen the elephant" once, were not so quick to desert the next time Federal troops intruded into their neighborhood. One of the most ironic pictures to emerge from the pages of this volume is that of Marlbourne plough hands in May, 1863, pausing to permit the passage of George Stoneman's blue-coated cavalry over their farm road and then proceeding to work as if nothing were amiss. Doubtless, there was more than a modicum of truth in the diarist's contention that conditions in the Federal camps left much to be desired.

If Ruffin remained sanguine of the ultimate triumph of Confederate arms on the battlefield, he was less certain of the ability of the southern economy to withstand the rigors of an extended war. Almost from the outset, he regarded economic problems as a greater threat to the survival of the Confederacy than Union military might. As early as December, 1861, he began to complain of soaring retail prices, and, as inflation approached runaway proportions, his apprehension increased. "The continuation of the Yankee blockade," he wrote in April, 1862, "threatens more danger to our cause, by the consequent scarcity & high prices of necessaries of life, than do the Yankee arms & armies & fleets." As the months passed, prices rose to unprecedented heights. By the spring of 1863, with corn selling for $11.00 a bushel, wheat for half that amount, and hay for $25.00 the hundred pounds, Ruffin was obliged to concede "that our country &

cause are now, for the first time during the war, in great peril of defeat." Little did he realize what lay ahead for southern consumers during the next two years.

Although the overwhelming preponderance of entries in this volume of the diary relate directly to contemporary events, there are a few unexpected dividends. For example, students of the slave South will find Ruffin's recollection of the Nat Turner insurrection especially significant. Describing the white reaction to that conspiracy as one of "extended & very general community-insanity," he relates how he interceded with the governor of Virginia in a vain attempt to procure a pardon for a slave in his county who had been wrongfully implicated in the plot. For his efforts, he incurred "much odium" from his neighbors and was threatened with "personal violence." Equally interesting is the diarist's authoritative account of a conspiracy among Virginia secessionists on the eve of Sumter in which plans were formulated to employ physical force, even to the extent of arresting Governor John Letcher and leading submissionists in the State Convention, if that dilatory body did not adopt a secession ordinance within a specified time. Ruffin also renews the attack upon Jeffersonian democracy which he mounted in the preceding volume. While crediting the "Sage of Monticello" with "kindly & benevolent feelings," an "amiable disposition," abundant "private virtues," and a "commanding intellect," he charged that, through his advocacy of universal suffrage and popular election of all executive and judicial officers, Jefferson had "caused more evil, and done more to destroy free & sound institutions" than any other man in our history. To believe in such nonsense might be "pardonable in boys at school," but for one of Jefferson's political sagacity and experience to embrace extreme democratic doctrines was, to Ruffin, incomprehensible.

More significant, perhaps, than Ruffin's assessment of Jefferson, is an extended analysis of his own life and public career, written early in 1863. With more than a trace of bitterness, he complained that his many public services—rendered as state legislator, agricultural reformer, editor of the *Farmers' Register*, member of the Board of Visitors of William and Mary College, president of the State Agricultural Society, and defender of southern rights—had never been properly appreciated, especially by those in his native state. It was the last role that he most cherished. For eleven years he had spearheaded the secession movement in Virginia, only to be rewarded with vilification, calumny, and public censure. Not until he was accidentally placed in the position of firing the first cannon against Fort Sumter did he receive the popular adulation he so craved, and even then it was muted in his own state. Although he did not claim such credit, he could think of no greater honor than to be remembered by subsequent generations as the patriot who had been "the chief cause of effecting the separation of the Southern from the Northern states." Thus did the dream of the fiery old southern nationalist live on. Appomattox was still two years away.

II

In general, I have adhered to the editorial practices adopted for the first volume. With minor exceptions, every effort has been made to reproduce the diary exactly as it was written. Occasionally, commas and apostrophes have been added in order to promote clarity. Words consistently misspelled by the diarist, of which there were approximately seventy-five in the 1,374 manuscript pages included within this volume, have been noted at the first instance and silently corrected thereafter. Deletions, though slightly more extensive than in Volume I, have been confined almost exclusively to trivial health and family matters; repetitious passages; mention of minor military engagements, especially in the West; and clearly erroneous information gleaned from newspaper reports. I have also eliminated some passages relating to inconsequential books read by the diarist during the war years, believing that the general pattern of his reading habits was adequately documented in the previous volume. Deprived of all new books and periodicals from the North or Europe after the outbreak of war, Ruffin was obliged to resort largely to second and third readings of older works—especially the novels of Sir Walter Scott. Moreover, as he observed early on, "the excitement of the war, & interest in its incidents, have absorbed everything else. We think & talk of nothing else—& nearly all reading is confined to newspapers."

By the close of 1861 Ruffin had so extended his journal as to convert it into a daily commentary upon news reports concerning every facet of the war. Individual entries had become appreciably longer, usually extending to several manuscript pages. However, the adoption of such a practice created certain problems. As the diarist himself recognized and complained about on numerous occasions, journalistic reporting during the Civil War was notoriously inaccurate. For example, estimates of Union casualties were almost invariably exaggerated in the southern press. Much initial intelligence concerning military movements and engagements was extremely distorted and unreliable. Consequently, in order to sustain an accurate narrative it has been necessary to check virtually all references in the diary to wartime events. Where the diarist was misled by faulty or incomplete reports, I have inserted clarifying footnotes. These contain specific references to the monumental 130-volume compendium, *The War of the Rebellion: A Compilation of the Official Records of the Union and Confederate Armies* (Washington, 1880–1901), where that invaluable source was directly consulted. Also especially useful in facilitating my labors in this regard were two reference works, E. B. Long, *The Civil War Day by Day: An Almanac, 1861–1865* (Garden City, New York, 1971) and Mark M. Boatner III, *The Civil War Dictionary* (New York, 1959). For biographical data on personalities mentioned in this segment of the diary, *The Biographical Directory of the American Congress, 1774–1971* (Washington, 1971) proved more valuable than any other source. It should be noted, however, that this volume does not include sketches of persons already identified in Volume I.

III

Perhaps no aspect of this project has been the source of greater personal gratification than the enthusiastic response to it by members of the Ruffin family. Since publication of the first volume in 1972, a number of the diarist's descendants have come forward to lend encouragement in various ways. Thanks to their interest and assistance, I have been enabled to construct a much more complete genealogical chart of the Ruffin family than that which appeared in the initial volume of the diary. And from them I have received a wealth of supplementary information relating to the elder Ruffin and his descendants. I wish particularly to thank the following: Mr. Braden Vandeventer, Jr., of Norfolk and his mother, Mrs. Braden Vandeventer (born Eliza Phelan Ruffin), of Virginia Beach, who supplied me with important genealogical data; Mrs. Edward Lorraine Ruffin of Houston, Texas, who furnished additional genealogical information; the late Edmund Sumter Ruffin, Jr., of Virginia Beach, who provided several interesting vignettes concerning the

Introduction

Ruffin clan; Mr. and Mrs. George R. Gilliam, who graciously received me and my son at Beechwood in August, 1975; Mr. Gilliam's brother, James S. Gilliam, who accompanied us on the tour of Beechwood and generously provided me with various Ruffin materials; and Mr. Julian Meade Ruffin II of Upper Marlbourne, Virginia, a great-grandson of the diarist, who held me spellbound with his reminiscences of life on the Ruffin farms in Hanover County. Above all, I am indebted to Mr. Ruffin's son-in-law and daughter, Mr. and Mrs. Sterling P. Anderson, Jr., also of Upper Marlbourne, who worked closely with me on the family genealogy, furnished the illustrations, and extended to me other courtesies too numerous to mention. On three separate occasions, they entertained me and my family at Upper Marlbourne and served as our personal guides in visits to many of the sites made famous by their distinguished ancestor. I shall forever be grateful for their invaluable assistance and their gracious display of true Virginia hospitality.

I wish also to acknowledge my appreciation for two grants from the University of Southern Mississippi Faculty Research Fund which facilitated the editorial work on this phase of the project. As usual, the staff of the Louisiana State University Press, under the capable direction of Leslie E. Phillabaum, has rendered every possible assistance and displayed remarkable patience in the face of several missed deadlines. I am particularly grateful to Martha Lacy Hall, who served as copy editor for this volume. Finally, I am indebted to James Latham, a graduate student in the Department of Geography at the University of Southern Mississippi, who displayed his cartographical skill by drawing the four excellent maps.

WILLIAM K. SCARBOROUGH

Hattiesburg, Mississippi
February, 1976

The Ruffin Family

CHILDREN AND GRANDCHILDREN
OF EDMUND RUFFIN

Edmund Ruffin—born January 5, 1794, at Evergreen, Prince
George County, Virginia; died June 18, 1865, at Redmoor,
Amelia County.* Married (1813) Susan Hutchings Travis
(1793–1846), daughter of Colonel Champion Travis and
Elizabeth Boush Travis of Williamsburg. Issue:

1   Edmund, Jr. (1814–1875)—attended the University of Vir-
     ginia; proprietor of Beechwood, Prince George County;
     captain, Prince George Cavalry, Confederate States Army.
     Married, first, Mary Cooke Smith (1816–1857), daughter of
     Thomas Gregory Smith and Anne Dabney Smith of King
     and Queen County, on December 15, 1836. Issue:

     a   Virginia (1837–1844)

     b   Edmund Quintus (1839–1853)

     c   Anne (1841–1863)—called "Nanny" by the diarist.
          Died unmarried.

     d   Thomas Smith (1843–1873)—married Alice Lor-
          raine, daughter of Colonel Edward Lorraine, on
          May 23, 1867.

---

*Surprisingly, there is considerable uncertainty concerning the precise date of
Ruffin's death. Most authorities, including biographer Avery Craven, give Sunday,
June 18, as the day of his suicide. This is supported by the diarist's obituary,
published in the Richmond *Daily Times* on June 20, 1865, and, seemingly, by
internal evidence in the diary itself. However, the latter is somewhat ambiguous; the
final entry is dated "June 16, 17 & 18," but we cannot be sure that it was actually
written on the 18th. Two other dates are in contention. Ruffin's tombstone in the
family burial plot at Marlbourne clearly shows June 15 as the date of his demise. This
date, which I am confident is erroneous, was also cited in a genealogical sketch of the
Ruffin family which appeared in *Tyler's Quarterly Magazine*, XXII (April, 1941),
242. However, Sterling P. Anderson, Jr., has recently provided me with the copy of a
letter—also published in *Tyler's Magazine*—from Edmund, Jr., to his sons, dated
June 20, 1865, at Marlbourne, which recounts the details of the diarist's tragic suicide
at Redmoor on Saturday, June 17, and his subsequent burial at Marlbourne on the
nineteenth. Despite the persuasive character of this letter, which has convinced Mr.
Anderson that June 17 is the correct date of Ruffin's passing, the weight of the
available evidence still seems to me to support the eighteenth.

e George Champion (1845–1913)—married Alice Cocke, daughter of James Cocke of Prince George County, in June, 1880.

f Susan (1846–1931)—married, first, William Willcox of Flower de Hundred, Prince George County; second, Edward C. Harrison (1847–1908) of Charles City County.

g Mary Smith (b. 1848)—married the Reverend Edward Valentine Jones (1844–1923) on November 23, 1873.

h John Augustine (1853–1926)—married Jennie Cary Harrison (1855–1909) on May 22, 1888. Resided at Evelynton, Charles City County.

Married, second, Jane Minerva Ruffin, daughter of Judge Thomas Ruffin of North Carolina, on April 25, 1861. Issue:

i Edmund (b. 1862)—married Lelia Beverley Harrison, daughter of Colonel Randolph Harrison of Elk Hill, Goochland County, and Williamsburg.

j Roulhac (b. 1864)—married Edith Jett of St. Paul, Minnesota, in April, 1894.

k Kirkland (1866–1932)—married Mary Dunn of Petersburg on April 4, 1894.

l Julian Beverley (1867–1930)—married Annie May Edmunds of Danville, Virginia, on November 14, 1894.

2 George Champion—died in infancy.

3 Agnes (b. 1817)—married Dr. Thomas Stanley Beckwith of Petersburg. Issue:

a Julian (1839–1862)—attended William and Mary College; killed in action at Seven Pines on May 31, 1862.

b Margaret Stanley (1842–1932)

c Thomas Stanley, Jr. (b. 1843)

d Edmund Ruffin (b. 1845)

e John (b. 1845)—twin brother of Edmund.

f Susan Travis (b. 1846)

g Agnes Ruffin (1847–1930)

 h Lucy (b. 1850)—died in infancy.

 i Charles (1851–1928)—Episcopal bishop of Alabama.

 j Catherine Devereaux—died in infancy.

 k Mildred Elizabeth (d. 1939)

 l Kate Devereaux (d. 1931)

4 Jane—died in infancy.

5 Julian Calx (1821–1864)—attended William and Mary College; proprietor of Ruthven, Prince George County; killed in action at Drewry's Bluff on May 16, 1864. Married Charlotte Stockdell ("Lotty") Meade (1833–1918), daughter of John Everard Meade and Rebecca Wormeley Beverley Meade, on May 26, 1852. Issue:

 a Julian Meade (1853–1938)—married Mary Ruffin (first cousin), daughter of Charles Lorraine Ruffin, on July 19, 1887.

 b Jane Skipwith (1856–1944)—died unmarried.

 c Bessie Callender (1859–1941)—married Roland Faulconer Broaddus on April 24, 1889.

 d Edmund Sumter (1861–1949)—born one week after the bombardment of Fort Sumter. Married Cordelia Willing (Byrd) Waller, daughter of Richard Willing Byrd, on April 30, 1895.

 e Rebecca Beverley (1863–1963)—married Henry Harrison Christian on June 14, 1905.

6 Rebecca (1823–1855)—married John T. Bland of Prince George County. No issue.

7 Elizabeth (1824–1860)—married William Sayre, who became resident manager of Marlbourne following the diarist's retirement. Died December 4, 1860, after giving birth to a son. The infant also died within a few weeks.

8 Mildred Campbell (1827–1862)—resided at Marlbourne until her marriage, on October 4, 1859, to Burwell Bassett Sayre, a Frankfort, Kentucky, schoolmaster and brother of William Sayre. Issue:

 a Ruth (b. 1860)—died three weeks after birth.

    b   Elizabeth (1862–1940)—married Admiral Hugh Rodman of Kentucky.

9   Jane (1829–1855)—married Dr. John J. Dupuy (first cousin), son of the diarist's half-sister, Jane Ruffin Dupuy, of The Glebe, Prince George County. Issue:

    a   Jane Ruffin (1855–1864)

10   Ella (1832–1855)—died unmarried.

11   Charles Lorraine (1832–1870)—twin brother of Ella. Married Henrietta Alice Harrison (1843–1925), daughter of Alexander Harrison and Mary Boisseau Harrison, on April 28, 1864. Resided at Rose Cottage, Prince George County. Issue:

    a   Charles Lorraine, Jr. (1866–1951)—married Mary Levering of Baltimore, Maryland, on April 24, 1895.

    b   Mary (1869–1938)—married Julian Meade Ruffin (first cousin) of Marlbourne, Hanover County, on July 19, 1887.

Civil War Chronology

1861

April	14	Federals evacuate Fort Sumter.
	17	Virginia Convention approves ordinance of secession.
	20	Federals evacuate Norfolk Navy Yard.
May	6	Legislatures of Arkansas and Tennessee approve secession ordinances.
	10–11	St. Louis riots.
	20	North Carolina Convention votes unanimously for secession.
	24	Federals cross Potomac and occupy Alexandria, Virginia; Colonel Elmer Ellsworth slain.
June	3	Confederates routed at Philippi in western Virginia.
	10	Battle of Big Bethel, Virginia.
July	2	Federal Brigadier General Robert Patterson crosses Potomac and invades Shenandoah Valley.
	4	Thirty-seventh Congress convenes in special session in Washington.
	11	Confederates defeated at Rich Mountain in western Virginia.
	13	Engagement at Carrick's Ford in western Virginia.
	17	Brigadier General Irvin McDowell begins advance on Manassas Junction.
	18	Engagement at Blackburn's Ford on Bull Run.

	20	Third session of Confederate Provisional Congress convenes in Richmond.
July	21	First Battle of Manassas.
August	6	Federal Congress adjourns.
	10	Battle of Wilson's Creek (or Oak Hills), Missouri.
	28	Federal expedition captures Fort Hatteras, North Carolina.
	31	Third session of Confederate Provisional Congress adjourns.
September	3	Confederates invade Kentucky
	6	Grant captures Paducah, Kentucky.
	11–15	Cheat Mountain campaign in western Virginia.
	20	Federals surrender Lexington, Missouri, to General Sterling Price.
October	21	Federals defeated in Battle of Ball's Bluff (or Leesburg), Virginia.
	29	Large Federal land and sea expedition departs Hampton Roads en route to South Carolina coast.
November	1	Major General George B. McClellan succeeds Winfield Scott as general-in-chief of Union Army.
	6	Jefferson Davis elected to six-year term as President of Confederate States of America.
	7	Federals land at Port Royal, South Carolina.
	8	Confederate commissioners James M. Mason and John Slidell forcibly removed from British mail steamer *Trent*.
	18	Fifth session of Confederate Provisional Congress opens in Richmond.
December	2	Second session of Thirty-seventh Congress convenes.
	11	Great Charleston fire.

23   Lord Lyons presents British ultimatum concerning *Trent* affair to Secretary of State Seward.

26   Lincoln administration agrees to surrender Mason and Slidell to British—end of *Trent* affair.

1862

January   11   Burnside expedition departs Hampton Roads en route to North Carolina coast.

18   Former President John Tyler succumbs in Richmond.

19   Battle of Logan's Cross Roads (or Mill Springs), Kentucky.

27   Lincoln issues General War Order No. 1, prescribing a general advance of the principal Union armies.

February   6   Fort Henry, Tennessee, falls to Federals.

8   Battle of Roanoke Island, North Carolina.

16   Surrender of Fort Donelson, Tennessee.

18   First Confederate Congress convenes in Richmond.

22   Inauguration of President Jefferson Davis.

25   Federals occupy Nashville, Tennessee.

27   U.S.S. *Monitor* sails from New York.

March   7–8   Battle of Pea Ridge (or Elkhorn Tavern), Arkansas.

8   C.S.S. *Virginia* (*Merrimac*) attacks Federal blockading squadron in Hampton Roads.

March   9   Duel between the *Monitor* and *Merrimac*.

14   Federals capture New Berne, North Carolina, and New Madrid, Missouri.

17   Opening of McClellan's Peninsula Campaign—troops from Army of the Potomac begin embarking at Alexandria, Virginia.

	23	Battle of Kernstown—beginning of Stonewall Jackson's Shenandoah Valley Campaign.
April	5	McClellan lays siege to Yorktown.
	6–7	Battle of Shiloh.
	7	Federals capture Island No. 10.
	11	Fort Pulaski, Georgia, falls to Federals.
	16	President Davis signs Confederate Conscription Act.
	21	Confederate Congress adjourns.
	24	Flag Officer David G. Farragut successfully passes forts below New Orleans.
	25	fall of New Orleans; Federals capture Fort Macon, North Carolina.
May	3	Confederates evacuate Yorktown, Virginia.
	5	Battle of Williamsburg, Virginia.
	9	Confederates evacuate Norfolk.
	11	C.S.S. *Virginia* scuttled off Norfolk.
	15	Federal naval force repulsed at Drewry's Bluff on James River.
	23	Jackson captures Front Royal, Virginia.
	25	Battle of Winchester, Virginia.
	30	Beauregard evacuates Corinth, Mississippi.
	31	Battle of Seven Pines (or Fair Oaks), Virginia.
June	1	Battle of Seven Pines concluded; Robert E. Lee assumes command of what will soon be known as the Army of Northern Virginia.
	6	Fall of Memphis.
	8	Battle of Cross Keys, Virginia.
	9	Battle of Port Republic, Virginia—conclusion of Jackson's Valley campaign.
	12–15	Jeb Stuart's first "Ride Around McClellan."
	16	Confederates repulse attack on Secessionville, South Carolina.
	25	Beginning of Seven Days' Battles east of Richmond.

26   Battle of Mechanicsville.

27   Battle of Gaines' Mill.

28   Farragut's fleet passes Vicksburg en route up the Mississippi.

29   Battle of Savage's Station.

30   Battle of White Oak Swamp (or Frayser's Farm).

July   1   Battle of Malvern Hill—Seven Days' Battles end as McClellan reaches Harrison's Landing on the James.

17   President Lincoln signs Second Confiscation Act.

29   C.S.S. *Alabama* departs Liverpool on maiden voyage.

August   6   C.S.S. *Arkansas* blown up at Baton Rouge.

9   Battle of Cedar Mountain, Virginia.

14   McClellan begins to evacuate Army of Potomac from Peninsula to Aquia Creek on the Potomac.

18   Second session of First Confederate Congress opens.

24   C.S.S. *Alabama* commissioned off Azores.

28   General Braxton Bragg begins invasion of Tennessee and Kentucky.

29–30   Second Battle of Manassas.

September 4   Lee begins crossing Potomac into Maryland.

13   Lee's "Lost Order" discovered by two Union soldiers in Frederick, Maryland.

14   Battles of South Mountain and Crampton's Gap.

15   Jackson captures Harpers Ferry.

17   Battle of Antietam (or Sharpsburg); Bragg captures Munfordville, Kentucky.

22   Lincoln issues Preliminary Emancipation Proclamation.

[xxxi]

<table>
<tr><td>27</td><td>First Negroes enrolled as soldiers in Union Army.</td></tr>
<tr><td>October 3–4</td><td>Battle of Corinth, Mississippi.</td></tr>
<tr><td>8</td><td>Battle of Perryville, Kentucky.</td></tr>
<tr><td>9–12</td><td>Stuart's second "Ride Around McClellan."</td></tr>
<tr><td>13</td><td>Second session of First Confederate Congress adjourns.</td></tr>
<tr><td>14</td><td>Democrats score victories in congressional elections in Ohio, Indiana, and Pennsylvania.</td></tr>
<tr><td>October 23</td><td>Bragg retreats into Tennessee through Cumberland Gap.</td></tr>
<tr><td>26</td><td>McClellan begins crossing the Potomac into Virginia.</td></tr>
<tr><td>November 4</td><td>Democrats register additional gains in congressional and state elections in New York, New Jersey, Illinois, and Wisconsin.</td></tr>
<tr><td>7</td><td>Major General Ambrose E. Burnside supersedes McClellan as commander of Army of the Potomac.</td></tr>
<tr><td>17</td><td>Major General Edwin V. Sumner's Right Grand Division reaches Falmouth, across the Rappahannock from Fredericksburg.</td></tr>
<tr><td>19</td><td>Lieutenant General James Longstreet's First Corps arrives at Fredericksburg.</td></tr>
<tr><td>December 1</td><td>Third session of Thirty-seventh Congress convenes.</td></tr>
<tr><td>7</td><td>Battle of Prairie Grove, Arkansas.</td></tr>
<tr><td>11</td><td>Burnside crosses Rappahannock and occupies Fredericksburg; Major General John G. Foster initiates ten-day Federal expedition from New Berne to Goldsborough, North Carolina.</td></tr>
<tr><td>13</td><td>Battle of Fredericksburg.</td></tr>
<tr><td>17–20</td><td>Federal cabinet crisis precipitated by friction between Secretary of State William H.</td></tr>
</table>

Seward and Secretary of the Treasury Salmon P. Chase.

20 Major General Earl Van Dorn raids Grant's supply depot at Holly Springs, Mississippi.

29 Sherman repulsed at Chickasaw Bayou, Mississippi, as Federal campaigns against Vicksburg begin.

December 30 U.S.S. *Monitor* sinks off Cape Hatteras, North Carolina.

31 Battle of Murfreesboro (or Stone's River), Tennessee; Lincoln signs bill admitting West Virginia into Union as thirty-fifth state.

1863

January 1 Effective date of Lincoln's Emancipation Proclamation.

2 Battle of Murfreesboro concluded.

11 Federals capture Arkansas Post (or Fort Hindman); duel between C.S.S. *Alabama* and U.S.S. *Hatteras* off Galveston, Texas.

12 Third session of First Confederate Congress convenes.

19–22 Burnside's futile "Mud March" along the Rappahannock.

25 Major General Joseph Hooker supersedes Burnside as commander of Army of the Potomac.

29 Confederate Congress authorizes Erlanger Loan.

31 Confederate gunboats attack Federal blockading squadron at Charleston.

February 3 Seward rejects French offer of mediation.

24 U.S.S. *Indianola* captured by Confederates below Vicksburg.

March 3 President Lincoln signs Federal Conscription Act.

	4	Third session of Thirty-seventh Congress adjourns.
	16	Yazoo Pass expedition against Vicksburg ends in failure.
	17	Engagement at Kelly's Ford, Virginia.
	18	Erlanger Loan opened in Paris.
	24	Steele's Bayou campaign against Vicksburg ends in failure.
	29	Grant begins marching army south from Milliken's Bend on west side of Mississippi River.
April	2	Richmond "Bread Riot."
	7	Federal naval assault on Charleston.
	11	Colonel Abel D. Streight begins raid into Georgia.
	16	Federal flotilla effects passage of Vicksburg batteries.
	17	Beginning of Grierson's Raid into Mississippi, which lasted until May 2.
	22	Federal transports and barges run Vicksburg batteries.
	28	Hooker begins crossing Rappahannock.
	29	Beginning of Stoneman's Raids during Chancellorsville campaign—concluded May 8.
	30	Grant crosses Mississippi River at Bruinsburg and commences final campaign against Vicksburg.
May	1–4	Battle of Chancellorsville.
	1	Federals capture Port Gibson, Mississippi; third session of First Confederate Congress adjourns.
	3	Streight's raiders surrender to Nathan Bedford Forrest at Cedar Bluff, Alabama.
	5	Clement L. Vallandigham arrested in Dayton, Ohio.

10 Stonewall Jackson dies of wounds incurred in Chancellorsville campaign.

14 Federals occupy Jackson, Mississippi.

15 Fire at Tredegar Iron Works in Richmond.

16 Battle of Champion's Hill, Mississippi.

17 Battle of Big Black River Bridge, Mississippi.

18 Grant lays siege to Vicksburg.

21 Federal siege of Port Hudson, Louisiana, begins.

25 Vallandigham turned over to Confederate authorities in Tennessee.

June 3 Lee begins moving Army of Northern Virginia out of Fredericksburg area as Gettysburg campaign commences.

THE DIARY OF
EDMUND RUFFIN

"It seems to me, that, but for the accident of Fort Sumter, my patriotic labors & efforts would [have] been unknown—& my name almost forgotten in my own country, & by the generation which I have so zealously & effectively labored to serve. I appeal to future generations for the due appreciation of my efforts, & their effects.

—'A prophet is not without honor, but in his own country, and among his own kin, and in his own house.'—St. Mark, vi, 4.—"

Edmund Ruffin, January 20, 1863

April–June

e~o

1861

RETURN TO VIRGINIA e~o RICHMOND PRE-
PARES FOR WAR e~o A VISIT TO THE TREDE-
GAR IRON WORKS e~o REUNITED WITH THE
PALMETTO GUARD–POLITICAL AND
MILITARY SPECULATIONS

April [22]. At 11 last night, set out for Richmond. By 10 to 11 A.M. entered the territory of N.C. still to us, in law, a foreign country, & part of the now hostile U.S. But everything seen on the whole passage through was not only peaceful & friendly, but evincing unanimity & enthusiasm for secession, & in favor of the C.S. . . . [1322] There joined us on the way, at the Florence junction, three companies of Ga. volunteers, who were greeted enthusiastically by the assemblages at almost every station. We left these companies at Wilmington, to wait for a special train. At Wilmington there was a great crowd, of ladies as well as of men, & at every station there were many persons waiting, to hear news & to see the passage of the expected troops for service in Va. or for Washington. R[oger] A. Pryor was along, on his way from Montgomery, & he was called out to speak to the crowds at sundry places, of which the latest was at Weldon, after 10.30 P.M. I also was called for whenever the people learned I was along, & was forced to utter a few sentences only, at three different places, of thanks & congratulation. . . . North Carolina is substantially a seceded state, & united with the C.S. & will so act—although the legal formalities have yet to be gone through.

April 23. We reached Richmond about 6 A.M. I went immediately to the Exchange Hotel & washed, shaved & dressed.—Had met

[5]

Mr. Cropper, on the train, just from Norfolk on business of the state, who gave me much & correct information about the doings of the Navy Yard, which corrections I will now state. Com. [Charles S.] Macauley, commander, ordered & attempted to effect, the destruction of the buildings & all the property at the Navy Yard, & the ships alongside. Most of the extensive barracks & workshops were burned, & also the great 120-gun ship Pennsylvania, & the Columbia, Raritan, Germantown, Merrimac & Dolphin, all afloat, all burnt to the water's edge. Also, two 74-gun frames on the stocks, & the houses erected over them to preserve [1323] them. Of all these, the Merrimac (first-class steamer) & the Germantown, only, were in good condition, & quite or nearly fit for sea. All the others greatly short of full repair & value. Nearly all the cannons were spiked, but imperfectly, with nails. Quantities of muskets, in cases or otherwise, were broken & thrown into the river—& all other valuables that could be broken & destroyed, even to a magnificent collection of astronomical & nautical instruments & charts &c. Most of the ships afloat had their cannon on, which of course were sunk, & in deep water. But these, it is thought, may all be got up. The Pawnee, of shallow draft (one of the Charleston fleet,) had come up to the Navy yard, with 400 to 1000 troops. The Cumberland frigate was lightened by having guns &c. thrown overboard, & then was towed by the Pawnee, with all the men, by Norfolk & over the obstructions placed in the channel below, & so escaped. Two officers only, by some accident remained, & were afterwards taken prisoners. There were but the few volunteer companies of Norfolk & Portsmouth embodied, under the command of the empty Major-General [William B.] Taliaferro, who commanded so inefficiently at Charlestown during the John Brown campaign. These had no cannon larger than 6 pounders—& could not have stopped the Pawnee & Cumberland, though I wish they had at least fired on them. But this would not have been done even if with suitable guns, because Macauley had announced that he would shell & burn Norfolk, if fired upon. I wish that the risk had been taken. Still, it is a great loss & defeat of the enemy, though effected by his own hands, in desperation of relief. There were nearly 2000 cannon, of which 1500 are scarcely at all injured. The great dry-dock was attempted to be blown up, but in vain, & was not hurt. Mr. [1324] Cropper, who made a cursory examination, thinks that three millions of dollars worth of property was destroyed (others estimate 5 millions)—but that 20 millions remain, but little injured, or to be recovered.—The arsenal at Harper's Ferry was blown up by the retreating Northern guard, & one of the workshops. But 5000 of best muskets remained uninjured, & were captured by the Va. troops, & most of the workshops in good order.—On the train yesterday, & to this place, came the "Hon[ora]ble Edmund Morison," secretary of the British legation in Washington, to which place he is going, having come from England by way of New Orleans. I have no doubt he is on a tour of political observation—& he had much to see yesterday & today. I became somewhat intimate with him.—The streets here offer more appearances of military preparations than even Charleston did. Volunteers in uniform are seen everywhere. Companies arriving from their homes, & others drilling in the Capitol Square. Numerous companies have been called into service. It is expected that an attack will be ordered on Washington—& apprehended that the enemy may attack the defenceless borders of our broad waters. 3000 kegs (100 lbs each) of gunpowder were taken below Norfolk in the U.S. magazine, & sent to Richmond or elsewhere. Cannon have been placed at different positions to prevent any of the enemy's vessels again ascending the river to Norfolk. Reinforcement of 1100 Northern volunteers lately landed at Fort Monroe—making the present garrison 1400 men.—The Northern government has proclaimed a general blockade of southern ports, but it is not yet carried into effect strictly anywhere. However, the capturing of vessels on both sides (in port) has been begun, & therefore vessels are afraid to attempt passing out of the Capes of Va. or elsewhere that the enemy's vessels are near enough to capture them.—The routes of travel, mail, & telegraph [1325] have been broken at several points (by bridges being destroyed) in Md. on both sides of Baltimore, & also of Washington. So we get but little news, & many false rumors. It seems however certain that there has been throughout Md a complete & wonderful change, in a few days, from a majority being for union, & submission to abolition rule, to an apparently unanimous & zealous support of secession. An agent has come on here from Md. to ask for cannon & small arms, & they have been furnished & sent on. . . . Col. Robert Lee, late a U.S. officer, & said to be one of the best, has been appointed general in chief command of the Va forces. He is now in Richmond.—I have been received here with marked appearances of welcome, & cordial regard, by all my acquaintances, & by very many who were

[7]

strangers before, & who have now sought my acquaintance, or saluted me, without an introduction. The latter are mostly transient sojourners here. All congratulate me & thank me for my recent services, & many express themselves in more especially complimentary terms, & say they are gratified that I, if alone, upheld the honor of Va abroad. There has been a complete & wonderful change here since I left. Now (apparently) all are earnest for secession, & resistance to northern domination. But very few of the still continuing submissionists, like [John M.] Botts, dare to speak their opinions.... My reception here today, by many individuals at least, has seemed to approach to something like the kind & friendly & favorable appreciation evinced for me in Charleston. And however far falling short of that, is in marked contrast to the treatment I have generally received in my own country.—I have met with very many friends & former acquaintances here, too many to mention. Among the most valued were Prof. [James P.] Holcombe, Lewis E. Harvie, W[illiam] G. Crenshaw & sundry other residents of Richmond. At night, Ex-Pres. Tyler, just arrived from home. Hon. Weldon Edwards,[1] Gen. Th. Green ... of N.Ca. here. Major [Walter] Gwynn, who left Charleston the night before I did, to offer his services here, was next morning after his arrival commissioned as Major General of Va. & sent to assume command at Norfolk. Gen. Taliaferro being thus superseded went home in disgust, to the great relief of the cause.

April 24. The governor has, by proclamation, called into actual service all the volunteer companies north of James river & below the Blue Ridge.—Called on Vice-President Stephens, who has been here some days, in conference with the Va. Convention & Governor. He lodges in this hotel. ... More reinforcements have been thrown into Fort Monroe, & the garrison now reported to be 5000 men. It is thought that the enemy designs to strike a blow somewhere [1327] in Va. & Richmond is deemed the most likely place for the attack. I do not believe that so bold an attempt will be made, or is even meditated.—The Convention continues to sit every day with closed doors, & nothing of the proceedings is known outside. I trust that they will act for a vigorous prosecution of the war, & the furnishing aid to Maryland.—Saw, for but a minute, Col. F[rancis] H. Smith & the late Commander U.S.N. [Matthew F.]

---

[1] A prominent legislator and ardent secessionist, Edwards was elected president of the North Carolina Secession Convention when it convened in Raleigh on May 20.

Maury, who has resigned, & come here. Both of these have been appointed by the Convention as counsellors of the Governor, & as such are closely employed.—Afternoon, Gen. [Milledge L.] Bonham & his staff arrived, with 450 of the S.C. troops. The remainder of the 2000 men will soon follow. They were received with evidences of much joy by the people here, & of attention to the General & officers of his staff, who came to this hotel.—Plenty of rumors today, all I suppose false, but no reliable news. . . .

April 25. Troops continue to come in daily, from all parts of Va, & 100 more from S.C. The latter are received with warm & enthusiastic welcome. Richmond has a much more military appearance than Charleston had at any time. There are now some 3000 volunteers here, & more coming. . . . Heard today that the Palmetto Guard are coming here—which I shall be very glad of. Saw yesterday Capt. Harrison H. [1328] Cocke, who has been, to a few weeks back, the most thorough, slavish, & base submissionist that I knew, & who now goes beyond me in extreme measures for disunion. For I was for seceding by due course of legal action. He *now* maintains that we ought not have waited for such action, but have gone out of the Union by summary & revolutionary steps. As soon as I saw him here, I was certain that he came to seek office, as Lincoln's government could no longer pay him as a "retired" navy officer, if living in Va.—& on inquiring learned that I had guessed rightly. . . . The Convention this day acceded to the new federal constitution, & agreed to become a member of the Confederate States. This most gratifying act was permitted to be published. All other proceedings of latter days kept secret. . . . I was introduced previously & today to sundry Virginians, former officers of the U.S. army & navy, who had resigned their commissions, & come here to serve this state. One of these, Col. [John B.] Magruder, very lately made his escape from Washington. He told me that mines had been dug under some of the principal public buildings in Washington, as he knew, & he presumed of all, to blow them up with gunpowder, in case of the government being compelled to retreat. . . . This is the night for Edmund's marriage.[2] I trust that it has not been postponed by his troop having been called into service.—About 10 P.M. a band of music came, to serenade the S.C. officers, & an immense crowd was soon collected in the street to call for & hear speeches. Gen.

---

[2] To Jane M. Ruffin, daughter of Judge Thomas Ruffin of North Carolina. See Volume I, 571.

Bonham was first called out, & Col. A[lfred] P. Aldrich of S.C. Then Gen. T. Green of N.C., R. A. Pryor, & myself. I spoke but a short time, in congratulation of the present unanimity & zeal for separation from the North, the action (of today) of union with the South, of the presence of S.Ca. troops, of the present danger & brave resistance of Md., & the necessity of our aiding Md., & on its soil, to defend Va. from the danger of invasion. I was heard with marked attention & respect.—This afternoon, as I was standing on the foot-way before the hotel, conversing with some others, the Vice-President passed. Having seen him before today, I merely bowed to him. But he turned to me, & offered his hand, saying that he must shake hands with me on the present joyful occasion of Va entering the Confederation of Southern States. I used the occasion to express my hope that President Davis would soon be here with a large army on his way to Maryland—& added that he need not confine his calls for men to the states regularly seceded & confederated, but might call on N.C. as one virtually seceded, & which I was sure would comply with the call, with any number of well armed volunteers. His reply was properly (as in company of others) guarded & general. But he clearly enough indicated that the President would pursue such general policy, & would be here soon—probably by next Wednesday. [1330]

April 26. . . . Went in the forenoon to see the Dupuys. After dinner, hired a carriage, & with three other gentlemen drove out to their respective encampments to see the Va. Military Institute Cadets, & the S.Ca. troops. . . . Charles returned tonight from Petersburg. He met with Edmund & Jane just from Alamance, on their way to Beechwood. The marriage took place at the appointed time, on 25th. I am rejoiced that it was not postponed by orders for the troop to go into service, as was very likely. As I had before announced to both Jane & Edmund, I shall not go to see them until they are somewhat used to their new position, & when I shall be in no danger of being *de trop* in the family circle.—When I went to M[ontgomery] Dupuy's today, his wife & my neices [*sic*] were employed in making shorts of blue flannel for the more destitute soldiers in service. My little granddaughter Jane was sewing on some of the easiest work of one, & was quite proud of her employment & aid.—This afternoon, I met on the footway the Hon. Wm. C. Rives. I have long despised his political character & conduct, in all his different phases & changes—& though we were fellow-

Welcome to Burke County Library,
Waynesboro!
You checked out the following items:

1. The diary of Edmund Ruffin
   Barcode: 31057902473498 Due:
   2010-10-26

students at Wm. & Mary college, & fellow-lodgers, & never had the slightest personal difference, for a long time I have preferred to avoid meeting with & accosting him, or exchanging salutations. When not to [1331] be avoided, without obvious disrespect, as on this occasion, my salutations were coldly polite, & his much more gracious & cordial. Of course, when meeting now, I should have made no allusion to the present state of Va, which he was one of the most thorough opposers of—a complete union-worshipper & sub-missionist to all northern oppressions. But of his own accord, as soon as we had shaken hands, he, (as many others of his stamp have done, since I arrived,) referred to the subject, & said in substance, "Well, Mr. Ruffin, affairs in Va are now in the state which you have been wishing for a long time—& which I, as conscientiously & earnestly, was entirely opposed to. But I have lately come as con-scientiously to your side, & I rejoice that we are all now together—" I answered merely by expressing my gratification at his & the general present position, & so we parted.

April 27. No telegrams or other news today, except by private and newspaper reports confirming what had been heard more generally before. The foreign U.S. troops already in Washington certainly 6000, & otherwise stated as in all (including the District troops) 15,000. But the city & district companies not deemed loyal or reliable. The public buildings all mined, & gunpowder placed, to be blown up if a retreat is necessary. Such preparations show that the authorities expect to retreat. The swinish northern & western volunteers quartered in the superb apartments of the Capitol, & cooking in the committee rooms, so gorgeously & foolishly deco-rated. The occupants will leave their quarters in fine condition, even if they should not be destroyed by the explosion of the mines. Reinforcements from the North are arriving daily—& it is there understood that there will be 100,000 soldiers concentrated [1332] at Washington. The latter reports I heard from Judge Rose, who left Washington two days ago. . . . Vice President Stephens left for Montgomery last night. Mr. [William] Boulware arrived here two days ago.[3] Had a long talk with him this afternoon. From him (& his

---

[3] Although the diarist's handwriting normally is not difficult to decipher, the letters *n* and *r* are almost indistinguishable and occasionally present problems. In the case of proper names whose identities are unknown to the editor, it has been necessary to hazard educated guesses. Thus, this individual, who was one of Ruffin's most intimate friends, was identified as William Boulwa*n*e throughout the first

literary taste is of high order,) & also from another gentleman today, I heard voluntary & uncalled-for expressions highly laudatory of my "Anticipations of the Future"—which nourished the hope that the work is not so entirely unnoticed & un-cared for, as had seemed to be.—Called on Mr. Tyler at his apartment & conversed with him for an hour.—Today gave to the "Dispatch" a short piece written yesterday on the 50,000 old muskets held & as useless by the state government. Yesterday arrived from Maryland, as agent of the revolutionary party, Col. F[rancis] J. Thomas, one of the active leaders, & a very intelligent man.[4] He was introduced to me by J[oseph] R. Anderson, & the object of his mission (to obtain arms) was stated to me. I urged him to get as many as could be of these old flint-lock muskets, & he afterwards told me today that he had obtained 6000 of them, & 49 heavy cannon from the state authorities.

April 28. (Sunday.) This morning Col. Thomas sought me, & we again conversed on his business & the policy for Md. He showed to me his credentials, & a letter in them by him to the Governor of N.C., to whom (as being personally acquainted with him) he asked me to write myself, in support of his request for arms, & to enclose his letter. This I did. Subsequently, he wrote in my room a similar letter to the Governor of S.C. & requested me to send it through Gen. Bonham. This I did also, bringing Gen. Bonham to its earnest support. Afterwards, I brought him & Col. Thomas together. [1333] . . . Two naval U.S. officers, in service at the Portsmouth Navy Yard, were left & taken prisoners, immediately after the affair there. They were brought to Richmond, entertained for some days, (on their parole,) at the Governor's house & table, & then discharged. Since, Gen. [Williams S.] Harney, on his way from St. Louis to Washington, by Rail-road, was arrested at Harper's Ferry, & also sent here—& subsequently was also set at liberty. While, on our side, this extraordinary indulgence is exhibited, southern U.S. officers, at the North, for merely offering to resign, & refusing to

volume of the diary. A recent perusal of the *Virginia Historical Index* has revealed that his name was really William Boulware, and he will be so identified in this volume. The editor regrets the error.

Boulware, whose pretentious residence, Traveller's Rest, was situated in King and Queen County about twenty-five miles from Marlbourne, was dubbed "Lord Boulware" because of his courtly manner. During the administration of President Polk he served as minister plenipotentiary to the Court of Naples. Letter from Sterling P. Anderson, Jr., September 4, 1974.

[4] On May 17, 1861, Colonel Thomas formally assumed command of all Maryland volunteers then in the service of Virginia.

serve against their southern countrymen & their states, are treated as criminals, imprisoned to be tried for "seditious language," & are to be tried by courts-martial. Private citizens, southerners & secessionists, at the North, have latterly been in danger of assassination by mob violence, & could only escape home by using scenery & disguise. Since the taking of Fort Sumter, & the secession of Va, the whole northern mind has been exasperated against the South—& the previous opposition to the administration, & to the dominant abolition faction, has been [1334] intimidated into acquiescence, or more generally has united in the violent policy of the abolition party. There now prevails throughout all the northern & northwestern states one universal howl for vengeance on the South, & for the most energetic policy of invasion & subjugation—& the leading paper, the N.Y. Tribune, openly advocates, after the conquest of Md. & Va., the sharing out the lands to the victorious northern soldiers.—Saw Capt. [John D.] Imboden, just from Harper's Ferry, & heard from him that the troops of that place were well prepared for any attack.[5] I fear it is not so here, or with the corps near Alexandria. The latter commanded by Ph[ilip] St. G[eorge] Cocke, lately made a general, & whose only military experience was of a short time as a West Point cadet, & lieutenant of U.S. army, for a short time afterwards. I fear that he is one of the sundry incompetents who have been put in high offices by the governor. [1335]

April 29. The Convention today elected 5 representatives from Va to the Congress of C.S. The selection is worse than I could have conceived possible, even by this body, with its submission proclivity. R. M. T. Hunter is the most able & least objectionable—but there are a dozen men in the state, at least, preferable to him. The others are W. C. Rives, Judge John Brockenbrough, W[aller R.] Staples,[6] &———Camden. The last I had never happened to hear of before.[7] . . .

---

[5] A lawyer and state legislator in civilian life, John Daniel Imboden (1823–95) commanded the Staunton Artillery when Harpers Ferry was occupied. He later saw extensive service in western Virginia, rising to the rank of brigadier general before being incapacitated by typhoid fever in the fall of 1864.

[6] Following his service in the Provisional Confederate Congress, Waller Redd Staples (1826–97) represented his state in the Confederate House of Representatives, 1862–65. Later, after Virginia was redeemed from the Radicals, Staples sat for twelve years on the Virginia Supreme Court of Appeals.

[7] The editor is as bewildered as Ruffin. No Camden is listed as a Virginia representative to either the Provisional Confederate Congress or the First and Second Confederate congresses.

April 30. Received a copy, completed, of my printed "Sketches of N.C. &c." from Raleigh,[8] & proceeded to read them over, to make out a list of the more important errors of the press, to be printed in an additional leaf. Also, began the Table of Contents, to be appended. The work makes an 8vo volume of about 290 pages. The Governor of N.Ca. will order it to be bound, for sale (for the state) & also gratuitous distribution of many copies.—This afternoon, Col. [Joseph B.] Kershaw & his staff, with 280 more troops from S.C. arrived.—The Md. legislature assembled on yesterday. I fear there is no prospect of an early act of secession—or of the government sustaining the recent action of the people of Md. If not, & Md. does not invite the aid of the Confederate States, our troops cannot be sent into Md., & then nothing will be done, & that state will, for the time, remain submissive to the North.—Dr. Garnett, a resident of Washington, left there this morning, & arrived here this afternoon. He is a very intelligent man, son-in-law of Gov. Wise. He gave me much information about Washington, & the northern troops there. He says, (as had appeared from the newspapers,) that the northern people are now united to a man against the South, & impelled by a fanatical spirit [1337] & thirst for vengeance. He thinks that the feeling has been produced by the attack upon & capture of Fort Sumter, the secession of Va, & exasperated still more by the threatened danger of Washington city. He represents some thousands of the northern volunteers in Washington as first-rate troops, & armed in the best manner—especially 1700 men from Rhode Island, whose numbers are to be increased to 3000. He thinks that Md. will not dare to secede—that the military preparations & strength of the northern government are far better than ours in Va. This may be—but still I do not think that, with this superiority, that government will dare to begin offensive operations, or to invade Va. Most of the volunteer troops there, from abroad, came to defend the capital of the U.S. but will not choose, & cannot be legally compelled, to invade Va, or even Md. The militia of the District are not relied upon, & half of them, or more, are better affected towards the South, than to the North, or to the Lincoln government. There were supposed to be 16,000 regulars & volunteers in service there, & the number rapidly increasing every day, by reinforcements from the North, coming by the rail-road from Annapolis.

---

[8] See Volume I, 471, 473, 474.

May 1. . . . Afternoon, the Hon. J[ames] M. Mason arrived, from Fredericktown, Md., where the legislature had lately assembled. The indications presented by the late newspapers are that Md. is overawed by the U.S. power, & is about to back down from the bold attitude lately assumed by the people of [1338] Baltimore & generally, & that the legislature & people will submit to the Northern tyranny. On my expressing this opinion to Mr. Mason, he opposed it entirely, stating his belief that both the legislature & people of Md were ready & would resist, & effect what would be equivalent to secession—but that it could not be done, in the weak, unarmed, & exposed condition of the people, in a formal & regular manner. He supposed that the legislature will appoint a "Committee of Public Safety," invested with abundant funds & undefined (ie. dictatorial) powers. I wish he may be right, but I fear that he is much too sanguine. Mr. M., I believe, was sent to Md. by the government of Va. on a secret mission—& he, with Ex-Gov. [Thomas G.] Pratt of Md, it is believed are now here seeking to obtain support for the secession party of Md. Md. must invite aid of soldiers before any can be sent to her territory by other states—& that has not yet been done. And unless there is an army, capable of maintaining its ground, it would be useless to send many arms, as they would probably be captured by the enemy.—More S.C. & Ga. & Va. volunteers have arrived & are coming here every day. J. M. McCue, of Augusta, arrived this evening from Washington, & reports a long conversation with Gen. Scott, in which the latter avowed the intention of the U.S. government to recapture Harper's Ferry, at any cost—& Forts Sumter & Moultrie, & every other stronghold & position of which the govt. had been dispossessed by the southern states.

May 2. . . . I received a letter from Gov. Ellis (by his secretary,) in answer to my last, stating that he had sent 500 first-rate muskets for the use of Md., & would be willing to send more, but did not know to whom to send them. Soon after, Major Davidson, of N.C., accosted me & requested a private conference & my advice. He told me that he was the agent of Gov. Ellis, & had brought on to R[ichmon]d 5000 muskets for Va. & 500 (those referred to by Gov. Ellis, as it seems,) for Md. But Major D., learning from the newspapers the apparent disposition of Md to submit, & there being now no party in arms opposing the northern domination, was doubtful whether to forward the muskets, & on that head desired my opinion

[15]

& advice. I advised him to retain them here for the present, & not to forward them, unless affairs were in more encouraging condition. This course he determined to take.—Afternoon, by previous arrangement, I went with Col. Kershaw & a number of other officers of S.C. to see the Tredegar iron works of Messrs. Joseph R. Anderson & Co. All of us were much gratified & astonished with the extent of the operations. There are 900 workmen employed, with water-power for every movement & labor to which it can be applied. Except some small proportion of the hands engaged in working one rolling mill, & making spikes & "chairs" for laying rail-road tracks, all of this vast force is now occupied in making cannon, mortars, balls & shells &c. for the Confederate States, or some of the several seceded states. While we were there, we saw the casting of a cannon to carry [1340] a ball of 130 lbs. weight. It is usual, at the casting, to give a name to each cannon—& this one was named the "Palmetto." Many such have lately been cast for the C.S., some of which we saw undergoing the subsequent finishing process of boring, outside smoothing & polishing &c. All of us, as must all who see this great work-shop, came away with greatly enlarged appreciation of the military resources of these southern states, in having this establishment to call upon.—Was introduced to Judge Wm. M. Cooke of Missouri, a young & very intelligent man. Had a long conversation with him on the political condition of Missouri. He is (as he told me) an agent sent to procure arms & aid. He says that the Governor ([Claiborne F.] Jackson) is a zealous & devoted secessionist, & a man of strong will, ability & much influence. The legislature & people also for secession by decided majorities. The city of St. Louis only is abolitionized in sentiment. Missouri, being surrounded on more than three-fourths of its frontier lines by abolition & hostile states, &, by the rail-roads, greatly exposed to the invasion of sundry . . . others, may expect immediate invasion & bloody war, if declaring for secession. There are no public arms whatever. It is necessary to have the people better prepared for defence before incurring these impending & great dangers, which will immediately succeed the passage of an act of secession.—Mr. James M. Mason came with me (on my previous invitation) to my room, & we had a long confidential conversation on the condition of Md. I first told him of Col. Thomas' mission, of whom he knew nothing. Then read to him Gov. Ellis' letter to me, & told him of the detention of the muskets. Mr. Mason has no official mission either to [1341] or from Md. But has been observing affairs there, & acting to encourage the secession movement, by his advice & influence. He told me that the traitor governor, [Thomas H.] Hicks, devoted to the northern power, was forced to call the legislature together, (which he had long & obstinately resisted,) only by his fears, & upon threats made to his face by prominent citizens, that they would put him to instant death if he did not immediately perform this duty—& that it was almost literally, as well as figuratively true, that he signed the proclamation to summon the extra session of the legislature under the muzzles of loaded pistols. Mr. M. is sure that both houses of the legislature & a decided majority of the people are for immediate secession.[9] But the state has no arms, & almost no military organization—& by its geographical position, is at the mercy of the Northern power, & the large army (now 27,000) already in Washington. Mr. M. had stated to leading members of the legislature (in Fredericktown) & of the secession party, that it was impossible for other states to send arms or other aid to Md., until the government & legal authority of Md. asked for them. Therefore, as well as for my other reasons, (the present danger of arms so sent being captured by the enemy,) he approved of my advice to detain the 500 muskets sent from N.C. . . . A telegram today announced that the legislature of Tennessee had passed the act of secession—subject, it is inferred, as in Va. to the future ratification by the people, of which there is no question. If this is true, there are now 9 seceded states—& N.Ca. may be counted as the tenth, for the state is virtually in the C.S., wanting merely the forms of law.—The Northern Government some time ago *proclaimed* the blockade of the ports of all the seceded states, & very lately added those of Va & N.C. But the actual blockade, by armed ships, has not been yet commenced anywhere, except for Va, which is now strictly blockaded—& the passage of all the lower rivers guarded & prevented. All of our transportation by water, near the Chesapeake, & for Norfolk, is entirely stopped.

May 3. Saw in the Charleston Mercury of 1st. a very complimentary notice of the reception in Charleston of the Palmetto Guard, when returned from service on Morris Island. In the list there published . . . of the members of the company who were engaged in

---

[9] Mason's assessment was a bit optimistic. Just three days before, on April 29, the Maryland House of Delegates had voted against secession by a margin of fifty-three to thirteen.

the seige [*sic*] & battle of Fort Sumter through the 12th & 13th ult. I am proud to see my name published as one of the privates of the company. I have been expecting the arrival of the company here would have been some days back, & my stay has been in part extended to meet them here. But he longer delay I fear may continue until after I shall have gone home. Took a John Brown pike (labelled,) which has been left for 9 months in the State Library, for exhibition, & arranged for it to be presented, from me, to the Palmetto Guard. [1343] . . . Afternoon, I went to the camp of the South Carolina troops, & saw their evening parade, & all of my acquaintances there, including Col. [Maxcy] Gregg, & Lieut. Col. Hamilton. Mr. [Leonidas W.] Spratt also, who arrived this morning. Though the weather was cloudy & disagreeably cold, sundry ladies were on the ground. Mrs. Wm. Rutherford & her sister Miss Sherrard were there, & seemed delighted to meet me. Mrs. R. told me that she wept (for joy or some other emotion,) when she read that I had fired the first gun in the battle of Fort Sumter. And three different gentlemen have before told me of the like effect so produced on their wives, [1344] all of whom were entire strangers to me, & whom I had never even seen.—Sought a conversation with Judge John Brockenbrough, one of the delegates to the Congress of the C.S., & urged on him several matters of policy for that body. These were the immediate authorizing of privateers—low duties on European goods, as the essential part of a war of tariffs on the North—& discriminating against the North, as a war or hostile measure—with some other minor points. He agreed with me in all my views—but requested me to write notes of my positions, & the reasons for them—which I did afterwards, & directed to him.—Received some days ago a letter from . . . Julian . . . . It contained the agreeable news of Lotty's having had another son, who is named Edmund Sumter. . . . Nothing new—but reports continue to confirm the increasing strength of the enemy in Washington, the seeming submission of Maryland, & the very exposed condition of Va, & most dangerously, because of the inducements for attacking Norfolk & the Navy Yard, & Harper's Ferry & the armory there. The northern people & their newspapers, even those previously advocating the South, now unite in urging war upon us, & extreme measures for coercion. I annex a sample from Harper's Weekly Journal.[10] Doubtless, if inclined, the North can do us great damage.

---

[10] After urging a vigorous prosecution of the war, *Harper's* predicted that "the practical effect" of such a policy "must be to liberate the slaves."

But no benefit to the North will be gained by it, even if there should be no retaliation. And the game will soon be found a very costly & losing one, independent of our having & using the power to retaliate, & to inflict equal injuries. [1345]

May 4. Left Richmond early, by the steamer. . . . Reached Coggin's Point & landed at 11 A.M. . . . Found all the family well—& my new daughter-in-law Jane seemingly at ease & happy in her new home and position. I felt greatly rejoiced to meet with her here, & as my son's wife. She & Nanny seem to be drawing towards each other in kindness & regard, & getting on as well in their new connection, which was awkward & threatening of evil to the one, & especially painful to the other. I do not doubt that each of them will strive to do her duty to the other—& if so designing & acting, they must soon learn to love each other. Mrs. Lorraine told me that every thing had gone on well between them, & in Jane's new position from the time of her reaching her new home.—[1346] When I arrived, Edmund was absent at the now weekly muster & drill of his troop of cavalry. After 3 P.M. he returned, with the report that the troop had been ordered to meet again at 5 P.M. at Garysville, thence to march to Hoods, where some cannon have been placed to mount a battery which has been ordered to be constructed there. A foolish & false report, as I am sure, of a northern armed steamer being on its passage up the river, to spike & destroy these cannon, caused the superior officer thus to call out the cavalry. . . . Found here a letter to me from Mrs. [Maria R.] Roper, written at my request, & giving an account of the incidents which fell under her personal observation in Charleston during the cannonade of Fort Sumter. This is a very interesting letter, which I value highly.—After tea, as the best mode of giving the ladies an [1347] account of the affairs & battle of Fort Sumter, I read to them the portion of my journal including these incidents, until bed-time.—There was today lying off this Point, a northern ship, with a crew of 18 northern negroes (under white officers,) which some weeks ago had been captured at City Point, without legal authority, the vessel held, & the negro crew imprisoned. Lately the governor has ordered the release of this ship, & sundry other northern vessels which had been in like unauthorized manner captured in our rivers—& permitted for this ship, its lading (of tobacco) to be completed for the North. And this after our (and other southern) ships & steamers have been captured & retained by the northern government, & when our lower tide waters are strictly blockaded, & Norfolk threatened by the northern

[19]

ships of war, & the army in Fortress Monroe! I cannot conceive an excuse for this extent of forbearance.—It was one of my reasons for leaving Richmond, that I was so fretted & disgusted with the appointments of officials, & with the inactivity & wrong doings of high public functionaries. I could not (& never can) bridle my tongue, & by speaking of persons as I deemed they deserved, & my free censures & opinions reaching their ears, I would be again building up for myself the load of disfavor & odium which I had before borne, & which my recent celebrity, & general applause, have served but partially to hide. If I live a year, & in society, I shall lose all my present popularity. I feel, in sincerity & earnestness, that I have now lived long enough—& for my own future place in the opinion & regard of my countrymen, it will be best for me to die very soon. But though desirous, for the reason [1348] stated, to get into private life, & seclusion, at home, I cannot now remain there but a short time. I must get back to Richmond to meet & welcome my comrades of the Palmetto Guard, when they shall arrive, & then remain a few days.

May 5. Sunday. Mr. Allen, the overseer, who is one of the troop, & had gone in it to Hoods, returned on leave this morning, & reported (what I was sure of from the first,) that the foolish ground of the call was false. Still, proper military duty & guard were observed, & the troop remained to guard the cannon from attack. . . . We all went to church. A very small congregation—as almost every man in the neighborhood, though not in the troop, had gone today to Hoods to see & hear. Before we had left the church after the services, Mr. R. F. Graves rode up, & announced that the cavalry had been relieved by the arrival of an infantry company, & discharged, & the men had returned to their homes. I went home to dine with Julian. Found Lotty doing well, & her infant son, (born April 19th.) a fine looking boy, & with no indication of ill health, except crying a great deal. . . . Returned at night to Beechwood . . . . Earthworks are to be erected at Hoods, to be mounted with 7–32 pound cannon, brought there from the Navy Yard. Negroes from the neighboring farms had begun to assemble there, & the work was begun this day. This would be very well, except that the work is under the direction of Capt. H. H. Cocke, who is incompetent & untrustworthy in other respects—though fortunately a superior in command arrived there with the relief company.

May 6. . . . The mail brought many papers, including 4 or 5 Nos.

of N.Y. Herald. While I was in Richmond, one mail only from north of Baltimore came through, which brought an accumulation of the previously delayed papers—of which, we received our share today. No news of any importance. Troops still moving to Va. from the more southern states, & to exposed points from other parts of Va.; & northern reinforcements coming on to Washington. I trust that Norfolk (for the Navy Yard) & Harper's Ferry, (for the armory) & Richmond, for the Tredegar cannon foundry, which were especial objects, are secured from danger of sudden attack. And I have no fears for the invasion of other places. I think that our policy is to threaten Washington, by having troops which might be concentrated there within a few hours, but not to attack the city. Fearing such attack, the Lincoln administration will not dare to [1350] leave Washington exposed, by withdrawing a large portion of the garrison to invade Va. I think we cannot employ the 30,000 U.S. soldiers now there, or 40,000 should they be so increased, better than by keeping them idle, & to be fed & supported at vast expense in Washington, & on the defensive. If other armies are raised, & (according to the programme of designed operations announced by Gen. Scott,) shall attack every fort taken from the U.S. & now garrisoned by C.S. troops, that will be for us the best & most advantageous mode of the war being conducted by our enemy. For it will require thrice as many men, & money, & loss of life, to attack fortified places as to defend them.

May 8. The newspapers report continued accessions of troops to Washington—& also, from the South to Va. A regiment from Louisiana has reached Richmond. The worst of the increasing military force at Washington is that the power of the North is more & more enchaining Md. . . . The Senate of Md. has under consideration a bill to establish a Committee of Public Safety. This is what I heard, from Mr. Mason, was designed & expected to be carried through. If effected, the next thing will be a request of Md. for military assistance, & the entrance on her territory of Southern troops. I am earnestly & impatiently anxious for such results. . . . When in Richmond, I read "The Sable Cloud," a new book on slavery, by the Rev. Nehemiah Adams.[11] It is a good argument [1352] in defence of

---

[11] Pastor of the Union Congregational Church in Boston, Reverend Adams had earlier provoked the wrath of abolitionists by publishing a mild, conciliatory work entitled *A South-Side View of Slavery* following a brief visit to the South in 1854. So vehement was the reaction of the northern press that Adams felt compelled to respond to these attacks by penning *The Sable Cloud*, which appeared in 1861.

the institution of slavery in the South, if addressed to Northern haters of the institution & of the South. But I found nothing to instruct me, & but little of interest or amusement. The next book I began there, & finished reading today, is also a new publication, & on a kindred subject—"Soulouque & his empire." It is an amusing sketch of the beginning & progress of the negro people & government of Hayti, & especially of the late despotic ruler, Soulouque.[12] But the manner of treatment is too slight, & unfinished, to impart full information.

May 9. Received a letter from Mildred. She is much alarmed at the prospect of war, & the actual effects of predatory or other invasion of us. We, who are among the most exposed to predatory incursions, are comparatively careless, & not at all alarmed—except as to the already begun & expected harassing calls into temporary service, & without any proper causes, of the volunteer companies, to the new fort at Hoods, or elsewhere. This day, the company to which Edmund's Evelynton overseer belongs, was called to meet, for service, at Charles City C.H. & so he is left there without an overseer—though, to guard against this, he had previously offered in vain $20 a month, extra, for a substitute for his overseer. While he went there, to make some arrangement, an order arrived here for him to detach a piquet guard of 24 troopers, to be stationed at the mill on Ward's Creek—where they will be as like to see any invading force as if stationed in Blackwater swamp. For this, Edmund issued [1353] orders as soon as he returned.—A long letter from my friend Willoughby Newton, on present affairs. I am glad to learn from it that his countymen have come to their senses, & to a just appreciation of his opinions & merits, so as to request of him, by unanimous vote, to be a candidate & to serve them in the next legislature. Recently, they rejected him for a seat in the Convention, electing in preference to him, & by large majority, a submissionist named Critcher, possessing not one-tenth of Newton's ability or moral worth.—It is reported from Montgomery that the Congress of C.S. have declared war against the U.S., but if so, it has not been officially made known.[13] No other war or political

[12] Emperor of Haiti from 1847 to 1859, Faustin Soulouque proved to be one of the worst of a long line of political incompetents and tyrants to whom the unfortunate people of that island state have been subjected during the last two centuries.

[13] The report was correct. On May 6 President Davis signed a bill, enacted three days earlier by the Provisional Congress, which recognized the existence of a state of war between the United States and the Confederate States of America.

news—except that new supplies of troops from the North continue to move on for Washington, & from the South to Virginia. Of the latter, there have arrived troops not only from Ga. & S.C. but since from Ky (400 individuals, without authority or arms) & organized corps from Ala, La, & Ten. . . . I have before inserted extracts from northern papers showing the general disposition & high authority for the war on the South being made one of brigandage & of utmost destruction & ferocity. But all threats & intimations fall short of what is indicated & indirectly recommended in the following quotation, which has been published in most of the southern newspapers:—"*Hellish Suggestion.* The Westchester Democrat, (of Pa.) reminds the Pennsylvania volunteers that Baltimore 'has always been celebrated for the beauty of its women' and that 'the fair were ever the reward of the brave,' and 'that [1354] *Beauty & Booty* was the watchword a[t] New Orleans.'" This suggestion was simultaneous with the declaration of the Washington authorities to reopen & force the way for the passage of troops through Baltimore, at all hazards and consequences.

May 10. Since the troops in service in Va. have been so greatly increased, I am much better satisfied with the delay of aggressive action on our part than when our numbers were much smaller & the organization far less perfect. Now the only three very important places in Va, Harper's Ferry, Richmond, & Norfolk with the Navy Yard, are well garrisoned. So many troops (probably 20,000, which in 24 hours may be increased largely) are within striking distance of Washington, & so threatening an attack there (which ought to be continually threatened, but never made,) that the enemy will not dare to diminish the garrison, whether of 30,000; or 40,000, to invade Va anywhere. If we are safe in this respect, as I now believe, we may well afford to wait. For by delay our army & its discipline will be improved, & the enemy's army in Washington more & more demoralized, & rendered more hateful, by its brigandage & atrocities, to the so far submissive population. The scarcity of provisions must soon be great in Washington—& the expense of maintaining troops there much greater than to the C.S. in Va. If the [1355] licentious conduct & atrocious excesses of some corps of the northern volunteers (from New York, & other great cities,) continue unchecked by the authorities, it must produce deadly hatred, & a dangerous desire for vengeance, even among the previous submissionists of Washington. Perhaps these excesses may be put down by

[23]

a repetition of the Sicilian Vespers.[14] The unrestrained pillage of the shops & propertyholders by the volunteers is the ordinary & regular procedure—& the exercise seems to be considered by the actors, as a series of pleasant jokes, more fitted to excite laughter than indignation. But far worse atrocities have been committed. Every inhabitant suspected of holding opinions favorable to the cause of the South, or of secession, is in danger of personal injury if not of assassination. Many have been driven away from their families or business or property—& all such have fled who could get away without utter ruin. One man was called out of his bed & shot. It is privately reported that rapes have been added to murder & general pillage. Yet even all this is scarcely so abominable as is the indulgent & almost approving manner in which these violators of law, decency, & military discipline, are spoken of by the principal journal of the abolition party—as seen in an appended article.[15] [1356] So far I have referred only to defensive measures. But, if Md. will have the strength & resolution to declare for the South, & invite Va. & the C.S. to aid her with troops, we can, with command of Harper's Ferry, & the rail-road thence to (or near) Baltimore, send enough troops to free Md, within a few days—or still sooner to retake the now occupied lines of rail-roads, & enclose Washington & its garrison, except as to the passage of the Potomac—which could soon after be closed, by earthwork batteries, well defended from assault. Such, taken altogether, it seems to me ought to be our war policy. And as everything now seems to be in proper aid of its execution, I trust that such is the policy designed by our military authorities.—The few items of news from Md. today state facts which indicate conflicting views of policy. At Fredericktown, the legislature, in preliminary secret meetings, & in secret legal session, are still considering the instituting the Committee of Public Safety, which is the measure designed for secession & resistance. On the other hand, there are strong popular remonstrances against the enactment—& Baltimore has actually disarmed nearly all of its before armed volunteers, & a leading paper (the Balt. American) advocates the delivery of all the state arms to the Washington government, including [1357] 2000 muskets furnished to Md by

---

[14] The reference is to a massacre of the French in Sicily in 1282 by which the Sicilians ejected their Angevin ruler, Charles I, and ended French domination.

[15] Reference is to an item in the New York *Tribune* recounting the irregular activities in Washington of the New York Fire Zouaves, commanded by Colonel Elmer E. Ellsworth.

Va.! I am feverishly anxious for the decision of Md. for resistance, & the immediate aid to her, on her own soil, by troops & arms from Va. & the C.S. . . .

May 11. Attended, with Jane & Nanny, the muster & drill parade of the troop at Garysville. Most of the ladies of the neighborhood there. It is a very good troop. Some fifty of the troop, & visitors, dined at Garysville. I, as well as all the ladies, returned home to dinner.—The declaration of war by the Congress of the Confederate States, made before in secret session, has been made public. This is very proper, & much needed. It will serve to remove all question as to our relations with the North. Before, while we were subject to all the penalties of a state of war, we did not avail ourselves of the accompanying benefits or rights. I trust that no longer will our authorities discharge northern vessels which have been captured, prisoners who had been taken, & even strongly suspected or convicted spies & emissaries of the enemy—or permit all northerners freely to pass through, or sojourn in the seceded states, unless they so acted as to induce suspicions of their hostile & criminal action, & then merely to compel their departure, without punishment.—The guns have been mounted at Fort Powhatan,[16] behind earthworks (*faced* [1358] with wood!) so foolishly constructed that they will be as dangerous to their defenders as to the assailants. To protect these works & the cannon, there are several volunteer companies encamped there, (one from this county,) & a piquet of our cavalry, of 24, to be kept stationed at Ward's creek, near Brandon Church, for no ostensible purpose whatever. . . .

May 13. According to our arrangement made yesterday, Col. Peterson & Mr. Baylor came to Beechwood before breakfast—& immediately after, I set out with them to visit the military [1359] post at Fort Powhatan, & to examine the new works constructed. We found there Capt. Pegram,[17] with whom I was acquainted, & I

---

[16] A new installation at Hoods on James River. On April 29, 1861, Major General Robert E. Lee directed Colonel Andrew Talcott of the engineer corps to select two points on the James River which, "in your judgment, should be fortified, in order to prevent the ascent of the river by the enemy." Fort Powhatan was constructed just below the confluence of the Appomattox River with the James and was upstream from the other site designated by Talcott. *War of the Rebellion: A Compilation of the Official Records of the Union and Confederate Armies* (Washington, 1880–1901), Vol. II, 788–89. Hereinafter cited as *Official Records.* All references are to Series I unless otherwise indicated.

[17] Apparently William Johnson Pegram (1841–65), younger brother of General John Pegram, and a noted artillerist who served with distinction in all the major

was introduced to Major Wilson, commanding officer, & several others. There are 7 cannon, 32 pounders, mounted, & all well as to them. But the earth & wood-work defences are even worse than I had anticipated from previous report. The bank or wall, of sand, is faced, both in front & rear, & on the sides of the embrasures, with upright piles of sapling pine, varying in size from 6 inches in diameter to 3, or less—driven into the earth by mauls, & of course very insufficiently buried. The sand in bags, which ought to have been made to construct the upright sides of the embrasures, & the front face of the embankment, (where the sand alone would not have served better,) have indeed been used—but placed *inside* of the surrounding wood piling. These piles are exposed to enemy's balls not only in front, & on all the sides of the embrasures, but even in the rear, by the tops there rising above the sand, & so being exposed to be struck by balls passing over the top of the sand. A cannon ball striking these piles, anywhere, would knock many of them out of the ground, & by the splinters, as well as the whole piles, thrown among the men working the guns, kill or wound many more than would the balls alone. Capt. Pegram told me that if he had to fight with these guns, he would prefer, even for the greater safety of his men, that all the defenses should be cleared away, & the guns be worked & fired from the open & entirely exposed platform. Capt. Cocke, incompetent, worthless for command as he is, & withal the most abject of submissionists & sycophants to northern [1360] power, (up to Apr. 11th) has been trusted with the charge of the construction of defences on all James river—& to his ignorance, or his neglect, or both, is owing this miserable job. And several companies are here, & the force is to be increased, to guard this battery, which is worse than nothing for defence, if vigorously attacked by a naval force. We returned to Beechwood to dinner . . . . The mail brought many papers, but little news. Confirmation of the declaration of (existing) war by the C.S. against the U.S.—excepting therefrom all the slave-states not yet seceded—& the enactment of issuing commissions to privateers, after 30 days' notice. I rejoice at the beginning of this important means of defence, especially in our peculiar circumstances, of having almost no ships, or ocean commerce. Maryland seems still more crushed & submissive. Some troops have passed through Baltimore, on the route from the North

eastern campaigns until he was mortally wounded at Five Forks, just a week before Lee's surrender.

to Washington, without any opposition, or even indication of displeasure, of the residents. The Lincoln government have possession of the Railroad from Baltimore to the Relay House, & have a strong force at the latter station. . . . Reinforcements continue to be poured into Washington, & additional southern volunteers into Virginia. Both sides are earnestly preparing for either attack or defence—& both seem desirous to avoid beginning by attack. The Palmetto Guard have arrived in R[ichmon]d—which I am glad of, as I had arranged with Nanny to go there tomorrow.—Gen. Beauregard's full official reports of the battle of Fort Sumter in today's paper. In bestowing commendations on the conduct of various officers, he brings in my name, (the only private mentioned except Wm. G. Young, also of the Palmettoes, who accompanied Col. [Louis T.] Wigfall in the small boat to the fort, when the flag had been shot down—) in a manner more complimentary, than exactly descriptive. He says—"The venerable & gallant Edmund Ruffin, of Virginia, was at the Iron Battery, & fired many guns, undergoing every fatigue & sharing the hardships at the Battery with the youngest of the Palmettos."

May 14. At 11 A.M. Nanny & I left home, in the boat, for Maycox & took the steamer for Rd. at 1 P.M. . . . On arriving at Rd . . . I called on the Governor, who was not in, to remonstrate against the performance, & also the further employment of Capt. Cocke. Then I went to see the Council of State (then in session) but could not have a hearing. Col. [Francis H.] Smith, however, on my naming my business, said it lay within the powers & duties of Gen. Lee. To him, I proceeded—accompanied by Wm. B. Harrison of Prince George, to introduce me, & who also concurred in my general views & positions. After some conversation, Gen. Lee suggested the propriety of having something in writing, as grounds for him to order the examination which I urged. I withdrew to prepare this, & soon wrote a short statement, & request for the superseding of Capt. Cocke, which Mr. H. united with me in signing, & which I delivered at Gen. Lee's office myself, so that he may have time to send some qualified examiner to the fort by the steamer going tomorrow. . . .

May 15. Had a conversation with Lieut. Gov. [Robert L.] Montague, who is a new member of the State Council, in which I set forth some of the greatest & most inexcusable delinquencies of the Governor—the attempt to sacrifice (by selling at $1.50 for each) the old flint muskets of the state—60,000—[1363] the omission to use them, when so much needed—the failure to arm steamers to protect our tide-water rivers—& the appointment of incapable & untrustworthy submissionists to important military or naval offices or commands—Gov. Ellis of N.C. had been here lately, to confer with our authorities, & went away early this morning, &, as is reported, utterly disgusted with Governor Letcher.—This afternoon, walked from Mr. Lorraine's with my three granddaughters & Alice Lorraine to the camp of the S.Ca. brigade, & witnessed the evening dress parade of both regiments.[18] I also saw the Palmetto Guard, the members of which company received me with great attention & even enthusiasm. Many of the men, both officers & privates, introduced to the girls, who of course were delighted to receive their attentions. After tea, I went to a meeting of Baltimoreans & Washingtonians, who to the number of nearly 200, are exiles & recently escaped from their former homes. Those from Baltimore were either concerned in the late fight with the Massachusetts troops passing through, or otherwise exposed to danger for their known secession views. Those from Washington had fled thence because of the tyranny of the ruling authorities, & the danger impending over all secessionists. The object was to organize a corps of volunteers in the service of Va, &, if possible, in direct aid of Maryland. Some jarring interests & opinions prevented the full execution of the design—but no doubt it will soon be effected. . . .

May 16. The news from England is that a minister has stated in parliament that, in reference to our sending out privateers, [1364] the Confederate states will be considered a "belligerent power." This seems equivalent to an acknowledgment of our independence. Also, it was stated that a British squadron would be sent to our coast to take care of British commerce. This also is in our favor.—Md. is trodden under foot by Lincoln's government, & made to "drink the cup of humiliation to the dregs." Baltimore is occupied by northern troops—& the very Massachusetts regiment which was attacked there by the residents with stones, has been sent back to be the garrison. All the arms have been delivered to the Washington government, including 2000 muskets sent by Va.—A

---

[18] The three granddaughters referred to were Nanny, aged twenty; Sue, aged fifteen; and Mary, aged thirteen—all children of Edmund Ruffin, Jr. Sue and Mary boarded at Mr. Lorraine's while attending school in Richmond, and Nanny stayed there when she accompanied the diarist to the capital city.

convention of traitors, led by [John S.] Carlile & two other members of the Va. Convention, has been held at Wheeling, & has adjourned.[19] It resolved for the separation of north-western Va. from the remainder of the state, & the adhesion of the fragment to the northern states.—The legislature of Md. has adjourned without doing anything.—There is an impression generally prevailing, & strengthened by approaches of U.S. troops, that Va is soon to be invaded, & especially a strong attack to be made to possess & hold Harper's Ferry. There are there some 7000 troops, under a good commander, Col. [Thomas J.] Jackson. Our governor is a great clog, & his inaction or wrong action is as bad in effect as if it was instigated by treason. I sent a telegram to President Davis urging him, for the salvation of our cause, to come immediately & assume the military command. But I cannot expect any effect from my urging, when so many of greater influence have urged the same. . . . I had been introduced to, & had some conversation with many of the refugees from Baltimore. I had at first inferred that they were of the "Roughs," that lawless, & desperate & numerous class which formerly held Baltimore in subjection, & who happened on the recent occasion to fight on the right side. But I was agreeably surprised to find the whole number whom I saw in their meeting last night, apparently respectable men, & most of them worthy & intelligent gentlemen. Some have had to flee, leaving their families, & nearly all have left property and business at the disposition of the military & abolition & mob despotism which now rules in & oppresses Baltimore & Washington. Two military companies have been nearly made up of these exiles here, & there is one other already in service at Harper's Ferry. I earnestly wish that all were organized, & at Harper's Ferry, & occupying the Maryland side. They would be armed & supported by the force on this side of the river, & make part of it—& form a nucleus to which all other like persons in Maryland might collect, & find means & support for their resistance. . . .

May 17. One of the benefits to the South which the recent general change of opinion of the before moderate or apparently friendly &

---

[19] Recently elected to the Thirty-seventh Congress, John Snyder Carlile (1817–78) was elevated to the United States Senate in July, 1861, filling the seat vacated by Robert M. T. Hunter. At Wheeling, Carlile advocated the immediate formation of a new state, but more moderate counsel prevailed and the birth of West Virginia was delayed for two years.

just men of the North [will bring], will be to assure us of the fact that we have no friends in the North—not one, of all who were so counted on, among the distinguished men, or prominent & influential presses of the North. The people of the South have long been deceived by their own politicians, & believed that the whole democratic party of the northern states was friendly & would be just to the South. Many of the leading politicians of that class were deemed to be especially our friends—& among them long & until lately was counted Stephen A. Douglas. But since the battle of Fort Sumter, the fanatical hatred of the abolitionists has extended to, (or been forced upon) all, & has become universal, & all our [1367] before supposed friends, whether voluntarily or coerced by popular opinion, now unite in crying for vengeance & subjugation on the South. Pierce & Buchanan, both of whom were made presidents of the U.S. by the undivided southern vote added to their minorities of northern supporters, have gone against us fully. Fillmore & Everett, Cushing & [Daniel S.] Dickenson [*sic*], & all others are now thorough supporters of the policy and the unconstitutional as well as blood-thirsty measures & designs of Lincoln's administration. I had long dissented from the belief of our having *many* friends in the North, or of the northern democrats. But there were two in whom I trusted as being just & friendly to our rights & cause—& they were the only men of whom I would have been willing to accept (& to prefer) as President. These were J[ames] K. Paulding & Dickinson.[20] The former died before being tested by recent events, & the storm of popular fanaticism which has swept away all others. Dickinson lives to speak—& in . . . his recent public declaration of opinions, he clearly establishes his right to be considered a zealous new convert & worthy disciple of the Greely [*sic*] school of politicians & haters of the South.—I am getting tired of staying here, having nothing to do, except to look over the newspapers of each day's issue, & to hear rumors (generally false,) of military matters, & to converse on the only & universal subject of conversation among all classes. . . . 600 troops from Louisiana arrived in a body today. Every day troops arrive, & they or others are

---

[20] A native of New York, James Kirke Paulding was a prolific author and had served as secretary of the navy in the Van Buren administration. He died on April 6, 1860. Daniel Stevens Dickinson (1800–66), a former Democratic United States senator, was elected attorney general of New York in 1861 on the Union ticket. During the war he joined the Republican Party and in 1865 was appointed United States attorney for the southern district of New York.

sent on to Harper's Ferry or other places deemed most exposed to invasion by the enemy. I have so much confidence in the extreme caution of Gen. Scott, (who requires that no proper preparation shall be omitted, before he will hazard an important offensive movement—) & in the cowardice of Lincoln & Seward, as to doubt whether they will dare to hazard making any serious invasion of Va. unless in the disaffected north-western counties. And if invading that region, I trust that the invaders & occupiers will not be opposed—but be left undisturbed to weary & wear out the hospitality of the residents who side with the North.

May 18. . . . After 6 P.M., drove with Nanny to the S.C. camp, to partake of a collation at Capt. [George B.] Cuthbert's tent, to which we had been invited, & where we met as other guests, J. R. Anderson & his lady, & some other of the ladies & gentlemen of Richmond. . . . It is reported from Montgomery, on reliable though not official authority, that the Congress has ordered the removal of the seat of Government to Richmond. This will be a great advantage in directing our military operations on the border, & in Va—& will also add to the appearance of our strength & confidence, in thus moving towards & near to capital & army of the enemy.—This forenoon wrote a short & severe article on the conduct of our affairs by the governor & others, & carried it to J[ohn] M. Daniel, editor of the Examiner, for him to publish as editorial, or as a communication, at his choice.

May 19. Sunday. Last night 300 N.Ca. troops arrived here. This morning, 600 more from La. Mr. Boulware arrived last evening from Norfolk, & reports the defences there [1370] to be very good, & safe from attack. Danger has been supposed there, more than anywhere else except Harper's Ferry, because of the facilities & means of the enemy, in the neighboring blockading squadron & large garrison of Fortress Monroe—& in the object of retaking the Navy Yard, & completing the imperfect work of destruction there. I do not believe that any invasion will be attempted there—still less at Richmond—& doubt it even at Harper's Ferry, or anywhere, unless of the disaffected counties in the North-west.—About 40 more Baltimorean refugees arrived last evening. Two military companies of the earlier comers have been organized, & one of them mustered into service here, preparatory to being sent to Harper's Ferry—where there was a like company previously in service. . . . Arranged with Nanny for our departure for home early tomorrow morning. . . . Also left a farewell letter to Capt. Cuthbert & the Palmetto Guard, enclosing $100 as a contribution to the funds of the company.—More exiles or refugees from Baltimore arrived this afternoon. [1371]

May 20. At daybreak, drove to Mr. Lorraine's for Nanny, & we hurried to the steamer, which was advertised to start at 5, but did not move until 6.15 A.M. Landed at Maycox wharf, & was met there by the carriage, (as it was raining,) & thence drove home. Edmund with his troop on duty—& on his return at night, heard that the troop was called out for regular service, at Brandon, & is to march there on the 22nd. This service, in such a position, is so useless, & absurd, that I trust it will not be continued long. . . . Our family circle passed a very pleasant & cheerful evening, notwithstanding the call of Edmund into service, & the ferocious threats of vengeance of all the North & its government. Received a letter from Mildred full of expressions of deep anxiety & sorrow on account of her anticipations of danger & evil to the southern country, & especially to her relatives & friends here—while we, on the place deemed in such peril, are without alarm or much apprehension of serious injury. I must write to her immediately, & try to quiet her fears. . . . [1372]

May 21. . . . Began to make a fairer copy of the portion of this journal embracing the preliminary matter & the siege & surrender of Fort Sumter, for exhibition to my children & near friends. . . .

May 22. Edmund set out at 10 A.M. for Brandon, the assigned post for the military service of his troop. He was [1373] accompanied by his son Thomas, not quite 18, but tall & stout enough for a soldier, who, if permitted by the vote of the company, will serve as substitute for his father's overseer, who is a member of the troop, & who, if so permitted, may stay at home & attend to the farm business. Edmund's overseer at Evelynton, his farm in Charles City [County], had before been called out into service, & marched away. A very insufficient substitute for him on the farm only could be obtained.—North Carolina has seceded, on the 20th, the day the Convention met, & also joined the Confederate States. The number now virtually or completely seceded & confederated are eleven. Virginia, Arkansas, & Tennessee want for their complete action only some legal forms. Maryland & Missouri would be with us, if they were not for the present time subjugated by the northern power & military force. I trust, & believe, that neither of these states will remain long thus crushed. . . . By the return of the servant who drove the wagon (to convey provision & furniture,) Jane received a [1374] letter from Edmund. Thomas was received, & is enrolled for regular service in the troop.

May 23. This is the day for the general voting upon the ratification or rejection by the people of the ordinance of secession. I rode early to the Brandon election precinct for this purpose, & after giving my vote, waited no longer than to see Edmund, who arrived soon after with his troop, to vote & return immediately to the camp. . . .

May 24. . . . No news today—so I infer that the threatened & expected [1375] invasion of the enemy yesterday, at several different points, in the hope of interrupting the voting, & preventing the ratification of secession, had not been attempted. For these northerners are such credulous fools as to believe still that the people of Va. are mostly opposed to secession—& that whether so or not, that they can conquer the South. The credulity of the North on this latter point is exemplified in an annexed editorial from a late N.Y. Herald, in which the ease & certainty of the conquest is coolly & amusingly set forth.[21] Another example is the annexed condensation of longer & detailed accounts in the northern papers of the slaughter of near a thousand men on our side, in the fight of Sumter, which is still generally believed in the North, whereas we had not one man either killed or wounded! . . .

May 25. The paper of today brought the important news that [1378] the enemy's forces (reported to be 6000) have crossed the Potomac, & occupied Alexandria, without opposition—the 600 volunteers posted there, retreating. There are various particulars stated, & also rumors of other incidents of the war, which, (as first & even later reports are so generally false,) I will wait for their confirmation before noting. One of the greatest vexations of the time is the numerous reports which are either entirely unfounded, or have a little truth mixed up with & undistinguishable from a much larger amount of falsehood. Even the news mainly true can scarcely be separated at any later time from the false additions, which are not even subsequently contradicted. . . .

---

[21] After detailing a series of grandiose operations, the *Herald* concluded: "The united forces of the federal government, having captured New Orleans and Richmond, will meet at Montgomery, and, after settling matters there, detach a few thousand men to Charleston by land to square the account about Fort Sumter. Thus will the great Southern rebellion be crushed out." Clearly, neither side had the slightest appreciation of the tribulations that lay ahead.

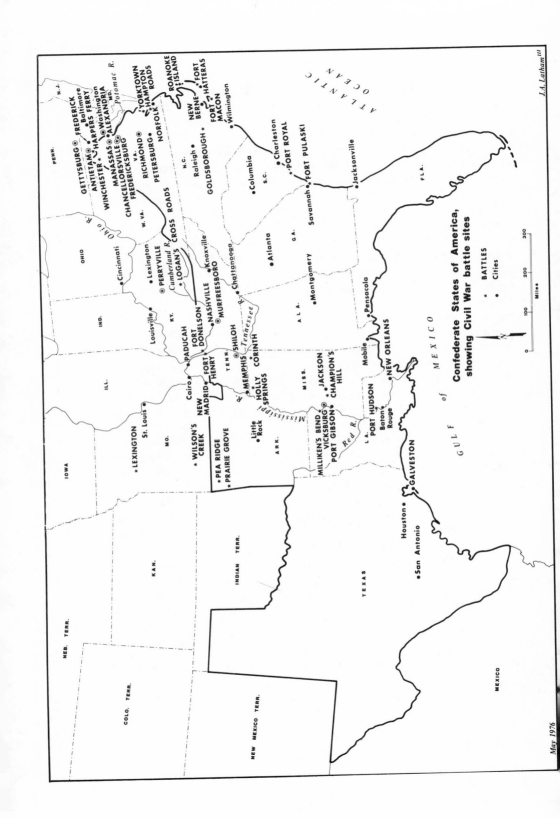

Confederate States of America,
showing Civil War battle sites

BATTLES ★
Cities ●

Miles
0   100   200   300

J.A. Latham III

May 1976

May 26. Sunday. . . . A report came [1379] yesterday, which seems confirmed today, of the discovery of a conspiracy for future & contingent insurrection by some of the slaves on several of the farms near City Point, & on both sides of the river. There have been the most ample facilities, at that place especially, for indoctrinating & deluding slaves with northern ideas, by their long continued & free intercourse with northern sailors, &, in latter times, with free negroes, forming crews of vessels, from the North. Besides this, the negroes have received very general, if faint & false, impressions that the northerners were operating for negro emancipation, or as friends, real or pretended, to the slaves. Still, I believe that the general feeling of the slaves towards unknown northerners is more of suspicion & fear, & dislike, than the contrary. But many, as in this case, have learned that Lincoln's election was to produce general emancipation—& of course, many hoped for that, & since for northern military carrying out of that measure. It seems that the leaders in this conspiracy had proposed, & designed, in the event of Lincoln's army coming to support their movement, to begin insurrection. But, with characteristic negro inertness & cowardice, it was only on this contingency of sufficient armed support from the North, that they designed to move. The accused parties were tried before a magistrate's court, on the very full & confirming testimony of a young negro woman & a negro boy, who had been acquainted with the deliberations, & which have been in progress for 6 or 8 months, & carried on at their night meetings for pretended religious worship. There was no doubt of the guilt of conspiracy & of intention. The offenders in custody were punished [1380] only by the infliction of whipping—30 lashes to each, except one, deemed the chief instigator, & the leader in their "prayer-meetings," who had 39 lashes. The slaves across the river, (on Dr. Epes' Island farm, & on Shirley,) had not been apprehended for trial—& among them were some deemed the most guilty. We informed our ladies of all these circumstances, & they do not seem to be alarmed or disturbed. A conspiracy discovered & repressed is better assurance of safety than if no conspiracy had been heard of or suspected. While I deem that there is not the least ground for alarm & that this conspiracy, if undiscovered, would have had no dangerous results—still we ought to be always vigilant, & be ready to meet attacks, whether from northern invaders or negro insurgents. In regard to the former danger only, as soon as Edmund was called into service, & I was here the only male of the household, I began, & shall continue, to

[35]

use means for defence which I never did before, in keeping loaded guns by my bedside. Still, as before, my sleeping apartment is in the small house in the yard, separate from the mansion, & my door (which is also the outer door,) never locked, or fastened on the inside, & my window perfectly exposed to access, because the servant forgets to close the outer shutters about half the nights. I do not like to adopt new safeguards, lest it might indicate fear of negro enemies, or distrust of our own servants. If the ladies had desired . . . I would have moved my lodging into the mansion, where they alone, & a female servant, sleep, when Edmund is away. I [1381] consulted him as to such removal—but he agreed with me that it was not needed, & that for me to propose it might induce fears that did not yet exist.

May 27. . . . The northern troops occupying Alexandria have been increased to 12,000, as reported, but they have made no farther advance. The first Virginian (or southerner) killed in warlike operations, & the only one yet known occurred [t]here. A Confederate States flag had been hoisted on the Marshall House (hotel) & long in sight from Washington. On the occupation, Col. [Elmer E.] Ellsworth, commander of a N.Y. regiment of Zouaves, hastened to pull down the flag with his own hands. James W. Jackson, the proprietor of the house, aroused from his bed by the intrusion, resisted the attempt, & shot & killed Ellsworth, & was himself immediately killed by Ellsworth's followers. May every drop of the blood of this first martyr in our cause be avenged by the slaughter of a northern invader!—Troops from Richmond (including the S.C. brigade) & from the South, have been pushed on to Manassas Gap Junction, & to Harper's Ferry, to oppose the invaders—& we may count upon hearing of a serious conflict very soon. The northern troops at Fortress Monroe have been increased to 7000, & must be designed for early offensive operations. . . . The annexed paragraph, an editorial of the N.Y. Herald, shows on what kind of troops, & of hostile operations, the people of the North rely upon, & are willing to resort to, to war upon the South—& of which the most influential northern journals & editors are not ashamed to speak of approvingly.[22] . . .

---

[22] In an apparent attempt to frighten the South, the *Herald* threatened to unleash 300,000 urban "roughs" on Virginia and Maryland and promised that "the character of the coming campaign will be vindictive, fierce, bloody and merciless beyond parallel in ancient or modern history."

May 28. Went to Cumming's shop, to receive the daily paper, & to meet the neighbors to arrange with others the setting on foot a voluntary night patrol. There is already a loose organization of the residents of the county who are exempt from military duty by law, & who already number more than 100 men & boys, & probably will be 150. My name has not yet been enrolled, but will be as soon as I can send it to the captain of this precinct. Latterly our public mail has been reduced from thrice to twice a week—& the general anxiety to obtain more frequent news has caused the neighbors, in concert, to send a daily messenger to Petersburg to obtain the daily newspapers for all the parties, & the bundle is brought to Cumming's shop for distribution, by 11 A.M. . . . My son Charles consulted with me & his brother Edmund about his wish to be enrolled (of course as a private) in the Palmetto Guard, so as to get into active service immediately. We approved—& he has made his indispensable arrangements in leaving his home & business, (though his presence at home was of little use to his business,) & came here this afternoon to announce to me his decision to set out tomorrow morning for Petersburg, & thence as speedily as possible to reach the position of the Palmetto Guard. This company, with all others of the S.Ca. brigade, had reached the Manassas Gap Junction on the Gordonsville & Alexandria rail-road, & within [twenty-five] miles of Alexandria. An engagement may be soon expected. But I think that the longer it shall be deferred, without gain to either side, the worse it will be for the invaders, & the better for the defenders of the country. If I had the direction of the campaign, & judging from my present imperfect lights, I would oppose to the invading army, now at Alexandria, a sufficient force to check them whenever required, but to suffer & even invite their advance farther towards Richmond—& at the same time to send 10,000 men from Harper's Ferry into Md. to raise the secessionists & [1384] to arm them, enable Md. to drive out the northern invaders, & when that movement was in progress, with fair prospect of speedy success, for our army to attack Washington from the Md. side. . . .

May 29. After breakfast, Charles took leave of us, to proceed on his way to join the army nearest to the enemy. . . . God grant that this step may be a new direction & turning point in his progress, leading to usefulness & honor. So far, he has lived for no good purpose, & has thrown away his time & opportunities. May he now deserve & achieve success, & acquire justly an honorable reputation, if not distinction & glory. But if not—an early & honorable death in fighting for his country's rights & defence is preferable to a useless & inglorious life extended to old age. . . . No news reports today. The telegraph wires [1385] from the different important military stations have been broken, as supposed by order of our government. This seems to indicate speedy & important movements.

May 30. A home guard, composed of persons exempt by age, infirmity, or profession, from compulsory military duty or service, together with those subject to, but not now in actual service, has been organized throughout the county. Though I do not approve of the particulars of the plan, & doubt its being efficient, I sent to the officer of this section to enrol [*sic*] my name. This afternoon, the neighbors assembled at the Church, to get up a more active company from this neighborhood. I attended—but on hearing the new plan, which I think rather more objectionable than the old one, I withdrew silently, & will continue in the old organization.—Edmund & Thomas came home before sunset. The occasion is that orders have been received from Gen. Lee, for the troop to move & encamp near Burwell's Bay, near the mouth of the river. Most of the troopers had leave to go home for this night only, to prepare for this move to more distant quarters.—Began today to teach Nanny to fire a gun, & to load & manage it. Could not prevail on Jane to join us. I am trying to persuade all the ladies of my acquaintance in this neighborhood to learn to shoot, & to become familiar with using guns & pistols. If this practice & usage was general, & it was known that every female, as well as male, kept fire-arms always ready, & knew how to use them, it would remove all of the small existing danger of insurrectionary or other attacks, of negroes—& would render our women an important [1386] portion of a "home-guard." . . .

May 31. Edmund & Thomas left us again, by 9 A.M., for the camp. The troop will move tomorrow to Burwell's Bay. The Surry troop also has been called out & mustered into service, & will proceed to Smithfield. Our ladies bear the calling away of Edmund with commendable calmness. The obligation of service in the field is for 12 months, if required by the authorities. I think that the active operations of war, caused by invasion or blockade by the enemy will not last half that time—& that their defeat & our manifest superiority for defence, will as soon enable us to disband most of the troops now in service. . . . New arrivals of troops continue from the South, & of new requisitions of Va, & are every day moving on to the neighborhood of Norfolk or Hampton, & to Richmond & the posts nearer to the enemy. The Tribune & Herald, the most influential papers in support of the administration, give out that Richmond is the object of the two armies which have invaded Va. I can scarcely believe that Gen. Scott & the administration at Washington are so infatuated as to attempt to march an army either 60 or 30 miles through our territory, after full notice of the invasion & intention. The former would be the least length of march (the rail-roads being broken up,) for the army from Alexandria, & the latter of that at Fort Monroe, from West Point. If the invading armies could succeed in reaching Richmond, which I do not fear, if they then could escape defeat & destruction, we will deserve to be crushed by the Northern power, & reduced to the present abject condition of Md.—The returns of the votes on the 23rd. continue to show almost unanimity for the ratification of secession in nearly all Va except in the North-western counties & in Morgan & Berkley counties, where there are large majorities against secession—& a unanimous vote in the "Pan-handle" counties. In nearly all the other counties of Va. the vote has been unanimous for secession.[23] In some of the towns & a few counties only have there been less than half a dozen union votes in each—& in Portsmouth only were there more—60 & more being there given, of individuals before employed in the U.S. Navy Yard, & [1388] mostly northerners by birth, or parentage.—I have finished my copying of the Fort Sumter writings & other extracts, & am now without any work to do, or any new or amusing reading, except the newspapers. The ladies here, though quite brave, & not fearing any danger while I sleep here, would be in alarm & great uneasiness if I were to be away for a night. So while they continue so apprehensive, & they have no other guardian, I must not go away.

June 2. Sunday. All went to church.—There are so many daily false rumors, that I defer mentioning them until confirmed. And thus, when the confirmation comes slowly, I forget to record it, or omit it because [1390] supposing that it had been recorded. In this way I omitted to mention the arrival of the monster ship the Great Eastern, in the port of New York, some weeks ago. It has attracted very little attention, & but little notice of the newspapers. This neglect is

---

[23] The total vote was 96,750 in favor of secession; 32,134 against.

in astonishing contrast to the *furor* of interest & curiosity excited by the first visit of this great steamer to these shores.[24]—President Davis arrived in Richmond on the 31st, & Gen. Beauregard since. The executive departments of the Confederate government are already established at Richmond, as the seat of the general government.

June 3. A letter from Charles dated 30th ult. He had been enrolled in the Palmetto Guard, & the regiment (Kershaw's 2nd S.C.) had advanced & was stationed at Bull Run, 20 miles from Alex., & 1st regiment (Gregg's) 3 miles farther on at Centreville.—19 of the North-western counties have voted almost as unanimously against the ordinance of secession as all the remainder of the state for it. The "Pan-handle" counties & Wheeling almost entirely disaffected & for the enemy. I should not be sorry if this most disaffected section should be occupied by 20,000 of Lincoln's troops, & would not have their occupancy disturbed for some time, [1391] until other matters were settled elsewhere. . . . All recent indications of English papers, & of the English & French governments, are that the equal rights of the Confederate States, as a "belligerent power" & nation, will be admitted & respected, including the right to use privateers against our enemy—& that the blockade of southern ports will not be recognized, unless it is "effective." Further, I do not believe that a general blockade, operating to prevent the exportation of cotton to Europe will be permitted, even if it could be made "effective." Our congress has already prohibited the export of cotton from the C.S. except from our sea-ports—which will operate to prevent all exportation to or through the U.S. & to Europe except in defiance of the northern blockade. . . .

June 4. Nanny & Juliana [Dupuy], under my instruction, practised pistol firing. Juliana did well, under the circumstances, & Nanny's performance was excellent. . . . The enemy are gaining, & occupying positions far with[in] our territory west of the Alleghany [*sic*], & committing great destruction of property, & atrocities, near Hampton & Newport's News [*sic*], including the inveigling & retaining [1393] at least 100 negro slaves in Fortress Monroe. These are serious matters—& much more so than any I apprehended until now. The great extent of disaffection & treason in the north-western counties, & the readiness of slaves to flee to the enemy, are both results which I did not expect. . . . A Washington (Lincoln) paper

---

[24] See Volume I, 446.

reports the troops of the enemy now in Va. & Md. to be nearly 60,000—& all in or threatening the seceded & slave-holding states, to be 95,000. This is probably a very exaggerated estimate, designed to deceive & alarm. An attack on Harper's Ferry is threatened, by forces from the west, from Pa. & from Md. Whichever side may be the assailant, I think that a serious conflict must take place within a few days. I trust that it may be begun by our forces, & by invading territory held by the enemy.

June 5. . . . No news, except the continued increase of forces on both sides, & the advance of the enemy's forces towards Harper's Ferry. I cannot imagine what is designed on either side. It would be madness in the enemy to attempt (as is set forth in the northern papers,) to pass on to attack Richmond from Alexandria & Hampton. I infer that Gen. Scott is under the [1394] absurd delusion general at the North, that the majority of the people of Va, & even of eastern Va, are favorable to Union with the North, & would declare for it, if protected by an invading army—& that this is the chief object of the advance to Alexandria & to Hampton. Probably more than one feint is designed. Also, I infer that a feint is designed by Gen. Lee, & that by his not strongly opposing these invasions of the enemy, he desires rather to invite farther advances, which, while he will prevent their complete success, he will throw a strong force into Md. & invite & effect the up-rising of the now crushed secessionists of Baltimore & all others of that state.

June 6. . . . The mail brought letters from Edmund, & one to me from Mildred, dated 25th. ult. . . . The encampment of Edmund's troop, at Burwell's Bay, is within 18 or 20 miles of that of the Northern post at Newport News, & the enemy's tents in view, though across the broad river. The enemy's force is strong, & they *can* be brought, in greatly superior force, to this side at any time by their war steamers. This is a disagreeable position, as a single troop of horse, & quite new in service, can do nothing for offensive measures, & nothing for defence, if attacked, except to retard the advance of the enemy, while retreating before them. Nothing can be more discouraging to raw soldiers than to know that, if attacked or engaged, they are bound to retreat. . . . The threats & boasts of the northern papers, & those presumed to speak the ideas of the administration, are not confined to the seceded states—but extend to France & England. The now evident intention of these governments to recognize the legality of our privateers, & not to recognize our enemy's paper blockade, has aroused the rage of the northern press, & the European powers are denounced, vilified, & threatened with war as the certain result of their intimated policy. Even if these published denunciations are regarded as mere insults, they must operate to incline these powers still more to be favorable to the Confederate States & their cause, & to regard the North as hostile to them, & wanting only the strength to declare war. [1397]

June 7. . . . There has been a fight at Philippi (Barbour Co.) between 1000 of Va. secessionists & a much larger number of Va. unionists & traitors & Ohio volunteers & U.S. regulars, who attacked & surprised our post. As usual, the advantage claimed by both sides—& no truth to be had.[25] . . .

June 8. . . . Set out to a called muster of the "Home Guard" of the exempts, in which I had enrolled my name. The threatening weather caused me to turn back before reaching the place. There are 5 such companies in the county, making [1398] in all between 150 & 200 old men & boys, armed with their own fowling pieces, & who design to be supplied with buck-shot. If the enemy should invade our neighborhood, we propose to act as a guerilla [*sic*] force.—The paper of today brings no new war incidents of importance, nor clear confirmation of previous reports. But from the continued & large reinforcements of southern volunteers to our armies, & other movements, I think that certainly there must be serious business very soon, in attacks on the invaders near Hampton, or Alexandria, or both. From the division of sentiment among the people of the north-western counties, & the hostilities already begun at Grafton & Phillippi [*sic*], there seems every prospect there of civil war, & scenes of neighborhood violence & bloodshed, such as existed in the Carolinas in the war of 1775. This, as well as the general war in which Va. is now engaged, is the result of the action of the submissionists in so long delaying the act of secession, & especially exasperated in the north-west by the super-added treasonable conduct of Carlile & a few other leaders in that region. . . .[1399]

June 10. Sundry papers by the mail, but nothing new of importance. It is very strange, & condemnable, that apparent spies, &

---

[25] The truth was that the Confederates, commanded by Colonel George A. Porterfield, had been routed by a unit from McClellan's command in this minor engagement which some regard as the first land battle of the Civil War.

resident northerners hostile to the south in sentiment, are allowed to go or remain, & not one yet punished—& also that outrages of murder, & destruction of private property, not justified by the laws of war, & perpetrated by the enemy's troops near Hampton, have not even been investigated or noticed by our authorities. . . . Afternoon, walked to the field where the mowing of clover for hay has been begun, & instructed the overseer & negroes how to cure it in cocks, on my plan. Also furnished the overseer with my printed directions, in my "Essays & Notes on Agriculture.". . .

June 11. The Petersburg paper stated reports that the enemy's camp at Newport News had been removed, & that heavy firing had been heard, indicating a battle. But this scarcely attracted my notice, [1400] regarding it as among the numerous false or exaggerated rumors, among all which it is rare that one statement is true. But in the afternoon a private letter (written at noon yesterday,) from Edmund arrived, confirming the statement, as at his camp the firing could be distinctly heard. Later, reports by steamboat passengers reached us, leaving no doubt of the general fact that the northern troops had advanced towards Yorktown, & attacked a detached portion of our troops in the peninsula, & had been repulsed & driven back, with considerable loss to the enemy, & but little to us.[26] We all were greatly excited by the reports, & remain in feverish anxiety to hear the corrections tomorrow. . . .

June 13. No confirmation of the last report of the second fight at Philippi, & no additional particulars of that near Hampton. Indeed, as to the latter, all accounts of the last two days have served to deny what had been before stated and believed as incidents, & to lessen the importance of the affair. I now expect that the final & true account will reduce both the slaughter of the enemy & the glory of our troops to very small amounts. It is astonishing what numerous & circumstantial false reports are printed, & all true facts so exaggerated or distorted that it is impossible to know what is the truth, even when there is any.—This was the fast day, proclaimed by President Davis. All our household went to [1402] church except myself & Juliana Dupuy. . . .

---

[26] This was the battle of Big Bethel, or Bethel Church, in which a Federal force, consisting of seven regiments from Benjamin F. Butler's command at Fortress Monroe, blundered into a Confederate unit of less than half its size and was sharply repulsed. Colonel John B. Magruder had general command of the Confederate forces, although Colonel Daniel H. Hill's First North Carolina Regiment bore the brunt of the fighting for the victors.

June 14. No more news by mail. But my nephew, Wm. Dupuy, who was in the late action, as a private in the Nottoway troop, arrived, for a few days' absence on leave, & brought us the first reliable accounts—though still uncertain as to numbers engaged, & still more so as to the enemy's loss. From 1500 to 1800 of our troops, under Col. Magruder, marched from Yorktown to the line of Elizabeth City, & threw up a surrounding intrenchment, which served for partial protection of the force—a N.C. regiment, some companies of howitzers from Richmond, with their field pieces, & two troops of cavalry—all raw volunteers. The enemy's force, 3000 to 3500 [4 regiments, & part of another, making 4900],[27] as understood, marched from Hampton & Newport News, & attacked three different times, & were repulsed—& the last time retreated rapidly to Hampton, followed, but too late for any effect, by our cavalry to near their position. Our loss, 1 man killed, 6 or 7 wounded. The enemy's not known, as they moved (in vehicles seized along the road, of all the residents,) most of their wounded, & also of the dead, as supposed. They had cannon & fired shells as well as balls. Several horses of our troopers killed. The enemy's loss variously estimated at from 100 to more than 500. They confess (as printed [1403] in Washington,) to 30 killed only.[28] Our men must have fired badly & the Yankees abominably, not to have killed more. But at any rate, the attacks were met bravely & coolly, & it was a gallant & effective defence for entirely new & raw volunteers. The fight, including the intermissions caused by the several repulses & retreats of the enemy, lasted 4 hours. Not more than 800 of our men could engage, (those only on the two sides off the intrenchment which were at different times attacked,) & all of the other infantry & all the cavalry did not fire a shot, or strike a blow. Whether 30 only of the enemy, or 300, were killed, it was a signal defeat, for such superior forces, attacking with confidence—& the very small loss on our side, strange as it is, is but in accordance with nearly all the preceding conflicts, in which our loss or damage was either nothing, or very slight. . . .

June 15. Letter from Edmund. He has obtained suitable boarding & lodging, & desires Jane to come—also Nanny & myself when we choose. It is arranged for Jane to go by the next steamer.—Full

---

[27] Inserted by the diarist at a later date.

[28] Total Union losses were actually seventy-six, including eighteen dead. Ruffin's figures concerning Confederate casualties are accurate.

private accounts, in detail, of the battle of Bethel Church. Also the official report of Col. [Daniel H.] Hill, who commanded the N.C. regiment, to Gov. Ellis, by which we learn that 1160 men on our side made up our whole force on the ground. . . .

June 17. . . . I went with Jane to the steamer, & placing her under the care of our neighbor H. W. Harrison, to visit her husband. . . . The battle of Bethel seems to excite even more the North than the South. It is as mortifying to them as gratifying to us. The Northerners are still gaining & encroaching in the north-western counties, & in the Valley, by aid of our disaffected or traitorous citizens. They have got footing along the Balt. & Ohio Rail-Road, by invasions from Pennsylvania, as far as into Hampshire. Gen. [George B.] McClelland [*sic*], who commands the northern forces in all the west, is said by Gen. Lee to be the ablest of all the commanders under Scott. His successful & extended advances on us seem to offer evidence of his talents.—History repeats the like great events & revolutions, with their causes, in different ages, & yet no warning is taken by one generation of the experience of another preceding. The most striking example of such repetition is presented in [1405] the now current events. The northern people are now fully engaged in, & eagerly pursuing, the vain attempt to conquer the seceded southern states, the same infatuated & insane policy which was used against them & us, the American colonies, by the Mother Country in our war of independence. The only important difference is in degree, & not in principle—in the power & prospect of success of England in comparison to the colonies, having been far greater than of the Northern section to the southern. Every impartial reasoner would pronounce, that however the North may injure, it never can subdue the Southern States. And even, if able, by possibility, to subdue them, no gain or benefit would thereby be acquired, which could compensate the cost of the war of subjugation. Yet the whole North seems now united & ardent in the mad pursuit of this conquest, at any cost, & without any reasonable prospect of success, or triumph, & still less of compensation! So far, in all the incidents of the war, the success or gain to the south has been most marked, & almost without exception. The only losses, in any of the Confederate States, have been the enemy's holding Fort Pickens & Monroe, & the two forts of Key West, (4 out of some 18, all others of which we have seized & hold,) & the recent advances of the invaders in Virginia. Even if we should be beaten in one or two important battles, it would be but temporary loss to the South. One or two important victories gained over the North would be to them ten-fold more disastrous. Md, Ky, & Missouri, [1406] being still in the United States, & neither having declared for secession, their losses & degradation, & their disturbed & insubordinate condition, are not to be counted as losses to the South, but to the North. Not being of us, we have not to supply men or money to defend our cause in those disordered border states—while the Northern power has to maintain costly garrisons to crush Md. & Missouri, & must do the same for Ky., or lose them all. The rebellious movements in two of these states, & the declared neutrality of Ky, all work in our favor. And when these states shall be driven by oppression to join us, as must happen, their change will serve to destroy all remaining chances for the success of the northern power in carrying on war against the South. . . . [End of MS Volume 7—p. 1407] Lately Stephen A. Douglas died.[29] Not many months ago, this able man & unequalled demagogue stood higher in popular favor, & in the prospect of gaining political eminence, than any other individual in this country. No other politician had so many devoted & zealous supporters—though he had not enough to beat the combination votes that elected the comparatively obscure Lincoln. Since Douglas coalesced with the abolition party, he had lost his previous high political position, & his later advancement to the presidency was hopeless. Probably chagrin & mortification for his political overthrow combined with disease & the fruits of long continued intemperance (part of his demagoguical [*sic*] policy & procedure,) to cause his early death. There was no more unscrupulous or dangerous politician.

June 18. . . . The newspapers confirmed a report received, but not credited before. Harper's Ferry has been evacuated & abandoned by our strong garrison—the buildings of the Arsenal burnt, & some grain, for which there was not means for transportation, also burnt—& the place left open for the enemy's occupation. The confidence in the strength of our army, & of that portion, & in the ability of our military chiefs, & in the wisdom of their policy, induces the general belief that this abandonment of Harper's Ferry, which looks like a great reverse to us, & will be supposed so by the enemy, is for some proper & important object, & that we shall soon hear of an attack upon & defeat of the enemy, either in Md,

---

[29] Douglas died in Chicago on June 3, 1861, at the age of forty-eight.

Washington, or in the Valley of Va. But nothing is yet known to us, of the particular design—nor even is known the direction of the march of Gen. [Joseph E.] Johnston with the large force which had held Harper's Ferry. It may be to unite with the main army at Manassas Junction, & attack the enemy in Alexandria, or to move westward. . . . This afternoon, about 6 o'clock, the overseer, & also others in the field, heard the firing of cannon, seemingly at regular intervals, in the direction of Richmond—unless it was distant thunder, which has [1409] been before so mistaken. I hope it may be a salute for some good news—though it is too soon for our armies to join, & gain a victory at Alexandria. . . . Some of the many recent accounts and comments on the battle of Bethel, in northern papers here appended. . . . Witnesses in our battery say that the enemy's soldiers fought bravely, advancing three times to the attack. Yet, even if our men were protected by their hastily raised breast-work (of earth) from their balls, why they did not assault & run over the sloping embankment, (as was easy to do,) I cannot conceive—unless from incapacity of [1410] the commander, or cowardice of the soldiers. But whatever was the cause of the loss, the repulse of the enemy was a glorious act of our comparatively small force—& the result a new example of the seeming manifest protection afforded to us & our cause, by the providence of God. So far, almost every incident of the war, & of the conduct of the northern government, & even those at first seeming most for our injury, has worked for our greater success. Perhaps, the recent crushing of Md & Washington, & even the invasion of north-western Va. may, by exasperating the people, also operate for our better union & more complete success.—The vote of the Va. Convention on the ordinance of secession just made known—88 for & 55 against. Among the latter, the bolder & more persistent submissionists are J[ohn] B. Baldwin, who has since been appointed by the Governor to be Inspector General, & J[ubal] A. Early, made a General. Most of the as abject & meaner submissionists, as [William] Macfarland, M[armaduke] Johnson (since a Governor's aid & Col. in rank & pay), T[imothy] Rives &c. &c. after making all previous possible opposition, at last voted with the majority.

June 19. This morning more cannon, & in greater number, heard towards Richmond, after sunrise. . . . Did not get my saddle (which had [1411] been lent to W. Dupuy,) until late—after which I rode after the reaping machine, & directed its proper performance. The overseer is not capable of directing this work of harvesting—& if he knew how, no one man is physically able to attend to so large a business. I should only make bad worse by interfering with details, except by advice to him—which I find to be of little effect—& by directing the operation of the reaping machine & relieving the overseer from this part of the duty. The absence of Edmund, & now of any female head of the family, & the absence of all previous arrangements for such contingencies, have produced great disorder & difficulties, & extend to Evelynton as well as this farm. Edmund is in military service, & for a year—& though his offer of service was in every sense voluntary—he being over the military age—his best overseer, at Evelynton, also called into service, & very insufficiently substituted on the farm by an inexperienced young man—the incapable overseer here also called, as a member of the troop, & only remaining at home by being substituted in military service by Edmund's son. All these will make up an amount of loss & sacrifice far greater than all the public charges required by the war, in taxes & service in arms. The same or similar private losses will more or less fall to every man & farm & household—but, as it seems, will be yielded ungrudgingly for the public good & our good cause. . . .

June 20. After breakfast, overlooking the reaping, in the absence of the overseer, employed in another field, until time to expect the private mail. . . . Received yesterday a letter from Mildred, which could only be conveyed by being sent by private hand to Nashville, to be mailed. In Ky. all letters to & from the C.S. are stopped by the U.S. postmasters, & sent to Washington. I do not know how I can now convey letters to Mildred—as she gave no instructions.

June 22. . . . The opposing armies drawing nearer together between Alexandria & Manassas Junction. They must come in conflict soon.—Gov. Wise has been appointed a general of the Confederate States, & has been sent, with some forces, to Staunton, to raise more, & arouse the western people to oppose the invaders. Being destitute of military experience, Gen. Wise must be in that important respect a very inefficient officer. But he has courage, energy, zeal, & unbounded ambition, & may do good service in inspiriting the people & acting through better qualified subordinates. His great power of public speaking to ignorant assemblages he will also fully exercise wherever he goes—& in this manner at least, his great though despicable talent & power over the masses will be put

[48]

to better use than ever before—when exercised [1415] solely with views to his own personal aggrandizement & power.—Count Cavour is dead. His great mind was the main constructor of Italian nationality under the rule of the former king of Sardinia. It is to be feared that the unfinished structure may be damaged, if not overthrown, in consequence of the loss of the wise & politic chief constructor & safe-guard. Garibaldi, great as he was in military operations, & disinterested, patriotic, brave & noble, has neither statesmanship nor discretion—& is nothing except as a soldier. It was lately reported that he, in the apparent lull of hostilities in the field in Italy, was coming to this country to aid the North. This was not credible. But if true, he is the very man to accept & support the anti-slavery fanaticism of the North, & to arouse, & bring to his support, & to direct, all the fanaticism, zeal, & confidence of the ignorant northern people. Thus, he might be their most efficient military leader. But even he would find in the southern people a very different class from his opponents in Europe.—The events of this war, so far, have been remarkable in character, & in general, of remarkable uniformity. The Northern government had possession of all the navy, of the regular army of veteran troops—& of all the fortifications & munitions of war, except such as our authorities or people seized upon in the beginning. On our side, we had not (& scarcely have now) an armed vessel—not a regular or trained soldier—& no military organization. In every skirmish or more important fight, except the shameful surprise of our troops at Philippi, we, with raw volunteers, have had the advantage. Even in the two surprises, at Philippi & at Fairfax C. H., our forces, though surprised, & at Philippi routed, caused most blood-shed—& at Fairfax [1416] C.H., the remnant of our men who stood their ground gained a decided victory. In these, as in all other fights in which our triumph was complete, it has been remarkable that the enemy scarcely killed any, & wounded but few of our men. In every engagement & skirmish, from the cannonade of Fort Sumter to the latest skirmish, all our killed have not amounted to half a dozen—& the wounded not more than in ordinary proportions. In every fight too, except in the surprises named, & at Alexandria, where no defence was ordered or attempted, all of our raw volunteers fought as bravely as if they had been veteran regulars. At Fort Sumter there was not much opportunity for the exercise or display of courage on the part of the assailants. But it was not less remarkable there that

[49]

our raw & but little practised men, who were not even artillery-men until in that service, fired with more accuracy than the veteran artillerists who composed the garrison of Fort Sumter. Such results, both of steady courage & discipline, I had not anticipated, hopeful as I have been of our general success. In regard to the enemy's successes & advantages gained, I have been disappointed in them only in one case, where the premises were understood. This is that any considerable number of slaves should have deserted to them, as is the case at Fortress Monroe. But that locality is the one where the continued supremacy of the North *seems* more certain to the ignorant slaves of the neighborhood—& also they have been long exposed to the contaminating influence of an abolition garrison & Yankee crews of vessels. I confess also to have been mistaken as to results, in the recent strong military power of the Northern government, & the successful [1417] advances of its armies in Va. But this is the legitimate result of new, unknown, & unsuspected premises—without which such results would have been impossible. The Congress of the U.S. only has constitutional power to make war, to raise armies, buy or build vessels of war, to declare & enforce blockades, to suspend the writ of *habeas corpus*, or to occupy an unresisting state by military coercion as a conquered country. Congress not only did not authorize any of these acts, but refused to act in regard to the most important measures. Yet, since the adjournment of Congress, the President has, in violation of the constitution, adopted each & all of these measures, & in fact is at the head, & wielding the power of an unlimited despotism, sustained by military force. It is a striking evidence of the ignorance of the northern people of constitutional obligations & rights, that there has been scarcely a voice raised against this great & complete revolution, & destruction of all free & limited constitutional government. But, wielding such power, & enabled to call any amount of military & naval force into service, it is not surprising that the Northern government has been able to threaten & partly invade our borders with large armies, superior in numbers to all we have yet opposed to their progress. Yet our opposed forces are not greatly inferior in numbers, & equipment, & [are] superior (in proportion to numbers,) in moral strength. Our levies, & our expenditures, have as much exceeded my anticipations as have the enemy's, for the causes stated. But our extraordinary efforts are authorized by law, & fully seconded & sustained by the ardent patriotism & public-

[50]

spirit of the people. And even if the Northern government shall (as it now threatens,) bring 500,000 [1418] men to attack us, we have abiding confidence in our ability to repel them & defend our country & our rights.—Latterly, there has been a marked change in the tone of the Northern papers. Some are advocating peace—& opposing all attempts to coerce the South—& some of the most influential of the thoroughgoing Northern editors, & still as truculent as before, are beginning to realize the difficulty of conquering the South, & also the suffering & losses of the northern people. . . .

June 25. The reaping machine again repaired & at work. Riding after it, & directing the operation, until it soon again broke, & was then given up entirely. . . . The opposing armies near Alexandria still drawing closer, but both using great caution, & each seeming to invite rather than to desire to offer attack. If I was not desired & obliged to stay here, with the ladies who would be otherwise by themselves, I would be glad to go to the scene which must soon be so interesting & important. I hope to obtain leave of absence.

June 28. . . . The opposing forces near to Alexandria have their out-posts within a few miles of each other—both sides intrenched. Though a general battle has been so long threatened, & more & more [1423] probable every day, I now think it is not likely to occur for two or three weeks. Gen. Scott's policy is caution, the most perfect preparation, & never to engage until he is completely ready for fighting, & with strong assurance of victory. He has more numerous forces, a portion of them regulars & therefore better than our volunteers—& better arms, & all necessary munitions of war. We have fewer men, but better than the northern volunteers—& reinforcements are arriving every day. We will have to lose a few soon by the expiration of their term of service—though among these is one of our best regiments, Gregg's of S.C. On the other hand, most of the early northern volunteers were for 3 months, & the time for a great proportion will expire in 2 or 3 weeks, & they are so disgusted with the service that few will re-enlist, except those entirely destitute. The new levies, substituted, will be still worse soldiers, at first. Our commanders are capable, & as cautious as Scott—& it seems to me that we have nothing to lose, & much to gain in strength, by postponing a general engagement for some weeks. By that time, the increased heat, & the beginning of the malaria season, (for northern constitutions,) will begin to operate fearfully on the invaders. In the mean time, there are frequent affairs of out-posts, & skirmishes, in nearly all of which our men have the decided advantage. The invaders' scouts & piquet guards are frequently shot, & all such are in great danger. Guerrilla fighting has been begun, & with great effect, near Alexandria & also near Hampton. Some of our people, acting alone, or in small parties, & at their own discretion, have crept upon [1424] & shot many of the sentinels & scouts. It is only necessary for the people generally to resort to these means to overcome any invading army, even if we were greatly inferior to it in regular military force.

June 29. . . . A letter delivered, by private conveyance, which ought to have come yesterday, states that Jane will not return before next Monday evening, & even that is spoken of doubtfully. . . . [This] determined me not to delay my departure, as I had designed, for a few days longer, but to leave by this evening's steamer. . . . At 4 P.M. left the shore for Berkley wharf, & before 5, was on the steamer. Reached Richmond, & as soon as securing my room at the Exchange Hotel, (nearly 9 P.M.) I hastened to Mr. Lorraine's house to see my granddaughters. . . .

June 30. Sunday. Saw & conversed with, among other friends & old acquaintances, Ex. Pres. Tyler, Mr. Boulware, [Alexander H.] Boykin of S.C., Judge [Arthur F.] Hopkins of Ala. The latter introduced me to his wife, [1425] who is going to Culpeper C.H. to aid the hospital comforts for our sick soldiers there. I gave to her a check for $20 in aid of her objects. . . . At 9 P.M. went with Judge John Robertson to call on President Davis, at his present lodging, at the Spottswood Hotel. We sent up our cards, but he was then engaged, & requested us to wait a while. I waited half an hour, & not hearing from him again, left for my hotel. It was mainly to offer, by my call, evidence of my respect now felt for the President that I made this call—& having done so, & failed to see him, I need not make another. In time back, I blamed him greatly, as all other of the most prominent seekers of the Presidency of the U.S., for his truckling to & flattery of the North, in speeches delivered on a journey in New England, & his indirect treachery to the South. In this political sin, I placed him next to Wise. But since the election of Lincoln, & the beginning of the secession movement, Davis has thrown off the previous corrupting influence, & has acted as a true & zealous representative & supporter of the South. He was the best man for his present office; & since [he] has been President of the C.S. his conduct has deserved the commendation & [1426]

respect which I now cheerfully accord to him. Wise also, who has done very far more & worse acts of treachery to southern rights, seems now among the most zealous of their supporters. And to him, also, I am willing to approve his being employed in high trusts, though I never can forget his former conduct, induced by his unlimited ambition.

July–September

᭙᰾᭙

1861

AGAIN IN THE RANKS OF THE PALMETTO
GUARD ᦞᬽ᩠ EYEWITNESS ACCOUNT OF FIRST
MANASSAS ᦞᬽ᩠ POLITICAL ARRESTS IN THE
NORTH ᦞᬽ᩠ A VISIT TO FORT MACON, NORTH
CAROLINA

July 1. Made my purchases & other preparations for my designed stay in camp. I bought two coarse blankets, & a small cheese, & with great difficulty found either—& the cheese with a half-barrel of hard crackers made up my stock of provision. . . . [A] curious & successful adventure was learned this morning by the arrival of the parties, & the prisoners, 40 in number, the crews of the steamer & three sailing vessels captured.[1] . . . Hearing that "Col. Thomas" was the leader, & concoctor of the scheme, I supposed he was the same person whom I met here as an agent of the Md. secession party, & set out to seek him, but in vain. He, hearing of my attempt, came to call on me, with an acquaintance to introduce him—& they sat in my apartment some time after I had retired. He was dressed in Zouave uniform, a Turkish dress, with his closely shaven head covered by a very small cap. He has been commissioned as a colonel in the service of Va. & expects to be able to raise a regiment

---

[1] On the night of June 28 a detachment from the First Regiment of Maryland Zouaves, commanded by Colonel Richard Thomas—not the Colonel Thomas encountered previously in Richmond by the diarist—seized the government steamer *St. Nicholas*, which was on its regular run from Baltimore to Washington. When plans for a demonstration up the Potomac River went awry, the steamer proceeded downstream to the mouth of the Rappahannock, capturing three sailing vessels along the way. The spectacular incident was an affront to northern sensibilities but had little military significance.

of Marylanders, & to perform more of such captures as he has now so well effected. [1427]

July 2. Left Richmond early in the train of the Central R.R. Mrs. Hopkins went also, & stopped at Culpeper C.H. where is the principal hospital of Beauregard's army. Several hundred patients there, the cases mostly of measles. Reached Manassas Junction, after a slow passage, at 4 P.M. There the regular train now stops. And as the irregular train, to Fairfax Station, was to be in the night, & no certain conveyance thence to Fairfax C.H. where the Palmetto Guard (& all Kershaw's Regiment) is stationed, I accepted an invitation soon offered to me by Col. [James L.] Kemper, to go with him in his carriage tomorrow forenoon, direct to the camp. Got quarters, with the promise of *half* of a bed only, at the hotel—of which the accommodations in every respect were miserable, & yet overwhelmed with guests at every meal. Sundry others, less favored than myself, slept on the floor, either on their own blankets or without, of the baggage & public rooms.—There are several regiments here, & Gen. Beauregard's head-quarters are here. I did not call on him, though before acquainted, a[s] I supposed him to be closely engaged, & that any visitor without business would be objectionable. This is an intrenched camp—earth-works being thrown up at various points, & a few pieces of heavy artillery I saw mounted at one. Gen. Beauregard studiously tries to conceal the strength & condition of his forces, & therefore I asked no questions of any one capable of giving information. They are scattered over many different places. But I suppose that there are not less than 30,000 men within striking distance of, or . . . near enough to be soon concentrated here or near Alexandria. Still the enemy's forces opposed, & in Washington, are much superior in number, & in position if we were to attack them. Both sides seem reluctant to attack, & to prefer to postpone a conflict, or [1428] to await attack behind their intrenchments. . . .

July 3. The occupant of the other half of my bed was a perfect stranger to me, but fortunately a very gentlemanly & polite old Frenchman from Louisiana.—This morning the 1st S.C. regiment, (Col. Gregg's) passed, returning home, having served its term, & for most of the men a second term, with the campaign on Morris Island. For public interests, the loss of this corps is much to be regretted, being one of the best in our service. But most of the men will soon return, as they say, & the regiment, re-organized under Col. Gregg,

& most of the same officers will be here [1429] again in a few weeks. . . . [1430] Col. Kemper called for me about 8, & we drove to Fairfax C.H. Went to the camp of 2nd S.C. Regiment, & the tents of the Palmetto Guard. Soon found Charles—well. Welcomed by my old acquaintances. Invited to dine by Capt. Cuthbert, at one of the hotels, but declined, preferring to pay for a very mean dinner at another. But I accepted his invitation to sleep in his tent for the present. . . . I had been asleep two hours, on a hard & uneven foundation, & covered by my blankets, when I was awakened by the movements of my companions, & found Capt. C. & all of his company about to march (with some others,) on a secret expedition. All that he could inform me of was that the march would probably be long & laborious—& supposing it quite beyond my physical powers, he had not before informed me. I disliked very much not to go with the company in this first chance for a fight—but, at my best, I would have broke down under a long march, & was then very unfit to do even as well as usually. So I decided not to make the attempt.

July 4. Heard early that some 800 men, with cavalry & artillery, under Col. Kershaw, had marched last night (12:15 A.M.), & about 7 those who could hear supposed they heard in our camp irregular cannonading, & even the sound of musquetry [*sic*], which could not be the regular salutes of artillery to Independence Day—which had been heard very early, either from Alexandria or Washington. On this, & feeling as able as usual, I went, with two other amateur [1431] volunteers, to join Kershaw's force, if we could reach it. We drove to our outer picket guard, 2½ miles distant, & towards Alexandria, & there heard that our men were certainly halted on the road ahead, & some miles farther. There had been no fight, but a deplorable firing, by mistake, on some troopers of the Fauquier Black Horse company, by which 2 or 3 troopers were killed, & several horses. The bodies had been carried into the village. Inferring that the scheme was frustrated, & that nothing more would be attempted, I & my companions returned, by our conveyances. . . . Within an hour after our return to camp, the troops followed—having marched 6 miles out, & as much back, & near to the enemy's picket guard, without seeing an enemy. Gen J[ohn] McQueen came to see me. He & sundry others are here, either enrolled, or as unattached & amateur volunteers, waiting for a battle. Among the latter class is Capt. [Allen J.] Green of Columbia, a fine artillery officer who commanded a company & a battery on

Morris Island. Among the regularly enrolled, & in the Palmetto Guard, is Gen. [Johnson] Hagood, a scientific military engineer by education, a General of militia in S.C. & late actual Colonel of a regiment of volunteers, which was refused leave, by Gov. Pickens, to march to Va. On this, he resigned, & came on alone, & entered, & is serving, as a private, in the Palmetto Guard.[2] One of those who accompanied me this morning was Mr. [E. J.] Meynardie, chaplain of the regiment, & a pious Methodist minister, who was well armed, & as anxious as any one to get into battle. . . . There are many instances of men of S.C. in high position in previous military service, or present [1432] rank, volunteering to serve as privates in actual service.—The unfortunate affair of this morning is worse than I had first heard. The two troopers were sent by their officer, Col. [Thomas T.] Munford, (part of the same expedition) from the advance to convey a message to Col. Kershaw—& were fired at, first by a lieutenant, under the supposition of their being enemies, as they galloped by, & then by many others, & killed. One other trooper, in his company, was wounded.—Report, first heard yesterday, of a fight on the Potomac near Williamsport, the enemy crossing in great force, & opposed by a few thousand men. Nothing reliable yet as to results.[3]

July 5. I know as little of the number of our forces as of the enemy's opposed to us. Strict orders have been issued that no one shall write, even in private letters, anything of the position or strength of the forces—& every means is used by our commanders to prevent any information going abroad. So I suppose that the strength of our army is less known to me, & to all, except the higher officers, than it is to Gen. Scott. But whether our forces, near to this the most advanced position, are 20, or 30, or as some say 40,000 . . . the enemy near Alexandria & Washington are 50 percent more numerous. Intrenchments have lately been ordered here at two

[2] After First Manassas, Hagood (1829–98) returned to Charleston and reentered state service. Commissioned a brigadier general in the Confederate States Army in July, 1862, he commanded a brigade in the Wilderness campaign and at Petersburg. Following the war he was active in the political and economic life of his native state and, in 1880, was elected governor of South Carolina.

[3] On July 2 General Robert Patterson crossed the Potomac at Williamsport, Maryland, and moved into the Shenandoah Valley, where he was directed to engage the Confederate army of Joseph E. Johnston so as to prevent the latter from reinforcing Beauregard at Manassas. Patterson's failure to accomplish this mission contributed to the Union defeat at First Manassas and resulted in the early termination of his Civil War military career.

particular points, & are now being constructed—but not finished, & no cannon for them. The enemy are at Falls' Church on the road to Alexandria, about 8½ miles from this place. . . . The first night I was here, Capt. Cuthbert insisted on giving up to me part of his sleeping accommodations, & even his couch I found very rough & hard. Last night, I had [1433] a straw bed, on the floor of our tent, which though thin & hard, served well enough in that respect. But the night was so chilly, that my two good blankets did not protect me from suffering with cold in the latter part of the night. The tent is open at both ends, & the draft of air was on my head. I should have been much annoyed by this, if I had not slept in my hat, which is a soft one, & allowed my lying on it in any position without inconvenience. Its broad brim was a good shield against the wind.—I am received in the officers' mess, in which Charles was before, & three other privates and non-commissioned officers. My addition make[s] the number nine in all. The mess occupies adjoining tents. I have received, for arms, (in preference to a rifle,) a rifled musket, & the accoutrements.—After dinner, walked with Capt. Cuthbert & Lieut. [T. Sumter] Brownfield to see the earth-works in progress—& now in part completed. Passing by Col. Kershaw, at his quarters, we stopped & conversed with him & other officers. While there, Gen. [Samuel] McGowan (Q.M. of Brigade)[4] rode up, & announced the order from Gen. Beauregard for every man to have 40 rounds of ammunition this afternoon. This seems as indicating some expectation of an attack. The forces here supposed to be 9 to 10,000, & those of the enemy in Alex. & nearer to us, on this side of the river, to be 15,000. In Washington perhaps 40,000 more. Report from a gentleman from Winchester that the northern army which crossed at Williamsport were in Martinsburg on the night of 3rd. after three skirmishes—Gen. Johnston had joined the first opposing & weaker force of Col. Jackson, & was encamped near Martinsburg & between the enemy & the Potomac, & had sent word for the women & children to leave Martinsburg. A battle expected to take

---

[4] A veteran of the Mexican War, McGowan (1819–97) had commanded a South Carolina brigade during the bombardment of Fort Sumter and at this time was acting as voluntary aide-de-camp to General Bonham. Commissioned a lieutenant colonel, Confederate States Army, in the fall of 1861, he served with distinction in the Army of Northern Virginia until Appomattox, rising to the rank of brigadier general and suffering wounds in four major engagements. After the war he sat in the South Carolina legislature and served as associate justice on the state supreme court.

place yesterday. Martinsburg & Berkeley county have a population mostly of tories. [1434]

July 6. The "Rump" Congress was to meet in Washington on the 4th., & though we are within 20 miles, & within 14½ of Alexandria, we have not yet heard anything of the proceedings.—This morning, about 300 men, including all of our company, at work on new intrenchments. The labors progressed well, & in 3 hours the breast-work was more than half completed, & will be finished, or fit for service, before night. . . .

July 7. Sunday. Still no later news from Gen. Johnston. Richmond papers of yesterday repeat what we before heard, & which seems reliable, that Johnston had cut off [Gen. Robert] Patterson's army from the Potomac, held him in Martinsburg, & had sent to Beauregard for re-inforcements. Col. Kershaw told me that a regiment had been sent yesterday from Manassas Junction. A battle must come off there today, if not sooner. Though our army is inferior in numbers, we are sanguine of its great success.—The battery at which our men worked yesterday was completed in the afternoon. Several others were also begun the same morning, & not being finished, the work is going on today. These intrenchments seem very proper, & necessary. But if so, it is strange that the construction should have been so long postponed. I worked myself a little in the trench, with a gravel shovel, (the implement which I used for throwing up marl,) to incite others to labor, & also to show that sleight more than strength served for the use. . . .

July 8. It is very difficult to buy a Richmond paper here, & at the extravagant price of 10 cents, even for the Dispatch, which is bought at the publication office for one cent. Our company is well supplied with Charleston papers. I wrote for the R[ichmon]d Whig yesterday.—All yesterday, nothing but contradictory reports, & none reliable, of the state of affairs in Berkeley county. It is surprising that we remain ignorant to this time.—Among the visitors here are Senator [Thomas L.] Clingman of N.C. & Col. [Laurence M.] Keitt & [William W.] Boyce, late M.C., of S.C. I went to see them this morning, & had a pleasant conversation on public affairs. Lincoln's message has reached us. He demands of his rump congress a loan of 400 millions of dollars, & an armed force of 400,000 men. This will convey to Europeans a very different meaning than was designed. They must infer that if such enormous preparations are needed, the conquest of the south is impossible. I have not yet been able to see the message.—Col. [Benjamin F.] Terry & Mr. [Thomas S.] Lubbock, both from Texas, are here acting as scouts & ameteur [*sic*] fighters "on their own hook," or at their own expense, & at their own choice.[5] I was introduced to Col. T. some days ago, & conversed with him on his manner of service. He is a handsome & refined looking man, neat in his dress, & genteel in appearance & manner, & very different in that respect from our soldiers, who from Brigadier Gen. Bonham to the privates, indulge in very careless & in many cases slovenly attire. Col. Terry has a very mild countenance & manners, & would be among the last persons to be supposed suited for the wild work he has undertaken. Yesterday afternoon he went out with his companion & another, Mr. Morse, a resident here, who acted as guide, to the Potomac below the Great Falls, at a ferry, where the river is very narrow, (about 150 yards wide,) [1436] & where a small piquet guard of the enemy was stationed on the other side. The guards & scouts of the enemy have latterly been in the habit of firing from a distance on every white man on our side—& wounded a poor man as he was ploughing in his corn-field. This piquet was concealed from view, but Col. T. could hear their voices, as they conversed with each other, & he waited in his concealment more than an hour before he saw one of them. At last one of the guards walked through an open space, as if on the look-out, & stopped & looked around. That moment was seized to fire on him by Col. T., from a rest, & the man fell instantly with a loud shriek, followed by groans which rapidly became more faint. His companions seemed to draw the body away, but they kept low & out of sight. Col. T. is confident that he killed the soldier, & that he died quickly, from his moans becoming inaudible. He & his companions then moved higher up the right bank of the river, &, on a bald hill, came in sight of a much larger number, the main body of the piquet, across the river, at some half mile distance. The enemy fired sundry shots at them, which went plenty far to strike them, but all were wide of the mark. After getting under cover, our men returned the fire, & with rifles of sufficient range—but also without

---

[5] At First Manassas, Terry and Lubbock, whose brother was the Civil War governor of Texas, carried out valuable reconnaissance missions while attached to the staff of General James Longstreet. Later, they returned to Texas and organized a cavalry regiment, known as Terry's Texas Rangers, which compiled a splendid war record in the western theater of operations. An early casualty of the war, Terry died leading his rangers in a charge at Rowlett's Station, Kentucky, on December 17, 1861.

effect, as they supposed, except making the piquet scatter at every fire. Col. Terry told me of these circumstances, at his hotel, & on my inquiring as to his arms, invited me to his room to see them. His equipment in rifles, pistols & Bowie knife is as perfect as possible. The breech loading (Moroc) rifles cost $130 each. I wish we had a thousand such men, & as well armed & equipped, to carry on guerrilla operations. Among [1437] the mountains & defiles of our upper country, & the swamps & ravines of the lower, with woods, they would be more effective to resist, than ten times their number of invaders, in their offensive operations. Capt. Cuthbert & others, speaking on this subject, greatly condemn these operations, & pronounce the secret shooting of a sentinel on his post as nothing less than murder. I should also join in as strong condemnation, if we were opposing an honorable enemy, carrying on honorable & legitimate warfare. But we are entirely wronged, & on the defensive. The aggressive war begun & waged against us is of the most atrocious character, & conducted on a system of brigandage & outrage of every kind. Near Hampton, private property has been either stolen or wantonly destroyed—houses burnt—fields laid waste—& slaves invited to flee to & be protected by them—& this latter act sustained by the heads of the government. This one procedure alone, independent of all pecuniary loss so produced to the owners, is threatening, in the designed consequences, to our institutions, & destructive to our well-being. On these grounds, I deem that the enemy should be treated as robbers, incendiaries, & murderers—& that every soldier should be shot, whom it is not as easy & certain to make a prisoner. The invaded country has a great advantage in carrying on guerrilla hostilities. And as we may profit greatly by such operations, & our enemy much less, if at all, it seems to me that it would be over-scrupulous in us, if refusing to avail . . . ourselves of this advantage, when our stronger enemy has so many superior advantages in other respects, & has no scruple in using them to full extent.

This is a pretty country, of undulating surface approaching to hilly. Most of the surface is cleared, & in small fields, within [1438] many small bodies of wood-land interspersed. The roads, wherever on inclined planes, are worn & worked deep, & narrow, & make dangerous defiles for the passage of troops, if confronted by artillery, or by infantry in ambuscade. The intrenchments recently constructed, & now in the course of construction & extension, are located with reference to these features of the country, & the probable routes of invading troops.

The camp of our regiment (Col. Kershaw's 2nd S.C.,) is in a pretty situation, a grove of oak trees, just outside of the village, & next to the enemy's camp at Falls' church, said to be 8 miles off, & 14 from Alexandria. We have much idle time, & wearisome, for want of employment or amusement—& this is the worse for myself, as, for want of bodily ability, I could not perform, & have not undertaken, any of the drill, guard, or fatigue duties. So all my time is on my hands—and nothing but conversation & the few newspapers, for employment or amusement. But there are many intelligent gentlemen among the privates of our (& no doubt other) companies, as well as officers, & visitors, to converse with. While there is perfect subordination to command, & respectful demeanor to the officers, in our company, & at all times, yet when off of duty, there is also equality & freedom of conversation, between our officers & privates, as when at home or in civil life. The captain's tent is a free & common resort for all the company. Our eating table which stands on one side of the tent, & the officers' seats, are, at other times, resorted to as the chosen place for conversation, & for writing letters—& there there is every night an assemblage for conversation, in which officers & privates, of our & other companies, meet as gentlemen & equals. [1439] After dark, & before 9 P.M., (when the fires & lights are put out, except at officers' tents,) clusters of men are collected around the lights at various tents, in conversation. Merry laughter is often heard from some distant group. Last night there was some good singing in harmonized parts. The lights, & the surrounding groups of soldiers, under the trees, present a very pleasing scene, & great variety of changing lights & shadows. . . .

July 9. . . . I went early to the village to collect verbal news, but heard none. Lincoln's message in the newspapers. Saw assembled, & the riding off, of a guerrilla party of 12, under direction of Capt. Terry. He was in his dress & equipment for service. He had on a dark gray flannel shirt, outside of his linen, vest, pantaloons of like gray color. He carried his formidable & breech-loading rifle, & two large revolvers & a bowie knife in his belt. His companions, except two, (who accompanied him before, & one of them the guide,) all seemed to be powerful men, well mounted, & all volunteers for the occasion. Among them were Col. Keitt & Capt. Green, both of S.C. All were well & variously armed. Most of them returned at night, having seen nothing, & after [1440] getting thoroughly drenched in a heavy rain which fell in the afternoon. No news from Johnston's army, except that what we heard before was false, of his advance on Martinsburg—instead of which he had fallen back to Winchester. His force is much smaller than Patterson's—& the present prospect of a general engagement there now seems less than has been here for two weeks.

July 10. No news. Invited this noon to Col. Kershaw's tent, with some 8 or 10 officers, where we conversed for half an hour, while they took a drink of whiskey or wine. I heard there some things which are anything but encouraging. An officer said that our powder (in the cartridges) was inferior in quality, & also many of the percussion caps defective. Some regiments have only the old muskets, formerly flint-lock, altered to percussion. These, however, I do not think as badly of as do others. I also gathered that our advanced force, at this place, (in all some 8, or 9000 men,) was not expected to withstand long the much larger number that the enemy can bring upon us on any day—but to fall back on our main body, at Manassas Junction, if not both joining at the intermediate position on Bull Run, the previous post of this advanced portion of the army. It is said that the northern forces in & this side of Washington, & all of which may be speedily concentrated on this advance of 8 or 9000, are estimated at 60,000. Our numbers are kept very secret from the public. But I cannot suppose that all at & near Manassas Junction & this place can exceed 30,000. It is inconceivable to me, & seems inexcusable, [1441] why our armies here & elsewhere have not been greatly reinforced. As yet, the volunteers have not been near all accepted, & no resort made to drafts of militia, or a call of militia in mass, at the most exposed & endangered points. I have confidence that our men, behind intrenchments, & with warning, could & would oppose 10 times their number of the northern forces—or be equal to them in open field, if only 2 to 3, or perhaps 1 to 2. But there is no reason why we should incur the risks of such unequal terms. The construction of earth-works in advance of our foremost positions still continues. The rear regiments of our advanced brigades have no intrenchments. Between Manassas Junction & this place, the engineers are directing the making of new roads, shorter or better than portions of the old.—This afternoon another heavy rain. The picket guards have to stand all such weather, & for 24 hours, without fire at night. Such exposure is worse to bear than all the labors & fighting. Some of our men, just relieved from their 24 hours service on picket guard, & thoroughly drenched, came into our crowded tent, & were refreshed by some of our hot coffee, much to their comfort.

July 11. No newspaper mail last night. But I saw a late Washington paper. This states that a forward movement of 40,000 men is to be made on us this week. We attach no credit to the report. This paper also contained a serious account, very amusing to us who knew the truth in part, of the little affair of Terry & two others only, on Sunday afternoon. This account admits that two of their picket guards were killed—which is one more than our men claimed or suspected. It also admits that the numbers of the enemy's out-post were 200, a German battallion [*sic*]. Still they claim (as usual) the advantage—as they increase our three scouts to a strong force of infantry [1442] & cavalry, & that firing was kept up on both sides for some two to three hours, during which they saw "several saddles emptied" by their fire, & they suppose that they killed at least a dozen of our men! Yet this report is not much more false than all that the enemy make of the many skirmishes which have taken place—& no doubt, many of them, without correction, will pass into future history.—This morning came to our breakfast the Rev. Mr. [Robert W.] Barnwell [, Jr.] of S.C., a visitor, Though a very young man, he is distinguished as a scholar & a preacher.[6] With him came Prof. [Charles S.] Venable, formerly of Va. & now of the College of S.Ca.—in service here as a private, & lately acting as military engineer.[7] . . .

July 12. Some field artillery pieces have been mounted on the intrenchments. Fatigue parties are cutting down trees in the woods in advance of our position, & on the different routes by which the enemy may attack us, to obstruct their progress. At the same time we hear that Gen. Bonham is impressing all the wagons that can be obtained, for which we can imagine no object except to move back

---

[6] The nephew of a distinguished former president of South Carolina College, Barnwell was chaplain and professor of religion and moral philosophy at that institution. During the war he performed valuable hospital work in Virginia until his death from typhoid fever in 1863.

[7] Venable had followed the famed Le Conte brothers from the University of Georgia to South Carolina College, receiving an appointment as professor of mathematics and astronomy in the fall of 1857. He accepted a commission with the Corps of Engineers in March, 1862, and served on the staff of General Lee during most of the remainder of the war.

the baggage & provisions, co-incident with this force falling back when assailed by the enemy. This movement would be greatly disliked by all of us, & in addition to all other objections, a retreat will be discouraging, unless after good fighting, & damaging severely the superior assailing force.—I am glad to see that the Governor has called out all the remaining militia, in mass, of this & 8 other adjacent counties. This will not only add much to our military force, but will throw some of the war burdens on the men who have been willing to stay at home & shun them. Also, for this county & Prince William, it will compel the many [1444] tories either to serve in the army against their northern friends, or to leave Va. & join them.—Col. Terry informed me, & asked my advice thereupon, that he had asked for a captaincy of Texas Rangers, which he knew [he] could raise, of men of the best description & capacity for guerrilla service. Instead of this, he had been offered by the President the Colonelcy of a regiment of such troops, to be raised in like manner. The offer placed him as he said "in a devil of a fix," & he was unwilling to accept the higher place, for several reasons—of which one was that he did not think he would be qualified to command a regiment, though very confident of his ability to lead 100 or 200 men in guerrilla service. I advised him & urged him to accept, & to bring into our service so valuable a force. Others did the like—& he set out for Richmond this day, (as before required,) to confer with the President on the subject.—The picket guard, large before, has been doubled in number. It is understood that the forces of the enemy between our position & the Potomac have been greatly increased. . . .

July 13. Late in last night a tremendous storm of heavy rain with thunder & lightning. If the enemy's increased force had designed an early advance, this rain, added to three others in the preceding three days, would, by making the roads soft, greatly embarrass the movements of artillery.—A newspaper report, seen this morning, from a Washington & northern writer, says that there are now 32 regiments near to Alexandria & on this [1446] side of the Potomac . . . & 38 on the other side—including, I suppose, all in Md. . . . The pickets were doubled in number last night, & for the future—& the call on our regiment alone is 100 men for this service alone. Our company furnished 50 for the next 24 hours. Another very heavy rain early this afternoon, which made two for the suffering of the picket of last night & today. . . . The pickets tonight are to be

[65]

advanced (in part,) more than a mile nearer to the enemy's post at Falls Church—whose forces have also been advanced, as well as greatly reinforced, as reported. . . .

July 14. Though the rain ceased last evening before 6 P.M. when the new guards marched to their posts, the weather continued damp, raw, & very cool. . . . The army opposed to us near the Potomac has lately taken position in advance in two other points besides Falls church, viz. Annandale, on the turn-pike road from Alex. & at Springfield, on the rail-road—each of the three positions being within 8 or 8½ miles from our camps. Our picket guards extend about half way to Falls Church.—There exists, & is permitted hereabout, a most extraordinary condition of things. Some hundreds of northerners long ago settled as Farmers, in this county, & mostly between this place & Alex. or Georgetown. They & their children have continued Yankees in everything but residence. Only five of their whole number are believed to be true to the South. All the others are [1448] tories—many, females as well as males, supposed to act as spies for the enemy, & traitors to our cause. Yet they have not been molested, &, by their position & connections, (many being between the two opposing armies,) have it in their power to serve the enemy, by daily information, to our incalculable injury. Yet this is suffered, & this traitorous population principally fills the section between our camps & the enemy's army. . . . Mr. Williams, whose acquaintance I have made here, is an intelligent old gentleman & a strong southerner. His farm was near to Alexandria, from which he had been driven by the near approach of the enemy. 4 of his young negro men had been forced by Gen. [Daniel] Tyler's orders & soldiers to accompany them to their positions.[8] One of these slaves, a very smart fellow, gained Tyler's confidence by pretending entire willingness to serve the enemy, & to shoot his master, if opposed to him in battle. He was taken into the Connecticut general's domestic service. Profiting by the facilities which this somewhat confidential service afforded, he soon made his escape, & got here to his master. He reported all that he knew, to Mr. Williams, & to Gen. Bonham of the position of the enemy's advanced position. He stated that his three fellow slaves,

---

[8] A graduate of West Point, Brigadier General Tyler (1799–1882) commanded the First Division, Connecticut Volunteers, at First Manassas. He later led a brigade at the siege of Corinth, Mississippi. Following the war he built the town of Anniston, Alabama, naming it for his daughter-in-law.

who had been forced to go with the Yankee scouts, were armed & put in uniform, & were regularly drilled as soldiers, in the enemy's ranks. Also, as a precaution for their recapture & punishment [1449] (as supposed) in case of their desertion, their heads were shaved. This converting the stolen or inveigled slaves into soldiers is a new feature of the atrocious policy of the enemy. It is an unmistakable indication of the desire, & intention, to facilitate & induce the insurrection of our slaves, & their being better prepared for military action, & provided with trained military leaders of their own class. . . . There are sundry indications of a sudden general movement being expected. Some days ago, all the men were ordered to have three days' provisions cooked in advance. This order has not been obeyed, for the sufficient reason that no regiment, company, or mess, had three days' rations in advance. Our mess, whose provisions are bought, was never so scarce of food, & now has not a full meal in advance. The sick have been removed to more distant hospitals—all the wagons impressed that could be found. This evening, orders were read for every one to reduce his baggage to the smallest quantity, & no more than he can carry, & to pack up all the extra baggage for early & sudden removal. At least this is the supposed intention of the order. I have feared for some days back, that the policy of Gen. Beauregard would require, in case of the enemy attacking us, the falling back of our advanced corps on the forces in our rear. I have full confidence in his good judgment & military knowledge, & am ready to submit to & to second whatever he may [1450] order. But I shall, in common I believe with all our army here, greatly regret the necessity for a retreat. It will encourage the enemy, who now, nearly double in numbers to every one of our threatened armies, are very slow, if not afraid to attack either one as posted—& will depress, if not discourage our men, & all those who can come to aid us. I believe that if our army had to choose, the voices of nine-tenths would be in favor of fighting here, against twice, if not thrice their numbers, rather than to retreat before fighting. With the support of our earth-works, we would hope, & expect, to repel if not defeat the enemy, if attacking our position with much greater numbers.

July 15. Sent off to the rear, by orders & aid of the authorities, the surplus baggage—with which went my trunk, & all my clothing except the outer suit on me, & two changes of other articles in my carpet-bag, my overcoat, (which serves also as my pillow at night,)

& my two blankets. Thus we are made as light as possible for a sudden march—the probability of which, or movement of some sort, seems to be indicated by various things. Most of the inhabitants of this village (around Fairfax C.H.) are moving away. Though the houses are few, & scattering, a large proportion are constructed of brick. These will make good positions for defence, should we have to fight the enemy while retreating, & through the village.— Lincoln's message, & more fully the report of his Secretary of the Treasury, recommend the confiscation of property of the rebels & traitors, that is, of all in the seceded states except tories, to the northern [1451] government. Various rumors, important if true, & of the most contradictory purports. . . .

July 16. Still more contradictory reports, & not one decided. But, I greatly fear that we have suffered a defeat, & heavy loss, of a large detachment of Gen. [Robert S.] Garnett's army, in Randolph county.[9]—Reports that large reinforcements have been sent from Washington to this side. Indications of a speedy advance of the enemy on this post seem now to be certain.

July 20. I have lately been separated from my papers, & all facilities for writing until this day, & thus have passed a longer time than ever previously without making an entry in my diary. I will now state, in the past tense, the important incidents of the last three days.[10]

The next following pages of the text were written hurriedly, in tents belonging to other persons, which I used thus by courtesy of the occupants, & where I was subject to frequent interruption during the limited times in which only I could thus bring up my diary. A consequence of these disadvantages was that I omitted noting many minor, yet not unimportant incidents, or remarks, in regard to matters fully seen & understood—as well as many more of more importance, not then understood, but which were sub-

---

[9] On July 10 General George B. McClellan launched his campaign against Garnett's much smaller Confederate force in western Virginia. Three days later, at Carrick's Ford, the Federals intercepted the retreating Confederates, and Garnett was killed in the ensuing skirmish. Meanwhile, Colonel John Pegram was caught at Beverly and forced to surrender his command of 555 men to McClellan on the same day. Total Confederate losses in the campaign amounted to nearly 700.

[10] The following two paragraphs comprise the first of fifteen notes inserted by the diarist at various times after he penned his initial account of the Manassas campaign (*e.g.*, see below, p. 560). Subsequent notes will be identified as they appear in the narrative.

sequently explained to me by the published official reports of commanding officers, or still later by the information of trustworthy eye-witnesses, who saw more than circumstances permitted to myself. To supply these defects, so far as then known, I copied this account of the battles of Bull Run & Manassas, with additions, & in a more full & satisfactory form, not long after the occurrences. That enlarged copy was written for my daughter, Mrs. Mildred Sayre, residing in Kentucky—& to her that paper was afterwards conveyed, by a safe private hand, together with a like enlarged copy from my diary of the incidents of the siege & capture of Fort Sumter. In consequence of later events, it is probable that those papers are either already lost, or destroyed, or may not be recovered. On that account, & being desirous to correct errors & supply defects, by my later information, I now shall prepare these notes. It would be a more easy & agreeable task, to do as I did before, re-write the whole, & so make of the whole materials a more corrected & regular & clear narrative. But as I may be misled by my frail memory, I prefer to preserve the original writing, without alteration, as, however defective, showing truly my first impressions, so far as they were stated at the time, or within a few days after the occurrences. Thus, though more awkward & inconvenient in structure, as a whole, there will be the advantage of all later additions, not noted at the times, being stated separately in these notes.

The most important explanations subsequently offered for my information or correction, were furnished by the several official reports of the battle of Manassas by officers on both sides. The most instructive of these, in regard to the matters I saw, & treated of, is the report . . . of Col. J. B. Kershaw, the colonel of our (2nd. S.C.) regiment, & acting commander of our brigade for the occasion. Also, for incidents of the 18th of July, at our intrenched post on Bull Run, Gen. Bonham's report gives additional information. For the rout of the retreating enemy at the "Suspension Bridge" over Cub Run, & the disastrous effects, the fullest published information I found in the two official reports of the Yankee commanders of brigades, Col. [Samuel P.] Heintzelman, & Col. [Ambrose E.] Burnside, whose troops were severally in or near the closely packed mass of men, horses, artillery &c. on which the firing from Capt. [Delaware] Kemper's guns produced effects so remarkable, & so disastrous for the fleeing enemy.

Early in the morning of the 17th. it was evident that important movements were to be made, &, so far as I heard opinions of the officers & soldiers, it was the universal wish that there would be a defence of our then position to the utmost of our power. The enemy's army was known to be advancing from Falls Church. Orders were received to strike tents, & hasten to put all the camp equipage & remaining baggage into the wagons. We had barely & hurriedly eaten breakfast, & packed up everything for removal, before our regiment (as all the others,) was mustered. Our regiment (2nd S.C.) had occupied the advanced camp, & from it our company, (the Palmetto Guard,) & another were immediately marched out towards the enemy, & diverging from the road, were posted in the edge of a piece of wood within 150 yards of the road, over which the passage of one body of the invading army was looked for. Previously, some of the advancing troops had been visible from the village, in a distant field, supposed to be flank guards. We had not remained long on our post before [1452] we saw Capt. [A. Burnet] Rhett's company of riflemen advancing rapidly along the road, & pushing on ahead of us. As learned afterwards, this movement was to bring in our piquet guard in safety. We were soon ordered to march—retracing our steps, & passing along the east of the village, passed through the extensive lines of earthworks. Although we had now heard that the enemy's advancing force, under Gen. MacDowell, was more than 40,000, we still supposed that we would fight before retreating. But in addition to the necessity caused by the great disparity of numbers, I afterwards learned that for some time previously Gen. Beauregard's *sealed* orders had been held by Gen. Bonham, to be opened only on the advance of the enemy, the purport of which was to retreat without resistance. This was a part of a general plan of operations, & probably designed to draw the invading army farther into the interior, & much farther from its supplies. Our march was rapid—much of it at first in "double quick" time, that is, a full trot, & nearly as fast as I could run. I had marched in the ranks from our camp, & kept my place, both when advancing & retreating, for nearly two miles. By this time it was manifest to me that nothing was designed then but to retreat—& also, that I could not hold out in such a rapid march for another mile. Therefore I asked & obtained leave, during a short halt, to ride on the caisson of Capt. Kemper's light artillery (of Alexandria,) the company which did such excellent service at the

[70]

Vienna station.[11] Temporary halts had been made in several different intrenchments, merely to be seen there by the approaching enemy, & to give them a notion that we meant there to make a stand. The cause of the haste was to prevent the enemy's out-flanking our little army, which [1453] they were attempting to do with one of their three separate columns . . . . A few cannon shot had been fired by the enemy, at such distance as to be of no effect, & to leave it doubtful whether they were aimed at us, or designed as signals. The day was very hot, & our men suffered greatly with heat. The men hurried only because so ordered—& the disorder of their ranks, which increased towards the latter part of the march, was caused only by the exhaustion of many rendering it impossible to keep up with the more enduring. When reaching near to Centreville (a very small village,) which offers an excellent position for an engagement with a pursuing & superior force, our army was halted, & remained in order of battle for some time, & afterwards at ease, & free to seek the little shade of trees, for the remainder of the day, offering battle to the enemy—who however did not appear in sight. In the afternoon, it was learned that they had also halted within 1½ miles of our position. Four pieces of field artillery (Kemper's, attached to our regiment,) were placed in position in a small intrenchment which our men had some weeks before constructed. At dark, both the cavalry & infantry were placed in line, behind & below the crest of the long eminence on which the artillery was posted, & ordered to retain their places. The horses were there fed, & the infantry soldiers slept by their arms—as I did, having rejoined my company on our arrival. The moon shined brightly early, but before midnight was obscured by clouds. At midnight orders were quietly given to stand to our arms. . . . After waiting some short time, & no enemy appearing, (as seemed to have been expected by Gen. Bonham, our commander,) the order was given to resume the retreat. Just before, signals, made by an elevated light, had been exhibited at our station, & which were seen at & probably answered from Manassas [1454] Junction, & by which information was given to Gen. Beauregard's head-quarters, & probably his orders, for continuing the retreat, were received. The whole force

---

[11] This was a minor action on June 17 in which Colonel Maxcy Gregg's First South Carolina Infantry, to which Kemper's battery was temporarily attached, ambushed a trainload of Ohio troops at Vienna, Virginia.

was soon in motion—I resuming my seat on the caisson wagon. Even to me, the passage was very tedious & disagreeable, with the jolting over the rough road, & my back aching for want of any support to lean against. It was far worse with the previously wearied walkers. The march to Bull Run, of 4 miles, occupied nearly 4 hours—& we arrived there & crossed over just before the dawn of day-light on the 18th. As soon as all of our regiment had arrived, (it having served as the rear-guard of the retreating army, as it had occupied the advance post when encamped near Fairfax C.H.) the companies took positions in the several intrenchments just below the public road, (at Mitchell's Ford), which had been thrown up when the army had previously occupied this position, before advancing to Fairfax C.H. Here we remained through the day—at first expecting the main attack of the enemy at this point, & which it seems was so intended by the enemy, & indicated in their first operations, though subsequently diverted. We had before heard that they had entered Centreville soon after we left it. It is strange to me that they did not attack our army in its march thence—by which they might have inflicted severe injury, even if failing to convert the slow & disorderly retreat of our wearied army to flight & a rout.

We had seen through the previous forenoon the smoke from the houses set on fire by the enemy at Fairfax C.H.—reported to be the Court-House, a Church, & one or more private buildings. By gross neglect, part of the tents of our company, as of others [1455] of the regiment, much of the private baggage, & nearly all the provisions, were not put in wagons, after we marched out of the camp, & were left & taken by the enemy.

It was learned early in the forenoon that the Yankee army, [or] a portion of it, had reached a position within a mile or two [of our] intrenchments at Bull Run. Kemper's field pieces & company recrossed . . . the stream & lowground, to give them a few shots. Our company & another also recrossed the Run, to support & defend the artillery, moving to their position in "double quick time"—as were made all the succeeding movements, both advancing & retiring. I had, because of my weakness & fatigue, given out all thoughts of moving with my company, & keeping up with them—& in addition, the stream could be crossed only by wading mid-leg deep. So I, and a lamed volunteer only, William Elliott, of our company remained in our intrenchment. Before these companies so ad-

[72]

vanced, the enemy's cannon opened against our intrenchments. We heard the balls whistle over us, & one of the shells exploded so near, that a fragment of it fell within 30 yards of the rear of the excavation for the bank. . . . Not one of their discharges did us any harm, or struck our works. Capt. Kemper, when beyond the Run, from an eminence, fired 6 balls or shells among the advancing enemy, causing their disorder & hasty falling back, & then, as previously ordered, retreated to re-occupy his previous position in the rear of some of the intrenchments, & on a level high enough for his pieces to be fired over the heads of our men in the trenches, if the enemy should approach near enough. The rear of the intrench-ment of our company, & others, was occupied in like manner by a company of the Richmond Howitzers, Capt. [John C.] Shields. Our riflemen were too far from the enemy to hurt them, though exposed to their artillery fire, & did not fire a gun, when across the stream, before following our artillery in retiring. At a later time of the day, on a false impression of the enemy renewing the early attack, & advancing on us, the same artillery & rifle companies again crossed over [1456] & not finding the enemy within reach, soon after again returned as before.[12]

The firing aimed at our intrenchments was soon after diverted to another quarter, &, as appeared evident, by the attack from our forces which were extended on our right. (The various positions of our troops, with the large reinforcements, extended for some miles along the west side of the stream, & both above & below the public road by the intrenchments we occupied.) Cannon reports were heard from below, & soon were answered by the enemy—after which they drew farther from the position of our regiment, & not another shot was fired at it during the remainder of the day. The cannonade grew more rapid, & soon musketry was added, which for a time rattled continuously. By the passage of officers & messen-gers, by our rear, we learned that the fight on our side was carried on by three Virginian regiments & the battalion of La. Washington Artillery, engaging (as supposed) the whole force there present, on

---

[12] The diarist is imprecise regarding time. Kemper, who early in the morning had posted two guns on Kemper's Hill, about six hundred yards in advance of the Confederate center at Mitchell's Ford, retired across the stream shortly after 12:30 P.M. Accompanied by Kershaw's regiment, he recrossed Bull Run at 4:00 P.M. and engaged the enemy briefly before again retreating to the south bank of the Run. *Official Records*, Vol. II, 459.

the left wing, of the enemy's army. The firing afterwards ceased entirely for a time, the enemy having been driven back, & our small force not venturing to pursue them across the Run. Subsequently, the Yankees returned & the fight was renewed as vigorously as before, & with like results. Then it was (about 3 P.M.), as before stated, that Capt. Kemper's Artillery, with two cannon, was again sent over the stream, & up the hill, & our riflemen to support them. Two round shot & 3 Shrapnel shells were fired, & the latter with obvious & great injury to the enemy, who rapidly scattered & disappeared from view—when the artillery again returned across the stream to its post. All at our post of course were [1457] bound to remain there, idle listeners to the exciting sounds of the battle, which was within less than a mile of us, down the stream.[13] At one time only could we see from the intrenchment of our company something of the conflict & the combatants. Between two pieces of wood-land the view from us stretched over a wheat field, as a broad vista. Through this opening, I could see the rapid passage of combatants, by the gleaming of their bright arms. The smoke from the cannon & small arms hung like a heavy cloud over-head, & dust elsewhere indicated the tramp of our cavalry on the arable bottom land. About 4 P.M. the combat again was suspended, by the second repelling & then entire & final withdrawal of the enemy. The fight had been maintained by a very inferior force (in numbers) on our side, & with great gallantry. Our whole number killed, wounded, & missing, is reported to be only 52—of which 2 were killed out-right, & 8 more died afterwards in the hospital. Of the enemy's loss we shall never have a true report. 72 dead were afterwards counted, without embracing the whole ground, & taking in none struck by Kemper's shot & shells, which operated at different places from the main conflict. The loss is variously computed—& it is believed that the whole killed & wounded of the enemy did not fall much short of 1000.[14] Nothing more was heard of them that evening. Small as was our loss, Gen. Beauregard (who commanded in person,) thought, as was reported, that more than half of it was caused by one of the Va.

---

[13] At Blackburn's Ford, where the major clash on July 18 occurred.

[14] This estimate is greatly exaggerated. According to the official reports of General Beauregard and Colonel Israel B. Richardson, the Union field commander, the Confederates lost fifteen dead and fifty-three wounded while Union casualties were nineteen killed, thirty-eight wounded, and twenty-six missing. *Official Records*, Vol. II, 314, 446.

[1458] regiments, by mistake, firing upon another. This deplorable blunder, of firing upon friends, has occurred sundry times already. And the day after, or night after that, some of one of our picket guards fired upon & killed one of their own body, placed in advance. Yet, to guard against such mistakes, all our men were made to wear badges, & which have been changed every day, to prevent the enemy using them as disguise. For the first day, (17th.,) it was a red badge, of the breadth & outline of an epaulet, on the right shoulder. For the next day it was transferred to the left shoulder. Last night, (19th.) the badge was yellow (the cloth being doubled, & turned over,) & on the right shoulder. Today, all these signs were discarded, & the mark of recognition, as friends, was the military salute, made with either hand held up to the head for some seconds. [Note 4 follows]

From all apparent indications on our side, as well as the early (& for some hours continued) fire from the enemy's artillery on the intrenchments of our brigade on the 18th., it seemed that our post, at Mitchell's ford, would be the object of the main attack. The intrenchments did not afford space for the men to spread themselves in single line, behind the breast-work of earth. We had room only by being arranged four deep. We were ordered by Capt. Cuthbert, & sufficiently drilled in the movement, if having to fire, that the men of the front rank, immediately after discharging their pieces, should fall back to the rear, to re-load, & the second, & third & fourth ranks successively advance & retire in like manner, each one moving up towards the breast-work, as the man before him made room. We were ordered, generally, to remain in the intrenchment, & behind the breast-work, to be protected from the balls from the enemy's artillery, which every now & then were aimed at our position, & passed over us. The shells we could not be protected from, if any should lodge within the open intrenchments, or explode over them. But, after the fighting began below, & so near to the post of our regiment, neither the exposure to the discharges from the enemy's batteries, nor the previous general orders of our officers, prevented our men standing on the rising ground immediately back of the intrenchment, to see as much as possible of the combatants. The situation, & the little that we could see, & the much more that we could plainly hear of the sounds of the conflict, presented a most exciting scene. . . . [end of Note 4]

A little before twilight, all of our regiment, with Kemper's company of artillery, were marched from our trenches two miles up the course of the stream, & made to take positions on the edge of the high land bordering on the lowground, which is there, as at the intrenchments, covered by forest, but un-thinned—whereas at the intrenchments we had occupied all the small growth had been cut away. It was dark before we took our places, halted in lines of separate companies, & were discharged, but ordered to remain in line, in open order, & to sleep by our arms. This was then supposed to be the most endangered point, & through which the enemy would be most likely to attempt to penetrate, [1459] & by surprise, at night. Rain had begun to fall fast—but fortunately it ceased soon—though not before I was wet to the skin where my woollen clothing was thinnest. . . . Light misty drizzle fell later, but fortunately not enough to penetrate woollen clothing, though all the upper surface was wet when I awaked & rose early in the morning, to seek the warmth of a fire. None had been permitted to be kindled in the night before, as it was especially desired to prevent the new occupation of this position being made known to the enemy. It was hoped that they would attempt to cross the bottom & Run here, without expecting opposition. Nearly all the intervening distance to our previous position below, at intervals, was also occupied by other companies—& each had, or soon after had, a low & slight bank thrown up against the old fence which divided the open & sloping ground & the wooded bottom, along which we were posted. Kemper's Artillery company occupied the top of the hill back of us—& this day (19th) they threw [1460] up two intrench-ments, & placed their 4 cannon behind them to fire on the enemy over the heads of the infantry advanced below. This day, (19th.,) when the other companies were digging & throwing up their slight defences, the Palmetto Guard & the adjacent company were for-bidden to make any, so as to leave a clear sweep for Kemper's cannon balls, where the passage of the enemy was most likely to be attempted.—To the men of our company generally, who were young & vigorous, though accustomed to good fare at home, the exposure of the last night was of less discomfort than the want of food. The provisions of our company & most others had been lost, & there was very little food on hand, or chance to eat, since our hasty meal on the morning of 17th before leaving Fairfax C.H. The very little bread brought in our haversacks made all our supply until the morning of 19th., when new supplies were furnished, & meals brought cooked from the wagon yard, two miles in rear of our lines. . . . When food came to us on the 19th., the fresh beef was too tough for my few teeth to chew, & besides had been salted so highly by the cook that it was made unpalatable; & otherwise I would have feared to eat it, as it would increase thirst, & our water was very scarce & also dirty—the muddy stream of Bull Run, contaminated with the washing & filth of all the troops stationed on the border, & a few adjacent small pools, of clearer but not much purer water, being our only sources of supply. I tried to drink as little as possible—& yet the very idea of the privation must have increased the want, & made me drink more than ordinarily. Our [1461] bread was hard crackers, of which only I could eat, & to eat which was slow & hard work, & very little of such bread sufficed for me. Our coffee was without sugar, & quite unpalatable, & could not be drunk by me. One thing only would have been good—some beef soup, which looked rich & tempting—but it also had been so excessively salted by the cook that I could not swallow a second mouth-ful [*sic*]. Still I suffered less from hunger than perhaps the best-fed soldier in the camp, owing to my peculiarity of constitution in this respect— or, I may say I suffered no hunger, & felt but little appetite. . . . The enemy remained quiet all the 19th & 20th, & the visible lines stretched out, (as reported by our scouts, the intervening trees hiding them entirely from our lines,) about a mile from us, on the hills across Bull Run & its wooded bottom land. The bottom here is narrow, & the land beyond, as on our side, arable, & rising gradually but quickly to high levels.

On the 19th. we had information that large reinforcements were hastening to join our army. That from Manassas (4 miles off,) had been sent on the 17th, & fought the main battle on the 18th. It is reported that Patterson's army, 30,000, had retired from Martinsburg [1462] to Harper's Ferry, as supposed to push on by the railroad to Washington, & thence to reinforce the enemy here. This allowed Gen. Jos. Johnston's army to leave Winchester—which was done so quietly & speedily that the designed movement was not suspected in Winchester on the 17th, & was completed to Manassas, & partly or wholly to Bull Run on the 20th, by the whole army, some 18,000.[15] Gen. Beauregard, it is said, aims to out-flank

---

[15] The figures given by the diarist are somewhat inflated for both armies. Actually, Patterson's army numbered 18,000 and Johnston's 12,000. Moreover, not all of Johnston's units had arrived in Manassas by July 20.

the enemy on both sides, while inviting attack (by seeming neglect of full defence) in the centre, & so to beat the invaders, & cut off their retreat. A signal victory over this large army would in effect close the war. Success is especially needed for us now, when the Yankees are so much encouraged by their recent success, & our great disaster in Randolph county. . . .

After an idle & tedious day, (the 19th.) enlivened only by the frequent successive & contradictory reports of movements of the enemy, &c., our regiment [1463] passed the night as before in order of battle, & slept lying by their arms. A night attack on our line was expected by our higher officers, & we sat, with arms ready in our hands, & in our lines, looking out for attack, & attempted surprise, for an hour before we lay down, by orders, in our ranks for sleep. I again performed my full share in this night's service & endurance, again sleeping on the ground, & in the open air. . . . This morning, the 20th, believing that no very speedy hostile action was to be expected, I determined to go to look out for my baggage, or for some information of it—& also to find a shelter for obtaining some rest. Having obtained leave, I rode in a light wagon, with some other passengers, to the wagon yard, & was able to recover from one of our wagons full of baggage only my small bag of clothing, containing also my writing materials. Thence I proceeded to Manassas Junction, & inquired in vain as to where was my trunk, sent off previous to the retreat. Returning, I again stopped at the wagon yard, where I had offered to me the use of a tent to write, & to lodge in—& there commenced the writing of the foregoing pages. Wrote until 10 P.M. before going to sleep on the blankets of some other of our company, as mine could not be found, & got out of the wagon.

July 23. Again I have been separated since early in the morning of Sunday, 21st, until noon 23rd, soon after which I resume my writing. I had resumed my writing early on Sunday morning, 21st, & had returned to it immediately after breakfast, [1464] when I heard the sound of cannon, indicating an attack by the enemy from across the Run. I hastily locked up my papers &c. & taking my musket & accoutrements, I walked towards our camp-ground, which is 1½ to 2 miles distant. When approaching to near the very high & open eminence between, (McLean's hill,) I saw Kemper's artillery at a distance going at a trot towards the Run on the public road at our first position.[16] I stopped for half an hour on the highest ground,

---

[16] Mitchell's Ford.

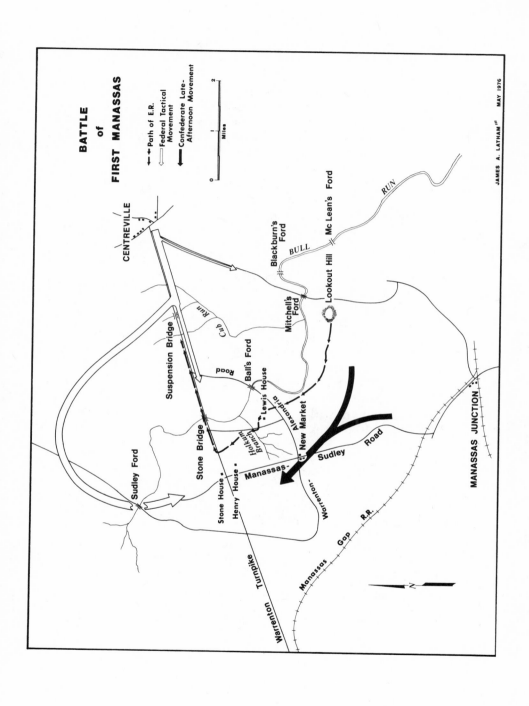

BATTLE
of
FIRST MANASSAS

Legend:
- ◄··· Path of E.R.
- ⇦ Federal Tactical Movement
- ⬛ Confederate Late-Afternoon Movement

Miles
0   1   2

JAMES A. LATHAM III   MAY 1976

Map labels:
- CENTREVILLE
- Suspension Bridge
- Cub Run
- Ball's Ford
- Lewis House
- Blackburn's Ford
- Mitchell's Ford
- BULL RUN
- Lookout Hill
- Mc Lean's Ford
- Holkum Branch
- Stone Bridge
- Sudley Ford
- Stone House
- Henry House
- New Market
- Alexandria
- Manassas-Sudley Road
- Warrenton-
- Manassas Gap R.R.
- Warrenton Turnpike
- MANASSAS JUNCTION
- N

(McLean's hill?)[17] which affords the most commanding view of the surrounding country, & especially of the opposite heights where the Yankee army was extended for some 6 miles in separate camps, & (as reported) in some intrenchments. They were throwing cannon balls & shells, from two places, supposed to be intrenched batteries, one on the height central of their & of our lines, & nearly opposite this place, & from another lower down, & which seemed to be near their extreme left & opposite our right flank. The central battery was the most active. The balls & shells seemed, to my view, to be aimed at our main or central intrenchments, which our regiment first occupied in part. There was no fire returned. Next I went to our camp & company, & found that the intrenchment, well executed, had been continued along its line, & learned from Capt. Cuthbert that, by orders, the work had been begun at 12 the preceding night, & completed early in the morning. As there was now no reason to expect attack here more than at a dozen other places for a distance of 6 or 8 miles, & as, also, if remaining here, I would be confined to one spot all day, between a high hill & thick woods, where nothing could be seen, I asked & obtained leave of Capt. Cuthbert to return to the hill, to look out & to see the battle at a distance, if, as expected, not reaching it myself anywhere. . . .

On returning to the height, I found other persons there as spectators—& in the course of my stay, saw [Leonidas W.] Spratt of S.C. & Duncan, a reporter for southern papers. Also the Rev. Capt. [William N.] Pendleton, an excellent artillery officer, who did good service lately, & with whom I was glad to make acquaintance.[18] About 9 or 10 o'clock Generals Johnston, Beauregard & Bonham came & were among the observers with spy-glasses.[19] . . . When

---

[17] Ruffin seems uncertain of the name of this eminence. Douglas Southall Freeman referred to it as Lookout Hill (*Lee's Lieutenants*, I, 56n), while neither Beauregard or Johnston, both of whom spent most of the morning there, gave it any name at all. According to Beauregard, it occupied a central position in the Confederate line of defence and was situated "about half a mile in rear of Mitchell's Ford." *Official Records*, Vol. II, 488.

[18] A graduate of West Point and an ordained Episcopal minister, Pendleton (1809–83) entered military service as captain of the Rockbridge Artillery. He was promoted to the rank of colonel on July 13, 1861, and appointed Chief of Artillery for Johnston's army. Later, he held the same post in Lee's Army of Northern Virginia with the rank of brigadier general, Confederate States Army.

[19] There is some discrepancy concerning the times of arrival and departure of the Confederate commanders at Lookout Hill. Beauregard stated that he and Johnston arrived at the position about 8:30 A.M. and remained until 11:30. *Official Records*,

these distinguished officers were observed, the many scattered spectators of the distant cannonade drew near to them, so as to make a crowd of 40 or 50 on a small space. Gen. Johnston quickly ordered that they should disperse. The order was given none too soon, as the next shot & sundry following from the enemy's cannon, opposite, were directed to this spot, & flew over-head. Subsequently, & long after the generals had withdrawn, other shot & shells were aimed at this hill, when not more than 6 or 8 persons remained to be exposed to the danger. But generally the discharges were otherwise directed, & as I thought mostly at our central intrenchments. The firing, from both the enemy's centre & left, was continued from 6. At 11 A.M. they had so fired 230 balls & shells, from the two batteries, or positions stated, without any fire being returned from our side—nor had there been any return from our batteries at 1 P.M. when I left—& I do not know that our opposite batteries returned the fire during all the remainder of the day. The nearest battery of the enemy to the hill on which I stood was about 1¾ miles distant—& 1 mile to our main intrenchment.

About 11 A.M. frequent firing of cannon was heard on our left, & apparently about 3 miles from my place—& the reports, from all three places, became so rapid & intermixed that the discharges from the batteries could no longer be counted by the gentleman (a chaplain,) who had noted the number previously. I have since learned that cannonading began, as well as musket firing, about 6 A.M. near the "Stone Bridge." But either the direction of the wind, the intervening woods, or something else, prevented the sound being heard by me, or by any one around me, (so far as I knew,) until about 11. Then it was soon manifest that battle had been joined in that direction, & was vigorously contested. It [1466] was supposed to be the object of both the opposed commanders to out-flank the army of the other. By doing this, McDowell might avoid our defences, & the main body of our army, & pass on to Richmond with an army too powerful to be resisted. The firing of the enemy did not cease at any point. But the only conflict was at the highest position.[20] The firing of cannon was very rapid. Once in a while the

---

Vol. II, 488, 491. Johnston estimated the time of arrival at 8:00 A.M. but agreed with Beauregard that the duration of their stay was three hours. *Ibid.*, 474. On the other hand, Bonham—the only one to refer to the site as Lookout Hill—recalled that his meeting with Beauregard and Johnston took place "a little after noon." *Ibid.*, 519.

[20] That is, upstream on the Confederate left.

sound of musketry would come to us in long maintained volleys, that sounded as continuous, and much like long continued rolling thunder. Confidence in our soldiers & our highest commanders had caused me to have but little doubt of our success, even if with a much larger number of our enemies. This, with the apparent movements of the opposed armies, satisfied me that we were beating the enemy's forces. After 12:30 P.M. I saw a numerous body of cavalry galloping by,[21] back of the hill-top, to the field of battle—I supposed that they were all the cavalry at the post—& inferred that the victory must then be nearly effected, & that the cavalry were sent to pursue the broken & fleeing enemy. Also large bodies of infantry were seen marching to the battle, which seemed an indication less favorable. The shot from the enemy's central battery were then directed to the moving troops, & many struck the ground near them during their passage. I became so excited with the sounds of the firing, & the supposed relative conditions of the opposing armies, which were invisible throughout to my eyes, & from my then position, that I determined to get near, & try to see the conclusion, & to view the field of battle immediately after the victory had been gained, & the enemy had retired from the conflict. The sun shone brightly, & the weather was very hot. Though the battle, as indicated by the sounds & smoke of the firing, had rolled far to the left (my left) of the first observed position, the direct distance was still about the same, or apparently from two to three miles. This was plenty near to see the troops with the naked eye, if they had not been always behind bodies of intervening wood, & also obscured by the smoke. Younger observers, with good eyes, did not see the men any more than myself. One [1467] of these, Dr. Jackson of Loudoun, had been with me for some hours, & we had made acquaintance without any introduction. I set out, with him, about 1 P.M. to go to the battle ground, across the intervening fields, & directed only by the smoke & noise of the battle itself . . . as neither of us knew the ground, & we had no path. We walked on quickly, & I, carrying my musket, became much heated & fatigued before getting near. To my surprise, there was no lessening of the firing as we came nearer. And though the clouds of dust raised in that neighborhood had before assured me that the cavalry had

---

[21] In all probability, this was a detachment of the Thirtieth Virginia Cavalry, commanded by Lieutenant Colonel Thomas T. Munford. *Official Records*, Vol. II, 534.

arrived there, there was no indication that they had had an opportunity to charge on the enemy. When getting quite near, on descending a hill gently sloping, where was the public road, I came up with a number of our soldiers, perhaps 100 to 200, standing without order or apparent object.[22] I learned on inquiry of those nearest to me, that they had been in the battle, & had left the field, some for slight wounds, but mostly because of exhaustion, & (as they said) by order, or by permission, to rest themselves & then to return. But none seemed to have the least desire to return. [Note 7 follows]

This was my first acquaintance, & without previous suspicion of such conduct, of the class of "skulkers" or "stragglers" from battlefields, & who since have been so noted, & so increased in numbers, & in detriment to the army & its fullest success. In my inexperience & simplicity, I at first believed what these men reported of themselves, as well as of the battle they had left. But I was struck with the strange fact, that of all these men reported as either wounded or worn down by exertion, not one was sitting or lying, as if to rest, but that all were on their feet. I had also yet to learn, that soldiers who skulk or flee from a battle, always report the most disastrous events, as if to excuse their cowardice, & to prevent any other persons from increasing their shame, by their own better conduct. Col. Kershaw's command, (which had marched on ahead of me, though I did not then know the fact,) passed by this same crowd of skulkers, & heard from them just such reports as they made to me, as I learned long afterwards.[23] . . . [end of Note 7]

In answer to my questions, I was told by some (& which seemed assented to by all) of these soldiers that our troops had been driven by the enemy for miles, (which was true, though they fell back gradually & in good order, & without ever ceasing to fight)—that the day was certainly going against us—that sundry companies & even regiments had been nearly cut to pieces—& that some of our separate bodies had fired upon each other, & very disastrously. In

---

[22] It is impossible to chart precisely Ruffin's movements during the early afternoon of July 21. After comparing a diagram drawn by the diarist (MS page 1468) with the most satisfactory map of the Manassas battlefield (*Official Records Atlas*, Plate III–2), I have concluded that the public road to which Ruffin refers was the one west of Lewis House which intersected the Warrenton Turnpike on the north and the old Warrenton-Alexandria road to the south. It is probable that the diarist encountered these skulkers at a point on that road just south of Holkum Branch. For the complete track of what I believe was Ruffin's route after leaving Lookout Hill, see page 79.

[23] *Official Records*, Vol. II, 522.

the few minutes consumed by these inquiries & answers, & occupied by doubts as to what I should do, I perceived that reinforcements of infantry were still passing on by us along the public road. Stunned as I was by the unexpected & gloomy reports, the sincerity of which I fully credited, I thought that these reinforcements might perhaps yet save the almost lost day, & that it was the duty of every man who could pull a trigger to lend his aid to their action. I hastily determined, feeble & then greatly fatigued as I was, & already suffering with thirst, (although twice drinking water from canteens of returned soldiers—) that I would go—& would try also to induce others, who had before retired, to return. Therefore I called out to those around me, & asked who would join me to go with the reinforcements [1468] to the battle. Not one replied, or made any indication of hearing, except by staring at me in silence. I said no more, but turned off & proceeded towards the battle. . . .

I had not gone on 100 yards from my setting out for the field of battle, before meeting other skulkers who had withdrawn later from the battle. I asked for the latest news, & heard from them repetitions & increase of our disasters, with the important addition that we had lost all our field artillery. This I knew must settle the matter—as the enemy, superior before, & successful now, having artillery in abundance & we having none, could speedily destroy our so weakened army. I confess, believing as I did this last report, so confidently asserted, to be true, I thought my advancing farther to be useless & foolish—& that, in the inevitable & speedy rout, or even an orderly though rapid retreat, I could not fail to be left behind, to the mercy of the pursuing enemy. I would have turned back, but for shame. [Note 8 follows]

I was not willing to return, & so soon, by & in view of the skulkers whom I had just before invited to go with me to the field. Therefore, though without a remaining hope of our retrieving the day I still walked onward, as fast as I could, but yet slowly, because of my fatigue. Other reinforcements were still marching on, & successively overtaking & out-stripping me. One of the regiments was the 19th Mississippi.[24] I had inquired frequently for my (Kershaw's)

---

[24] The diarist is mistaken about the identity of this unit, since no such regiment is listed in the Confederate organization at First Manassas. From the time of day and location on the field, it seems probable that this was Colonel William Barksdale's Thirteenth Mississippi, attached to Brigadier General Jubal A. Early's Sixth Brigade. Commencing his march about 2:00 P.M. from a point near the McLean House, Early

regiment, & at last met with a soldier who knew it, & informed me that it had marched on to the field some length of time before. He pointed out to me, some distance ahead of us, in the winding column of advancing reinforcements, the company of Secession Guards, (Capt. [W. W.] Perryman,) belonging to our regiment. This company (as I afterwards learned,) had been, in the morning, on detached service, & therefore received orders late, & after the other companies had marched. This company was made conspicuous by its spectacular uniform, of blue flannel shirts, worn outside. I thought that I would try to keep in sight of this company, & when it halted, I would join it, if my own company & the regiment were elsewhere. . . . [Shortly thereafter] I was . . . overtaken by one of Kemper's field pieces . . . which I was sure was on the route to the battle-field, or to wherever it could do the best service. There were but a few of the artillerymen along, & they were mounted on the gun-carriage & caisson. The officer in command, Sergeant Stewart, knew me, & as passing, invited me to take a seat, the only one then vacant, on the cannon, which invitation I gladly accepted. The carriage stopped barely long enough for me to mount & bestride my seat, & then resumed its rapid progress. We had not gone but little farther when there was a second stoppage, & as I inferred, to receive new orders but of which I heard nothing. Immediately after, the carriage was turned short around, & was driven as rapidly back through the cornfield to the public road I had left, & thence up the hill on that road, in the direction opposite to the hill where the skulkers were seen, & to the table land . . . . Here, on the public road, & (as I thought from the sounds,) within a few hundred yards of the rear of the Yankee musketry, our party halted again, & the men alighted. I most gladly took this opportunity [to] dismount from my very uneasy & also precarious seat on the cannon—&, with leave asked & granted, seated myself on the gun carriage. My previous ride had been as disagreeable to me, as my position must have been ludicrous to any one enough unoccupied to be an observer. The surface of the corn-field was rough, from the marks of

traversed approximately the same route over which Ruffin had moved earlier from Lookout Hill to the scene of battle on the Confederate left. According to Beauregard, Early was in position west of the Manassas-Sudley Road by 3:30 (*Official Records*, Vol. II, 496), so this would place the meeting with Ruffin at about 3:15. It was Early's timely arrival on the extreme left that turned the tide of battle and precipitated the general Union retreat, which, according to Captain Kemper (*ibid.*, 535), began about 4:15.

the ploughing left on a hard clay soil. The public road was still rougher, with numerous stones sprinkled over the surface. Yet over all, & down-hill & up-hill, our team was driven as rapidly as they could well draw. With such severe jolting it was of course very disagreeable & even painful riding, & difficult to hold to my seat. But these difficulties were doubled by the smooth & highly polished surface of my brazen steed, by my having to carry my musket in my right hand, & my left being deprived, by . . . former injury, of half its natural strength & fitness for any use.—What the previous movements & also the present halt meant, I could not conceive. But I had full confidence in Capt. Kemper's courage & discretion & that he was doing what was most proper for the occasion. Expecting the guns, (for I saw the other three not far off,) to be moved onward every minute, I was afraid to leave my seat lest I might be left on foot again. . . . [end of Note 8]

. . . I did not deem it proper at such a time to occupy the attention of Capt. Kemper, who was at a little distance, or any other stranger officer, to answer my questions. And so I remained under my latest impressions, that defeat was inevitable, & indeed supposed that a retreat had already been begun, until hearing that it was the enemy that was retreating, & that our army had, at last, by aid mainly of the reinforcements, turned the tide of battle, & gained a glorious victory, though, as at first reported, at deplorable cost of life on our side. [Note 9 follows]

While the artillery remained halted here, for half an hour or more—(& which delay then seemed to me unaccountable, whether the next movement was to fight or to retreat—) & before there was any perceptible abatement of rapidity in the firing of musketry nearest to us, I plainly heard shouts from the combatants. These I then supposed to be from the Yankees, whose line was then nearest to us. But soon after I learned that the shouts proceeded from our line beyond, & upon the joyful occasion of the enemy's ranks giving way, & their rapid retreat being begun.

It was some weeks later, from Col. Kershaw's official report, [that] I learned the cause of Kemper's Artillery company being so quiet. They had been so exhausted in the previous service, that they had been ordered to withdraw from the battle, to rest.[25] [end of Note 9]

---

[25] See *Official Records*, Vol. II, 535. The period of rest probably extended from about 4:30 to 5:00 P.M. At the latter hour Kemper's battery joined Kershaw's brigade in pursuit of the fleeing Federals, as the diarist recounts below.

We were soon joined by other troops, mostly from South Carolina, & began to march, where I did not know then, but as it appeared afterwards, in pursuit, or on the track, of the fleeing enemy for a few miles only. This movement was by Col. Kershaw's brigade only, with Kemper's artillery & some troops of cavalry[26] attached for the purpose. Our way was along roads passing first through a part of the field of battle, & afterwards getting into the turnpike road & crossing the "Stone Bridge" over Bull Run, still continued along the route of a portion of the fleeing enemy. Our progress was slow, with several stoppages, the reasons for which I did not then know, but supposed because of the weariness of our men. We saw many of the killed, though our route was at first only on the out-skirts of the hardest contested ground. Muskets & other arms were scattered along the road, & many were broken by being passed over by the artillery carriages. Wagons had been sent out from our former camp, as early as my arrival, to remove our wounded. At the first stoppage, on the top of a hill, I saw our cavalry pursuing the enemy in a different direction, as was supposed, on the route to Leesburg. While remaining still, there was some opportunity for the meeting & greeting of acquaintances belonging to different companies. Some old & some new acquaintances of mine, of Col. [Wade] Hampton's (S.C.) Legion thus approached me. This body, or rather a small portion of it, 600, had arrived but the night before, had just before been recruited, & without any opportunity for drilling or acquiring discipline, had at once been engaged in this severe conflict. They had suffered severly [*sic*]. It was then understood that nearly half had been killed or wounded. But it was not near so bad as that.[27] On our resuming the march, I passed by this corps, & they gave three cheers in honor of me. The same was done later by the Palmetto Guard when I passed them. I had before heard that no one of our company had been killed, [1472] & only 12 (afterwards known to be but 6) wounded. . . . [Note 10 follows]

The causes of these halts, of which I had no conception at the time, are explained in the . . . official report of Col. Kershaw. The first delay was to send for & obtain leave to pursue the fleeing enemy. Another was in obedience to orders sent to wait for rein-

---

[26] Thirtieth Virginia. *Official Records*, Vol. II, 532, 534.

[27] The Hampton Legion suffered 121 casualties, or 20 percent of those engaged. Among these was Hampton himself, who was wounded slightly in the final Confederate attack of the afternoon. *Official Records*, Vol. II, 567.

forcements, then on the way. Another was, when first coming in sight of the fugitives, to form the line of battle for engaging them—which was useless as the flight was not suspended, or soon resumed. . . . On the route, we met some 40 Yankee prisoners, under guard, who had been captured by the advance, & were sent to our rear.—Seeing that muskets were scattered everywhere on the track of the fleeing Yankees, (over one of which we were following,) & that our artillery carriage wheels were frequently passing over & destroying them, I requested a soldier, on foot, to pick up & hand me one—which he did together with a cartridge box. It was a new Springfield musket. I carried this also through the remainder of the march, & my riding on the gun-carriage. So, for the remainder of the time I had the care & trouble of two muskets & their appurtenances. I intended to take this musket home as a memento—as every body else took anything left by the Yankees that they chose. But, on reflection, I thought it wrong—& the next day, I gave up the musket to Col. Kershaw when I was on my way home. . . . [end of Note 10]

As we proceeded farther, the indications of the haste & desperation of the fleeing Yankees became more numerous. There were but a few of their dead bodies (I think 3) along the road after crossing the Stone Bridge, as far as we went. But the road was strowed with articles which were thrown away by the fugitives—arms, accoutrements, havresacks [*sic*] (mostly well filled with hard biscuit or crackers,) knapsacks filled, & loose articles of clothing, blankets, drums, & brass musical instruments &c. This road is an old turnpike from Alexandria to Fauquier. According to the former foolish mode of road-making, this was in perfectly straight stretches, up & down hill, & here it was straight for miles ahead of us towards Centreville. Of course this was the greatest advantage to our use of artillery, as shots correctly aimed along the road, at the retreating foe, if in reach, might do damage as long as they could go. After our detachment, which consisted of Col. Kershaw's then command, had followed a few miles, & it was after sunset, (or when darkness was beginning to approach,) the foremost guards announced that the enemy's troops were in sight & not far ahead—cavalry as at first supposed. By order, two of Kemper's guns were unlimbered, & quickly ready for firing. I, having before obtained the captain's permission, fired the first of these guns—either 10 or 12 being thus directed, & rapidly fired off. We could not see the effect there from our position—but soon some of the enemy were seen escaping by a lateral road to our left, from the position first fired at. [Note 11 follows]

It was a mistake that these fugitives were (as I at first supposed) a portion of those fleeing from the direction to which our first guns were aimed. I have since learned so much of what then occurred, which I did not understand at the time, that it will be best for me to write a more extended & correct account of all that happened here.

When our advance guard gave the information of the enemy being ahead, & near to our front, (it proved to be about half a mile,) our front, to which Kemper's artillery had previously been changed, was at the crest of a long hill, down the gentle & uniform descent of which the turnpike road extended in a perfectly straight course, to the Suspension Bridge, over Cub Run. . . . The line of our march in pursuit, along the turnpike road, had been the same track of one large body of the routed & fleeing Yankees.[28] These had reached the bridge over Cub Run, & there filled the road with a closely packed crowd of soldiers, artillery trains, baggage wagons, ambulances &c. The first wagon had just been driven upon the bridge, to pass over, when the first gun (my gun) was fired from Kemper's battery, loaded (as I learned afterwards,) with Shrapnell [*sic*], or spherical-case shell. As the official reports of the Yankee commander afterwards stated, some of the shot from this first discharge, (which he said was from a "masked battery,") struck one or more of the horses of the foremost wagon. In their pain & fright they suddenly turned, upset the wagon so as to barricade the whole width of the bridge & effectually precluded any other wheel-carriage, or horse, from moving on. The whole mass of fugitives immediately got out of the track, & all escaped who could, on foot & as quickly as possible. The rapidly succeeding discharges of our cannon, aimed as correctly as the first down the slope of the straight road, kept up & increased the panic & the headlong haste of the Yankees. No doubt they instantly left the road, it being the line along which the balls were flying. The stream could be forded, by men or horses, but the banks were too steep for the passage of carriages. Thus all the wagons & artillery were abandoned, & everything else left by the terrified fugitives, who, by their various tracks, proceeded to Centreville, which is some three-quarters of a

---

[28] This was the First Brigade, First Division, commanded by Brigadier General Erasmus D. Keyes.

mile farther on.—But these were not all, nor even half of the number of the routed enemy then in our close neighborhood, & of whose presence & approach we did not know, until just before turning our guns upon them. While our pursuit of one large body of Yankees had been along a road nearly straight, there was another & much larger body which when fleeing from the battlefield passed over Sudley's ford (above the Stone Bridge,) & thence by the circuitous road which joins the turnpike a little before it reaches the bridge over Cub Run.[29] Old Gen. [George] Stuart [*sic*], of Md.,[30] was a prisoner, &, as such, came with this immense & confused crowd, & which he supposed numbered at least 20,000 men. This crowd had arrived within a mile, or less, of the turnpike & the bridge, & still nearer to the head of our column, unseen by us, & their presence unsuspected, (so far as I heard,) when Kemper's first cannon was fired towards the bridge—& which also gave to the other & larger crowd of fugitives notice of our being near. Instantly, they also scampered from the road, & took, through the woods, & across Cub Run, the shortest course to Centreville. It was not until after this crowd had heard our first firing, & in panic terror was dispersing, & escaping through the woods which were alongside & beyond their road, that Kemper's guns were turned towards them & fired. It was against this part of the Yankee army, that the Palmetto Guard was sent out to skirmish . . . & exchanged some shots with the last remaining of the fugitives. The skirmishers soon returned, & our column turned back, & was on the march returning, before the news arrived from the bridge of the complete disappearance of the enemy. Then a general halt was ordered, & we waited for an hour, or more, before moving on again, & not until after the first 7 or 8 pieces of the enemy's captured artillery had been brought back, & sundry wagons &c. which accompanied our column to the camping ground. A sufficient force was left to bring off the remaining captured artillery—which was not finished until after midnight.—The sudden though very slow backward movement of our force, im-

---

[29] This was the same route by which the main body of Union troops had advanced early that morning in their attempt to turn the Confederate left.

[30] Captured in midafternoon by a detachment from the United States Second Dragoons, General Steuart remained a prisoner only a few hours before being recaptured in the confusion at the Suspension Bridge. *Official Records*, Vol. II, 384, 525. General Steuart should not be confused (as the index to the *Official Records* does) with George H. ("Maryland") Steuart—apparently his son—who was also present at First Manassas, as lieutenant colonel of the First Maryland Regiment.

mediately after our successful cannonade, & when both bodies of the enemy were in rapid retreat, seemed then strange. Though night had begun, it seemed as if the pursuit might have been continued to good effect. The explanation is afforded in Col. Kershaw's official report. He had just received a "peremptory order" to return past Bull Run, & encamp.[31] . . . Col. Kershaw's report differs from my digest in some unimportant particulars—& awards to my feeble efforts much more of effect, & applause, than they deserved *as performances*. Nevertheless, the exaggeration of the due measure of praise does not prevent the whole being highly gratifying to my self-love. Col. Kershaw's account of the firing on the bridge, with the connected reference to myself, is as follows:—"The main body of the enemy were retreating by the Sudley's Ford road, which comes into the turnpike at the Suspension Bridge, on the south side of the Run. Capt. Kemper fired from one gun on the column retreating by the former road, & from the other, along the turnpike. The effect of the firing was most disastrous. The reserve which we were pursuing meeting the main body of the enemy coming by the other road, just at the entrance of the bridge, completely blocked it, & formed a barricade with cannon, caissons, ambulances, wagons & other vehicles, which were abandoned, with horses & harness complete, while the drivers fled. Many of the soldiers threw their arms into the creek, & everything indicated the greatest possible panic. The venerable Edmund Ruffin, who fired the first gun at Fort Sumter, who, as a volunteer in the Palmetto Guard, shared the fatigues & dangers of the retreat from Fairfax C.H., & gallantly fought through the day at Manassas, fired the first gun at this retreating column of the enemy, which resulted in this extraordinary capture. At this point, I received a peremptory order to return to Bull Run, & take my position at the Stone Bridge—"[32] [end of Note 11]

. . . We returned at 10 P.M. to encamp in a new position, in a field alongside the road, across the Stone Bridge, in which the battle had been begun in the morning. No tents were pitched, or in place—&

---

[31] The order was from Beauregard, who, in his official report, explained that the pursuit had been "recalled in consequence of a false report which unfortunately reached us that the enemy's reserves, known to be fresh and of considerable strength, were threatening the position of Union Mills Ford." *Official Records*, Vol. II, 497.

[32] See *Official Records*, Vol. II, 525. Captain Kemper also mentioned Ruffin in his report. *Ibid.*, 536.

indeed most belonging to our company & regiment had been left behind at our camp near Fairfax C.H. & were, with the other combustible articles, burnt by our men in charge of them, & not captured, as we had at first supposed. [1474] We lay on the ground by our arms. Fatigued as I was, I slept soon & soundly—but awaked with cold half an hour before daybreak, when I arose, to get warm by exercise as there was no fire, as yet, nor had there been any permitted earlier. . . .

There had been brought in 18 cannon, leaving three which our firing had dismounted, making 21 in all. Most were rifled, & all were of brass, except one very long iron rifled piece,[33] which had required 10 horses to draw it. More than 100 horses had been there captured & brought in, with several wagons laden with various articles, including sundry trunks of officers' baggage. At a later time, I heard that here & previously elsewhere, we had captured 61 out of the 63 cannon which the enemy had brought from Washington.

This day (22nd) was overcast, soon drizzling, & from noon to 9 P.M. steady slow rain. Our company was sent out to examine the battlefield, & collect the articles left, & look out for & attend to what was directed as to the wounded & dead. . . . I borrowed a horse of Col. Kershaw, & rode over one portion of the field of battle to see the dead bodies. [Note 13 follows]

The portion of the battlefield I examined was the part nearest to the turnpike road & the Stone Bridge. It was an open field of some 30 acres, nearly surrounded by woods. In this open ground, & on the highest level, was the humble dwelling house in which, (as I was told,) occurred the killing of the old woman who owned it,[34] by a cannon shot, as she lay sick in bed, & incapable of being removed, while the battle was raging around her residence. [end of Note 13]

It was a horrible sight. The dead, (nearly all then left being of the Yankee army,) were scattered over this whole open ground, a field of some 30 acres, & probably extended in like manner for some three miles, over which, from its beginning to end, the conflict had passed. The countenances & postures generally indicated the suffering of agonizing pain. Many were of the noted Zouave regiment [1475] commanded by the late Col. Ellsworth, who had been killed by the martyr Jackson on the taking of Alexandria. Of this villainous corps, it is said that much the greater number were killed. They

---

33 A 30-pounder Parrott.
34 Mrs. Judith Henry.

were conspicuous by their red trousers, & otherwise peculiar Turkish dress. Clotted blood, in what had been pools, were under or by almost every corpse. From bullet holes in the heads of some, the brains had partly oozed out. The white froth covering the mouths of others was scarcely less shocking in appearance. I saw not more than 5 or 6 of the wounded still alive. All of these lay quiet & motionless, until looking up as I approached very near. The first to whom I came had a tin cup of water near, but, as I thought, not within his reach. I alighted from my horse, & asked if he wished to drink, offering the cup to his lips, which he accepted. I was pleased to see that nearly all, if not quite all whom I afterwards saw, had been in like manner provided with a cup of water by the kindness of some of our men. . . . I spoke, in compassionate tone, to each of them, saying that it would not be much longer before the removal of our dead would be completed, & then that the wagons would remove them. To one, I added that, when placed in the hospital, he would be cared for as much as our own wounded men. To this he replied that he believed it, for he had been very kindly treated since he had been lying there. Hundreds of our soldiers were indulging their curiosity in viewing the dead, as I was, & many accosted the living—but none whom [1476] I saw, in hostile or injurious words—unless to ask why they came to invade & to fight us, who had never offended them. But any questioning, or conversation, was probably painful to suffering men—& this injury was offered more because of thoughtlessness than malice. To a group of our soldiers who surrounded one of the wounded Yankees, talking to him, I suggested that probably it might be offensive or hurtful, & they all immediately & quietly drew off. No one more bitterly hates the northerners as a class than I do, or would be more rejoiced to have every invading soldier killed—but all my hatred was silenced for the wounded, seen in this long continued & wretched state of suffering.—In one part of this small section of the battle ground, I counted 12 horses (mostly if not all of artillery,) within a space which I supposed not to exceed an acre. Within 80 yards of that space, there lay 11 others, within a quarter acre. Elsewhere there were 5 near together, in each of two different places, & one or two in several other spots.—On this field I saw Capt. [Robert] White, of Lexington, Va., a former acquaintance, who commanded a company of 65 youths, all students of Washington College. Of these, either 5 or 6 had been killed. Their lives were of no more value than those of men of mature age. But I cannot help feeling greater regret for such cases, of mere boys. There is somewhere else in service another company made up of students of the University [of Virginia]. Another, of the students of Hampden-Sydney College, commanded by their President, the Rev. John Atkinson, surrendered as prisoners of war in the late disastrous defeats of different portions of our army [1477] in north-western Va (Randolph Co.) of Gen. Garnett's army . . . .

After viewing this scene of horror, I rode to see the scene of the last night's capture of the enemy's artillery. It is at Cub Run, a large stream within a short distance of Centreville. . . . There had been removed to our camp, besides the artillery & heavy laden wagons, a portable forge, apothecary's shop & medicines, some light [1478] wagons, & numerous smaller matters. There still remained admirable ambulances, with mattresses, left unused, while our own wounded men were being jolted today from 4 to 6 miles to Manassas, in common road wagons. Many extra wheels for the artillery & ammunition wagons had been brought on, & were scattered along the road. The completeness of preparation for every want & every contingent accident was admirable. In such preparation Gen. Scott excels—& I believe his ability for such provision is his chief merit as a military commander. [Note 14 follows]

. . . When I arrived at the place (about 12 M. on 22nd.) the early mist & drizzle had increased to steady slow rain. The bad weather prevented my staying long, & I did not dismount from my horse, for closer examination, or ride outside of the road. . . . One chief object of my visit was to learn the number . . . killed by our cannonade, of which some extravagant reports had been brought to the camp. I saw there but three dead bodies, (according to my present recollection,) and of these, two, if not all three, were lying in a wagon, which otherwise was empty. Hence, I too hastily inferred that these dead bodies had been brought there from the battlefield, when wounded & dying—& that, in fact, our firing on the bridge, however damaging in other respects, had killed none of the Yankees. This was a great disappointment to me. I should have liked not only to have killed the greatest possible number—but also to know, if possible, *which* I had killed, & to see & count the bodies. It was not until some months afterwards that I learned from several trust-worthy eye-witnesses, who were present (in the cavalry sent on) immediately after our firing, or early the next morning, that there were about 7 dead bodies then lying in the road. Neither of these witnesses remembered to have counted the exact number—but all were sure that there were not fewer than 6, nor more than 8. All these must have been killed by our cannonade—& also I am persuaded that a good proportion of them fell by my first fire. For, by the official report of the Yankee commander, all fled immediately after their receiving the first shot—& it is not probable that the fugitives remained longer in the line of our fire, along the road. It is plain enough why most of the dead bodies should have disappeared before my arrival. While lying in the road, they would necessarily be some hindrance to the labors of the men engaged in taking away the artillery & wagons, & therefore would be moved out of the track. Those dead bodies which I saw had thus doubtless been lifted off the road, & laid in an empty wagon standing there, as the quickest mode of putting them out of the way. The others probably were first lifted to the sides of the road, & next removed into the bushes, of which a few yards of width made an effectually concealing screen. . . . The three brass field pieces, which had been dismounted, still remained on the ground. Of course, there could be no question of these having been dismounted by some of the balls from Kemper's artillery. For, even if there had been no other and direct evidence, it is certain that if these guns had been dismounted previously, on the battlefield, the panic-stricken & fleeing Yankees would not have encumbered themselves, & retarded their progress, by bringing with them dismounted cannon & their broken carriages. . . . [end of Note 14]

Before I turned back, the rain had become steady & soaking, & the clay soil of our camp was soon a saturated mire for an inch or two deep. Our Quarter-Master's & Commissary's departments seem the very reverse of Scott's, totally without system & proper regulation. Through this steady & long continued rain, our regiment was without tents, separated from its baggage, & the baggage & bedding at our last camp exposed to all this rain—without supplied fuel & even food, for 30 hours during & after the hard service of the previous day. Yet there was no murmuring, or complaint, except such as might have been made of bad weather or other inevitable causes of privation & suffering. After dark, when the rain had ceased, such tents as remained to us, & our wet blankets & wet or damp clothes, arrived—but added nothing to comfort for that night. . . .

[95]

July 23. Having before determined here to close my military [1479] operations, or attempts, & to escape from the hardships & privations which began to show effects on my strength & appearance, though yet without the slightest sickness, I this morning took leave of my friends & comrades, & set out for Manassas, in a small wagon, with Professor Venable, now a private soldier, & several others going for different objects. Along our road, we passed several dead bodies of men & of horses. The odor of putrefaction already was offensive in their close vicinity, & it will be a very offensive & disagreeable duty, if not injurious to health, to bury the remaining bodies after this time. At Manassas, called on my friend William Gilmer, who is in the Commissary department, & took dinner with his mess, & supper. I enjoyed these meals. They were the first of inviting character which I had seen for a week . . . . Having recovered my clothes bag & writing materials, I used the leisure of this day to write much of the foregoing pages, & to bring up my notes to the current or very recent time.—As my only place for lodging, I, like other designed passengers, spent the night in the rail-road car, with very scant accommodation, & opportunity for ease & for sleeping.

July 24. At 6.30, the rail train set out for Gordonsville & the train there for Richmond. The whole people greatly excited about the recent battle & victory. All are speculating upon what will be the consequences. My opinion is that this hard-fought battle will be virtually the close of the war. . . . Reached Richmond after 5 P.M. . . . Saw Mr. Sayre & Mr. Boulware, & conversed with both as well as answered inquiries of many other persons. It was with difficulty that I could withdraw from questioners, & get to my room, to wash, & to resume my writing late at night. Saw Col. Gibbons, of Frankfort Ky, who is going home tomorrow, & who was good enough to offer to convey a letter to Mildred—[1481] which I accordingly wrote. I have not received a letter from her for a long time, & fear that both her & my latter letters have been stopped on their passage. I was sorry to learn from Col. G. that the disposition for abject submission is more general in Ky, & less prospect for resistance to northern despotism & oppression, than I was prepared for by even my observations last September. After writing my letter, resumed the bringing up my diary until 12.30 before going to bed. This was the first time of my sleeping in a bed, or in a house, or of taking off my day clothes, since my first arrival at Fairfax C.H. And comfortable as was the change, I soon awaked, & being unable to sleep again, lighted a candle & resumed my writing at 2.45 A.M.

July 25. Having heard last night (though incorrectly) that Edmund was at home, on furlough for this week, I waived my intention of stopping a few days in Richmond, to hasten to Beechwood—to which I proceeded by steamer by 5 A.M. Arrived at Beechwood (by Maycox, & boating & walking afterwards,) before 11 A.M. Found that Edmund had returned to his camp last Saturday, & Jane with him. Nanny & the younger girls here, & John & Mrs. Lorraine. . . . All of my family well. All eager to hear my news of the army & the battles, which I have already told in part to so many inquirers that I am wearied with the repetition . . . . Col. Richard Thomas, of recent notoriety & gallant adventure, has been so imprudent as to proceed on a steamer on the Chesapeake, to reach Baltimore. He was recognized, captured, & is confined as a prisoner. I wish that he may not have incurred deserving the legal character of a spy, & the penalty of death, which the Lincoln administration would be delighted to be authorized to inflict, because of his prior adventure. . . .

July 26. The mail—but nothing new of importance. It is strange that no *certain* report of the advance of our army, or its operations otherwise, have [*sic*] been received later than I heard on the ground on the 22nd—that is of Gen. Bonham having occupied Centreville. If the whole army was to advance towards Washington, there has been full time to have heard of its reaching the Potomac. We have rumors to that effect, & others indicating still more the bad condition of the enemy—but nothing that can be relied upon as true. The newspapers are full of narratives & statements of the incidents of the two battles—(the first of which is called of "Bull Run," & the second of "Manassas"—) of which nine-tenths are false. It will be some time before we shall learn the truth, or even approach it, as to the enemy's numbers engaged, & losses. Our present estimate is that the enemy had 35,000 men actually engaged & we 15,000. The enemy's loss is estimated at 3,500 to more than 4,000 in killed & wounded, & near 1000 prisoners have already been brought to Richmond. Our loss is estimated at about 300 killed & 1200 wounded. No prisoners known of.[35]

Immediately after breakfast, rode to Ruthven. All well. . . . Lotty

---

[35] As usual, the diarist is close to the mark regarding Confederate losses but high in his estimate of Union casualties. The latter actually numbered 460 killed, 1,124 wounded, and 1,312 missing or captured for a total of 2,896. Confederate losses were 387 killed, 1,582 wounded, and 13 missing for an aggregate of 1,982.

seemed delighted with my arrival, & received me most kindly & affectionately. I brought, myself, the first news of myself & Charles heard since I left home.—Returned in the evening, to be ready to leave for Burwell's Bay in the morning, to see [1484] Edmund & Jane before she leaves for Alamance. . . .

I cannot believe that the last three days, of which nothing of our army operations have been heard, were idly spent by our military authorities. The reports from Washington state that the Yankee army has retreated to Alexandria, & that its pickets extended no farther than two miles this side of that city. If so, our advanced posts must be very near. Gen. Beauregard had before used great care that no information of his positions, strength, & prospective operations should be conveyed in writing from the army. Since the last battle, it is forbidden to all persons to visit our camps & military positions. I trust that we shall first hear of the completion of some important movement. I wish that it may be (passing by Alexandria) the seizure & occupation of the heights of the Potomac opposite Washington, & the bombardment of the city, or other better means for driving out the President & Congress. Next—I trust that the war may be still farther "carried into Africa"—by invading Maryland & thereby inducing insurrection against the existing despotism—& next, a dash upon Philadelphia, & the laying it in ashes, as proper & complete retaliation for all the atrocities committed in detail by the Yankee forces wherever they have invaded [1485] our land—plundering of private property & persons—house-burning—destruction of other private property—stealing slaves, & forcing as well as inciting them to join their forces. For all these violations of the laws of civilized warfare, we cannot retaliate in the same manner, as invaders & occupiers of northern territory—& if we could so operate, I would not have it done. But it would be a proper & efficaceous [*sic*] retaliation, worthy of national revenge, & of our national dignity, to strike the one great blow of destroying some great northern city, as full settlement & acquittance for the past northern outrages. After that, the enemy might choose whether the war should be afterwards conducted according to the laws of war, or in violation of them. We would prefer the former course—but may not be the least successful of the two parties, if waging a war of destructive retaliation & vengeance.

July 27. Went in the boat to Maycox wharf, & thence, at 9.30, went on the steamer. Many passengers, most of them soldiers going to their several camps along the river. At Fort Powhatan, the cannon had been removed, & were then on board a vessel at the wharf, to be carried to Mulberry Island, & there mounted on a new intrenchment. This post will be dismantled as a fortification, & I presume will no longer be held as a camp or garrison. Capt. Harrison H. Cocke, had before been superseded in his command, or general direction of the construction of fortifications on this river. Saw Col. Pryor on board, going to his command at Burwell's Bay. All the newspapers of today on board. Not a word yet of any movements of our army later than the day before I left our camp near Bull Run. The secrecy must be by design, & surely our general must be doing something of importance for [1486] assuming the offensive on the Potomac, or beyond.—Landed at the Stone House wharf, the lowest place to which the steamer now goes (for fear of the Yankee armed vessels,) & which is two miles above the camp of the Prince George cavalry. I found a buggy waiting for my arrival, with an invitation to go in it to Mr. Wrenn's mansion, a mile farther than the camp, & where my son & his wife were then staying. Arrived there after 3 P.M. & found the family & guests at dinner, in which I joined. My nephew Dr. J. J. Dupuy there, & my grandson Thomas. . . . I was most kindly welcomed, & urged to stay here during my visit, instead of at the camp, as I had designed. I have no choice but to accept this invitation, as Edmund is now staying here with his wife, when not required by duty to stay in camp. This family has been very kind & attentive in its hospitality to him & his family throughout—& such has been the general conduct of the neighborhood to the volunteers of the post. This mansion is large & handsome, & in a beautiful situation, very near to the beach & broad water of Burwell's Bay. The enemy's camp, at Newport News Point, is about 20 miles below, on the opposite side of the river. After dinner, rode with Thomas to the camp, & saw my acquaintances of the company—& also my grandson George, who is there on a visit to his father & brother, & is quite delighted with the novelties of camp life. Supped with the mess, partly on excellent fresh fish, & afterwards returned with Edmund to Mr. Wrenn's where we slept. I witnessed the afternoon parade & drill of [1487] the troop—which indicated good drilling & proficiency in the exercises. I hear that my grandson Thomas is a good soldier, & is delighted with his military life.

July 28. Sunday. This day, by direction of the Congress of the

C.S., has been appointed for general thanksgiving services, for the great mercy of God afforded in our late victory. Elsewhere, where there are facilities for proper & solemn services of religious worship, no doubt they will be very impressive. Here there were no services. . . . After dinner, rode with Edmund & George some three miles down the river, by the encampment of the remainder of the regiment (all commanded by Col. Roger A. Pryor,) & a fort recently erected on Day's Neck. It was constructed in a very elaborate & perfect manner, & the earth-banks turfed—very different from the hastily raised & rough banks of sand or clay which I had seen before. But this will be of no more utility because of this extra finish & beauty. And I fear that it will be of little protection—as the nearest part of the ship channel is 2000 yards distant. I have no faith in our artillery firing accurately enough to prevent the passage of the enemy's vessels, at upwards of 2000 yards distance. What is the width of the channel, & how much farther passing vessels may keep from the fort, I did not learn. Heavy artillery were landed, to be mounted on this [1488] new fort. . . .

July 29. . . . I arranged to return by the steamer today, to Richmond. . . . Spent some hours at the camp, & left the landing on the steamer between 2 & 3 P.M. Reached Richmond between 10 & 11. The two principal hotels so full that I could not obtain a bed in either—& got one on the floor of a common room at the Columbian Hotel.

July 30. Met with many of my acquaintances from distant homes, some of them members of the Congress of C.S. which met here on 20th. Among the latter were J[ames] A. Seddon, Burton Craige,[36] Thomas Ruffin, A[braham] W. Venable, & Judge J[ohn] Perkins. Attended in the hall the opening of the session; but, as usual, the congress went immediately into secret session, & all others had to leave. Wm. H. Harrison of Amelia came in the train from Manassas Junction, he having been to Fairfax to see his sons. He tells me that our army is quartered in various places in Fairfax, & nowhere in advance of the posts we held before our retreat, except at Vienna. There is nothing known to indicate what movement Gen. Beauregard intends to make. . . . Saw Spratt, & sundry other southern

---

[36] Like his colleague, Thomas Ruffin, Francis Burton Craige (1811–75) was a North Carolina congressman from 1853 to 1861. As a member of the North Carolina Secession Convention, he introduced the ordinance of secession which was adopted unanimously by that body on May 20, 1861.

[1489] men. Among them Gov. Hammond, who is in bad health, & on his way to the Springs. . . . This morning changed my lodging to the Exchange Hotel & a single bedded room, just vacated. . . .

July 31. Saw Mr. Calhoun[37] & other gentlemen just from Manassas Junction & our farthest out-posts, at Vienna & Falls Church. Our army seems to be fronting & so threatening Washington. But I trust that there will be no attack on the enemy there, or even against them at Alexandria & Arlington Heights. Another mode seems to me so much preferable, & now available, that I have hopes it may be adopted. I understand that our force at Aquia creek has been increased to 8000 men. More are near. We have a large steamer in Aquia creek, armed with a few cannon, & which can carry 1000 men across the Potomac each trip, & from 4000 to 6000 within a night. I would send over into the opposite & entirely friendly part of Md. as many as could be sent without discovery or effective attack by the enemy. Of the main army, I would send 30,000 across the Potomac from Vienna, to march upon Baltimore. The two separate corps would concentrate there. As soon as even 20,000 men would so enter Md., Baltimore would rise against the Yankee power, & conquer the garrison. All Md, except the extreme west, would soon follow, & insure our success. If but 20,000, or even but 10,000 of our troops were left to watch the enemy's forces, the latter would not dare to march into Va, with two armies of ours in their rear in Md, & the majority of all Md rising against them. The militia of the section aided by reinforcements now continually arriving from the more southern states, would rapidly enlarge our 10 or 20,000 remaining forces, & be enough to protect Richmond & the state. If Md rose in the rear, Washington would [1492] fall of itself without direct attack—& Lincoln & his government would flee from it as fast as possible.—Telegraphic report that a proposition for peace was moved in the Rump Congress (House of Rep.) & was voted for by 42 members. Before the last battle, such a proposition would not have received 10 supporting votes.—This afternoon, when walking in the Capitol Square, I met & was passing a gentleman & lady. He accosted me very cordially, as if acquainted, & seeing that I did not know him, named himself as Mr. [John H.] Reagan, & introduced the lady to me as his wife. As usual I not only had entirely forgotten him, but could not remember that I had ever met with him be-

---

[37] Presumably Andrew Pickens Calhoun of South Carolina, eldest son of John C. Calhoun.

fore—as no doubt I did, in Washington last summer. Yet Mr. Reagan was then & is now a functionary of high position—late U.S. Senator from Texas, & now Post-Master General of the C.S. & a member of the Congress.—At night had some political conversation with Judge Perkins, on our former almost despairing efforts to promote disunion—& the subsequent speedy, & unlooked-for fruition of our schemes. In reference to the recent peace proposition in the Rump Congress, Judge P. thought that the successful passage of the resolution of speedy peace would be a much greater evil to us than any to be produced by continuance of the war. He said that our party, (the most thorough southern,) had at first to fight against *union* with the North, & we had beaten our opponents. Then we had fought & again beaten the different schemes for *compromise.* Then we had to fight *re-construction* of the Union. And now we are threatened with the great danger of *conciliation.* If peace should soon be made, before the South is completely separated in feeling & in regard to the ties of habits & of business from the North, that former business [1493] connection will be renewed, & the commercial dependence of the South on the North will be almost as great as formerly. I think these views & fears are well-founded. I shall be glad if recent or subsequent disasters shall sicken the North of its scheme of conquest, & induce the cessation of aggressive & offensive operations of war—& the sooner the better. But I will be glad if the re-establishment of peace, & amity, by treaty, shall be deferred for years after, so as to prevent all possibility of the renewal of our former business connections & commercial vassalage—& also that we may previously make treaties of peace, & of preference of benefits, with other friendly nations, and discriminating against the trade of the unfriendly, & especially of the Northern States, as our worst enemy, whether in war or peace.—Made acquaintance with Dr. Montrose A. Pallen, a refugee from St. Louis, he having to leave his abolition city, & his wife & young children, at very short notice. He is in our military service, until he can properly get into that of Missouri, battling for the South—as seems now to be beginning.[38]—Met with Col. Gregg, (& also his secretary, A[lexander] Haskell,) who has waited in Richmond for the return of his

---

[38] Later in the war, Dr. Pallen went to Canada and created something of a stir when, in a letter to Secretary of War Stanton, he complained of the alleged mistreatment of Confederate prisoners in four northern prison camps. *Official Records,* Series II, Vol. VI, 718.

regiment from S.C., when re-organized, to return to the seat of war.

August 1. Left the hotel before 5 A.M. & on the "Schultz" steamer, just repaired & replaced on the river, returned home. Was landed on Coggin's Point, & walked to Beechwood house by soon after 10 A.M. Found Mrs. Lorraine only at home—Nanny & the younger girls having driven to the Court-House to join with other ladies in forming a sewing society, to make clothes &c. for the soldiers in the hospitals. . . . My time already [1494] heavy on my hands, for want of some regular employment. Reading one of a number of novels &c. gathered in a bookstore in Richmond, to kill time. Trashy stuff probably, in general. I learned from two of the principal booksellers in Richmond that their supplies by purchase, (heretofore entirely from northern cities,) were all stopped, & not yet substituted by any other mode, either of importation from Europe, or home publication. But in compensation, (as to the public, & not as to the booksellers,) nearly all demand for books had ceased as completely as the supply, except as to military works, for instruction in tactics—several of which have been republished in the S[outhern] C[onfederacy]. The excitement of the war, & interest in its incidents, have absorbed everything else. We think & talk of nothing else—& nearly all reading is confined to newspapers. . . .

Aug. 3. A private report (not in the newspapers) of scaling ladders being sent down the river for Yorktown. I had heard when in Richmond that they were in requisition. Some movement of Gen. Magruder has seemed to be impending lately—but I cannot believe, (as this seems to indicate,) an attack on Fortress Monroe, & by storming or escalade! Also, we hear, from Petersburg today, that two regiments of infantry, the Petersburg dragoons, & a company of light artillery, have been ordered to Burwell's Bay, from Suffolk. The government war steamer lately "Yorktown," with 8 64-pounder guns & 180 men, is lying at City Point, ready for sea, &, as supposed, waiting for a favorable time to run by the blockading squadron to sea. Putting these things together, it seems likely that either an attack, or more likely a feint, on Fortress Monroe is designed, so as to detain & occupy the enemy's large force there, & prevent a large portion of [1496] them being sent to reinforce those in Washington, as was expected since their late defeat, & the complete frustration of the scheme of their two invading armies meeting at Richmond. Gen. Butler can do nothing by offensive movements now, & therefore it is useless to keep at or near Fortress Monroe more than a strong garrison—or say 3000 men, whereas he has had 10 to 20,000, as supposed. If by feints, & even by bringing our troops across the river at Burwell's Bay, by aid of the Yorktown, all these superfluous forces of the enemy can be detained at Fortress Monroe, it will so much facilitate the attacks which I trust are designed by our army near the Potomac—& as I hope, by invading Md from Aquia creek, & by the main army above the falls. . . .

Aug. 5. Rode for the mail. It is confirmed that Gen. Wise, after gaining some minor advantages, had been compelled by the superior force of the enemy to abandon the Kanawha [Valley], & retreat to across Gauley river, burning all the bridges af[ter] him.[39] I had just written an argument for the present withdrawal of all our forces from this disaffected region, which I will [1499] send for publication tomorrow. . . .

The telegraphic reports of the enemy, sent from the battlefield of Manassas, were all in their favor, & reporting the successive steps of a great & glorious victory—until a late hour of the day & conflict, when the reverse result could no longer be misunderstood or concealed. I will insert some extracts from editorials of the principal New York papers of July 22nd—from which may be inferred the universal rejoicing & glorification of the northern people, & the stunning [1500] effect of the later true report of the battle. . . . As in regard to all their previous defeats, the enemy's reports, by way of excuse, make a loud clamor about our numerous defensive breastworks, & "masked batteries." It so happens that our forces did not fire a single shot from any intrenchment through the whole engagement. The only use made of such defences was by the enemy, in intrenchments behind which were mounted batteries of heavy siege artillery—from which they fired from 6 A.M. to 1 P.M. (& I believe throughout) [1501] at our forces, & earthworks in which our men stood idle, & to which long continued cannonade from the enemy's batteries, with ball & shell, not a return fire was made by us, either from our batteries or otherwise. One or more of these batteries of the enemy, after firing harmlessly for 8 or 10 hours on our batteries & troops, were finally abandoned, together with the artillery there mounted, & seized by part of our pursuing troops the same afternoon. . . . [1502]

---

[39] Under pressure from Federal forces commanded by Brigadier General Jacob D. Cox, Wise evacuated Charleston, Virginia, during the night of July 24 and retreated toward Gauley Bridge. Cox occupied Charleston on the following day, and by July 30 he had moved up the Kanawha Valley to the vicinity of Gauley Bridge.

Aug. 7. . . . The mail. No later news yet of our army on the Potomac. It is reported that the enemy's troops have evacuated Newport News—as had before been done with Hampton, & all outside of Fortress Monroe. I fear that the withdrawn force has been sent to reinforce Washington. I am in most anxious expectation of hearing of Gens. Beauregard & Johnston advancing into Md.—& our government adopting the policy of "carrying the war into Africa." . . . My grandson George returned home from his father's camp. Jane set out for Alamance today. [End of MS Volume 8—p. 1503]

Aug. 9. The mail. The remains of Hampton were burnt by the Yankee army before retreating to Fortress Monroe, on the 7th.[40] Their troops have also evacuated Newport News, & have gone thence to sea—& not as I expected & feared, to reinforce Washington. Nothing in the papers about the movements of our armies.—Received a letter from Mildred at last—which was sent by private hand to Va. to be mailed. Some of her letters, as well as some of mine, have failed, & doubtless were intercepted & sent to Washington, & read & retained by Lincoln's infamous administration. All public modes of transmission have failed, & are untrustworthy—& so we must depend on rare private conveyances for our letters hereafter. I began my answer, although it may be months before I can sent it.—My communication (signed "Peter the Hermit") appeared in the Dispatch of 8th.[41]

Aug. 11. Sunday. At church. No use in my going, so far as relates to the sermon. I took a near seat to the minister, & tried to hear him—but in vain. . . . Began yesterday to make a copy (corrected) of my diary embracing the incidents connected with the battle of Manassas, as they appeared to my observation, for Mildred when I can convey it to her. Getting interested in my task, I copied for some hours.

Aug. 12. The mail. It appears that Hampton was not burnt by the enemy, but by order of our General, Magruder, for military objects. Also, Newport News is not evacuated.—Afternoon, Mrs. Lorraine, Nanny & I drove to visit Mrs. [Martha] Cocke of Tarbay—& at her invitation, remained [1505] to tea. . . . Mr. Hansburgh also came there—& both he & Mrs. Cocke are very agreeable company to me.

[40] The diarist's initial intelligence proved to be erroneous. The town of Hampton was actually fired by order of Confederate Brigadier General John B. Magruder. *Official Records*, Vol. IV, 571–72.

[41] See entry for August 5.

But when meeting with 5 or 6 persons, the general conversation, not addressed to me, I rarely hear—& when more than one person speak at once, even if one addresses me, & in loud enough voice, I am equally incapable of hearing. . . . It is time for me to give up all company & association out of my own family. I am wearied of life, & of all that it can now offer for my enjoyment. If death would come suddenly, & without notice or pain, I wish it could be before I am a day older.

Aug. 14. . . . Our Congress has authorized the President to accept the service of any number of volunteers, to 500,000. The rump congress of U.S. had before authorized Lincoln to [1506] raise 500,000 volunteers (or drafted militia,) 40,000 regulars, & to borrow $500,000,000. Another most important & sweeping enactment, if it could be made valid, is that ordering the absolute confiscation of all the land, slaves, & every description of property, possessed by all rebels (that is, by all persons except our few tories & traitors,) in all the seceded states. This act is not only of the almost universal confiscation of all property of all proprietors in the Confederate States, but includes virtually a decree of general emancipation for all the slaves. Yet no one seems to care for this enactment—& I thought so little of its expected operation, that I had forgot, until now, to note it, as an important item of political news. The practical operation of negro abduction, wherever the Yankee army has complete sway, is much more important. Gen. Butler, in a published letter to the Sec. of War, boasts of having now 900 abducted slaves of the neighboring country in Fortress Monroe, & that his plans are to obtain greater numbers. The Sec. of War has formally sanctioned this policy, & also President Lincoln—the latter further receiving into his domestic service one of these fugitive or stolen slaves.— Finished copying the extracts from a previous portion of this diary, with corrections & extensions, making the whole article 49 pages. . . .

Aug. 15. Missouri may now be counted as one of the seceded & Confederate States, though as yet divided & the scene [1507] of both civil & other war. The Confederate forces, under Gen. [Benjamin] McCullo[c]h (the noted Texan Ranger,) had some weeks ago entered Mo. from Ark., & have been aiding the secession party, & successfully, to fight against the invading U.S. troops & the German mercenaries, of which class is mainly recruited the Union volunteers of St. Louis, & the abolition states which nearly surround Mo.

The Governor & the Legislature, & most of the people of the state, are for secession. But the Convention, elected as ours was, to represent the submission party & sentiment, had a majority of submissionists, & further, the secessionist members were either serving as part of the armed defenders of the state, or, in many cases, prevented [from] attending the Convention, because in danger of unlawful arrest, & violence, from the U.S. military authorities. Thus, the southern & true men being excluded, the remaining submission "rump" Convention has erected itself into a revolutionary & despotic government—which has, by enactments, deposed both the Governor & legislature, elected another governor, their suitable tool, & has assumed to itself all legislative & other powers. On the other hand, the previous & lawful Governor, [Claiborne F.] Jackson, (claiming to be authorised by the previous general & dictatorial powers conferred on him by the legislature,) has proclaimed the provisional independence of the State, & called upon all its citizens to oppose the forces & the authority of the U.S. & their abettors. The Congress of the C.S. also has appropriated $1,000,000 to be expended as deemed best by our President, for the aid & support of Mo., through the state authorities. Though the reports of all recent military operations, & of several conflicts, are still contradictory & unreliable as to details, there can be no doubt of the general results being favorable to our side. . . . [1512]

Aug. 16. The mail today brought no *certain* news of importance, but many reports, & indications of prospective movements. The chief direction of military matters at Washington seems to have been taken out of Gen. Scott's hands, & Gen. McClellan appears to be the real commander in chief of the U.S.A. & especial direction at Washington. It is manifest that an attack on the U.S. forces there, & in Md, is greatly feared, & active measures have been adopted, & are in progress, to strengthen the U.S. forces at & defences of Washington, & also to guard the lower Potomac counties of Md from invasion from our side. A large detachment of the enemy's troops on the upper Potomac lately forded the river into Loudoun [County], & there pursued their accustomed course of robbery, outrage & arson, without any effective resistance. . . . The latest reports, & some of these coming through the telegrams to the north, continue to give support to the before reported success of our forces in Mo. so that I begin to confide in their truth as to the general facts. It is thus asserted that Gen. McCulloch had a long & hard-fought battle with the U.S. army, both in large force, & had [1513] beaten & routed them, with great loss—including the killing of Gen. [Nathaniel] Lyon, the U.S. commander.[42] He was, as Capt. Lyon, the agent & commander in the first illegal & treacherous & successful attack on the militia of Mo. & the consequent massacre of unarmed citizens, & women & children in St. Louis.[43] For this service, he had been promoted, at one step, from a captain's to a brigadier general's commission in the U.S. regular army. Whether the report of this victory is true or not, the U.S. commander in chief in the west, (the noted Fremont,) seems much alarmed for the safety of St. Louis. That abolition city is the strong-hold of the northern power, & its capture will be the death-blow to it in Mo. If also it can be laid in ashes, it will be well-deserved for the abolition & northern preferences of the majority of its inhabitants, who are either foreigners (Germans) or northerners.

Aug. 17. Last winter, I determined to write & publish nothing more—or to be known as mine—under the mortifying belief that my writings neither attracted attention of or produced benefit to the public, nor added anything to my own reputation or appreciation. To conform to that rule, I even withheld from publication the two last numbers of a series of articles which I had just before written on Florida, & of which the first had already been published in the "Southern Planter." I have continued to act under this rule of seclusion from publication, or putting myself or my name in print, where to be known. But at several times I have been tempted, by passing events, to write short articles for the newspapers. These have all been anonymous, in reality as well as in form—& the authorship concealed from all except the editors, who of course require to know their correspondents, & especially where charges are made on [1514] the responsibility of the writer. Also, the further to conceal my still writing for the press, even to this small extent, I sent these pieces, in turn, to different papers. All were promptly published, & copies have been appended to this diary, as the articles appeared. It was not that I was unwilling, or afraid, to be the

---

[42] This was the battle of Wilson's Creek (or Oak Hills), fought on August 10 in rolling country some ten miles southwest of Springfield. As a consequence of their victory in what proved to be the major battle in Missouri during the war, the Confederates gained control of most of the southern portion of the state. Casualties were heavy on both sides.

[43] This incident, which occurred on May 10, left nearly thirty civilians dead or mortally wounded.

known author & proclaimer of the opinions or charges set forth in either or all of these pieces, that I sought concealment—but because I wished that I should no longer be known as addressing my opinions to the public, through the press, or otherwise. The last of such communications, or rather a series of two numbers, I wrote yesterday & today, on the subject of "Retaliation" on the enemy for atrocious & systematic violations of the laws of civilized warfare. This I will send to the "Whig" by next mail.—Reading the "Village Notary," a novel of Hungarian authorship, & manners & condition. . . . [1515] Among the wounded prisoners now confined in Richmond is my former acquaintance Col. [J. Egbert] Farnham of New York, who was a field-officer of the noted Zouave regiment, & in command of it in the battle of Manassas. Col. Farnham was one of the officers of the slaver Wanderer—& thereby, & also by his subsequent trial & acquittal in Savannah, acquired much notoriety.[44] At these former times, he professed to be thoroughly in favor of the South, & of course of the institution of & necessity for negro slavery. But Col. Farnham the slave-trader, like all the more exalted northern former advocates for the south, has gone entirely against us.—I have found in . . . one of the official reports of the enemy's commanders of brigades (Col. Burnside's,) further testimony of the powerful effect of the 10 or 12 discharges from guns of Kemper's battery on the entangled trains passing over the bridge at Cub Run. According to this account, the trains were crossing, & might have crossed & escaped, if one shot, (which I should infer was mine, that being the first,) had not struck & stopped a train, & caused the wagon to be overturned, & so blocked up the passage. Whatever damage was thus caused, was certainly by those few discharges from two of Kemper's guns—as no others, of any kind, or at any time, were fired upon that place.

Aug. 20. Finished reading the "Village Notary"—a strange but interesting romance of Hungarian manners, & a very dark picture of Hungarian policy & law, & the administration of law & justice. . . . Began & finished the "Enchanter" by Bulwer—& began "Mary Barton."[45] [1517] Still, as I cannot read all the day, or when not at meals or in bed, there were other heavy & wearisome hours. There

---

[44] See Volume I, 268, 270, 379.

[45] Written by Elizabeth C. Gaskell and published in 1848, *Mary Barton* was an historical novel which portrayed sympathetically the life of factory workers in Manchester during the early Victorian period.

are no subjects of any interest for conversation in our family circle, & no subject for us on any others except the political & military state of the country, & the incidents of war news. The only enjoyment remaining to me is to receive the triweekly mail, & to read the newspapers (& very rarely a letter,) which it brings. The newspapers received usually occupy me for the remainder of that day, & sometimes longer—& then I have nothing to kill the remaining dull time, until the arrival of the next mail.

Aug. 21. . . . The war mania at the North, which seemed universal after the capture of Fort Sumter, is subsiding. Until lately, no individual or editor dared to raise his voice against this general madness, supported by mob violence. Now there are no less than 152 northern newspapers which are opposing this popular current, & advocating peace with the South. Yet even these publications are examples of the general ignorance in the North of the sentiment & condition of the South. Nearly or quite all of these papers, & also public meetings holding like views, recommend the calling of a general convention of all the states (northern & southern,) which is expected to adopt some plan of compromise, such as that of the "Peace Congress" or of Crittenden's Resolutions, & so satisfy the seceded states, & bring them back into the [1519] former general Union! All these advocates of compromise, peace, & union, are blindly ignorant of what every southerner knows, that no terms of compromise, no guaranties, that the north can offer, or even that we ourselves might prescribe, would induce the seceded states, or any of them, to return to the Union, even as it stood formerly. But now, the former government & constitution of the U.S. have been completely revolutionized by the Lincoln administration, & submitted to without a complaint or objection by the people & states of the North—& the government is now an unlimited despotism, & the rulers the basest scoundrels & low fools, that ever directed the policy of a great nation. Every man in the South who understands & values free government, & who heartily supported the acts of secession & the principles therein maintained, would prefer to the present government of the northern people, to be extended over the South, not only a limited monarchy like England, but even a despotic one like France, or even Russia.—Finished reading "Mary Barton," as well as the newspapers brought by the mail. Of these, we receive here the [Richmond] Daily Dispatch, Daily Express,

Triweekly [Charleston] Mercury, & semiweekly [Richmond] Enquirer & Whig—besides exchanging some of these with Julian for his Charleston Courier & Richmond Examiner. . . . Two . . . laws recently enacted by the rump congress exhibit the atrocious hatred & malignity & not less the political blindness & ignorance of the northern people, in regard to the South. These two acts, designed [1520] to promote the conciliation and submission of the South, provide 1st, for the general confiscation of all the lands & other property of the seceded states, including the general emanicaption of slaves—& 2nd, for the abolishing of all civil & constitutional government, & the substituting of martial law, despotic rule, & including [1521] the subjection of every citizen of the seceded states, (other than their few tories & traitors,) to the penalty of death, as rebels & traitors to the northern-states & power.

Aug. 23. . . . Plenty of new rumors, and of indications of impending war events—but nothing certain of later occurrence & also of importance. According to rumors, & earliest reports (which I always discredit,) affairs in Missouri since the victory at Oak Hill continue to be very favorable to the southern cause. The congress of C.S. has passed an act to admit that state into the C.S. as soon as its legal wish shall be expressed—& recognizing Gov. Jackson as the head of the legal government & authority. Upon whatever grounds, Gen. Fremont & the northern party are in great alarm for their ascendancy in & possession of St. Louis. The Lincoln administration also are seriously alarmed for the safety of Washington, on account of the recent increase of our forces along the Potomac, & indications of their threatening to enter Md., long as that movement has been expected & hoped for on our side in vain. A call from the Washington government has been made on the governors of ten northern states, to send on to Washington immediately all of the recently embodied volunteers, even though the regiments be incomplete in men, & not equipped. . . . Sundry acts both of mob violence & of illegal military authority in the North & West have served lately to suppress newspapers that advocated peace with the South. Some have been stopped by order of the commanders of the Yankee forces—of which two were in St. Louis. Of other papers, the offices & materials have been destroyed by mobs. In Massachusetts, in addition, one editor, for urging peace, was tarred & feathered, & made to ride upon a rail, until recanting & begging pardon on his knees.—Gen. [John E.] Wool, (75 years old,) has superseded Butler in command of Fortress Monroe.[46] The blockading naval force there has lately been much increased (to 15 vessels,) so that some movement is expected in consequence—& one *guess* is the invasion of the south side of James river. This is very improbable. . . . There has been a remarkable & very proper silence of all our newspapers latterly as to the movements & designs of our forces. But some of them are beginning [1523] to speak out, & to refer to operations & conditions already published at the north, & to complain of the 4 weeks of inaction since our great victory. It was afterwards evident that, if our army then had pursued the panic-stricken & fleeing northern army, ours might have taken Washington. Since then, the greatest weakness of the beaten enemy (added to by the discharge of all their oldest volunteers, whose time of 3 months had expired—) has been continually lessened by reinforcements & supplies. Our army & positions also have been greatly strengthened—but not so much as the enemy. It seems now to be understood that our commanders have in view the plan which I have long desired to be carried out, the invasion of Md, both above & below Washington. It seems now that Mathias Point is being strongly intrenched, & heavy cannon mounted, which will command the passage of the channel. If this is all true, & we can stop the vessels of the enemy, we may send troops across the Potomac into the most friendly part of Md.

Aug. 24. . . . Col. Farnham was not (as stated) brought to Richmond or made a prisoner. He was taken to Washington, & has since died of his wound.

Aug. 25. Sunday. At Church. There met Charles, who had come home, on furlough for 12 days, from his camp at Fairfax C.H. . . . Heard from him what he knows of the army, which is very different from what I had inferred. I know, by experience, that a private [1524] soldier, or even an inferior officer, can know but little of the condition, strength, & probable movements of the army to which he is attached. Still even this serves to correct both my own expectations, & the concealments, or designed misstatements of the newspapers, designed to deceive the enemy. Charles tells me that all Beauregard's army—consisting of 8 brigades & some other corps, & supposed to amount to 40,000 men—is all posted at & near

---

[46] Butler had been detached to assume command of a military expedition which captured Fort Hatteras, North Carolina, on August 28.

Fairfax C.H. But it seems that no further forward movement here is in view now, inasmuch as none of the reinforcements have gone there, but all to the armies farther west. Johnston, with his army, had left this position, & had marched to the upper Potomac, in face of [Nathanial P.] Banks' army, (before under Patterson,) in Md near Harper's Ferry. Gen. Lee is present & in command across the Alleghany, & there it seems most of the reinforcements have been sent. Hence I infer that the movements of our forces on the Potomac are merely defensive, or feints, & also Magruder's—to keep the Yankee forces threatened, & quiet, on the Potomac & in Md, & at Fortress Monroe, while a strong offensive effort will be made in the north-west. I would have preferred the leaving that disaffected section to the possession & rule of the Yankee power, for some time. But as the reverse policy is adopted, I trust that the designed blow may be fully effective.... Charles, on the suggestion of some friends in Richmond, designs to [1525] apply for a commission in the regular C.S. Army. I most ardently wish that he may succeed— though I have but little hope. I do not think that my name & influence will help him much, if any—though I will try to exert it as far as I can conscientiously. I deem him competent—& whatever has been objectionable & blamable in his habits, would not affect his worth & usefulness as a military officer. I have no doubt that by his partial military education, & otherwise, he is better qualified to fill a captaincy than most of the individuals who have been & will be appointed to that rank, & of sundry (as Pryor, Wise, Floyd & Bishop Polk,) who have been appointed colonels & generals. This is the first case in which I have ever asked for office, whether for myself or any other of my family—& I feel reluctant & even ashamed to do so now.

Aug. 26. . . . At 5 P.M. crossed the river to the Berkley wharf, & went on the steamer at 6.15. Reached Richmond at 10.30. No bed at two hotels—& I was about occupying a sofa for the night (near midnight,) when the clerk was enabled to find me a bed.—Saw Mr. Boulware, A. W. Venable, & other acquaintances.

Aug. 27. Obtained a good room, though very high. Among other acquaintances, saw Mr. Tyler, J. A. Seddon, Judge Brockenbrough & Mr. [Charles B.] Williams. I have conversed with no one as to Charles' designed application, except Seddon, who expresses himself much interested in its favor—& for the present I expect to leave it entirely to his care. I furnished him the names of all the members of Congress whom I suppose would aid [1526] the application on my account.—I was in the hall of Congress a short time before the hour of meeting, to see any of my friends who might be present— but as soon as called to order, & the prayer ended, the body, as is done regularly, went into secret session, & all spectators had to leave. . . . At the hotel today I met with Mrs. Roper of Charleston, & Judge [Arthur F.] Hopkins & his lady, of Ala. Also three of my comrades of the Palmetto Guard, who had come here to attend others who are sick, & in the hospitals. Arranged to visit them tomorrow. At night met with Mr. Hayden of La., with whom I had made acquaintance & spent pleasant times at Old Point, & also was with at the White Sulphur Springs. . . .

Aug. 28. Went after breakfast to visit the members of the Palmetto Guard who are in two hospitals. None of them were acquaintances of mine. All were doing well, & wanted no attention. These hospitals are maintained by associations of [1527] private individuals in Richmond, & seem to be well kept. I gave to the funds of the St. Charles Hospital $25—& will give to the other (a small one) $10.—Got from the office of Secretary of War a permit to see the Yankee prisoners, & went in the afternoon. There are about 1300 here, nearly all taken at Manassas. They are confined, under sentinels, in several large buildings before used for tobacco factories. Two were occupied by the wounded. Nearly all doing well. But one poor fellow was dying—in the agony of death—whose leg had been amputated on the field of battle. In the other buildings, there was no appearance of discomfort or sorrow. Some were reading, some playing cards—& most amusing themselves as do idle soldiers in their barracks. One floor is occupied by officers only. Except a few of them, they appeared as slovenly & rowdy as the private soldiers—& the N.Y. member of congress, [Alfred] Ely,[47] as low as any. One of the exceptions was Col. [Michael] Corcoran,[48] who seemed as a gentleman in both dress & manners. The apartments are clean & well ventilated, & free from any offensive odors, even in the hospitals. The men have good provisions, & in plenty, &,

---

[47] Ely (1815–92), a second-term Republican congressman, had ridden out from Washington to witness the battle and was captured by the Eighth South Carolina Infantry Regiment during the pursuit down Warrenton Pike. *Official Records*, Vol. II, 531. He was imprisoned in Richmond for nearly six months.

[48] Corcoran, who commanded the Sixty-ninth Regiment, New York Volunteers, during the battle of Manassas, was captured by the Thirtieth Virginia Cavalry in the pursuit near the Suspension Bridge over Cub Run. *Official Records*, Vol. II, 497.

notwithstanding the pain of confinement, probably most of them prefer this life, for a time, to their previous military duties & privations.—Met with Professor Venable, Mr. [P. G.] Evans of N.C.—& F[rank] G. Ruffin, who invited me to go to his house to tea, which I did. He & his wife now board in the city, to which he is confined by military duty.—Late at night Charles arrived. . . .

Aug. 29. Read the city newspapers in the morning, & the northern exchange papers in the Enquirer office in the afternoon—which made my chief occupation. Saw Mr. Seddon at night, & heard that he had obtained the ready signatures of 27 members of congress in support of my application for Charles' commission. He will present my letter, with theirs, to the President, as soon as he is well enough to see any visitors on business. As I can do nothing more in the matter, I shall leave tomorrow morning for Alamance. . . . A gentleman from Portsmouth, sent up today on this business, told me that a naval expedition, (as known some days ago,) had been sent from Fortress Monroe southward—& that it was feared that it was to seize Roanoke Island—that it had been effected. 400 men had been sent this morning from Portsmouth, [1529] through the ship canal, to defend the place, if in time. . . . Heard of another private conveyance to Ky, & used it to write . . . to Mildred. It was not until after having written & sent off this letter that it occurred to me that I may have endangered Mr. Sayre's property and person by my "treasonable" expressions. Some of my letters, & also Mildred's, had before been stopped, & I suppose examined by the authorities at Washington. And if Ky. shall be reduced to the present condition of Md., the fact of such correspondence, & the inference of such opinions, would be enough to cause my daughter's husband, if not herself also, to be imprisoned without limit. [1531]—This evening saw Mr. Evans of N.Ca., & was inquiring of him about the fortifications of Hatteras Inlet & other parts of the seacoast of N.C. He introduced me to Col. [W. Bevershaw] Thompson who as engineer had constructed the earth-works on Hatteras Inlet, the most complete of any, except the forts constructed of masonry. I had designed a visit to this place, & perhaps others—& one object of my inquiries was to learn the modes of access, & for accommodation while there. This was before I heard of the enemy's movement thereabout.

Aug. 30. At 5 A.M. left the hotel for the R.R. station, & soon after on the train for N.Ca. on my way to Alamance, the residence of Judge Ruffin. . . . The Petersburg newspaper of the morning, received

[115]

there, stated the attack & capture, by the naval expedition lately sent from Fortress Monroe, of the forts at Hatteras. But though the statement was made with much particularity of detail, Mr. Evans & Mr. Winslow, two intelligent N. Carolinians on the train, did not give any credence to the report. On reaching Weldon however, other reports received by telegraph from Newbern, compelled our reluctant belief of this unexpected & great disaster—caused by neglect & carelessness of the N.Ca. [1532] government. There were but few cannon mounted, & none heavy enough—& 750 men (in three positions) which were thrice as many as needed for use—& the ammunition was exhausted after a gallant but fruitless defence of some 12 hours. The two forts[49] (earth-works) & all the men except a few, were surrendered to the enemy. The evil consequences of this loss are incalculable. As soon as armed vessels of light draft are sent into Albemarle & Pamlico sounds, all their borders & the towns thereon will be exposed to the enemy.—At Weldon, made the unpleasant discovery that my hand-trunk, & only baggage, which had been checked in Richmond as far as Weldon, had, by some mistake, not been brought so far. In ascertaining the facts, & endeavoring to effect the recovery, so much of my time was lost, that the direct train for Raleigh left me—& the more circuitous train by Goldsborough had also set out before I knew that I might use it as an alternative. So I was left to stay at this miserably dull place until the next train, which was for Goldsborough, at 9 P.M. Set out then, & after 12 reached Goldsborough, & soon after went to bed.

Aug. 31. Roused before 5 A.M. for breakfast, & on the train for Raleigh before 6. From passengers from Newbern [1533] heard the accounts from Hatteras confirmed. Great alarm general. Nearly all the women & children have already fled from Newbern—& it is generally believed that that town, & also Washington, Edenton, & Elizabeth, will be in great danger of being burnt by the enemy, & all the lands on the sounds being plundered. I do not doubt the disposition of the enemy for all this & more—but I do not believe any such depredations possible, for some time, or until many more light draft armed vessels can be brought into the sounds. Preparations are making to hasten large bodies of troops to the exposed places.—Reached Graham station at noon, & there met Sterling

---

[49] Forts Clark and Hatteras.

Ruffin & his uncle James—in whose carriage I returned with them to Alamance. Found all well, & all the resident members at home, except Mrs. Ruffin. All seemed delighted to see me—& especially my dear Jane and Patty. A visitor for the day was the Rev. Dr. [Alexander] Wilson, a neighbor whom I had never met with before. He is a Presbyterian clergyman, & a teacher of great ability & reputation, & a man of great worth & intelligence.—Plenty of subjects for conversation, to a late hour, in the recent news, & in questioning me concerning my late military adventures.

September 1. Sunday. Many more newspapers have been suppressed in the northern states, & it seems that the policy is to be carried out of suppressing [1534] all that are not subservient to the war policy & despotic measures of the administration. In some cases, where the popular sentiment was sufficiently strong & general, it was left to a mob to demolish the printing office, & in some cases maltreat the editor or proprietor. In other cases the regular military authority stopped the publication by formal order of the military commander. In the city of N.Y. & as to very important publications, where either of the preceding courses might be too severe a test of the public sentiment, another way has been used, less odious in appearance, but nearly as effectual for suppression. This is for the government spies & agents to search out & stop all copies of "disloyal" publications sent by public conveyances to their subscribers & purchasers. Thus, by cutting off all furnishing of any such paper abroad, it must necessarily soon stop for want of purchasers & supporters. In this manner have been treated 5 of the most able & respectable opposition papers in the city of N.York— the moderate Journal of Commerce, the Christian Observer (the valued paper of the Presbyterian sect,) & the Freeman's Journal, the Catholic organ. It is not only that the very few advocates or apologists for the South & southern institutions are so treated, but others who have merely opposed the policy of attempting the subjugation [1535] of the South by war, & the flagrant violations of the U.S. constitution by the Lincoln government, & the despotic power thereby acquired & exercised. It seems, from the steps already taken, that every press, & publisher, that does not go all lengths in support of the enormities of the administration, is to be crushed. Further—"disloyal" individuals in their words—or even private opinions—who have done or attempted no *act*, have been imprisoned, without charge of the offence, or limit of time, (the writ of *habeas corpus* being entirely disregarded,) in Fort Lafayette, surrounded by the water in N. York harbor, which is converted into an unapproachable Bastile for holding these state prisoners. Suspicion is enough for the arrest & solitary & hopeless confinement of any one. All the Maryland prisoners, who were deemed too near home when imprisoned in Fort McHenry, & possibly unsafe, have been brought to this island Bastille in New York, & many others added to them. Latterly, ladies of high position have also been arrested, & imprisoned in a secure building in Washington fixed for their confinement. Mrs. [William] Gwin, wife of the Senator of California,[50] was absent, but had her trunks broken open & searched, & "treasonable" papers found & abstracted. Mrs. [Rose] Greenhow,[51] & Mrs. [Philip] Phillips[52] & her grown [1536] daughters have been confined—& several others were about to be arrested & confined. Another exercise of unlimited despotism has been made by Gen. Fremont, (the noted swindler candidate of the abolitionists in 1856, for the Presidency,) now Commander in Mo. He has raised a forced loan from the banks of St. Louis for $250,000. Also, the specie funds of the Springfield bank, ($25,000,) just before that town was occupied by our troops, were seized (*to save them*,) by the Abolition general, & carried off. Still later, $160,000 more has been drawn as a so-called "loan" from another bank in St. Louis. Now, as a certainty, not a dollar of these sums will be repaid before the occupancy of Mo. is settled—& if the abolition party cease to rule there, not a cent will ever be repaid. These & all other exer-

---

[50] A native of Tennessee, William McKendree Gwin (1805–85) served one term in the United States House of Representatives from Mississippi before moving to California in 1849. There he was immediately elected to the United States Senate, serving until March, 1861. During the war Gwin was involved with both the Confederacy and the Mexican government of Maximilian.

[51] A Washington society matron, Rose O'Neal Greenhow was the most celebrated female spy for the Confederacy. It was she who apprised Beauregard of McDowell's plans for the First Manassas campaign. Arrested with Mrs. Phillips and several others on August 23, 1861, she remained a prisoner until the spring of 1862, when she was exiled to the South. After a triumphal tour of Europe she was drowned in a boating mishap off the North Carolina coast in September, 1864.

[52] The wife of a prominent Washington lawyer and former congressman from Alabama, Mrs. Phillips was later released, only to run into additional difficulties after the Federal occupation of New Orleans. She was arrested in that city in June, 1862, and incarcerated on Ship Island, Mississippi, by order of Major General Benjamin F. Butler. Because of her maternal responsibilities—she had nine children—she was again granted clemency after a confinement of three months. *Official Records*, Ser. II, Vol. IV, 105, 516.

cises of illegal & unconstitutional power—to punish opposers, crush opposition, & enrich the despotic & plundering government, all work wonderfully at first to strengthen its power in the contest with the South. But even the slavish submissionists of the North, & still more of Md. Mo. & Ky., must thus be brought, after a time to fear, & next hate, & finally to oppose the progress & policy of this now unlimited despotism. [1537]

I have long held the opinion that the people of the northern states were not only immeasurably inferior to those of the southern in the understanding & appreciation of constitutional government, but that, as a community, they had no comprehension of what is the true meaning of a constitution of government, or of rights secured by a constitution. And there are few individual exceptions to this rule, even among their wisest statesmen—none in the great inferior mass. A northern politician regards the constitution of his state, & of the United States, as being like the by-laws of any petty corporation or association—as presenting the [1538] indispensable regulations & arrangements for the working & government of the association—such as what officers shall serve, & their number, powers, the times & places of their election—the manner of assessing & imposing taxes, &c. &c. But they never get rid of the idea, that the majority of the people have an inherent & indefeasible right to over-rule any provisions of the constitution, or to disregard it—& that, for this & for any other purpose, that the will of the majority shall govern, is not only deemed right, but it is lauded as the true & only democratic rule, or principle of free government. They never can conceive that a constitution of government is adopted for the very purpose of controlling majorities, & preventing them from oppressing minorities. But notwithstanding this low estimate of mine of the northern political intellect, I had not supposed it possible that the northern people—a free people until recently, & long under a free constitution—should have consented, & even approved & applauded, the complete abrogation of their chief constitutional safeguards of personal liberty & rights, & the establishment of an unlimited despotism by usurpation & force. No free people, however ignorant, has ever before submitted at once, & willingly, to such deprivation [1539] of their liberties & rights. Indeed, no enslaved & oppressed people, having any privileges established by custom, (as have all, even Turks & Russians,) would have submitted to these privileges being abolished, as the northern people have the destruction of their most solemn & precious constitutional safeguards, the writ of *habeas corpus*, the liberty of the press & of speech, & the exclusive right of Congress to raise & maintain armies. Yet all these rights have fallen, within a few months, before the ostensible *dictum* & will of a president, who is neither wise, nor brave, nor even very popular, but a low & vulgar black-guard & buffoon. Other countries have yielded their constitutions & liberties to great statesmen, warriors, & popular leaders—such as Caesar, Cromwell, & Napoleon. But, until in this case of the northern states, no people have so yielded, without even alleging objections or unwillingness, to such arbitrary rule & usurpation of a fool, or of others not much better, acting in his name. For it is most probable that President Lincoln not only did not himself project & plan his despotic usurpations, & the overthrowing of constitutional government, but that he does not even know that it has been done, or that he has effected a complete & momentous political revolution. He is a tool in the [1540] hands of others, having more sense than himself indeed, but not enough to direct the revolution they have inaugurated. Terror—fear of the power of the government to confiscate the property & imprison the persons of opponents at will—may for a time silence opposition, & even prevent the indications of it being seen. But it must grow silently, & when strong enough to dare to speak, will soon overthrow the low & brutal despotism that now rules, though it may be to establish one more powerful in its place. . . .

Sept. 2. Among the many books which are piled on the tables in the sitting room—Judge Ruffin's books, & even hundreds of newspapers, which must not be moved, or if moved must be exactly replaced—I picked up & looked into the 7th vol. of [John G.] Lockhart's Life of Walter Scott, & became interested enough to read for the third time the affecting details of the gradual ruin of his great intellect by disease. Perhaps I have been, & am still more now, the more impressed with his deplorable fate in this respect, because fearing a somewhat like end for myself—which may God in his mercy save me from, by an earlier & sudden death. . . . Scott, of course, like all other Britons, deemed slavery the worst of evils, & thought that one of the most beneficial operations of the Christian religion was its overthrowing of slavery—which however it did not do. He mentions earlier in his diary his conversing with Mr. Jacob, the political economist,[53] & hearing his scheme for the relief of the poor of England—which was to compel them to labor, under [1542] the compulsion of military discipline. Scott thought it would be a very good plan, except that its being put in operation would inevitably produce a rebellion. It did not occur to his mind that, even if there was no danger of this evil of rebellion, the consummation of Jacob's plan of compulsory labor would be nothing more nor less than slavery—but of a kind much worse for the slaves than would be our kind. Slavery of class to class is always harder than of individual to individual. . . .

Sept. 3. . . . Skirmishes of out-posts have taken place in Western Va. & on the Potomac, & in all of which the advantage has been on our side. Our out-posts have been farther advanced towards Washington. The reports thence (of the enemy) say that our campfires are visible from the Georgetown heights. It is generally believed that every appearance there indicates a speedy battle, in which the whole of Beauregard's forces will be opposed to the enemy near & in Washington. I do not believe it still. I trust [1543] that he is making there a very strong feint, to threaten Washington, & to draw & keep the enemy's forces there, while our army will cross the Potomac, above or below, or both, & succor & raise Md. by passing in the rear of Washington. . . . Kentucky must choose her course, whether with the North or the South, within a few weeks. Then civil war there, & defeat of the Submissionist party & Yankee forces, as in Mo. Although the Submissionists are twice as many, at least, as the Secessionists, I have no doubt of the success of the latter when they resort to blows, or force, even if there should be no aid to either party from abroad. As a general rule, the Submissionist party embraces, & is largely composed of, the old, the timid, the cowardly, the imbecile & the mean-spirited. In the Southern or secession party will be found most of the youthful, the ardent, the patriotic & public-spirited citizens. In a contest between bodies so constituted, one man of the latter is more than equal to two, or perhaps three of the former. Also, there are thousands of the young men of Ky, voluntary exiles now, & bearing arms for the southern cause in other states. As soon as they [1544] shall be permitted to strike for their own land, they will hasten to return, in organized

---

[53] Presumably William Jacob (1762?–1851), merchant, statistical writer, and comptroller of corn returns to the Board of Trade from 1822 to 1842.

bodies, aided by the C.S. government. Such men, so arrayed, will exercise double the force of any other auxiliaries.—A law has recently been made by the C.S. congress which is like to have important effects in counteracting the enemy's blockade. Heretofore, certain harbors only, embracing all the deep, & convenient for peaceful navigation & trade, have been legal "ports of entry"—to which only foreign vessels were authorised to bring in & land cargoes—& to some one or more of which only they could be directed from foreign countries. If a foreign vessel, finding the port of its destination obstructed by blockade—or any more so named ports—were to attempt to enter, & discharge at, some other unaccustomed & not legalized port, & fail, & be lost or captured, the insurance would be forfeited. If succeeding, the vessel & cargo was subject to forfeiture under our former & general revenue law. Now the privileges of ports of entry have been extended to our whole sea-shore & all the inlets. All these have a sea-shore extent of 3000 miles. It was before impossible for all the navy of the U.S. to blockade all the previous ports of entry. It will be impossible to blockade or even to watch one half now opened to foreign vessels, or other discharging vessels of shallow draft. If European vessels cannot enter the unfrequented & shallow inlets, they may transship in the West Indies [1545] to small vessels. Thus, even if European powers were not to refuse to obey the illegal paper blockade altogether, (as I trust they will soon,) their traders may easily elude, while they still appear to respect, the restrictions. The general condition of things will now be brought about which I predicted in my "Anticipations of the Future," in which it was supposed that no operative blockade of our sea-coast can possibly be effectually maintained.—In my present visit to this family, I have been rejoiced to learn positively, what I had inferred long previously, that the heavy affliction of Wm. R., in the loss of his leg, & his being thereby confined a prisoner to his chamber, has brought to him the more than compensation of reformation of his before intemperate habits—or rather of extreme intemperance on the rare occasions only when he left & stayed from home. Though by this grievous propensity & error he has wasted & lost the bright prospects of his youth & prime of manhood—all the utility & profit of his great natural talents & excellent education—still, to himself & to all his now affectionate & attentive & respectful family, his reformation, with all the consequent changes, is most happy & blessed. . . . In this house, & family circle, I am situated differently from any other, except of my own children. While I am sure that my presence is most welcome & gratifying to all, I am not only nominally, & in part, made *at home*, but to the fullest extent. While every needed attention is paid to my comforts & supposed wishes, & every suspected want anticipated, I am in all other respects treated & left to act as if I were one of the household. Judge Ruffin reads, or writes, or goes abroad on his numerous calls of business, just as if I was not here—the other members of his large family all do the like as to their employments or engagements—& I am left, just as I would wish, to interfere with no one's business or pleasure, & to read, (for which there are plenty of books,) or write in my room, or to converse, without requiring the notice of, or annoying any one. This course is just what I like, & always ask for, when visiting where I can make so free—but which I never could obtain so perfectly anywhere as here. . . . Judge Ruffin is in much better health than when I saw him last, & better than I had ever expected to see him again. His cough still continues, though less troublesome. In other respects, he seems well, & walks as briskly, & takes exercise as in his former healthy & active life.—According to the rule I had laid down for myself in writing this diary, I have avoided stating any report of news until it was apparently so authenticated, or confirmed by later news, as to be deemed trustworthy. And even with such care to obtain truth, I have not avoided being deceived in many cases, & stating baseless falsehoods, or gross exaggerations. Yet by omitting all early rumors of war news, carrying with them considerable credence, & therefore at first important, though afterwards contradicted, I miss even adverting to matters which cause to me & the public much excitement & interest before their emptiness is made known. If, on the other hand, I were to record the daily rumors, as brought by the newspapers, I should add pages to each of these meager daily entries—& have afterwards to deny, or to remodel, almost every report. Of course, this would be too troublesome, besides being otherwise objectionable. Yet, for a change, & for a short time, until again omitted, I will state the *important* new reports only. If the reports of unimportant matters also were embraced, I should have to write twenty pages for one heretofore.[54]

---

[54] After this date the diarist increasingly follows this new policy of noting, and commenting upon, unauthenticated newspaper reports, thus resulting in longer entries and the inclusion of much erroneous information. In the interest of clarity and accuracy—and because of space limitations—much of this material will be deleted.

Sept. 4. Reports—& from Yankee writers or northern papers. The
N.Y. Herald states that the Southern troops now [1548] in actual
service in Va are nearly 300,000—of which 180,000 are near &
threatening the Potomac. (These are enormous exaggerations,
which I trust the Yankees will believe.) The same correspondent
predicts the speedy attempt of our forces to cross the Potomac
above Washington, & thus invade Md. . . . More ladies in Washington have been imprisoned by the government, or are confined to
their houses under strict *"surveillance"* of the police. In addition to
the other followings of the worst despotisms of Europe, there has
been established in the North a system of extensive *"espionage,"*
which is acknowledged & applauded, by leading papers, as necessary for the present condition of things in the more disaffected
localities of the North. [1549]

Sept. 5. . . . Gen. Beauregard's official report of the retreat from
Fairfax C.H. & the battle of Bull Run (July 18th) has lately been
published.[55] I learn from it some things in regard to our Brigade
which I did not understand before. The enemy attempted by two
different plans to cut us off, & were near doing so, first at Germantown, & next at Centreville. When our corps was ordered to leave
the latter place, after midnight, the enemy's forces had then been so
advanced on our right & left, that they had surrounded us on three
sides, leaving open only the route towards Bull Run. This fact
increases the wonder that the enemy did not overtake us in our very
slow & often obstructed retreat, in which our regiment, the rear
guard, had so often to wait for the preceding troops to advance, that
it occupied 4 hours for us to march the 4 miles to our position in the
trenches across Bull Run. I also detect an inaccuracy in Gen. B.'s
report, which I am surprised should be [made]. [1550] He states as
the commencement of the engagement on the 18th., that the enemy
"appearing in heavy force in front of Bonham's position, *about
meridian*, opened fire with several 20-pounder rifle guns from a
hill, over 1½ miles from Bull Run. *At the same time*, Kemper,
supported by two companies of light infantry, occupied a ridge
about 600 yards in advance of the Ford (Mitchell's) with two
6-pounder guns. At first the firing of the enemy was at random, but
by 12.30 P.M. he had obtained the range of our position, & poured
into the brigade a shower of shot, but without injury to us" & c.
Now, though I did not take the time by my watch, I am confident

---

[55] See *Official Records*, Vol. II, 440–47.

that the firing of the enemy's cannon at our intrenchments, & the *first* movement of Kemper's artillery & the supporting infantry was as early as 8 A.M.[56] . . .

Sept. 6. The mail. . . . Gen. Fremont has proclaimed Mo. under martial law—& for a large designated portion of the state, he declares subject to the penalty of death *every man* found in arms against the U.S., & that absence from home shall be assumed as presumptive evidence of such crime—the confiscation of all property, real & personal, of such offenders, & the emancipation of all slaves of such owners. If this does not extend the insurrection, & speedily free the state from the power of the Yankees & tories, I do not know what will. . . . Read a few chapters, (& all the general & political,) & looked over the remainder of "Spain & the Spaniards," a new book of travels by J[ames] J. Pettigrew.[57] It is written well— but it seems to me as if designed full as much to display the abilities & acquirements of the author, as his professed subjects. However—there are two leading subjects of nearly all books of travels, or at least in well-known countries, which afford me no gratification—the descriptions of scenery, buildings, & paintings, & the personal adventures of the author. The exceptions are when the scenes [1552] are of countries little known, as of the frigid or torrid zones, & then they should be general—& when the author's personal adventures serve well to exhibit manners & customs & peculiarities of the people. However, little as I liked this book, it served to increase my previous high appreciation of the abilities & acquirements of the author.

Sept. 7. Our main newspapers (from Va.) failed to come today, but the scant supplies of news from other papers were added to by some verbal reports brought by passengers on the train. Gov. [John M.] Morehead, just from Beaufort, stated that an attack of the enemy on Fort Macon had been & still was expected every day, from indications given. With artillery of heavy metal & long range, good artillerists, & enough ammunition—& bomb-proof casements for protection of the garrison—I would have great confidence in any

---

[56] The reports of Colonel Kershaw and Captain Kemper confirm the diarist's recollection that two guns from Kemper's battery were posted on the north side of the run in the early forenoon. *Official Records*, Vol. II, 452, 459. See note 12 above for further clarification of this incident.

[57] A noted Charleston lawyer, Pettigrew gathered material for this book during an extended tour of Europe in 1850.

attack of the enemy being repelled. But I fear deficiencies in all these requisites for safe defence. . . . I had intended, as soon as ending my visit here, to go to Beaufort, or rather to the port thereof called Morehead—& to Fort Macon. For the latter, or both, it may now be too late. But I design to set out for the purpose by [1553] the Express train on Monday morning (9th.) . . .

Sept. 8. Sunday. No preaching or public worship—& Judge Ruffin does not, as always formerly when there was no minister's service, read the morning service & a sermon. . . . In the afternoon, took leave of my good friends, & drove to the "Shops" station, to stay the night at the hotel, & to take the train for Morehead & Fort Macon early tomorrow morning. I would not let my destination be known—as I knew that Jane & Patty would make a fuss about the supposed danger of getting so near the enemy, & to a fort & locality expected daily to be attacked. . . . If the fort is properly fitted for defence, I shall be glad to be in it, should a speedy attack on it be made. But if unfitted for defence against long-range cannon & bomb-shells, I shall have no inclination to risk being taken prisoner there by a surrender of the fort, as at Hatteras [1554], or even to remain so near as the railroad at Morehead, which would be one of the first points seized. The passengers by the Express train from Morehead, which arrived here tonight at 8, report that no attack had been made by the enemy on Fort Macon, & that one war-steamer only was blockading the harbor. . . .

Sept. 9. Arose at 3 A.M. & started on the train at 4. Detained at Raleigh station an hour, & then reached Goldsborough before 11 A.M. where I had to wait until 3 P.M. for the train to Morehead. . . . I fear that I am about to get out of the region of newspapers—as I know Beaufort was. None came here today for sale, & I was indebted for the sight of one to a passenger from Petersburg. . . . Arrived at Morehead, (where I stopped) the *prospective* town for Beaufort harbor, (as the old town of Beaufort is on shallow water—). Capt. [William F.] Lynch, of the C.S.N. & formerly U.S.N., & the Dead Sea explorer, is staying here, & in command of all the C.S. naval forces from James river to Cape Fear river. He soon introduced himself to me, & also Gen. [Richard C.] Gatlin, who commands the land troops of this station.[58] When stopping half an hour

---

[58] A graduate of West Point and veteran of the Mexican War, Brigadier General Richard Caswell Gatlin (1809–96) had assumed command of the Department of North Carolina on August 20, 1861. He supervised the coastal defenses of that state

in Newbern, saw Judge [John R.] Donnell & others, who received me with much attention.

Sept. 10. Breakfast—without any fresh fish, which is the only possible attraction to this place—& otherwise a poor hotel. Immediately after breakfast, hired a boat & sailed to Fort Macon, 2½ miles. Two English ships are now at the wharf, which came in with full cargoes, long after the Yankee blockade was proclaimed, but before a blockading ship had appeared. It is only since the capture of Fort Hatteras that a Yankee steam frigate has been lying off the mouth of the port. Col. J[ohn] L. Bridgers, the commandant of Fort Macon, is my old agricultural acquaintance of Edgecombe [County, N.C.].[59] He is, I was sorry to find, in bad health. He received me very kindly, & showed me all of the fort, & explained the means for defence. The fort is very strong, in construction, cannon, & everything for defence, if attacked. Its position perfectly commands the channel, the outside of which is only 1000 yards from the fort. The whole width of water, to the opposite Shackelford's bank, is less than 1½ miles. The channel also is crooked & difficult, & would keep a ship [1556] long under the fire of the fort. There are 35 cannon mounted, mostly 32-pounders—& two of 8 inch Columbiads, (64-pounders.) A large rifled cannon has just been landed, & will soon be mounted. There are 47 cannon not mounted, & not needed, mostly 24-pounders. The fort consists of two distinct concentric circumvallations, separated by a broad ditch, or moat it would be except that it has no water unless from extraordinary & rare high tides. This moat is raked by several cannon pointed from interior embrasures. If the whole outer fortification should be occupied by the assailing enemy, & also the moat, the interior fortification, or citadel, if bravely defended, might be impregnable. The apartments are bomb-proof. All the cannon, directed against the water & land approaches, & on both the enclosing platforms, are placed *en barbette*, or pointing over the parapets—the gunners protected from shot by breast-works, but exposed to bomb-shells. This is but slight exposure, under the circumstances. But this is about to be lessened, by coverings to be constructed of rail-road

---

until a serious illness obliged him to resign from Confederate service in September, 1862.

[59] Colonel Bridgers had already received a citation for gallantry while serving as a captain in the First North Carolina Regiment in the engagement at Big Bethel, Virginia, on June 10, 1861. *Official Records*, Vol. II, 92–93.

iron-bars. Col. Bridgers provided me with a saddle horse, & rode with me along the ocean beach nearly two miles, & past the anchorage of the Yankee steam frigate (supposed to be the Susquehannah,) now blockading the harbor. It is anchored about 3 miles from the fort—&, as Col. Bridgers supposed, near as far from the nearest part of the beach, where we rode. . . . Since lying here, the frigate has [1557] made no other hostile movement or indication. I have no idea that any attack will be made on Fort Macon, under present circumstances. About 6 miles west from the fort, along the "bank," there is a regiment of infantry, to prevent the enemy's landing. . . . The walls, or parapets, of Fort Macon are low, & present but a small object to the cannon of an assailing force. Except for the flag-staff, & the cannons' rising above the level of the parapet, the fort would not be distinguished at a mile's distance from a natural mound—differing from the numerous sand-hills only in being more regular in surface, & in being green instead of white. The fort is near the northern extremity of the southern sand-reef. Except near the fort, where it has been levelled, this sand-reef is a succession of low hillocks of loose sand, with a few scattered tufts of low vegetation. The surface is well adapted to conceal skirmishers. The reef is very narrow for some miles, only a few hundred yards wide.—Having seen & learned all that seemed desirable, I returned to Morehead to dinner—& would have been glad then to leave this very dull place if a conveyance had been offered earlier than tomorrow morning.—From all that I have heard, from the naval officers here & others, I come to the conclusion that the surrender of Fort Hatteras & its garrison was unnecessary & inexcusable. The naval officers however do not say so, or attach any blame to Com. [Samuel] Barron, the commander—but seem disposed to apologize for him on account of the difficulties. Even if it was a necessity to [1558] lose the forts (which were only recent earth-works,) it could have been foreseen in the intervening night, & the cannon might have been spiked, the extra muskets & stores destroyed, & the garrison have marched out along the reef, until to be securely embarked & removed by our small armed vessels, then close by in the Sound. The worst feature of the whole affair was that the reinforcement sent from Norfolk, of more than 300, was landed late in the afternoon, & in the night before the surrender, just to be given up as prisoners. The battery at Beacon Island (inside of the reef,) of which the guns commanded Ocracoke Inlet, was evacuated by its garrison (who escaped), the cannon spiked, & the carriages burnt. None of the enemy have yet appeared there to occupy the place, or to claim the cheap conquest. They hold & have strengthened Fort Hatteras, & are secure there against any naval attack that we have force to attempt. But still I think that the fort may be recaptured by a land force, landed at a distance on the sand-reef, & concealed by the sand-hills, & storming the intrenchment in a dark night, when the heavy cannon would be of little more effect on the assailants than so many muskets. The attempt would be greatly aided by the previous occurrence of a heavy & long continued gale, which, with the accompanying usual rains, & sometimes overflowing waves, would go far to distress the garrison & damage the defences—& no supplies or reinforcement [1559] could be given by the enemy, for some days after the subsiding of the wind of a severe storm. I shall look to the approaching & usual equinoctial gales for something to be done.

Sept. 11. Left Morehead after early breakfast, & reached Goldsborough at 12 M. There found that the next train to Weldon would be after 10 P.M., & I had to wait this tedious time with very little amusement. It was the day of the regimental militia muster, which brought to me all of my previous acquaintances in the county, & sundry strangers who sought my acquaintance. . . . 150 of the Yankee prisoners from Richmond, including most or all of the officers, were brought, under guard, in the train of cars, on their way to Fort Sumter, or Castle Pinckney, for safe & more convenient confinement. A special train went to Va. full of troops from the South, & also several companies came on by the night train. Indeed, they are still pouring on almost every day, & the number now in our service must be very great—probably more than 200,000 volunteers, & still more coming on.—A very recent change in the times of the trains running to & from Weldon, & the cessation of the night train to Petersburg, have broken the connection, & I shall be again delayed, for more then 12 hours at Weldon. This is not the worst. If the trains had run as always before, & as I counted upon, I should have reached Petersburg very early on the 12, in time to take the Schultz going down to Coggin's Point—which will not again offer until the 14th. As the Wilmington train could not connect at Weldon, there [1560] was nothing to be gained by speed. Therefore, & as there was a heavy freight of troops & commodities, the running was very slow—so that it was dawn (12th) when we reached Weldon. I had been very inconveniently seated, & had obtained little rest or sleep.

Sept. 12. Immediately after arriving at the hotel at Weldon, I lay down, & endeavored to sleep—but to little purpose—& awoke fully roused, & arose after 7 A.M. Here met among the detained passengers several of my acquaintances—among them Gen. [James] Simons of Charleston,[60] & Capt. [William K.] Bachman of Columbia, commanding a Charleston German company of volunteers, on the way to the seat of war. By accident heard that Lieut. [W. L.] De Pass of the 2nd S.C. Regiment was here, detained by illness, & I hastened to call on him. He was severely (& as then thought, desperately,) wounded on the head by a musket or rifle ball at the battle of Manassas, & the concussion so affected his brain that he immediately became insane, & continued so for some days. After getting better, (& his wife having come to him,) he got as far as this place, & while stopping was seized with other illness which has left him prostrate. His wound is mostly healed. It was a gash to the bone 5 inches long. It has healed up to the middle 2 inches—which is still a very ugly suppurating wound.[61]—Had to wait until 2 P.M. for the train to start. As now I have lost the trip by the Schultz, & it is very costly to hire a carriage from Petersburg, I shall go on to Richmond, & stay a day before taking the next passage of the Schultz—which steamer only will land passengers [156] on my son's farm at Coggin's Point. . . . Did not reach Richmond until 8.30. Soon after supping, returned to my room to read newspapers.

Sept. 13. I saw & conversed with W[illiam] S. Ashe of Wilmington (here in the service of C.S.,) & also sundry other persons on the subject of Fort Hatteras & Beacon Island. Mr. Ashe agrees with me in regard to them, & as to the feasibility & means for recapturing Hatteras. John Tyler jr., who is acting chief clerk of the War Department, was one on whom I urged my views, & especially as to the ease & the necessity of reoccupying Beacon Island, because I thought he might operate to attract the attention of the Secretary of War. In answer, he told me in confidence that secret measures had

---

[60] Brigadier General Simons had earlier commanded the troops on Morris Island during the bombardment of Fort Sumter.

[61] De Pass apparently recovered fully from his wound, for in January, 1864, he was commanding Battery G of the Palmetto Battalion Light Artillery in the Third Military District of South Carolina. *Official Records*, Vol. XXXV, Pt. 1, p. 558.

already been taken for the re-occupying & holding Beacon Island. Saw Mr. Spratt, who is to repeat tonight a lecture he has delivered before descriptive of the battle of Manassas, & which I will go to hear. Saw some intelligent soldiers lately from the army near Alexandria & Washington—& from their accounts I doubt whether any early general engagement is to be expected. . . . At night went to hear Spratt's lecture on the battle of Manassas, which was admirable. Met there & was introduced to Gen. [Edmund] Kirby Smith, who was severely wounded in the battle, & has nearly recovered. Also Dr. [M.] Laborde of S.C. who has been acting as surgeon, & who very lately was at our advanced post at Munson's Hill. I asked him what prevented our general commencing offensive movements. He said that both subsistence & transportation were deficient—but a still greater obstacle was the great amount of sickness, near or quite one-half of the whole army having been unfit for duty when there was most sickness. There had been improvement since.—Fremont's proclamation, declaring (besides death to the offenders, & general confiscation of all their property,) the emancipation of the slaves of all "rebels" in Missouri—that is of every man who sides with his state & the South—is in designed operation an edict of general emancipation. For more than half the slaves belong to secessionists, & so are directly proclaimed emancipated. And if this edict of martial law could be effective, & all these slaves became free, it would be impossible for the others, belonging to submissionists, to be held in subjection [1563] to their masters—& so all would become free, & the institution of slavery be abolished throughout Mo., with all its like influence on the neighboring slave-holding states of Ky, Ten, & Ark. One would think that this important & lawless act & policy would be enough to detach Ky from Yankeedom, but it seems not. On the contrary in the legislature, which represents the submission party only, submission has just crouched lower than ever. That body, recently assembled, has directed the Governor to demand the withdrawal from the state of all Confederate forces, & refused, by the same majority of nearly 3 to 1, to include in the same prohibitory order, the troops embodied under Lincoln's authority.[62] . . . This base subserviency must have

---

[62] Allegedly in response to threatened encroachments by the Federals, General Leonidas Polk ordered Confederate troops into Kentucky on September 3, thus ending the self-proclaimed neutrality of that state. Three days later, Union forces under General Ulysses S. Grant occupied the important river town of Paducah.

much effect, added to the emancipation proclamation for Mo., in bringing to their senses the moderate & deluded union men of Ky., who are not ready for complete submission. There will soon begin civil war in Ky., as in Mo., the opposed parties being supported by armies from the North & the South. When fighting begins, the present small minority of secessionists will be soon stronger than the majority of submissionists. The same terrible trial as of Mo. will be passed through—& in both states the same result will be reached of triumph for the southern side.

Sept. 14. Left Richmond early, & by the Schultz steamer reached Beechwood by 11 A.M. Edmund had not come home, & his coming now very uncertain, as there is some alarm of an attack there by the enemy—which I deem without foundation. Gen. Magruder has lately called for 10,000 more men to reinforce his army about Yorktown. This indicates that he either expects an attack, or designs to make one himself. . . . The following letters[63] will serve to exhibit samples of the ordinary predatory conduct of the Yankee troops, permitted by the government, & of the government directly in the treatment of the prisoners now confined in Fort Lafayette, mostly without being charged with any crime, & without any remedy to obtain trial, or relief. There are now 60 of the (male) state prisoners in this Bastile, all of them men of respectable & some of high social position. [1565] Among them are C[harles] J. Faulkner, late U.S. minister to France,[64] & Mr. [James G.] Berrett [*sic*], mayor of Washington city,[65] & Mr. [George P.] Kane, Marshal & chief of the Baltimore legal police.[66] Whether all are treated as badly as the

---

[63] Appended to the diary in the form of newspaper clippings, the first purports to be a letter from a Vermont soldier describing depredations in northern Virginia just two days before the battle of Manassas. The other two letters, written by Baltimore police commissioners, are highly critical of prison conditions at Fort Lafayette, New York.

[64] A former four-term congressman from Virginia, Charles James Faulkner (1806–84) was appointed United States minister to France by President Buchanan in 1859. Upon his return to the United States in August, 1861, he was detained by Federal authorities and incarcerated in Fort Lafayette for four months before being exchanged for Alfred Ely, the New York congressman who had been captured at Manassas. He then entered the Confederate army, serving as a staff officer with General Thomas J. Jackson.

[65] Sent to Fort Lafayette on August 25, 1861, Berret was released three weeks later by order of Secretary of State Seward after he took an oath of allegiance to the United States and resigned his post as mayor of Washington. *Official Records*, Ser. II, Vol. II, 596.

[66] It was Kane who, on the night of April 19, 1861, following a confrontation

writers of these statements can not be known. But all are equally at the mercy of the despotic government, & deprived of any hope of trial, or termination of their confinement, except when the government may choose to release them. There are also 14 ladies, of high position, now imprisoned & guarded within the walls of the Bastile for females in Washington. [1566] . . .

Sept. 15. Sunday. . . . Julian showed me a letter from Mr. B[urwell] Sayre, asking advice as to the direction of Mildred's bonds & securities still remaining invested in Va, to the amount of about $8000. By our (C.S.) recent retaliatory law, sequestrating or confiscating all property of residents of northern & hostile states, Ky., as [1567] well as Mo. Md. & Delaware, are exempted. I began to write to Mr. S. (as Julian had done before,) to give *my* views of the *business matter* only. I think he can, as heretofore, collect the interest, & even transfer the principal, while this exemption continues—& it will become fixed, if Ky. shall become a member of the C.S. But, in the (to me very improbable) contingency of her continuing finally in the northern U.S. & of course at war with the C.S., the exemption must be repealed, & all stocks & funds of hostile Ky. owners in the C.S. be confiscated.

Sept. 16. Finished my letter to Mr. B. B. Sayre, & also wrote to Mildred. Her last letter instructed me to direct my letters under cover to a friend of Mr. Sayre's in Nashville, Ten. who will forward them by private conveyance, when such offers, to Frankfort. . . . [1568] Seven more men, of high position, in Md., have been arrested & imprisoned. Among them are Henry May, M.C. from Baltimore,[67] several members of the Md. legislature, [Benjamin C.] Howard, the candidate of the peace party for the Governorship,[68] the Mayor of Baltimore, & the editors of the "South" & the

---

between Baltimore secessionists and the Sixth Massachusetts Regiment, ordered the destruction of all railroad bridges leading out of Baltimore toward the North. Arrested a month later by order of Major General Nathaniel P. Banks, he was held in confinement for seventeen months before being released in November, 1862. *Official Records*, Ser. II, Vol. I, 648, 666, 748.

[67] May (1816–66), arrested in Baltimore on September 13, 1861, by order of the secretary of war, was paroled one month later. *Official Records*, Ser. II, Vol. II, 790.

[68] The diarist was misinformed concerning Howard. There is no evidence that Benjamin Chew Howard (1797–1872), former congressman, veteran United States Supreme Court reporter, and unsuccessful candidate for the governorship of Maryland in 1861, was ever arrested by the Lincoln government. The reports apparently confused him with Frank Key Howard, editor of the *Exchange*, who was arrested in Baltimore on September 12, 1861, and remained in custody for some months thereafter. *Official Records*, Ser. II, Vol. II, 778–79.

"Exchange" newspapers. In Baltimore, all print-sellers, having displayed at their windows photographs or other portraits of President Davis, Gen. Beauregard &c have been compelled to withdraw or give them up. Men wearing neckties of red & white stripes, (called "Secession Ties,") are stopped in the streets & compelled to pull them off. A dealer who had children's socks of red & white stripes was made to remove them from sight. Two little girls of 5 & 8 years old, having some article of dress of these denounced colors, were actually arrested in the street, at their father's door, & carried to the station house. If any refuse to obey these commands, they are enforced by the alternative of imprisonment—of course at the discretion & mercy of the despotic government. Can such pitiful & contemptible, as well as galling, tyranny be tolerated long? I should infer not, even if every southern state were not as completely subjugated & crushed under oppression as Maryland is at this time. Let the oppressors beware when the day of retribution & vengeance shall arrive! . . .

Sept. 17. Dull & wearisome time. Nothing to engage or employ me, or to amuse—except for some hours after the receiving the newspapers, thrice a week. Nothing else to read, except old books, previously read more than once, & more usually 3 or 4 times.—To-day came here a requisition from Gen. Magruder on the people of this county, as well as on all the neighboring counties, for one half of their men slaves, to go to the neighborhood of Williamsburg, to work on the intrenchments. It is designed to construct a continuous & strong intrenchment across the peninsula, where it will be 9 miles long. Those persons who had before contributed hands to construct fortifications elsewhere, (as Edmund had,) are [1570] to be excused of sending one-fourth of their adult male slaves. But of all others, one-half are required—& *all* the adult male free negroes, of which there will be 150 in this county. 50 cents a day is promised for each laborer while in service. This demand, as yet, is an appeal to the patriotism, & voluntary action of the slave-holders. But the Secretary of War, who authorises the call, asserts the right to *impress* this amount, or all of such labor, if necessary. In answer to the demand, I shall wait for Edmund's presence & action, as he will be at home, for a few days, next Saturday, & can then act for himself. There are several things connected with this matter that are incomprehensible to me—besides the extended demand, & its employment so late as this time. Gen. Magruder has 12,000 troops—& although many are sick (1800) still the remainder are numerous enough for defence in arms, & for *easy* construction of all needed intrenchments, even if there had not been (as there has) numerous slaves before so furnished & employed. Next, if a continued intrenchment is required, why is it not as near the enemy as Yorktown, where its extremities would still be above the batteries on York & on James rivers. And again—if proper to be as far back as at Williamsburg, (as is said,) why is an intrenchment of 9 miles length required, when it is not there more than 3 miles from one to another of two narrow but navigable creeks, with soft muddy bottoms & marshy borders, which could not be either safely navigated or crossed by an invading army? . . .

Sept. 20. . . . At night, read aloud to Mrs. L[orraine] & my granddaughters the latter part of "King Lear," (in "Family Shakespeare") of which I had so read most of the previous portion the last night we were here together. . . .

September 21. Wrote a 2nd Codicil to my will.—After 8 P.M., Edmund arrived, on a short furlough. Soon after, Charles came. . . . It is understood that the three separate armies of the enemy in the field in Western Va, severally under [Brigadier General Joseph J.] Reynolds, [Brigadier General William S.] Rosecrans & [Brigadier General Jacob D.] Cox, together amount to more than 40,000—& that each corps is superior to our force opposed to it. I greatly fear that this superiority of force, aided by the disaffection of a large part of the population, augur for us renewed defeats & disasters. I am confirmed in my opinion that we should have left this disaffected region to the occupancy & tender mercies of the Yankee troops & government, until we had been victorious every where else within our claimed territory. . . .

Sept. 23. Charles left this morning before daybreak, to take the train in Petersburg for Richmond—& afterwards for the army whence he came by leave. He ought to have gone long ago. . . . In the afternoon . . . a visit by the two Misses Selden of Westover, & their brother.—No important news, but many small skirmishes & rumors of indications of impending important matters. Sundry of the secessionists of the Md. legislature (just about to meet) have been imprisoned by the Lincoln government & the purpose plain to so prevent the expected act of secession. Other members of that party have fled to avoid the same fate. . . . In Ky., the forces arrayed under the southern & northern flags are face to face (if not already engaged, as reported—) & civil war must soon be in full blast. The army which came from Ten. is commanded by Gen. Buckner, a

Kentuckian—& the advanced portion is composed entirely of Kentuckians, & recent residents. . . . In Frankfort, the capital, & where the legislature (3 to 1 of Submissionists,) is now in session, civil war must . . . soon be arranged, & the parties distinctly separated & opposed. This dreadful condition of things will be begun at the worst possible time for poor Mildred—whose confinement in child-bed will be about the same juncture.—In my want of anything new to read, except newspapers, I have latterly been reading some of the plays of Shakespeare which I had not read twice before, & of which the first reading (of the whole of the plays,) was before I was quite 10 years old. Of these I have now again read Julius Caesar, King John & King Henry VIII. Whenever [1576] I read Shakespeare's plays, & especially the historical plays, I am astonished & disgusted with the excessive proportion of weak & foolish & ridiculous parts, compared to the small sprinklings of beautiful & noble passages, & paintings of striking characters. In looking for another volume among my disordered collection of books, I found [Henry] Fielding's "Tom Jones," which also I had not read since the first time, when I was under 12 years old—& began to read this. In both works, not read for 55 years or more, I was surprised to find so little of the incidents, or narrative portions, of which I did not retain some recollection—&, of all such parts, more remembrance than would have been if I had first read the same only two weeks past. Still—though the chief incidents of the narrative are remembered, & the minor ones are recollected as soon as they are touched upon in this late second reading, they appeared so different in coloring from what they did formerly to my childish mind, that there is something of agreeable novelty in this late & new view of the subject. In addition, Fielding's keen satire, & his admirable insight into & sketches of human nature, a reader so young as I was could not appreciate, & scarcely understand the application of.

Sept. 24. Rode to the Post Office to mail a letter. The Government has not yet provided postage stamps, & it is sometimes very troublesome to pay postage in advance. . . .

Sept. 25. Our armies in Western Va have had to fall back, to concentrate, before the superior numbers of the opposing Yankee armies.[69] The reign of Terror supreme in Md. Five ladies have been

---

[69] Thus ended the Cheat Mountain campaign of September 10–15, 1861, in which General Robert E. Lee made a rather inauspicious debut as a field commander.

arrested & imprisoned, & 38 members of the State Legislature. [1577] This to prevent that body assembling, & passing an ordinance of secession, as was expected. . . .

Sept. 27. . . .Another & much larger naval force has set out from Hampton Roads, (on 23rd.,) & gone to sea—8 large ships of war, & sundry transports, supposed to convey a large army.[70] This expedition has been threatened some time in the northern papers, but the place for departure, & destination only surmised. It was understood to be designed for the southern coast, & for another Hatteras operation on a much larger scale. Among the sundry points for attack suggested, it seems most probable that the point aimed at is Brunswick on the coast of Ga, a deep harbour—reached by rail-road, & in a thinly settled section. The means for defence there must be very slight. It is thought that a chief object of the enemy is to possess & fortify a good sea-port, & by means of it to obtain the supply of cotton for European demand, & so prevent the European powers refusing longer to be deprived of cotton by the pretence of blockade. The rumors have latterly strengthened, (& even from Yankee sources,) that Spain, France, & England will not long delay recognizing the independent nationality of the C.S., & refusing to recognize the legality of the Yankee blockade of our ports, where a real blockade has not been maintained. And such has been maintained only of the waters of Chesapeake bay.—Besides the previous [1579] arrest of sundry members of the Md. legislature, there were enough others seized & imprisoned on the day for the meeting of that body (in Fredericktown) to effectually prevent a quorum, & to prevent the secessionists, who made up the majority, passing an act of secession, as expected if they should act as a legislature. All the officers of the two houses also were arrested. This most highhanded & undisguized [*sic*] act of usurpation & despotism is concurred in & applauded by the Union members of the legislature, & by some of the prominent newspapers of that party. The Reign of Terror has already been commenced in Ky. The Louisville Courier has been put down by military order—& Ex. Gov. [Charles S.] Morehead & two other Secessionists have been seized, carried off, & imprisoned beyond the limits of Ky.[71] . . .

---

[70] This report was premature by more than a month. Not until October 29 did the long-heralded Federal land and sea expedition depart Hampton Roads for Port Royal, South Carolina.

[71] A former two-term congressman, Charles Slaughter Morehead (1802–68) was elected governor of Kentucky in 1855 on the American Party ticket. A typical

Sept. 28. Edmund returned to his camp.—Finished reading "Tom Jones," & began "Joseph Andrews."[72] . . . A newspaper of today . . . upon Yankee authority, (which in such cases only may be trusted,) reports an important battle, & defeat of the Union army, & taking of Lexington, Mo. by Gen. [Sterling] Price commanding Mo. Secessionists.[73] By this (their own & the only report,) the enemy lost in all, & mostly as prisoners, 3500 men, 3000 horses, & a quantity of arms &c. and $250,000 in gold, which had been before plundered (or "borrowed") from the banks. Fremont is denounced for not preventing this disaster, as it is asserted that he had 50,000 men in array at St. Louis, & in Northern Mo., under his command, & from whom to send reinforcements to Lexington. This general will probably now sink, as Gen. Scott did, in the favor of the Yankee government & people, from the highest to the lowest position.— [1580] Nothing yet heard from the Yankee naval expedition, since its setting out on 23rd, whence I infer a far southern destination, as La. or Tex. There was a storm on the 27th, but I fear not severe enough to endanger this fleet. I feel great anxiety to hear the first report of its reaching land. It is certain that the enemy, by their naval superiority & complete supremacy, may inflict on us great injury, at numerous points of our extensive coast, where it is impossible that we can (at all of them) oppose sufficient defensive force. But, they will not always be successful, as at Hatteras—& on the whole, this predatory & piratical warfare will cause to them more loss than their success will repay. . . .

Sept. 30. . . . Our three armies in western Va have been concentrated, under Gen. Lee, & all have fallen back to Meadow Mountain in Greenbrier. Our whole force there, as reported, but 15,000, & the whole forces of the enemy said to be 50,000. The latter is incredible—but no doubt the Yankee army & Va armed tories greatly outnumber our troops. Gen. Wise has left (or been recalled from) that service, which is [a] matter of rejoicing. I wish our service was rid of him & all the other civilian & untaught generals, who have

---

southern planter-politician, Morehead also had extensive agricultural interests in the lower South. Arrested in September, 1861, on a charge of disloyalty, he remained in custody at Fort Lafayette until the following January. After traveling in Europe throughout the remainder of the war, he returned to the United States and settled on one of his plantations near Greenville, Mississippi.

[72] Also by Henry Fielding.

[73] After an eight-day siege of Lexington, Colonel James Mulligan surrendered his army of 3,600 Federals to General Price on September 20, 1861.

shown no more talent for commanding than they have had experience. . . . The progress of the war, & all connected matters, only, now are greatly interesting to me. And to know the issue is the only thing now left for me to desire my life to be continued longer. I have done all that can be done by me, whether for my deserving children or my country. My remaining life will be a burden to me, if not to others, even if my infirmities of body & mind[74] do not grow worse, as they certainly will do as long as life shall last. There is scarcely a day that passes of which the wearisomeness & sense of what is disagreeable do not outweigh my gratifications. I feel neither energy nor inclination to seek for change, or for other gratifications—though mere uneasiness drives me to go abroad, to find, & soon to fly from other annoyances. Writing formerly occupied [1583] the larger portion of my leisure time, pleasantly for myself, &, as I long deluded myself in believing, beneficially for public interests. The slighting neglect of the public at last relieved me of that delusion—& I have therefore ceased both to publish & to write. When I go abroad, to Richmond or elsewhere, I meet some friends whom I am gratified to see—& receive from many others, & especially strangers, greetings of kind favor & eulogy, which are gratifying to my self-love & vanity. But that is all. The difficulty of my hearing, with persons not knowing it, or unaccustomed to talk to me, is even more an obstacle to conversation in public, & in mixed companies, than at home. In cities, I can find books enough. But the circumstances forbid application to reading—& even if otherwise, under no circumstances can I read 12 to 16 hours of the day—as I might have done with pleasure, & for days together in the early part of my life. In short, I see nothing before me but days & nights of decreasing capacity & means for enjoyment, & increasing sources & causes of pain. Would that I may be soon relieved of the continuance, by a sudden, unexpected, & painless death! If a cannonball, at Bull Run, or Manassas, had then been the means, it would have been the most desirable termination of my life.

---

[74] By this time, the diarist had become afflicted with a hearing impediment so severe that it was difficult for him to engage in general conversation. Moreover, he had become increasingly concerned about his inability to remember what he had read. The partial deprivation of these two great pleasures—conversation and reading—accounts for the extreme air of despondency reflected in this entry.

INSPECTING CONFEDERATE BATTERIES ON
THE POTOMAC ❧ SOJOURN IN THE CON-
FEDERATE CAPITAL ❧ THE PORT ROYAL
EXPEDITION ❧ EXCITEMENT OVER THE
TRENT AFFAIR ❧ A SPECTATOR AT THE
VIRGINIA CONSTITUTIONAL CONVENTION
VISIT TO THE RICHMOND ARMORY

October 1. After breakfast, rode to Ruthven, intending to remain some days.—I had finished reading "Joseph Andrews" two days ago. Resumed "Sam Slick's Yankee Stories" by Judge [Thomas C.] Haliburton.[1] Julian has obtained the service of an overseer, who began his service today—which I rejoice at, as Julian's confinement to his business is injurious to his health as well as comfort. His previous overseer left that service to go into the army. It is a week ago since both Julian & Edmund sent to [1584] the army near Yorktown their quota of slaves, to work for 6 weeks on the fortifications.

Oct. 2. No important news, except that which is perfectly mysterious to me, the drawing back our out-posts from nearest Alexandria—not only, as heard before, from Falls Church, but since from Munson's & Mason's Hills—& all, as reported, now concentrated about Fairfax C.H. I cannot believe that this is designed for a real

---

[1] A native of Nova Scotia, Thomas Chandler Haliburton (1796–1865) is credited by some authorities with founding the American school of humor. After a tenure of nearly thirty years as a judge—first, on the court of common pleas, and later, on the supreme court of Nova Scotia—Haliburton moved to England in 1856, remaining there until his death. He also wrote *The Letter Bag of the Great Western* (1839), which the diarist read after completing *Sam Slick*.

retreating movement—& our generals can scarcely expect to practise on the enemy the same trick as before at Bull Run. I had hoped
it was the preparatory march for invading Md. But the movement is
too open, & too long in making, to deceive the enemy. It is reported
that President Davis has gone to Beauregard's head-quarters. It is
now understood that the President, & he only, has been opposed to
our armies moving across the line, or invading Md, & thus ostensibly taking offensive action. If so, I cannot conceive his reasons.
Every one would oppose our making really aggressive war, by our
invading, for conquest, any portion of the non-slaveholding states,
or even any slave-holding border state, which did not take part
either for us or against us. But for both these actions we are called
upon to enter Md, to aid our friends, & to put down their & our
enemies. Besides, hasty & destructive incursions on the enemy's
territory may be & would be the best though indirect measures for
defence of our own. I would not desire (if even so practicable) to
conquer & retain any of the territory of Pennsylvania. But, if feasible & also safe, I would push on an army to burn & sack Philadelphia, in retaliation, & then to return. This would be the best policy
to keep the Yankees to their own territory, & so to guard ours from
their aggressions. It is true that the state government of Md. has not
declared secession—& under her [1585] traitorous governor, & the
crushing military despotism of Lincoln, no free action of the state
government is possible. If waiting for the action of the state government, we may wait forever. And we have not waited for such
either in Mo. or Ky. before sending in Confederate troops for our
self-defence, and to aid the uprising of the down-trodden secessionist party. In Md., every such claim is stronger—& why we have
not carried the war into Md., long ago, but more especially since the
battle of Manassas, is to me incomprehensible. . . . Our before three
separate corps in western Va. have been united, under Gen. Lee, at
Meadow Bluff & Sewell's Mountain, & there, though much fewer
in numbers, await the coming of the enemy under Rosecrans. This
general has latterly shown more ability than any of the whole
Yankee armies—& seems to have out-generaled all three of our
opposed commanders. . . .

   Oct. 4. Left Ruthven for Beechwood . . . . In Ky., the reign of terror
is begun. Sundry distinguished citizens, who had never avowed or
committed themselves to secession doctrines, have been either
arrested, or forced to flee to avoid it. Among the latter are Senator

[John C.] Breckinridge, & J. Preston[2]—both of whom have joined the Secessionists. Gov. [Beriah] Magoffin is closely guarded—& one report is that he also has escaped, & is raising the people in opposition to the legislature that is the tool of Yankeedom. . . . While at Ruthven, read most of Haliburton's "Slick Stories," & "Letter Bag of the Great Western," & began to dip into [Mary] Somerville's [1589] "Physical Geography,"[3] which I brought home with me to continue.—It is even now doubted whether the naval expedition sailed on 23rd ult. to attack some part of our southern coast, as reported. But it is reported by N.Y. papers that a later expedition left N.Y. for the same purpose. . . . I have a letter for Mildred on hand, & add to it now & then. But now there is no prospect of either conveying it to her, or receiving any communication from or concerning her, until all western Ky at least shall be a portion of the C.S. & under regular government. Weeks must now have passed since the time for Mildred's crisis of personal pain & danger—& I can receive no information whether she is safe from the perils of child-birth, or whether———

Oct. 7. This forenoon left Beechwood for Richmond. . . . Arrived at Richmond, & the Exchange Hotel after 6 P.M. Saw Col. John Preston (Aid to Gen. Beauregard) just from the army—& though of course he could not speak of any matters designed to be kept secret, I inferred that there was nothing of importance expected there immediately. . . . [1591]

Oct. 8. As usual since the war, I met with many strangers at the hotel who sought introductions to me, or introduced themselves. I am more especially thus complimented by persons from other states. . . . Met, accidentally & separately, with the Secretary of State, [Robert M. T.] Hunter, & of the Treasury, [Christopher G.] Memminger. Both accosted me with much cordiality of manner, & especially the latter, who invited me so earnestly to call on him, that I shall do so—though I avoid rather than seek the company of men high in office. My time spent pleasantly enough in conversation with various persons & in reading late newspapers. Took tea, by

---

[2] The diarist apparently means *William* Preston (1816–87), former congressman and late minister to Spain, who was a staff officer under Breckinridge until Shiloh and later rose to the rank of major general in the Confederate army.

[3] Published in 1848 by the brilliant English scientific writer Mary Somerville (1780–1872), probably the most distinguished woman of her generation, this book went through six editions.

invitation, with Daniel H. London. Met with & was introduced to three gentlemen recently from Ky. . . . Heard, in confidence, that the President had ordered the sending to Ky the aid of 6 pieces of artillery, & some troops. . . . My trunk, which had been so long lost, was this night restored to me, when I had despaired of again hearing of it. It was sent from Manassas Junction. . . . [1592]

Oct. 9. Newspapers, & conversation with various persons. Among these were three more gentlemen of Ky., Judge Moore & Messrs. Burns & Menifee, who are here as commissioners for the secession party, & who, having completed their business with the authorities here, will set out tomorrow for eastern Ky, there to establish another camp & organization. I had an interesting conversation with them, & obtained much information as to the condition of political & military affairs in Ky. The prospects are represented as very encouraging. Though even now, the submissionists & Unionists are by far the most numerous, they have but little zeal, energy, boldness & courage, compared to the Secessionists, who include most of the young, the enthusiastic & energetic. But few natives volunteer on the Union side, & much the greater number of the Lincoln troops in Ky are from the adjoining north-western states.—Capt. Franklin Buchanan, whom I formerly knew & visited in Md., called on me today. He was until lately a staunch union man, & a captain in U.S. Navy. But he could not submit to the despotism of Lincoln, & has resigned his commission & come over to the South, & has been received as an officer in the non-existent navy of the C.S.[4] Saw Mr. Godfrey, a member of the Palmetto Guard, & another gentleman very late from the army. They report that arrangements seem to be made for a battle, yet there is no strong probability that any general engagement will take place. One who lately left Lee's army reports that there is much sickness, great want of supplies, & consequently, the army almost disor-

---

[4] A native of Maryland, Buchanan (1800–74) was one of the most distinguished naval officers to enter Confederate service. He had served as the first superintendent of the Naval Academy, had commanded the flagship in Commodore Matthew C. Perry's expedition to the Far East in the early 1850s, and, when the war broke out, was head of the Washington Navy Yard. He was commissioned a captain in the Confederate States Navy on September 5, 1861, and, several months later, assumed command of the Chesapeake Bay Squadron. Buchanan commanded the *Merrimac* on March 8, 1862, when she made her initial appearance in Hampton Roads, but was wounded and did not see action against the *Monitor* on the following day. In August, 1862, he was promoted to the rank of admiral.

ganized. It is getting to be a prevailing opinion that Rosecranz [*sic*] has out-generalled our commanders. . . .

Oct. 10. Called on Mr. Memminger, at the Office of the Treasury Department, & sat & conversed with him for a short time. I was careful not to so occupy but a few minutes of his time. Saw Ex-Pres. Tyler, who had arrived last night—& also my old friend Colin Clarke of Glocester [*sic*], & Col. E. Tayloe of King George— D[aniel] De Jarnette of Caroline.[5] Reading the last newspapers, & looking over books in Randolph's bookstore. Spent the evening with my nephew A. M. Dupuy & his wife, at their house.—Yesterday & today, obtained letters of introduction from Prof. [Albert T.] Bledsoe to Gen[eral]s [Theophilus H.] Holmes[6] & [Isaac R.] Trimble,[7] & from Col. Preston to Col. [Wade] Hampton—officers commanding on the Potomac. The battery at Evansport, above Dumfries, is nearly completed. Vessels passing up or down the Potomac must pass nearer to the cannons of this earth-work than to any other. When the passage shall be stopped, unless the enemy submit to it, they must bombard the most effective of the opposing batteries, & especially this one at Evansport. Nothing but its being still masked, by the trees & bushes, & the enemy being ignorant of its existence can have prevented an attack before its completion. Thinking that a battle, of artillery, if of no other arms, will soon occur here, I shall try to be present.

Oct. 11. . . . [A] report . . . came from Fredericksburg, that 12 to 15 armed [1594] steamers of the enemy had attacked the incomplete battery at Evansport, at 3 A.M., & that the cannonading had continued since. This, with other particulars, was stated so confidently that I believed it, & therefore hastened my departure. I left in the only daily train for Fredericksburg & Aquia creek, at 4 P.M. Mr. De

---

[5] Father of Daniel Coleman De Jarnette (1822–81), United States representative from Virginia, 1859–61, and a member of the First and Second Confederate congresses.

[6] A North Carolinian and West Point graduate, Holmes (1804–80) commanded the reserve brigade at First Manassas. He later commanded a divison at Malvern Hill and served for a time as head of the Trans-Mississippi Department, rising to the rank of lieutenant general.

[7] Isaac Ridgeway Trimble (1802–88), a West Point graduate and former railroad superintendent, was in charge of constructing Confederate batteries along the Potomac. He participated in several eastern campaigns as a brigade commander before suffering severe wounds at Second Manassas. He recovered in time to serve in the Gettysburg campaign, but was again wounded, and taken prisoner, while leading one of the three divisions in "Pickett's Charge."

Jarnette came on with me. On reaching Fredericksburg, we learned that the whole report was false—& that the only foundation for it was that a small unarmed vessel descending the river had been fired upon by musketry—& that the fire had been returned by some cannon shots from an armed steamer of the enemy, several of which are always off Aquia creek. Orders have been given that the batteries shall not fire on any vessels until ordered from Head-Quarters. Of course there can be no immediate cannonade, though it may be expected as soon as the batteries are completed, & all their cannon mounted. Such being the case, I preferred not to call on Gen. Holmes, at his quarters 7 miles farther, at the very unsuitable hour of 9 to 10 P.M., but to take the tomorrow's forenoon train. So we went to stay the night, & the other intervening time, at the Plantern's [?] Hotel, the best public house, but still a very poor one. After conversing with some new-made acquaintances for an hour, & writing these notes in my room, I went to bed at 9.30 P.M. for want of amusement.

Oct. 12. Nothing to do, or to see, while waiting for the train to [1595] set out—which was not until 12.30. Stopped at Brook Station, 7 miles, the Headquarters of Gen. Holmes, who commands this military district of the Potomac army. I was introduced to him, & delivered my letter. He received me with great kindness, as well as courtesy—& invited me to take dinner with him before I left, which I did. As I stated my wish to get to Evansport as soon as possible, or to its vicinity, Gen. Holmes offered me the loan of a saddle-horse, to be retained by me for my return, or, at my choice, on my arrival to be delivered to the quarter-master for Evansport. I accepted this offer; but soon after heard that a four-mule wagon was going on the way as far as Dumfries, with medical & hospital stores, & in which would go Dr. [W. H.] Geddings, a young army surgeon whom I had renewed acquaintance with at Fredericksburg, & who had served as a private in the Palmetto Guard at Morris Island. For this, as the easier mode of travel, I declined the offer of the horse—& we set out in the wagon at 3 P.M. The road is very hilly, rough, & in bad condition. We reached Dumfries after 8 P.M. (18 miles,) & stopped at the wretched public house. On entering, I found the public hall occupied (as if for their lodging,) by 5 or 6 soldiers—& the other, or sitting-room, full of company. On asking if I could obtain lodging, I was told the house was full. Luckily for me, Dr. Garrett, (son of Col. H[enry] T. G[arrett] of Westmoreland,) was a lodger. He invited me into his very small bed-room, in which he was sitting with two other military physicians. He set out immediately to search for lodgings for me, relieving me of all trouble of the attempt, which could scarcely have been successful, at that time, in this wretchedly decayed little village. He soon reported that he had [1596] secured for me comfortable lodging, so I was relieved as to this prime requisite. After supper, at 9.30, I was shown to my room, in an adjacent private house—& though it was furnished very plainly, it was neat & the bed comfortable. I did not suspect until the next morning that I was indebted for this room to the hospitality of Dr. Hill, one of the young surgeons, who had given it up for my use, & sought other lodgings for himself. Much as I regretted his thus being deprived of his room, I could not then undo the arrangement—& he declared that he suffered no inconvenience in his exchange.

Oct. 13. Sunday—though I did not know it until it was learned by accident, after some hours. It was arranged that I was to drive with Dr. Hill, in an ambulance, to the batteries near Evansport, & 3 to 4 miles from Dumfries. But after the Dr. had finished his morning duties, it was found that one of the horses was lame—& so I had to ride on the other, & to go alone. These three batteries are the highest fortifications up the Potomac, (except Fort Washington in Md, occupied by the enemy). No. 1 is immediately below the mouth of the Quantico creek, & on the river—5 heavy cannon, 4 of them Dahlgrens of 94 lbs. & 1 rifled 32 pounder. No. 2 is a few hundred yards lower along the river side—& has 6 cannon, 42 & 32 pounders. No. 3 I did not go to. It is a mile lower, & has 2 cannon only. The earth-works are well constructed, & strong, & very nearly complete. A number of men were on work on both, finishing. I was told that the work would be completed in two more days. The armament is complete now, & the works fit for a battle. I believe that our commander, [1597] Gen. [Joseph E.] Johnston, has no expectation or desire for very early putting these batteries to use. The work was going on in the usual slow way of soldiers' work, & there seemed no desire to hasten it. The work is still concealed from the view of passing vessels, by the small pine trees & bushes not having been yet cut away—& it is presumed that the enemy know nothing of the construction. But I cannot believe that they are so ill-informed by their spies—or even by their ocular observation. Vessels pass every day—& today there was an unusual number. 5

[146]

or 6 steamers, mostly large, passed down. The first one, (not of large size,) kept off as far from the batteries as the channel permits, about 1¼ miles, & our observers with glasses saw that the men were standing to their cannon. The other steamers followed, at different distances of some miles apart, quite carelessly & slowly—& one came within half a mile of the batteries. There were also some ships & smaller sailing vessels—mostly going downward, but a few sloops & schooners coming up the river. There will never be so good a chance for sinking vessels, after the batteries are allowed to fire. It is said that Gen. Johnston has ordered that no vessel shall be fired upon, without his order to that effect, or unless the batteries are seriously attacked, & required to fire for defence. This is quite right, if the crossing of our army into Md. is intended, & of which no previous expectation should be given, or resistance to it induced by such hostilities. The obedience to the literal tenor of this order very foolishly & mischievously gave a recent advantage to the enemy. A few nights ago a large & new wood-vessel, which might have carried a piece of artillery & 1000 men across the river, was taken into the narrow Quantico creek, & there anchored. The night following, an enemy's steamer sent boats into the [1598] creek, which passed within 300 yards of our soldiers at the battery, but (under the general order) were not challenged or fired upon, until when returning, after having set fire to & partially burnt the vessel. As returning, the boats were fired on by musketry—but without damage, so far as known. They certainly succeeded in their design. There are three regiments at or around these batteries—& several other regiments within a few miles, besides some 10,000 (as guessed) within 15 or 20 miles below & 10 miles above.—Col. (late U.S. Senator) Wigfall commands one of the neighboring regiments, & I met him with sundry other visitors at the batteries. I did not see Gen. Trimble, or deliver to him my introductory letters. But I was introduced to sundry inferior officers, & very courteously treated. After dining with Capt. Martin of Arkansas, I rode back to Dumfries. I could not be worse off anywhere for amusement than in this miserable decayed village. The mail comes but twice a week, & the one which will come tomorrow will bring no later news than I read in Rd., the morning before my departure.... I made another effort, in vain, at the other hotel, to obtain a bed. Upon ... reflection, I came to the conclusion that there was no more cause for the putting the batteries in use in any early time to come, than in the few last days, when they were completed sufficiently for all purposes of offensive or defensive hostilities—& that under this expectation, [1599] & my very uncomfortable quarters, it was useless for me to stay any longer. There is no public or regular mode of travelling from this place; & hearing that there was an army wagon to go the next morning, in which the military officer in charge offered me a seat, I determined to use the opportunity.

Oct. 14. Set out at 7 A.M. in an open two-horse wagon, over an exceeding bad road. At Aquia creek, 9 miles from Dumfries, I met Gen. Holmes, riding, accompanied by two other officers. We stopped to speak, & he asked me why I was returning so soon. I stated the reasons of my very uncomfortable position, & my belief that there was no intention of soon stopping the passage of the enemy's vessels, or probability of there being an engagement. He answered that as to the first, I was mistaken—for he was then going there to order the stoppage of vessels—but that he did not think that the perfect execution of that order would produce an engagement. That is, the enemy would submit to the blockade, without attempting to take the batteries, which enforced the blockade. This general opinion had been expressed to me by Gen. Holmes when I saw him previously. Even to see the enemy's vessels stopped, without fighting, or with the slender chance for it, I would then have been glad to return with Gen. Holmes—but I had no mode of conveyance, nor did I meet any on the road. So I returned to Fredericksburg at 2.30 P.M. I paid a long & pleasant visit to my friend [Alexander] Little, editor of the F[redericksburg] News, whom I had been able to see for but a short time as I went on. With him, I went to see Capt. [Matthew F.] Maury, at his residence in this town—& found him as always, agreeable & instructive. . . .

Oct. 15. Left in the train at 6 A.M. & reached Richmond before 10. Proceeded immediately to make inquiries & contingent arrangements for my renting & furnishing a room. My object is to spend a large portion, if not the much larger portion of my time here, until I get tired. And as it is entirely too expensive for my income to pay $2.50 a day for board at a first-class hotel, (& lately raised to $3, if a fire is had in my lodging room—) I aim to try the mode of renting & furnishing a room, & employing a servant for such times & services only as I will need.—At 2 P.M. heard of the arrival of a telegram at the War Office, that 7 of the enemy's steamers had begun to bombard & cannonade the fortifications at Evansport, which was re-

[148]

turned by our cannon—& after the battle had continued for some hours, the vessels drew off. So if I had remained 27 hours longer, I should have witnessed a battle, though I fear it has not done any damage to the enemy's vessels, as none was reported. . . . An iron-clad English steamer, the Bermuda, has lately entered Savannah, in defiance or evasion of the blockade, with a full cargo of gunpowder, rifled cannon, Enfield rifles, & munitions of war, blankets, shoes &c. It is said that $300,000 will be cleared upon the importation of the cargo. I saw some of the rifled [1602] cannon which have been brought to Richmond. . . .

Oct. 16. Hired a room for 3 months, at the rate of $87.50 for the year, & bought, or ordered, the essential furniture. It is in a house of 4 apartments on Clay St., between 8th & 9th. The other 3 rooms are occupied by as many lodgers like myself. I will try whether a residence in Richmond, for a considerable portion of my time, will make its passage more tolerable. And if the trial shall be unfavorable, I can abandon it without suffering much loss.—Col. Preston is still here, & Capt. [Samuel W.] Ferguson, another aid-de-camp of Gen. Beauregard, has also arrived—which is another indication that no battle on the Potomac border can be expected soon. There are many & loud complaints, in the army, & throughout the country, & published in numerous newspapers, of the slowness of our commanders, & especially of the army of the Potomac. Indeed, the defensive policy, or the waiting for attack, seems to be general with all our commanders. The only important exceptions have been the battles of Springfield & Lexington in Mo. & the late advance of troops into Ky. . . . [1603]

Oct. 17. Left Richmond, in the steamer Schultz, before 6 A.M. . . . A fierce quarrel has taken place between Gen. Fremont & the Blairs, backed by their respective friends, & the President opposed to Fremont. The latter, so far, has not obeyed late orders of the former, requiring certain of Fremont's measures to be altered—& it seems not unlikely that Fremont, urged by his ambition & self-conceit, & by his stronger-willed wife, [1604] may drift into greater extent of insubordination, if not rebellion. It may be that he thinks himself capable of establishing for himself a separate dominion, extending from the Mississippi to the Pacific. His wife, (the true daughter of Thomas H. Benton,) is the very woman like Lady Macbeth, to urge a weaker-minded husband to ambitious & desperate courses.—Our army under Gen. Lee, intrenched on

Sewell's Mountain, was faced by the Yankee army under Rose-crans, on another height, for some days, the latter supposed also to be intrenched, as well as being greatly superior in number. At last, Rosecrans decamps in the night, & is out of reach before his departure is known—or whether his movement is a retreat, or with a view to attack elsewhere, with greater effect, because unexpected. When our troops move to his deserted camp ground, they discover, from its limited extent, that the occupying army was not more than half as many as we supposed, & that there had been no intrenchments for defence. Clearly, Rosecrans has shown greater generalship than Lee. . . . Landed on the Point, & walked to Beechwood, reaching there before 11 A.M. All well & at home. . . . Edmund has obtained boarding for his wife within two miles of his camp, & she is there residing.—Yesterday there arrived by mail, at Richmond, a figure of a palmetto tree, of which the sole material [1605] is strips of palmetto leaves, beautifully & yet strongly constructed, with a miniature photograph likeness of Gen. Beauregard attached. With it, was a separate card, on one side of which was written my name, & on the other—"To an aged patriot, whose love of country is only equalled by his gallantry in defending it.

> Miss M. I. L. of Charleston
> South Carolina"

I do not recognize these initials, & have no idea to whom I am indebted for this compliment. . . .

Oct. 19. Rode to Ruthven, & remained through the night. Finished reading the 5th vol. of Macaulay's History of England. What a loss was his death to the literary world! He was the most attractive writer within my knowledge. His style & manner of treatment invested with interest, & rendered charming, details of history which in other hands would have been dry & repulsive.

Oct. 21. Having made all necessary preparations & arrangements for going to a new temporary home, set out at 10.30 A.M. for the Point, to await the steamer for Richmond. The wind is strong from the east, & tides . . . high. Before the steamer passed, the tide rose to the fringe of small growth above ordinary high tide. This prevented my signal flag being visible (I suppose) to the steamer; & I was so engaged in reading that the steamer was rather above opposite before I saw that it was near, & when my making a plainer display of my signal was too late. . . . Now I must wait until the next trip of the Schultz, on 23rd. The other river steamer passes up in the night, & at very irregular & uncertain times. . . . The new batteries at

Evansport have operated to blockade the river there. No vessel was sunk when passing, & most passed by under the fire. But the passage is too hazardous to be used. . . . A great number of sailing & steam vessels (supposed some 50) are assembled on the broadwater, where safe, below Evansport, kept there by the batteries above. It is not said that any battery lower than Aquia, (which is too far from the channel to damage passing vessels,) prevents passage below. If not, I do not understand why all these vessels do not descend the river, & those bringing supplies for Washington, go to discharge at Annapolis. . . .

Oct. 22. . . . Finished reading "Amelia"—which I had read only once before, when I was under 14. These two interesting novels of Fielding, "Tom Jones" [1609] and "Amelia," & admirable except for their coarse heroes, & their moral, are alike in their general character & purport, in the characters & portraiture of their most estimable & attractive heroines, & in the propensities, weaknesses, good dispositions & vicious acts of the several heroes. . . . Tom Jones & Booth are but examples of a numerous class of men (& women too,) who are generally esteemed as among the best & kindliest in the world, & who indeed show nothing of what is bad in character & conduct, until they are subjected to temptation, & then they may become as detestable in conduct as under other circumstances they had been deemed estimable & excellent. Such persons have naturally kind feelings & good impulses, by which they are entirely directed, & not in the least by principle, or by reasoning upon right & wrong. A spendthrift seeks only his own selfish gratification, whether to indulge his appetites or his vanity & love of ostentation, or his kind feelings for the gratification of other persons, whom he pities or loves. A spendthrift, while still having plenty of money to spend, is usually very liberal, or even lavish, to others—& yet for the same selfish indulgence & impulses. When no longer rich, or having any means of his own for spending, no man is more likely than the most "generous" spendthrift to seek to acquire [1611] the property of others, to continue the same indulgencies, & to be unscrupulous in the use of falsehood, fraud, & swindling tricks for success. . . . At night, read aloud "The Dream," a very interesting play of Joanna Baillie's,[8] which it seems to me is well suited for the stage. Yet I never heard of its being acted.

---

[8] Perhaps best known for her play, "The Family Legend," Joanna Baillie (1762–1851) was a distinguished Scottish dramatist and poetess. Her tragedies have been described as "the best ever written by a woman."

Oct. 23. Having made my preparations again, again took leave and went to wait for the steamer, which arrived today unusually late—after 2 P.M. . . . The papers on board the steamer gave intelligence, which though very concise & general, was official & seemed reliable, that we had gained a great & glorious victory, near Leesburg, of four regiments of ours against twelve of the enemy's.[9] I will not state particulars until they may be supposed correct. Arrived at Richmond after dark, & drove to my newly rented room on Clay street (between 8th & 9th.). Found that my larger trunk & furniture (bought previously) had been brought, including a mattress & cot. I brought blankets, sheets & a pillow with me—so that enough of necessaries were ready for me to begin my solitary & very plain lodging & boarding forthwith. . . . After giving orders to the servant, I walked to the Exchange Hotel, & found sundry acquaintances, as usual, in the Hall & other public rooms—among them, Mr. Boulware, Judge Hopkins, W[illiam J.] Robertson & Daniel (both of Court of Appeals,) [1612] George Fitzhugh &c. Everybody interested & talking about the recent small battle & great victory near Leesburg. Returned to my room at 9, & read until 10, when I first used my narrow & cramped bed. The gas light is too dim & too high, which will be a great inconvenience if it cannot be remedied.—The Lincoln government is making vigorous efforts to possess Kentucky. Numerous troops are already there. They occupy Paducah, which commands the mouth of the Tennessee river, Smithland, which commands the mouth of the Cumberland, & Henderson & of course Louisville. They have between 20 & 30,000 troops on the railroad between Bowling Green & Louisville. Latterly our forces in Ky have done nothing. It is understood that Gen. [Albert S.] Johnston is fettered by being ordered to keep on the defensive, because the government of Ky has not joined the Southern Confederacy. J. C. Breckinridge, Humphrey Marshall,[10] &

---

[9] In this engagement, also known as the battle of Ball's Bluff, Confederate forces commanded by Brigadier General Nathan G. Evans ambushed a Federal contingent led by Colonel Edward D. Baker and drove them into the Potomac River, thus winning a spectacular but strategically unimportant victory. Baker, a former senator from Oregon and intimate friend of President Lincoln, was killed in the battle, which was fought on October 21.

[10] A nephew of the noted abolitionist, James G. Birney, Marshall (1812–72) had rendered important public service as a lawyer, four-term congressman, and former minister to China (1852–54). Appointed brigadier general, Confederate States Army, on October 30, 1861, he served in the West Virginia—Kentucky theater until June, 1863, when he resigned to accept a seat in the Second Confederate Congress.

W. Preston, refugees from Ky, are here on political business.—Yesterday I found among Edmund's books, & began to read, "Party Leaders" by [Joseph G.] Baldwin, & finished it today, while waiting on the beach for the steamer. It is an interesting & instructive work. The author succeeds much better than I could have supposed of any contemporary, or any party man, in treating with impartiality of opposing political leaders. Still, I think that I can learn, from his expressions, [that] the author was a whig who had previously been a federalist. His account of Randolph is especially well drawn, & does justice to his political character. He is too favorable to his private character & disposition. Jefferson fares worse in his hands—though not much worse than he deserved. Jackson is too much favored—& made both a greater & a better man than he was.

Oct. 24. Took my breakfast at an eating house, & then went to gather the news from all the city papers. These I find at Randolph's [1613] bookstore, & others, besides these, at the public reading room, to which I shall now become a subscriber by the year. The reports of yesterday seem to be confirmed, of the battle near Leesburg. . . . Every one is excited & delighted by the news, & nothing else is talked about. 520 of the prisoners arrived today, 130 more being left at Manassas to follow. Later reports that the losses of the enemy were much greater than at first reported, & ours less. It is even stated that the losses, in killed, (& drowned,) wounded, & missing or prisoners are as 2000 of the Yankees to 160 of ours.[11] . . . At night, saw Mr. Johnston, brother of Gen. [Joseph E.] Johnston, & who is just from our army. He says that our commanders will not leave their secure intrenchments to attack the enemy in theirs—& therefore it will depend on the enemy's option [1614] to make an attack & bring on a general engagement, or not. This, I think, they will not venture to do, & still less after the severe check that Gen. Evans has given to them.—Since the firing from the batteries on the Potomac (near Evansport) was begun, it has been continued. Large vessels cannot pass, except at almost certain injury, & great risk. Sundry of the enemy's armed steamers have passed, but all were struck, & more or less damaged, though none stopped. The Pawnee war steamer received 6 or 7 balls. Two sailing vessels only have been captured, which were conveying hay & other army stores to

---

[11] As usual, the estimate of Confederate losses was accurate, but that of Federal casualties grossly exaggerated. Actual losses were 921 Union, of whom 714 were listed as missing or captured, and 155 Confederate.

Washington. But few vessels attempt the dangerous passage. . . .
Met my former Morris Island acquaintance, Capt. Jones, now a
Colonel. He & I were the only persons, in all our batteries fighting
with Fort Sumter, who suffered the least bodily harm. He was
knocked down by a sand-bag being knocked over by a cannon ball
on his shoulders, & I had my hearing destroyed in one ear & greatly
impaired in the other, by the noise of our own artillery.

Oct. 25. . . . For some time back the northern papers have
threatened a formidable naval & land force being in preparation for
an early attack on the southern coast. It was reported that there
would be 60,000 land troops or more embarked. The particular
destination unknown. Today a Ga regiment & a battalion left here
for Goldsborough N.C., which would seem to indicate that our
authorities expected the blow to fall on the N.C. coast. It was before
reported that the Yankee forces at Hatteras had been increased to
8000 men. There have been recent large additions to the Yankee
naval force in Hampton Roads.—Saw [James D. B.] De Bow, who is
just from Charleston S.C. & from [1615] him heard two items of
good news, which yet are private. Our newspaper editors have
been so discreet as not to publish them, & the Yankees have not yet
found them out. Mason & Slidell, our ministers accredited to England & France respectively, have sailed from Charleston some
two weeks ago. Also, the steamer Bermuda, which got into Savannah in defiance of the blockade, has left as successfully, taking to
England a cargo of 1500 bales of cotton. The profit to the chief
owner of the cargo, [George A.] Trenholm of Charleston,[12] of this
"British" steamer, on the cargo brought in, was full $100,000 & on
the whole cargo, $270,000—& the cotton carried out will sell for
100 percent advance. These enormous profits, with the easy evasion of the blockade, will doubtless induce many other adventurers
to pursue the same course. . . . Saw W[illiam] B. Preston, who was
lately from Beauregard's camp. He told me that the effective force
(ready for service) now in the army of Beauregard, (excluding
Holmes' command on the lower Potomac,) is only 40,000 men. I
had supposed that there were at least 70,000 in the whole. The
enemy's opposed forces estimated by Beauregard at 80,000.—The
enemy's vessels in Hampton Roads two days ago amounted to 40.
This stated by Lieut. [George T.] Sinclair C.S.N. who came up

12 Trenholm, a prominent Charleston merchant, succeeded Memminger as Confederate secretary of the treasury in July, 1864.

yesterday to bring a Yankee Lieut. Hale U.S.N., who professes to be a deserter from the enemy's fleet,[13] but who is suspected [1616] of being sent to our lines as a spy. Until his true character is known, he is imprisoned. On his report, (& Sinclair believes his whole statement,) the present naval expedition of the enemy is designed for the coast of N.C. & first to seize upon Beaufort & the Rail Road, & then Newbern. Enough attention has been paid to Lieut. Hale's statement for the govt. to exert increased vigilance & preparation for defence for that coast. . . . Received a letter from Julian, enclosing $755, the remainder of the interest to Oct. 2nd, due for myself & my granddaughter Jane Dupuy. Bought a C.S. bond for $500 out of it—though I do not think I can spare as much out of our half-year's income.—The war caused a general suspension of specie payments by the banks. This, by depreciating all paper money, by 15 perc[en]t, caused the legalizing the emission of notes by banks of denominations as low as $1—& of various corporations & individuals the illegal issue of notes for the fractions of a dollar. This had become an intolerable nuisance, & still increasing. At last, the government has issued postage stamps of 5 cents—& these are bought for Confederate States notes, issued to serve as currency. I shall avoid the use of these small bills, by using postage stamps as currency for small sums, & for change in larger payments. If such use could be general, besides the convenience to the user, it would be no little gain to the government, not only in the use, but in the destruction of these small bills.

Oct. 26. . . . The Potomac is now completely blockaded by our batteries at Evansport, & no Yankee vessels of size have passed for the last two days. Very small vessels, of shallow draft, may still pass close to the Md. shore, & possibly others larger in fog or darkness. But for nearly all purposes, the enemy's vessels are stopped, until they can take these batteries.—*Reported* that the Yankee fleet assembled in Hampton Roads, which left yesterday, did not go southward as expected confidently, but up the Chesapeake bay. Nothing since heard from it. Heard that as many as 18,000 troops have been brought to guard the sea coast of N.C. If so, I trust they will at least retake Hatteras, & re-occupy Beacon Island.—At the hotels tonight saw several acquaintances from the south—among them Col. [Charles] Haskell of Charleston, & Gen. Th. Green of

---

[13] Specifically, from the U.S.S. *Minnesota*. *Official Records*, Vol. IV, 686.

N.C. & Gen. Bonham from the army. Col. Haskell last from Beauregard's camp. He & all other visitors there concur in the opinion that there will be no battle, unless the Yankee army attacks ours, of which there is no prospect at present. . . .

 Oct. 27. Sunday. . . . This [1618] morning, at the Spottswood House . . . saw . . . & renewed acquaintance with Mr. Breckinridge, late Vice-President U.S. & the candidate of the unanimous South, for the Presidency. He appeared glad to see me. Humphrey Marshall, another of the distinguished refugees from Ky., also was introduced to me, at his own request. I should before have called on these gentlemen, but that I supposed their time was fully occupied, & that my visit would scarcely have been desirable, as they now say. They, with W. C. Preston, late U.S. Minister to Spain, are here, negociating [*sic*] with the President for succor to the southern men in Ky. Mr. Marshall told me that every man of distinction in Ky, who was known to be a secessionist in opinion, had been imprisoned, if not avoiding it by flight. And that numerous arrests & imprisonments had been made of men of secondary position, of like principles. Later, saw Judge Moore of Ky, just arrived from [Brigadier General Felix K.] Zollicoffer's camp.[14] He says they can raise any number of volunteers in Ky, but have no arms for any. . . .

 Oct. 28. The great expedition (or Yankee Armada) certainly set out on the 25th—& to sea, & to the south. Where it will land is uncertain. Guesses vary as to attacking the N.C. coast, with Beaufort, Newbern & the Atlantic Railroad—or Charleston—or New Orleans—[1619] or ports in Florida or Georgia. It is reported that there are 60 vessels of all kinds in the fleet, conveying 30,000 land forces, including a regiment of cavalry. Oh! for a tremendous storm for their destruction! But the weather never seemed more like being settled fair. . . . I should think that our reporters of our battles were the greatest liars in Christendom, if the Yankee reporters (including the commanders & official reporters,) did not out-lie ours by ten to one. They regularly convert their signal defeats & disasters to signal victories or successes. Except the battles of Fort Sumter, Bethel, Manassas, Springfield, & Lexington, which could not be so misrepresented, they have claimed the advantage in every fight & skirmish that has occurred during the war. . . . Yet they have not gained the advantage in any battle, & scarcely in any skirmish,

---

[14] Zollicoffer was operating in east Tennessee and Kentucky at this time.

except at Philippi, Rich Mountain, Hatteras, & some few small affairs in the Va Mountains. And in all of these cases, the enemy had an overwhelming superiority of numbers, & the aid of tories & traitors, & in our mountains, also of a disaffected population. But on our side, there has been gross exaggeration, if not entire falsehood, so generally, that I do not believe in any success when first reported, without strong testimony as to the general result—& not even then as to the details. And the true facts, in detail, are so long appearing, if they ever appear, that we can not then separate the truth from the falsehood. . . . I gave $20 to the fund for the Alexandria regiment of volunteers, including Kemper's artillery. I had before given the same amount to the Maryland regiment. All these are political refugees, driven from their homes by Northern domination.

Oct. 29. The enemy's fleet did *not* set out from Hampton Roads until yesterday—& even now its direction of course is not known. Mr. A[braham W.] Venable, whom I saw today, told me that he saw & counted 93 vessels of all descriptions & sizes of the enemy lying in Hampton Roads on the 27th. . . . Met at the hotel & conversed with Lieut. Gov. [Thomas C.] Reynolds of Mo., whom I knew before. Also J. J. Hooper of Ala. now Secretary of Congress, Geo. Fitzhugh, M. R. H. Garnett, late M.C. U.S., & Fendall Gregory. . . .

Oct. 30. Saw Lewis E. Harvie. We united in regretting that Pryor had no opposition as a candidate for Congress for our district. I have strong objections to him, besides that of his being now in service as Colonel of a regiment. If such plurality of offices is not illegal, it is extremely objectionable. No man can fill both places at the same time. The higher the military office, the greater is the objection. An officer of high grade cannot be spared from his command, if he is good for anything. Again, he will be tempted & induced to seek popularity with his soldiers to secure their votes for his election to Congress, & so prostitute his service & duties to advance his self-interest.—Mr. Magruder, brother of the general, has just returned from visiting the camp at Yorktown. He has learned that the defences are deemed in good condition, & secure from any attack. The only weak point is a battery on York river, to blockade the passage, where there are but 2 cannon mounted, & will soon have 8. . . .

Oct. 31. The sailing of the great Yankee Armada from Hampton Roads, which had been several times announced prematurely, is said now to have taken place on the 29th, &, as supposed, destined to seize upon & hold, or more probably to ravage & abandon, some portion of our southern coast. It conveys an army of robbers, house-burners, wanton destroyers of property they cannot use or remove, slave-stealers & inciters of negro insurrection, ravishers & murderers. This war made upon us by the northern people & their rump government is unjust, unprovoked by any legitimate cause, & entirely aggressive. Even if it had [1624] been carried on with humanity, & with all respect to the laws of war between civilized nations, it would deserve to be met by feelings of hatred & desire of vengeance for such great & undeserved wrongs, & by every legitimate measure of retaliation & revenge. But the manner in which our enemies have warred against us, & always in invading our own territory, has been as atrocious as the motives & designs were unjust. In fighting against such enemies, on our own invaded soil, & especially in regard to their merely predatory & incendiary, & insurrection-seeking incursions, we would be justified in refusing to make any prisoners, & putting to death, as felons, robbers & murderers, all who may be in our power in battle. I earnestly wish that this policy would be adopted by our government, & proclaimed to the world. And if the enemy knew that such would be their treatment, I believe that they would not dare to invade our territory. . . . I heard yesterday that Gov. Letcher had promised to supply of Va. arms 1000 stands to J. C. Breckinridge, & as many to H. Marshall for the use of regiments to be raised by them in Ky. This evening I again met with Marshall, & asked him if this news was true. He told me it was—& further, that he would be appointed a Brigadier General, & would have two Va existing regiments to move to Ky under his command, in addition. I was glad that he was to have arms for, & the command of, a regiment of Kentuckians to be raised by himself—for he had a military education, & is a man of ability & popularity. But I am sorry that he is to be placed in a higher command. I am utterly opposed to making generals of civilians, unless in extraordinary cases of men who have shown that they have a natural genius for [1626] military command.—Saw Mr. Gourdin, just arrived from Charleston S.C. He told me that the ocean steamer Nashville had set out from Charleston, in evasion of the blockade, for England. There went in it some of our naval officers, supposed to take command of a C.S. government vessel of war, to be bought in England. Also Mr. G. informed me that the

Gordon steamer, which carried Messrs. Mason & Slidell to the West Indies, has got back safely into Savannah, with a cargo of goods. . . .

November 1. . . . Was introduced to Capt. A[lbert] P. Hill, of Miss., at the Spottswood House—who was wounded in . . . [the] battle [of Leesburg] in the right arm. Though but a flesh wound, it prevents his making any use of that hand. I offered, together with any other service, to be his amanuensis for any letters he desired to have written—& he used my service to write to his wife. . . . Met again Capt. Franklin Buchanan, late of U.S.N. & now of C.S.N. He has been to our batteries at Evansport since I was there, & informs me that they are greatly strengthened, & safe from any attack. The little armed steamer George Page, now the Richmond, which has so long been confined in Aquia creek, has gone up to Quantico creek, where protected by our batteries, & [1627] can be very serviceable in cruising in the river, & assisting the completeness of the blockade. Latterly no armed or other vessel of the enemy has attempted to pass the batteries. Already the army in Washington is straitened for supplies, & especially for provender for the numerous teams & cavalry horses.—Finished reading & glancing over . . . Madame d'Arblay's (Miss Burney's) Diary & Letters.[15] There is much that is very interesting in this work—but much more that is too prolix & too much drawn out, & not a little that is insufferably tedious, if not disgusting for its servility & sycophancy to the great merely by birth & rank. . . . I am nauseated with her servility & toadyism, which caused her to represent (as doubtless she fully believed,) that the very large & very commonplace family of George the Third was admirable, without exception, for graces & perfections of person, manners, mind & heart. . . . [1631] Rain at night with high wind from north-east. May the storm increase, & wreck every vessel of the Yankee fleet!

Nov. 2. The wind blew strongly through the night, but changed to south-east. This morning, still blowing strong, & raining slowly, until 11 A.M. when the wind moderated & soon ceased, & the rain also ceased. I fear that the wind continued for too short a time to

---

[15] An English novelist, Frances (Burney) d'Arblay (1752–1840) created a sensation in the literary world with the publication of *Evelina* at the age of twenty-five. Her second novel, *Cecilia*, was also a success, but subsequent works were only mediocre. Much of the material in her *Letters and Diaries* concerns her tenure as second keeper of the robes for the English royal family during the 1780's.

raise a sufficient storm for the armada of robbers, even if it extended to their then place on the ocean.[16] To 5 P.M. no telegraphic report of the ships being seen from the land—& no indication heard of the designed place for the attack.—This forenoon, wrote three more letters for Capt. Hill. . . . At dark, called to see Capt. Buchanan, to return his visit to me made some time ago.

Nov. 3. Sunday. A very dull day to me. . . . After staying in my room, reading & partly sleeping, for some hours, I began to write & finished, & then copied, an article of three pages, entitled "Civilians for Military Commands"—in which I aimed in general terms to denounce a gross abuse of Pres. Davis' administration.—Went to Capt. Hill's room, & wrote for him three more letters from his dictation. He will set out for home tomorrow morning.—Not a telegraphic dispatch giving any report worth notice for three days, & no other news of the Yankee Armada—except that some 37 of the vessels had passed in view of Currituck beach. Passengers on the train which left Charleston on the 1st. state that the storm was heavy there that morning, & continued with them through the day. This beginning was 12 hours earlier than here—& gives stronger ground for hopes of damage to the enemy's fleet. . . .

Nov. 4. Telegraphic dispatch to the government, that two of the enemy's gun-boats had been wrecked & beached on the coast of S.Ca. Afterwards, another report added a steamer to the wrecks. Also a verbal report that the Baltimore Sun of 2nd. stated that Seward, Cameron, Blair, all heads of departments, & Gen[eral]s Scott & McClellan, had resigned. I do not give the slightest credit to this report. Not one of them would be willing to relinquish [1633] office for the alleged cause, (difference of opinion as to offering battle to our opposed army—) & I will ensure that Scott will never resign his salary of $17,000. If the report were true, it would be good for our cause merely as displaying such extent of discord among the high authorities. But otherwise, or if considering each case alone, there is not one of all named, except Gen. McClellan, whom I would not be sorry to be displaced. For I judge that the continuance in office of each of the others is the better for our cause.—Offered my writing to Hugh R. Pleasants, who is a regular writer & assistant

---

[16] The storm, in fact, did strike the fleet off Cape Hatteras, causing considerable damage and confusion. However, only one transport was lost, and the expedition, consisting of seventy-seven vessels and twelve thousand troops, proceeded toward its destination—Port Royal Sound, South Carolina.

editor for the "Dispatch," who approved & accepted it to be inserted as editorial.—Met in the street Commander M. F. Maury, & had a short & (as always,) agreeable conversation with him. . . . Yesterday, after having read the first half of a novel which was so foolish that I could read no farther, I began "The Caesars" by [Thomas] De Quincey.[17]—Since the war has made this city a stopping place for troops, & still more since it became the capital of the Confederate States, the Main street is always [1634] crowded. When new telegraphic reports of interest are affixed to the Bulletin boards before the Dispatch & Enquirer offices, as was the case this afternoon, a compact crowd of persons, waiting for their turn to read, blocks up the footway, & is kept full by new arrivals until dark.—Wrote another short article—a page & a half, on the treatment of prisoners of war. . . .

Nov. 5. My article given to H. R. Pleasants yesterday for the Dispatch, appeared this morning in that paper, as editorial. Gave the later writing, for the same use, if approved. My published article . . . denounces the system & policy of the President in making military appointments—& it so happened that at the same time appeared, in the Whig, a communication denouncing in strong & bitter terms particular acts of injustice & nepotism. These were, the slighting neglect of Gen. [William H. T.] Walker, one of the best officers in the army, which has caused him to resign[18]—& the appointing to supersede Walker, & as a general, [Richard] Taylor the brother-in-law of the President, & a man without military experience or knowledge.—No more new reports of losses of the enemy's fleet, except of one store-ship wrecked on shore. Confirmatory accounts of the other three wrecks, & of 73 prisoners secured from them, in N.C. Part of the fleet seen from Tybee island, appearing to be off Port Royal (Beaufort) harbor in S.C. . . . Finished

---

[17] This work, by the prominent English author Thomas De Quincey (1785–1859), was described by William Dean Howells as "one of the greatest historical monographs ever written."

[18] A graduate of West Point and veteran of the Seminole and Mexican wars, William Henry Talbot Walker (1816–64) resigned his appointment as brigadier general, Confederate States Army, on October 29, 1861, ostensibly because of ill health. However, he immediately accepted a commission as major general of Georgia troops. Reappointed brigadier general in the Confederate army early in 1863, he performed brilliantly in the West and was promoted to major general in May, 1863. After more than a year's service as a division commander, he was killed in the battle of Atlanta on July 22, 1864.

"The Caesars," & began another volume of De Quincey's writings, Miscellaneous Essays. Called to see Capt. Maury, without finding him. . . . Wrote another article, 3½ pages, in favor of giving no quarter to invaders. [1635]

Nov. 6. My second article appeared as editorial in the Dispatch. Telegraphic dispatch, deemed reliable, announces that 8 war steamers of the enemy's fleet have attacked our batteries (earthworks) which defend Port Royal harbor, S.C., & that by our fire, one of the steamers was disabled & on the ground, & another so damaged as to be towed off. [1636] Afternoon—the above report contradicted, except as to the fleet (or part of it,) being off Port Royal harbor. Gen. Lee left Richmond this morning to take command of the forces there.—Gen. Scott has retired from service, but retains his salary. Reported that Fremont has been removed from his command. . . . This is the day of election of Electors of President & Vice President, & of members of Congress. Great interest in the latter election here. John Tyler had a large majority in Richmond, where two of his competitors, [William H.] Macfarland & [James] Lyons, had their strongest support. The secession votes would be divided between three candidates of that party, Tyler, Lyons, & Baker. This gave the only chance for Macfarland to slip in, as he a late submissionist & whig, would get all the votes of secret submissionists, & whigs who have not abandoned their old party preferences. Macfarland too, as president of a bank, carried the votes of those who prefer a chance for getting loans, to maintaining any political principles.—Copied my piece & sent it to the Dispatch as *editorial*, & am very doubtful whether it will be adopted.

Nov. 7. Tyler has received much the largest vote in Richmond, which was Macfarland's strongest ground, & is supposed to be elected. McClellan succeeds Scott as Commander in Chief—which post, however, Scott had been virtually ejected from, & superseded by McClellan as to the armies near the Potomac, ever since the battle [1637] of Manassas. . . . Telegram this afternoon that there had been firing between the enemy's fleet off Port Royal & our small flotilla, & also our land battery. . . . We all are waiting in most anxious expectation, to hear the full accounts of the disasters suffered by this great armada in the late storm, which came upon it in precisely the best time & proper locality, for its greatest damage & loss. . . .

Nov. 8. Every body in a state of excitement & anxiety to hear the

[1638] news by telegraph from the enemy's attack on our batteries at Port Royal harbor, where, by the last report, a battle was going on. I waited for the next report until 1 P.M. Then there came a telegram to the government, not from the south, but from the west, announcing a severe engagement, & a great victory to us, at Belmont in Mo. on the Mississippi river, immediately across from Columbus in Ky. . . . Soon after came news, & very bad news, of the issue of the battle at Port Royal. The cannonading of the fleet had compelled the garrisons of our two batteries, at Hilton Head & Bay Point, to evacuate them. The telegram did not state that the enemy had landed, & occupied the evacuated works, but that is inferred. . . .

Nov. 9. So great was my anxiety to hear further accounts from S.Ca. that I remained downtown, after reading the newspapers, until nearly 2 P.M. merely to hear of any telegrams. In vain. No news, nor even a report from any quarter, to 6 P.M.—The principal editor of the Dispatch, after keeping my article for three days, returned it, but not until I had applied for it several times. I do not find fault, & am not surprised at its publication being denied. But I am displeased at its being kept so long, without a reason or explanation. I shall make some changes which the lapse of time & change of paper require, & send it to the Charleston Mercury. [1639] Before this being returned, I today wrote a short article & sent it to the Charleston Courier. It is in amusing or ridiculous contradiction to my resolution to write no more for publication, (& there can be scarcely a motive to write otherwise,) that I have written & sent to the newspapers four pieces within the past week. But all of them, except the short one written today, which required to be a communication, were written under editorial disguise & concealment. If adopted by the editors, I have a reasonable assurance that any new writings of mine do not show signs of dotage, & also that they will not be known by the public, & by but few individuals, as mine, & so may be judged without either favor or prejudice.—I procure any books I want from Randolph's bookstore, on loan—but am careful not to abuse the favor. I also am a subscriber to a newspaper reading room, with a miscellaneous library attached, from which, by right, I can carry to my home any volume for two weeks. . . . Began tonight the "Marble Faun."[19] . . .

Nov. 11. It is strange that nothing more has been heard, since the

---

[19] Published in Boston in 1860, this was a novel by Nathaniel Hawthorne.

first report, of the enemy's movements in Port Royal harbor. On the 8th. the telegram came that our batteries had been evacuated & the enemy's ships had passed above. Nothing since, not even whether any or all of their land forces had disembarked. But though I hope they have landed, & will attempt to march into the country, & to Charleston, this delay of any such movement, which I infer from hearing nothing of it, is indicative of their weakness, & in aid of our successful opposition—unless indeed the attack there is a feint, & the main attack is to be made elsewhere. Finished reading the "Marble Faun"—interesting, & well written—but like most other of Hawthorne's fictions, unnecessarily mysterious, & with mysteries left unexplained. By such course an author may increase the interest of his narrative, but causes equal disappointment to the reader in the end.—On going into the State Library, to consult the large map of S.C., I was introduced to Judge [Thomas B.] Monroe, late Judge of the U.S. Court of Ky, & now an exiled fugitive, because of his southern principles.[20]—A company of Artillery, with their commander, left here today for Ky.—After 8 P.M. I again went down town to inquire for news, & at the Exchange Hotel, met George Fitzhugh, De Bow & D. London on the same pursuit. An armed vessel of the enemy has shelled the little & quiet town of Urbanna, on the Rappahannock. 140 bomb-shells were thrown into it, to very little purpose, except to give this additional evidence of the disregard [1641] of all laws of civilized warfare. . . . The wrecks of the enemy's vessels on our beach seem reduced to two—the Union steamer which was beached near Beaufort harbor N.C. & the Osceola steamer, near Georgetown S.C. Yet but 43 vessels of all sorts, not many more than half of the whole fleet of 80, have appeared in sight off Port Royal. What can have become of the other 37? Perhaps gone on another & more distant expedition. . . . Telegram from Augusta, Ga. states as the understanding there that the *black flag* is raised in Savannah, Charleston & Be[a]ufort, indicating the intention of giving no quarter to the enemy. If this is true, the public sentiment is in advance of my recommendation (sent to the Mercury). If false, (as I suppose,) the report will serve more extensively as a feeler, to draw attention, & to test public opinion on this policy.

Nov. 13. . . . It does not appear yet that any of the Yankee army has

---

[20] Judge Monroe was seated in the Provisional Congress of the Confederacy as a representative from Kentucky on December 16, 1861, and served for the remaining two months of that body's existence.

landed in S.C., except a few to occupy the evacuated earth-works. Yet the nearest planters to these posts have already burnt all of their cotton, & two of them, Messrs. [William] Pope[21] & [Ephraim] Baynard,[22] have also burnt all of their buildings, including mansions. Perhaps they were too hasty, as they might safely have waited until the enemy had landed in force, before applying the torch. Still they showed a noble spirit—which, when the self-sacrificing deeds are known, will astonish the people of the North & of Europe. . . . The [Virginia] Convention met today, but there was no quorum, & so adjourned to tomorrow.—I have not heard from Mildred since her last letter dated Sept. 7th. Her position in Frankfort, & in the now disturbed condition of Ky., must be very difficult & painful. My first & chief anxiety is for her. A secondary one is that the fear of the despotic & treacherous power there dominating may have required her to destroy the two manuscripts which I sent to her,[23] & which I would be very sorry should be lost. [1644]

Nov. 14. . . . The Yankee cruisers have been carrying on their marauding & negro-stealing operations to great extent on the Rappahannock. We have suffered thus from transient incursions, & in the neighborhood of the permanent occupations of the Yankee armies, as near Fortress Monroe, Alexandria, Fairfax county &c. But the route of any of their large & for the time unopposed armies is worse. The annexed extract is from a publication & writing of Thurlow Weed, a thorough abolitionist & Lincolnite. He is describing & commenting on the conduct of Gen. Fremont, & of his army, in the march through Missouri.[24] This testimony of staunch Lincolnites may be believed, even if all from our side were suspected of gross exaggeration. . . . It is true that the black flag was raised in Charleston & Savannah. And I am surprised to hear so many persons advocating this policy of giving no quarter to the predatory invaders. An amusing example of the growth of this opinion was an

---

[21] Known as "Squire Pope," he owned three plantations on Hilton Head Island as well as other units in Beaufort District. Pope took refuge in Sandersville, Georgia, where he died on March 10, 1862.

[22] Census figures for 1850 reveal that Baynard owned at least 576 slaves on his extensive properties in Beaufort and Colleton districts, South Carolina.

[23] The diarist refers here to his extended accounts of the battles of Fort Sumter and First Manassas, which he had forwarded to Mildred several months before.

[24] According to the attached newspaper clipping, Weed charged that Fremont's march through Missouri was marked by "spoliations and ravages which disgrace the age of civilization."

editorial article in the Dispatch of yesterday, which even goes beyond my article which was rejected [1645] but a few days ago, for advocating this course. The editor now adopts my opinion, & so nearly uses my words, that I cannot but believe that he "stole my thunder." The particular matter referred to is the recent condemnation of some of our captured privateersmen as pirates, & to suffer death by hanging. This, I am confident the Lincoln government will not dare to carry out. But, to prepare for it, our President has had selected by lot as many (13) Yankee prisoners of the highest military grades, to suffer the same fate.—The Convention, with difficulty & delay, made out a quorum, but did nothing more. There is as little zeal in this whole body, as respect for it by the public. No news by telegram, not even an incredible report.—Saw Thomas Ruffin jr. (son of the Judge,) who has himself been lately made a judge, & leaves his military command to begin his judicial duties.[25]

Nov. 15. This is the day of general fasting & prayer, or so requested to be by the President's proclamation. All houses of business are closed and everything appears as if on Sunday. In all the churches, sermons suitable to the occasion, & on the war. . . . The Yankees of the naval expedition at Port Royal are landing predatory parties on the exposed islands, & stealing slaves, carrying them off by force. But it does not appear that any considerable or permanent landing of troops has been made. A portion of the fleet has been seen from Fernandina, passing southward. . . . Afternoon, made a visit to Mr. Tyler, at his room at the Exchange. I took supper at that hotel, & saw several acquaintances, members of the Convention, & others. Among the latter, whom I am always glad to meet with, was James W. Cook of Greensville.—Yesterday finished reading [James Fenimore] Cooper's "Mercedes of Castile"—a poor romance, & only interesting in the portion occupied by Columbus as one of the principal characters. Tonight finished 2nd vol. of De Quincey's "Literary Reminiscences"—the 1st not being on hand—a very interesting book.

[25] Appointed judge of superior court by Governor Ellis of North Carolina, Ruffin held court only a few times before rejoining his regiment, the Thirteenth North Carolina, in May, 1862. As he explained in a letter to his father, "No. Carolina has been a generous State to you and yours, and I could never bear the idea of this war being fought through and no son of yours being in the fight." J. G. de Roulhac Hamilton (ed.), *The Papers of Thomas Ruffin* (Raleigh, N.C., 1920), III, 236. As lieutenant colonel commanding the Thirteenth North Carolina, Ruffin later won commendations from his superiors for his valiant leadership in the engagement at South Mountain during the Maryland campaign. *Official Records*, Vol. XIX, 1030.

Nov. 16. Attended the session of the Convention today. Mr. Tyler was nominated for President, (the previous occupant, the submissionist [1647] [John] Janney,[26] having resigned,) but he declined, on the ground of his being a member of the provisional congress, which meets on the 18th. Then Lieut. Gov. [Robert L.] Montague was nominated, & also James Cox of Chesterfield who like our member from Prince George, T[imothy] Rives, was a base submissionist, & also a base demagogue, & a drunkard to boot. Montague was elected receiving two votes to Cox's one—most of the former extreme submissionists being among the latter's supporters. It was decided that the body will proceed to amend the present infamous constitution, & it is understood that the amendments will go to undo or to lessen the evils of universal suffrage & popular elections of judicial & executive functionaries which the demagogues who made that constitution fixed upon the commonwealth. Previous to the organization, I was requested by several members to occupy a chair on the floor on one side of the President's seat—& after the adjournment, the President invited me to continue to attend the sessions, & to occupy the same seat. . . . My nephew George Dupuy arrived this evening from his residence at Eddyville in S.W. Kentucky, & I took tea with him at his brother's. From what [1648] I heard from him, I infer that the tories in East Ten. will soon be put down by the loyal inhabitants, who are much the more numerous, & are rapidly gathering.[27] Also the prospects of the southern-rights men in Ky. seem more promising, & quite favorable . . . . Mr. Woodfin,[28] also just arrived, from his home on western border of N.C. near to Ten., supposes that three-fourths of the population of East Ten. are opposed to secession—& if a Yankee army could get there, to enable them to embody & organize forces, that a reaction would be caused there which would be difficult to put down. . . .

Nov. 17. Sunday. . . . The only news received by telegram is of remarkable character. Messrs. Mason & Slidell, our commissioners sent to England & France, & who embarked at Havanna [*sic*] in a

---

[26] Janney, a Whig of the Clay variety, was a sixty-one-year-old lawyer from Loudoun County.

[27] Beginning on November 8 and continuing for several days thereafter, Unionists in east Tennessee attempted to harass Confederate forces in that area by burning railroad bridges and attacking isolated outposts. The uprising was poorly managed, however, and was soon quelled.

[28] Probably Nicholas W. Woodfin, who served as superintendent of saltworks for North Carolina during the war.

British mail [1649] steamer, (a government vessel,) were followed by a Yankee ship of war, the steamer stopped on the ocean, & the two commissioners, with their secretaries & baggage, were taken out, & brought to Fortress Monroe, where these gentlemen are now prisoners. Gen. Wool so informed Gen. Huger at Norfolk, who sent the news to the Sec. of War. Such an insult has not been offered to the British government in the last century. I am glad of it—hoping that the insult will be resented. Mr. Boulware, (with whom I had a long conversation on various subjects,) thinks that the affair will be smoothed over by Seward, for this government, declaring (falsely) that the outrage was unauthorized, & contrary to positive (the written) instructions—& by offering the most humble apologies, after having effected the object of the capture. Every body excited by this occurrence. The enormity is increased, & I trust the effect in England will be increased, by the ladies of the commissioners' families being sent on to Europe, as entire strangers, without their husbands & parents. . . .

Nov. 18. . . . The C.S. Congress met today, & after organizing, adjourned. Had a conversation with Musco[e] R. H. Garnett on the amendments of the Va. Constitution desirable to be enacted & ratified by the people, & also how much of these it would be impolitic to propose, lest the people should refuse them, & in doing so, also disagree to what might be taken by them, if alone. He thought that the Convention was prepared to put down the popular elections of executive & judicial officers, & to prevent the voting of all foreigners (of course including Yankees,) not before naturalized, after the close of the war. But he thought it hazardous, & therefore impolitic, to propose to restrict the present right of suffrage, even to tax-payers, lest it would produce a clamor and opposition, which would cause all amendments to be voted down by the people. . . . Finished Irving's "Alhambra."—The capture of our commissioners continues still the subject of chief interest & remark. The question has been raised whether such official passengers were not "contraband of war," & therefore liable, under the law of nations, to be captured in a neutral ship. . . .

Nov. 19. Yesterday I asked the editor of the Enquirer to republish the annexed tribute to James Keelan, (from the Abingdon Virginian,)[29] & to open a list for pecuniary subscriptions for his aid—

[29] The appended clipping reveals that Keelan was the lone defender of a railroad bridge at Strawberry Plains, Tennessee, when it was attacked by a party of sixteen

which Mr. Boulware (who happened to pass at the time) & I began by giving each $10. The Rail-road bridge which this brave fellow was watching alone, & saved, is the most important one on the Tennessee railroad, in a tory neighborhood, [1652] which, if destroyed, might have been the means of letting the Yankee forces from Ky. occupy the railroad, & East Tennessee. I would have given more, but for the supposition that a contribution of this small amount would be more apt to induce others, than a larger sum for the beginning. I had before given the like amount to the mother of [Private Henry L.] Wyatt, the only one of our soldiers killed at Bethel, & in consequence of his self-exposure, & to the widow of [James] Jackson, who killed Col. Ellsworth at Alexandria, & thereby forfeited his own life. . . . Attended most of the session of the Convention. By an overwhelming majority, it was decided to admit as members 11 persons who had been each voted for by a few soldiers in camp from the north-western counties, to supply the places of as many traitorous members who had been before expelled from this body. The votes to elect had in one case been as few as two, & in all were very few. The counties for which representatives are so made, are disloyal, adhering to or occupied by the enemy, & in which no election could have been held. The measure is altogether illegal, & very dangerous to the cause of free government.—I did not attend Congress before its early adjournment, but heard that it did nothing except to receive the President's message. [1653] . . . Met with Messrs. Holcombe & [James A.] Seddon, the latter a member of Congress, & the former of the Convention, & also elected for the next Congress. These are two legislators of high statesman-like talents, sound principles, & patriotism untainted by corrupt self-interest & ambition. I fear that there are but few if any others representing Va in these two bodies who deserve the same praise.—At night I went to visit Mr. Holcombe, to suggest some of my views as to amendments of the constitution, as I had before to Mr. Garnett. We all agree in the ends to be desired. But all of these members doubt the expediency of now attempting any restriction on the present universal suffrage—even of the payment of the smallest tax—for fear that the unpopularity of that restriction may cause all amendments to be rejected by the people, including such as, if offered alone, will probably be ratified. These are the putting

Unionists. Though desperately wounded, he drove off the attackers and saved the bridge.

down the other abominable features of the present constitution,
filling all executive & judicial [1654] offices by popular election in
name & appearance, but really placing them in the hands & at the
disposal of demagogues, who operate through unauthorized conventions, & use the ignorant & deceived people merely as tools, for
their own advancement & interest. I have always thought, & have
often asserted, that [the] Va. Convention of 1851 was mostly filled
by demagogues, nominated & elected by their dishonest arts, &
that they framed the constitution to strengthen & promote their
own political action & policy as demagogues, & to establish de-
magogueism as the ruling influence & power in the state, which has
been done effectually by their work. That convention was indeed a
weak body—not representing the actual talent any more than the
patriotism & virtue of the state. But there was scarcely a member
who was so deficient in intellect as not to know that he was voting to
enact features of government that were contrary to the interests of
the people, & detrimental to the preservation of enlightened, pure,
& free government.—Read the President's message, & then resumed De Quincey's Literary Reminiscences, of which I have now
the 1st volume, after having read the 2nd.—I suggested to Mr.
Holcombe some provisions which seemed to me proper to be
adopted, in case the Convention should make any change in the
right of suffrage, by requiring a property qualification. First, not to
use the term "property" at all, which is used so plausibly & successfully by demagogues to mislead the people, but instead of the
possession of property of any stated amount, to have *"tax-paying,"*
even though of the smallest assessed amount, as a requisite for
voting. Next—not to let a recent payment of tax to suffice. For that
would be paid by the candidate [1655]—& so the designed exclusion of the lowest & basest portion of the people would serve only
to increase the corruption of voters & of elections. The requirement
should be the payment of the last year's tax (the latest then completed,) & that within the limit of time prescribed by law. Candidates could not begin to buy votes so soon, & no person could then
vote who had been a delinquent as to paying his portion of the last
collected revenue of the treasury. Further—if by possibility, the
Senate could be so constituted as to represent property, or taxation,
then, to shut out the probable jealousy of large slave-holders, &
their deficiency of military service in proportion to their share of
representation, I would subject all male slaves (& also free negroes)

of military age to military service, not as soldiers, but as laborers in aid of military operations, defence, or support. They should be subject to draft, as if they were white & free, & in equal proportion. Thus a rich planter who owned 50 male slaves of the military age, would furnish from them, for the military terms of volunteer or militia service, as many laborers as 50 free white men would of soldiers—for each tour of duty, or throughout a war. The richest or most productive agricultural sections of the state (as the borders of the great rivers,) will have the largest slave population, & the fewest whites to defend their own slaves. If, as would be necessary, heavy demands were made on the poor non-slaveholding population, for soldiers to defend these especially defenceless localities, it will kindle dissatisfaction & jealousy, & give ground for the demagogue clamor of the poor being required to defend or [1656] protect the slaves of the rich. If my plan were adopted, there would be no ground left for such complaint, as the slaves would render service as much as the soldiers—& the very service that soldiers like most to avoid. Mr. Holcombe approved of all my suggestions, & seemed struck by the last, as being entirely a new suggestion, and, as it appeared at first, also a valuable one.

Nov. 20. Attended the sitting of the Convention. An attempt made to exclude foreigners & especially Yankees, who are not citizens of the C.S. at the close of the war, from acquiring the privilege of suffrage, for a long time or altogether—& failed. . . . Went twice today to see Cook, who is sick at the Exchange. . . .

Nov. 21. At the session of the Convention. Discussion & action on the right of suffrage. From all indications, there will be no improvement made in this feature of our abominable constitution—nor much, if any, in any other. Also at the opening of the session of Congress, (also in the Capitol,) but had to withdraw immediately, as the body went into secret session.—Afternoon, called on Seddon. Found several other gentlemen at his room. Our conversation on the proceedings of the Convention, & the principles of a constitution necessary to secure free government. When all had gone except myself, Wm. B. Preston came in, & joined in conversation on the subject of the capture of our two ministers on board a British government mail steamer. These two able men held very different views as to the consequences, which I will state the heads of. Mr. Preston thought that the act would be disavowed & apologized for by the Lincoln government in the most abject manner, & any mode of satisfaction readily agreed to that England would demand. Whether it would be sufficient to make the proud English people, & government, pass over the outrageous insult to their flag, he doubted. I said that I had at first expected that humble course of denial & apology from [1658] this most base & lying administration. But if so intended, the very first act, after learning of the imprisonment of Messrs. Mason & Slidell, would have been to order their unconditional release, & with every show of courtesy to them, & of regret for their arrest. This they could well afford to do, after having gained all that could be gained by their capture & detention. Mr. Seddon believed that the Lincoln government meant to maintain the ground they had taken, not only at the risk of war with England, but because they wished their act to bring on that war. That they had learned that to conquer the Southern Confederacy was impossible. They wished to get out of the war—but to propose it would ruin the leaders of the abolition party, & cause them to be driven, in disgrace, from place & power, without any hope of re-establishment. The leaders preferred the greatest loss to their country to their own personal loss & ruin. They therefore desired war with England, & to take the initiative step, when they could, without being condemned, withdraw from warring on the weaker foe, the Confederate States. This supposition would explain the hostile & threatening & bullying tone . . . which Seward, & the leading northern newspapers, had used in speaking of England, & the chances of war with that power. Mr. Preston thought that the only ground on which this view could be correct, (& which, if existing, would render it very probable,) was that Seward had already ascertained (from diplomatic information) that war must come, on the blockade question, between the U.S. & England, & if so probably with England & France [1659] united in their common cause of quarrel. If having such information & belief of the future, Seward & his associate leaders & rulers might well suppose that they would stand a better chance to maintain their popularity, & the support of the people, by boldly taking the initiative step, & "bearding the British lion," by making it a quarrel for England alone, to get rid of France as her ally, than to wait for both England & France to begin the war, on account of the wrongs inflicted on them under pretence of a blockade which was notoriously ineffective. After this conversation ended, Mr. Preston began on a subject which he said had brought him to consult with Seddon, & to urge on him to use his supposed greater influence with the President. I moved to leave, but he requested me to remain, & so I heard a very alarming state of things in the south-west. Preston lives in & represents Montgomery county in the Convention—& he & Seddon are . . . two State members of the Provisional Congress. He stated that [Brigadier General John B.] Floyd had only 4500 men, & had been compelled to retreat before Rosecrans with more than double that force, before he had received, recently, large reinforcements, by three steamers which came up the Kanawha. Our forces in Southeastern Ky. had fallen back into Wise Co. Va. pursued by the much stronger Yankee army, into the border of Va. as now understood. These overwhelming armies are within less than 70 miles of the Va & Ten. Rail Road, of the great salt-works, & of the valuable lead mines & works in the South West of Va. Zollikoffer's [*sic*] force, at Cumberland [1660] gap, was much smaller than the Yankee forces threatening him, from Ky—& in East Ten. & along the route of the Railroad, the population disaffected, & the bridges there recently burned by the tories. Our main army in Ky under Gen. Johnston was 250 miles distant from where its service was required, & without railroad facilities for the direct route. All these things are indeed very alarming—& Mr. Preston seemed to be correct in his opinion that to drive back the enemy from the south-west of Va & Ky, & to secure the endangered rail-road especially, were objects paramount to any others for which the troops were held back which were necessary to give us the superiority over the enemy's armies. Two regiments only have lately been sent for this purpose, which reinforcement is entirely inadequate.—Heard from gentlemen just from Charleston what were the latest reports there from Port Royal. It was said that the Yankees had taken 1500 negroes (whether with or against their will,) & 2000 bales of sea-island cotton. These numbers were not relied upon, & both supposed to be exaggerated. But the worst is, & is reported by Mr. Memminger, that the slaves remained on the plantations because they refused to obey their masters' orders to leave. This seems to me to indicate a mutinous disposition which was not suspected, & a wide-spread influence of the previous teachings of abolition emissaries & agents. . . .

Nov. 22. Attended the sitting of the Convention. But little done, or interest in the debates. The congress again sitting [1661] with closed doors. . . . Saw Capt. F. Buchanan, just arrived from Charleston & Savannah. He says our defences are strong—that the enemy have not landed but a small force—& that they do not command the country beyond the extent of the range of their heavy cannon. They have stolen some cotton & some slaves. But the published statements of both are much exaggerated. . . . Finished the 1st vol., (having read the 2nd previously,) of De Quincey's Reminiscences—a charming book of literary gossip, & the most interesting one I have read for a long time. Began [John G.] Wilkinson's "Ancient Egyptians."[30]

Nov. 23. . . . The disastrous effects of the storm & high tide on Fort Hatteras, & the enemy's troops there, are minutely described [1663] in the . . . N.Y. Tribune. It is just the result that I expected would occur, whenever a violent storm happened at the same time with a very high tide. It is a remarkable & inexcusable neglect of our officers commanding troops at Newbern & Roanoke Island (if having vessels,) that they did not before keep prepared to attack, & did not attack the enemy as soon as possible after the highest tide. They could have made then but feeble resistance, & might have been completely destroyed. [1664] At the Convention, but did not stay long, as there was nothing interesting in the Proceedings. Congress not sitting—& when it does sit, it will be with closed doors.—Today received, by Express, 8 copies of my "Sketches of Lower North Carolina"—now first issued, though I saw the printed sheets, & sent the Title page, Contents, & a list of errata, which were all then wanting, some 7 or 8 months ago.

Nov. 24. Sunday. Saw Major Blewett, who has just arrived from Columbus, Ky. He says we have 17,000 men there, & the commanders are in continual expectation of attack by the much more numerous forces at Cairo. . . . More losses of slaves from the Northern Neck—which narrow peninsula, between the broad waters of Potomac & Rappahannock, it is feared will be occupied & laid waste by the Yankees.—Sat conversing with Mr. Boulware at the Exchange for two hours—& afterwards we paid a visit to Mr. Tyler.

Nov. 25. Attended the Convention.—Saw Judge Perkins of La. & W. Porcher Miles of Charleston,[31] among the newly arrived mem-

---

[30] Considered the most important published work of the English explorer and Egyptologist Sir John Gardner Wilkinson (1797–1875), *Manners and Customs of the Ancient Egyptians* was first published in three volumes in 1837. The diarist read a later two-volume edition.

[31] William Porcher Miles (1822–99) was one of the most distinguished men in the

bers of Congress.—Thin ice this morning first seen.—Report, with
more evidences of truth, that the enemy's force has been greatly
increased between Alexandria & Occoquon [*sic*], & that the intention is indicated of crossing the creek & attacking the batteries at
Evansport. [1665] A gentleman who has just escaped from Baltimore says, in addition, that the scarcity of supplies at Washington
make the taking of these batteries, & breaking the blockade of the
Potomac, a matter of necessity—& that public opinion in the North
also demands offensive operations of McClellan's army.—At night,
at the Exchange Hotel, I met with Gen. Steuart (the elder,) of Md, a
refugee, who for the second time introduced himself to me. The
first time was soon after I had fired the first cannon discharged from
Kemper's battery at the enemy's retreating forces then at the Suspension bridge, over Cub Run. Gen. S., who was on the field of
battle as an amateur, was taken prisoner early in the day, & accompanied that portion of the enemy's army that retreated by the more
circuitous route by Sudley's mill, & thence by the road which
entered the turnpike from the the left just before reaching the
Suspension Bridge. He told me that thousands of the routed &
fleeing army (he guessed as many as 10,000,) were crowded together in retreating within range of our cannon (though concealed
from our view, by some intervening wood, as well as the approaching twilight,) when our field-pieces fired on the other crowd of
fugitives at the Suspension bridge, & caused all the damage & loss
to the enemy there which I have stated formerly.[32] But I now learn
from Gen. Steuart that if our balls had been directed against the
other much more numerous crowd in which he was then confined,
great slaughter would have been inevitable. He said that the actual
effect on that part of the fleeing [1666] army, of our firing . . . was to
cause the whole body to flee with redoubled speed, & leaving the

---

nineteenth-century South. After a progressive term as mayor of Charleston—during
which he reorganized the police force and instituted the drainage system described
earlier by the diarist—he was elected to Congress and served until his state withdrew from the Union. A strong supporter of slavery and secession, he was a member
of the South Carolina Secession Convention and represented his district in the
Confederate Congress throughout the war. Named president of the University of
South Carolina in 1880, he resigned that post two years later to assume the management of his father-in-law's extensive sugar holdings in Ascension Parish, Louisiana.
During the next two decades he resided at Houmas House, the former home of John
Smith Preston and John Burnside, and was one of the giant figures in the Louisiana
sugar industry.

[32] See above, page 89.

road to take the most direct course to Centreville, which course was above the suspension bridge. After firing our 10 or 12 balls at the enemy at the Bridge, it was first made known to us that another body was on our left, & some discharges were made in that direction—but too late. All were then in the most rapid flight, & their prisoner was left without any thinking of retaining him. It was then that ... Gen. Steuart accosted me, & stated his name & his capture. ...

Nov. 26. No telegram, & but little other news. It is understood that 13,000 men have been landed from the Yankee fleet, & that they are constructing fortifications on Hilton Head & other adjacent outer borders of Port Royal Harbor. They have not ventured to penetrate the land even for a few miles, or to occupy any ground outside of their camp. Parties have gone to Beaufort, (which has been abandoned by all the white inhabitants,) but they have not remained through a night. J. Jenkins Mikell, Mrs. Hutchinson [sic],[33] & Mr. J[ames] Legare, on Edisto Island have burnt their crops of cotton with the houses containing it. This noble sacrifice will [1667] probably be made by all other planters on the sea-coast. When the men & also the women can make such sacrifices for patriotism, the subjugation of such a people & country is impossible. ...

Nov. 27. ... Attended the Convention. Some [1668] of the worst features of the Constitution have been repealed, the popular elections of Judges & all county functionaries, except justices of the peace. The election of these, & of Governor & Lieut. Governor are still left to the popular vote. But some provisions in regard thereto have been adopted, & others seem likely to be adopted, which will greatly lessen the present evils of popular elections in these remaining cases.—Finished Wilkinson's "Ancient Egyptians." This book is not what I had anticipated, a description of the wonderful antiquities of Egypt—but is still more remarkable. ... Wilkinson gives rude out-line copies of some 500 ... selected pictures, from which are presented to the reader a more complete account of the ancient Egyptians than we have of their living successors. These pictures, instructive as they are, are of very low order as works of art. Indeed, they are generally very like, & not greatly superior, to such drawings as many children make for their amusement. ...

---

[33] An appended newspaper clipping identifies her as Mrs. Hopkinson.

I did not read Wilkinson's two 8 vo. volumes through, nor perhaps half of their contents. For I soon took to looking at the pictures, & merely read the accompanying remarks & explanations when they were needed, & the particular subject was interesting.—Began the "Pathfinder."[34]

Nov. 28. Saw the Rev. James Owens[35] & R. B. Rhett, members of [1670] Congress. With the last, had a conversation, & learned that the commander at Port Royal, [Thomas F.] Drayton, was one of Pres. Davis' favorite incompetents, made a general.[36] I infer that the bad defence was owing to him. The neighboring planters, except two or three, did not burn their crops of cotton, because they had been assured of the defences of the harbor being strong enough to keep off the enemy. Gen. Lee, who has since gone there & taken command, though reputed to be an accomplished & great officer, (deemed the best in the U.S. army, before he resigned,) is, I fear, too much of a red-tapist to be an effective commander in the field. The people & late residents now volunteers in service, or fugitives, wish to burn their cotton & the town of Beaufort, & have asked authority & aid from Gen. Lee. But he will give neither because he deems the acts "unmilitary"!—The invaders have occupied Tybee island [Ga.].—We are feverishly impatient to hear of some one or more of the great battles which have been expected—in Mo., in Ky., & on the Potomac. I begin to think that all indications afforded by the enemy of their attacking our army on the Potomac are but feints to conceal other designs & operations, & to enable them to diminish their army to invade the South, while they keep our army on the watch for a daily expected attack, and at its full force, & even increasing. . . .

Nov. 30. . . . Called on Col. [Charles] Dimmock, Superintendent of Va. Armory, to make inquiries. In this establishment, defective

---

[34] Published in 1840, this was one of the *Leather-Stocking Tales* by James Fenimore Cooper.

[35] A delegate from Florida to the Provisional Congress of the Confederacy.

[36] A graduate of West Point, Thomas Fenwick Drayton (1808–91) resigned from the army in 1836 and returned to his native South Carolina where he prospered as a planter, railroad executive, and state senator. Commissioned a brigadier general in the service of the Confederacy, Drayton had charge of the military district around Port Royal at the time of the Union landing. Ironically, his brother, Captain Percival Drayton, commanded one of the attacking Yankee vessels. Drayton later led a brigade under Longstreet at Second Manassas and Antietam, but because of his age and fundamental incompetence, his military career was undistinguished.

arms are repaired only. With a letter of introduction from Col. D., I then went to the former state armory, lately transferred to the C.S. government, & where the complete manufacture of muskets is carried on. The Minie rifled musket is the only weapon made—all precisely alike, so that the parts of any one will as well suit for & fit any other. Col. [James H.] Burton, the superintendent,[37] with much politeness showed me the whole establishment. The machinery used was all captured at Harper's Ferry. There is a separate machine for making almost every part of the musket—a few of the smaller irons only being wholly or partly made by hand. 250 muskets are now turned out weekly—or 13,000 a year—which will be increased to 15,000 a year.—Members of the legislature are beginning to arrive—& among them, met with my friends [William] Tate of Augusta, & F[ranklin] Minor of Albemarle. Also saw Capt. Maury, who has been absent since I saw him here last. He agrees with me in the opinion that the enemy will not attack us on the Potomac, & for a better reason than mine. He said, why should they attack us where we are strong, & stronger than anywhere else, when they can attack us, by aid of their navy, in hundreds [1673] of places where we are necessarily weak, if not incapable of all resistance, & the enemy can concentrate a powerful force.

December 1. Sunday. Took breakfast at the Exchange, which by their lately raised rates, costs $1. Saw more acquaintances who are members of the legislature, & lately arrived—among them Col. [Samuel M.] Reid, & my most valued friend Willoughby Newton. Alex[ande]r Boteler of Jefferson, elected to fill the place in Congress vacated by Mason,[38] arrived here but a few days ago. He had but barely left, when an outrage of the enemy was perpetrated at his residence, which he related to me. His mansion is near Shepherdstown, & within a mile of the Potomac. His daughter's husband, Mr. Shepherd, who belonged to our army, had visited his wife for the first time in two months, & was the only white male on the prem-

---

[37] Formerly master armorer at Enfield, England, Burton had been brought to Richmond in October, 1860, by Joseph R. Anderson, owner of the Tredegar Iron Works, to assist in equipping the Virginia armory with musket machinery. Later in the war, he was superintendent of the Confederate armory in Macon, Georgia. *Official Records*, Ser. III, Vol. I, 10; Ser. IV, Vol. II, 958.

[38] A graduate of Princeton and former one-term congressman, Alexander Robinson Boteler (1815–92) was seated in the Provisional Congress on November 27, 1861, following his election a week earlier by the Virginia Convention. He also represented his state in the First Confederate Congress.

ises. Late in the night, about 100 of the Yankee soldiers surrounded the house—another hundred (as was afterwards learned) having been stationed as guards on their route from the river. Mrs. Boteler had been kept in continual alarm, & her husband, though not in the army, had, some months ago, been made a prisoner, & had escaped. Being awakened by the noise, she arose from her bed, & went to a window to look out. Always in fear of such visits, she kneeled on the floor so as merely to show her head over the window sill, as she parted the curtains to look down into the yard. Her chamber was on the second floor. As soon as her opening the curtains partly exposed her to view, a volley of balls (some 20) were fired at & into the window, which struck & shattered the ceiling of the chamber. None of the balls struck Mrs. Boteler, but one [1674] so nearly grazed her cheek as to leave a painful sensation. The soldiers immediately forced their way into the house, seized & made prisoner of Mr. Shepherd, & searched the house thoroughly from garret to cellar, searching for Mr. Boteler. When, in answer to inquiries, they were told that he had gone to Richmond, an inferior officer said, insolently, that his capture would only thereby be postponed, as they would have Richmond in a few months. It was a remarkable exception to their usual course of plunder & destruction, & especially in that neighborhood previously, that this party made no plunder, or destruction of property. This might seem as some mitigation of their outrage. But, on the other hand, that circumstance proves that the party was under regular & strict command, & therefore the firing into Mrs. Boteler's window, & at her head, must have been, not the unauthorized acts of disorderly soldiers, but by the command of their officer. The commander was understood to be a Capt. Buchanan of Indiana.—Went with Newton to his room, & had some conversation with him on important matters which will soon be before the legislature. One is a reorganization of the militia, & new militia law, just adopted by the Convention, & which I urged on Newton to try to repeal by the legislature. It is worse than the old system in at least one important respect, & I do not see that it is much improvement in any. Another is the gross outrage on right & justice which the Convention has now before it, of selecting by vote of that body, "representatives" (so mis-called,) for some 40 disaffected counties in the north-west, where either the disaffection [1675] & traitorous disposition of the greater number of voters, or the presence, or the fear, of the enemy's armies, prevented any election by the people being held. In the greater number of these counties, illegal elections were held, by which "representatives" were sent to the *bogus* legislature at Wheeling. To elect nominal "representatives" from these counties, by the Convention, would be a greater outrage than that body has actually committed in admitting 11 new members from the most disaffected counties, who had only a few votes (one had two votes only) of soldiers of their counties in distant camps.—Returned to my room at 12; & read until 4 P.M. Went again to the hall of the Exchange to see friends, & to hear news—of which none had been received today. Again in my room at 6, & read until 9 P.M. Finished the "Pathfinder," & began to read Lepsius' "Letters from Egypt &c."

Dec. 2. . . . Another naval expedition has been sent from the North to our southern sea-coast.[39] I saw an acquaintance from Charleston who supposed that the enemy near Port Royal had not yet got possession of more than 500 bales of cotton, (& that by plunder only,) & would not get more than 2000. Even this small measure of their gains was owing to the fact that Gen. Drayton was our commander, & that his plantation was the one on which our principal fort (on Hilton Head,) was built. This incompetent general, like sundry others, owes his promotion to his having been at the West Point Military Academy with President Davis. Oh! that our President had never studied at West Point!—The legislature met today—so the Convention adjourned before 12, & met again at 7 P.M. I went to the night session, & heard nothing of any interest.—Snowing at night, & the ground white when I came home before 8. . . .

Dec. 3. The snow very thin. . . . At the Convention by 10, its hour of meeting, but it [1677] immediately went into secret session. When the House of Delegates met at 12, I went into the gallery, but could hear so little of the debates, that I soon left, & will not go again.—Deposited $20 in aid of the subscription for the Hampton volunteers. Most of these, residents of Hampton & the neighborhood, have had their houses burnt, & all or most of their moveable property stolen or destroyed by the enemy.—The people of the occupied or most exposed sea-islands of S.C. are continuing the noble sacrifices of burning their cotton & the houses containing it,

---

[39] This force left Hampton Roads on November 27, 1861, en route to Ship Island, Mississippi, where the Federals were establishing a base for operations against New Orleans.

& also their other houses, when they would otherwise shelter or aid the enemy.—Heard, as certain, that the President has made Col. [Henry] Heth, a young man of but 36 years old, a Major [1678] General, & will send him to Missouri, where, by his higher rank, he will supersede Gen. Price, the most successful of all our commanders.[40] This act of the President's is very unpleasing to his best friends & thorough supporters, & is strongly denounced by some others, who support & generally approve of President Davis, but who will not be silent on his errors, of which this is the very worst. . . . In the afternoon, I went to Seddon's room, where I conversed with him & James C. Bruce.[41] At 5.30, I went to see Judge Perkins & his lady, at their rented house, to which I had been kindly invited. Conversed for an hour with Judge P., [1679] with much interest. He called my attention to the strong & gratifying contrast of the circumstances under which we now met, with those of Aug. & Sept. 1860, when we were together at the White Sulphur [Springs], concerting plans to preach disunion, & when we had not half a dozen there to sustain us in these sentiments & wishes.—Attended the night session of the Convention until I was tired. The subject was the outrageous proposition for the Convention to elect "representatives" for some 25 counties & districts of the northwest, whose elected members have joined the Yankees.—After writing my diary, as usual now at night, I read until after 10.

Dec. 4. The Convention has referred the election of "representatives" for the disloyal counties & districts to the two houses, severally, of the legislature, & giving them power to act therein. The

---

[40] The rumored elevation of Colonel Heth (1825–97) to the command of Confederate forces in Missouri was frustrated largely through the efforts of that state's congressional delegation. *Official Records*, Vol. LIII, 762–63. Instead, after serving under Floyd in the West Virginia campaign, he was promoted to brigadier general in January, 1862, and ordered to Lewisburg, Virginia, to assume command of all troops in that district. After service in West Virginia, Kentucky, and Tennessee, he was transferred to the Army of Northern Virginia early in 1863. Promoted to major general following Chancellorsville, he commanded a division at Gettysburg, where his unit suffered heavy losses on the first day, and in subsequent campaigns in the eastern theater.

[41] Educated at the University of North Carolina, Harvard, and the University of Virginia, James Coles Bruce (1806–65) was the proprietor of Berry Hill estate in Halifax County and reputedly one of the largest slaveholders in Virginia. Nevertheless, he was a proponent of gradual emancipation and a staunch Unionist in the Virginia Convention until the outbreak of hostilities at Fort Sumter. During the war he contributed at least $50,000 to the Confederate cause.

intended superseding of Price by sending Heth as a Major General seems to be universally condemned. It is supposed that the Congress will refuse to confirm Heth's promotion—which of course will frustrate the scheme as to him. An editorial in the Enquirer this morning (no doubt being the views of the President,) states that dissensions between Price & McCulloch made it necessary to put an officer over both. This would be perhaps proper in such case. And no one could object, if a general previously of superior grade, & also of established & high reputation, (as either of the two Johnstons,) were sent, & not this young colonel, recently but a captain of U.S.A., & whose only known ground for the designed great promotion & distinction is that he was educated at West Point. . . . It has been for some months announced that England, France, & Spain, combined, were preparing an expedition to Mexico, to take military possession of the sea-ports, & to indemnify themselves for the claims they severally have on Mexico. This act of intervention, it is generally supposed will not end there, but that the three allied powers will establish a protectorate over Mexico, or perhaps set up monarchical government under some European prince. Of course, the U.S. government is extremely opposed to these movements, & also to Spain's previous re-annexation & forcible occupancy of Dominica. But now the U.S. [1681] government can do nothing in opposition, but will complain & threaten. I trust that this will offer new causes of hostile feeling, if not of hostile action, between Lincoln's government & the three European powers.—After dinner, I went to Newton's room at the Exchange, & with him to Franklin Minor's, where I also met my friend Tate, Capt. M. F. Maury, & half a dozen others. Our conversation mostly in condemnation of the movement of the Convention, empowering the Legislature to elect "representatives" for all the disloyal counties, & in discussing the arrest of Mason & Slidell, & the probable consequences.—At 6, returned to my room—& for lighter & more amusing reading at night, began [James Fenimore] Cooper's "Satanstoe," [42] as a diversion to Lepsius. Found it rather tedious.

Dec. 5. . . . Attended the Convention in both its morning & evening sessions. Nothing interesting.—Read several interesting articles republished from different London papers, on our affairs.

---

[42] The first and most distinguished of the *Littlepage Manuscripts*, this historical novel, published in 1845, depicted the life of the New York gentry in the mid-eighteenth century.

December 6, 1861

The English have heretofore received all their information of the Southern States through the medium of Northern newspapers & reporters—& of course greatly to our prejudice & disadvantage. [1682] They are beginning, as these articles show, to find out how deceptious & untrustworthy these sources are. Thus, they have believed heretofore, that the Yankees would certainly conquer the South, & that the Union would be reconstructed. But these results, so confidently promised by the North, are now discredited in England—& the current of popular sympathy is turning in our favor, despite of the anti-slavery fanaticism of England.

Dec. 6. . . . At the Exchange hall, saw Gen. [John B.] Clark, M.C. of Mo.[43] whom I formerly knew in Washington. Also Mr. [Henry C.] Burnett & Mr. [William E.] Simms, Commissioners of Ky.[44] Heard that Mr. Burns, with whom I had become acquainted some two months back, had been killed in battle at Jay Creek, in Ky.—John Cochrane, the former northern friend of the South . . . was in Richmond last February, (after 5 or 6 states had seceded,) & delivered a street speech, of which . . . [an] extract is published in the Dispatch of today.[45] Now it ought not to be inferred from the violent opposition of his former & his present creed that Cochrane's opinions or his principles have undergone a singular & extraordinary change.

---

[43] John Bullock Clark (1802–85), veteran Missouri militia officer and former United States congressman, was seated in the Provisional Congress of the Confederacy on this date. He later served as a senator in the First Confederate Congress and as a representative in the Second Congress.

[44] Along with William Preston, Henry Cornelius Burnett (1825–66) and William Emmett Simms (1822–98) comprised a commission sent to Richmond by pro-Confederate Kentuckians, who had passed an ordinance of secession at Russellville on November 18, to seek recognition of their government and admission to the Confederacy. *Official Records*, Ser. IV, Vol. I, 743. Both Burnett and Simms were former members of the United States House of Representatives, and both served as Confederate States senators from 1862 to 1865. Burnett, who had presided over the Russellville convention, was also a member of the Provisional Congress.

[45] A former two-term Democratic congressman from New York, Cochrane (1813–98) was at this time colonel of the Sixty-fifth New York Infantry, stationed in Washington, D.C. In a recent speech in that city he had advocated arming southern slaves and had told a cheering crowd: "If necessary to save this Government, I would plunge their whole country, black and white, in one indiscriminate sea of blood, so that we should, in the end, have a government which would be the viceregent of God." Such sentiments were in startling contrast to those expressed in Richmond less than a year earlier, when he had assured Southerners that "before New York would permit such a thing as coercion of the South, her streets would run red with blood." Cochrane was promoted to brigadier general in July, 1862, and saw action at Malvern Hill, Antietam, and Fredericksburg before resigning on account of physical disability in February, 1863—his thirst for blood presumably quenched.

He is simply a common specimen of the *species* democrat, & *genus* Yankee. [Daniel S.] Dickinson, [Caleb] Cushing, & all our other northern "friends," might have been more discreet & reticent on both occasions than Cochrane. But if either tempted or compelled to speak out, all would have uttered similar expressions, first & last. Neither are such strongly opposed doctrines, uttered by the same individual, to be taken as [1683] evidences of his being especially false or hypocritical. Able Northern politicians in leading, & their ignorant followers, by whatever party names they may call themselves—democrat, whig, republican or abolitionist, are all thoroughly democratic in an extended sense. That is, they are ready to submit to, & to uphold the will of the majority, just as soon as they know clearly which is the majority. I have even seen in northern papers applauded in good faith, & as entirely commendable, the conduct of a Pennsylvania whig, who declared himself a democrat as soon as he knew that the democratic party was certainly the majority of his state. This change, for this reason, which would have been deemed infamous in the Southern states, was praised as patriotic & truly democratic by the party which gained the consent, & was scarcely condemned by the party which lost him. So Cochrane would have stuck to his first declarations as long as he hoped to have the majority of the North, or of his state, to concur with him. But as soon as he knew that he was in a hopeless minority, he hastened to join the majority, & to go as far as the most extreme. . . . Tired of "Satanstoe," & returned .it, & began Cooper's "Deer slayer."

Dec. 7. The Convention actually adjourned finally last night. The end of this at first base submissionist body, & since long-usurping of functions which it had never been entrusted with, is hailed with joy by every one, but by a majority of its members, who not expecting ever to hold political power again, were most reluctant to surrender it. Still among their many sins, they have adopted some very beneficial & real amendments of the state constitution—& every one of which is either a complete return [1684] to a before abrogated feature of the oldest constitution of 1776, or an approach thereto. Still we have left the infamous features of popular election of Governor, & of county magistrates (though both evils are somewhat mitigated,) & of suffrage nearly universal. The demagogues' constitution of 1851 destroyed all of the principles of free & republican government. But the two evil principles now left are enough to bring about that destruction more slowly.—The burning of the cotton crops & houses continues to spread on the sea-islands of S.C. & soon there will not be a bale left, or enough of unginned cotton to make a bale in all these islands, except on the few plantations within the enemy's picket guards. This act of self-sacrifice is more patriotic & noble than any that has occurred in modern times. It will strike with dismay the Yankee powers & people, who confidently expected to secure all this cotton, either by plunder or by purchase. The people of Europe will learn these facts with astonishment, & draw from them the like inference that the world learned from the burning of Moscow by its own inhabitants & proprietors. Every individual planter in lower South Carolina severally & independently executes for himself a self-sacrifice which one Retoschepin [*sic*] only served for among the million of residents of Moscow.[46] Such a people may suffer defeats—but they cannot be conquered.—President Lincoln's Message to his rump congress in the Dispatch today. In it he recommends the recognition of the independence of Hayti & Liberia, & establishing diplomatic connections with them. He [1685] also plainly indicates the emancipation of slaves generally, by purchase from the "loyal" proprietors, &, as may be supposed from the course now pursued, by forcible abduction & plunder from the southern states in general, or by the incitement of general insurrection, by general proclamation of emancipation. He makes no reference to the capture of our ambassadors—nor to the immense destruction of cotton by burning, caused by the success of the Yankee army & navy. The losses of an enemy, the effect of warlike operations, are usually deemed gains & subjects of triumph to their antagonists. But though the burning by the owners of cotton, rice, & other crops will probably amount to the value of millions of dollars, not an expression of joy, or even a reference to the facts, has yet been heard from the north.—By previous invitation, I dined with Judge Perkins. Besides himself & the ladies of his family, I met there Judge John Robertson, Mr. J. A. Seddon, & Gen. G. W. Randolph.[47] Spent the time very pleasantly.

[46] The reference is to Fyodor Vasilievich Rostopchin, governor of Moscow, who in mid-September, 1812, ordered the burning of that city in order to forestall an extended occupation by Napoleon.

[47] A grandson of Thomas Jefferson and son of former governor Thomas M. Randolph, George Wythe Randolph (1818–67) organized a militia unit known as the Richmond Howitzers shortly after John Brown's raid. Following the outbreak of war he saw action in southeastern Virginia, rising to the rank of brigadier general. In

At 7, went to the Exchange to inquire for news, but heard of none.

Dec. 8. Sunday.... Spent most of the day in my room, reading.... Finished "Deer Slayer," which like most others of Cooper's novels (though not all,) is interesting, but like all of them, containing a great deal of foolishness.

Dec. 10.... At 5 P.M. went with W. Newton to the room of F. Minor, to meet Capt. M. F. Maury, & hear him state his scheme for building steam gun-boats, to defend our rivers from the Yankee ships of war. His plan has been [1689] approved by the State Convention, & also by the C.S. Secretary of the Navy, who promises to urge its execution. The boats are to be launches, moved by steam, & to carry two heavy guns each.—A convention of the secessionists of Ky. has declared the independence of that state, formed a provisional government, & elected a governor & council to exercise full state powers—& also applied for admission of the state into the Confederate States. Our congress has agreed to it—& so Ky. as well as Mo. are in the S[outhern] C[onfederacy] if we can hold them by beating their tory inhabitants as well as the Yankee armies from abroad. The secession of Mo. was effected by the legitimately elected legislature & Governor. But I fear that the secessionists of Ky. are still a minority, & that the admission of the state into the C.S. is unauthorized & premature. However, it could not be avoided, without doing worse. If our government had declined assuming the offered direction & command of the secessionists of Ky, the northern power would have remained in the ascendancy.—Began to read vol 1 of [Charles] Darwin's "Voyage of a Naturalist round the world."

Dec. 11.... I met & conversed with Judge [William M.] Cook[e] of Mo. with whom I became acquainted some time ago, & who is now here as a member of Congress from his state.[48] He informed me of difficulties & necessities of the southern party & their armies in Mo. which served to explain incidents for which I could not account before.—I had supposed that there were now scarcely any submissionists in lower Virginia, & that these few, who are com-

---

March, 1862, he was appointed secretary of war, succeeding Judah P. Benjamin, but resigned in November because of ill health and increasing friction with President Davis.

[48] After serving as a colonel in the Missouri State Guard under the command of General Sterling Price during the summer and fall of 1861, Judge Cooke was elected to the House of Representatives in the First Confederate Congress.

pelled to be silent, & who at least profess to be now zealous secces-
sionists, were to be found among the upper class of politicians, &
not among the lowest & most ignorant class, who, deprived of their
submissionist leaders, are usually ready to follow the majority. But
I learn that there are many of the lower classes on our tide-waters,
who are so disaffected that, though not daring to act for the enemy,
they will be ready to surrender, & to obey, as soon as the enemy can
invade & command their locality. The persons who make up this
disaffected class are either without property, or whose small capital
was vested in small vessels carrying wood, oysters, or whose labor
was used for supplying such vessels, & who were mostly
employed, before the war, by Yankees, who owned, or freighted,
almost all the vessels trading in or navigating our rivers & creeks.
These people have no property interest in the commonwealth.
They have been taught by our demagogues to distrust the wealthy,
& even all property-holders, & to envy them their possessions.
They are too ignorant to know the value of our political institutions,
& of African slavery even to the poorest citizens. Their previous
association & affiliation [1691] & business connections have been
much more with Yankees than with their own countrymen & even
their near neighbors. In addition, the rupture of the former union &
the consequent war bear very heavily on this class, & more especially on the Potomac river, & other waters most exposed to the
enemy's power. Their business & means for support have been
greatly impaired, if not entirely broken up. Their markets, whether
for catching or carrying oysters, or cutting or carrying wood, have
been cut off. It has been necessary, to prevent the wholesale escape
of fugitive slaves to the enemy's ships & garrisons, to arrest or to
sink the small vessels & to seize or destroy the boats on our tide-
waters, (& which measure was delayed too long—) & these vessels
& boats belonged mostly to this disaffected class, & in many cases
constituted almost all their property & means for subsistence.
Then, contrasting their new condition with the condition of the like
class in Maryland, they saw that these, their near neighbors, enjoyed not only all their former sources of profit, but had them greatly
increased by having a monopoly of the supplies. True, the state of
Md, & all its property-holders, were crushed under Lincoln's despotism. But this low class saw nothing in that (even if they knew it,)
to hurt their interests. Mr. Newton thinks that such sentiments are
far extended in the Northern Neck—& that these people think, &

sometimes say, that the object of the secession & the war is to protect the negroes of the rich men, who own all the negroes & all the good land—& that they own neither, & have no interest in fighting, or opposing the North. He supposes that there are very many of this class, thus feeling [1692] & thinking, who will not, as militia, oppose the invasion of the enemy with good-will, & will be even glad to surrender to & obey them, & to aid in establishing their supremacy. There are very many of this class in our Eastern Shore counties, who will welcome their occupation by the enemy, & who, doubtless, will find present benefit to their business pursuits & profits, even though every property-holder is robbed of his crops & his slaves. Of this class, a somewhat different & lower variety inhabit the sandy reef of North Carolina about Cape Hatteras & Ocracoke Inlet, the members of which have lately so readily taken the oath of allegiance to the U.S. government. This is not so much an indication of their preference, or disaffection, as of their indifference. These people are all wreckers by profession & for profit, & fishermen for subsistence. Many of them are Yankees by birth, & those who were born there have had much more association with Yankees than with their own countrymen. Probably they have little regard for either—& care not what government they swear allegiance to, so they thereby secure their present safety. Yet, with the few miserable wreckers, the Lincoln authorities have acted the contemptible farce of setting up a new state government for North Carolina![49] The only functionaries named in their recent proclamations are the Governor & his Secretary. Of the latter no one here had ever heard. The Governor, Marble Nash Taylor, is a methodist preacher, who was assigned to that region lately—was with our garrison at Fort Hatteras, & preached there a strong southern & secession sermon the Sunday preceding the attack on the fort. As soon as Fort Clark was evacuated, this man made signals to the enemy's vessels [1693], & deserted to them, carrying to them all the knowledge he had of the deficiencies of our troops and defences. The loss of employment & of profits by this low class of citizens on the tide-waters of Va. is not their only grievance, nor ground of contrast, unfavorable to themselves, with their neighbors of

---

[49] The diarist is partially in error here. A local convention, meeting in November, 1861, did repudiate the ordinance of secession and "elect" Marble Nash Taylor "governor," but the Lincoln administration never extended recognition to this fraudulent government.

Md—& now also of the like class in our Eastern Shore counties, since occupied by the enemy. In common with all other citizens of the seceded states, these have to pay enormous prices for all the ordinary necessaries & comforts of life, except grain & bread—as sugar, coffee, salt, leather, shoes, & clothing, all of which now sell at from 50 to 400 percent advance on former prices—& at which former prices most of these articles can still be bought in the U.S. & all territory subjected thereto. All these, to men without property, knowledge, or political principle, & caring merely for present interests, are sufficient reasons for their being disloyal, & ready to submit to the subjugation of their country.

Dec. 12. . . . . Received a very affectionate & interesting letter from Nanny. She has paid a visit of three weeks to the neighborhood of her father's camp . . . & Jane, & her niece Fanny Hamilton, have come with Nanny to Beechwood, to stay through Christmas. They all urge me to go there to see them, & I must do so before many days pass. . . . Telegraphic dispatch of extensive & destructive fire in Charleston S.C., & still in progress. The calamity is certainly very great, but the full extent yet unknown.

Dec. 13. No further account of the fire today. From the reports of last night, it seems that one-fifth of the city had been burnt, & among the thickest built & most valuable part. It is an awful [1694] calamity, even if it extended no farther. . . . Gen. Price has sent part of his army into Kansas, to retaliate on the plundering & burning & murdering villains under [James H.] Lane[50] & [James] Montgomery, who had before invaded Mo., & there carried on the same atrocious mode of warfare which they had used in Kansas, with the addition of stealing slaves from Mo. John Brown had been one of Lane's subordinate officers, & was not more a robber & murderer. Yet Lane is a U.S. Senator of Kansas, & a general of Lincoln's appointment, & in his special favor. . . . It may be inferred that if the invading Missourians get the upper hand of these villains . . . they will exact a most bloody retribution. I trust that Lane & Montgomery [1695] will be hanged, without even the formality of a drumhead court-martial, & that no quarter will be given to their

---

[50] A former congressman from Indiana, James Henry Lane (1814–66) moved to Kansas in 1855 and became the leader of the Free State faction. He was elected to the United States Senate in 1861 and served until his death five years later. At this time he also held an appointment as brigadier general of Volunteers, though this appointment was canceled in March, 1862.

followers.—Received yesterday 42 more copies of my "Sketches of Lower N.C." which I am distributing among my friends & some literary men, libraries &c.—Read in Randolph's bookstore, yesterday & today, "The Southern Spy," a political pamphlet lately published, on current events. It is written by Edward Pollard, late of Washington, & now in Richmond.[51]

Dec. 14. . . . I sent on to the Mayor of Charleston my checks for $300, as my contribution for the relief of the sufferers by the fire. I had but about $20 left in hand, after depositing $100 for a sight check—& have made the other $200 payable on Jan 10th. 1862, by which time I can raise that balance. Five churches were burnt, & some 4 or 5 other important public buildings. The Courier estimates the total loss at from 5 to 7 millions of dollars. I trust that this is much above the true value. But, however the estimate may be abated it is a most awful calamity. . . . In a late message of Gov. Letcher to the Convention, he states that Virginia has sent 40,000 volunteers into service—& that she has furnished 67,000 muskets from her arsenals to her troops & to other states. He estimates the value of arms, vessels, machinery &c. captured by us at the Navy Yard at Portsmouth & at Harper's Ferry, to be worth between 20 & 30 millions of dollars. This is indeed much. But it ought to be known that these 67,000 muskets were mostly of the old flint pattern, which though now found to be good, Gov. Letcher, in conjunction with the military board, had condemned as worthless, & actually agreed to sell for [1697] $1.50 each. It is a much more serious charge against the governnor, & a just one, as I think, that by his neglect to seize & hold the Balt. & Ohio Rail-road, & the Northwestern rail-road—or, if unable to hold them, to destory them, which might easily have been done before an invading enemy appeared, he allowed the enemy's forces to hold these rail-roads & to enter Va. from the Ohio to the Allegheny. The whole costly & disastrous war in the Northwest, & the enemy still being there the master, I charge to this neglect of the Governor. . . . Finished Vol. 1 of Darwin's "Voyage of a Naturalist &c." Could not find the 2nd—& began Charles Lamb's Writings, "Essays of

[51] A native of Albemarle County, Virginia, Pollard (1831–72) was probably the most prolific southern writer of the Civil War period. This work, subtitled *Curiosities of Negro Slavery in the South,* was published in 1859. From 1861 to 1867 Pollard edited the *Daily Richmond Examiner.* He became a bitter critic of President Davis and is best remembered for his work, *The Lost Cause,* published in 1866.

Elia.".... Yesterday saw Gen. [Nathan G.] Evans, on his way to join our army in S.C.

Dec. 15. Sunday. Went to church, under the supposition that a collection would be taken in this and all the churches today, for aid to the Charleston sufferers. But it is to be done next Sunday.... This morning met with Gen. Ben. McCulloch, who arrived here last evening from his command in Arkansas.—Met with Mr. Thomas Ryan of Charleston, one of the Palmetto Guards, on his way home. His whole property was in buildings, all of which were burnt in the late fire. Yet he did not appear depressed. This war operates to make men prepared to bear up under the heaviest pecuniary losses. Our captain, Geo. B. Cuthbert, who was a planter near Beaufort has had his whole crops of cotton &c. burnt (& willingly,) & all his slaves, like all others there, made free of control, & will be lost to the owners, if the Yankees can so arrange the matter....

Dec. 16. .... I am getting more anxious to get to Prince George, & now think that I will go on the 19th.—Propositions, by resolutions and by petitions, continue to be made in Congress of U.S. for the emancipation of all slaves in the "rebellious" states, in addition to the sentiments uttered in favor of the same general object, in Lincoln's Message & Cameron's Report. It is true that there is an ostensible difference between Lincoln & the more moderate abolitionists on one side, & Cameron & the more violent on the other. The latter advocate openly the general emancipation of all slaves (if proclaiming it can effect it,) in all the seceded states—only promising compensation to the "loyal" owners—& also putting arms in the hands of all revolting or fugitive slaves, to fight against the whites of the slave-holding states. I trust that the most extreme & violent party may carry the victory, (as is usual in revolutions,) & that it may enact & endeavor to enforce its policy. It cannot do us more harm than the pretended moderate policy—& many slave-holding unionists in the border states will [1700] be driven, by self-interest, to oppose the north with the policy of immediate & general emancipation, with servile war set on foot, who might still submit to the emancipation schemes of the more moderate, (as they have done all along,) & which schemes would be equally as effective, or more so, with a little more delay.... A novel mode of warfare has been begun, & is now in progress by the Yankee government. 25 old whale ships have been laden with stone, in northern ports, & sunk in the shallowest parts of the deepest channels to different southern ports, by which obstructions the enemy believe they will permanently close these ports to all vessels drawing more water than is clear of the stone. I have only seen by their reports that they have thus obstructed Ocracoke Inlet—but the entrances to Charleston & Savannah are named as among those to be subjected to this "stone blockade." Another such fleet is preparing, in addition to the first. Perhaps some ports may be so obstructed, [1701] & require the stone to be removed hereafter. But they will be of but temporary effect where the bottom is of shifting sand, as at Charleston, or soft & varying alluvial sand as at the mouth of the Mississippi. And the existing inlets of the sand reef of N.Ca. might even be perfectly & permanently closed by walls of stone, & other passages would soon be opened elsewhere, by the force of the water & storm tides.

Dec. [17th]. . . . Very good & exciting news received first by telegram from Kentucky, & later & more fully from northern newspaper items republished in Norfolk. The report of the arrest of Mason & Slidell had been received in England, with general indignation of the people. A popular meeting in Liverpool, (when the mail steamer landed,) with great unanimity, denounced the procedure, & called on the government [to] resent the insult to the flag & nation. Nothing yet heard to indicate the course of the government. . . . Though the northern newspapers pretend to find pacific indications, the northern government & people must think that there is strong probability of their having on their hands a war with England. If so, that opinion will serve as a new & more potential reason for hazarding [1702] a battle with us, before they will have another foe to combat. Besides, if they could soon gain an important victory over one of our armies, it might operate (or so the Lincoln government will think,) to deter England from making war. On these grounds, I now think (in opposition to my previous opinion,) that there will soon be a serious attack made on some one or more of our armies. And this attack may be from Fortress Monroe & Newport News, as large reinforcements of men & horses have lately been landed there, & Gen. Magruder has called to his aid all the militia, not before in service as volunteers, from the counties of Charles City, Henrico, Hanover, King William, King & Queen & others. If Gen. McClellan means to attack us near the Potomac, (of which I have been utterly incredulous for some time back,) he has not a day to lose. For dry weather has put the roads & earth in good order for artillery, which will be altered by the first rain.—At the Exchange saw among the new arrivals, Mr. Boulware, & Messrs. J[osiah] Collins, W[illiam] Pettigrew, & J[osiah T.] Granberry of N.Ca. . . .

Dec. 18. Before 2 P.M. another telegram announcing arrival of a later steamer, 5 days later from England, at Halifax N.S. confirming & adding to the yesterday's reports. The [1703] main & all-important addition is not yet certain, which was that the British government had sent orders to their minister at Washington to demand the release & restitution of Messrs. Mason & Slidell, and if that should not be accorded, to demand his passport. It is true & certain that the Steamer was detained to receive a special messenger with dispatches, & it was believed by all that the above was their purport. But there is no doubt of the arrest of our ministers being generally deemed an insult to the flag & people of England, requiring exemplary satisfaction & atonement, or war. At night, received from Norfolk republished articles from English & New York papers giving details. . . . The people of Richmond, & visitors, more excited & more rejoicing at this news than at any time since the battle of Manassas. I walked from my room 4 times downtown, to learn the news, besides at other times making, separately, two distant visits to friends in an opposite direction. . . . At night, at the Exchange, again saw Gen. McCulloch, & had some conversation with him. Heard from him of a recent fight & splendid victory of the regiment of Col. [Benjamin F.] Terry, my Texas acquaintance at Fairfax C.H., over a body of the enemy in Kentucky. But though only 3 or 4 were killed on our side, the brave Terry was unfortunately one of these few. Gen. McCulloch spoke of him in very high terms of praise, & thought that he could scarcely be replaced by his equal.—Made my preparations for [1704] leaving tomorrow morning, before day-break. . . .

Dec. 19. . . . The steamer left the wharf at 6.30. On the way I heard of a most afflicting & fatal accident at Mrs. Martha Cocke's, close to Beechwood. Her youngest son, Nathaniel, about 17 years old, was shot & killed by the undesigned discharge of a gun in his own hands, when he was about to go out to shoot partridges. When I reached Beechwood all the family had gone to Tarbay to the funeral. . . . Cotton in New York, at last known sales, was 36 cents. This is an advance of 9 cents since the Yankee fleet "opened the cotton port" of Port Royal. The (to the Yankees) totally unexpected incident of the burning of the cotton crops &c. by the planters & owners must have been the principal element of the recent & most rapid advance of price. But for the wretchedly mismanaged defence of our forts there, by the incompetency of the commander in chief, Gen. Drayton, & their hasty & unexpected evacuation, the more complete & more glorious result would have greeted the conquering [End of MS Volume 9—p. 1707] invaders of every cotton house & bale being [burn]t, & every other house & crop, by the hands on orders of the owners. As it was, owing to the very speedy retreat of our troops from the forts, the plantations nearest to the enemy's guns & troops could not be safely burnt—& as much cotton thereon may be left for their stealing as may amount to 3000 bales, or less than two ordinary ship cargoes. All the other exposed crops have been burnt by their owners, with the cotton houses & machinery, & generally all other of their crops, plantation houses, & mansions, which, if left, might have been of service to the enemy. These noble acts of patriotism & self-sacrifice have not been equalled in modern times, except when the Dutch cut their dykes to let the sea overflow their country, rather than permit its being occupied by their invaders. . . . The water passage into Port Royal harbor was too broad to be effectually defended by any forts, & therefore I am not condemning the commander because the enemy's ships passed the forts, & so rendered their possession by our troops untenable. But the firing from our forts was very bad, & sundry cannon were dismounted by their own recoil, & others *spiked* & rendered useless to us by the awkward use of the priming wires. Yet, for their effectual spiking, before leaving them, there were no files on hand. This miserable mismanagement & inefficiency of the military operations, is in strong contrast with the general & noble conduct of all the numerous individual proprietors whose plantations were exposed to the enemy, [1708] & who could, & [did, b]urn their crops & houses. But I cannot understand why the town of Beaufort was not burnt, when abandoned by every white resident. The enemy did not occupy it until very recently. Among the noticeable facts were these: the principal fort (or earth-work,) had been constructed on Gen. Drayton's plantation—& his brother, a captain in the U.S. navy, commanded one of the steam war-ships that attacked the fort.

Dec. 20. The mail today brought no important news. It does not appear that Lord [Richard B. P.] Lyons has yet made (if he has received such orders,) a peremptory demand on Lincoln's government for restitution of Mason & Slidell, or satisfaction to England.[52] The tone of the Yankee press, & people so far as heard from, & of the government, as expressed by its organs, is defiant, & as if determined to resist the supposed demands of England. The government organs profess to discredit any extreme action by England, & the probability of war. But mercantile prices indicate the belief of business men that war is imminent. Immediately after the late accounts from England, U.S. & other stocks fell in N.Y. from 6 to 10 percent. Saltpetre rose 15 cents on the pound. Cotton (middling) ordinary upland has since sold at 40 cents, & a superior lot of upland or short-staple at 42. The banks of New York were about to suspend specie payments—& reported since that the measure had been consummated. This suspension will be universal. The necessity for it indicates a reflux of gold to Europe. Exchange on England has risen to 112. . . . The report, universally believed, that Pres. Davis intended to supersede Gen. Price by Col. Heth, promoted to be a Major General, has been contradicted by the President.—The last sales of salt in Richmond at $25 the sack, & $28 afterwards asked. $8 for a single bushel some days earlier. Silver money is at 30 percent premium, & gold 40. . . .

Dec. 21. . . . Read [Joseph] Addison's comedy, "The Drummer," & began "Gulliver's Travels"—both of which I had read over 55 years ago, & the latter a second time since.

Dec. 22. Sunday. . . . Rode to Ruthven. All at home & well. My young grandson, Edmund, who was so long sick, & like to die, is as fat as a prize pig, & entirely free from all ill health, except some remains of the whooping cough, which all the children here have lately gone through. I stayed through the night.

Dec. 23. Rain last night, & part of the forenoon. Strong N.W. wind, & raw & cold.—The mail. . . . Another arrival from England, bringing reports of unabated agitation there, & determination of the popular mind to resent the insult to the English flag, & of extended preparations for war.—Afternoon [1712] returned to Bee[ch-wood]. . . . It is not to be denied that in the last two months most of

---

[52] Lord Richard Bickerton Pemell Lyons (1817–87), the British minister at Washington, in fact had outlined informally his country's demands, calling for the immediate release of Mason and Slidell, in a meeting with Secretary of State Seward on the preceding day. However, Lyons did not deliver the official British note, which demanded a response within seven days, until December 23.

our people have been lowered in their sanguine hopes of signal success over our enemy, & a speedy & triumphant end of the war. But while there is general & great disappointment, in these respects, (& of none more than myself,) there are no indications of discouragement, or doubts of our final success, or of any disposition of any previous secessionist to yield in the least to our enemies. If the previous submissionists, & late professed converts to secession, entertain such disposition, they have not dared to express it. The general change to despondency, or to less hopeful expectations, grew out of the complete naval supremacy of the Yankees, and our utter inability to prevent their naval expeditions either ravaging or occupying our unprotected coast lands in any of hundreds of places, as they have done in lower Virginia, at Hatteras, & at Port Royal harbor. On the part of our enemies, who in all their views seem to be demented, they are still sanguine of success, & deem our subjugation, or voluntary submission, as sure as we do their failure to effect either. I make no reference to the late news of England's probable engagement in war with the North, which of course must affect calculations on both sides. . . . So far from . . . there being any ground for despondency on our part, I think we have every reason to be as hopeful of our final triumph, a[s] when we expected but a short & slight struggle—though we may, & probably will, have to attain that end through much greater losses than I had at first supposed even possible. In every considerable battle of land forces we have been victorious, & in nearly every minor fight & skirmish. In the few affairs in which our forces were beaten, the enemy were greatly superior in numbers, or were guided & aided by our traitors, or had both of these advantages. In the beginning of warlike operations, the enemy held, & still hold, the entire navy & regular army, most of the arms & munitions of war, & occupied all the forts & arsenals in the southern states since seceded, from 18 to 20 or more in number. Of all these, they now only retain two on the main land, with Key West & Tortugas. All the others are ours. They have since seized & still occupy portions of the eastern border of Va, no where as much as 12 miles in width, & they have plundered & wasted other like exposed places. They hold Fort Hatteras, & their later conquest of sea-islands in S.C. & a few desolate & small islands of Ga, Miss. & La. In all these [1714] occupations, except in Va, the expenses of the enemy's expeditions & conquests have been far greater than all the benefit they derived,

& also the damage & loss of property caused to the residents & proprietors. In regard to more extended & important occupations of territory, the Confederate States have not only continued to hold all the seceded states, with the above named exceptions of small portions, but have extended conquest over much of Ky & Mo., against not only the submissionists & tories of these states, but large armies from the North, in both. Eastern Tennessee, which was in sentiment with the North, has been quieted. North-western Va, which was not less disposed to submission to the North, is the only extensive territory within our claimed boundaries, (of any first seceded states,) which is still of disputed occupancy & loyalty. Whatever is now ours in Ky & Mo. is the gain of our arms—& so much loss of the enemy's previous quiet possession. And in Md., which we have not yet entered, & have effected nothing directly, the enemy can only keep the possession, & maintain its political power, by the presence of an army of 30,000 northern mercenaries. Our defence of Port Royal harbor in S.C. was the feeblest & most disgraceful of the war on our part—& scarcely anything has yet been done there to repel & injure the enemy. And there the losses of the people have been also the greatest. Yet counting these losses at the highest mark, they will scarcely amount to 4 millions, which was the estimated cost of the naval expedition to the Yankee government. The operations of war are to be computed more correctly by their cost, & by the loss they inflict on the opposite party, than in any other mode. And even if the naval & predatory expeditions of the Yankees shall be uniformly successful, to the extent of occupying detatched [*sic*] spots [1715] of territory, seizing much property, & causing [the] destruction of much more—but that the expense of such expeditions also amount to much more than all their plunder & all the damage to property, the enemy will be more injured & weakened thereby than ourselves.

The enormous expenditures of the northern government, & the great numbers of men in arms have very far exceeded any anticipations on our part, because the cause & the means were not anticipated, or even thought of as being possible. The cause & the means of such enormous power are both presented in the sudden & complete revolution by which all free government has been suspended in the northern states, & an arbitrary despotism established. The very large southern & peace party in the north, (large & strong enough, if left to operate constitutionally, to paralyze the war

& majority party,) was struck down & silenced by terror, & forced to add all its power to the conquering party. The despotism commands & wields the undivided force & entire wealth of the whole northern people. The leaders of the political party in power care nothing about their country's welfare in comparison to preserving & promoting their own political power & individual interests. The incurring a national debt more onerous than that of Great Britain, & even being defeated in the end by the South, are small damages in the estimation of Lincoln, Seward, &c. compared to their now losing their places, & their influence with their political party. Their yielding to the South would be the death-blow to their political existence & personal gains—& therefore any greater calamities to their country will be met in preference. These inducements, & their [1716] means, have brought about the prodigious (& formerly would have been deemed incredible) armaments of the North. And while the Southern Confederacy & its government have no aid from either such causes or motives, & have only the support of the patriotism & courage of the people, we have made nearly corresponding efforts for defence against the enormous military power of our foe. And though our whole armament of land forces has probably never, at any time, equaled two-thirds of that of the enemy, we have beaten them almost everywhere by the superiority of the material of our armies. Our troops are all volunteers, in the fullest sense, & have in their ranks, the most worthy of our people. Most of the enemy's soldiers are also nominally volunteers—but are mostly foreigners compelled to enlist to obtain bread. Such mercenaries are not stimulated by patriotism & courage, as our troops are—& have never failed to give way, or to be beaten, when fighting equal numbers, & with equal advantages otherwise—& often when superior in every advantage except courage. The enemy being able to oppose to us 3 soldiers to our 2, & with greatly superior arms & equipment, they may even defeat us in a larger proportion of future land battles than they have done heretofore—& maintain their complete supremacy on the water & much of our coast line. But our subjugation or submission will be impossible in any event. And by what has already been done by the Yankee government & armies, a more deadly hatred has been produced than exists between any other hostile nations. If the aversion & hatred entertained by both peoples were known in Europe, it would suffice to put an end to all the existing belief in the probable submission of the South, & the reconstruction of the former United States.—Such were my views previous to the late [1717] news from England, & without reference to our having any foreign aid in our defence against the North. But if England will merely raise the blockade of our ports, & remove the complete naval supremacy of our enemy, we will be well able alone to cope with them on the land, & successfully defend all our territory, & drive our invaders to seek security at home.

Dec. 24. My chief occupation today was writing the last pages, & reading Gulliver's Travels. I find but little amusement in conversation in ordinary company, & the less in proportion to the number of persons present. For the more there are, & especially of young people, the less occasion is there for any to address their words especially to my dull hearing. And when two or more are talking or making any other noise at once, I can hear nothing clearly, no matter how loud the talking may be. Thus, the larger the company, & the more cheerful & talkative they are, the more lonesome & unamused I am. I left the sitting room & the gay party of young people at 9, that my silence & grave manner might not cast gloom over their mirth, & because solitude is more tolerable to me when alone, than in a crowd.

If there should be no interference in this war by England, in our favor, it is certain that we shall suffer greatly by the predatory attacks, & especially by the naval attacks of the northern power. These injuries however will be confined within the limits of their armed occupations, or incursions by overpowering armaments. To their disposition & intentions of damage there is no limit. Already, by either the action of the rump congress, or by proclamations [1718] & general orders of the military commanders—& by more complete & stringent enactments now before the congress, & certain to be adopted—every secessionist in the 13 Confederate States, which means every man not a tory or traitor to the South, is liable & doomed to execution & death, as a traitor to the northern government & people. And every species of property, in these states, real & personal, of course including slaves, is already confiscated, unless proved to belong to adherents of the North. The public declaration of universal emancipation of slaves, in one form or another, has already been published, & is enforced, by their abduction, & encouragements held out to armed insurrection wherever their military rule is complete. Secretary Cameron has avowed the adopted policy of putting arms in the hands of the fugitive or insurgent slaves, & admitted that he had sent surplus arms to S.Ca. for that use. But these edicts of general confiscation of property, of emancipation of slaves, & of their being armed for insurrection, by the northern government, have caused no increased alarm to the southern people, & indeed have had very little general operation on southern minds, except to increase feelings of indignation & hatred. . . . How long the war will continue will be measured by the powers of the contending parties to bear up under their respective expenses. [1719] It is admitted by northern authorities that the expenses of the U.S., necessary to carry on the war, average two millions of dollars per day—& of their army, that for every soldier, the annual cost is equal to $1000. . . . If northern madness does not end sooner, the war must end (or become passive,) as soon as the northern credit fails so that no more loans can be made at home—for none have been or can be negotiated abroad. What are our expenses & resources I do not know. But our means (in actual productive property,) are greater, & our expenses very far less than those of the North.

Dec. 25. Christmas day. Julian, Lotty, little Jane & Mrs. Meade came to spend the day.—The mail. Seven ships of the "stone fleet" of the enemy have been sunk by them in the main channel leading to Charleston S.Ca. Another portion had previously been sunk in Ocracoke inlet. This fleet cost upwards of $600,000. I wish they would extend the operation to ten times that expense. The mode of warfare, in its object to ruin our ports permanently, is of a piece with the other practices of the Yankees. But the effect . . . in these cases, if not in all, will be as small as the malignancy of design is great. . . . This morning finished Gulliver's Travels, & began to look over & read some of the papers of the "Spectator" of Addison in his collected works.

Dec. 26. After breakfast, walked to Ruthven. When not conversing with Julian or the ladies, reading in Burns' poems.

Dec. 27. The family & visitors of Beechwood expected to dinner, & most of them came. After a very cheerful day, we returned to Beechwood, the young people staying until after ten.—The mail. The tone of the principal northern papers has so changed, that they recommend to the government more or less of yielding to the demands of the British government. It is not yet known what demands have been made. Every indication from the English papers, of all parties, is that full satisfaction will be obtained, or war will be made. I cannot believe that the Lincoln government can confess itself so mean & abject, after all its late boasting, as to surrender Mason & Slidell—nor can I believe that England will be satisfied with less. . . .

Dec. 28. . . . A newspaper of today brought from Petersburg. Later reports from Europe state all England to be unanimous & earnest for reparation for the Mason & Slidell arrest, or otherwise for war with the U.S. Canada in like temper—& in both countries preparations for war in active progress. The principal newspapers of Lincolndom are now disposed to surrender our imprisoned [1723] commissioners. Disgraceful as would be so complete a backing out of the recent pretensions & boasts, I begin to fear that it is possible. Lord Lyons does not seem to have presented the *ultimatum* of his government, or to have received any inadmissible answer from Lincoln's. Interviews have taken place, but it seems quietly, & without any marked issue. Special messengers have been sent with dispatches to England, both by Lyons to his government, & by Lincoln to his minister there. The understanding in England is that the ministry are unanimous for demanding full reparation of the U.S. In France, the press, of all parties, deprecates war, & hopes that the difficulty will be adjusted, by the U.S. surrendering the prisoners & apologizing—but maintain unanimously that England will be right in insisting on such redress. . . . Read (a second time,) a "Review & Refutation of Helper's 'Impending Crisis,'" by [Gilbert J.] Beebe, a N.Y. country editor. This pamphlet is a good argument & exposure of the false positions of this infamous book. Heretofore no one has taken the trouble of thoroughly sifting such a mass of falsehoods. The conclusions were so illogical & monstrous that readers scarcely questioned the premises, when, as in most cases, they were presented as statistical facts, copied from the census reports, or so understood. Even if they had been so, & ever so sound, the deductions of Helper would have been false in most cases. But, as Beebe has shown, Helper falsified statistics continually & grossly, to suit better his desired deductions—& he has escaped detection generally, because no opposer deemed it possible that even so infamous a writer could dare so to falsify statistical facts reported & before the public in the census reports. Continued to read Spectator papers.—[1725] For want of other occupation & amusement, I have latterly extended the form of my diary so as to include most of the most striking of current events, & also my reflections thereupon. I have in this way lessened the extent of my wearisome hours. I would be glad to still farther extend my diary, so as to make it also a journal of the war & political changes of the country. But that is impossible, because of the first reports of all war facts being so generally exaggerated, distorted, or altogether false. . . . However, I will try. But such attempt, (even though rejecting without notice, or waiting for confirmation, of the least credible reports,) must be more a record of my first & contemporaneous impressions made by the statements in newspapers, than of the true & exact occurrences. . . .

Dec. 30. By previous arrangement & appointment, Mrs. [Fanny Roulhac] Hamilton[53] was to go to the camp near Burwell's Bay to join her husband, by the steamer today, & Jane had arranged to go with her, to join her husband. They left this morning in the carriage for the Hood's wharf, where they went on board the steamer. My grandson George went with them to the wharf, & saw them on board. This previous appointment prevented our family going to the funeral of Mrs. Edw[ard A.] Marks—she & her husband our much esteemed neighbors—for want of conveyance. I only went, on horseback, calling by Ruthven, & thence went in Julian's carriage, with him, Lotty, & Mrs. Meade. A very large attendance for the country. . . . Returned . . . to Ruthven to dinner—& I sent my horse home, intending to stay some days. . . . It was before stated, incorrectly quoting Gov. Letcher's message, that Virginia had furnished 40,000 volunteers as soldiers in the southern cause. The mistake did much less than justice to the noble efforts of this state. The whole number of soldiers of all arms furnished by Va. to the Confederate government has been 60,000, in 70 regiments. I suppose that this enumeration includes the ordinary militia, which in a few cases of pressing need, have been called into service, in mass, for particular counties, & for short terms of service. But much the greater number (probably 50 to 55,000) were volunteers for not less than 12 months' service. Yet one-fourth of Va. being disloyal, or occupied by the enemy, furnished very few soldiers. . . . Our army in Fairfax has gone into winter quarters, & I suppose all prospect of a general engagement is at an end. For a month back the weather has been remarkably dry for the season, & the roads good, & the

---

[53] Niece of Jane Ruffin, wife of the diarist's eldest son.

earth dry & firm. There could not have been a more favorable time for the use of field artillery. And as Gen. McClellan did not offer battle in that time, it cannot be expected later. The first winter rains will make the earth too soft for artillery for months. . . .

Dec. 31. Began yesterday, & continued through most of today, to read the "Fortunes of Nigel."[54] [1732]

---

[54] Published in 1822, this was a romantic novel written by Sir Walter Scott.

1862

RECOLLECTIONS OF THE NAT TURNER IN-
SURRECTION ᏫᔄᎧ AN EVALUATION OF THE
PUBLIC CAREER OF JOHN TYLER ᏫᔄᎧ GRIM
NEWS FROM THE WEST ᏫᔄᎧ AGAIN IN THE
CONFEDERATE CAPITAL ᏫᔄᎧ INSPECTING
C.S.S. *VIRGINIA* IN DRY DOCK ᏫᔄᎧ MCCLEL-
LAN ADVANCES UP THE PENINSULA

January 1. After breakfast, walked from Ruthven to Beechwood. . . . The conical balls of the Minie, Enfield, or rifled muskets,
with which the enemy's troops are so generally provided, make
much worse wounds, than the smooth spherical balls which are
used for most of our muskets & rifles. This is a serious disadvantage,
which is but one of the consequences of our generally inferior small
arms. . . . Nothing definite yet heard of the state of negotiations on
the Mason & Slidell case. It is supposed that no *ultimatum* has yet
been sent by England. Before that will be done, there will be heard
there the accounts of the universal rejoicing, boasting & threatening of the U.S. press, people, & government, & also before will be
known the present change to a tone of yielding & abject humiliation to the demands of England. I trust that these earlier & bolder
indications may cause England to first announce a declaration of
war by the artillery of an overwhelming naval force. Either the
national virtue or scrupulousness has increased wonderfully since
the times when England captured the Spanish treasure ships
previous to a declaration of war, & bombarded Copenhagen &
captured the Danish navy in previous profound peace, if now
expecting or designing to make war, that power does not make use
of the great & peculiar advantages [1733] now offered in the
situation of the navy of the U.S. It is now divided into sundry
separate blockading squadrons, each one in the outer harbor of

some fortified southern port, & the position & nearly the force of each squadron well known in England. It would be only necessary to send, without previous notice, a decidedly superior naval force to each position, & every Yankee blockading squadron would be destroyed or captured, or be itself blockaded, & hopeless of relief or reinforcement, until compelled to surrender. This England can now easily effect, & within a few weeks time. The temptation to utterly crush the naval power of a dangerous rival seems to me too strong to be resisted, when the folly & arrogance of that rival has furnished abundant cause for war. . . .

Jan. 2. Finished looking over Addison's Spectator papers. I was disappointed & surprised to find so little in them to amuse or interest me. I read them with much more interest when I was a boy. But then I had access to but few books, or I probably might not have read the Spectator.—After Breakfast, walked to Ruthven. Finished Nigel. This is one of the very few romances of Scott which I had not before read twice, at least. My not [1734] having read this one again, since its first publication, was owing to my disgust excited by its plot & principal characters. This feeling is undiminished—but in other respects, this book is among the secondary romances for interest to the reader—though not to be compared to the author's greatest productions, such as "Old Mortality," "The Heart of Midlothian," "Guy Mannering," "The Antiquary" & "Ivanhoe." The part of James I is the chief object & end of the "Fortunes of Nigel," & it is admirably designed for interest, & probably for truth to great extent. Certainly the author has not spared his subject in describing his pedantry & folly, his cowardice & meanness. Still Scott's thorough toryism & sycophancy to royalty induced him to give some undeserved graces & claims of favorable consideration of this most despicable of Kings. . . . Besides the too favorable delineation of this meanest & basest of royal scoundrels, the plot & characters of the author's hero & heroine are most distasteful to me. . . . Began to read "Peveril of the Peak"[1] . . . At night, as usual, our conversation mostly on the war, & political state of the country—& especially on the probable course of events in respect to the present embroilment of England & Yankeedom. Not only on this, the now most important point (unless Lincoln satisfies England,) but in others, we must be on the eve of important events. On Green river,

---

[1] Another novel by Sir Walter Scott.

Ky., at Columbus, [&] in Mo. great battles seem to be impending. And in central & northern Ky, if numerous reinforcements should join [Brigadier General Humphrey] Marshall's army on its northward march, the results may be of the most important kind. Oh! that he may have the numbers, strength, & ability, & also the equipment & supplies to enable him [to] move on to Cincinnati & lay it in ashes as a first & deserved retribution for the iniquities of our invaders!

Jan. 3. At last comes the now unquestionable report that Lincoln's administration has yielded our imprisoned commissioners to the peremptory demand of England! Such an act of abject humiliation has not been parallelled [*sic*] by any civilized nation in the last century. This is a bad turn of affairs for us, as removing the otherwise certain occasion of England making war on our powerful & malignant [1736] enemy. But it remains to be seen whether England will be pacified & conciliated by this act of submission—& will forget that the now humble apologist, lately, & in regard to the same act of insult & wrong-doing, played the part of the boastful & threatening bully, before changing to that of the timid poltroon. It is natural to nations as well as to individuals to presume on the fears & submission of an adversary. This was not the only existing ground of complaint for England. It may well be doubted whether that nation will be so magnanimous or so forbearing, as not to be more urgent in other demands for justice, because this one has been so easily enforced. The details of the surrender have not yet been published here. . . .

Jan. 4. . . . . Finished the latter (& main) portion of "Peveril of the Peak." Historical romances, Scott's included, serve less to increase knowledge of true history, than to mislead as to its events & still more as to the characters of the persons introduced. In this romance, as in Woodstock, Scott has as much disguised truth to favor the selfish, unprincipled [1737] & base Charles II, as he did in "Nigel" to lighten the load of infamy of James I. But there is one important respect in which Scott's romances throw much light on the obscure statements of history, which seem incomprehensible because their causes were not exposed by the historian as vividly as by the romancer. Nothing that I had read in history had served to explain the mystery of the "Popish Plot" in the reign of Charles II. After all the explanations of history, it remained to me incomprehensible why persons of character, or of high position or family, should be condemned to & suffer death as plotters & traitors, upon not only most insufficient & improbable evidence, & even that given only by the basest of common informers, infamous in their lives, & manifestly perjured as witnesses—& that, on such evidence, jurors would convict, & judges sentence, & the king fail to pardon persons against whom no fair observer could find ground of serious charge of guilt. Scott . . . in describing imaginary scenes & characters, has explained what history & true narratives had left hidden & inexplicable. Nations & communities sometimes become insane, as well as individuals. At this period, the protestant people of England had one of these fits of insanity, of which, as in this case, terror & fear are the essential elements & causes. The unfounded belief of a general "popish plot," encouraged, for their own purposes, by able & vile leaders, spread through all of the most ignorant. It became not only unpopular, & even odious, for any one to discredit or doubt the existence of such a general plot, but for any one to do so was enough for him to incur suspicion of being concerned, & subjected to all the dangers [1738] of arrest & trial as a plotter & traitor. The same suspicion, or at least of being a concealed papist, & well-wisher to the plotters, would attach to any one who as magistrate, Judge, juror, witness or attorney, seemed to disbelieve the obviously false witnesses, or to give the accused the benefits of a fair & legal trial. The only (& very obvious) course for perfect safety to any individual was to join clamorously in the general cry, & to become persecutors to save themselves from being persecuted. Such would be the speedy course of all the timid, the unscrupulous, & the selfish. I have myself witnessed, on a small scale, the occurrence of insanity of a community—& which enabled me to understand how the "popish plot" & its concomitants could have existed in England. My experience of a more circumscribed state of insanity of a community, was in lower Va. & N.Ca. following & caused by the insurrection of slaves & their massacre of whites in Southampton County in 183[1].[2] The true facts were enough to inspire terror. These were that the slaves in a neighborhood had begun in the dead of night to kill the sleeping whites—& in some 12 or 14 hours had massacred nearly 70, mostly women & children. But these facts were greatly magnified in every early report—& no exaggeration was greater than every hearer's imagination would readily offer. In

---

[2] Reference is to the Nat Turner insurrection.

the absence of all information of the peculiar causes which excited this out-break, & which confined its first operation to but 7 actors, in one locality, every hearer would naturally suppose that it was a wide-spread conspiracy, & as likely to extend to his slaves, & to endanger his family, as anywhere. The insurgents & murderers, with their subsequent recruits (voluntary or by compulsion) [1739] were either killed or captured within 48 hours, except a few captured later. The whole conspiracy was crushed, & every participant suffered death. There was full proof that the knowledge of the design was confined to three persons only, until within a few hours of the beginning of the massacre, & that it could not have been previously divulged elsewhere, or to others. Yet terror & fear so affected most persons as to produce a condition of extended & very general community-insanity. The unreasonable & unfounded belief was built upon false & absurd particular statements of alleged facts, that there had been a wide-spread, if not general, conspiracy of numerous slaves, from the centre of Va. to the south of N.C. Many slaves, who certainly had never heard of the insurrection until after its complete suppression—& some 100 miles & more from the scene—were charged with participation, & tried & condemned to death, on testimony of facts, or from infamous witnesses, which at any sober time would not have been deemed sufficient to convict a dog suspected of killing sheep. If any more moderate or sane person, in a private or public capacity, endeavored to defend, or to demand a just trial of persons so charged, he incurred odium, if not personal danger, as a favorer, if not approver, of murderous insurgents, & midnight slayers of sleeping men, women & children. Sundry of the slaves so suspected were killed without form of trial, or in the few cases of acquittal, after being discharged. But generally, the magistrates who tried the accused, & the states attorneys who prosecuted them, dared not do justice, or were laboring themselves under the general insanity, & incapable of knowing either justice or proper evidence. [1740] In one of these cases, a slave in this county (Prince George,) was charged with knowledge of & participation in the conspiracy, & tried, & convicted, & sentenced to be hanged, by the unanimous voices of 4 magistrates, (not an ignorant & impassioned jury.) The facts alleged against the prisoner might have every one been true, without involving him in the crimes charged. In addition, the witness, a white man of the lowest class & character, would not have been worthy of belief, even if the statements had been of importance. I exerted myself to get up a petition to the governor (which I wrote) for the pardon of this convict. There was scarcely any person to whom I applied who did not belive the man innocent, but who still did not refuse to meddle with the matter so far as to sign the petition—to which I could obtain but 11 signatures besides my own. With these, I went to Richmond, & offered the petition to the Governor, ([John] Floyd, the elder—) but even he did not dare, or deem it politic, to grant the petition, or to pardon in any such case. But previous to my application, he had commuted that & all other of such sentences to death of persons manifestly innocent, to "transportation" & sale beyond the limits of the United States—but which practically was merely banishment from & sale beyond the limits of Va. This, however great a moderation of the sentence, still was as unjust—& I urged, in vain, that justice required the full pardon of the unjustly condemned & innocent prisoner. But doubtless it was more politic to yield something to the prevailing insanity of the public mind. For even if for no other reason, if the negro had received a full pardon, & been permitted to go home, he would have been secretly or openly murdered by some "fellows of the baser [1741] sort," who in times like these always rise in power & in influence—& who could then have committed such a murder, even openly, with impunity, under the claim of patriotism & protection of the vital interests of the community. I did not escape incurring much odium for my having gotten up & urged the petition for pardon of the convict—& even intimations were uttered that I ought to be punished by personal violence. Some who thus joined in condemning me had previously confessed to me their belief in the entire innocence of the convict.

Jan. 5. Sunday. All of us went to church except Lotty, who was unwell.—This is my birth-day—which did not occur to me until past noon. Yet one would think that the arriving at the age of 68 was an event not likely to be so long forgotten.—Returned from church to Ruthven.—A letter received from Edmund. He informs me that he will be on a Court-Martial for two weeks, in session at Smithfield—& during that time, being free of other military duties, he will spend every night with his wife, at Bruce Gwynn's. I am much inclined to go there, & am trying to persuade Julian to go with me,

& so to indulge himself with a few days' relaxation. But he is so averse to leaving home, that he regards it rather as punishment than pleasure.

Jan. 6. Light snow & sleet last night, which barely whitened the ground. Cloudy & cold. The cold weather admonished me of the imprudence of my contemplated trip to Nansemond, & I gave it up. . . . Walked to Beechwood. Found, as expected, that the young visitors from Richmond had gone home this morning.—The mail. . . . In the London "Times," a commentary on Lincoln's Message to his Congress, treating it most deservedly with the greatest contempt, in regard to both its matter & manner. The tone of the English papers, received by the last arrival, seems to indicate that the mere release of our Commissioners to an English steamer will not satisfy all the complaints of the British government. Some of the papers denounce the recent act of sinking a fleet laden with stone, with the intention of destroying the navigation of our harbors, as an offence against the commerce & rights of the world. . . .

Jan. 7. . . . Finished [1747] "Waverley," & began "Guy Mannering." At night, read aloud to Mrs. Lorraine & my granddaughters the first Act of "Twelfth Night," for a sample, & trial of their liking.

Jan. 8. The mail brought no important news. Mason & Slidell, with their secretaries, embarked on a British war steamer sent for them, & left their prison in Boston for England on the 1st. . . . The annual report of the U.S. Secretary of the Treasury estimates the expenses of the government for the year 1862 at 655 millions of dollars, if the war should last so long—but predicts that it will be ended (by defeat & surrender of the South,) by midsummer!—At night, read more of "Twelfth Night" aloud.

Jan. 10. The mail. . . . According to latest northern reports, there were 20 ships of the enemy's "stone fleet" sunk in the channel over Charleston bar alone. Yet it does not say much for the efficiency [1749] of the Yankee blockade, even with this novel aid, that since, 4 vessels from foreign ports, with cargoes, passed the blockade in one week, & three of them in the same day, & reached Charleston safely. One of them came in in open daylight, & under the fire of the blockading ships, without being struck.—Reported that 20 of the light draft vessels of the naval armament lately assembled at Annapolis are in Pamlico Sound—& expected to attack Newbern or Washington, N.C. . . . I will append a report of a *sermon* delivered lately, at the Church of the Puritans, New York, by the Rev. Dr.

[George B.] Cheever—who stands next to the Rev. H[enry] W[ard] Beecher as a ferocious denouncer of negro slavery & of slaveholders.[3] This sermon, regularly delivered on the Sabbath, in a church, & by a professed minister of the gospel of the "meek & lowly Jesus," was applauded [1750] by the audience as if it had been a political meeting. The blood-thirsty Marat continually clamored his demand for the massacre of 300,000 of the people of France, (which he estimated would include all the aristocracy of birth, rank, & wealth,) & which sacrifice he deemed necessary, & certainly to be effective, for the safety, the disenthralment, & the regeneration of the nation. But this clerical & pious modern Marat, Dr. Cheever, demands a far greater sacrifice of blood & of lives, (to say nothing of all other sacrifices to his worshipped Moloch of Anti-Slavery,) than did his great exemplar. In demanding the sentence to death by hanging, of Mason & Slidell, as traitors, (& of course all other "rebels,") & of all slave-holders, the modern Marat would exceed the demands of the older by some millions of lives—& so deprive him of his heretofore peculiar supereminence in thirst for blood, that his great predecessor would appear an angel of mercy compared to the Rev. Dr. Cheever. But though his recommendation of the slaughter of nearly the whole male white population of the "rebel" states (he does not expressly include the women & children—) may not find favor with the ruling powers, & of course *cannot* be approached in practice, because physically impossible—the actual policy of the Lincoln government will probably not be only extended beyond the limits of civilized warfare to what has been already avowed or executed. It has been recommended in northern papers, & will doubtless be attempted should occupancy afford opportunity, that the "levees" or dykes, which shut out the floods of the lower Mississippi, shall be broken, & millions of acres of the most fertile lands in the world, & all its crops, be so overflowed. . . .

Jan. 13. The mail. The great naval armament of light-draft armed vessels assembled at Annapolis, has moved—mostly to Hampton

---

[3] A militant reformer and antislavery zealot, George Barrell Cheever (1807–90) was pastor of the Church of the Puritans from 1846 to 1867. In the sermon to which the diarist alludes, Cheever attributed the late crisis with England to the failure of the Lincoln administration to repudiate slavery and called on the President to issue a proclamation of general emancipation. He also advocated the extermination of southern slaveholders in general, and Mason and Slidell in particular.

Roads, where some 4 to 6000 land troops were disembarked at Fortress Monroe. 35 of the vessels were there. It is not known where the fleet is destined. It is rumored to be the Rappahannock—another report is that it has gone to sea & southward—& it is not yet confirmed whether the advance squadron, as before reported, actually was in Pamlico Sound.[4] Besides of this strong armament, important military operations seem impending in South-western Ky. & on the upper Potomac. Gen. Jackson's army is in motion. . . . It is supposed that he has marched to attack the Yankee army at Romney.—The N.Y. & northern banks have *formally* suspended specie payments, as was done in effect some time back. Exchange in N.Y. on England has risen to 115, which must cause gold to be exported. The banks of the north have refused to receive the U.S. treasury notes—& the banks & capitalists have also refused to lend more money to the government. . . . Schemes are before Congress to issue treasury notes (irredeemable for many years, & yet to be made a legal tender,) & to impose direct taxes, to supply the defect of loans. I must think that this [1753] failure of all credit in the money market, & the manifest inefficacy of forced paper issues & direct taxes to supply the deficiency of 400 millions, is the beginning of the certain end of the discomfiture of the North. The raising even 100 millions by direct taxes would be impossible—& the very attempt w[oul]d produce wide-spread disaffection, if not physical resistance, through all the northern states. To attempt to force into circulation 300 to 500 millions in Treasury Notes, made a legal tender, & already at 4 percent discount, will be to repeat the incidents of the issue of the American "continental currency," & of the *"assignats* of the French revolution. Since the people of the North became demented, & permitted the rule of the existing despotism, I have not doubted that they would urge on the war with tremendous power, & to the incalculable damage of the South. But I did not deem the final success of the North in the least probable, even if the heretofore enormous means could continue. If every seceded state were overrun, & occupied by the Yankee

---

[4] This naval expedition, carrying some 15,000 troops under the command of General Ambrose E. Burnside, departed Hampton Roads on January 11 and arrived at Hatteras Inlet, North Carolina, two days later. A lack of shallow-draft vessels precluded an immediate landing. and not until February 7 did Burnside begin to land his troops on Roanoke Island. The badly outnumbered Confederate defenders surrendered the following day, thus giving the Federals control of Pamlico Sound as well as an important base for operations against eastern North Carolina.

troops, as Maryland is, it would require at least half a million of soldiers to garrison their conquests, & the expense alone would render the permanent occupation impossible. But I looked to the certain failure of the borrowing-credit & money resources of the Northern government as indicating the limit of their ability to carry on this iniquitous war of aggression & invasion. And though the first indications of the actual failure are but just announced, I am confident that the worst consequences must rapidly follow. . . .

Jan. 14. This morning we all were equally surprised & pleased to find that my grandson Thomas Ruffin had arrived, late in the last night, from his camp, on a furlough for 7 days. He brought the welcome news that his father will come home, on furlough, in 8 days. I had intended to go to resume my sojourn in Richmond tomorrow—but now will wait for Edmund's arrival, & part of his stay at home.—Snow or fine hail last night, & at intervals today. Cloudy & gloomy. Finished "The Abbot," & some omitted chapters in the "Fifty Years &c." of Vincent Nolte.[5] Began "Old Mortality." . . .

Jan. 15. The third great naval expedition (under Gen. Burnside,) which had assembled at Annapolis, has sailed in two divisions by Hampton Roads, & thence the first part to sea on the 12th. On the 13th. there was a heavy storm on our coast, & still violent wind, with snow & sleet the following day—giving ground for hope that the fleet, mostly of small armed steamers, may have suffered much damage. The second division was in Hampton Roads on 13th. . . . For some time back there have been intimations in northern papers, & more plainly now . . . that one general grand & simultaneous assault was to be made by all the enemy's armaments, from the Potomac to Missouri & Kansas, & perhaps also along all our coast occupied or threatened by their fleets. If such was the design, I do not think it would be so notified to us by northern papers. And I wish that such is the design, & that it will be attempted. For the more extensive that may be such a combination of great military movements of aggression, the more apt will be failures of some, if not all, in making the time for each movement to depend on the beginning of others. They have already found it sufficiently

[5] Born in Italy of German parentage, Vincent Nolte (1779–1853?) was a merchant and traveler whose book, *Fifty Years in Both Hemispheres*, later inspired Hervey Allen to write the best-selling historical novel, *Anthony Adverse*. *The Abbot* is another of Scott's romances.

difficult to move one great army into action —& impossible, so far, with [1756] success. But to move at the same time to the attack, 5 or 6 great & separated armies, (let alone the coast invading armies,) will be so far beyond the ability of Gen. McClellan & his subordinate commanders, that I cannot believe they will make so gigantic an effort. . . . Some freedom, or greater licence of speech, is beginning to be shown in the rump congress, despite of the oppressive tyranny of the administration or executive branch. There are indications of three parties being already in action.— The fanatical abolition [1757] party contends for making *general emancipation* of slaves the avowed object & policy of the war. The larger number disclaim & profess to oppose this (open & avowed) policy, & set forth *union* as their sole object, and for which they as zealously support & urge on the war. These two new parties embrace all of the old abolitionists, & the greater number of their former opposers, the democrats. The third & much the smallest *peace* party, (represented in the congress now by less than 20 votes,) is composed wholly of the few former democrats who have not, by corruption or fear, gone over to the support of Lincoln, or of abolition. I have no question that the peace party throughout the northern states is much more numerous than it now dares to show. Disheartening defeats or perils to the North will soon serve to display this now concealed strength of political opponents in their own ranks.

Jan. 16. A clear, bright, & mild morning, but the earth very sloppy with melting snow. Rode to Ruthven, to stay some days.

Jan. 17. Last night, about 7 P.M., several of the household heard the firing of cannon, from the direction of Richmond—of which the unusual time excited some interest.—Finished reading "Old Mortality," for not less than the fourth time. This, in my opinion, is the most admirable of all Scott's romances.—The mail. Nothing about the supposed firing of cannon last night—so it could not have been heard. . . . Cameron, U.S. Secretary of War, has resigned. I am very sorry for it. He is a fanatical abolitionist, & supported the extreme policy of that party. Such measures to be used by the Yankee government I deem best for our defence & suc[c]ess. . . . [1759]

Jan. 18. . . . Began the "Black Dwarf." Having accidentally dipped into one of Scott's romances, I was induced to continue by the unexpected interest, & to resort to others—so that if my stay here &

at Beechwood was made long enough, it is probable that I would go through the whole number, as the most interesting reading. I had before read the poorest of these works at least once, most of them at least twice, & the best three or four times.—My ordinary almost sole amusements of reading & conversation have been varied in the latter few days, & very agreeably, by my resorting to knitting gloves, with one barbed needle, which I had practised in my boyhood, & never since. Indeed, the art, then common among boys, has since been disused & is known of by very few persons. I had resumed it to instruct Julian, & it was also taken up by Lotty, [&] her two older children, as well as myself. . . . This kind of knitting is pleasant employment, & if I could obtain suitable yarn, I would use it to kill some of my wearisome hours, besides the present job on hand. [1760]

Jan. 19. Sunday. At Church. Thence went to Beechwood. At night, came from Tarbay Thomas Cocke & Miss Miller, the new teacher of Mrs. Cocke's daughters. She is a very pretty & sweet looking young girl, but is so silent that none here have yet found out any other attractions. . . . Finished the "Black Dwarf."

Jan. 20. John Tyler is dead. He died in Richmond on the 17th., full of years & of honors—& to the last fortunate in dying after a few days' illness.—The 3rd Yankee armada (or a portion of it,) has been seen at Hatteras, 45 vessels, &, later, a part of them had entered Pamlico Sound. Their direction was not known (& was subject to wide guesses,) until the fleet sailed southward out of the capes of Va.—& even then its particular destination was unknown. Now there can be little doubt of its being the towns on the N.C. Sounds. . . . The occupation of Romney by our troops confirmed, & the previous retreat of the enemy being so hasty as to leave a great quantity of stores &c. The latter admitted, to some extent, by Yankee reports. The counties of Berkley, Morgan & Hampshire now cleared of the enemy. . . .

Jan. 22. . . . Edmund & his wife expected at home this forenoon. A letter from him to the purport that he will not be able to come until some time [1762] in next week, & then uncertain. I had delayed my departure for a week to await his return today. As he has not come, I will leave tomorrow. . . . 125 vessels of the Burnside fleet reported to have reached Hatteras Inlet, & 100 of them inside of the Sound. One or more speedy attacks expected from this numerous flotilla of light-draft steamers (mostly,) & sailing vessels . . . on Newbern &

other towns on Pamlico & Albemarle Sounds. Nothing yet known to us of any losses of the Armada in the storm which lasted for 48 hours while it was between Cape Henry & Hatteras Inlet. . . . Price of salt in Petersburg, $36 the sack, of 4 bushels. I have seen the price by the single bushel elsewhere stated at $12. At Charleston, the cargo of the Ella Warley (which ran the blockade) was sold at auction & by wholesale. Among the numerous articles (selected abroad to suit the market,) Rio coffee (the most inferior kind of coffee,) sold at 57 to 63 cent the pound; Tallow candles, 18 to 30 cents the lb.; Whale oil, $3.60 the gallon; Sole leather, 85 cents the lb. These are among the highest priced articles. But all that we have to buy from merchants, or which are not produced at home for sale, are at greatly enhanced prices. [1764] But ours are not the only blockaded ports. The closing of the lower Mississippi river is a closing of the main & only cheap outlet for exports to all the Northern States on the upper Mississippi & Missouri rivers, & to great extent also to the states on the Ohio. The only markets now left for all these fertile north-western states are the northern Atlantic States—& the only routes to them are by railroads which are very costly for bulky & distant transportation, or the circuitous routes by the lakes, as costly, & also stopped by ice for 5 months of the year. The articles of import to these northwestern states are brought to them more cheaply than to us (by running the blockade,) & are of cheaper transportation in proportion to their light weight. Still, they must be enhanced—if only because, as with us, the railroads cannot convey the greatly increased freights offered. But . . . our blockade of [the] Mississippi is much more distressing to the Yankee states above, in preventing nearly all export of heavy agricultural products, which cannot pay rail-road charges, & for which, besides, there is no sufficient demand in the eastern Yankee states. Their great & natural market, on the lower Mississippi, is entirely cut off. Consequently, the only products of these north-western states, being agricultural, have neither available transportation nor markets—& are at prices too low to reimburse the actual expenses of culture or production. Thus, the Yankees' blockading our sea-ports, or otherwise keeping at war with us, serves as effectually to blockade all their territory on the upper waters of the Mississippi, & at least as much to distress the inhabitants. This is an important view of the war question which is considered [1765] but by few persons. There are now 8 western Yankee states thus held blockaded, &

some 3 or 4 territories. And this disadvantage to the northern power, in all times of war with the South, & our power of causing damage, & of control, will increase with the future growth & increase of production of the north-western states. . . .

John Tyler died, at the ripe age of 72, in Richmond, after but a few days of sickness. His accustomed good fortune attended him to the last, in the time, manner, & place of his death. His latest public duties were those of a member of the Confederate Congress. That body being in session, as well as the Va. legislature, enabled & induced more evidences of honor & veneration for the dead, than had ever been given to any preceding statesman or patriot, on the like occasions of death & funeral ceremonies. The Governor of the State announced the death of John Tyler, in a special & appropriate message, to the legislature. In both the Senate & House of Delegates suitable resolutions of sorrow & eulogy were passed. And in both bodies, & in the Confederate Congress, some of the most prominent members, of all former parties & of different present opinions, delivered speeches of highest praise and honor of the deceased. Among these voluntary eulogists, the old Jackson & "hunker" ("whole-hog") or thoroughgoing spoils democratic party was especially represented by James Barbour, an able, crafty, & selfish politician; the as thorough whig, & as dishonestly faithful to all the baseness of that party, by W. H. Macfarland; the old states-rights or Calhoun [1764][6] division of the democratic party, in R.M.T. Hunter; the old nullifiers of S.C. & the early disunionists, in R. B. Rhett; the true, patriotic, & disinterested few, who scorned party shackles & party names, in Willoughby Newton—& even the recent (if not still at heart) thorough submissionists to the North, in Wm. C. Rives. Yet there was not one of all these now eulogists, who at some former times had not strongly opposed & denounced the then political course of Tyler, &, with some of them, to the extreme limit of political enmity & hatred. In addition, the funeral obsequies were attended, with every mark of respect by the two legislative bodies, & all officers of both the confederate & state governments, to the city Cemetary [*sic*], where the body was interred near to that of President Monroe, & over which a tomb is to be erected by order of the legislature, by the State of Virginia.

---

[6] Misnumbered by the diarist. Should be page 1766.

Of all politicians who have reached high positions, John Tyler, as a public man, was the most fortunate. From the age of barely 21, he was continually in successive public stations, & always rising with every change, until the career apparently closed with his service as President of the United States. Before his being elected Vice-President, by the Whig Party, he, in siding against its leaders & policy, had forfeited all his former popularity with the Jackson or democratic party, & indeed had acquired its especial strong dislike. When the accident of President Harrison's death raised Tyler to the Presidency, he soon lost the support of the great body of the Whig party, by his refusing to carry out the policy of its leaders, at the sacrifice of his own former states-rights & old republican creed & principles. And by failing to maintain their principles to the letter, he had failed to secure or retain the support of the purists of the states-rights school, who [1765] even though acting with either the democratic or Whig party, as either was deemed to be nearest right for the time, held both these great parties & their leaders in impartial dislike & contempt. Tyler served his term as president, not only without the support of any party, but with all parties in strong opposition to him. . . . The President had in Congress scarcely a dozen supporters, advocates or apologists, (called, in derision, the "Corporal's guard,") & these were supposed to be mercenaries, bought over by the hope of pay. Tyler's highest official position was thus made the most difficult, & even humiliating. Yet considering his great difficulties, his administration was most useful & fortunate for his country's political interests, & it should be deemed (in all higher matters,) most honorable & glorious to himself. Though long before well acquainted with Mr. Tyler, & always on good outward terms of amity, I had never thought highly of him, & even disliked him as a public man for those very manners & qualities by which he sought & gained general popularity. In his extremely embarrassing position, & early great difficulties as President, I was induced by our political views & objects to draw towards his support, to try to influence him to sustain his old & good principles. I learned to think better of him in his conduct in his highest & most responsible office than [1766] I had as to any of his previous inferior positions. When he had served his term as President, he retired (for the first time,) to private life. Wonderful as had been his previous ability, or lucky success, in acquiring popularity, all that he had possessed seemed then gone forever. He had left no partisans & but few apologists—& there was scarcely left to him the semblance of respect from any portion of the public—or even of his near neighbors & former intimate private friends. No doubt he suffered most severely under this infliction—more severe to him than to almost any other man, because he had lived for & upon popularity. No doubt he eagerly & unceasingly desired to recover his lost ground. But, with admirable tact & discretion, he kept all such feelings to his own thoughts. He exhibited to others neither resentment, discontent, complaint or even consciousness of being treated with neglect, injustice, or ingratitude. How different, & how much worse, would *I* have acted in his then situation! I should have returned these undeserved manifestations of hostility, or of ingratitude, with scorn, contempt, & hatred. I would have so increased & kept alive & increasing, the hostile feelings of all other persons to me—& I should have become a miserable misanthrope, living & dying without a friend. But far wiser, & more politic, was John Tyler. Even with all his large share of self-esteem & vanity, & his very sanguine disposition, he could scarcely then have expected ever to recover popularity, if even to rise to the possession of ordinary respect & kindly consideration. But this did not alter his course. As always, he met all persons with courtesy & kindness of manner. He remained generally at home, or went abroad only when [1767] required by his private business, quietly & with no more pretension than if he had never been more than a plain & unpretending farmer in private life. He thus lived down enmity & dislike. He acted towards his ill-wishers & scarcely-covert enemies as if they were his friends, until he made them so, or at least to appear as such. Still, respect & regard to him as a private man were all that were reached for a long time. The first public attentions again offered to him were by our State Agricultural Society, (& chiefly by my influence,) in several times inviting & more than once inducing him to deliver addresses at the annual meetings. Even then, it required much management to procure these compliments, & also a respectful & favorable attention of the audience. Stranger than all his previous acquiring & long retaining of popularity, & of high political position, when these had been long completely lost, both have been lately recovered. When the late (& deserving to be held infamous) Convention of Va. had at last adopted the ordinance of secession, & finally elected the full delegation to the Confederate Congress, John Tyler was elected one (of the latest chosen) of these representatives. He had before been elected, by the people of his county & electoral district, to a seat in that Convention. Neither of these honors could be deemed very great in themselves, (though they should have been,) because the Convention was mainly constituted of inferior men, or of unsound political principles—& the delegates chosen by that body to the provisional Congress, embraced men of very moderate abilities, & others (as Rives, Macfarland &c.) who were selected because of being submissionists [1768], because the Convention was still of that disposition secretly. But these, or almost any election by the popular vote, or a popular assembly, was [*sic*] most remarkable for one in Mr. Tyler's previous position. Also, he was deputed by the Convention to the "Peace Congress" at Washington, & by that body was elected its President. This honor was induced less by the favor of his few friends in that body, than the servile respect of his Yankee enemies paid to his former rank. Next, & more remarkable than all these, he was nominated to represent his own (the metropolitan) congressional district in the next constitutional congress. In this district, part of which he had represented in the Congress of the U.S. half a century ago, he had been most abhorred, because he had been there previously most favored—& more generally & strongly had he been hated in the city of Richmond, the "Gibraltar of Whiggery." Yet against very influential opposing candidates, Mr. Tyler was elected, & by a greater vote than that of all the opposing candidates put together, not only in the whole district, but also in the City of Richmond. Within a few months after receiving the last of these honors, he died in the public service. His best friends ought not to wish that his life should have been protracted.—It may seem hereafter, when time shall have made John Tyler's measure of ability more correctly known than now, unaccountable & wonderful that a man so moderately endowed in natural power of intellect, & still less by study, should have acquired such high & many political distinctions—& still more, after the most complete prostration of his popularity, he should have recovered it to great extent—& really have attained a higher place in the public estimation than he held at any previous time. These results were owing to the combination of a virtue & a vice, which worked together admirably for the attainment of the one great object, [1769] popular favor. John Tyler was in natural disposition most kindly & amiable. If there was a place in his heart for hatred or malice, or even strong resentment or ill-will towards the worst of his numerous enemies & maligners, there was no such expression from his lips. . . . Few men have lived who have had reason to resent the hostile conduct or expressions of as many others. Yet I have rarely heard from Mr. Tyler, freely & unguardedly as he seemed to speak, unkind or hostile expressions of any persons. All this procedure was owing to his truly amiable & benevolent natural disposition. But added to this, he was by taste & education a thorough electioneer, or seeker of popularity at all times, & of all persons. This he pursued as the means for gratifying his insatiable ambition. Under both his virtuous & vicious influences, he acted so as to conciliate enemies [1770] & to secure friends everywhere. And most signal was his success.

Jan. 23. I had intended to go to Richmond today. But the sky was lowering, & threatening rain, the wind high, & the boat leaky, & as the steamer for today does not stop except at a wharf, I should have been obliged to cross the river to Berkley wharf, & then probably wait 2 hours or more for the very irregular passing of the steamer. So I gave up my departure—for better weather, if not now to wait for Edmund's coming home.—Walked to Ruthven. Afternoon, snow & rain at intervals. At night, wind still increased, & from northeast—giving ground for hope that the enemy's armada, even though within the sand reef at Hatteras, may suffer severely.— Reading Rob Roy.

Jan. 24. The wind continued as strong & still from north-east through the night, & unabated to 2 P.M. There must be a terrific storm on the sea-coast, & the tide raised so high that the former disasters of the Yankee garrisons of the earth-works at Hatteras must be repeated, & made still worse by the cold weather. May the worst of possible disasters befall the vile invaders & their vessels along all our coast! The violence & direction of the wind continued until after dark, accompanied by very light drizzle. Wind moderated before 8 P.M.—The mail brought very bad news—of the worst defeat our arms have suffered during the war. Reports, (though none of official character,) have been received from both sides—& strange, & altogether opposed to all past experience, the reports from the enemy's side state our losses to be less than do our own accounts. It seems that Major Gen. G[eorge B.] Crittenden, by his higher rank, had superseded Gen. Zollicoffer in command of the army in Ky, which had gradually advanced from E. Tennessee to

[221]

Somerset, [1771] near which the army was intrenched. Gen. Crittenden, with 8 regiments, & 6 pieces of artillery, leaving his fortified camp, advanced some 10 or 12 miles & attacked the enemy's force (under Gen[eral]s [George H.] Thomas & [Albin F.] Schoepff [*sic*],) in their strong intrenchments. There was heavy losses on both sides, as admitted by both reports. Gen. Zollicoffer, (then second in command,) was killed—when, our troops lost confidence, & retreated in haste & disorder, pursued by the enemy. 275 of our men, as reported by the northern account, killed & wounded, were left on the field of battle—or 500, as our own reports state. Probably the missing were included in the latter estimate.[7] Our flying army left & lost all their artillery, stores, baggage &c., & crossed the Cumberland river, which was not far off, in progress towards Tennessee. No other particulars known. Major Gen. Crittenden was one of the sundry officers of high rank taken from civil life, & without military experience, as has been done so inexcusably, & in many cases by Pres. Davis. In addition, as I heard in Richmond when Gen. C. was there, he is a drunkard. If the truth shall ever be known, I infer it will appear that his ignorance, & his being drunk at the time, caused this great disaster, & the panic of the army under his unworthy command, & which previously had been led on with success & honor by Gen. Zollicoffer.[8] It is to me a sorrowful & disheartening reflection, that so many of these inexperienced & incompetent commanders, who, at most, had but a West Point education in their boyhood, are now entrusted with the command of our troops, & the honor & safety of our cause. In the now very important commands about the N.Ca. coast, the three generals in different commands [1772], Jos. R. Anderson, [Henry A.] Wise, & [Lawrence O.] Branch were all appointed from civil life, were all without military experience or knowledge,

---

[7] This supposition was correct. Confederate losses in the engagement, usually known as the battle of Logan's Cross Roads or Mill Springs, totaled 533, of which 99 were listed as missing. Federal casualties were about half that number. This defeat, suffered on January 19, was the first in a series of military disasters which would befall the Confederates in the Tennessee-Kentucky area during the spring of 1862.

[8] The diarist was not alone in his condemnation of Crittenden. The latter was arrested and censured following the debacle at Logan's Cross Roads, and in October, 1862, he resigned his commission. It is not true, however, that the Kentuckian lacked military experience. A graduate of West Point, he was a veteran of both the Black Hawk and Mexican wars and had served continuously in the regular army from 1846 to June, 1861. He was the son of John J. Crittenden, the distinguished former senator from Kentucky, and his brother, Thomas L. Crittenden, was a Union general.

& the latter two without even military education.—It is strange that nothing certain has yet been heard of the enemy's fleet of 100 or 125 vessels reported before to be at Hatteras inlet, & mostly in Pamlico Sound. . . . Great anxiety is felt for information of its true position, & the effects of the two storms. . . . The election of C.S. Senators for Va. resulted in the choice of R. M. T. Hunter & Wm. B. Preston. I am rejoiced that Wm. C. Rives judged so badly of his chances as to be one of the candidates, & that he was able to command but 23 votes in both the Senate & House of Delegates. . . .

Jan. 25. . . . Finished "Rob Roy." Looking over C[harles] Campbell's "History of Virginia." Began to read (3rd time) "Anne of Gei[e]rstein."⁹

Jan. 27. Finished "Anne of Gei[e]rstein."—The mail. . . . This is [1775] the fifteenth day since the whole of the third Yankee armada (Burnside's expedition) sailed out of the capes of Va. southward—& nothing (true) has yet been heard of a single vessel. In the two storms which have since occurred, & the last a very severe & prolonged one, these numerous small, mostly frail, & heavily laden steamers & transports, must have suffered heavily, & could scarcely have avoided many shipwrecks. But if so, it is very strange that no wrecks have been thrown ashore. (One such only is reported.) The fleet must have taken a course far from the coast, & for a far southern destination—I suppose the Mississippi river.—But if so, it is nearly as strange that nothing has been heard of the fleet & its safety, by vessels meeting it, & bound to northern ports. The longer that it will be before any account of the situation is heard, the more ground there will be to infer great disaster & loss. May it be equalled in proportion only by the loss of Pharaoh's host in the Red Sea! . . .

Jan. 29. The mail. Letter from Edmund stating that his return home is still delayed to next Friday (31st) or Saturday.—Sundry reports of important matters but nothing certain. It is again stated, & apparently on good testimony, of eye-witnesses, that the Yankee fleet was at Hatteras just before the last storm—but strange to say, nothing positive has been heard of it since, (in 7 days,) & it is again doubted, & disbelieved by some, whether the fleet was there, or had been there. . . .

Jan. 31. The Yankee fleet *is* in Pamlico Sound, & at Hatteras.

---

⁹ Published in 1829, this is another novel by Sir Walter Scott.

Though that fact has been asserted several times, & truly, as it now appears, it was contradicted by what seemed more trustworthy evidence, & disbelieved. What is even more strange than that long continued uncertainty, is that the fleet had actually arrived at Hatteras Inlet before the greatest violence of the first of the two storms. What we now learn, & rely upon for general facts, is derived from northern reports. These admit (in general terms) great losses of their fleet by the storms. . . . 8 of the residents of Portsmouth (near Ocracoke) had been seized by order of the Yankee commander to serve as pilots in the Sounds. But they refused to act, even when threatened with death, & finally were discharged. This speaks better for the southern feeling & loyalty of this portion of the "bankers" at Ocracoke than could have been expected from the previous conduct of those near Hatteras. But even at Hatteras, the union sentiment is reported by the Yankees to be very feeble. The want of native & good pilots is stated to be a serious difficulty to their progress. If this deficiency shall continue, there will be many more of their vessels lost on the shoals of the Sounds, among which the navigation is extremely difficult, & impossible except with good pilotage. . . . There must be important military events in Ky. very soon, & probably [1781] some have occurred already. Gen. Beauregard has been withdrawn from his command in the Potomac army to act as second in command to Gen. A. S. Johnston in Ky. It seems that the grand combined plan of operations of the whole Yankee armies & fleets is being attempted in Ky—& probably the fleet at Hatteras being shattered by the storms prevented the attempts being extended, as was doubtless designed, to the interior of N.C., if not also in Va, on Norfolk, & elsewhere. The northern papers, deeming that no harm to their cause can now be done by such publications, have stated the intentions of their forces reaching Weldon, by the Roanoke & otherwise, seizing the connections of all the N.C. rail-roads, & so cutting off the supplies for Richmond & the Potomac army. But though they may have 100 armed vessels (mostly steamers) in Pamlico, & may send there as many more, I have but little doubt of their meeting results more disastrous than triumphant. Two weeks have already been spent, unopposed & almost unseen by any Confederates, [&] have served merely to get their fleet inside of the Hatteras Inlet, without attempting any farther advance. . . .

What the great Burnside armada may hereafter effect remains to be seen. But so far, including its 12 or 13 days of unknown presence & inactive hostility, all of these great & enormously expensive expeditions have been of the least possible efficiency or benefit to the enemy. The first one, under Butler, captured the sand forts at Hatteras—& excepting (long after) to visit & ostensibly occupy Beacon Island & Portsmouth, neighboring parts of the undefended sand reef, that great armament has made no advance in N.C., & gained not the slightest additional advantage. The fleet & army [1783] (whether part of the same, or another expedition,) also under Butler, has since occupied Ship Island [Mississippi] & Biloxi, but has done nothing else, & attempted nothing on the Gulf of Mexico. The second great armada captured our forts at & opposite Hilton Head . . . & since, that strong force, naval & military, has done nothing in all the neighboring parts of S.C. . . . The third great armada, with its (reported) 100 to 175 armed vessels, & 20,000 or more land troops, have a magnificent part to play, as set forth by the northern papers. But I feel confident that its future operations will also be failures. In addition to these later demonstrations, there have been the grand army at & near Washington, of 200,000 men kept idle, & besieged, by our much weaker opposed army of the Potomac. The great armaments at St. Louis & Cairo, & the numerous army in Ky near Green river & the Louisville railroad, all have remained inactive for months. It is true that we have suffered, by these sundry armies & fleets, all the expenses of the armaments called or kept in service to oppose them—& also the destruction of cotton in S.C. & of other property there & elsewhere, because of the expected or actual inroads of the enemy's forces. But all these expenses & losses, great as they are, must fall far short of the unremunerated losses of the enemy. Our opposing armies also have been as [1784] inactive as the invaders. But we were generally the weaker, & everywhere on the defensive, & necessarily waiting for the enemy to attack.[10]

February 1. Rain last night & to noon today. Though through very bad weather for setting out, Edmund came home on furlough, bringing Jane. All found great joy in the family reunion. . . .

---

[10] President Lincoln was also struck by the prolonged inactivity of the Union armies. Accordingly, four days before this journal entry, he had promulgated General War Order No. 1, which prescribed a general advance by Federal land and naval forces no later than February 22, 1862. The order was heeded in the West, but not until mid-March did General McClellan begin moving his huge army to the peninsula between the York and James rivers for his ill-fated campaign against Richmond.

Feb. 3. Snowing fast the early part of the day. . . . The mail. No full account yet of the losses of the Yankee armada—though doleful general statements of miscarriage, disaster & disappointment of aims in the northern papers. Some 6 or 8 vessels only named as being certainly wrecked. These reports state that much the greater number of the vessels had been aground portions of the time since their arriving at Hatteras Inlet, or after having got through into the sound—that pilots could not be induced to serve—& no water could be found deeper than for 7¼ feet draft of vessels, instead of 8½ reported & counted upon. The vessels that could pass over clear, had made no advance—& reinforcements were required to enable this numerous fleet & strong army to advance, & effect any of the objects. . . . A late arrival from England, which left after the surrender of Mason & Slidell had been announced, brings strong indications of an early recognition of the Confederate States by England, &, as there supposed, by France also. The London "Herald," the organ of the opposition or Tory party, most strenuously urges this recognition, & advocates the cause of the C.S. against the North.

Feb. 4. . . . Left for Richmond before 12, crossing the river to Berkley to go on board the steamer. Reached Richmond by sunset. Left my carpet-bag at my room, & ordered it to be prepared for my lodging, & went to A. M. Dupuy's. . . . Left early to go to the Exchange Hotel to see friends. Met with but few acquaintances, because the legislature was holding a night session. . . .

Feb. 5. The rump government has made another back-down, in arriving at & announcing the determination to treat our captured privateersmen as other prisoners of war, instead of hanging them as pirates, as had been positively declared. I was sure from the beginning that they would not [1786] dare to carry that threat into execution, for fear of the certain retaliation. . . . Gave to the State Ordnance Department, for public use, a large rifle sent by my son Edmund, & from me, the U.S. musket which I brought from Manassas—one of those thrown away on the field of battle by the fleeing Yankees. . . . Afternoon, visited at their rooms Newton & Tate, & saw Th. Preston & other friends at the Exchange. At night, went to see & hear the musical performance of that natural prodigy, the blind negro boy Tom.[11] This is the second week of his nightly

---

[11] Born to slave parents in Georgia about 1849, Thomas Greene Bethune, better known as Blind Tom, began giving concerts and musical exhibitions about 1860.

public performances, & his second visit in this city—& yet the African Church, the largest room in Richmond, was crowded. I will say no more now, as I design to call on his master tomorrow, & learn more of Tom in private. Returned to my room at 9.30, & read "Essays of Elia" (resumed) until sleepy.

Feb. 6. A steady slow rain through the forenoon. This will prolong the wet & miry condition of the earth, & prevent the threatened aggressive land operations of the enemy. Other demonstrations have been made by their water expeditions, conveying land forces, on the Tennessee river. Some gunboats had fired on our Fort Henry, 90 miles up that river from its mouth, & a short distance below the rail-road from Paris [1787] to the river, & bridge across. That portion of the Memphis & Ohio R.R. only was not finished in 1860, & I do not know whether it is completed now. In conjunction with this slight (& harmless) cannonade of the fort, land troops were disembarked two miles below. It is understood that our means for defence thereabout are good.[12] . . . This forenoon, I went to the room of Mr. Oliver, the master of Blind Tom, to see the latter in private, & to make inquiries. I endeavored to draw Tom into such conversation as he is capable of, but to little purpose. He seems to be an idiot, of unusually low order of intellect even for an idiot. When I went in, Mr. Oliver was assorting a great number of bank notes on a small table, aided by his negro man servant, who was the only person present besides. Tom was sitting by, & as long as I saw him, when not spoken to or answering, was always making contortions of his features & ridiculous grimaces & motions of his hands or body. Afterwards, while I was talking about him with his master, (to which he seemed to give not the least [1788] attention,) he arose, & amused himself, as a confined monkey would, by walking about in the very contracted vacant space of the room, & throwing his limbs & body into fantastic attitudes. These tricks, & also his apparent stupidity, may possibly be affected, & taught him, to make his performances more wonderful. I might even doubt whether he was entirely blind, if judging only from what I myself witnessed. But it is impossible, if any such arts of deception had been prac-

---

Although blind and idiotic from birth, he displayed extraordinary talent in playing and improvising on the piano.

[12] Unknown to the diarist, Brigadier General Lloyd Tilghman had surrendered Fort Henry to a Union naval force commanded by Flag Officer Andrew Foote shortly before 2 P.M. on this date.

tised, for years of his travelling & exhibiting, but it would have been discovered. Besides, Mr. Oliver is said to be a respectable planter of Ga, & his condition, & also Tom's, at home, before the public exhibitions were begun, must have prevented such deception afterwards, without its being exposed. There is however one & a very useless deception attempted in the bills. The age of Tom is stated to be 11 years. He is evidently 14 or perhaps 15, & his voice indicates that he has reached the period of puberty. He has true & even exaggerated features of the negro type—& his profile is almost as much like pictures I have seen of the Ourang Otang [*sic*]. During his musical performances, his mouth is generally open, & the expression of his countenance stupid. As to his execution, my imperfection of hearing, & the worse impairing of my sense of musical sounds, in both tone & tune, prevented my fully appreciating & enjoying his playing as *music*. . . . I sat very near, & saw well, & heard as plainly as my infirmity permitted. I could not detect any error of execution in Tom's playing elaborate & very difficult operatic & other long pieces—some of which were from the operas of Cinderilla [*sic*], Norma & Lucretia. Some few of the shorter pieces (including one from Norma,) I have long known, & could not detect a mistake in them. He played "Home, Sweet Home," as arranged by Thalberg, with extremely complicated & difficult variations, & with perfect success, so far as I could judge. It was affirmed, & any persons from the audience invited to come to the instrument as performers & afford the proof, (which however none complied with—) that if any good performer would play the *Primo* of any piece, either before unknown to Tom, or even then improvised, that he would accompany it correctly playing *Secondo*—& then, changing seats, would play correctly the Primo that he had then heard but once & for the first time. But, as no one offered for the purpose, no proof of this marvel was afforded—nor of the lesser, that he could repeat correctly any piece of music, (not very long) that he had heard but once. There were some other very wonderful performances, but which I thought less of, as they were merely tricks of dexterity or skill, in performance, but not producing anything admirable as music. Such were his playing a rapid tune with his back to the piano & his hands behind him, & of course his left hand to the treble, & the right to the bass: playing (in usual position) one air (Fisher's Hornpipe) with his right hand, another (Yankee Doodle) with his left, & singing a third (Dixie) all at the [1790] same time, neither tune having any accordance of conformity with either of the others. I omitted another & much higher kind of musical talent, his composing. Several of his compositions have been published. I have heard only one of them, which I deemed a pretty fair composition, or of middling merit. Mr. Oliver gave me copies of several [of] these printed compositions, as well as accompanying engraved portraits of the inspired musician. That term is not misapplied. For the marvellous talent for music possessed by this boy, idiotic, & also blind from his birth, must be the gift of a new sense, or supernatural increase of the ordinary sense of hearing & remembering musical sounds.—Went to the hall of Congress a short time before the session, & saw & conversed with several of my acquaintance who are members, especially Rhett, [Robert W.] Barnwell,[13] [James A.] Seddon. Rhett speaks in strong terms of condemnation of the dilatory & otherwise improper conduct of the President &c. in carrying on the war, & general administration. There is no doubt sufficient grounds for such censures; but their sharpness is added to by Rhett's feelings of neglect & disappointed ambition. He, & many others of the earliest & staunchest movers of secession, & defenders of southern rights & interests, now that the great measure has been brought about, have to experience that the conduct of affairs, & the honors & rewards of office, are withheld from the men of their class, service & merit, & are given to "eleventh hour laborers," & in numerous cases to those who were submissionists to the last moment of free choice.—Afternoon called on & conversed with Newton & Seddon at their rooms, as well as saw other friends in the public rooms of the hotel. . . .

Feb. 7. The Burnside fleet has been again heard of, & in motion. A number of the vessels, reported as 50 or more, were seen going on towards Roanoke Island, & as supposed, to attack our fortification & forces there, which, until reduced, will command the passage from Pamlico & Albemarle Sound.—The correspondents of the northern papers, who are Yankees & Lincolnites residing in Europe, all concur in the opinion that England & France are about to recognize

---

[13] A graduate of Harvard and former president of South Carolina College, Robert Woodward Barnwell (1801–82) had a long and distinguished political career. He was a member of the United States House of Representatives from 1829 to 1833, served briefly in the United States Senate in 1850, and at this time was a representative from South Carolina in the Provisional Congress of the Confederacy. From 1862 to 1865 he was a member of the Confederate States Senate.

the nationality & independence of the C.S.—& that the Emperor of France is especially anxious for the measure. As all these writers, & the papers for which they write, are as much northern & abolitionist as can be, & of course very reluctant to come to such conclusions, their opinions on this point must be reliable. . . . The mail brought newspaper reports that a large land force had landed some miles below Fort Henry, [1792] on Tennessee river. Later, a telegraphic despatch came from Nashville stating that the fort had been attacked by an overwhelming force, & after two hours fighting, our troops had evacuated the fort, & were retreating to Fort Donelson on the Cumberland river, (13 to 16 miles distant). The enemy had burnt the rail-road bridge, which, as well as the passage of the river Fort Henry had commanded. No further particulars. It is a great disaster. In this part of the great general plan of offensive operations, the enemy has been eminently successful. This success gives them the free passage of the Tennessee above, until other means of repression are established—& cuts off our use of the railroad (which before *was* completed,) from Memphis to Bowling Green.—In Congress Hall before the session began—when, as always, the session is secret. Afternoon, visited the hall of the Exchange, but heard nothing more—& called to see Mr. Owens of Fl. & [William W.] Boyce of S.C. (members of Congress,) at their lodgings. At my room at 7 P.M. . . .

Feb. 8. Heard that Gen. Jeff. Thompson, the famous guerrilla leader,[14] was in town, & called on him at the Spottswood House. Though I did not know that I had ever seen him before, he recognized me as a former acquaintance. I was surprised to find him so young looking a man. He does not appear more than 30. . . . Afternoon, Wm. H. Harrison, of Amelia, called on me, & we were together [1793] for an hour, as long as his hurried time permitted. When we walked down town together, we found a telegraphic despatch posted, to the purport that the enemy's fleet, to the number of 54 vessels, had attacked our earth-works on Roanoke Island yesterday evening, doing no harm except burning, by the

---

[14] Mayor of St. Joseph, Missouri, before the war, Thompson organized a partisan force—soon to be known as Thompson's Swamp Rats—shortly after the bombardment of Fort Sumter and led a series of raids against Federal forces in Missouri throughout the remainder of the year. In March, 1862, he joined General Earl Van Dorn's command in the Trans-Mississippi Department, and in the fall of 1864 he commanded a brigade in General Sterling Price's ill-fated Missouri expedition.

bomb-shells, some of the houses. The fire had been returned from our guns, & as thought, a vessel was set on fire. Night put a stop to the firing, but it was expected to be renewed this morning. . . . I learned today from Col. Blue, whose houses were burnt & other property wasted at Hanging Rock, in Hampshire, that the enemy had not (as supposed) been driven entirely out of that county by the approach of Jackson—and more lately, they have come back, to three different places, within from 8 to 13 miles of our advanced post at Romney, where they now threaten an attack. . . . Great uneasiness is now felt, (& great hopes formed by the enemy,) on the ground that most of our army is composed of 12 months volunteers, whose terms of service will end in April & May, & who, when discharged, will be replaced by raw recruits, if not drafted militia. The legislature of Va has been debating on the means to meet this danger for our state troops, for some weeks, & to little purpose as yet.—Began to read lately, & finished today, "Cause & Contrast," a new book by [T. W.] McMahon, on the slavery question & the war. Also finished tonight, the "Essays of Elia," with much glancing over & skipping. I do not admire this as much as is done by writers of highest literary ability & taste. It is true that the comic & peculiar manner of the writer is admirable. But the matter of which he treats is often unimportant & trifling, or only of local & temporary interest.

Feb. 9. Sunday. Twice down town to see the people & to hear the news—& neither to much purpose. In the ladies' parlor, at the Exchange, saw Mrs. Gen. Gaines,[15] who received & greeted me with much cordiality. When I saw her formerly at the White Sulphur [1795] Springs, in 1860, I found that her conversation offered too much of a good thing, & indeed, after half an hour, *tete a tete*, I was so tired as to try to avoid her afterwards. But now she is just from Washington, & has much to talk about that is interesting. And as I have nothing to do, & but little to amuse me, I shall call on her specially, to hear more of her conversation.—Most of the day, & at night, reading in my room—Joanna Baillie's "Plays of the Passions," in her collected works.

Feb. 10. The worst disaster of the war! Roanoke Island has been

---

[15] Presumably the widow of Edmund Pendleton Gaines (1777–1849), one of the most noted military figures in the United States during the first half of the nineteenth century. The daughter of New Orleans merchant and territorial delegate Daniel Clark, she was Gaines's third wife, having married him in 1839.

captured, & all our troops, nearly 3000, captured, except 25! This occurred on the 2nd day (8th) after long continued & hard fighting. The enemy had 53 vessels & 15,000 men. Though the telegram states sundry particulars, I will wait for later information before confiding in them. Of the main great fact there is no doubt. Possessed of this island, & having plenty of small armed steamers of shallow draft, the enemy can threaten every town & farm on the two sounds & their many deep & broad rivers, & command them, if not defended by 50,000, even if they cannot ascend the narrow upper waters & reach one or both of the rail-roads. . . . Accidentally met with & was introduced to MacMahon the author, & Alexander Dimitry,[16] a man of high literary attainments, who was lately U.S. Minister to Central America.—The legislature, at last, has passed the military bill. Under the pressing necessity for keeping our already disciplined men & organized corps in the field, the heavy sacrifice of citizens [1796] is required of serving in the army for the war, or for three years—from which the volunteers now serving are not exempt, but only will have credit for their first year of service. If new volunteers do not offer in sufficient numbers to fill the present vacancies in the respective companies, & further to raise each to 100 men, then there will be drafted from the militia now at home, & from the now serving volunteers who shall not re-enlist, as many as will be needed for the purpose.—My account with publisher & bookseller, J. W. Randolph, settled to Dec. 31, 1861. In 3 preceding years there have been sold of my several publications, only as follows: Essay on Calcareous Manures, 20 copies, Essays & Notes on Agriculture, 31—both yielding to me $6.65. Of 4 different pamphlets on Slavery, Af. Colonization &c. at 3½ cents, $37.86: Anticipations of the Future, but little more than 400 copies have been issued in sales & *gifts*, yielding to me as two-thirds owner & publisher, $144.12. The whole after deducting my own purchases ($120.75) from R. in that time, returning to me about $75. [1797]

Feb. 11. The various reports of the disaster at Roanoke Island seem to make reliable the following principal statements: . . . The

---

[16] A native of New Orleans, Dimitry (1805–83) was the first English editor of the New Orleans *Bee* and the first superintendent of education in Louisiana. During the 1850's he worked as a translator with the State Department in Washington and in 1859 was appointed United States minister to Costa Rica and Nicaragua. Resigning his post upon the outbreak of war, he returned to the South and served as assistant postmaster general of the Confederacy throughout the conflict.

fight was obstinately & well contested by our small force of 2100 against 15,000 of the assailants. Finally, our men were over-powered. Only about 50 escaped to the ocean sand reef, & all the others, having no boats, surrendered. . . . Our army earned honor & glory—but every thing else was lost. It seems to me an unpardonable neglect in Gen. [Benjamin] Huger, the commander of the District, at Norfolk, not to have strengthened this post, when the fleet had been weeks in Pamlico, & its destination almost certain. If he had sent half his forces from Norfolk, it would have been perfectly safe, as if Norfolk was to be attacked, it could only be by this army of Burnside's, or by other forces in cooperation with these. Three companies there were from Richmond, which has spread sorrow into numerous families here. Our little flotilla retreated to Elizabeth City, on the Pasquotank. The enemy's vessels pursued. The vessels were abandoned, & (not burnt, as they should have been, but) captured. Elizabeth City, a town of 3000 inhabitants, was burnt, & I suppose with nearly all the wealth it contained, by its inhabitants [1798], or by order of our military commander, to prevent the enemy getting possession, which we had no other means to prevent. . . . Our advanced force has been withdrawn from Romney, & the enemy immediately reoccupied it. While before they were in that county, (Hampshire) the Yankees burnt 85 houses, & besides their other numerous acts of plunder & lesser outrage, rapes were committed on five respectable females. . . .

Feb. 12. . . . More, & contradictory reports of the details of the recent disasters in N.Ca., which need not be noted until the truth can be known.—Gen. Beauregard had reached Columbus [Ky.]. I trust that he will command with ability, & to good effect.—The grand plan of combined operations of the Yankee fleets & armies does indeed seem to be now closing around us, & to powerful effect. I should feel much less uneasiness, indeed scarcely any, if we were but sufficiently supplied with arms & gunpowder. But both are deficient, & made & kept so by the blockade of our sea-ports. Their strong iron-clad steam gunboats are proof against musketry, & nearly so against such few cannon as we can oppose to them from land batteries only—being almost without vessels—& so their light-draft war-steamers can penetrate into our country as far as our long navigable rivers extend—as recently of the Tennessee, & the various tributaries of the sounds of N.C. Even if we had abundance of the best arms & ammunition, it would require a ten-fold more numerous force to defend every endangered & important locality, than that by which the enemy, supplied with every naval requisite, can choose the point for attack, & bring against it an overwhelming superiority of aggressive forces.

Feb. 13. . . . Mr. Th. C. Johnson, a member of the Senate of Mo. (St. Louis,) & now a refugee, introduced himself to me today, (as very many strangers do,) & from him I heard that the President had sent orders by telegraph for 20 regiments, from Texas & Arkansas mostly, to move into Mo. There the gallant Price & Thompson barely maintain their positions, in their far separated camps.—The first reports of the great destruction of life among the Richmond companies at the late fight & defeat have been contradicted, & it is now believed that very few were killed. Though thus the great distress & anxiety of their families is much alleviated, still there is very general panic here, & still more in Norfolk, from which place all women are fleeing who can leave. I saw tonight, at my nephew's, two elderly ladies who had just arrived from Norfolk, bringing [1801] all their slaves, some 20. Heard from them that the Merrimac war steamer is at last completed, & will be out of the dry-dock tomorrow. This is one of the several ships of war burnt & sunk by the Yankees when they abandoned the possession & fled from the Navy Yard, in panic, immediately after the secession of Va. It was raised, & the lower structure has been covered with thick iron plates, so as to render the steamer (as expected) nearly invulnerable to shot & shells, & a most formidable agent of offensive warfare on any of the enemy's ships of war. It is hoped that its qualities for attack & defence will soon be put to trial. . . .

Feb. 14. Previous report confirmed that the enemy have captured Edenton—& also the town of Hertford. Neither burnt, as should have been by the inhabitants. And the burning of Elizabeth City was but partial, as the Yankee forces, after landing, & the tory portion of the residents put out the flames. Land troops have been landed in considerable numbers both at Elizabeth & Edenton. No doubt they will proceed to capture Plymouth, & other places near. The Yankee gunboats attacked Fort Donelson on the 12th aided by land forces, supposed to be 10 to 12,000. The fighting continued on 13th to nearly 3 P.M., when the enemy drew off. The attack expected to be renewed next day.—Every successive northern report repeats, with increased confidence, that France will certainly & soon recognize the C.S. [1802] or interfere in the war. There is nothing however direct from the French government, to authorize that opinion of the northern press, & the European correspondents thereof. . . . The Rump government of the North, like a desperate gamester, is risking everything on a single chance of the game. If their present war expenses continue for a year longer, the northern people & government will be irretrievably ruined. They know this well. But their only hope . . . & which they now are sacrificing all their wealth & credit to realize, is to conquer the seceded states, & to reinstate their enormous expenses & losses, by the confiscation of all the property of the people of the South.—Finished 10 of Joanna Baillie's dramas. Five others I had read previously. . . .

Feb. 15. . . . No farther accounts from Fort Donelson, except varied confirmations of the decisive repulse of the enemy's attacking force on the 13th. after two days fighting. . . . Annexed is an extract from a late speech in the rump congress, by Thaddeus Stevens, a leading member of the abolition party, in favor of general emancipation, & of arming the slaves. Resolutions in favor of both measures have been passed almost with unanimity by the Senate of Maine. Resolutions for general emancipation, it is said in Northern papers, are about to be introduced in the U.S. Senate by [Charles] Sumner of Mass. I wish heartily for the success of these propositions, so far as to be adopted by Yankeedom, & enacted by its Congress. The legal shape of enactment will be no worse in practice than what is now done by the Yankee military officers—& the recognition of the policy by formal act of the government will shock & repel many Union men in the border slave-holding states.—A telegram to the President this afternoon, reports that the enemy's attack on Fort Donelson was again renewed yesterday—the third day—8 steamers coming within 200 yards of the fort & there firing ball & shells, without [1805] doing the least damage. Our fire was returned to such good purpose that, after some hours of hard fighting, the vessels were compelled to retreat, after, as was supposed, our fire had inflicted considerable injury. These attacks, repulsed for three days in succession, constitute a glorious result, whatever may be the amount of damage to the enemy's fleet & men, of which the reports are probably, as usual, greatly exaggerated.

Feb. 16. Sunday. . . . Two later telegrams repeat & confirm the general report of the successful repulses of the enemy's armed steamers attacking Fort Donelson—with the addition, that our troops outside, under Gens. Buckner and Floyd, were pursuing the enemy's land forces, under Gen. [John A.] McClernand, who were retreating into Ten. Great anxiety to learn later incidents, as well as the reliable particulars of what has been reported in general. . . . Later report unfavorable—that the enemy had been reinforced from Paducah, & had in turn pursued our army to their intrench-ments. Nothing more heard from Fort Donelson or our army there, though I waited anxiously at the Telegraph Office from 7.30 P.M., the time of opening on Sundays, to nearly 9.—Yesterday began to read "Notes" by De Quincey, a volume of his works before omit-ted.—My anxiety, (as of most others,) is intense to learn the later events of the battle on the Cumberland. The armies on both sides were large, & the enemy, at [1806] first more numerous, had re-ceived strong reinforcements. Reinforcements to our army also were ordered from Bowling Green. The battle will be very impor-tant, & of momentous consequences, whatever may be its result. Before the check & retreat of our army, there was every appearance of its gaining a great victory. God grant that it may be so yet!— Though no official or authentic account has yet been received (or made public,) of the defeat at Roanoke Island, yet, from comparing the numerous reports of persons who escaped, I now think that, instead of the fight having been bravely contested, & highly honor-able to our soldiers, that it was disgraceful in all its parts, except to the few companies, including the three from Richmond, who seem to have fought well, & suffered all of the little loss of blood. Eight only were killed on our side,[17] & of them were two of the captains of these companies—O. J[ennings] Wise of the Richmond Blues, & Capt. [Roberts] Coles, of the Albermarle company. Probably our very inferior & mostly raw forces, of 2100, could not have ulti-mately beaten off 15,000 who attacked them, aided by the cannon & mortars of 53 war steamers. But, after keeping them off one whole day, & our forces having earth-works to protect them, & cannon to fire, it was disgraceful & inexcusable in the commanding officer to surrender unconditionally, when no more than 8 men on our side had been killed. It is said that the N.Ca. troops, raw & undiscip-

---

[17] This estimate is low. Colonel Henry M. Shaw of North Carolina, the immediate field commander, listed Confederate casualties as twenty-three dead, fifty-eight wounded, and sixty-two missing. Nor did the two Virginia regiments suffer dispro-portionate losses. Their casualties were six dead, twenty-eight wounded, and nine-teen missing; the remaining casualties were borne by the North Carolina regiments. *Official Records*, Vol. IX, 173.

lined, skulked & scarcely fought at all. Nothing was done rightly & properly for preparation. One of the great omissions was that no boats had been provided for retreat across the shallow water to the adjacent sand-reef, so that only about 50 men escaped from the island. Not a word of blame, or [1807] of the facts indicating cowardice, has been uttered in our newspapers—though much censure is indicated on the want of preparation for efficient defence. . . . An English vessel lately ran the blockade, & reached New Orleans with 15,000 Enfield rifles, & munitions. But since, 3 other British vessels laden with cannon & munitions have been captured by the blockading squadrons. Our scarcity of gunpowder is so great, that it is necessarily used of bad quality. I have heard this reason alleged for the very inaccurate firing from our forts on the Potomac, & for some other important failures or omissions. . . .

Feb. 17. A telegram from Gen. A. S. Johnston, received yesterday at the War Department, which I did not see until this morning confirms our success at Fort Donelson on 15th with additional particulars. The enemy's forces (*reported* then to be 50,000,) had returned to the siege, & *invested* our lines completely. Our troops attacked them at 5.30 A.M., fought 9 hours, repulsed them & drove them back, the enemy leaving 1240 killed & wounded. Our loss 500. We also took 6 pieces of artillery & 300 prisoners. Heard from Mr. Pritchard, the telegraph news agent, that as late as 1 last night, attempts were made to convey a government dispatch to that army, & by three different routes, in vain, the communication being broken. Today a dispatch from Nashville to the Ordnance Dept. states that its subordinate there had moved off from there the Percussion-Cap Factory, but could not transport the shells &c. This message indicates great danger to Nashville, & as a condition thereto, that we had either suffered [1808] or expected defeat on the Cumberland. I have heard nothing since. . . . This forenoon, sat some time with Mr. Boulware, who arrived yesterday.—This day, the term & being of the Provisional Congress ended. Tomorrow the Congress under the Constitution will assemble—& on the 22nd, the President will be inaugurated for his constitutional service.

Feb. 18. Fort Donelson has fallen! That naked but all-important fact is all that is learned. It was to be expected, even before we knew (or believed) as is stated now by northern reports, that besides the powerful flotilla of armed steamers, there were (by the northern reports,) 40,000 land forces to begin the battle, increased to 50,000

[237]

by reinforcements before the last of the four days of fighting outside of our intrenchments. We had before heard that Gen. A. S. Johnston's army had left Bowling Green, which place had been forthwith shelled, burnt & occupied by the enemy. Northern reports also state that [1809] Springfield, Mo. had been abandoned by Gen. Price, after a short skirmish, & much of his stores captured in the camp by the enemy. These defeats, & especially that at Fort Donelson, bring awful peril to the South, & certain & immense loss. Nashville is now open to the attack of a naval force, if not also of land forces sent by rail-road.—Read the northern accounts of their victory at Roanoke Island, in which they give more credit to the defending force than I am sure it deserved. Today I saw Gen. (late Col.) George Randolph, who has just returned from that neighborhood on official duties. He confirmed my opinion, which I formed solely on the general fact that our army had surrendered when but 8 of our men had been killed. Gen. R. says that the acting commander, Col. [Henry M.] Shaw, was incapable, & most of the N.C. troops acted most cowardly. . . . Now we have been driven out of all our posts in Ky, except Columbus, & all Mo. except Gen. Thompson's small partisan corps. I am of opinion that we have no general who knows how to manage a large army [1810] in battle, & scarcely to keep it well provided & efficient on a march or in camp. The most effective fighting that has been done in the war was in Mo., by Price, McCulloch, & Thompson, at the head of small armies, & acting independently, & almost without aid, as well as command, from the Confederate or state government. I believe that even now, except at a few points, where a large army under one head is needed to face & oppose a stronger assailing or threatening force, it would be better to resort to small bodies under independent commands, (so that they were well commanded,) to carry on the war as [Francis] Marion did formerly, & Price recently. . . .

Feb. 19. . . . Still more of disastrous news. We know nothing of the particulars of our losses at Fort Donelson except through northern reports. According to these, announced in the rump congress, our loss in prisoners is 15,000, including Generals Johnston [1814], Buckner, & Pillow. . . . The enemy, with their whole naval force from Port Royal, are steadily making advances towards Savannah. Unless both well & bravely defended, the capture of that city is probably not far ahead.—Our ministers have reached London & Paris. From both countries, & especially France, reports continue of recognition of the Southern Confederacy being expected soon. I am inclined to believe that the knowledge of our late heavy disasters will be more likely to hasten than retard that action by England. This whole former U.S. has always been hated by the English rulers, on political grounds. The southern states were further odious as slaveholders, & upholders of the institution of negro slavery. The Northern states were viewed with jealousy, as dangerous rivals in navigation, manufactures & commerce—& also hated & despised (very deservedly) for offensive Yankee propensities & habits. Now, just so long as England could do without our cotton, she would be content to leave the northern & southern states to weaken & damage each other, & the more the better, until the North shall be ruined in finances, & so reduced as no longer to rival England in trade or naval power—& until slavery should be destroyed in the South, by northern action. But England rejoices in the division of the former great & growing U.S., & has no intention of allowing, through her neglect, the possible reconstruction of the former union, [1815] & (to England) its dangerous power & rivalry. Therefore, I infer, that if the subjugation of the South was believed to be probable & impending, England will immediately recognise our independent nationality, raise the blockade, &, if needed, go to war with the stronger & before triumphant Yankee power—& all to forward & maintain her own selfish interests.—A French ship of war came into Hampton Roads some weeks ago—& since, others have arrived until there are now there 5 frigates. This seems ominous of designed interference. . . . Mr. Jones, who rents & resides in this house, today saw wagons carrying to the Depot, to be sent to the Peninsula, many long ladders. This, in conjunction with the reported readiness for service of the Merrimac, & the probably reduced garrison of Fortress Monroe, seem to indicate an intended attack on that post by Magruder's army. . . . For some days my reading has been in [Heinrich] Barth's Travels in Africa, & Suetonius' Lives of the Twelve Caesars.[18] Both dry.

Feb. 20. . . . Burnside's gunboats have been cruising about the mouths of the rivers, & as high as the southern end of the Albemarle & Chesapeake canal, leading to Norfolk. But it does not seem that except Roanoke Island, he occupies any ground. His occupying

---

[18] The African explorer, Heinrich Barth, led an expedition from Tripoli to the Niger River and Lake Chad in the early 1850's. Gaius Suetonius Tranquillus (70–121?) was a Roman biographer who wrote during the emperorship of Trajan.

forces left Elizabeth & Edenton after a short time. Having heard no later confirmation, I doubt whether Hertford was entered by them.—It is strange that for 48 hours there has been no telegram from Nashville, or from our troops thereabout. Afternoon, there came reports from Nashville, but telegraphed from Atlanta, that all four of our generals, with their commands, has [*sic*] escaped from Fort Donelson, & all had reached Nashville safely, except Buckner's corps, which had been intercepted, but had fought its way through the enemy, though scattered, & that most of the men had arrived, & the remainder expected. . . . Heard that [Henry S.] Foote had made a strong speech [in the Confederate Congress] in condemnation of the conduct of the war, & especially in condemnation of the Secretaries of the Navy & of War.[19] . . .

Feb. 21. It is understood that the telegraph communication from Nashville has been suspended by order of our military authorities there—which is ominous of evil.—I now infer that the scaling ladders sent to Gen. Magruder are not for so arduous or desperate use as attacking Fortress Monroe by assault, but may be for the fort at Newport News, should the Merrimac cooperate successfully. But the action of the latter is still some weeks off. I saw this evening the commander, Capt. Buchanan, who told me that all the guns were not yet on board, nor had he been able to enlist as many sailors as were required for the crew (they being very scarce,)—& when ready in both these respects, there would be required time enough to practise the men at the guns. . . . I attended for two hours the session of the House of Representatives. The debate was a continuation of what was begun yesterday, & would have been interesting, except that I could hear but very little of it. Yet, by favor of the Speaker, (Mr. [Thomas S.] Bocock,) I had a chair near to the side of his, & the [1818] best place for me to hear, but for the buzz of talkers outside of the door. There was a perfect jam of spectators within.—Learned that Nanny had come to Rd. yesterday evening, & was at A. M. Dupuy's where I went to see her this evening—& arranged to go with her & the other ladies tomorrow to witness the

---

[19] Foote (1804–80), whose differences with President Davis were personal as well as political, soon became one of the most vociferous critics of the Davis administration in the Confederate Congress. A former United States senator from Mississippi, he had defeated Davis in the gubernatorial election of 1851. He moved to Tennessee shortly before the war and represented that state in both the First and Second Confederate congresses.

ceremonies of the inauguration of President Davis. Great numbers will be in Richmond as visitors on this occasion, to be added to the 20,000 of the ordinary floating population of the city, since it has been the capital of the Confederate States.—Our recent heavy & repeated disasters have made the North wild & crazed with rejoicing. They already pronounce the rebellion crushed. But, instead of discouraging the people of the South, or causing them to despair or deem resistance hopeless, they seem to have derived from these misfortunes a new impulse to patriotism & to the disposition to sacrifice every private interest to that of our country. The volunteers in service have not since been more reluctant to reenlist for the war—but, to the contrary, the re-enlistments have been much more rapid & extensive than the previous rates.

Feb. 22. A steady slow rain to this time (10 A.M.) without abatement, promises a very inauspicious day for the President's inauguration. Farther accounts of the battle of Fort Donelson go to confirm the Yankee report of our great loss of prisoners, which they state, officially, at 15,000. They also report (after heavy reductions from some of the items in their first reports,) their capture of 3000 horses, 12,000 muskets &c., all our artillery, & an immense amount of munitions & stores. While they admit "great slaughter" on both sides, [1819] they make the ridiculously small statement of 400 killed & 800 wounded to be all of their loss.[20] . . . The last reports, by telegraph & otherwise, are that Gen. Buckner, on the 17th. [*sic*] after 4 preceding days of hard fighting, raised a flag of truce, & offered to surrender upon terms—& these being refused, he surrendered unconditionally. Our loss of prisoners, arms, horses & stores very great—perhaps not less than by the Yankee report. . . . Gen. A. S. Johnston, with his army of 25,000, had evacuated Nashville, & retreated 30 miles southward—& that city with immense stores, is believed to be occupied by the enemy.[21]

Feb. 24. . . . Nothing heard direct from Nashville, & it is not certain whether the enemy have occupied it, or have yet to do it. . . . No official or other full report from Fort Donelson, on our side. . . .

---

[20] Actual losses in General Grant's command at Fort Donelson were 500 killed, 2,108 wounded, and 224 missing for a total of 2,832. Confederate casualties were about 1,500 in addition to the number—variously estimated at from 5,000 to 15,000—surrendered by General Buckner on February 16.

[21] This report was slightly premature. Federal troops under General Don Carlos Buell did not enter Nashville until February 25.

But the unaccountable yet certain fact is that, after three days of brave & hard fighting, against an army & naval force of thrice their number, this army of 12,000 or 13,000 should have surrendered (& by previous determination,) prisoners of war, instead of endeavoring to escape, either secretly in the night, or even, if no other resource was left, by cutting their way through the enemy's ranks. Gen[eral]s Floyd & Pillow, with some 800 men, did escape in the night, after the surrender was determined upon for the next morning.—There seems great disposition to despond, with many persons. But the volunteers in service have received from the recent great disasters a new stimulus to their patriotism. The reenlistments for the war have been increased threefold by this impulse—& it is expected that much the larger number [1821] of all in service will volunteer for the war.—The great cause of the enemy's success has been their iron-clad gun-boats, carrying very heavy cannon & mortars. Their armor has rendered them almost invulnerable, & their offensive armament makes them fearful & powerful agents of destruction. Still stronger & more powerful vessels of this class are now in preparation at St. Louis & at Brooklyn.—Received a letter from Edmund with the most welcome report that his wife had given birth to a son on the 16th inst—& both mother & child doing well.—When I saw Gen. J. Thompson, I offered to him, & he seemed glad to ac[c]ept, the musket which I obtained from Manassas, to be put in the hands of some one of his brave men, for the service of our cause in Missouri. But an engraved plate, with my name &c. which Col. Dimmock, of the State Ordnance dept., had previously ordered, was not ready on the only day that Gen. Thompson remained. Therefore I offered to send it after him, when a safe conveyance could be used. Such a one I heard of today, in Col. [George G.] Vest, a M.C. from Mo.,[22] who is going to Gen. T. & will set out tomorrow, & who readily agreed to carry the musket. I was sorry to learn that Gen. Thompson's little army of temporary volunteers had nearly all disbanded—though he expects to have them again, or a brigade of other recruits, as soon as they can be put

---

[22] A native of Kentucky, George Graham Vest (1830–1904) moved to Missouri in the mid-1850's and, when war broke out, sided with the pro-Confederate forces in the state legislature. After serving briefly as judge advocate on the staff of General Sterling Price, Vest entered the Confederate Congress in 1862 and remained a member of that body for the duration of the conflict. In 1879 he was elected to the first of four successive terms in the United States Senate, where he pursued a generally conservative course highlighted by his opposition to the protective tariff.

to good service. Price's successive armies, & Thompson's on a smaller scale, have been made up of men who served as long as convenient, & went home when they pleased.—After calling on Judge [William M.] Cook[e] & Col. Vest, at their room, I retired to my own by dark. . . . A very heavy gale of wind most of the day, which even in this city caused much damage. Several hundred feet of the Rd. & Petersburg railroad bridge, crossing James river, were blown off.

Feb. 25. No telegraphic news, & little of any other—except northern rejoicings over their late successes. The telegraph wires were doubtless broken on every route by falling trees &c, & the railroads had previously been damaged in various places by the quantity of rain, causing land-slides, or washing by floods. It is whispered, from earlier information not published, that Gen. Beauregard has announced the necessity of evacuating Columbus—& that as soon as the roads are firm enough, the enemy will advance in force on Winchester, & that our Potomac army must retreat from the lines of Manassas. It is said too that our horses in service have so suffered for want of long forage, & the team horses from abuse in addition, that they have died in great numbers, & few will be fit for use, when the state of the weather & the earth will permit it.— There is a general disposition to find fault—& censure is mostly directed against the Secretaries of War & Navy. I think that it is more deserved by inexperienced & incompetent & drunken officers in command of armies or military posts, & by the President for appointing such officers. . . . Finished reading "The Twelve Caesars" & reading & skipping over 1st vol. of Barth's Travels, & began Thackeray's "Paris Sketch-Book." . . . Wrote to Edmund informing him that I shall go to his camp on the 28th—& to Julian, asking him to go with me.

Feb. 26. Still no telegraphic despatches, & no news, except northern. From the latest European advices, there seems no disposition shown in either the British parliament or the French legislature, (both lately assembled,) to interfere in this war, by recognizing our independence, or raising the sham blockade.—Attended the session of the H. of Rep. for more than two hours. The President's regular message to Congress was sent yesterday. Neither that nor his inaugural speech on the 22nd. gave any indication of the [1824] war policy to be pursued. In the afternoon there began another steady rain. I waited down town until after 6 P.M. to go to a public

[243]

meeting at 7.30—but the rain so increased that I supposed there could be no meeting, & I came home.

Feb. 27. Still no reliable news. Reported, as expected, but still uncertain, that the enemy have reached Nashville. Attended the session of Congress for an hour—but hearing nothing, & the proceedings not being of much interest, I left. . . . To my surprise, I learned that the meeting had been held last night, & an interesting debate—& the business was adjourned to this evening. I had been appointed on the Committee to draft resolutions, which I attended at 4.30 P.M., & the meeting at 7.30. The object was to discuss the policy of the Confederate government buying all of the cotton & tobacco of the last year's growth now on hand, & causing to be burnt all that was in danger of being seized & stolen by the enemy, & to continue so to burn all that may be hereafter exposed & in danger. The assemblage was very large. The resolutions, in favor of the policy stated, were advocated, in long & eloquent speeches, by the Rev. C. K. Marshall of Miss.,[23] the author of the proposal & of the resolutions, & Judge [James W.] Moore of Ky.[24] The resolutions were adopted, without a dissenting vote. Great enthusiasm [1825] was displayed by the meeting. After the vote had been taken, other speakers were called for. Gov. Foote of Ten. spoke until 11, when I left, because I had to fix for my leaving before daybreak—& another speaker had previously followed, & the audience was but little reduced in number. . . .

Feb. 28. . . . Walked to the Exchange to take the omnibus for the steamer, which left the wharf at 6.30. When passing Maycox, I looked in vain for Julian, to whom I had written to meet me there, & join me in my visit. . . . Opposite the batteries at Mulberry Island & Hardy's Bluff, we passed the armed steamers Patrick Henry & Jamestown, which have been anchored there for some time. Reached the Stone House wharf, & landed, at 4 P.M. [1826] where my nephew Dr. Dupuy & my grandson Thomas Ruffin were waiting for me, with a horse for my use. We rode two miles along & down the shore, whence we could see the two Yankee frigates lying above Newport News, & which blockade James river. A Yankee steam gunboat also was still in distant view, which today had been

---

[23] Marshall was a prominent Methodist clergyman from Vicksburg and a zealous champion of the southern cause.

[24] Moore was a member of the Confederate House of Representatives from 1862 to 1865.

up the river within 5 miles of our lower (& useless) fort, on Day's Neck, under a flag of truce, but which had not been met, or responded to, & so had returned. At a mile from the shore, in the pine woods, I found the winter quarters of the "Prince George Cavalry," my son's command. He, & also others of my acquaintance, received me with warm welcome. The log houses in which the company are now quartered, were built by the hands of the men, & are neat & comfortable—& kept warm by good fires. The only discomfort is that the roofs, made of bad pine slabs, have many cracks, which admit rain in rainy weather, & too much cold air. But notwithstanding my feeling the small cold draft unpleasantly on my face & head throughout the night, I slept soundly, after eating a good supper, with unusual good appetite. . . . Ever since the capture of Roanoke Island &c. a further advance of the enemy has been looked for, either on the rail-road, or Norfolk, & most probably first upon Suffolk. But except the early movements on Elizabeth, Edenton, & the burning of Winton, the Yankees have done nothing—& these were nothing of military benefit or progress to them. They have retained occupation of no place except Roanoke Island. Probably they are waiting for reinforcements for their next & heavier blow. Whether any adequate or less means have been provided by our authorities to meet this danger, I do not know, & much doubt. Tents & two days' provision [1827] of hard bread were sent to this company, some days past, with orders to be ready to move at a moment's warning.

March 1. A cold morning. Ice. . . . As no newspapers were printed anywhere today,[25] we have no later news than I had yesterday from Richmond. . . . Edmund received a letter from his wife with the gratifying news to me as well as to him, that she & her infant continue to do well.—Slow rain nearly all day, & heavier in the night.

March 3. The steamer did not arrive, by which we were anxiously expecting newspapers by 5 P.M. (usually.) After dark, heavy rain, which delayed our mail from Smithfield from 8, the usual time, to 10.30 P.M. We sat up awaiting it with great anxiety, & received one paper only. . . . It is *inferred* that the enemy have occupied Nashville, after it was evacuated by our authorities, but nothing is stated directly & clearly. The N.Y. Herald publishes the confident expec-

[25] Presumably because the preceding day was designated by proclamation of President Davis as a day of fasting and prayer throughout the Confederacy.

tation of the Yankees soon getting possession (by plundering of course,) of two millions of bales of cotton, in the south-west, & in Ga. & S.Ca., & thereby supplying the existing demand not only of the North but of Europe. The Paris correspondent of that paper (a Yankee,) states the existence & increase of great distress in France, owing to the interruption of the supply of cotton, & of other trade with the Southern States, & the certainty of the early interference of the French government in the war, unless the supply of cotton is soon re-opened. The northern papers are doing all they can to operate on the European mind in this respect, by exaggerating the recent northern victories, & adding as their consequences, the most monstrous & absurd lies of the great amount of cotton that will thereby be secured by the northern troops, & of the great union or submission sentiment produced by these successes, & exhibited by our troops, as well as by the population of the southern states, or of all the localities reached or threatened by their maurauding [*sic*] expeditions. . . . Martial law over Norfolk & Portsmouth, & for 10 miles distance therefrom, was proclaimed by the President on Feb. 28th—& the like measure has today been proclaimed as to Richmond. This measure, I trust, will permit & induce the arresting & punishing of disloyal residents, spies & traitors, who have heretofore escaped all punishment, & almost all constraint. Indications of the needed change are given in the news from Rd. today, that the noted former whig & submission leader, John M. Botts, with some five other of his disciples & inferior unionists & tories, have been arrested, their papers seized, & they imprisoned. Not doubting the treasonable sentiments & disposition of all of these, & very many more, I earnestly hope that full evidences of their treason may be obtained, & that they may have summary trial & punishment by a court-martial. The distillation & also all selling of spiritous [*sic*] liquors in Richmond are forbidden by the same proclamation of the President. This measure will be most salutary, if it can be made operative. For some time back the great assemblage of soldiers, generally without command, & their drinking, have made Richmond a sink-hole of drunkenness, rowdyism, & crime. . . .

March 4. Camp life, especially in bad weather, is dull even for the soldiers, who have duties to perform—& still more so for visitors who have nothing to do. Books are scarce here. . . . The only incident of each day, impatiently looked for, & of great interest when arriving, is the getting of newspapers from the mail at Smithfield, which is from 8.30 to past 10 P.M. Nothing of any novelty tonight, or importance, except the certainty of the general fact that the enemy have accepted the offered capitulation of Nashville, & hold that city. . . .

March 5. Attempted to leave this morning for Richmond—but the steamer had not arrived, so that I had the trouble of riding to the wharf by daybreak, & waiting there some hours, for nothing, but to come back again.—Five new recruits have just enlisted in the Prince George Cavalry, raising the actual number to 78—& four more are engaged but not yet arrived. No reenlistments of the old members have yet been formally made, as their service [1831] continues to May 18th. But it is supposed that nearly all will reenlist for the war. Edmund has determined to do so, if the company desire him to continue to command it—& this is understood, & also that if he should retire, there will not enough of the men reenlist in the same company to preserve its integrity & existence. Even for this important & patriotic consideration, & with all the stimulus afforded by the recent reverses & disasters of our armies, I was surprised that Edmund should think of continuing his entirely voluntary service beyond the year for which he had offered it. For he was past the military age before his service, or his volunteering it, had begun—he has no ambition for office or rank—his business & his house-hold matters require his presence at home as much as any other man's—& further, his comfort, his happiness, & all his selfish wishes, are embraced in his own family circle. His sacrifices made for serving his country's cause are as great as those of any other person within my knowledge. But should the event show that he is not wanted by his company to command it, & thereby to preserve it, he will not hold himself bound to continue his service, for which there will not be, & has not been, any legal obligation.

March 6. Again set out before daybreak for the wharf, & this time the steamer came, & I embarked for Richmond. And it was well I was no later, as this is the last trip of the steamer, & this only took the passengers as far as City Point. This & the other river steamer thence returned under military orders, to take troops from Mulberry Point on their route for Suffolk, & will be so employed for several days. This looks like an attack of the enemy was expected there soon. I went from [1832] City Point by rail-road to Petersburg, where I dined, & wrote letters . . . & at 4 P.M., proceeded to Richmond. Snowing before our arrival. . . .

[247]

March 7. Ice & very cold & strong wind. But little snow left. Columbus, Ky., has been evacuated. This was expected, & supposed necessary, after the loss of all other places in Ky.—From last European accounts, & the published correspondence of Lords Russell & Lyons, there seems no present prospect of England opposing the Yankee blockade, or recognizing the independence of the Confederate States. The abolition fanaticism of England seems to over-balance its commercial interests. The hope that the Yankee [1833] government, if not prevented by European interference, will destroy negro slavery in the C.S., out-weighs all . . . England's causes of complaint against the North, & the great benefits which would accrue to England from the independence & tranquillity of the South.—Attending to sundry little matters of business, preparatory to my closing my sojourn in Richmond, & returning to Beechwood. . . . Attended the session of Congress, until the doors were closed. An act was passed to authorise the President to order the burning of cotton & other crops &c. when in danger of being seized by the enemy. This is very well—but the measures enacted or authorized are imperfect, & fall far short of the plan & policy proposed by the popular meeting held here last week, & which seemed to have met with very general approval by the public.— Notwithstanding that Gen. Pillow has published a long account of the battles & final surrender of Fort Donelson, we cannot learn anything near the main facts, & all-important tests of the result, as to the numbers of the enemy's forces, the number of their killed & wounded, & the number of our men taken prisoners. Enormous differences in all these are still reported. All the enemy's iron-clad steamers, except two, were disabled by our heaviest artillery— though they seemed invulnerable to less than 64 to 128 lbs. shot. Through three days of fighting, the success & glory were to us—& even the final surrender, under complete exhaustion of our men, to triple their numbers, does not detract from their bravery, though it may from the competency [1834] of the commander. But it seems to me that nothing can excuse Gen. A. S. Johnston for not having reinforced the army at Fort Donelson from the larger army at Bowling Green, which retreated to Ten. during the very time. I hold Johnston as condemnable for this, & almost as inefficient, as Gen. Huger in permitting the loss of Roanoke Island & its whole army.[26]

---

[26] Despite his exalted rank and reputation, Albert Sidney Johnston suffered a precipitous decline in popularity following the debacles in Tennessee. The editor is

March 8. Saw Mr. Wm Sayre in the street. He seems very despondent, & thinks it easy, & not improbable, that the enemy will come up the Pamunkey—in which case, he is sure that they will destroy every thing destructible at Marlbourne, on account of its connection with me. I cannot compliment myself so highly.—We no longer hold any portion of Ky, except an island (No. 10) in the Mississippi, to which it seems the garrison of Columbus retreated, & will fortify. I should think that we had had enough of risking armies in fortifications in reach of the enemy's naval forces. An island is the place most exposed to their attack, & the least capable of being reinforced, or of the garrison escaping in case of defeat. The enemy are investing New Madrid, which is now almost the only part of Missouri that we still hold.—Paid my bills for rent &c. to be ready to leave on Monday morning (the 10th). . . .

March 9. Sunday. Last night, on my way home, I heard a report of important events, to which I gave no credit, & did not spend a further thought on it. But this morning, I learned that these & other additional facts have [1835] been received in telegraphic despatches to the War Department, which I have since read, & therefore must be true, unless by mistake of the official reporter. Even if but the main statement is true, the occurrences are as glorious & beneficial for our arms, as they are novel & remarkable as incidents of warfare. The iron-clad vessel Virginia, reconstructed on the bottom of the former U.S. frigate Merrimac, at last steamed out of port yesterday at 11 A.M., & proceeded at once to attack the two sailing frigates which were lying just above Newport News. These frigates opened fire on the Virginia, which was not returned until she had approached near. After a severe fight the U.S. frigate Cumberland (44 [guns]) was sunk, & the other, the Congress, either was driven or drifted on shore, aground, & there hoisted two white flags. Two other steam frigates, of largest size, supposed to be the Minnesota & Colorado, advanced from off Fortress Monroe, & also the floating iron-clad battery lately arrived there, which was reported to be something like, & a match for the Virginia. These attacked the Virginia—and the Minnesota was driven aground on a shoal, & the floating battery also, somewhere; & the Colorado retreated under

---

reminded of the comments of a Louisiana overseer who, at about this same time, denounced the unfortunate Johnston as "an old ass" and asserted that he "ort to be Hung for not making a Stand at Nashville." Magnolia Plantation Journals (MSS in Henry Clay Warmoth Papers and Books, Southern Historical Collection, University of North Carolina, Chapel Hill), February 19, 1862.

the guns of Fortress Monroe. Three or four small gunboats accompanied & aided the operations of the Virginia, & also the Jamestown & Patrick Henry armed steamers soon joined. To these latter was left the care of the Minnesota after she grounded, & they were firing on her, while the Virginia proceeded to cannonade & shell the fort at Newport News. The fort responded but feebly, as its heavy artillery, & most of the guns are directed towards the landside [1836], no attack from the water-side having been apprehended. These events, or even half as much, would make a great & glorious victory. But I trust that they will be the causes of other successes of still more important benefit. If the Virginia is indeed as nearly invulnerable as was expected from its peculiar form & defensive armor, & as powerful in attack—& both seem confirmed by the first trial—Newport News may be cut off from assistance by water, & invested on the land side by Gen. Magruder, & compelled to surrender—although several of his regiments had before left for Suffolk.—This evening, other dispatches confirmed the above statements in the general, with some variations & additions of particulars. The Virginia & the Patrick Henry (which latter received a ball through the boiler,) had gone to Norfolk. Very few killed & wounded of our men. The loss of the enemy supposed to be very great. The frigate Congress was burnt. . . .

March 10. At 8 A.M. Left in a carriage, & went by my nephew's house to take up Mrs. [Rebecca Dupuy] Epes,[27] to go to Petersburg on her way home. We arrived there at 11 A.M. But as I had not expected to arrive before the afternoon train, & had so appointed, I had to wait six dreary hours before setting out for Beechwood in the carriage. . . . Heard in Petersburg later news & more [1837] particulars of the naval engagement—both from the latest papers, & from passengers who left Norfolk at 12 today. The Cumberland Frigate was sunk by the Virginia, & the Congress driven on shore, when she struck her colors, & raised the white flag, & was boarded by boats from our vessels, which removed 23 prisoners. But while under the white flag, & our men on board, the guns of Newport News were fired on the Congress—& the frigate was therefore set on fire, & burnt & sunk. The Minnesota (first class war steamer,) got aground & was supposed to be greatly damaged. But at last she was got off. In the previous effort to draw her off, a steam-gunboat burst

---

[27] The diarist's niece.

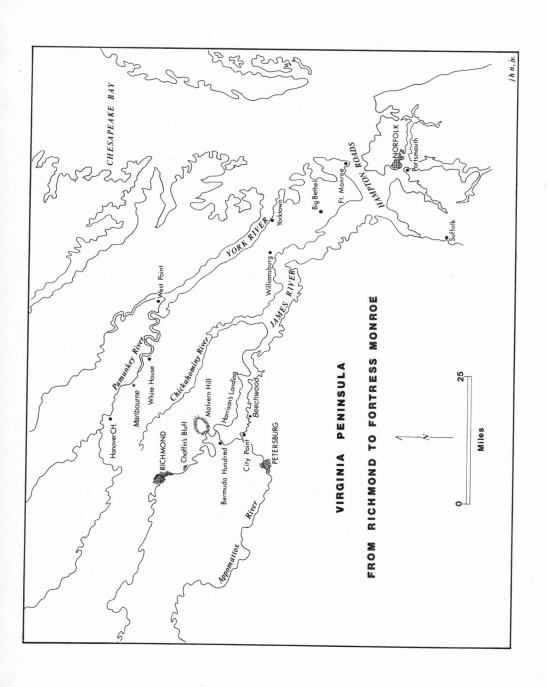

CHESAPEAKE BAY

NORFOLK
Portsmouth

HAMPTON ROADS

Ft. Monroe

Big Bethel

Suffolk

Yorktown

YORK RIVER

West Point

Williamsburg

Pamunkey River

JAMES RIVER

Chickahominy River

HanoverCH.

Marlbourne *

White House

RICHMOND

Chaffin's Bluff

Malvern Hill

Harrison's Landing

Beechwood

Bermuda Hundred

City Point

PETERSBURG

Appomattox River

jh n. jr.

VIRGINIA PENINSULA

FROM RICHMOND TO FORTRESS MONROE

N

0   25

Miles

its boiler, took fire & was burnt. Another gunboat (the Reindeer) was captured & carried to Norfolk. The Virginia & Patrick Henry went to Norfolk yesterday, which made me believe that the former as well as the latter was damaged, & needed repairs. This was so. Many outer plates of the armor were displaced by the balls, & leaking caused by the jarring. But it is said that all needed repairs will be made in a few days. Our total loss was 7 killed & 17 wounded—& most of these by the small arms from Newport News fort. The enemy's loss must have been very great—*guessed* at more than 600. The Cumberland was sunk so quickly that it is believed that most of her crew must have been drowned. This frigate carried cannon of the largest size & greatest power, & most formidable even to the armor of the Virginia. Even if limiting the measure of success to what is certain—the destruction of the two first-class sailing frigates Cumberland & Congress, & under the guns & fire of [1838] [the] fort at Newport News, & subsequently of the reinforcement of the first-class war steamers Minnesota & Colorado, & of the Erics[s]on floating battery,[28] this is one of the most decisive & remarkable naval combats & victories in the annals of warfare. The great success, with so little loss, of the Virginia, is the more wonderful, because the plan & construction of the vessel was a new & untried experiment, & not made at choice, but erected on the bottom of the frigate Merrimac, which, among others, was burnt & sunk by the Yankee forces when they abandoned the Navy Yard. Also, the armament & equipment had been completed but a few days, the crew but recently enlisted, & with great difficulty, on account of the scarcity of sailors, & there had been no opportunity of trying the powers of the vessel, or of trying the guns at actual firing. The trial of either would have notified the enemy of the designed operations. The first movement of the vessel, & in the first two hours after starting, was to get close under the guns of the enemy's frigates, & its first guns fired were in answer to theirs.— Like all other true southerners, I have been greatly delighted & excited by this great naval success. Yet, on other grounds, I have felt more gloomy & depressed today than at any time before. The

---

[28] This reference, of course, is to the new Union ironclad, U.S.S. *Monitor*, which steamed into Hampton Roads on the evening of March 8 and sallied forth on the following morning to engage the *Virginia* in the celebrated first-ever duel between ironclad vessels. Clearly, the diarist was not yet cognizant of the details of the latter engagement, in which the threat posed by the *Virginia* to the Federal blockade was effectively neutralized.

Governor's proclamation published today, announces that the Confederate government has called upon Virginia for 40,000 men in addition to the previous requisition and proper quota of 65,000. To supply this call, the governor summons into actual service *all* of the remainder of the militia, from all eastern & central Va, indeed from all except the disloyal counties, or others occupied by the [1839] enemy, & a few others of the loyal mountain counties, whose militia are to hold themselves ready to obey a subsequent summons. It is to be hoped that this general call to the field will be obeyed readily & patriotically. But its being necessary indicates great & dangerous pressure on Va by the several threatening armies. And the whole military population being at once in the field must cause immense private injury & loss, in the cessation of labor, & removal of nearly all superintendence. Few will lose more by this measure than my two sons, Edmund & Julian, they from home in service, & their overseers also, & no others to be procured. It is reported that the late reinforcement has raised Burnside's army to 40,000. The Yankee army under Banks is pressing on upon Winchester. I heard, from private information, (as such things are properly kept out of our newspapers,) that our army of Manassas is falling back from its very strong positions, nearer towards Richmond. I look to the possibility of all Virginia being overrun by the enemy, as has already happened to Kentucky. But even if so, I feel as far as ever from yielding to subjugation, & as confident as ever in our ultimate success.

March 11. Immediately after breakfast I rode to Ruthven, to advise with Julian about the previous call for volunteers, & the present levy in mass. I had before, as well as his brother, urged him not (as he proposed & wished,) to volunteer for the war. Every man cannot leave home—& his family & business engagements oppose his doing so with peculiar strength. Besides, his constitution, frame, & health [1840] are feeble, & therefore he is ill qualified to bear the hardships of a private soldier. As every other one of my sons & grandsons within the military age, & two who were without the limits, (besides myself,) are in the field, this certainly was enough for our family—& Julian attended in part to his brothers' business, in addition to his own. Besides, in proportion to his small means, he has been very liberal in his pecuniary & voluntary contributions in aid of the war & its suffering soldiers. Still, he felt as if subject to censure & reproach if he did not, at every sacrifice, volunteer to

[253]

serve in the field. This intention I & others of his nearest friends had before prevailed on him to give up, & to agree to stand the chances of the draft, & if drawn, to hire a substitute, if possible. But now that all will have to march, & he in the common militia, incapable & untrustworthy in the field, I found that he had come back to his previous wish to avoid this position by volunteering in his brother's company. I again argued against this course, setting before him the certain ruin to his farming business if left without any supervision or direction, he having not even a trustworthy negro to leave in charge—& he agreed to seek out & hire a substitute if to be obtained, & steps were immediately taken to obtain one close by, who is not of the military age, but well suited otherwise.—Returned to Beechwood immediately after dinner. . . . The interesting current events, & the condition of the commonwealth & prospects of the war, & our own connection therewith, give unusual interest to the conversation of our family circles, both at Beechwood & Ruthven.

March 12. Nothing new in the papers today. Further facts of the falling back of our forces from the lines of the Potomac, & advance of the enemy. Great complaints of the misconduct of Gen. A. S. Johnston, which have even reached Congress. I hope he may be superseded. The more full accounts magnify the immense losses of public stores by the disgraceful surrender of Nashville—though, even if that surrender was inevitable, there were two weeks of previous notice & enough time to have carried off & saved everything. . . .

March 13. Threatening clouds & a little rain prevented my going to the Court House, to vote for the last amendments to the state constitution—but for which the polls will be open two more days. Afternoon, [1842] rode to Ruthven, & remained all night. Julian had been to the general muster of the militia, & heard that the call of the whole into service had been suspended, or postponed until the order shall be renewed.

March 14. Returned to Beechwood. The newspapers bring no confirmation of the report (which had been deemed certain) that the general call of the militia had been suspended. Already, in preparations for it 6 days of loss of labor, & of trouble, have been caused to every man subject to the call—& if it should be carried into effect, even for but a month, it would, in loss & distress, cost millions to the people, without any adequate object. Our positions on the Potomac, & in Fairfax, have been evacuated, & occupied in part by the enemy's forces. It is reported that we have evacuated Winchester. The enemy occupy Charlestown, in Jefferson, & Martinsburg. Burnside's fleet & army at last have been heard from. 75 vessels have ascended the Neuse to within 14 miles of Newbern, & had begun to land troops there, driving in our cavalry pickets. It may be inferred that their next movement will be to seize upon Newbern & the rail-road there.—There has been a great battle in Ark. near the Mo. line, between our army under Gen. Van Dorn, with Price & McCulloch subordinate to him, & the Yankee army—each estimated at about 30,000. The fighting had continued for 3 days, (the 5th, 6th, & 7th,) with great slaughter, & without decisive results, as, so far, both sides claimed the advantage.[29] On our side, Generals McCulloch & [James] Mackintosh were killed, & Price wounded. . . . The later & additional accounts of the late battle of Hampton Roads serve to increase the measure of our remarkable success. . . . The accounts of the more important events of the 8th. agree more nearly [than] usual—& the northern accounts, if undisputed, would not detract very much from our claims. But the northern & southern reports are altogether opposed as to the single combat of 4 hours, on the 9th, between the Virginia & the Monitor (or Erics[s]on Iron battery.) Each party asserts that the other was beaten & retreated, badly damaged. The Virginia certainly was not crippled, as asserted by the Yankees. But it seems like a drawn battle that both the opposing vesse[l]s should have drawn off—or if either of them retreated because of inferiority, that the other did not pursue & continue the attack. I fear that this indecisive result indicates that the Monitor is no contemptible antagonist for the Virginia. [1845] The Monitor has one superiority over the Virginia, in its greatly less draft of water. And though having but two guns, the enormous weight of shells & balls they can throw, 183 lbs. & 350 lbs., & the Virginia being but slightly injured by them (& by all the cannonading,) offer ample proof of its invulnerability to ordinary artillery.—The alarm at Washington at

---

[29] The battle of Pea Ridge or Elkhorn Tavern, the largest engagement west of the Mississippi during the entire war, was in fact a Union victory. On the decisive third day (March 8) Federal forces commanded by General Samuel R. Curtis ousted the Confederates from Pea Ridge and drove them toward the Arkansas River. Union losses totaled 1,384—nearly 13 percent of those engaged—while Confederate casualties numbered about 800 out of an army of 14,000.

the first day's performance of the Virginia was very great, & the joy for the (supposed) victory of the Monitor was great in proportion to the previous terror. A northern paper has the following passage in the letter of its Washington correspondent. "[Lieutenant John L.] Worden, who commanded the Monitor, is now the lion of Washington. His head & eyes were closely bandaged. He is led from place to place, & attracts universal interest. When introduced to Lincoln, a flood of tears gushed from his [Lincoln's] eyes. Lincoln grasped his hand with warmth, & said 'We owe to you, sir, the preservation of our navy. I cannot thank you enough.'" . . . [1846]—Reading the "Heart of Mid-Lothian." . . .

March 15. Rode to the Court-House to vote for the amendments to the constitution. These, on the whole, will improve the constitution greatly. But it still has enough of bad features remaining. Saw a paper of today, which contained no news—but some statements which may serve to explain why the Virginia retreated on the 9th to Norfolk, without having destroyed the Minnesota or beaten the Monitor—& without being beaten or disabled, as the Northern accounts assert. The great draft of the Va. prevented its getting within two miles of where the Minnesota lay aground—& in running against the Cumberland, the Va not only loosened (as before stated,) but *lost* its iron prow, which is its main offensive means. I infer that the latter incident caused the Va withdrawing to Norfolk for repair. . . .

March 16. Sunday. At Church.—It is not yet clearly understood whether the general summons of the militia is to be carried out or not. But they are not to go immediately into service, & not without further orders.—At night finished the "Heart of Mid-Lothian."— Heard today from Mr. Graves, who is just from Norfolk, (& who also saw the battle from Lambert's Point,) that the Virginia finally *did* draw off from the Monitor, after a long & close engagement, (on the 9th.) & proceeded to Norfolk to repair damages. The cause was that her iron prow, or sharp beak, was broken off in running against the iron side of the Monitor,[30] & thus not only a main means for attack was destroyed . . . [but] also the damage caused leaking. But there

---

[30] This damage was actually incurred when the Confederate vessel rammed the *Cumberland* on the previous day. During the two-day engagement, the *Virginia* also lost her starboard anchor, all her boats, two gun muzzles, and suffered extensive damage to her steam-pipe, smokestack, and armor plating. *Official Records*, Vol. IX, 10.

was no truth in the northern report that the Va. was greatly injured, & required to be towed to Norfolk. It also was slightly aground once during the action. It draws 22 feet water, while the Monitor draws 8 only. The Virginia was expected to be repaired in a few days more, & again ready for action.

March 17. Rode to see the farm work, & then to get the mail, & to Ruthven. Bad news entirely, of the enemy's advances in every quarter. . . . [1848] From Newbern, the capture of the town confirmed, after a defeat of our troops . . . . Fernandina had before been evacuated & occupied, with its strong fortifications, & without a blow in defence. Also St. Mary's, & Brunswick have been seized. So that every coast town in Ga., except Savannah, & several in Florida, are in the hands of the Yankees. In every one of these disasters I have no doubt that a sufficient cause was that our commanding generals were men without military talent or experience of military action. On the Potomac our army is falling back. The enemy occupy Leesburg, Centreville, & our upper fortifications on the Potomac. . . . Gen. Jackson, (according to orders,) has evacuated Winchester, which place was occupied by Banks' army. I have great confidence in our generals Jo[seph] Johnston & T. J. Jackson—& I still hope that they will gain a victory, (by concentrating their forces,) over one or the other, if not both, of the separated & superior armies which are advancing upon their retreat.—It is reported that the enemy's forces have advanced from Ky. to within 25 miles of Knoxville. Oh! for a J. Johnston or a Beauregard, a Bragg, or a Price, at the head of every army we have in the field, or in command of every important position held!—Remained with Julian at his work through the afternoon, & stayed at Ruthven through the night. [1849]

March 18. Returned to Beechwood, passing by & viewing the farm work. I mean to go to & see the work every day, unless prevented by other engagements or bad weather, hoping that even such slight supervision may be of some service—& also to better enable me to undertake a stricter charge, when the overseer shall be called away in military service. . . .

March 19. Began yesterday & finished today the arranging & stitching together my letters of 1861, separating, as heretofore, the letters of members of my family from those of other persons. Reading again the letters of Mildred received since Nov. 1860. Nothing heard from her since her last letter, dated Sept. 7, 1861,—though I have written to her 5 or 6 times since, & as long as there seemed any hope of communication.—Went by the P.O. to Ruthven, where the other members of my family had gone before. Julian in Richmond, on business necessary to be settled before he leaves home. . . . Reported that New Madrid has been evacuated. Our forces falling back at all points from the Potomac & Shenandoah. . . . Though several official reports have been published, we still are ignorant of the amount of our loss, & of that of the enemy, & of their amount of force, at Fort Donelson. . . . The remarkable high rise of the rivers, & the long continuance thereof, served greatly to aid the enemy's armed steamers in assaulting Forts Henry & Donelson, in the expedition to Florence, & in the later occupation of Nashville. All these would have been far more difficult, if possible, at an average height of water—& absolutely impossible at a low state.—Julian returned late at night, having had but 3 hours to be in Richmond. He heard, by verbal reports, that the Virginia would be again ready for action in a day or two—& that the propriety of the removal of the seat of government from Richmond, on account of danger from the approaches of the enemy's armies, had been discussed in secret session of Congress. Julian sold gold, to a broker, at 55 percent premium—& heard that those who bought from brokers had to pay 70 percent—or, that $30 in gold only was obtained in exchange for $100 in Confederate States or Bank Notes. . . .

March 20. Rain from early last night, & drizzle or mist all day, which detained me at Ruthven. Julian went again, by order, to the Court House, & with all the remaining militia, (reduced by volunteering & numerous exceptions to about 40 only,) ordered to meet on 21st. at Disputanta on the R.R. to proceed to Norfolk.—This day read nearly through [William Gilmore] Simms' "Life of Marion". . . . The acts of this hero, & of his brave & patriotic followers, are especially interesting at this time, when the like condition of the country already is upon Md, Ky, & Mo, & may soon overspread Va. Yet, S.Ca., when Marion & his men first began their resistance, continued & successful, to British dominion & oppression, was even more helpless & hopeless, weaker & more completely trodden down under the conqueror's & oppressor's feet, than is now the case with Kentucky, or even Maryland. In Missouri only, thanks to Price & some other partizan leaders, there have been such acts as will free the country. Oh! for a Marion in Kentucky, & men worthy to emulate his brave & devoted followers.

March 21. . . . The cotton in Newbern (which I suppose was not much,) was all destroyed by our authorities. Also the naval stores, which were more valuable. So, though we lose them, our enemy will gain nothing of the cotton &c. which they seek to plunder, & would be rejoiced to buy. They have now several cotton ports in their possession, & they have not been able to obtain a single bale of cotton by the will of the owner—& scarcely enough for two ship-loads, by all their acts of plunder. They claim to have got at Nashville, $100,000 worth, which at N.Y. prices would be not more than 1000 bales. All the remainder they got at Port Royal, & most of it by gathering from the fields.—Scarcely any news today, & no telegraphic reports for the last two days. . . . In remodelling his cabinet, Pres. Davis has translated Benjamin from the War to the (vacant) State Department, & made George Randolph Secretary of War. Returned to Beechwood. . . . Gunpowder is very scarce, & enormously dear. For private use, & by retail, it was long ago $2.50, & since has been $3 the pound. Whether lower now I do not know. Sundry new factories have been set up, & one in Petersburg. It was a gratifying fact that from this, part of the "Virginia's" powder was supplied before the late battle, & a full supply has been so furnished since.

March 22. Packed in a box my most valued manuscripts, private family letters, & copies of some published articles. Shall send it to Ruthven for greater safety, in case the Yankee plunderers should reach this place, & burn the houses. After dinner, went to Ruthven, carrying John.—At last, a letter has been received (by Julian,) from Mr. B. Sayre, giving news, good & bad, of Mildred. His letter of Jan. 19th had been two months on its passage—& my last one, received before he wrote, was nearly three months older. When he wrote, Mildred's infant daughter was 3½ months old, & well. Mildred had been very well for more than a month after her delivery, but since had suffered greatly from attacks of neuralgia in [1854] her head, &, at the same time, rheumatism in her lower limbs. . . .

March 23. Sunday. From Ruthven to Church, & thence to Beechwood. A yesterday's paper received by chance, tells of more disasters, or dangers. The enemy's gunboats have occupied Jacksonville, Fla., & it is feared that they will occupy New Smyrna, a more southern port, little used or known. It has lately been obscurely intimated that several different vessels had eluded the blockade, & brought valuable cargoes of arms & powder into southern ports. It now seems that they went to New Smyrna, & it is feared that, by unpardonable neglect, the cargoes have not been removed, & now may be captured by the enemy. Such is our usual management. . . . The enemy's troops have landed in force near Savannah & the rail-road thence to Charleston. I omitted to enter for yesterday that the march of the militia of the state (*en masse,*) has been suspended, to await further orders, & so Julian & the Beechwood overseer have not been yet taken from home. . . . The northern people are wild with joy at our retreat from the Potomac lines . . . . On the other hand, & notwithstanding their almost unbroken series of victories & successes for two months, some of the northern papers are uttering most dolorous lamentations over the intolerable costs of their triumphs. . . . [1856]

March 24. . . . The mail brought but little news. Our armed steamer Nashville has again gone to sea, from Beaufort N.C., & in the same manner as it came in, under the view & fire of the blockading Yankee war vessels, & without being struck.—Among the unvarying series of disasters to our armies, in defeats, & captures or evacuations of forts, there have been sundry skirmishes & guerrilla affairs in which our soldiers, in small parties, have been successful. . . . Capt. [John H.] Morgan, of Ky., has been rendering much good service near Nashville, on the out-posts of the numerous & triumphant Yankee army occupying that city, & which has met with no opposition since its conquest of Fort Donelson, except from this company. Every night some of the enemy's pickets have been killed or taken prisoners by Morgan's company, to the number [1857], as reported, of nearly 100 already. Morgan seems to be the only Kentuckian who promises to emulate Marion—& he does not operate in Ky., & doubtless because there are not enough true patriots & brave men there, in any locality, to conceal & favor such action. Were it otherwise, & the people of Ky were true to the South, they are far better able now to carry on guerrilla operations, & to the destruction of the Yankee power, than were the people of S.Ca. when Marion began his noble & successful course, for defending & saving his subjugated country from its powerful & before unresisted oppressors.

The annexed message of Lincoln's, recently sent to his Congress, was approved, & the resolution[31] adopted by the House of Repre-

---

[31] In an effort to consolidate Union control over the border slave states, the President had submitted the following resolution to Congress: "*Resolved,* That the

sentatives by a vote of 88 to 31, & will doubtless also be passed by the Senate. A general emancipation & confiscation bill, to emancipate all the slaves, & to confiscate all the other property of all secessionists in the seceded states, is before Congress, & will also doubtless be enacted. So much the better. I do not doubt that, whether now enacted, or denied, & protested against, this policy will be adopted & carried out by the Yankees, if they shall be enabled to do so by first subjugating the South. And [1858] that it is much better for our cause that their future policy shall be avowed & made known as soon & as generally as possible. If any southern men, after such undisguised avowals & enactments, shall, under any possible extent of disaster to our arms, be willing to submit, or will believe in any promises of favor from the North, they will well deserve to meet their certain fate of enslavement & impoverishment. . . . [1860] The Yankees have occupied Paris, Ten. & the main body of Gen. Buell's army, reported to be 80,000, is moving towards the Mississippi river, near Corinth, & our army, under A. S. Johnston & Beauregard, is meeting. A great battle seems probable thereabout soon. Our army, weakened by the defeat at Fort Donelson, must be inferior in numbers, & also composed in part of new & raw levies. The objects are momentous—the possession of the navigation of the Mississippi, & the command of the great system of rail-roads connected with Memphis.

March 25. . . . I have been wishing to make a visit to Norfolk, & have determined to do so now, inasmuch as the call of the militia has been suspended, & the overseer not withdrawn, for the present, from Beechwood. I shall set out on the 27th—& Julian, notwithstanding his business & his home-staying disposition, is much [1861] inclined to go with me. We suppose that the Virginia is now again prepared for action—& I hope, by going now, to witness its next engagement. If all ready now, it will not go out except in calm weather. . . . To our great surprise, Edmund arrived on horse-back soon after [dinner]. He is ordered to go to Richmond on military business, & with that, has leave to extend his absence to 10 days, & will use it to visit his sick wife in North Carolina. . . .

March 26. At 11 A.M. Edmund left to get on board the steamer for

---

United States ought to co-operate with any State which may adopt gradual abolishment of slavery, giving to such State pecuniary aid to be used by such State in its discretion, to compensate for the inconveniences, public and private, produced by such change of system."

Richmond. Soon after, I packed my travelling bag, & rode by the P.O., to [get] the mail, to Ruthven. There heard that Gen. Huger had positive[ly] called out the militia of his military district, & that Julian mus[t] proceed on the 28th to Norfolk, on military service, for an indefinite time. At first, I resolved to give up my trip to Norfolk. But afterwards, thinking that I could not be wanted here immediately, & if to be of any service to my sons, it would be better after a short time than now, I came back to my first intention to go. . . . The Yankee army occupying Winchester, about 18,000, appeared to retreat, & so deceiving Gen. Jackson, he returned & attacked them, some miles from Winchester, with only some 6000. After a sharp contest, he was defeated, with the loss of 200, & retreated. How many the enemy lost is not known. Jackson must have been deceived—& that deception [1862] compels me to give up the hope & expectation that, by a combined movement, Gens. Johnston & Jackson would fall first upon Banks' army, & defeat it, & next move upon the Potomac army.[32]—Large bodies of troops have been sent to reinforce those between Newbern & Goldsborough—some have gone from Johnston's army, & some from Norfolk. None of these movements are in the newspapers. . . . On last Friday, the Dispatch contained a letter from Col. Blanton Duncan, a refugee from Ky,[33] of[fer]ing $2000 towards a subscription for [bui]lding another iron-clad steam vessel on the plan of the Virginia, for the especial defence of James river & Richmond. I responded to it immediately by the annexed letter . . . .[34] The ladies of Richmond have since held a public meeting to forward this object, & there are indications that [1863] it may be effected.—After dark, unexpectedly arrived from the camp near Norfolk, John

---

[32] The diarist was unnecessarily gloomy in this assessment, although he, of course, could have no inkling that the engagement at Kernstown on March 23 was to mark the beginning of Jackson's brilliant Shenandoah Valley campaign. To be sure, Jackson was deceived at Kernstown, where he led 4,200 men against Brigadier General James Shields's division of 9,000 and was repulsed with the loss of one-sixth of his command. But his attack had the desired effect of withholding support from the armies of Banks and McDowell for McClellan's Peninsular campaign, which was just getting underway.

[33] Duncan, a rabid secessionist from Louisville, had raised a regiment of Kentucky Volunteers at the outset of the war and later served as a volunteer aide to General Joseph E. Johnston at First Manassas. *Official Records*, Vol. LI, Pt. 2, p. 66; Vol. II, 478.

[34] In his communication to the *Dispatch*, the diarist heartily endorsed the project and pledged $500 to the proposed fund.

Meade, the son of Mrs. Meade & brother of Lotty, on furlough of 7 days only, & the first time in his 11 months of service. He reports that portions of the militia had already arrived at Norfolk, & were being drilled.

March 27. At 4 A.M. I arose, & by 5 set off, in a buggy, for Disputanta, 9 miles distant, on the Rail Road. At 7.30, on the train from Petersburg, & reached Norfolk by 11.30 A.M. Took lodgings & board at the Atlantic Hotel. Met with Dr. [Jessie J.] Simpkins, & informing him of my wish to see the Virginia, he offered to go with me, & introduce me to some officer of the Navy Yard. While waiting a short time for him to come, I used the delay to go into t[he] office of the Albemarle & Chesapeake Canal Co., close by, [to] see Mr Marshall Parks, & found not only him, but Lt. [William H.] Murdaugh. Both were my companions in our cruise in Currituck & Albemarle Sounds, some years past.[35] On my saying that I was going to the Navy Yard, they said that they also were about to go, & in the same little steamer, Calypso, in which we made our former voyage. So we joined Dr. Simpkins, & all were soon landed at the Navy Yard. Lt. Murdaugh was one of the defenders of Fort Hatteras, & there had his arm badly broken by one of the shells thrown by the Yankee fleet. . . . Under his guidance, than which there could be none better, I took a general view of the Navy Yard & its contents, which I had not seen since the partial destruction by the Yankee forces, at the time of their evacuating it, & fleeing in drunken terror to [1864] take shelter under the guns of Fortress Monroe. The wrecks of the huge Pen[n]sylvania, the Columbus, & another large & old ship of war, lie where they were then burnt & sunk, & are not worth raising or repairing. The Merrimac, the Germantown, [&] Dolphin have been raised, & repaired for different purposes. Three new gunboats (steamers) are well advanced in construction, & 4 more are in Norfolk, nearly or quite completed. The former Merrimac, now the Virginia, which performed such remarkable & great services lately, was the chief object of my visit & examination. It is in the Dry Dock, receiving some additional improvements. The repairs of damages received in the fight have been made. It is under[stoo]d that it could go into action in a day or two. The repairs of the Patrick Henry have not been completed. That steamer & the Jamestown, (now called the Thomas Jefferson,) are lying here— & also the small gunboats Raleigh, Beaufort, & Teazer, all of which

---

[35] See Volume I, 210–13.

had some share in the battle, but none had much effect except the Virginia. The sides of the Virginia are entirely under water, (when it is afloat,) & the sides & ends of the deck slope upwards from the sides at angles of 35 degrees to the horizon. The 10 cannon are about midway of the slope of the deck, 4 on each side,& a heavier pivot gun at both head & stern, & each of which pivot guns has three port-holes to use, varying the direction by a quarter of a circle. The port-holes are open only when the gun is fired. At all other times they are closed by iron doors, as thick as the heavy plating [1865] of all the deck & upper part of the sides. The upper ridge of the deck is truncated, presenting a flat surface of some 5 or 6 feet wide, which is a grating formed of square iron bars, about 2½ inches thick, & the open intervals being no wider, for ventilation, & the escape of smoke. There is very little of the smoke from the guns which is left inside—being kept out by the small size of the side port-holes, & the quick closing of the shutters for the pivot guns. I conversed with the lieutenant (Semmes [*sic*])[36] & the chief pilot, Capt. [Lewis] Par[r]ish, & heard many incidents & explanations of the battle, & operations. We returned at 3.30 P.M. After dinner, Mr. Hathaway, the e[d]itor of the "Day Book," the only paper now pub[lish]ed here, called to be introduced & to converse with me. He invited me to go to his office, (which is close by the hotel,) whenever I pleased to read his exchange newspapers. . . . After tea, I visited my former hospitable & kind hosts, Mr. & Mrs. [Charles] Rowland, with whom I passed a pleasant time in conversation, until near 10—before which time it is necessary to be out of the streets, or to have the military countersign, or otherwise any one is liable to be arrested by the guards, & confined for the night.—It seems that the evacuation of New Madrid was effected by our troops with but slight loss, except of the heavy artillery, which, as usual, was left & lost. Island No 10 [1866] is above New Madrid, on the river, but south of it. It is well fortified—& the enemy's gunboats & batteries have been cannonading & bombarding it vigorously for some days, with little effect. But notwithstanding the ability of our garrison for defence & resistance, I expect to hear of the surrender of the besieged place, either because the supplies have been cut off &

---

[36] Lieutenant Charles C. Simms assumed the duties of executive officer of the *Virginia* when Lieutenant Catesby ap Roger Jones succeeded the wounded Buchanan as captain of the vessel during the first day of the engagement in Hampton Roads. *Official Records*, Vol. IX, 11.

have failed, or the ammunition exhausted—together with the difficulty of holding a position so high up the river when all others near have been abandoned.[37]—One of our first commissioners to Europe, Mr. [William L.] Yancey, has returned, & has taken his seat in the Senate of the C.S. In a speech he delivered in New Orleans, [he] declared the hopelessness of our expecting the intervention of [Eng]land, to raise the blockade, or to render us any friendly aid. I have before stated my reasons for the same opinion, founded on the supposed wish of England that the northern & southern sections shall continue to damage & weaken each other as long and as much as possible, short of the entire subjugation of the South, & consequent reconstruction of the former U.S. dominion, under the power of the North—which final result, & such recovery of political strength to a hated & feared rival, I am sure England will not permit by her continued non-intervention. But, from Mr. Yancey's remarks, & some other speculations of my own mind, I now go farther in my views of the policy of England. Her ministers & rulers rejoice in the operation of this war on the South as the expected means for crushing our institution of negro slavery. And although this measure (as even Lord Russell must now see,) would involve the destruction of the great supply of cotton [1867] to England & to Europe, with unheard-of suffering to the manufacturing population, England is willing even to face this calamitous condition to her own & general interests, for another reason than her fanatical hatred of negro slavery & the desire to destroy it in these southern states. By that destruction, & the consequent destruction of our great product of cotton, England would be left the then greatest cotton producer for sale (in India) in the world. And though the quality of the cotton would be poor, & the supply insufficient, England, being the producer, would hold a monopoly as against the other manufacturing countries of Europe. Brazil would be her only competition in production of cotton—& against that feeble power, she can wel[l ex]pect to act a like part, directly or indirectly, in crus[h]ing its slavery system & therefore its production of cotton, leaving England, by means of *her* East Indian slaves, the only great grower of cotton for sale in the world. These ends would well be worth to England all that her people may suffer by the protraction of

[37] The diarist's expectation proved to be correct. Island No. 10 capitulated to the forces of General John Pope on April 7, thus bringing the Federals a step closer to control of the Mississippi River.

this war. And I am now convinced that the policy of that country, or of its rulers, is directed not less by fanaticism for the extinction of negro slavery in the C.S. than for the destruction of cotton culture throughout the same region, which will be impossible, for exportation, without slave labor. . . .

March 28. After breakfast I went to the passport office to obtain [1868] a passport for the surrounding country, including all the camps & batteries. It was readily given, the blanks of a printed form being filled with a description of my person &c. I next crossed to Portsmouth, & thence walked to the Naval Hospital to visit Capt. F. Buchanan, my old acquaintance, & the heroic commander of the Virginia in its recent engagement. When admitted, by leave of his surgeon, I found him still confined to his bed, though his wound gives him but little pain. I conversed with [him] for more than an hour, & heard many interesting explanations & incidents of the fight. When I blamed him for having so greatly exposed his person, in firing muskets from the top of the grating, which I said was unjustifiable in [a] commander on whose life so much depended, he said that he [coul]d not help so exposing himself, for it occurred while the Va. was aground, when his direction was indispensable, & when below the deck (or roof) he could not see, or regulate the movement of the vessel. Besides the short time when it was actually aground, it was more often than clear touching & removing the soft bottom mud, which though not stopping the vessel impeded & injured its steerage. The iron prow was of cast-iron, & broke off, (as Capt. B. had predicted,) when it was first used, to run into the Congress.[38] After that, in the fight with the Monitor, the striking part of the Va. was merely of wood. The Monitor first retired from the battle, half a mile distant, & cast anchor on a shoal when the Va. could get no nearer. As it would have been merely wasting ammunition to continue firing at that distance, the Va then went back to the Navy Yard for its needed repairs. The prow is now made of hammered iron. It did not seem to me to project more than 1½ feet— & its extremity is not pointed, but is about 12 inches by 2. But I was told that this [1869] was sharp enough, & the prow plenty long. Capt. B. thinks that the vessel has been strengthened & rendered more operative for assault, by the alterations made. Capt. [Josiah] Tat[t]nall is appointed to take command now, & he arrived from Savannah last evening.—Went to the Day Book office to glance over

---

[38] Ruffin means the *Cumberland.*

today's papers—a very hasty & unsatisfactory mode of reading. . . .
Great battles must soon come off in three if not four places—near
Newbern—near the Mississippi—of the armies of the Potomac &
Shenandoah—& perhaps also in the Peninsula. It is reported, but
not credited, that large reinforcements [hav]e lately been landed at
Fortress Monroe, & that Wool [has] 50 or 60,000 men to throw upon
Magruder. It was reported today that a battle was then going on in
the Peninsula, & that Gen. Magruder had before asked for reinforcements from this place, which could not be spared. The reported fighting was not believed here. But it is understood that a
few days ago as many as 27 transport vessels filled with troops
landed them at Fortress Monroe.[39]—The heavy mortar fleet, which
was prepared at New York, has left Key West, for New Orleans, by
Lake Pontchartrain, according to the Northern papers. There are 21
mortar vessels, 8 steamers, & one store-ship, with 2000 men—sea
& land.—A younger brother of Capt. Buchanan, much beloved by
him, who also was an officer in the U.S. Navy, remained in the
northern service, & was on board the Congress when it was attacked & burnt. He was one of those who escaped.[40] Of course I
heard no allusion to this subject from Capt. F. Buchanan. . . .

March 29. Telegraphic dispatch, & afterwards the newspapers
from [1871] Richmond reported that Magruder's army had been
attacked on 27th, & fighting then going on. No accounts later than of
the 27th. . . . I had arranged to go today by the 2 o'clock steamer to
the camps & batteries at & near Sewell's Point—but when the time
had nearly arrived, slow rain had begun, which, with a previous
easterly wind, indicated a spell of foul weather. So I had to postpone my intended trip. I had waited until then to see my son Julian,
who came as appointed, at 11 A.M. There were but 31 men left of the
whole militia force of Prince George, [&] which remainder (after
the volunteering & exemptions,) ca[me] on the train today. . . .
Com. Tat[t]nall, who now commands the Virginia, boards & lodges
here, & I see him at meals, as quiet & apparently as much at leisure,
as if he had no public business on hand. I infer that while he is here

---

[39] On March 17 General George B. McClellan had begun transferring his massive
Army of the Potomac from Alexandria to the peninsula formed by the York and James
rivers. This formidable logistical movement was completed early in April, and on the
fifth of that month McClellan began his siege of Yorktown, thus inaugurating the
major campaign in the East during the spring of 1862.

[40] Actually, Paymaster McKean Buchanan was killed in the encounter between
the *Virginia* and the *Congress.*

(& he was at tea this evening,) there can be no very early movement of the Va. in view. Of course there will be no public notice of its setting out, before it is seen, & it is expected every day. It is still in the dry dock, but can be taken out in an hour. Improvements are going on.

March 31. The papers unusually deficient in news. No confirmation of Magruder's battle, & of other important matters, & therefore false. . . . I fear that there is no probability of the Virginia going out in a few days. I have arranged, with Capt. Doyle, & some others, who had kindly invited me, to go tomorrow morning to the camps at Sewell's Point.—After dinner, I walked to the camp of the militia, to see Julian. Found him sound asleep, he having served a[s] a sentinel for the preceding night. Except standing guard & answering at roll calls, [they] have had no duty to perform, & no drilling of these lately a[rri]ved. It seems as if it was designed, or at least there was no care to avoid, keeping the militia as untrained & useless as when first called into service. . . .

1862

CONCLUSION OF NORFOLK VISIT ❧ NAVAL
ACTION ON THE JAMES ❧ ANOTHER
SOJOURN IN RICHMOND ❧ AN END TO
LABOR FOR "OLE MARSE" ❧ EVACUA-
TION OF MARLBOURNE AND BEECHWOOD ❧
ON THE BATTLEFIELD AT SEVEN PINES ❧
J. E. B. STUART SEEKS A GUIDE ❧ THE
SEVEN DAYS' CAMPAIGN

April 1. At 9 A.M. set out in the government steamer which
runs regularly to Tanner's creek wharf, where I landed, & found a
horse waiting for my arrival. Rode to Capt. Doyle's camp, about a
mile, & which is less than half a mile from the beach of Hampton
Roads, opposite Newport News. Capt. Doyle had not returned, &
did not until the afternoon—but I found a hearty welcome &
hospitable entertainment from his three lieutenants, & partakers of
his quarters. Lieut. Johnson had a lunch in place of dinner,
immediately after which we rode to view the sundry fortified
entrenchments of Sewell's Point. They extend, with intervals, for a
considerable distance, & in the principal work there are about 40
heavy [1874] cannon pointed—some rifled & of long range. Some
of the works have bomb-proof casemates, but not for the greater
part. The lowest battery, (as yet masked,) is at the nearest part of the
beach to the "Rip Raps," or Fort Calhoun, (now "Fort Wool,") on the
artificial islet, opposite to Fortress Monroe. Two other forts I had
passed between Norfolk & Tanner's Creek, Pinnen's Point &
Craney Island. I was surprised to see so many ships & other vessels
lying off Fortress Monroe, after the sailing of perhaps 100 more
which had come in for shelter during the late easterly wind. All
these last had gone out, leaving only the Yankee fleet, & vessels
aiding that service, except a very few, among which are two French
war-steamers, & a British frigate just arrived. The Yankee fleet

presented a for[es]t of masts, stretching almost continuously from above the Chesapeake College, [to] below Fortress Monroe. It was impossible to count the vessels, though aided [by a sp]y-glass. But, at a rough guess, I supposed there were nearly 100 still [t]here. This morning there had come in 5 large steamers, & 4 tugs, each towing 3 large schooners, &, as supposed, all bringing reinforcements of troops, & supplies for troops. The army must now be very large, & it must be designed to begin aggressive operations in earnest, & most likely, a large part of the late Potomac army has been brought here, & the "march to Richmond" will be again attempted, up the peninsula. Gen. Magruder's army, above Yorktown, is greatly inferior in number, even with all the late reinforcements sent to him. The firing of cannon, at irregular intervals, and seemingly on the peninsula, has been heard yesterday & today—but no indication of a regular engagement.—This morning, there were some indications, (in the movements of the smaller armed steamers,) that the Virginia would soon come out—& I had strong hopes that the daily report that it was to be the next morning, was true at last. But when Capt. Doyle arrived, he told me that he had heard from the chief engineer that a strengthening & extending of the iron armor was in progress, which would require perhaps some weeks to finish. The vessel, on an emergency, [1875] could go into action at any time—& stronger for offence & defence than before—but the probability is, without some additional need, it will not go into service until this additional armament is completed. On this ground, I shall cut short my visit to this place, from which I had hoped to see the engagement, & shall return to Norfolk by the earliest steamer tomorrow, & get home by the next train.—The masts of the Cumberland above water present a conspicuous object, where that frigate was sunk off Newport News. . . .

April 2. At 9 A.M. walked to the wharf to meet the stea[mer,] but, owing to its going first to put out freight at Craney Island, it did not take off the passengers at Tanner's creek until nearly 11 A.[M.] [Reached] Norfolk before 12, but too late to get off by the train of this day. . . . The fortifications to defend Norfolk are more numerous than I supposed. There are intrenchments & cannon mounted at various places, from Town Point & the Navy Yard, both above Norfolk, to even with the Rip Raps, opposite Fortress Monroe—& there is no part of the channel of the river in which an enemy's vessel could be in which at least two contiguous forts or batteries

could not open a cross fire on . . . at once, & to good purpose. . . .
After dinner, [1877] I walked again to the militia encampment to
see Julian. The number in that one camp has been increased to 900,
by later arrivals from sundry counties. Yet no drill has been begun
for them, & no duty, except to keep a camp guard, & to answer to
roll-call three times a day. Yet so strict is the confinement to the
camp ground, of about 6 acres, & so few have leave of absence to go
out of it, that, if obtained in turn, it would be but once in 100 days
that any man can go to Norfolk, for business or recreation. The close
confinement is for no purpose, & the service for no benefit to the
country. And, if continued in same manner, no length of time will
make the men of any improved use as soldiers. However, those
earlier in service are drilled. The whole business of this call of the
militia, in mass, has been of the least possible use for the milit[ary]
aid of the country, & at very great & unnecessary annoyance [&]
heavy loss to the men—& still worse, if continued, will be ruinous
to the agricultural labors of the country. No white man is left at
home, of the military age—(& many before had volunteered of over
45 & under 16—) unless of the exempt for alleged or real bodily
infirmity, or legal excuses, who are many more than ought to be.
There are but few farms having any superintendence—& of course
there will be little work of the negroes, & enormous pillage &
waste. If this state of things continues, the usual production of Va.
will be reduced by half. If, instead of this useless & ruinous measure, there had been a strict draft of one-half of all the remaining
militia, without any exemptions except for real bodily infirmity &
incapacity, or for necessary & indispensable other public & official
service, then all the drafted men who could not leave their business
might have hired substitutes, or overseers, out of the postponed
class, the military [1878] service might have been supplied with
capable & good recruits, & yet enough men, of the right sort, left at
home to prevent the agricultural labors & production of the country
suffering greatly.—My seat at table is next to that of Com.
Tatnall—& so, by frequent neighborhood, without any introduction, we had come to exchange silent salutations when meeting
there. Today, at dinner, he spoke to me, about the raw weather only,
but as if to invite conversation. He asked me if I had seen the
Virginia, to which I answered yes, & added that I had hoped before
this time to see it in action . . . . Of course I did not make any inquiry
of him—[but] he smiled & answered that the vessel would be "out

[271]

in a few days." He remarked on the singularity of the condition of things, in which hundreds of people had come from a distance to witness the expected engagement, & thousands here were eagerly looking out to attend the great duel. At tea, we had more conversation, though on other subjects, of his leading. On his referring to his late stay at & near Savannah, I remarked on the very slow progress of the enemy's forces in attacking that place, & especially since they had commanded the passage of the river between the city & the fort. On this, he expressed an opinion that I was struck with the force of. He said that he had long been convinced that the enemy had no intention of making any serious attack or invasion of the southern Atlantic coast—but merely to so threaten it, & at various points, as to draw our armies to the defence, in great force, & in various places, & so to divert our attention & our strength from the west, where the enemy [1879] had their good soldiers, & where was their real & great object for attack. This seems not only good policy, but serves to explain the dilatory operations of the enemy's sea & land forces in North & South Carolina, Georgia, & Florida. But great as their forces have been there, & little as they have done, it is obvious that they have kept employed in watching them twice as many of our troops, scattered in various positions, & yet not strong enough anywhere to repel an attack of as many as the enemy could easily concentrate on one point. The impolicy of our plan of defence had been plain to me, even when I thought that the ene[my] really designed the invasion of the interior from the co[ast.] We had better have left them free to plunder & ravage [our] whole tide-water shores, of country, & even of the towns that were not (as Norfolk is) important military or naval positions, & kept our armies concentrated in the interior, than to have attempted to defend the numerous indefensible parts of our coast within reach of the fire from the enemy's vessels, & against which we had nothing of naval armament to oppose. If we could have drawn their army 50 miles from their vessels, it would be conquered. And if they dared not to leave the borders of the navigable waters, it would be an admission to the world that the conquest of our territory in general is impossible.—When I mentioned to Com. Tatnall the great number of Yankee vessels that I had seen yesterday off Fortress Monroe, & which I supposed to be as many as 100, he answered that there were about 150. I heard today, from good authority, that one of the pilots [1880] of the Virginia went down by land this morning, to make observations of what was to be seen from our shore.

April 3. Immediately after breakfast I went over to Portsmouth, designing to call again on Capt. Buchanan, at the Naval Hospital. But meeting with Lieut. Van Zandt, of the Ordnance Dept., I was induced to go again with him to the Navy Yard. Under his guidance, & with the aid of his explanations, I again visited the Laboratory, & different operations of manufacturing cannon, shells, & fixing ammunition, all very interesting. I saw the elongated shells & solid shot prepared for the 7-inch rifled Dahlgren guns of the Virginia. There were two new improvements in some ([of t]he latest) of these projectiles, deemed of important operation & [effec]t. One is a brass saucer-shaped appendage . . . to the bomb-shell, [o]r solid elongated shot . . . which, like the shot itself (or shell,) is not so broad as the diameter of the hollow of the cannon, so as to pass down it freely. But when the powder . . . explodes, its pressure causes the concave brass circular piece . . . to be flattened, & of course its circumference to spread out, so that it fills completely & closely the grooves of the rifled tube, & ensures the accuracy of the discharge. The other improvement is in the shape of the point or striking part of the shot or shell. The ordinary shape is a rounded point . . . . If this is fired against, & strikes against, the iron-clad side of a ship, precisely perpendicular to the plane, it will enter, if there is propelling force enough to make any projectile enter. But it is obvious that very few of all the shots fired can strike precisely perpendicular, in all directions, to the plane struck—& if not, this rounded point, or even a sharper point, [1881] must be disposed to glance [off the target].[1] . . . I next again viewed the Virginia . . . . The after-part of the vessel, to which the rudder is attached, seems to me its weakest & a very hazardous part. The whole is a projecting horizontal process, stretching out 12 feet or more in the rear of the hull & armor of the steamer, & the rudder under the after-part. It is true that the whole of this extension will be 6 feet under the water. But if it should be run into, or across, by the Monitor, (as was before attempted, but

---

[1] Unfortunately, a large tear renders the upper half of this and the seven succeeding manuscript pages illegible. As a consequence, the entries through April 9, 1862, necessarily will be fragmentary. The editor infers from what can be reconstructed on MS page 1881 that the improvement to the striking part of the projectile, which the diarist is about to describe, was the addition of a steel tip.

failed,) or by any other vessel, it seems to me that the rudder would be damaged, & the ship thereby disabled. It seems to me also that either of these vessels might be seriously damaged, if not captured, if the other would resort to throwing some combustible fluid, set on fire, as oil of turpentine ejected from a fire-engine, into the upper openings, when the two vessels were in contact. . . . The most exposed part of [the hull of the] Virginia was the angular sides, where the slo[ping deck or ro]of joins the upper part of the side . . . on which (below the angle,) there was only iron plating of one inch thick. It is true that the water was some 18 inches above the angle, & the upper line of the thin iron plating. But a ball having suitable direction might strike, with fatal effect, some feet below the water. To this danger, the Virginia was exposed when in action, & Lieut. [Catesby ap Roger] Jones told me today that a shot reaching her there would have sunk her. To guard against this danger, additional thick plates are now being spiked on perpendicularly . . . . This work was about one quarter done when I was first there. In the week since, it has been advanced another quarter. And if it is carried fully around, it will not be finished in two more [1883] weeks. . . . Met today [with] Lieut. Ro[bert B.] Pegram,[2] who has just arrived, & who invited me to visit him, which I did after tea, & spent a pleasant time. In conversing about the Virginia, I found that in the opinions of Lt. Pegram & another naval officer (whose name I could not hear,) the after-part of the vessel was deemed more liable to danger, & to destruction, than I had inferred. For not only might the striking thereon of another vessel endanger or disable the steering apparatus, but also damage the propeller, which is the moving power. These officers also think that this weak part may be protected by a covering of strong timbers, coated with an armor of iron. I shall not be surprised if this improvement, after being neglected to the last hour . . . shall then be adopted, & [thus detain the Virginia in dry dock for] two months or more. . . .

[*April 4.* Learning of s]ome new indications of intention to take [out the Virginia, &] also wishing to visit other persons in the [area who had k]indly & earnestly invited me, I went again [to the camps at Se]well's Point. This time I went first to the quar[ters of Quar-

---

[2] Lieutenant Pegram later commanded the *Merrimac* No. 2 (C.S.S. *Richmond*), which was completed in Richmond in the fall of 1862 and manned by the crew from the original *Merrimac*. *Official Records*, Vol. XVIII, 385.

ter-]Master Doyle . . . & made it my head-quarters. . . . After dining with the mess of Q.M. Doyle, (which included Col. Chamliss, Lieut. Col. Blane, & three other officers,) I walked to visit the camp of the Lynchburg Beauregard Artillery, (with some of whom I supped on returning,) . . . .

April 5. After breakfast, at 9 A.M. walked (refusing a horse,) to the wharf, to wait for the steamer. After unusual delay at Craney Island, we got to Norfolk wharf after 11.30, & barely in time for me to reach the train, which left at 12—everything having been arranged for my sudden [1885] departure, previously. R[eached] . . . [Ruthven by sun]set. . . . On board the steamer [I was introduced] to & conversed with Col. Vincent of New Orl[eans] . . . . He informed me more particularly [of what I had heard] generally before, that an iron-clad steamer . . . superior to the Virginia, had been built in [Norfolk &] was expected to be ready for service in another [few days?].[3] [If] the expectations of fitness & time be realized, we may tr[ust that such] a vessel will clear out the blockading squadron . . . & serve as the most important means for defence against the squadron now threatening invasion from up the river.

April 6. Sunday. Went to church with Lotty. There met with the Beechwood family, & to my great gratification Nanny had arrived from Richmond, & my nieces Juliana & Anna Dupuy, & my grand-daughter Jane R. Dupuy, had come with her. . . . I went to Beechwood. As I had before heard, Edmund had returned to his company, staying on his return from Richmond but one night at home. His overseer also gone to the army, & his son George, 16 years old, & totally without experience, the only one to give orders. Tomorrow morning I shall begin to aid him, & after seeing to & advising about arrangements here, will go then to see what I can do for the general direction of Julian's farming, which is still worse off. . . .

April 8. Heavy rain last night . . . . [Nearly] all ploughing & preparing for crops so [interrupted by] the unprecedented quantity of rain through [the last month that] there had been little farm work done—[& with so many of] the farmers & overseers being away, there will [be little] done in farming. Added to this, many of the

---

[3] Presumably the C.S.S. *Richmond*, which was under construction in Norfolk at this time. Following the evacuation of that city on May 9, the vessel was towed up the James River to Richmond, where work on it continued for some months. *Official Records*, Vol. XI, Pt. 3, p. 335.

m[ost valuable hands] have been impressed into the public service. [At Marl]bourne, half the male slaves had been taken to [construct] entrenchments for Johnston's new positions, & 4 mules impressed permanently.—Heard that Edmund's troop had been (lately) sent across the river, among other reinforcements for Magruder's army in the peninsula. . . . Edmund has subscribed $1000 towards the fund for building an iron-clad steamer, by gratuitous contributions. Still earlier, Julian had subscribed $100.—Mist in afternoon, increasing to steady drizzle at night. Cold. [1888]

[*April 9*]. . . . Drizzle still continues this morning. . . . Yesterday morn[ing, I fi]nished [Hugh B.] Grigsby's "Discourse on Littleton Tazewell"—[a fitting] tribute to the memory of one of the most remarkable men [as well as in]tellects that Virginia has produced. . . . Gen. Beauregard sometime ago made an appeal to the southern planters to give their plantation bells to the Confederate government to be cast into cannon. This appeal has been effectively responded to, not only by many wealthy planters, but also by numerous churches, of various or all denominations, giving their church bells for this patriotic object.—Liverpool salt at last sales in Petersburg sold at $40 for the sack of 4 bushels. The continuation of the Yankee blockade threatens more danger to our cause, by the consequent scarcity & high prices of necessaries of life, than do the Yankee arms & armies & fleets, otherwise.—[End of MS Volume 10—p. 1889] Rain so threatening that I was confined to the house before it began to fall steadily at 3 P.M. This prevented me (& I suppose every body else) from attending the called meeting of the exempts of the neighborhood.—The mail, with great & good news. Thanks to God! The previous report is confirmed of a great battle & complete victory to us, between the Yankee army in Tennessee, under Gen. Grant, & ours under Gens. A.S. Johnston & Beauregard. Their combined forces attacked the enemy at Shiloh, near to Pittsburg on the Tennessee river, on Sunday 6th, & after severe fighting for 10 hours, drove them in full flight to the river. They were thus fleeing, & our forces pursuing, at the last account & the end not reached. So far, the enemy's camp had been occupied, & all the baggage & provisions there captured, & most of the field artillery. How many were engaged on both sides, & how great the respective losses, was uncertain. But a short dispatch from Gen. Beauregard states the victory as "complete." I wait for more full & correct information as to these & other particulars. We had the great loss of our commander, Gen. A. Sidney Johnston being killed, but fortunately for him, after his victory was assured, & he died in the pursuit of the flying enemy. . . . I regret & heartily repent that I, in common with the public in general, had blamed & harshly denounced Gen. Johnston for not having succored & saved Fort Donelson, or the gallant army that defended it, & were made prisoners. There appears in today's paper the only vindication of his conduct [1890] which he had uttered, & which would not have been written, & would not have been made public now, but for the peculiar circumstances in both cases. He & Pres. Davis were old & warm friends. On this ground, while nearly all others were condemning Gen. Johnston, the President wrote to him a private & friendly letter inquiring, as a friend, as to the facts. This elicited an answer, which, after his heroic death, the President communicated to Congress, & which was read before that body, & spread on its journal. It is mild & modest, & does not give evidence of how deeply he must have been wounded by the censures which were cast upon him, & to which he made no reply. His letter states two facts which alone would go far to acquit him of having neglected Fort Donelson, even for securing other objects—& entirely from having refused succor, or even being permitted to know that it was needed. First—the number of his whole army, at Bowling Green, had been designedly exaggerated by reports made to deceive the enemy, & instead of being 50,000 or 60,000, as generally believed, was but about 30,000. Of these, he furnished to Fort Donelson, before the attack, 16,000—& had left but 14,000, including all unfit for duty. And the reports of every day of the fighting, from the commander at Fort Donelson, asserted continued success, even to the last dispatch of the last day at night, which declared success— though the next morning at dawn, the fort & troops were surrendered to the enemy. I had heard it intimated before (though there is no such intimation in Johnston's letter,) that [General John B.] Floyd & the other generals were so sure of success, that they did not want to lose or to divide the glory, for themselves, by calling for strong reinforcements, & thereby bringing [1891] Johnston, as well as his remaining force, to assume the command. But, whatever may have directed his course before his retreat from Nashville to Ala., he appears since, & speedily, to have planned & executed a most masterly & successful military movement. . . . There was some skirmishing on the 5th between our force under Magruder in the

Peninsula, & the strong Yankee army (now commanded by Gen. McClellan,) supposed to be 50,000 or more, supported by a flotilla of Gunboats in York river. They were repulsed, both by land & water—& no attack has been made since, to last evening. It is doubtful whether the enemy design any serious attack there. It is more probable that they are acting as they have done on all the more southern Atlantic coast, making attacks merely in supporting distance of their war steamers, & feints to induce the employment of large forces on our part to oppose them, thus kept idle & at expense, while more serious attacks are made elsewhere. A letter from Edmund informs us that his troop was ordered across the river to reinforce Magruder on the morning of the 6th, & set out immediately. All of us now in this house have some near relatives in Magruder's army—my nieces having two brothers there, & Mrs. Lorraine a grandson—& all here, except myself, suppose the enemy's attack to be in earnest, & a battle imminent. Yet all these ladies bear very composedly the supposed situation of danger, which, if as probable a year ago, would have distracted them with alarm & uneasiness. So much are we hardened to danger by use & habit.—Since the reverses & disasters of our armies, the Yankee people & government have become confident [1893] of their speedy & complete success, & their leading papers have boasted that the southern rebellion is virtually crushed, & that in a few months, order would be restored in the complete submission of all the revolted states. . . . The claims of superiority of the northern forces over the southern, are not far wide of the truth, so far as numbers, arms, naval power, & the present means for applying force are concerned in the question. But our superiority to our enemy is in the much higher moral & intellectual grade of the Southern people, & of the superior principles by which they are actuated, & the holy cause which supports their patriotism & courage. The southern people are defending their just & dearest rights, their property, their families, their very existence, against the fierce & violent assault of enemies who are impelled mainly by the greedy desire to rob us of all that we possess, to our complete impoverishment & ruin, & at the same time glut their fanatical hatred in our blood, & remunerate their ruinous expenditure, & loss, incurred in their flagitious war, by the confiscation of all the property of the south. Their impulses, & reasons for pursuing the war with vigor, are indeed strong—but they are [1894] but those

[278]

which actuate banditti & pirates in their pursuit of plunder by means of murder. The impulses which direct our defence are still stronger, in the necessity for preserving all that our enemies aim to take from us—& the means must be the patriotism & courage which directed the like resistance by the patriots who followed Marion, [Andreas] Hofer,[4] the first great William of Holland, & Leonidas. If physical force, & present means for using it, can overcome moral superiority, patriotism, principle, & the courage thence inspired, then the North has, even now, every prospect of success. But on the reverse grounds, in which I & most others of my countrymen confidently trust, there can be no question of the final & complete triumph of the arms of the South.

April 10. North-east wind all last night, & steady rain. The earth very wet, & the air very cold. Terrible prospects for farming, after a winter & spring so generally wet, & now so late. . . . Rode to Mr. Edward A. Marks', for his advice, & thence (under guidance of his son Charles,) to find the residence of Charles Harrison, a recently discharged soldier, & who before was an overseer, to see whether he would suit, & would serve in that capacity at Beechwood. Saw him, & had some explanations & negotiation, but nothing decided as yet. . . .

April 11. A clear day at last—but still N.E. wind & cool. Rode to the work here, & at Ruthven where I dined & returned at night.— The succeeding events after the great battle & our decided victory at Shiloh in Tenn., were unfavorable to us, instead of the results of the victory of the first day being doubled, as I had sanguinely expected. Gen. Buell's column of 30,000, from Nashville, arrived in time to reinforce the fleeing army of Grant. The battle recommenced on the next day, & was contested for some hours, when (as reported) both armies drew off, & ours fell back to its previous position at Corinth. It seems that our army lost nothing in this second battle with a greatly superior force opposed, except, as a consequence of that superiority, that Gen. Beauregard could not remove *all* of the great quantity of artillery, stores, camp equipage &c. which he had before captured, & which, during his pursuit, had been left behind him in the enemy's former camp. He, however, saved all his prisoners, (said to be from 4000 to 6000,) & much of the

---

[4] Hofer spearheaded a valiant uprising against French domination in the Austrian state of Tyrol during the Napoleonic wars. In the end, however, the rebellion failed, and Hofer was executed in November, 1809.

booty, & destroyed or spiked the artillery that could not be moved off. His army marched to Corinth in good order & not opposed—though the enemy's forces soon reoccupied their before captured camp. . . . Latterly, our authorities have contrived to keep the press silent as to reports which the enemy ought not to know, & to restrain the telegraph—& the commanders of armies have expelled or silenced the indiscreet correspondents of our newspapers. By this needed & proper reform, we are deprived of much information of facts, as well as of most of the false reports. For these reasons, we are in the dark as to the state of things in the Peninsula, near as the opposed forces are to us. [1897] It is understood that Gen. McClellan is there in command of an army not less than 50,000, & by some reports made 100,000. After a slight skirmish on the 5th. there has been no fighting since, & McClellan's army, instead of continuing to advance, is entrenching for defence, a few miles below Magruder's advanced line. What is the present force of the latter I have no information. It was said to have been 15,000 before this late movement of McClellan, but has been rapidly & greatly reinforced since, & troops have been going down James river to his aid in numbers during the last few days, so as to fill all the river steamers, to the exclusion of all private passengers down the river. The "Virginia" has been out of the dry dock some 4 or 5 days, & is lying in the Elizabeth river above Craney Island. This coming out so soon, & then waiting, both surprise me. The additional plating which was going on could not possibly have been completed so soon—& why the vessel should come out, & so notify the enemy to expect its attack, before being ready, I cannot conceive a good reason for.—The attack on Fort Pulaski [Georgia] has begun, & when heard from, the enemy's vessels & batteries had been throwing balls & shells for two days at the Fort. . . . The U.S. law emancipating all [1898] slaves in Washington & District of Columbia has passed both houses of U.S. Congress by great majorities. Also the resolution recommended by Lincoln, proposing emancipation by purchase in the border slave states. In both cases "loyal" owners are to be "compensated," or it is so promised in the laws. . . . [1900]

April 13. Sunday. All at church. Wind still blowing from N.E. & cloudy, threatening more rain. Heard that Gen. Lee (the C.S. Commander in Chief, lately appointed, & to reside at Richmond,) & Gen. Jos. Johnston, passed City Point yesterday on their way to our army in the Peninsula. This indicates that our highest authorities must expect serious work there, & very soon. Would that our army may be strong enough to attack McClellan's! The Virginia & some of our gunboats went out into Hampton Roads at last, on the 11th, & captured & sent in four unarmed vessels (transports,) of no great size or value, without firing a gun at either. The Va. also threw a few balls towards the Monitor, where the latter lay at anchor near Fortress Monroe. The latter answered the fire, but did not move to go nearer the Virginia, which then retired to Elizabeth river, & anchored. The delay of attempting any important offensive action, so long after the Virginia went out, as being ready for service, taken in connection with the recent indications of serious warfare on the Peninsula, makes me suspect that the Virginia is kept inactive to be ready to defend James river from being invaded by the Yankee war vessels—& perhaps to attack Newport News & the enemy's army there from the water, should our forces be able, & our commander aspire, to drive the enemy there in retreat, after defeating them in battle. . . . My nephew George R. Dupuy & his lately married wife, who had been expected for some days . . . arrived. They resided in Kentucky, & being secessionists, had to marry & [1901] flee immediately. Their coming very gratifying to all of us, & especially to George's sisters. . . . Heard from my nephew some facts which will not appear in our newspapers. Most of our troops lately sent so hastily from Va. to Goldsborough N.C. have been already and as hastily recalled, & sent to the Peninsula. A large body of troops, mostly called from the late Potomac army, is assembling at Richmond, which will amount (as understood) to 30,000, for the defence of that city during the present danger of its being attacked.

April 14. So closely engaged here that I had not time to go to Ruthven. At 4 P.M. went to the Church to the postponed called meeting of the neighbors to establish a Home Guard—but two only besides myself attended, so nothing was done. I shall not request a meeting again—but will be ready to act if any others will hereafter move. The mail. Some good news, but much more of bad. Fort Pulaski has surrendered, after being almost knocked to pieces, numerous breaches made through the walls & even into the magazine, under a tremendous cannonade & bombardment from the enemy's batteries continued for two days. Yet not one of the garrison killed, & but few severely wounded. The garrison of about 500, & everything else, captured. . . . It is also reported that Island No. 10 has been evacuated, or captured. . . . No certain accounts of fighting in the peninsula —& the delay & inactivity of McClellan's now large army, (reported as 100,000 or more,) augurs favorably for our prospects. Reinforcements have continued to be sent rapidly to our army there—& though it must still be very far inferior in [1903] numbers, (& we always are in arms,) to the enemy, I have strong confidence that we will repulse if not beat the enemy. It now seems manifest that a serious attempt is now in progress to capture Richmond. If the enemy could send a strong flotilla by our defences, up James river, or even up York river, it would be their best, & a very probable means for success. And that this has not been attempted up James river, we probably owe to the successful battle of the "Virginia," & its being now ready for action, & present. Its former remarkable & distinguished victory probably disconcerted the designed approach of Burnside's army to Norfolk, from N.Ca.

April 15. Rode before breakfast to Ruthven, & saw the work going on. Returned to meet with the man whom I had been negotiating with to serve as overseer at Beechwood. I found his demands increased, & increasing, according to his supposition of the necessity for his aid & service, & I at once refused, & closed the matter. I do not now see any prospect of engaging an overseer. . . . I was much in the field. I am glad to find that the strong repugnance I felt at first to attending to the business, (putting aside my wish to serve my sons' interests,) has already given way, & I already feel much interest in seeing & directing the operations at Beechwood. I cannot say that I experience the like pleasure as to those of Ruthven as yet, because nothing is done right there, though I try to attend to them as faithfully.

April 16. Nanny & all our visitors went to dine at Ruthven, as I did, but except 4 hours, I was nearly all day after breakfast in the fields where corn-planting is going on. The mail. The [1904] newspapers brought but little news. Our private letters, from Edmund & Thomas, to Nanny, George, & myself, were very interesting in the details of the service on the peninsula of the Prince George cavalry. Of course the writers could not see or know much of general operations. The company had been greatly exposed, day & night, in the rainy spell of last week. They were serving on picket duty on the western side of a mill pond, about 300 yards wide, at head of Warwick river (& 6 miles from Yorktown,) the enemy's pickets being on the opposite side. There was frequent interchange of shots, & also of words, in vituperative or contemptuous speeches between the opposed pickets. Some few on both sides had been killed & wounded (none in the P.G. cavalry,) but the inferiority of our arms, for long range, rendered our fire much less powerful than of the superior guns of the Yankee pickets—though they were not more successful in aim & effect.—Now that Fort Pulaski has been taken, there is nothing to prevent the enemy's approach to Savannah—& I expect to hear of its surrender very soon. The rump Congress & the northern papers claim the battle of Shiloh as a great victory, & are rejoicing, & giving public thanks for it. May they have more such victories! And yet, the northern reports of their losses there (in the two days,) even exceed the loose, &, as I supposed, exaggerated statements of our reporters. Different papers admit their loss, in killed, wounded & missing (prisoners,) to be 15 to 20,000; & the Baltimore American (a thorough Lincolnite paper,) states, more precisely, 23,000 as their loss.[5] . . . Our Congress has passed the law ordering into military service all men not over 35 years old, & not exempted. I do not yet understand how this law will affect those now in service (involuntarily) who are between 35 & 45.—It is understood that nearly all the former Yankee army of the Potomac has been removed to the peninsula under McClellan, & that there is no considerable force in Va. near to the Potomac, though [Brigadier General Daniel E.] Sickles' & other marauding troops have been laying waste the counties opened to them by the retreat of our Potomac army—which also has been mostly withdrawn to the peninsula under Johnston, who is now in command there. It seems to me that, in this changed condition of things, in the country between the Potomac & Rappahannock, either side might be struck heavily & disastrously by a sudden & bold stroke from the other. If either could have a good & well commanded force of but 20,000, with it, the one might reach Richmond or the other Washington, with no opposition on the way.[6] I am very glad that Gen. Johnston's presence & higher rank supersede Gen. Magruder's chief command in the Peninsula. Though the latter is a good officer, he is said to be intemperate.—

---

[5] Actual losses at Shiloh were about 13,000 Union and 10,700 Confederate. The combined forces of Grant and Buell on the second day numbered 62,000, as opposed to the effective Confederate strength of 40,000.

[6] It was precisely the latter possibility that prompted Lincoln to withhold General Irvin McDowell's First Corps from the Peninsula, thus precipitating an acrimonious exchange between McClellan and the President.

Northern accounts make McClellan's forces in the peninsula more than 100,000. Our army is reported to be now 60,000. Both were lately continually receiving reinforcements. With this great army, & with one certainly inferior opposed, [1906] Gen. McClellan must fight, or be disgraced in the opinion of the people of the North. He has already been denounced in the harshest terms by the N.Y. Tribune, & other abolition presses & politicians, for his long delay to act while at Washington, & for his alleged incapacity.—Full one-half of the territory of Virginia is now either under the present domination of the enemy, or exposed to the incursions & outrages of their marauding corps, without defence. If in the impending great battle which must soon occur in the peninsula, our army shall be defeated & routed, Richmond must fall, & probably all the remainder of Virginia be left open, & unresisting to the complete domination of the enemy. On the other hand, if we shall give to McClellan an overwhelming defeat, it will go half-way to end the war, if Beauregard will gain another great victory, for the other half. Momentous as is the present crisis of our affairs in Va, & with the enemy's & our forces at 100,000, or more, to 60,000, besides their naval forces, I look to the issue not only with hope, but almost with confidence. And whether well-founded, or not, such must be the general feeling, & of women who are mothers, wives, daughters or sisters of soldiers in our army, as well as of men in like relations, & citizens generally. Of course all feel great interest & anxiety. But I do not see any indications of despondency, or of terror. The females of this household seem to be more concerned & perturbed at the recent great exposure of their near relatives in this army, to rain & cold, & the other causes of suffering & probable sources of sickness, than because of the impending battle to be fought against a well-equipped & well-commanded army, of nearly [1907] double our numbers & physical power & means.

April 17. Warm for the last two days. Rode early to Ruthven to direct the labors. It is disheartening to me to find that so little is done, & no agents by which anything better is to be expected. Thieving also has been begun there, & here. This there is no means for me to prevent, or even to check. Returned before 12. The work here at least is done well—though probably not near enough of it by any of the hands—& if half a dozen are skulking out of sight at a time, I do not know them, & should not miss them. . . . My nephew George Dupuy left us today to make a short business visit to the

South, leaving his wife until his return. He sent to me from Petersburg the news that there was a partial engagement yesterday on the peninsula, about 5000 on each side, in which our troops repulsed the enemy. Our loss, about 20 killed & 75 wounded. . . .

April 18. The mail, (which includes the Petersburg & Richmond papers of same day,) brought confirmation & details of the partial engagement of 16th, but there had been no fighting since. Island No. 10 has been surrendered to the enemy, with part of its garrison, & all its heavy artillery &c. . . . The Yankee authorities have ordered a salute of 100 cannon to be fired for rejoicing, & solemn thanksgiving to be offered by the chaplains for every regiment in the army, for this victory & two others which they claim: viz. the battle of Elkhorn, or Pea Ridge, in Ark. in which our army under Van Dorn & Price in effect beat them severely, & for the later battle of two days at Shiloh! or Pittsburg Landing as they call it. . . . For a week or more, steamers have been passing down this river every day, in our view, carrying troops to reinforce our army in the peninsula.—Rode to Ruthven & the work there, & returned. From breakfast to nearly dark, most of my time is spent at the work of one or both of these farms.—A requisition has been made for half of every proprietor's male slaves in this part of Va. to go next Tuesday to the army in the peninsula, to perform labors in aid of the military operations. Arranging for complying with this draft, for both farms.

April 19. Early writing to Edmund—& received two letters [1909] . . . dated 16th & 17th, & one from Thomas. They were under arms & close by, during the engagement of the 16th, but prevented seeing the fighting by intervening woods, & had the enjoyment of the excitment of the occasion. Edmund's account agrees very closely with the more concise & general statements published. We had many soldiers & laborers digging & throwing up breastworks. The enemy attacked them, by wading across the millpond, or river, knee deep, drove off our working party, & occupied their position. But they were soon opposed by some of our regiments, driven back & pursued across the water in the course of the fight for three hours, & effectually repulsed, with, it was thought, much heavier loss than ours—which was 80 wounded & 25 killed—among the latter Col. [Robert M.] McKinney of N.Ca., who commanded one of the regiments,[7] & fell as bravely leading it on. . . .

---

[7] Colonel McKinney commanded the Fifteenth North Carolina Regiment in this engagement at Dam No. 1, or Lee's Mill, which proved to be the most serious encounter during the siege of Yorktown.

April 19, 1862

The French ambassador to Washington went to Norfolk in a French war steamer, & thence by rail-road to Richmond. It is supposed that his business with our President is to obtain permission for the free exportation & passage from Richmond of the very large amount of tobacco bought there & held by [August] Belmont, a citizen & resident of N.Y., to supply the French government. Others suppose a more important object (to us,) either to offer mediation between the South & North, or to arrange for our recognition.—An [1910] amusing example of the systematic lying, for policy & effect, appeared yesterday in the papers. Com. [Andrew H.] Foote, commanding the U.S. naval force which so long besieged & finally compelled the surrender of our fortifications on Island 10 (after evacuation by & retreat of the greater number of the garrison,) in his official report, gives our losses in detail, & no doubt made them fully as great as could be with any appearance of truth. Another account in the N.Y. Herald, elaborately particular & minute in details, & therein carrying every appearance of being made out with full knowledge of all the facts, was published just before, which is so outrageously & ludicrously exaggerated (taking Foote's report as true,) & so plainly a designed falsehood, that even the mendacious character of the Herald does not prevent astonishment that such incredible lies should be put out. But the cause is apparent, in the same paper, in the advertisement of the regular steam packet for England to leave N.Y. next day. This report of the latest victory for the North will go to England, &, until the arrival of the next following packet, some 15 days later, will in England pass for truth. When exposed, the editors of the Herald will offer neither excuse nor contradiction—& feel no shame, but, like Seward & Lincoln, in their official lies, take credit for having attempted to gain, or succeeded in effecting, a profitable object by these means. . . .

April 20. Sunday. Set out for church, but all of us were turned back by the renewal of rain. Afternoon, rode to Ruthven to stay the [1912] night. Mrs. Callender (Lotty's elder sister) there, from whom I heard many matters of news, or opinion, from Petersburg, which are not allowed to get into the papers. Also she had brought a paper of yesterday. The Yankee land force (said to be 5000) had advanced to Falmouth opposite Fredericksburg, & their gunboats had ascended the river to within a few miles. Our small military force had retreated, after burning the three bridges across the river, several steamers & other vessels lying there, laden with corn. Fredericksburg had surrendered, under threat of being shelled, but had not been occupied by the enemy, who were rebuilding one of the burnt bridges, before entering. No opposition to them expected. The opposed armies in the peninsula have continued to be reinforced. . . . Since the partial engagement stated, in which we obtained decided advantage, there has been no fighting. But both before & since, there has been slow cannonading from both sides, apparently to prevent the labors of intrenching by the opposite party, & to cover the like operations of their own. . . .

April 22. Sent off 9 men from Beechwood & 2 from Ruthven to Williamsburg, in compliance with the military requisition.—The ground too wet for any ploughing or preparatory labors for tillage—& the low-ground too wet even for grubbing, & it is too cold for wet ditching there, even if there were ditchers left.—Heavy shower at 12 M. intermixed with hail. . . .

April 23. Rode to Ruthven & returned to dinner. Ploughing here, & returned to cleaning out ditches in lowground.—A large body of Yankee troops have landed at Aquia creek, which will increase the body near Fredericksburg to 35,000. These of course are designed to move upon Richmond. Also Banks' army in the Valley has pressed our small opposing force under Jackson to retreat to Staunton. Thus Richmond is threatened from three points, & it is doubtful whether the main attack is designed from the army in the Peninsula, or by way of Fredericksburg. I very much fear that the great army of McClellan in the peninsula is but making a feint, & after drawing nearly all our opposing force there, will suddenly embark, & join the northern invading army, where we are comparatively defenceless, & would not have time to change our strong position. I long for the attack to be made [1916] & the great battle to be fought in the peninsula. If we do not gain a victory there, & very soon, Richmond will be in greatly increased danger, & if Richmond is taken, all the remainder of Virginia will be overrun, & defenceless. . . . The Yankee mortar flotilla has been bombarding the forts on the Miss. below New Orleans (100 miles) for three days, with an enormous expenditure of ammunition, & so far with no damage to the forts, & but little to the garrisons.—The C.S. Congress adjourned to August, on 21st, leaving much important business unfinished, as to indicate that the hasty removal of the members was owing to the fear of the occupation of Richmond by the Yankee

[287]

army. The French Minister to U.S. left the day after, & proceeded by Norfolk to Washington. It has not been made known what was the object of his visit.

April 24. . . . This [1917] is the day to elect a member of Congress for this district to supply the vacancy caused by the resignation of Pryor, who had been recently promoted from a Colonel to be a Brigadier General. After seeing the work here & at Ruthven, I rode to the C.H. & voted for J. A. Seddon. Very few voters at home—& most of these of the least worthy description, the most worthy citizens being mostly in the army. A government like ours of universal suffrage will always be a government of & by *the worst* of the people. And at this juncture we are still worse off, as the best portion of the whole voting mass is abstracted, & practically disfranchised. . . .

April 25. The mail brought but little news. The powerful mortars of the much boasted Yankee flotilla had been bombarding the two forts on the lower Mississippi (Jackson & St. Philip,) for several days, at an enormous expenditure of ammunition, & to little purpose. The besieged estimated that 1000 tons of shells had been thrown, & at Fort Jackson 5 men only had been killed, & 10 wounded. No report from St. Philip, but that believed to be as little hurt. . . .

April 28. Before we left the church yesterday, a report from Petersburg reached us, which, though of momentous disaster, I deemed too incredible to deserve notice. It is too true. New Orleans is in the possession of the enemy, & without resistance! Some or all of the vessels of the mortar fleet had passed the forts below which they had before been bombarding without damage. They steamed up the river to within shelling distance of the city, & demanded its surrender under the alternative of it being bombarded . As in the latter case, general burning & destruction of property would be inevitable, & no artillery of ours could meet with success these powerful mortar steamers, the authorities deemed it necessary [1920] not to oppose forcible resistance. . . . This disaster is to us most momentous—& still worse consequences must certainly follow. There is not now even the insufficient defence of a fort, or land battery of heavy artillery, to interrupt the progress of these mortar vessels up to Fort Pillow (70 miles above Memphis,) & wherever these powerful & almost impregnable vessels can reach within two miles, every town will be at their mercy. No amount & bravery of our mere land forces can successfully oppose even a single one of these mortar vessels. They will soon compel the surrender of Natchez, Memphis, & every other town on the Mississippi, & the lower & deep waters of its tributary rivers. The still remaining forts, below & above, cannot long hold out, when there can be no army to support either of them—&, when they are taken, the whole length of the Mississippi & its great tributaries through the Confederate States, will be open to the armed vessels of the enemy. Our communication with Texas is completely cut off, & soon will be with Louisiana, Arkansas & Missouri. To damage the enemy is one of the most usual designed operations & gains of war. In that respect, the Yankee power has struck a most heavy blow, [1921] & obtained a great triumph. But the direct profits, on which the North will count as certain consequences of the military possession of New Orleans, & the lower Mississippi river, will yet be found wanting. The government & people of the North will expect, & ascertain, that the port & river will be open as formerly for their trade: That cotton & all other southern products . . . will be willingly & eagerly sent by their producers & owners to be sold at the present high prices to northern merchants, or southern renegades, & shipped from New Orleans to Northern or European markets: That peaceful commerce will be restored, & all the heretofore shut-up products of the northwest will descend the river & find purchasers & shippers in New Orleans. I expect very different results. The cotton & tobacco, which would be the most eagerly sought booty where available, will mostly be burnt. The more safe portion, which might be sold to the enemy, will be held back, if not destroyed by the patriotic owners. I trust also that in like manner as at Port Royal & Nashville, few of our people will buy the products brought from the North, however cheap, & tempting in their recent destitution. Also, every freight & trading vessel on the Mississippi, belonging to the North, will, if captured, be lawful prize to our forces—& unless well armed, every one may be easily captured, or burnt, & by but a few bold men, in the long voyage, & necessary numerous stoppages for fuel, on the river. River privateers (in rowboats) & water guerrilla parties will make the trip of every freight vessel extremely hazardous. And this may be even if the enemy shall hold every town on the rivers in sullen & unresisting submission, & no open military resistance be shown anywhere along the banks of the rivers.—Heard through private information [1922], more confirmation of the troops of McClellan being in the course of withdrawing from the peninsula. A large passenger steamer today came up this river full of soldiers, which clearly indicated that our troops also are being sent off to oppose the enemy's expected approach elsewhere. . . . It is a great misfortune that a general engagement did not take place where the great armies have been lately opposed. And though I suppose that our commander (Johnston,) ought not to have attacked a larger & better equipped army, strongly intrenched, & supported by a naval force, still I do not abandon all hope, that during the withdrawal of the Yankee army, its remaining portion may be attacked, & also the aid of [1923] the "Virginia" made available. . . . Though the Yankees may occupy not only New Orleans but all other towns on the lower waters of the Mississippi, they cannot hold them long, if nothing forbids but the climate & season. In May, all these places will be sickly for northern constitutions, not acclimated—& by July they will be pestilential. . . . Besides this cause of loss, there will be plenty of what Gen. Buell in Nashville termed "assassination," including the nightly shooting of picket guards, & the other operations of guerrilla bands, besides the actual stabbing or shooting of Yankee soldiers, by individual action & private vengeance.

April 30. . . . Fort Macon, after being bombarded until no longer defensible, surrendered to the enemy. . . . The later reports from New Orleans serve only to increase the mystery & the wonder of the occupation of that city. It has not been formally surrendered. No Yankee has landed, except the bearers of a flag of truce to demand the surrender, & the hoisting of the U.S. flag, & removal of the C.S. flag—all which the Mayor refused to aid in having done. . . . So silent (by government policy) have been our papers on matters desirable to keep the enemy ignorant of, that the number & strength of the forts on the Mississippi near to New Orleans, & the number of the garrison of the city, are altogether uncertain. And as the telegraph at N.O. was broken up, & the operators fled, as soon as the near approach of the vessels was certain, we have learned nothing of details since. . . . The spirit & loyalty of the people of N.O. seem to be everything that could be desired. The "Home Guard" & the "Foreign Legion" (both probably composed of men exempt from legal military service,) keep guard & maintain order. . . . [1927]—Gen. [Mansfield] Lovell, on whom dark suspicions seem to lie, even of treason, was not born in the North, but resided there before the war, & until after the battle of Manassas. Then he either sought or was invited to command in our service, was appointed at once Brigadier General, & placed in this most important command, & since has been made a Major General.[8] Whatever may be his military abilities, a man so slow to side with us ought never to have been so received & trusted. This was one of Pres. Davis' numerous very bad appointments. Gen. [Benjamin] Huger was another. He was in the U.S. army, & did not leave it for the service of the South until after the Secession of Virginia & long after his own state, South Carolina, had seceded, & was arrayed in arms in defence against the government Huger still served. In addition to this sufficient demerit, Gen. Huger ought to be broke for his neglect & inefficiency, & especially for the result of both in our disaster at Roanoke Island.[9] . . . The recent disaster at New Orleans, & the probable consequences, have operated to depress my spirits more than all the previous losses to our arms & cause. I cannot now help admitting the supposition of the *possibility* of the subjugation of the southern states & the ruin of their cause in the establishment of the despotic rule of the North, which will be worse than any domination effected in modern times except that of the English under Cromwell over Ireland—& not exceeded in the infliction of loss to the conquered, [1929] even by the triumphs of barbarian hordes that successively laid waste the Roman Empire. But whatever may be my despondence, it does not dispose me (or I trust our people,) the least to submission—but rather increases the determination to resist by every possible effort, & at every sacrifice. Rather than submit to Yankee domination, such as it would be after victory, & our complete submission, it would be better for all to be killed in battle. If we are to be held as subject provinces, I would prefer that our despotic ruler & master should be any power of

---

[8] Lovell, the Confederate military commander in New Orleans, was a native of Maryland, who, following service in the Mexican War, had moved to New York City where he engaged in iron manufacturing and served as deputy street commissioner until September, 1861. Upon the recommendation of Joseph E. Johnston, he then received an appointment as brigadier general in the Confederate army. Although later cleared by a court of inquiry of responsibility for the loss of New Orleans, Lovell was so stigmatized by this Confederate disaster that he did not receive another command during the war.

[9] Ruffin's appraisal of Huger was not unjustified. Indeed, the latter was later relieved of his command in the East following a congressional investigation which held him responsible for the debacle at Roanoke Island.

Europe, even Russia or Spain, rather than the Northern States. . . .

May 2. Last night heavy rain, with thunder & lightning. The first warm day. Westerly wind. I believe that, with a few intermissions, none of which exceeded 24 hours, the wind has been easterly for some weeks. Such continued or repeated rains have prevailed since Christmas, as never known before—& the quantity of water fallen not less than in frequency.—No definite or important news by the mail—& absolutely nothing from New Orleans since its incomplete surrender. . . .

May 3. Last night, another thunderstorm, & very heavy rain. The earth seems more surcharged with water than at any previous time of this very long wet time. All the previous work, & all orders given last evening, unsuitable or improper, because of the increased wetness of the lowground, & depth of water in the ditches to be cleaned out.—Last evening we heard . . . that Edmund was to be at home last night, or very soon after. This kept us in anxious expectation, until he arrived tonight, & bringing his son Thomas also, who has been very sick, with dysentery, but is improving. He was so ill that he would have been sent to a hospital—but those near were filled, & there was no conveyance to any at a distance. Under such circumstances, he would have (as customary) been permitted to find shelter in any private residence. But none near was available, & none so proper, and scarcely more accessible, than his own home, while he is unfit for service. Much sickness prevails among our troops. So numerous were the sick waiting for transportation at the landing, that the three or four large steamers (employed exclusively for the army,) could not remove them, & of course no other person could get a passage. So Edmund & Thomas had to go to W[illia]msburg, & thence by slow land travel to Evelynton, & thence by boat to home. Edmund has resigned his commission, &, owing to the late "conscription act" of the C.S. Congress, closed his military service sooner than he had lately expected. When he accepted the command & aided in raising the company of cavalry, & soon after offered [1933] his & the company's service for 12 months, he was over 45, & of course exempt from all military service. Some months before the end of this year of service in the field, it seemed essential to the safety of the country that the 12 months volunteers then in the field should continue to serve. By that time, first one & then the other overseer of Edmund's two farms had been called out, & there was no chance to keep either, or to obtain substitutes

... for them, either as overseers or soldiers. In this, & other respects, no one could suffer more in his business than himself, by continued absence from home, & few as much in family matters. Still, as his continuing to command was supposed an indispensable condition to the company being maintained in its integrity, by the greater number of its members re-enlisting for the war, he (much to my surprise,) made the new & greater sacrifice of entering with most of his men in that engagement. Subsequently, & before the new organization of the company had been made, or the election of officers, the C.S. law was passed requiring all men from 18 to 35 years of age to serve. This would ensure a sufficiently numerous army, & enough therein of the before trained soldiers (the first 12 months volunteers,) to make the efficiency as great as could be otherwise from volunteers. This act abrogated all previous voluntary action of the soldiers—compelling the subsequent service of all men of 35 & under, even though they had not re-enlisted, & discharging (after some time,)all over 35, even though they had re-enlisted. Under these new circumstances, Edmund did not think himself called upon to continue & increase his great sacrifices of interest & feeling, when he could add in his own person but one more individual to the army. [1934] The company he commanded, both by previous re-enlistments & by the later conscription, had been preserved in existence, & would remain in service. Because of its good discipline & character, it had latterly been increased by new recruits from 70 to 102. Before the time for electing new officers, & when assured that his re-election, if consenting to serve, would have been certain, (there being not more than 6 or 7 offended & opposed,) he addressed the assembled company, & stated his reasons for resigning office under the new organization, & declining being a candidate for re-election, & requesting that no votes should be thrown upon him. Though his withdrawal was very unwelcome to nearly all, the men were satisfied with his reasons, & afterwards adopted resolutions expressing their respect & approbation for his conduct during his service & command. As soon as the new elections were made, (1st Lieut. Marks being made captain,) Edmund resigned, & was no longer connected officially with the company or the army. . . . Our army on the peninsula is certainly falling back towards Richmond. This is necessary to lead on the enemy's army out of the support of their steamers, armed with heaviest artillery, & of supplies of food &c. by water transportation.

We cannot attack the enemy, intrenched strongly, & having a powerful flotilla able to join in the battle, except under very great disadvantage, besides that of the superior number of their land forces. If they can pass our batteries, & push their flotilla past our army, in York, or still more if in James river, they might reach Richmond earliest. Besides these reasons applying here particularly, it is supposed that our government has at last changed its policy for carrying on the war—& instead of vainly defending rivers by forts, & seaports in reach of the guns of the enemy's naval forces, it is designed to concentrate our forces in the interior, & invite or compel the enemy to fight there, even though all our water lines be overrun.

May 4. Sunday. . . . Heard from private information later than Edmund's, that the retreat of our army, & partly dismantling our forts on York & James rivers had been begun—but as secretly as possible. Also, that Norfolk is to be evacuated by our forces, & left undefended. Of course it could not be held againt the enemy's land & naval forces, after our leaving the peninsula. [1936] Our loss of artillery, & even light baggage, will be enormous, on account of the roads being so wet & damaged. The machinery at the Navy Yard is already being moved up to Richmond by the Rail Road. . . .

May 5. Forts Jackson & St. Philip have surrendered. 13 of the enemy's steamers carrying heavy mortars had gone up to N. Orleans, & the U.S. Flag was at last hoisted there. The whole Yankee squadron which attacked the forts & threatened N.O. consisted of 46 vessels, carrying 286 cannon & 21 mortars. . . . The Yankee army commanded lately by Buell, & now by Halleck, has slowly approached Corinth, & there was a heavy skirmish between portions of the two armies on the evening of the 3rd. Our men fell back. The great battle expected the next day, or very soon thereafter.—The former report of the Yankees' withdrawing from the peninsula, as we now know, must have been false. A newspaper of today publishes the fact of our army falling back, & the designed evacuation of Norfolk. Three of the armed steamers in York river had passed our batteries at Yorktown & Gloucester Point, (probably then dismantled,) & had reached West Point, at the junction of the Pamunkey & Mattaponi rivers. . . . At this gloomy time, after so many & great disasters to our arms, & successes & continued advances of the enemy, there is no public exhibition of despondency, or indication of any of our people, before loyal, to submit. Every one must now view as a not improbable event—to be avoided only by our giving McClellan's army a signal defeat before Richmond—that our capital will be taken, & all the remainder of Virginia over-run & laid waste by the enemy, & the prominent citizens, as approached by the invaders, made fugitives to escape arrest & [1938] imprisonment. Still I hear of but very few faint hearts, of either men or women, amidst the general determination to make all sacrifices needed for resistance to the last. The last newspapers, of all parts of eastern Virginia, in strong editorial articles, admit the possible contingency of every sea-port of the S. Confederacy & every fort & military position on the navigable rivers being captured by the enemy's naval forces, by which (& by aid of which only,) we have been defeated in almost every attempt to defend such places. But they also maintain that our whole coast may be occupied, & all our sea-port towns taken, or burnt, & that the Yankee power will then be as far from subjugating the South as ever. Of this, there is no doubt, if our people are true to themselves. But, unless we can soon give great & overwhelming defeats to the two great armies of the enemy, we may prepare to undergo the worst suffering of an invaded country. . . . The legislature meets today. I wrote a letter to Willoughby Newton stating the monstrous abuse of the confinement in camp (for it is not employment or any use,) of the militia called out *en masse*, & the great injury to public as well as private interests thereby caused—& urging him to try to put an end to the most absurd & useless, as well as hurtful procedure.

May 6. All our visitors left us for Petersburg, on their way to Nottoway, & also Edmund for N.Ca. He is to return in a week. Before they had left, I went to Ruthven, to arrange for the delivery of the sale corn. On my arrival, I was surprised & much rejoiced to find that Julian had returned home the night before. The militia had at last been released from [1939] their useless service, or rather confinement. The sickness among the body (at first 900,) in which Julian had been included, was very great, & many deaths. At one time, there were five deaths in 24 hours. The diseases were measles & mumps aggravated, & pneumonia caused, by exposure, on guard duty, to the very wet & stormy weather. When, by discharges of newly exempted men, & enlistments in, or drafts to other companies, the number had been reduced to 460, there were at one time more than half (255) so sick as to be under medical treatment, besides slighter indisposition of many. Of those well, so many were required to attend upon the sick, that 5 only were left for all guard duty. Even at last, Julian thinks they would not have been discharged . . . but for the designed evacuation of Norfolk, which made it necessary to get rid of them in some way. Thus ends this most absurd & useless measure, which has been a great expense to the public, & greater loss & injury to the individuals, & without any actual benefit whatever.—After dinner I returned, & Julian & Lotty also came to Beechwood . . . . Heard that some of our troops of the peninsula have already got more than half way towards Richmond—& that Gen. Magruder & other officers were today at Westover, on their route. The apprehension of all this part of the country, below Richmond, being subject to visits & ravages of the Yankee armies, on their foraging & marauding parties, is in prospect. [1940] All the country north of James river, & south of Rappahannock, will be exposed to McClellan's main army—& on this side of James river we may expect the advance of Burnside's army from lower N.C. by way of Norfolk & Suffolk.

May 7. . . . On the 4th, the Yankee advanced guards drove in our pickets below & near to Williamsburg, & were then repulsed by a body of our cavalry. Another & more considerable skirmish took place next day, in which an Ala. regiment fought & repulsed a much larger body, though with considerable loss on our side. That of the Yankees not known.[10] The retreat of our army must have been badly conducted, & the pursuit of the enemy was very close. The main body of the Yankee army, following ours, passed through Williamsburg, & is passing on between the Chickahominy & Pamunkey rivers. Our army will make a stand between these rivers, nearer to Richmond. We have many indications of the enemy's army being near us—perhaps now within 20 miles, though separated by the James as well as the Chickahominy from this place. . . . The armed steamers Jamestown (or Thomas Jefferson,) Patrick Henry & Teazer passed by today, towing several unfinished vessels, which I suppose are the gunboats from Norfolk. The Jamestown & P. Henry returned downward this afternoon.—Our ladies, with Thomas, went in the carriage to visit our nearest neighbors, at Tarbay & the Parsonage. Every family in this neighborhood is considering the questions of whether to flee before the enemy's arrival, & to move off slaves or other property, or to leave things generally as they are.

---

[10] The Confederates lost 1,700 and the Federals more than 2,200 at Williamsburg—heavy casualties for what was basically a rear-guard action.

In any case, it will be necessary for males who would be in danger of being captured & imprisoned, to hide themselves when Yankee soldiers are at hand. Such would be all persons who had served in the army, & all others, however incapable of service, who had taken active & prominent parts in the political work of secession. As all my friends suppose that I would be an especial object for Yankee hatred & outrage, I must try to avoid being captured by them. I have no fear of being hanged, though that fate was promised to me in the N.Y. Tribune—but protracted imprisonment I may count upon, & that would be to me much worse than sudden death. But, until the Yankee vessels occupy James river, or until Burnside's army from lower N.C. shall invade us on the south side, & advance towards Petersburg, I do not think that here we risk much by remaining at home. In either of these not improbable contingencies, if occurring before Edmund's return, I shall have to direct what the emergency [1942] may require for the safety of his family, & his moveables, as well as to prevent my own capture by marauding parties. I trust that an earlier general engagement, & our defeat of McClellan's army, (separated from support of his naval force,) may save us from the incalculable sacrifices of even attempting partially to remove our families & property.—In Nashville, under the rule of the traitor Andrew Johnson, "Military Governor" of Tennessee, by Lincoln's appointment, the crime of secession is to be treated as treason, & by the courts of law. 900 persons in that city have already been indicted for treason, & their trials in progress. So much the better. I am very sorry that the general confiscation act for the South which had passed in the House of Representatives of U.S.C., has, because of constitutional difficulties, been laid on the table in the Senate, & so the policy remains suspended. . . .

May 8. Julian rode by, to inform me that he was on his way to Marlbourne, if able to get there, by way of Petersburg & Richmond. Both armies now passing up the peninsula towards Richmond, may already prevent all private travel as far as Marlbourne. . . .

May 9. The second fight below Williamsburg was much more important & bloody than at first reported. . . . Our loss in killed & wounded was heavy, & that of the Yankees much more so. After driving back the enemy for more than a mile, & completely repulsing them, the previous march towards Richmond was resumed by our troops . . . . We hear, every day, reports of cannon from one or other of the armies across the Chickahominy. Certain information that 3 Yankee gunboats had ascended James river, & fired on the forts below Burwell's Bay & at Hardy's Bluff. The first had been previously evacuated, & the second they silenced. One of the river freight steamers, sent down with stores for the Chickahominy, was [1944] afraid to go so low, & returned with the report of this movement. Of course, if the enemy's gunboats (one of them iron-plated,) could ascend to & above our highest fortification, there was nothing to prevent their going much higher, or even to Richmond. Under these circumstances, I sent a messenger to Evelynton to hurry the departure of the vessel which had been taking in the sale corn, for Petersburg, & to forbid its calling here for the 800 bushels of Edmund's & Julian's, which had been got ready, & partly transported from Ruthven to the barn here, for this very vessel. It seemed to me too hazardous to detain the cargo already in, to add more . . . . But my change of orders was for the worst that could be. Before night, the vessel had passed on, & I heard that the enemy's gun-boats had returned to Newport News. Their advance (at risk of encountering the "Virginia,") & their subsequent hasty retreat, were equally unaccountable. Both have been since explained . . . .

May 10. One of the former small canalboats, for Albemarle Sound, commanded for the Canal Company by a New-Jersey man, had been sold to the government, & used as a tugboat. Very improperly, trusting to the declared southern feelings of the captain, he was continued in command. He was lately sent from Norfolk to Sewell's Point landing, with supplies for the posts, to return immediately. On coming out, he hoisted a white flag, & steered for Fortress Monroe, & delivered his vessel to the enemy. This spy & traitor & deserter gave information of all he knew of Norfolk, including the intended evacuation, the already partial dismantling of the forts, & that the Virginia was then in the drydock, & could not get out & ready for action for some time. The expedition up the river, (rendered safe by the necessary absence of the Virginia,) was immediately set about—& also a more powerful flotilla subsequently attacked with shot & shells the forts at Sewell's Point. The attack & defence had continued [1945] for some time, when the Virginia, having been got ready & hurried out, appeared coming out of the Elizabeth river. Immediately, the whole Yankee fleet, which consisted of two frigates, the iron-clad Monitor, Stevens' iron-clad floating battery, & some gun-boats, fled over to Fortress Monroe. The 3 gunboats which had visited our forts up James river had returned thence still earlier. So after this alarming indication of the enemy being about to come, & in safety, up James river, we may again dismiss that fear, & trust to the Virginia as our safe-guard, at least until Norfolk is given up, & that, or any safe harbor, shall be out of reach of this vessel.—I rode to the Court-House today, to deliver 4 of Edmund's mules which had been impressed for the service of the army. One fourth of all the mules & draft horses of this county have been so taken, & paid for at appraisement, in this & other neighboring counties. Saw a paper of today. A general engagement of Beauregard's & Halleck's great armies commenced yesterday near Corinth, at noon, & was continued to the time of the telegraphic dispatch some hours later, & then still in progress. So far, the report was favorable, that our troops had made the attack, & had driven back the Yankee army. May God grant to us a complete & great victory! A report, very similar in general purport, of Gen. Jackson's (Stonewall's) army—that he had attacked & was forcing backward the Yankee army opposed. . . . [1946]

. . . Evening, I rode to Ruthven. Julian arrived at 8 P.M. from Richmond. He had seen Mr. [Willoughby] Newton very late in the night of his arrival in Richmond, & heard from him that he had just learned from President Davis & Gen. Lee that a Yankee gun-boat had reached Westover. This false report was fully believed by Gen. Lee, & of course, on his authority, by Messrs. Davis & Newton. The last, hearing Julian's intention to proceed to Marlbourne, informed him, in confidence, of this news, which was kept private, as its promulgation would have produced a general panic in Richmond. Mr. Newton was perfectly assured that both he & I, if captured by the Yankees, would be put to death, as original & zealous & prominent disunionists, who preached our doctrines years before another individual in Virginia dared to support us openly. He forthwith arranged for his own speedy flight, as soon as the approach of the enemy should be [1947] very near. Thus impressed, by such high authorities, Julian went on to Marlbourne, as he had designed, in the mail coach, before day-break. But instead of remaining until next day, he set off to return to Richmond after seeing Mr. Sayre for two hours only. . . . He brought from Petersburg the last telegraphic dispatches, & good news so far as learned. Stonewall Jackson had beaten the Yankee army opposed to him, & was pursuing them in their hasty flight. . . . The battle between Beauregard & Halleck did not become general, as the latter refused to engage, & retreated, probably to draw our pursuing army within the range of the artillery of his gun-boats, & to secure his army by their aid & protection. . . .

May 11. Sunday. At church. Much excitement among our neighbors, & some families have moved away. But no apparent indications of terror or despondency. A neighbor who arrived from Petersburg brought the verbal report that the evacuation of Norfolk by the military had been begun, & the destruction of the Navy Yard. . . . I believe McClellan will not offer or accept battle with our army now in the peninsula, but will remain still, & intrenched, until Burnside's army can unite in the attempt on Richmond, & also the army [1948] which now holds Fredericksburg, & which is supposed to be already between 30,000 & 40,000 in number.—I greatly regret Edmund's absence at this time, & anxiously await his return next Tuesday.—In the afternoon, Dr. Harrison & Mr. Hansburgh rode here to give the startling information that three Yankee gun-boats (one iron-clad,) had been seen slowly ascending this river, & at 1 o'clock had reached Hoods, which is 8 miles by land & 12 by the river below this house. They had been observed, with a spy-glass, & distinguished by bearing U.S. flags, by a respectable & intelligent young man named Hammond, who had watched their progress from & by Upper Brandon, & who went on immediately to Petersburg to convey the information, & to telegraph to Richmond, &, on his way, so informed Dr. Harrison. The vessels seemed to be making an examination, or *reconnaissance*, & drew together & paused, as if for consultation, off Hoods. If continuing, even very slowly, they would have passed this place before we heard the news. But nothing was seen of them tonight, nor heard of afterwards to bed-time. This movement, in face of the "Virginia," is very daring & astonishing.[11] It cannot be supposed that so small a force will land, or attempt to do open injury anywhere. But, aided by information & guidance of some negro deserter, a party might easily land in the night, & capture & carry off any especially obnoxious & noted residents . . . . The ladies here deemed me to be in especial danger of such an attempt—& that my presence here would be more likely to expose the house to the visit & outrages of a marauding party, than to afford them aid or protection—& on both these accounts they urged my speedy departure. My presence certainly can be of no service to guard or protect the family &

---

[11] Unknown to the diarist, the *Virginia* had been scuttled off Norfolk earlier in the day.

property. But I will not leave before Edmund returns, unless Yankees should actually [1949] come, or be seen approaching this residence. This news, though producing excitement & uneasiness, did not cause any manifestations of alarm of distress even of our females—who indeed seem to become more brave as danger of the enemy's presence increases. We have an unusually strong garrison here at present, in the two convalescent troopers, Thomas Ruffin & William Dupuy, & myself, besides my younger grandson George & my brother, upon whom no reliance for defence or aid could be placed. But no defence could be made by any or all of us, or attempted, against a regular military party, with any hope of success. And if so invaded, the two soldiers, (& also my son, if at home, as recently an officer in the army,) if captured would certainly be made prisoners of war, & I might be in much greater danger, of long & protracted imprisonment & the worst of treatment, to which, speedy death by shooting or hanging would be preferable. We prepared & loaded our fire-arms—& for the first time I even locked my room door (which is also an out-door,) & closed & fastened the very frail window shutters, when I went to bed.

May 12. The passage of the Yankee gunboats is confirmed—with the exception that they did not come nearer than three miles below Hoods. There they remained some hours, & then returned, without making a landing anywhere—though receiving 10 or 12 absconding & fugitive negroes from two plantations below, at & near Hog Island.—Troops from Fortress Monroe landed below all our forts & batteries, & marched to & occupied Norfolk & the Navy Yard. This was expected, & so published, a week ago. But, notwithstanding this general expectation & notice, the occupation seemed as if made by surprise—&, as usual, our evacuation & retreat was accompanied by enormous losses of cannon, stores, &c. But the worst loss of all is our most noble war steamer Virginia. [1950] It was in Elizabeth river, & the tide too low for it to pass out—& was burnt, & blown up, to prevent its being captured by the enemy. The dry dock was also blown up, & all the combustible parts of the other structures of the Navy Yard burnt, including several steam gunboats, & some of them ready for action. There must have been the worst possible management. If Gen. Huger had been cashiered, or shot, for his criminal neglect of Roanoke Island, or if Pres. Davis had sent a capable & faithful commander to supersede him then, this evacuation, though necessary, & not to be avoided, would have been

[301]

made without such horrible sacrifices. We want a delinquent commander to be shot. And Lovell & Huger both deserve it. Now, after the destruction of the Virginia, this river is entirely open to the Yankee war-steamers, & all the bordering country & the slaves exposed to their depredations.—Rode to Ruthven to dinner. At 5 P.M. attended a hastily called meeting of the neighboring residents, to consult & arrange for securing all the boats on our shore, & on the river adjacent, to prevent their being used by slaves to escape to the enemy's vessels. At the request of the meeting, I wrote to the Secretary of war, to obtain legal sanction & authority for our action in the matter.—The last report states Jackson's victory at McDowell, in Highland Co., 36 miles from Staunton, to be "brilliant."[12]. . . Their army in full flight westward, & ours in hot pursuit. . . .

May 13. The carriage was to go this morning to Petersburg for Edmund & his wife—& I arranged & was ready to go & return in the carriage, mainly because of my great anxiety to see him. . . . But I was prevented going when the carriage was ready at the door by our learning the close neighborhood of Yankee war steamers. Information had been sent to us, by a neighbor, just before, of a report that 5 of the Yankee gunboats were off Hoods at 10 last night. But I supposed this to be one of the continually occurring false rumors, & should not have paid any attention to it alone. But we had scarcely left the breakfast table when (at 8 A.M.) it was announced that the Yankee vessels were in the river in front of this house, & Berkley wharf. Through the only clear opening in the screen of trees which conceal this house & yard from the river, & nearly the river from us, we saw five [1953] steamers—three of them of large size, & having masts, one small, & the fifth like a long & deeply floating ordinary raft of logs, with the usual small house for the crew, in the middle, & which was only known as a steam vessel by its discharge of steam, & its being in motion. They were stretched along a line of more than half a mile, & moving so slowly as at first glance to seem still. The low raft-like vessel was manifestly the famous iron-clad Monitor. The small steamer was foremost of the line—& five row-boats were soon after seen ahead, apparently sounding the channel over Harrison's bar. The flags of the steamers were flying. But the

---

[12] The report was accurate. At McDowell, on May 8, Jackson defeated a portion of Fremont's army and pursued the Federals toward Franklin in the western part of the state. It was Jackson's first major victory in the Valley Campaign.

atmosphere was so hazy, (as it was also yesterday,) that we could not, with a spy-glass, distinguish the character of the flags—which however was not required to make it certain that they were vessels of the Yankee fleet, let loose from all fear & constraint by the destruction of the Virginia. These are evidently exploring the river, & with great caution. At 11 o'clock they were still in sight from our garden, not having gone 5 miles since they were first observed opposite the dwelling. But before 12, all had disappeared, above Indian Fields Point. I rode to Coggin's Point on this farm before 9 A.M. to get the closest view—but could distinguish but little more than that it was the Yankee flag flying. . . . Others who saw better, noticed that the largest steamer seemed crowded with men. Afternoon, Julian & Mr. Hansburgh came & stayed until near bed-time, to meet Edmund, who arrived at dark, but alone. Jane was coming with him, & came as far as Raleigh. There they heard of the destruction of the Virginia, & inferring the consequent free means of access of the enemy's vessels, troops, & marauding parties on & along the borders of James river, Edmund deemed it best [1954] for his wife & her infant to return to Alamance.—The price of paper is now more than $20 the ream for such as this sheet, & my stock is nearly exhausted. Of inferior foolscap paper, I had a large supply, the remnant of my old printing establishment. But this (as nearly all paper made 20 years ago,) is too rough for writing on readily with steel pens—& also is without lines, which I cannot well dispense with. The still blank portion of an old formerly blank book offered a supply of lined paper; but that is still more rough. . . . [Still] I must resort to it when I have no more suitable paper left for my journal.—The return of Edmund especially gratifying to all of his family at this time of difficulty—& still more to me, that he should be at home to reassume the management of his own affairs. . . . Julian had seen a copy of a note which [Commodore John] Ro[d]gers, the commander of this Yankee flotilla, had written & delivered at Sandy Point, addressed to the ladies & men resident on the borders of the river. The purport was to promise that private property should be respected, & no injury inflicted on any who would remain quiet at home—& to advise all to so remain at their homes. Though I am sure that these promises are made only for policy, & that they will be all violated, & the usual outrages perpetrated, as soon as the invaders deem it safe to do so, yet this offer & pledge of safety gives some assurance to us for the present time. They feel doubtful & unsafe in this new position, & therefore play the game of moderation & conciliation, until the Yankee [1955] domination is established—when here, as elsewhere, plunder, abduction of slaves, confiscation, arson, imprisonment & murder will be the order of the day. But before this system will be begun here, the enemy must feel secure in this river & through its bordering lands. And that may be prevented altogether, if McClellan's great army should . . . soon be defeated & drawn off.

May 14. . . . Yesterday, the Yankee gunboats stopped at City Point, & a force landed & held the place some hours, before again embarking & proceeding up James river. Our military guard burnt the wharf & a store-house full of tobacco.—The Navy Yard at Pensacola & our other military posts there have been evacuated.—The two armies are within three miles of each other in New Kent, between the Chickahominy & Pamunkey. It is feared that McClellan will not fight, except within supporting distance of his gunboats on York river, or until he receives the reinforcement now available for him by way of James river. If Johnston cannot compel a battle, & obtain a victory, & very soon, I now think that Richmond will most probably be taken—& if so all the remainder of Virginia will be over-run by the enemy, & at their mercy for a time. Our military affairs are grossly mismanaged, & nowhere worse than at the seat of government. The river is no where yet blocked up to stop the passage of the enemy's vessels to Richmond—& yet vessels laden with valuable mineral cargoes have been sunk uselessly in improper places, to great loss, & without the least good effect. . . .

May 15. . . . At Beechwood, more boxes packed, with blankets & other most portable articles which can be spared from early use, to be moved to Ruthven, or elsewhere away from the river, the bordering farms being supposed to be in most danger of marauding parties of the enemy, &, as we think, the only places much endangered for the present, or while the Yankee vessels have command of the passage of the river, & have not occupied any neighboring land. . . . Since the mail of yesterday, we have heard nothing certain, or reliable, of the progress of the Yankee gunboats, & nothing from the opposed armies. Surely, if our commanders mean to fight, this is the time, before the enemy brings a stronger naval force, & another army embarked thereupon, into James river, McClellan, while expecting these powerful reinforcements, though already he is much the strongest, certainly will not attack. And if our general will not, or cannot attack, I now begin to fear that there will be no great battle, but another retreat on our part, & next the surrender of Richmond, & the over-powering of the remainder of Virginia.—If nothing is heard by tomorrow's mail to change my mind, I shall go to Richmond the day after—to personally witness what is there going on, &, if of any use, to give my feeble aid to the defence of our capital, & in what may be the last struggle for Virginia. Should we be defeated, all in Virginia will be lost for the present time. And I & most adults of my family, destitute & helpless, may have to save ourselves from imprisonment, or death, by flight to the south. But before thus surrendering, or retreating, without fighting, I hope that our army may fight bravely until destroyed, & that Richmond may be bombarded & laid in ashes, because refusing to surrender.

May 16. This the day appointed by the President's proclamation & request for the general observance of public worship, prayer & humiliation. All of us attended church, though cloudy, & showery at intervals.—The mail. Obstructions have been placed across the river at Drury's [*sic*] Bluff, 6 to 8 miles below Richmond, though not until the last moment, & then in the most costly manner. As part of the barrier, the valuable [1958] steamers Northampton, Curtis Peck (passenger & freight vessels,) Jamestown (armed sea-steamer,) a sailing vessel costing $24,000, a gunboat & several canal boats were sunk. A land battery adjoining, on the bluff, had been partly constructed & armed, & fully garrisoned, when the Yankee steamers appeared, & immediately began the attack. From some 400 to 500 yards below, the iron-clad Galena threw shell & ball at the unfinished fortification, & was fired at in return for 2½ hours. Our garrison had 4 to 6 men killed, & 7 or 8 wounded. A plunging ball from our works struck & penetrated the deck of the Galena, & set the vessel on fire, (as supposed,) during which the whole flotilla drew off out of gun-shot, & went down the river. The fire was extinguished, & I suppose, without much damage,[13] as all 5 of the vessels are reported to be now anchored off Jordan's Point, five miles above Beechwood, but out of our view. The spirit of the state & general governments, & of the people of Richmond, appears to

---

[13] The *Galena* took eighteen shots through her sides and deck and was seriously damaged in this four-hour engagement on May 15. The other Union vessels—*Monitor, Naugatuck, Port Royal,* and *Aroostook*—suffered little or no structural damage. Federal losses were twelve killed and thirteen wounded. *Official Records,* Vol. XI, Pt. 1, p. 636.

be excellent. Declarations have been published by the Va. legislature & Governor, by the President, & by the city authorities & also by a popular meeting, all pledging themselves to the defence of Richmond to the last, & in defiance of the possible bombardment of the city. Nothing more from the two armies, still facing each other a few miles apart, near New Kent C.H. . . .

May 17. After breakfast, with Lotty & two of her children, drove to Petersburg. Thomas [Ruffin] & William [Dupuy] overtook us, going on to join their companies. Yesterday, I had heard of a foreigner, Wenderberg, & naturalized citizen, who owns a farm & residence at the mouth of Bailey's creek (below City Point,) having hoisted the U.S. flag in full view of the Yankee steamers, when they were passing up. He denies that it was the U.S. flag—but admits that the Belgian flag was hoisted at his house. This traitor is understood to hold a clerkship in some department of the government at Richmond. I wrote a statement of the reported facts, giving the authorities, & gave a copy to the Provost Marshal in Petersburg, & urged that he would send forthwith & arrest the offender—which he promised. Afterwards I sent the same to the Secretary of War. . . . At 4.30, left for Richmond. Got a room at the Exchange Hotel—& fortunately in close proximity to my friends Newton & Tate. Soon saw these, with Andrew Hunter, in Newton's room, & had an interesting conversation about the state of affairs. It had been reported, & I believed it, because so reasonable now, that McClellan had fallen back, to embark his army on James river, now under his control up to our obstruction, & would approach Richmond by water, & with all the aid of his naval forces, & of (perhaps) a land army coming up on the South side of the river. But the latest reports are that Johnston [1971][14] has fallen back to this side of the Chickahominy, & to positions from 6 to 9 miles from Richmond—& that the Yankee army has advanced. The pickets of the two armies are on the opposite sides of Chickahominy swamp, & frequently fire on each other. The Yankees have occupied Waterloo, the farm of Braxton Garlick, on the Pamunkey, 10 miles only from Marlbourne, & 16 of his negroes have absconded to them. This learned from Garlick's son. I fear & expect, that Marlbourne will be as much exposed to the depredations of the invaders, & large loss of slaves to be incurred there by my children also.—Saw Mr. Boteler, & heard later & most gratifying accounts of Stonewall Jackson's

---

[14] Misnumbered by the diarist. Should be page 1961.

operations, & matters connected therewith. . . . Gen. Jackson with his main force is marching down the valley (northward) & the main Yankee army, under Banks, retreating before him. Mr. Boteler tells me that guerrilla bands are increasing, & will speedily still more increase, under the recent encouraging measures of both the [1972] state & confederate government.—Saw my friend W. H. Harrison. Since I met him here last, he has had the heavy affliction of losing by death his daughter Lelia, a sweet & interesting girl of 19. I can well appreciate this loss, & sympathise with the father. . . . 10 of Dr. Gaines' negroes (of course, the men,) have gone to the enemy, from his farm & residence on the Chickahominy, 8 miles from Richmond. Our general has had the bridges over the Chickahominy burnt.

May 18. Sunday. Heard that the enemy occupied Garlick's two farms on the Pamunkey, 10 & 12 miles from Marlbourne. From Newcastle, the farm adjoining Marlbourne, all the negro men & boys, except 4, had gone off together to the Yankees. I expect next to hear of like losses from Marlbourne. The number, & general spreading of such abscondings of slaves are far beyond any previous conceptions.—It is believed that the crews of the Yankee gunboats which attacked Fort Drewry suffered greatly by the fire of our sharp-shooters who were concealed along the bank, at favorable positions, for some miles below the fortification. . . . Attended public worship at St. Paul's Church. When coming out, I saw my former colonel, now General Kershaw, & had a few minutes conversation. His brigade (before Gen. Bonham's,) which includes the 2nd S.C. regiment, & the Palmetto Guard, is now within two miles of Richmond. . . . On my expressing my fear that McClellan would still avoid a general engagement, Gen. K. said that I need not fear, for a battle was certain. . . . This evening, with Mr. Tate, walked to St. John's Church, on Church Hill.

May 19. Still no news through the newspapers, though plenty of verbal reports of the enemy & our forces in the neighborhood. Yesterday morning, Mr. Newton went in his own carriage to Summer Hill, where his wife was, & invited me to go with him. As he was to pass within two miles of Marlbourne, I concluded to ride with him so far, & walk the remainder of the way, & join him to return this morning to Richmond. For several [1974] reasons, I have felt a repugnance to visiting that, my once loved home, since Mildred left it. But deeming that my presence & suggestions, & information, might be of service in the present difficulties, & Mr. Sayre's uncertainties, I thought I would embrace this opportunity to go, notwithstanding the alarm of the approach of the enemy. I had paid my bill, & was ready to set out, when I learned that the same carriage would not return, & that I might have to put Mr. Sayre to the trouble of sending me back specially. This, added to the other objections, caused me to stay. It was well I did. For Mr. Newton, because of the near approach of a scouting body of 200 Yankee cavalry, had to leave hastily at 11 last night, & to return by Hanover C.H. The Yankee cavalry had stopped at Ingleside, on the stage road, 1½ miles below Marlbourne, to graze their horses & rest, & then passed by the Old Church & the Marlbourne gate (within 400 yards & open view of the mansion). Whether they stopped at either place we do not know. But nothing would have been easier than to seize me, if I had been there, in bed. They passed to Haw's shop, 5 miles above Marlbourne, & there captured some 30 horses belonging to the Confederate government, & on the way to Richmond. . . . The legislature adjourned today, after having had nothing to do for some days earlier.—Mr. Boteler (M.C.) in conversation gave me some interesting information in regard to Gen. Jackson, from whom he has late letters. In general, Jackson augurs well of the prospects of his army. Mr. B. saw the President today, who appeared to be greatly depressed in spirits, & for suffering which to appear, Mr. B. thought him much to blame. I fear that Mr. Davis is far from being the right sort of leader for our country in our present difficulties.— Saw Dr. J. Garnett, [1975] a member of the [Va.] Senate, who resides 5 miles below Richmond on the Chickahominy. A large portion of our army encamped on his farm yesterday, & immediately it was laid waste, & the house & everything to eat & drink plundered, even worse than is usual with the Yankees when occupants. This is most deplorable, not only for the enormous losses of the suffering individuals, but still more for the indication of bad discipline & demoralization of our troops.—At night, saw Col. Hill Carter of Shirley, from whom I heard that the Yankee gun-boats had not gone far below Harrison's bar (on the evening that I left Beechwood,) & that this morning three more, making 8 in all, were visible from the next residence below his, Wm. N. Harrison's, which is about 3 miles above Berkley. . . . None of McClellan's army have yet crossed the Chickahominy, & I again fear, & confidently believe, he will not make that advance, or accept the battle which Gen. Johnston is now offering him between the Chickahominy & Richmond.

May 20. Yesterday, & previously, I had in vain sought to obtain some information concerning the 12 negro men of my son Edmund, who had been brought into public service by requisition of Gen. Magruder, & of whom nothing had been heard since the retreat of the army from Williamsburg, except that these & other laborers had been sent to Richmond. The only thing that I could hear from any official authority was that all these hands had been discharged & sent home—which I did not believe, & have since found to be false. This morning [I set out], mainly on this search, & in part to see the fortifications at Drewry's Bluff, & the chain of obstructions across the river there, where the Yankee steam flotilla was lately [1976] fought with & repulsed. The only conveyance, to & fro, was walking to Rocketts (seeing no omnibus,) & steaming thence in one of the government tugs, which are carrying stone to complete the obstruction, or supplies for the fort or garrison. On arriving, I found my old acquaintance James Jones, of Chesterfield, a lieutenant of the garrison—who I supposed, as one who aided to furnish slaves, would know more than any other about what I was inquiring. He was confident that there had been no slaves there from Prince George. I had seen, at a wharf just above, my friend Wm. C. Knight, who invited me to call & stop with him at his house close by. I got a passage across the river at the works, from the right to the left bank, & walked a mile to Knight's residence above. When near, I saw a number of laborers on the bank, at their dinner, & I accosted one & asked whether he knew any thing of those I was seeking. I was heard & immediately replied to by two of them, & heard that they and all the others were at work on a new fortification on that side of the river. They were extremely anxious to return home—but for that I had no power. So I recommended patience to them, promised to write home & inform their master how & where they were, & told them that I expected they would be soon discharged.—The fortification is in a strong position, along the crest of a high bluff. But 3 cannon were useful when by them only the Yankee gunboats, iron-clad & others, were so well handled. There are now 11 mounted, & the defences much strengthened. I was misinformed as to the officers thinking that the enemy will not renew the attempt. On the contrary, they confidently expect it will be done, in much stronger force. And in addition to the war steamers, approaching by the river, that land troops will attack in the rear. The scouts sent out have [1977] already seen as many as 14 war vessels below, about the mouth of the Appomattox. . . . Dined with Knight—& afterwards, with him, returned to the works, & finding a tug just leaving, I returned in it to Richmond. My several walks today made nearly or quite 6 miles. . . .

May 21. . . . Today I met Capt. Cuthbert in the street. He is quite unwell, & staying in town on that account. I conversed with him on a painful subject, on which I had lately written to him (from Beechwood,) but he had not answered. Still hoping that my worst fears & suspicions [1979] might prove unfounded, I did not before even refer to them in this private record. But as there is no room left now for doubt, & my last act in the case has, in consequence, just been finished, I will state the main features of the ungrateful subject, & then dismiss it. When my son Charles came home last November, on furlough, I was much displeased with his conduct, in his manifest avoidance of communication with, & even the presence of myself & both his brothers' families—which seemed caused by his consciousness of doing or designing wrong. His leave (rigidly construed) had already expired, & he delayed returning on frivolous excuses, & was manifestly very reluctant to return at all to his company, the Palmetto Guard. As he could not get out of military service altogether, his pretence was the wish to exchange his service to his brother's troop of cavalry—for which he had obtained leave—which very troop he had formerly belonged to, & had very lightly & improperly resigned his membership & office in. I combatted this foolish fickleness & causeless desire of change, & urged him, on considerations of duty & honor, as well as of expediency, to return immediately to his post. This was at last done, but so slowly & reluctantly, that I did not know, even when he set out, whether he would go there or not. I did not disguise the appearance of my displeasure, though I said no more on the subject, after the first interview, which I had to go in search of him to obtain. There was but little written intercourse & in general terms between us after, & that I encouraged only by one short letter—& soon all ceased. Nor did Charles write to his always kind & indulgent brothers but very rarely & in answer only. So we heard very little of him, & mostly by accidental & indirect verbal information. In this way, I heard that he had gone to his company—was in a short time permitted to leave again on account of alleged bad health—& with the exception of one short interval of service, has not been in camp from last November [1980] to this day, & is still absent, (yesterday, & once before lately at this hotel,) & has for months back appeared in good health to those who merely saw him. The earlier time of his leave of absence he had spent at Warrenton in Fauquier, & more lately at Greenwood hospital in Albemarle. I did not like to make inquiries, because the inquiring would show my strange ignorance of his position & my suspicions, & serve to attract attention to his absence, & increase his disgrace. But when, at last, scarcely doubting, I wrote to Capt. Cuthbert to ask to know Charles' true position, whether disconnected from the company, & if so, on what ground. When meeting Capt. C. today, he obviously did not like to speak out, in respect to my feelings. But it was manifest that he thought there was no excuse for the long absence, whether sick or well. I repeated, what I had before written to Capt. C., that if my son was delinquent, I begged that he should not be indulged in wrong-doing, or exempted from coercion, or punishment, in tenderness to me. I wrote, & placed in the Post Office, a final letter to Charles, saying what I deemed necessary to urge him, for shame, & the liability to disgraceful coercion & punishment, to return forthwith to his post, & his self-assumed military duties. And that unless he will so act . . . to avoid my presence & communication. Whether he will receive the warning—for though he is in Richmond, & knows that I am here, I do not know where he is—or if receiving, whether he will obey it, is to be seen. But he has already so disgraced himself, & me also, in this matter, that this conduct takes away all the little hope that had not been before dissipated that he will ever act in such manner as not to add to my pain & sorrow. His honorable death would be to me a blessing, compared [1981] to his continuing to live & act as he has done.

May 22. . . . Edward Stanly, formerly a whig M.C. of N.Ca., since removed to California, & was there the defeated abolition candidate for the governorship, has been appointed "Military Governor" for N.C. by the Lincoln government, & has reached N.Y. on his way to his post. Newbern, which he formerly represented, will probably be the seat of his government. It is to be hoped that the base traitor & renegade will meet his proper reward, by the halter. Andrew Johnson, the "Military Governor" of Ten., in Nashville, is always attended by a strong guard of Yankee soldiers, to protect him from righteous assassination. . . . This afternoon, I called upon & conversed for an hour with Capt. Cuthbert. He is very thin, & [1982] seems much weakened & indisposed. . . . Afterwards I returned the visit of Gen. Steuart, of Md., who had introduced himself to me soon after he had been re-captured by our men near Cub Run, & lately had called to see me at my room.

May 23. . . . Of the movements of our armies in Va, & in some cases of the enemy, our newspapers say little, & most that we hear is from private & uncertain sources. It is so reported that Jackson has continued his course down the valley, & had reached New market, within 50 miles of Winchester. There is also a rumor that McDowell's army, occupying Fredericksburg, is moving to reinforce McClellan. I do not doubt that such reinforcements are expected & waited for—& that McClellan will not offer or accept a general engagement until he has every expected & available aid & superiority. It is understood that he now has 146 regiments. Our army is supposed to be 70 or 80,000. Both estimates probably unreliable—but no doubt that the Yankee army is larger by many thousands than ours. Yet all of our army & citizens are eager for a general & fair battle.—Several light skirmishes lately between outposts, but the enemy has not advanced across [the] Chicka-hominy—& I am confident will not, in the direct route towards Richmond. . . . No truth in the rumored movement of Yankee troops from Fredericksburg.—Firing was heard this afternoon, indicating as was supposed & earnestly hoped, the beginning of a general engagement. But it ceased after an hour or two—& was probably a serious skirmish, apparently on the farther side of the Chicka-hominy.—Heard from Petersburg, this evening, that the Yankee fleet off City Point had increased to 23 in number. Also, by message from Mr. Comer, a proprietor there, that all the negroes (men of course) about City Point had absconded—not to go to the Yankees, but to hide from them. Probably there are some cases of both kinds. . . . [Mr. Newton] sat with me, & we conversed for some time tonight. Acting lately on the committee on the "State of the Country" he has been in communication with the President, & he is better informed than most persons as to the numbers of the military corps. He estimates McClellan's army at 120,000, & ours in the peninsula, opposed, at 85,000—our army in the neighborhood of Petersburg at 30,000; which may expect attack from Burnside's army, & any other force which may be brought up James river. Our army this side of Fredericksburg is 16,000, threatened by the Yankee army said to be 30,000, but whose num[b]ers Newton thinks exaggerated. It is now thought that this army (McDowell's) will not attempt to advance on Rd. by land, but will come by water up James river, to land on either one side or the other. Another body of Yankee troops, about 15,000 is at Warrenton Junction—which may be used to reinforce or to unite with either of these larger armies, or perhaps Banks', in the Valley.

May 24. . . . The skirmish yesterday was near the northern end of the Mechanicsville Turnpike, & 7 miles from Richmond—between one of our regiments & two pieces of artillery, & three regiments & 3 pieces of artillery on the enemy's side. The artillery only was engaged on either side, the infantry only supporting. The enemy drew off. No loss on our side. That of the enemy not known.—All are expecting, for every succeeding day, or hour, the commence-ment of the two great battles, near Richmond & at Corinth. Here, there is a universal feverish anxiety for the engagement, in the fear that McClellan will be able & choose to refuse battle until his overwhelming numbers & slow approaches may cut off the supplies of our army & of Richmond, & so compel another falling back of the army, & the necessary consequence of the surrender of the city. Such a retreat of our army would be worse than a well-fought battle & our defeat. May God grant that these fears are unfounded!—Mr. H. K. Burgwyn & Mr. Boulware arrived here today. With the latter I had a long & earnest conversation on the present state of affairs, in which Newton afterwards joined, in my room. These two very intelligent friends of mine occupy the oppo-site extremes of discouragement approaching dispair [*sic*]—be-cause of the wretched administration of state, & conduct of the war—& of sanguine & undoubting hope, & anticipation of success. Mr. Boulware has adduced sundry facts in addition to all I knew or believed before, of the incompetency & mismanagement of our leaders, & inferred that the continuation would be as bad as what has gone before—that Gen. Johnston [1986] had no reason to delay a battle for the last 10 days, or last 20 miles of falling back—& that either from choice, or compulsion by McClellan, Johnston will permit the fatal results which I have latterly feared, a further retreat of his army, & the necessary consequent surrender of Richmond, & evacuation of all lower Virginia. Mr. Boulware says that if it were possible to suspect treason, he could account for the conduct of affairs only in supposing treason in some high & powerful official.

[313]

Newton on the other hand thinks that our affairs have been generally well managed, that our military success has been as great as
could have been expected, & that a great battle will certainly be
fought, & forced on [McClellan] by Johnston, as soon as could be, &
very soon, & a signal victory obtained. I also have full faith in our
beating the enemy, if fighting very soon. But I doubt it greatly, if put
of[f] for a week longer, & despair of it (for the present time,) if not
consummated within two weeks. I learned something new from
both these gentlemen, which I trust may indicate the intention of
fighting immediately. Our troops from near Fredericksburg have
been ordered here, & 3000 of them arrived last night, & I suppose
as many will come on today, & all the remainder tomorrow. With
this reinforcement to act along the Pamunkey, our engaging the
enemy generally ought to begin tomorrow morning, or at latest the
next day. If delayed longer, the stronger Yankee army at Fredericksburg will have time to follow on, & perhaps the already much
strengthened flotilla on James river, still more increased, may land
another army below our river batteries, & within 10 miles of Richmond. I shall most anxiously expect to hear the booming of the
cannon early tomorrow morning, indicating a general battle joined.
If so, we will triumph. If not—either then or very soon after—may
God save us, for I shall expect no [1987] help or safety from our
highest civil & military rulers.—Cannon heard at intervals
throughout the whole day to nearly 5 P.M. It was (so far as heard
from) artillery only engaged, & firing across Chickahominy swamp.
The effects probably will not compensate the waste of ammunition. . . . Newton came into my room after I was in bed, & we
conversed for some time on the present state of affairs. Hopeful as
he is, he thinks that he & I ought not to risk the possible contingency of the enemy's victory here, & the consequences of being
taken prisoners. Especially he urged me . . . to remove to some safe
retreat. I had not thought so seriously of my own personal risks,
though thinking more gloomily than he of the misconduct & probable danger of public interests. . . . At any rate I will risk waiting
longer to witness the issue of the impending conflict. Newton had
heard that the enemy already had taken a part of the Central Rail
Road, between this city & Hanover C.H. & were destroying the
track—that 6000 of our troops were ordered to march on them &
more coming after from Fredericksburg. We thought that, on these
grounds, a battle was to be expected to-morrow morning early, & I

asked him to notify me as soon as he should hear the sounds of the cannon.

May 25. Sunday. I kept my gas light burning very dimly, & Newton came in at 2½ A.M. to let me know that he heard frequent reports of cannon, which, of course, I was unable to hear. But I was satisfied that he was not mistaken, & after a time of joyful wakefulness & thinking, I fell again [1988] to sleep, expecting to hear the full roar of extended conflict later in the morning, when arising. Yet it was a mistake of his sense of hearing—for to 9 A.M. we have heard no confirmation of cannonading in the night.—On Sunday we have no newspapers, & rarely bulletins or telegrams—& it is therefore especially the day for false rumors. I was grieved to hear, & seemingly on good authority, that Jackson's army was ordered here. This implies that until that movement & reinforcement is completed, there will be no battle sought here by our leaders. On my saying so to Mr. Burgwyn, he said that there would be still another & latter occurrence to wait for, as he had been informed, that is, the bringing the North Carolina army, of 25,000 men, on the rear of Burnside's army which is about Suffolk & ready to move towards Petersburg—& that the whole would be a grand operation of admirable military strategy, extending over a space more than 100 miles wide. It may be so. But I have no faith in these great & extended operations, requiring combined movements, delays, & so many necessary conditions for success. I believe that we owe most of the misconduct & disasters of this war especially to these things, viz. West Point "red-tape" & strategy. I heartily wish that our civil & military affairs were in the hands of leaders who knew nothing of either.—Still can hear nothing certain of the state of things at Marlbourne, except that Mr. Sayre has fled from it, & was, when heard from, at Hanover C.H. Gen. Lee's family (ladies & children) had been making a temporary home at Marlbourne some weeks ago.[15] The report at Hanover C.H. is that *all* on the farm were under guard as prisoners to the enemy. This cannot apply to the negroes—& the only whites are the ladies of Gen. Lee's family. If

---

[15] Mrs. Lee, who often manifested a rather casual attitude toward social proprieties, proved to be a source of embarrassment to the remaining Ruffins on at least one occasion during the first part of her sojourn at Marlbourne. One morning, so the story goes, she washed a pair of the general's trousers and hung them to dry from a second-floor bedroom window, where they fluttered in the breeze much to the amusement of startled neighbors. Interview with Sterling P. Anderson, Jr., August 29, 1974.

they are guarded, it must be designed for their protection. Dr. Macon, one of the most distant neighbors below, was certainly taken & held by the Yankees as a prisoner. It is reported that several other persons near to Marlbourne have been treated in the same [1989] way. If there is a body of Yankees occupying the farm, in addition to the main army being so near, & unopposed, everything there will be lost. . . . The enemy have certainly occupied & destroyed part of the track of the Central R.R. between Chickahominy & Hanover C.H. The neglect to protect this, if it was neglect, is so glaring that I infer it was left unprotected as a bait to draw the enemy in force farther to the interior. As there are two stems from the junction of the two railroads to Richmond, this obstruction of the Central R.R. does not cut off any supplies—as the cars bringing them may be as well sent by the Rd. & Fredg. R.R. to Richmond.—At night heard the most gratifying report of another battle & victory of Stonewall Jackson, said to be sent by his own telegram. No details given, but only to the purport that "God had blessed us with another victory—& that many prisoners, &c. had been captured, & the defeated troops routed."—Capt. Cuthbert came to see me this evening. He is much improved.

May 26. After doubt having been cast upon the whole report, Jackson's recent success is confirmed, & repeated. At Front Royal, he captured two regiments. Pursuing the remainder to Winchester, he there captured 2000 more Yankees—& in both affairs, secured quantities of munitions of [1990] war, &c. Our loss, about 100 killed & wounded.[16] In fleeing from Winchester, the enemy attempted to burn the town, but they were so hurried that it was saved. Jackson was in pursuit of the routed army.—Heard the particulars of the bad news from Marlbourne, indirectly, & soon after from Mr. Sayre, who had just arrived here from Hanover, C.H., a full statement of the present condition of affairs on the farm. [1991] As I before stated, 200 of the Yankee cavalry had passed through the neighborhood, on Saturday 17th, stopping at Ingleside & Old Church, within half a mile of Marlbourne House, & passing on above to Haw's Shop, where they captured some 70 of our army horses, then

---

[16] Confederate losses at Winchester actually numbered 400. For once, however, the diarist's estimate of Federal casualties is not much exaggerated. Banks lost a fourth of his command (2,019 out of 8,000), more than 1,700 of whom were captured by Jackson on that fateful Sunday of May 25, two days after the lesser engagement at Front Royal.

on the way to Richmond. Very soon after, larger bodies of troops followed, & spread through every public road leading towards Richmond & to almost every farm in that neighborhood. Their vessels also ascended the Pamunkey as high as Retreat landing, 6 miles below Marlbourne. Whenever the Yankee forces passed, or stopped, it was the regular practice for the soldiers to tell the negroes that they were free, that the northern army had come to make them free, & that they should no longer work for their masters. In some cases they were commanded to cease such work. The slaves almost universally readily received these instructions, & availed themselves of the offered privileges. Up to the night of Saturday 17th, not an indication of disobedience or discontent had appeared at Marlbourne. The next day, 12 young men & boys of that farm went off to the enemy. The following day, Monday, all that remained struck work. Mr. Sayre reasoned with them, & endeavored, in mild tone & manner, to show to them the wrong & folly of their course. But in vain. They heard his remarks & answered any questions respectfully, & not one exhibited any insolence of words or manner, or any indication of hostility, or unkind feelings. But it was evident that all were convinced that they had in their reach the negro's heaven, of being relieved from labor, & were not at all troubled by any misgivings or fears of how they were to be fed & supported in idleness. The owners generally, & Mr. Sayre for one, made no attempt at coercion, & yielded to the necessity of the case. My former black overseer, Jem Sykes, who for the last seven years of my proprietorship, kept my keys, & was trusted with everything, even when I & every other white was absent from 4 to 6 weeks at a time, acted [1992] precisely with all his fellows. Mr. Sayre, deeming it useless for him to remain, & that, because of his opinions & zeal, he would probably be held as a prisoner if captured, arranged for leaving. The keys & care of the barn he placed in the hands of Jem, & the especial charge & trust of the large stock of hogs & cattle, & sheep & mules. The hogs & cattle & sheep were in good condition, many of them fat. The head ploughman & another remained & continued to feed & water the mules. And all the property, without the slightest available obstruction or limit, was in the power & at the will of these & indeed of any one of these (some 60) slaves of the farm, in a state of open & avowed rebellion, although of quiet resistance to authority. Owing to the want of means for transportation, two-thirds of the last crop of wheat, & all the corn,

(9000 bushels of which had been sold in March to the government, but not received,) were in the barns. All these, with the splendid growing crops of wheat & clover (to say nothing of the corn,) . . . are at the mercy of any pillaging or hostile or mischievous negro, not only of our own gang, but of the whole neighborhood, all being in the same lawless state. The wife & two grown daughters of Gen. Lee, our Commander in Chief, had before been permitted to use the larger vacant part of the Marlbourne mansion for their temporary home. And thus, strangely enough, these ladies are living in a place commanded by the enemy, & almost within their lines, & on a farm on which & throughout the whole neighborhood the slaves are in general rebellion. Yet Mrs. Lee does not seem the least alarmed. Mr. Sayre had written a letter to Gen. Lee, giving a full account of all he knew of the enemy's movements, & was riding to Summer Hill, 4 miles above, to visit the family (Mr. Newton's) & learn the news, & especially to have this letter conveyed to the Post Office at Hanover C.H., the only route then open to Richmond. On rising a very steep hill, he suddenly found himself meeting, & too close to avoid, a regiment of Yankee cavalry. There being no chance for his [1993] escape, or even for destroying or getting rid of the letter which it might be dangerous to be found on him, he boldly rode up to the commander, who exchanged salutations with him, & accosted him very politely & courteously. Mr. Sayre said (for explanation) that he was on his way to visit a neighbor, but would prefer to return homeward, as this unexpected body was moving towards his residence, & he deemed it better that he should then be at home. The officer (who introduced himself as Col. [Richard H.] Rush of Phil[adelphi]a)[17] urged & repeated his invitation to Mr. S. to proceed on his designed visit. But he was unwilling to risk his being stopped & searched by the rear-guard, & thought it much safer to be in company with the courteous commander. He rode back for two miles slowly by the side of Col. Rush, who conversed with him in the most gentlemanly manner, asking & also answering questions. He inquired as to the state of opinion, the possibility of reconstruction of the former union (on the ground of "every con-

---

[17] Son of the distinguished diplomat and statesman, Richard Rush (1780–1859), Colonel Rush commanded the Sixth Pennsylvania Cavalry. In his official report of a reconnaissance to New Castle and Hanovertown ferries on May 22, Rush mentioned his encounter with Sayre, remarking that he "learned much from him." *Official Records*, Vol. XI, Pt. 1, p. 650.

stitutional right being guaranteed to the Southern States,") &c. and received such answers as could only come from a firm, zealous & sanguine secessionist. Mr. S. declared that reconstruction was utterly impossible—& that if possible . . . scarcely any man of respectable position, or who had any influence, would desire it. The reasons for these views were asked & given, & heard without the slightest evidence of impatience or ill-feeling. In regard to the conduct of the invading troops, Col. Rush advised Mr. Sayre how to obtain protection for his property exposed to marauders. He said that the army was well supplied, & that except for needed supplies, nothing would be taken, by authority, from the residents. What supplies should be needed would be seized—& whether paid for or not would depend on whether the owner was "loyal" or disloyal to the U.S. Of course Col. Rush must have excepted slaves, from the general statement of property being so far secure from seizure. Mr. Sayre told him that he had lost 12 slaves, who had gone to the enemy's camp, "and" he added "I am told that if I were to go to Gen. McClellan [1994], & ask for their restoration, he would have me imprisoned." To this Col. Rush made no reply. Soon after, they passed by the Marlbourne gate, the mansion in full view at some 500 yards distance. Mr. Sayre observing that that was his residence, bowed adieu, & Col. Rush said he hoped they would meet again, to which Mr. Sayre assented, with the addition of the meeting "being under happier circumstances." The Regiment had been on a reconnoitring expedition, & proceeded towards the stage road. A camp for 10,000 men had previously been marked off in the field just above Ingleside, but no troops had then occupied it. That afternoon for the first time, the Yankee sentinels were extended to the Marlbourne gate, but still did not enter the enclosure. Mr. Sayre then thought he could stay no longer. That night he made his last arrangements—& next morning he mounted his horse, & rode across the fields & woods to the road outside of the farm, & thence to Hanover C.H. . . . The Marlbourne mansion having been offered & serving as a temporary home for the family of Gen. Lee might have increased the danger of the property, with many of the brigand leaders of the Yankee armies. But with those of better disposition, & anything of a gentleman's character, this circumstance may, as seems to be the fact, secure more protection to the dwelling place at least, because it is so occupied.—I forgot to state, as one of the conditions of the existing strange state of things, that Mr. Sayre, previous to the arrival of the enemy's advance, had shared out all the bacon (for the year) among the negroes, & given out to them all their allowance of summer clothing, & even their shirts for next winter, which were ready. Of course they will send corn to the mill, & supply themselves with meal (& flour,) at their discretion. They are admirably fitted out for a *strike* from labor. [1995] Thus, at one blow, there is, for the present time at least, an utter destruction of the property of the valuable Marlbourne farm & of all that was on it. Whether anything, except the naked & desolate land, incapable of being put to use, will ever be recovered by the owners, will depend on whether the enemy shall be very speedily & effectually beaten, routed, & driven off, in the expected battle. If our army shall be defeated, then all the Marlbourne property, as well as all other farming property elsewhere, will be entirely lost to my family. My own reserved fund, principal & interest, was secured on the Marlbourne farm & property—which was deemed such ample security, that it was not desired, & only included by accident, that my sons & Mr. Sayre, the present proprietors, also gave their personal security, jointly & severally, for the debt due to me. But, though in point of legal obligation, I am thus individually secured so long as they, or either of them, possess other funds equal to my claim, still I will never be thus benefitted at their loss. Whatever may be my sons' loss, I will share equitably with them—& if their loss of the property shall be total, I will be no farther charge to them as a creditor, beyond what will be necessary for my bare subsistence for the short remainder of my life.—On my mentioning Mr. Sayre's conversation with Col. Rush to Mr. Boulware, he said that he knew who he was very well. He is the son of Richard Rush of Phil[adelphi]a, & a high-toned gentleman, married to a Virginia lady. His two brothers were fellow students of Mr. Boulware at Princeton College, & his intimate & valued friends. . . . This evening, with Mr. Sayre, I sat with Messrs. Boulware, Burgwyn & Newton in the parlor, & had an animated discussion of the President's administration, & of the retreating & inactive conduct of the war, & especially the recent delay of a general battle, so universally desired by both our soldiers & citizens. The two former & I joined in condemnation, & Mr. Boulware with great bitterness. Newton alone defended the President. The conversation induced him & Burgwyn to go to call on the President, & to learn, if possible, something of his views. They did so, & after returning, they joined the others in my room, where we continued our conversation until 11.30 before separating. They learned by their visit that at least one great ground of our complaints was at last removed, by Gen. Huger being superseded in command—though not disgraced & cashiered as he ought to be. They also heard confirmed from the President that a portion of the Yankee army had crossed over & remained [1999] this side of Chickahominy—amounting to 5 brigades, unless designedly deceived by the enemy as to their number—& that as soon as the number was known to be enough, an attack would be made on them, & an attempt to secure the whole detachment. An early general battle promised in general terms only.

May 27.... Heavy cannonading was heard here today from the direction of the upper part of Chickahominy. At night it was reported that there had been two skirmishes—the one at Hanover C.H., in which we gained decided advantage, repulsed the enemy repeatedly, & secured (& sent in to Richmond,) 60 or more prisoners—cavalry. The other skirmish was on Chickahominy, near the rail-road, & the results not known. The firing ceased before 6 P.M.—There has been daily expectation here that the general engagement would begin the day following, but founded only on the general wish, & opinion of the expectancy. But this evening there is prevailing both in the camps & city, a much stronger belief than before, that the great battle will be begun tomorrow. Jackson's late victories, & his onward course still in progress, will tend to encourage & stimulate our army, & discourage the Yankees.... At night, we had another sitting of the same persons as last night, Messrs. Newton, Boulware, Burgwyn & myself, with some others, & our conversation was made more cheerful by the continuation of the successes of Jackson, & the prospect & hope of the general engagement here tomorrow....

May 28. Our hopes were vain, & no sounds or rumors of battle were heard this morning.... A report that Yankee troops had seized & held the Junction of the Central & Fredericksburg rail-roads, of course commanding the Richmond ends of both.—At 10 A.M. I attended a public meeting, called by the Mayor, to induce the enrollment of persons exempted by age or infirmity to form a guard to aid in defence of Richmond. About 80 names were signed, & mine among them, but with the explanation & reservation stated on my part, that I would serve so long as I should remain in Richmond, but be free to go elsewhere, to meet other & stronger claims of my family or my country, whenever I deemed it proper.—By 5 P.M. the loose rumor of the morning strengthened to the certainty that the Junction had been taken by the enemy, & slowly it came out that the afternoon firing [1995][18] heard yesterday was near Hanover C.H., when our troops (Gen. [Lawrence O.] Branch's brigade,) had been badly beaten by a much larger force of the enemy. That this force should have been allowed to get there from below, independent of surprising & beating our force, indicates gross neglect of our leaders.—Mr. Burgwyn gone home, much to the loss of our little circle. . . . At night, Mr. Richard Yeadon arrived from Charleston S.C. I introduced him to Newton & Boulware, & together we sat & conversed until I retired after 9. . . . Notwithstanding all the exciting incidents, reports, & comments, of this time & place, & the company of some of my most valued friends & most intelligent associates, I find my stay here very dull & tiresome. This must be owing to my having lost the capacity for enjoying conversation [1996] & society. I can remember well that, in the earlier time of my life, at any time, & without any unusual interest of news & events, my meeting with a few valued friends & intelligent companions, was alone enough to make every hour of several days pass pleasantly.

May 29. Throughout last night, numerous troops, with their trains, were passing through the streets. This morning I learned that they were from Petersburg—& that the great body of all our forces on the south side of James river has already arrived or moving on to this city. It is now believed that Burnside & his army are already with McClellan. Several regiments, from Petersburg & Drewry's Bluff, arrived here after 9 A.M. & were waiting for orders. Large reinforcements have been sent to Ashland. It is now understood that McClellan is pressing onward in that direction, & that he will aim to surround Richmond, & cut off all the approaches for supplies, by canal or railroads. The Yankee gunboats, Tuesday, went up the Appomattox, throwing shells as the[y] went on both sides, to near Port Walthall, which is the terminus of a branch of a rail-road connecting with the Richmond & Petersburg R.R. & which is not more than some 3 miles distant. It will be an object to seize that railroad, the Danville R.R. & the James R. Canal, as they have already seized the other canals, railroads & rivers. It is supposed that our general will force the great battle, making the attack

---

[18] Misnumbered by the diarist. Should be page 2001.

near Ashland—& many persons expect that the preliminaries of the battle will begin today. God grant it may be so!—The last news from Jackson was that he had reached Martinsburg, & had there added greatly to the previous captures of spoils, had destroyed the Bal. & Ohio R.R. at that point, & that Banks' men, fleeing in small parties, & in utter disorder, had [1997] crossed the Potomac. If our generals here can give to McClellan a complete & stunning defeat, it seems to me that Jackson, with the available accessions of arms & men, may invade & raise Maryland, & push on to Washington, & capture that city.—Received letters from both Julian & Edmund. The latter sends the information that 8 of his men have absconded from Beechwood, & one other hired out in the neighborhood, who belongs to my daughter Mrs. Beckwith. We may expect that we shall thus lose all the slaves that can have access to the enemy's army or out-posts.—Troops have continued to arrive from Petersburg, throughout the day—& have been ordered from N.Ca. Again, as usual, the battle which has not come today, is more strongly than ever expected tomorrow morning.—A letter from Capt. Cuthbert informed me that Charles had returned to his company, & was performing his duty. Immediately I went to the Post-Office, & finding there, still uncalled for, the letter which I wrote to him on 21st, I took it out, & will withhold it.[19]—The newspapers seem to be shut out from war reports as much as possible by the government, & in consequence the public is in the dark as to events close to Richmond. Except that Gen. Branch's brigade suffered a defeat, near Hanover C.H., we are still entirely ignorant of all other facts, & even as to whether the Junction & Ashland have been occupied by the enemy, or not. The Examiner, the paper which finds most fault of the President, & the commanding generals here, states our loss at from 500 to 1000—while the Enquirer, the most laudatory of the high authorities, declare[s] that our loss was very small.[20]

May 30. . . . The approaches of Halleck's army continue, but

---

[19] Apparently Charles's reformation was only temporary. At a later date the diarist inserted the following note: "Some months later, the grounds for it being renewed & continued, this letter was delivered—& without effect."

[20] The *Examiner* proved to be more reliable in this instance. In his official report, Brigadier General Fitz John Porter, commanding the United States Fifth Army Corps, claimed that Confederate casualties exceeded 1,000. General Branch admitted the loss of 66 killed and 177 wounded, exclusive of Colonel James H. Lane's Twenty-eighth North Carolina Infantry, which sustained heavy casualties. *Official Records*, Vol. XI, Pt. 1, pp. 680, 742.

very slowly, towards Corinth. I think that delay there is our best policy—as it serves to increase the sickliness of the locality (very bad already,) for the enemy, & also by the falling of the river, the enemy's large gunboats will be prevented navigating, or by the withdrawing them, endanger not only the receiving of supplies, but will make defeat doubly perilous to the army. . . . To this hour (at night) it is not known what were the circumstances & the extent of our losses in the fight three days ago near Hanover C.H., so near to us that we heard the sound of the cannon. Nor do we know certainly, (though I now believe) that the Junction & Ashland are held by the enemy. . . . A heavy rain this afternoon, for an hour—which will prevent a battle tomorrow, even if before designed by our commander, which I fear was not the case. The great interest felt for Gen. Jackson's movements, & for the hope of his marching into Maryland & attacking Washington, almost equal the interest in the great struggle for life or death—glorious victory or ruinous defeat—which we have been expecting continually for a week or more. . . . Gen. [David F.] Hunter's proclamation, emancipating at one dash all the slaves of S.Ca., Ga. & Fla., has been repudiated by another proclamation by Lincoln. But it makes no difference. Whatever may be enacted, or proclaimed, or denied, the great purpose in view, & practically carried out, is general emancipation of all the slaves—& as an incident, the arming them against their present owners.—Late at night Mr. R[obert R.] Bridgers of N.C. (M.C.) came to my room. From him I learned that Burnside could not have come to reinforce McClellan, as he was in Newbern last Sunday, & (as supposed) his army also. . . . Mr. S[amuel] Gresham had just arrived, & had heard that McDowell's army when last (& lately) heard from was posted 10 miles west of Fredericksburg. Therefore their supposed large reinforcements to McClellan's army have neither been yet received.—At night, a violent thunderstorm, with heavier rain than in the afternoon. These rains will cause the ground to be too soft for the use of field artillery, & the swamp to be flooded & impassable, & so will postpone the great battle still longer. [2000]

May 31. . . . 1 P.M. At 10.30 A.M. I heard in the street that a fight was going on, or soon to begin, down the Chickahominy, & on this side. I hastened to the State Library, to seek for information, & in vain, & then to the top of the Capitol, as the best place to see & hear. The road to Williamsburg, or street, stretches off directly from my

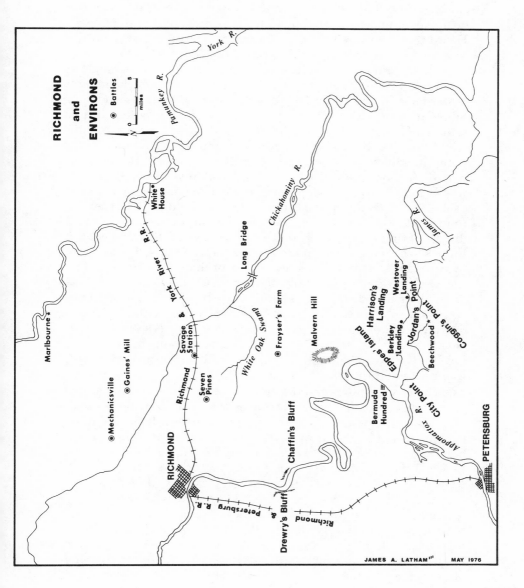

RICHMOND and ENVIRONS

● Battles

5 miles
N

York R.

Pamunkey R.

White House

Chickahominy R.

Long Bridge

Marlbourne

Mechanicsville

Gaines' Mill

Savage Station

Richmond & York River R.R.

Frayser's Farm

White Oak Swamp

Malvern Hill

Seven Pines

Harrison's Landing

Westover Landing

Berkley Landing

Jordan's Point

Epes' Island

Coggin's Point

Beechwood

Bermuda Hundred

City Point

James R.

Appomattox R.

RICHMOND

Chaffin's Bluff

Drewry's Bluff

Richmond & Petersburg R.R.

PETERSBURG

JAMES A. LATHAM III   MAY 1976

[325]

position. On it, there soon passed on a regiment of cavalry, & soon after a long train of artillery, & many ambulances & wagons. Another long train of ammunition wagon[s] drew out into the turnpike on one side, & stopped there, as if to wait until needed. Heard that a large number of our troops were previously on the route, or before posted in that direction. I could learn nothing reliable as to the enemy from any source. But it was among the street rumors that a large force had crossed the Chickahominy yesterday on the Long Bridges, that the tremendous rain-flood soon following swept away the bridge[s], & prevented their return or reinforcements coming to their aid. The sky was overcast, & little could be seen. Smoke apparently from the firing of cannon was seen indistinctly, & at intervals, & in the extreme distance of the horizon of woods. But the color of the leaden sky & of the smoke was so nearly alike that they could scarcely be distinguished from each other. I could not hear the [cannon] reports.—4 P.M. At 3 I returned to the roof of the Capitol & remained an hour. I was told that the firing of cannon had been heard from 2 P.M. frequently. From 3 to nearly 4, the reports were very rapid, as stated by auditors by my side, & even I could hear many of the louder reports. The smoke also was plainly visible, though [2001] the atmosphere was no brighter. The distance was supposed to be 16 miles, & intervening woods obstructed the view, & the wind was unfavorable for hearing. Before 4, the reports became much less frequent—& supposing that I had seen & heard as much as could be, I left the extremely crowded & confined position which I had occupied.—10 P.M. By 5 P.M. I returned to the Main Street, to observe the people eagerly seeking news from the battle. Every person coming in was surrounded while he reported what he knew. If three persons met & seemed to be earnestly conversing, every by-stander would press to them, & perhaps a dense crowd of one or two hundred be formed, before it could be made known that there was nothing to learn. Before 6, the sounds of the cannon had become so much louder that I could hear them in all the noise of the street, but could not determine the direction. I walked to Clay Street, where the table land reaches the abrupt & steep hill-side, & there heard the loudest firing to come from a very different direction. . . . Afterwards I heard that the whole of this new & heavy firing was from the Yankee intrenchments at Mechanicsville, to which our artillery on this side of the swamp did not even respond. After tea, with Mr. Newton . . . I again went among the excited crowds in the streets & in the halls of the hotels, & also we went to the War Office, to gather the latest rumors of the battle. They were too many, & too variant, to be noted. But they generally agreed in these main incidents: McClellan had crossed over yesterday with a very large force (from 45, to 60,000 as reported,) & after the rain . . . last night threw up intrenchments, about [2002] three miles from the swamp. Our troops attacked them there, and drove them back two miles, towards the swamp. It was supposed that notwithstanding the high water, & the temporary bridge having been destroyed, that the enemy constructed a pontoon bridge, & brought over reinforcements during the battle. Why our commander did not call into action more soldiers, seems strange, as there were thousands within two miles of the field of battle, unemployed. There was much carnage on both sides. But the balance of advantage was ours most decidedly. We took two field batteries. The firing ceased at dark. My great fear is that the enemy may be able to retreat across the swamp tonight, over the pontoon bridge. Or, if he holds his ground, & brings over reinforcements, the battle will be general tomorrow. If he can neither escape nor receive reinforcements, we ought to be able to capture all that are not killed.—After writing the above, Mr. Boulware came into my room, & afterwards Mr. Newton, from both of whom I heard additional reports. Mr. Boulware had been near to the contending armies, & upon the battlefield after the armies had passed off. He described the roads & other ground as deep in mud & water, that he could not keep his legs out of water, & that if he had not rode a strong horse, he could not have got through the miry roads. He saw our troops marching through pools knee-deep in water. . . . The enemy had rebuilt the bridge on the rail-road over the Chickahominy, & by it brought their reinforcements today. This gives them a degree of strength that will leave no thought of their retreating tonight, or avoiding a further contest. . . . [2003]

June 1. Sunday. Arose soon after 5, & went out expecting to hear that the battle had been resumed. Only a few cannon reports were heard before 6. I took early breakfast, & having obtained a horse, at 7 A.M. rode off for the neighborhood of the battlefield. Before getting on 3 miles, (or 1 mile past Rocketts,) I had met many wounded soldiers, in ambulances & wagons, & some walking. But few seemed to be otherwise than slightly hurt. Nearly all of the severely wounded had probably been sent in by the rail-road train.

There were numerous soldiers along the road, doing nothing, & many others, met later, bringing the wounded off the field on stretchers, to the carriages. Then & afterwards, there were hundreds, who for this & other pretexts must have been skulking from the fight. The firing of musketry became audible to me, & increased as I drew nearer. Though Mr. Boulware's description had prepared me to see a bad road, it was worse than I had any idea of. Upset & broken vehicles were left in numbers in the deepest quagmires. Perhaps for half the length of the road I passed over, from one to half a dozen new tracks had been made on the margin ground, whether through the fields under crops, or the woods—all flat & sloshy, & the ground "rotten" from the quantity of rain. These new tracks, in some spots, soon were made successively worse than the old road, before avoided as impracticable. In many places, my horse could scarcely recover his feet out of the deep mire under water, & I had several narrow escapes from being dropped by his falling, in deep mud-holes. Of course, the moving of artillery was almost impracticable—& but little use was made of any so long as I stayed. I went rather farther than the Yankee camp, & intrenchment, from both of which they had been driven yesterday. That position is about 8 miles from the Capitol, or 6 from the nearest part of Richmond, at Rocketts. When I arrived there, the firing was farther [2002][21] on, & I was enabled to ride over & view some half mile in extent, along the road, & in the fields on both sides of the field of battle of yesterday. It began to be manifest, by the dead bodies of men & horses half a mile this side of the intrenchment—& around that, & through the camp of the Yankees, the dead still lay thickest. Even outside of that space, around a small log house in an adjacent field, I counted 11 dead bodies, & two severely wounded Yankees, within a space of less than a quarter acre. Most of the dead bodies were Yankees, as known by their blue uniform—but some were our soldiers, distinguished generally by gray uniforms, & always by the white badge on the head used for this occasion. One of the dead I saw, decently arranged, was Capt. [T. A.] Perry of Florida. Later I heard of the deaths today of Gen. J[ames Johnston] Pettigrew of S.C. & Col. [Tennent] Lomax of Ala., both very valuable officers & men.[22] The dead bodies lay very much thicker than those I saw on

---

[21] Misnumbered by the diarist. Should be page 2004.

[22] The report of Pettigrew's death was erroneous. Severely wounded and taken prisoner on the first day at Seven Pines, he was subsequently exchanged and

part of the battlefield of Manassas. There, on the next day after the battle, there was nothing to attract attention but the ghastly killed, or the remaining & suffering wounded. Therefore, as well as for the novelty of the scene, it was full of horror. But today, though the exhibition was still worse, because of the more numerous cases, the ground was also used for the movements of the troops for the action of today, & as the promenade of the hundreds of visitors, who, however deeply impressed with the sight of the ghastly dead, were more interested in the battle still in progress, & in the connected incidents. Among the visitors, there were many officers from other posts, & also I saw Mr. Yeadon (who had come yesterday also,) Gov. Letcher, & the Secretary of War,[23] who came later. . . . The camp of the enemy, where most of the tents were standing, besides being sprinkled with dead bodies of Yankee soldiers, & their arms, had scattered & thrown over the ground by our searching soldiers, everything of food, clothing, & conveniences, which soldiers collect & carry with them. There were innumerable articles which would have been important to any of our soldiers. But very few were appropriated, though free to all, because but few could carry more baggage than they had already.—The fighting today was almost exclusively with muskets & rifles—& though not far in advance of my different positions, as I moved about or remained still on horseback, the combatants were always in woods, & concealed from my view. Sometimes no firing was heard for a considerable time. And for the last hour before I left (at 2 P.M.) I did not hear a report except a few of field artillery throwing balls & shells, & from both opposed sides. Earlier in the day, balls & shells had passed over the heads of those who, with me, were standing or riding in the rear of [2004] our then engaged troops, with the loud whistling of the missiles that manifests their dangerous proximity. But of the few late discharges from the enemy's ranks, which I supposed so distant as not to be worth regarding, one of the fragments of the exploded shell passed so close & immediately over my head, as I sat on horseback, that it struck the ground within 15 yards behind me. . . . These latter discharges, from both sides, were slow, & there was no other firing audible there. I could not understand anything

returned to service in the eastern theater. He survived "Pickett's Charge," in which he commanded a division, only to suffer mortal wounds two weeks later in the retreat from Gettysburg.
[23] George W. Randolph.

of the movements of the troops, the design or the results of our or the enemy's operations—nor even whether we had gained or lost by all the fighting of the day . . . . It was understood that our own loss was heavy. Of that of the enemy we had no means of estimating. Under these circumstances, I saw no use in staying longer, & left about 2 P.M., having been then 7 hours in the saddle, to which I am but little accustomed of late. It took me two hours more, of slow riding, to get back to the Exchange, wearied & almost broken down, & scarcely able to walk up to my room.—I saw my grandson Thomas Ruffin & my nephew Dr. Dupuy on the ground. Though not engaged in the ranks, they, with many other troopers, were equally busy & more disagreeably employed, by orders, in helping to collect & bring together the arms scattered over the field. . . . I have postponed to the last the notice of a most deplorable loss in my family, if true. A young man of the Petersburg regiment, named Carr, introduced himself to me to inform me that my grandson, Julian Beckwith, had been severely, if [2005] not mortally wounded yesterday. The ground on which it was reported he had fallen, was then thought to be in the power of the enemy—& so a search for the body was impracticable. . . . Some hours later, I again met with Carr, who accosted me & stated that he had been enabled to visit the place, & had found the dead body—killed instantanously [*sic*] by a musket ball received in front, in the forehead. Though I know nothing of the informant, (who says he is a cousin of Dr. Beckwith's) I cannot suppose it possible that he can be guilty of a cruel deception, or that he can be mistaken. The long existing alienation of myself from Dr. Beckwith & his wife, my daughter, & other circumstances, have made me almost a stranger to their children.[24] Julian was not even known to me personally, when I met him accidently lately in Norfolk, at two or three short intervals. I cannot, under such circumstances, feel anything like parental affection for grandchildren almost unknown to me, & the children of parents alienated from, or inimical to me. But while these conditions lessen or prevent grief as for a beloved child, they serve to increase the painfulness & difficulty of my position in other respects. I could not even take upon myself to communicate this great affliction to the parents, (which Carr will do,) not only for other obvious [2006] reasons, but because I do not yet relinquish all hope that the information is mistaken. God grant that it may be so! . . .

[24] See Volume I, 121, 353.

June 2. No sounds of cannon this morning. . . . The fighting & the movements yesterday, which, though close by, I could not understand, seem to have been little more than a heavy skirmish. The enemy attacked our troops, who then occupied the Yankee camp, as if to retake it. After a severe contest of some hours, the enemy were driven back into dense woods, more wet & sloshy than is general in all that neighborhood, & into which our commander did not pursue them far. The fighting closed at 10 A.M. After that, as I stated, there was nothing more than a few cannon shot & shells exchanged, probably without effect. . . . Nothing more heard from our forces at Corinth. Silence & delay there are good for our prospects. Reports from the enemy's camp, published in northern papers, give gloomy pictures of their army before Corinth, in actual sickness & prospective low water of the Tennessee. The Yankee commander is advancing by regular & very slow approaches. . . . Newton & Boulware came & sat with me an hour in the afternoon. . . . Newton told us of the existence of wide-spread discontent with the administration, (as we all knew & most of us shared in,) & further that there are numerous persons even ready for lawless revolution. The flame is fanned for the benefit of [John B.] Floyd, by his partizans, & he is to be the leader & the beneficiary of any revolutionary movement, if discontent & murmurs can be worked up to that extreme. Much as I have been dissatisfied with the misconduct of the war, I shall be utterly opposed to any lawless opposition to the President. And if any one is to attempt to play the part of Bonaparte or Cromwell, Floyd is one of the last whom I would trust or follow. He is an able man—but utterly wanting in principle, & even common honesty.—Our army has fallen back to a position some miles nearer to Richmond, & about in a line with our fort on Drewry's Bluff. Thus it seems that we have gained nothing, in position, by the bloody battles of the two preceding days. Heard, from Midshipman Phelps, who brought a dispatch to that effect, that 9 of the enemy's gun-boats have again ascended the river to a few miles below Fort Drewry. Another attack may be expected soon. The fort is much better armed & protected than it was before. [2008]

June 3. . . . The name of my grandson, Julian R. Beckwith, is in the list of killed in the battle of May 31st. I am thankful that his death was instantaneous & painless—& that he was killed facing & while firing upon the enemy. He fell in the assault upon the enemy's intrenchment & camp, & on the spot where there was much carnage.—I had been informed yesterday evening that Judge Thomas Ruffin jr (the son of the old judge,) now a Lt. Colonel in this army, had been very sick, & would be moved this morning to the city. I went to see him in the forenoon, & again after dark. He is too sick to converse, or to speak at all without pain, or to enjoy hearing others. As he was well attended to (at a good boarding house,) & I could be of no use, I returned after sitting nearly an hour, at each visit. I shall continue to visit him twice a day, & to offer any services I can perform. His physician is alarmed for his life. Tonight his condition was better. . . .

June 4. Rain last night, & very heavy this morning. This will further suspend active military operations. The enemy's camp, again on the miry ground which our army had first driven them from, & next fell back from, must be made much more uncomfortable, & tending to produce disease. But they seem superior to us in every sanatory as well as economical & industrial arrangement in aid of warlike operations. We thought that our having [2009] burnt the bridges, & the subsequent high flood of the Chickahominy, had precluded the possibility of the enemy's force on this side being reinforced speedily. On the contrary, they had immediately repaired Bottom's Bridge & the rail-road Bridge & track, & had been receiving over them (the trains running,) reinforcements & supplies to any desired extent. Our army is intrenching the new position. Gen. Lee now commands on the field, Gen. Johnston having been disabled by a slight wound.[25] . . . Gen. Wool, occupying Norfolk, (which after being evacuated, surrendered without resistance, & whose remaining population consists of non-combatant men, women & children only,) has inaugurated the novel & atrocious policy of subjecting the inhabitants to choose between the alter[n]atives of taking the oath of allegiance to Lincolndom, or to starve. He has forbidden, & excluded as completely as possible, the receiving by the inhabitants, or the sale to them, of all supplies of food & other necessaries, whether from the North, or the surrounding & usually supplying country. . . . Under such severe duress, the Yankees boast (whether truthfully or not,) that 1800 persons in Norfolk (probably including Yankee-infected Portsmouth) have already taken the oath of allegiance. Rather than to

---

[25] The press apparently minimized the gravity of Johnston's condition. Struck in the right shoulder by a musket ball and in the chest by a shell fragment, he did not return to active service until November, 1862.

suffer death by hunger, perhaps all may submit to this enforced relief. But what would even that extent of success effect in increasing the number of friends & supporters of Northern domination?—The atrocious general-order of [Benjamin F.] Butler, in which he ordered that [2010] every lady of New Orleans who should "insult" Northern authorities or soldiers, by word, gesture or look, (that is, in any manner exhibit their feelings of dislike & detestation,) should be deemed & treated as a common strumpet,[26] has excited universal indignation, which has been strongly expressed in various modes. . . . The new position of our army (opposed to the enemy) is on the Charles City road, & reaching to James river at the forts. Most of the ground is as flat, wet, & miry, from the last rains, as the encampment left, & now occupied by the Yankees. Gen. Lee has thrown up breast-works along the new lines. Judge Ruffin is something more composed, & better. I again went to see him morning & at night. . . .

June 5. No certain news. Reported that McDowell's army from Fredericksburg (diverted from reinforcing McClellan,) & Banks' army from Md., reinforced, are making a combined movement to fall upon & crush Gen. Jackson's army at Winchester. Also reported in northern papers, that when Halleck's slow approaches reached Corinth, the post was found vacant, & Beauregard's army gone further southward.—My grandson Thomas Ruffin came to town from his camp today, & spent some hours with me, including taking dinner. He has recovered his usual state of good health—which is more than was to be expected, under such great exposure, & his previous sickness. His company, & I believe the whole army, have no tents—& he has had to bear, without any protection save a water-proof cloth, all the many & some very heavy rains, & in some nights on wet ground, either miry, or overspread with rainwater. Such hardships must greatly increase the amount of sickness— which, altogether, serves to kill or disable ten times as many soldiers, as blood shed in battle. [2012] Among the late arrivals of my acquaintance, I saw M. R. H. Garnett, Gen. Bonham, & W. S. Pettigrew. . . .

June 6. Yesterday there was some firing of artillery on the lines, & some few killed, of men & horses.—The evacuation of Corinth is confirmed. It had been completed some days before the Yankee general knew it. This retreat will involve our loss of Memphis. . . .

---

[26] This directive, Order No. 28, was promulgated by Butler on May 15.

The rain-flood in James river is very high—higher than since 1847. It has swept away part [2013] of the pontoon bridge, constructed two miles above the fort, & fears are entertained for the safety of the obstructions across the river opposite the fort. . . . Mrs. Greenhow, who has been kept imprisoned for 10 months in Washington, for her southern principles, & under charges of treasonable acts against Lincoln's government, has at last been released, & sent here under flag of truce from City Point. She is boarding at this hotel. I was introduced to her & conversed with her today. She is very intelligent, [&] speaks remarkably well. Throughout her long imprisonment, she was subjected not only to the confinement & restraints & hardships of a convict, but to indignities far more galling to a lady who had always occupied a high social position. Her patriotism & courage no doubt rendered her very troublesome to her jailors & their masters—& I infer that she was at last released to get rid of her.

June 7. Still the papers bring no news, & there are no telegrams for public use. A later verbal report to Lynchburg is on the bulletin board, but I do not believe in it. It is that Gen. Jackson has fought & again beaten the Yankees, one of the three corps that are approaching him from different directions. These are the corps of McDowell & [Brigadier General James] Shields from Fredericksburg, that of Banks, reinforced, from Md—& one from Fremont's forces in the Allegheny region, united with [Brigadier General Robert H.] Milroy's broken force.—Since Mr. Sayre left Marlbourne, on 24th ult., I have not heard a word from that place, or from elsewhere in the neighborhood. This morning's paper contains an extract from a northern paper, showing that the residence of Mrs. Gen. Lee has been searched by Yankee soldiers, but there is nothing stated as to any other acts of violence or depredation. Though the name of the locality is not stated, & the distance from Richmond is erroneously given as 7 instead of 15 miles, there can be [2014] no doubt of Marlbourne house being the place in question, as that is the recent & present residence of Mrs. Lee & her daughters. . . .

June 8. Sunday. Sundry rumors in the streets, of Jackson's army, but none reliable . . . . One report (which seems trustworthy,) is that 15,000 men have been sent from the South to reinforce Jackson. I wish that 20,000 would be sent from this army. For I am satisfied that McClellan does not mean to attack, until he is aided by another army coming from the north, (which McDowell would have

MARLBOURNE, Hanover County, Virginia, 1936
COURTESY OF VIRGINIA STATE LIBRARY

The diarist with four of his children—(left to right) Julian, Ella, Charles, Mildred—*circa* 1850–1855

COURTESY OF MR. AND MRS. STERLING P. ANDERSON, JR.

brought, if Jackson had not drawn him off,) & a fleet on James river, & perhaps another army landed on its southern bank. And if, as I fear, our leaders will not attack, we might spare 20,000 men to Jackson—& with them he would, by an aggressive movement, defend Richmond better than would be done by double the number added to our army here. . . . Accounts from Charleston state that the enemy have made progress in Stono river [2015], & on John's & James Islands, & a large fleet is off Charleston. An attack on the city deemed imminent.

June 9. Plenty of reports in the papers this morning, but mostly so contradictory that most of them cannot be trusted. . . . But dismissing all these, I trust that the latest telegrams, received last night by the Governor, may be true. These are that Jackson, retreating towards Staunton, (with his prisoners & immense train of captured booty,) had been attacked by Shields, & had repulsed & was pursuing his routed forces; & that another corps of Jackson's army, under Gen. Ewell, had received an attack from Fremont, & repulsed him as effectively.[27] . . . Some picket skirmishing, & firing of artillery yesterday, which, so far as known, resulted in our favor—some 40 of the enemy's pickets having been killed.—The northern papers give extended accounts of the battles here of 31st ult. & 1st inst.—& (like McClellan's report,) claim a great & glorious victory for the northern arms. This is almost a matter of course. All these accounts admit heavy losses of the Yankee army, varying in different reports from 3000 to 4800. But they claim that our loss was very much greater. There has been no official report of our loss. But by estimates made for each regiment engaged, & of the wounded in each hospital, the total loss has been computed at less than 2500.[28] . . . Julian arrived here today, coming to [2017] invest some of his other stocks in Confederate States bonds. He remained only from 11.30

---

[27] For once, these early reports of Confederate successes were essentially correct. Climaxing his brilliant Shenandoah Valley campaign, Jackson defeated Shields on this date at Port Republic, thus complementing Ewell's victory over Fremont at Cross Keys the previous day. Presumably news of the action at Port Republic (which was over by 11:00 A.M.) reached Richmond during the afternoon or evening of the 9th (rather than "last night," as noted by the diarist). Federal losses at Cross Keys amounted to 684, compared to only 288 for the Confederates. At Port Republic the casualties were more nearly equal—1,018 Union (of whom more than half were listed as prisoners) to 804 for Jackson.

[28] This estimate was far too low. With about 42,000 effectives in each army at Seven Pines, the Federals lost slightly more than 5,000, while Confederate casualties totaled 6,134.

A.M. to 2.45 P.M. & returned in the afternoon train. . . . Charles was in town today, on leave, & came to see me.

June 10. Additional telegrams to the Governor confirm the before stated late successes of Jackson, with later continuations of the like kind. . . . Notwithstanding that McClellan & the northern newspapers generally claim a great victory on the 31st & 1st, the N.Y. Tribune admits a "reverse," & a letter writer in the camp (regular correspondent of the Herald,) speaks of their advantage in a very subdued tone . . . . I have no doubt that Gen. McClellan thinks with this writer, that he needs 50,000 more men—& until he gets them, he will not attack. I have before expressed the equivalent of this opinion. But for the victories of Jackson, & the consequent panic for Washington, which caused McDowell's army of 40,000 to be diverted to assail Jackson, that army would have advanced upon Richmond from the North, united with McClellan, seized the Central & Fredericksburg railroads, if not destroyed the navigation of the James river canal—& so have left nothing to complete the surrounding of Richmond, & the cutting off all its lines of supply, but the Danville & the Petersburg railroads, which, when occupied, [2019] would make the defence of the city, & supporting of the army, impossible. Our commander is equally fearful of attacking McClellan in his intrenchments. Therefore, I am confident that the long & daily expected great & decisive battle is not likely to occur for weeks, if ever. If Jackson cannot prevent, in time another army may advance by way of Fredericksburg, as McDowell designed—& a strong flotilla can at any time ascend James river, & land an army to aid in attacking the forts, or otherwise reinforcing McClellan. With such aids, he will attack, if by that time defence will not be impossible for our army.—A bloody riot has occurred in Norfolk, caused by the attempt of a Yankee soldier to kill a free-negro, acting as servant to one of their officers. The negro, in defence, & after flight, shot the assailant. Thereupon many soldiers assaulted, with their bayonets, every negro whom they saw in the streets, killed two, & wounded 10 or 12, before the rioters were suppressed. This is but an indication of the strong aversion & hostility that will grow up between the Yankee soldiers & the negroes. . . . Heard that three more of Edmund's negro men, from Evelynton, had absconded, & gone to the enemy's gunboats—whence all such were sent to Fortress Monroe. Gen. Wool has been removed from the command of Norfolk—& his policy of starving the residents into allegiance to Lincoln has been set aside. . . . I had hoped that Edmund might come to Richmond today, as his business requires it. If he does not come by tomorrow, I shall not remain here longer.—Heavy [2020] rain this morning—& after a cessation, drizzle until night.—Col. T. Ruffin has been reported to me as a little better each of the two preceding days—& so much better today, that I trust all danger of his disease is at an end. . . .

June 11. . . . Heard that reinforcements from Ga. & also from this army, are today on the way to Jackson. In the afternoon, Gen. J. E. B. Stuart came into my room & introduced himself to me, to ask for Mr. Sayre. I told him that Mr. Sayre was at Beechwood, & could not be communicated with immediately, but that I should go there tomorrow. He then informed me, in strict confidence, that some secret movement of his command was designed upon the enemy in Hanover, & he wanted Mr. Sayre to show him the roads and accompany the expedition.[29] For this purpose, he then telegraphed to Petersburg, with orders to convey the dispatch by express to Beechwood, in hope of bringing Mr. Sayre here tomorrow forenoon. This had not been done an hour before Mr. Sayre unexpectedly arrived. As soon as I informed him, he got his passport, & I left him seeking a horse to go immediately out to Gen. Stuart's camp, on the Brook turnpike, a few miles from Richmond. I trust that a successful & bloody dash may be made on the scattered Yankee forces in Hanover. Mrs. Gen. Lee has reached Richmond, from Marlbourne, & I called on her to learn what had taken place since Mr. Sayre's leaving. In addition to the previous loss, before stated, of all the slaves, either by going to the enemy, or by staying at home idle, & in quiet rebellion, [2021] the Yankees have taken all the farm mules, & all the corn in the barns, & all the fodder. No depredations as yet on the mansion. But now that Mrs. Lee & her daughters have left, no doubt it will be pillaged, if not burnt. Mr. Sayre brought as bad news from Beechwood. In addition to the 8 men who before absconded from that farm at first, & 3 from Evelynton, 14 more slaves went off from Beechwood, mostly men but partly women & chil-

---

[29] Stuart was about to embark upon his celebrated "Ride Around McClellan." Departing Richmond at 2 A.M. the next morning (June 12), the dashing young general led twelve hundred hand-picked cavalrymen on a dramatic four-day reconnaissance mission in which they ultimately circled McClellan's entire army on the peninsula. Their route took them through the Marlbourne neighborhood on Friday, June 13, when there were minor skirmishes at Haw's Shop and Old Church.

dren.[30] Not a single man is left belonging to the farm. Among them were two cripples & a dwarf, who had never done, or been required to do, as much work as would pay for their support. Even if no further direct losses are incurred, or depredations committed, the large crops of wheat at both Marlbourne & Beechwood must be lost, for want of hands to save them. My children are thus deprived at once of half of all they were worth in property—though not in equal proportions. Edmund, who was by very far the richest of all the family, is much heavier a loser than in proportion to his larger property.—At night Mr. Newton called, as usual, at my room, for us to exchange our latest news. He told me that the reinforcements sent to Jackson amounted to 25,000 men, of which the first 9000 were expected to reach him tonight. I had just seen a telegram that the Yankees on James island had attacked our forces, & had been repulsed. We lost about 65 killed & wounded. . . . Another conflict expected. We had before heard that 16 regiments of the enemy were on James island, & within a few miles of Charleston.—A letter from Edmund . . . & a few lines from Nanny to send me $20 to be given in aid of the wounded soldiers. I have not been in any of the hospitals, because I am incapable of rendering any service to the sick, [2022] & think that the numerous visitors who do no good, must do harm, & are in the way. But I have not the less aimed to furnish means to those who did the better part of personally nursing the sick & wounded, by contributing in money such amounts as I could spare. To this particular object I had lately increased my whole contribution to upwards of $120, & now directed Nanny's $20 in the manner I had deemed best for the object.—Mr. Sayer called late to tell me that he had not been able to procure a horse, but for the next morning, when he will go very early to Gen. Stuart, & will then reach him 6 hours earlier than if he had come in obedience to the telegram. I should now be glad to wait here for the conclusion of this designed expedition of Gen. Stuart's. But I had arranged every thing for my departure for Prince George—& moreover, at $21 a week for miserable board, I have already spent

---

[30] This mass exodus—consisting of six men, six women, and two children—took place on the night of June 8. Within less than a month (May 26 to June 22), a total of sixty-nine Negroes, including all the men, absconded from Beechwood and Evelynton. On June 23, with farming operations at a complete standstill, the younger Ruffin carried the remaining fifty-nine women and children to Petersburg. Edmund Ruffin, Jr., Plantation Diary (MS in Southern Historical Collection, University of North Carolina, Chapel Hill), June 9, 23, 25, 1862.

here nearly $70, & have not enough cash in hand left for five days more board. It is true that I have, to draw upon, a certificate of deposit of $500, which I had prepared & held to pay to the gun-boat fund. But under present circumstances, & especially as *now* that the Virginia has been destroyed, & James river is in the hands of the enemy, the building & using an iron-clad gunboat here would be but giving it to the Yankees, or to destruction, I deem that I & my sons are no longer bound by our several former offers to aid the enterprise, when it was feasible to protect James river. So I shall use my designed contribution for my own expenses, or any other purposes.—Col. T. Ruffin is so much better, indeed astonishingly improved lately, that he, with his family, will set out tomorrow afternoon for N.Ca.

June 12. Arose at 3.30 A.M., & before 5 on the train going to Petersburg. Arrived there, I got Mr. Sayre's horse, which he had left to await his return, at a livery stable, & rode to Beechwood . . . . The telegraphic dispatch had been brought at 3 o'clock in the night, by two soldiers in a hired carriage, & who returned immediately. Edmund, without understanding the object, (until I informed him today,) had deemed it necessary to be silent as to the contents. This was enough to put Mrs. Lorraine & my granddaughters, (after their first alarm was over,) in a fever of curiosity—which was still more heightened by my arrival, & my resisting all their inquiries for explanation.—The state of the farm, & house-hold, is bad indeed, & prospects worse, after the recent heavy losses of slaves—added to 12 other men, from both Beechwood & Evelynton, being still in the public service near Richmond, if they also have not escaped. The table is reduced in proportion, from the formerly customary bountiful & varied fare. Nevertheless, humble & limited as was the bill of fare, I made a much better dinner than I had enjoyed since my leaving home.—No movement of McClellan lately. He must have been severely checked by the battles of the 31st & 1st, & has been urgently demanding reinforcements. It is to supply them, in part, I suppose, that the garrisons of Norfolk & the neighboring country have been so reduced as to seem, with other measures, to indicate the expected evacuation. The fortifications have been destroyed, & also all not destroyed by our troops of the Navy Yard. The rail-road from Norfolk to Suffolk has been torn up entirely, & the rails removed to Norfolk, for shipment to the North. This shows that there is no march by land contemplated through Suffolk. This necessity of McClellan for more troops I think also explains the present eagerness of the Yankees to obtain supplies of negroes, & also what use they are put to. They are shipped to Fortress Monroe, & I suppose are there drilled as soldiers to take the place of the garrison, & permit most of those to be sent to McClellan. [2024] If it is true that McClellan absolutely requires strong reinforcements before he will venture to advance farther, it is probable that he will not find an opportunity to advance at all. And if not, the advance of the malaria season, & the increase of his sick list, will compel a retreat, which will be equivalent to a disastrous defeat.—A two-masted steam gun-boat passed by up the river about 2 P.M. But the passing of Yankee gunboats, tugs, or other steamers has been so frequent, that it causes no excitement, & scarcely attracts notice. What they are doing, except receiving absconding slaves, is difficult to guess. Persons have rarely landed & in but few places. No depredations have been committed (except in taking off slaves,) & no benefits gained. . . . Troops on their way to reinforce Jackson were moving through Richmond yesterday—& I met a number moving to the same destination (from Ga.) in Petersburg this morning. No intimation has been given in the newspapers of these movements. And many other army movements which I could learn from verbal information in Richmond, are entirely unknown to those who have only the newspapers as sources of information. This advantage I shall miss. [2025]

June 13. Frequent & loud reports of cannon were heard this morning, from soon after sunrise to past 8 A.M. They were heard as far back as 5 miles from the river, & in the supposed direction from the armies on the Chickahominy.—After breakfast, I rode to Ruthven. . . . Found Julian at work with nearly all his hands, in the garden, & he working with his own hands as hard as any other laborer. The first really warm day.—The mail brought no telegrams, & little other news. Fredericksburg, as now appears, was not evacuated, or has been again occupied. 2000 Yankee troops there. The Petersburg Express reports, on private information, that the riot of Yankees & negroes in Norfolk was much more serious than at first stated. The free negro who, in self-defence, killed the Yankee soldier, came from the North as an officer's servant. In revenge, or for retaliation, the soldiers of the regiment of the soldier who was shot, came from their camp into town in numbers, & assailed with deadly weapons every negro, without any discrimination, whom they saw in the streets, & of whom none would have escaped either wounds or death, except by flight. Several were killed outright, & more than 100 wounded before the riot was quelled. No publication of these occurrences was permitted in Norfolk, (where indeed the only newspaper had before been suppressed, because not submissive enough—) & all correspondents of northern papers were ordered not to write any account of the matter. . . .

June 14. After breakfast, returned from Ruthven to Beechwood. . . . The change from the bustle & excitement of Richmond made this a dull & tedious day.—

This war, as now made by the government & people of the north on the Confederate States, is stimulated & sustained entirely & solely by the expectation of the general, almost universal, plunder of the property of the invaded country. If the expected conquest is effected, & all the property of the secessionists (that is, of full 19/20 of the white inhabitants) of the Southern States shall be confiscated to the benefit & profit of the conquerors, then the Yankee nation will indeed be gainers by their war, & can pay off the enormous debt incurred, & secure vast riches besides. And though to every thinking man of the North, the complete subjugation of the whole south, & the consequent power to confiscate & plunder all its property, must now seem very doubtful, if not hopeless, yet all northerners (with their manner of reasoning,) may hope to conquer & retain possession of the border slave states. And the whole property of the "rebels" of these states only, after emancipating the slaves, & killing or driving off the present possessors, would indemnify the Yankee nation for expenses which otherwise must be ruinous, & productive of general individual impoverishment, & national bankruptcy. It is in the now hopeful expectation of this mode of compensation, & salvation from utter ruin, that [2029] this war is waged by the North, without any just or honest cause, or justification. The prompting motives, the encouragement, & the manner of the warfare, are precisely such as influence pirates, who rob & murder, without scruple or limit, unoffending persons, merely to obtain possession of their property. With the exception of Cromwell's conquest of rebellious Ireland, & the general confiscation of all property of the Irish, there has not been such effects or results of war since the conquest of Italy by the northern barbarians. And in design, & avowed intentions, & in absence of just cause or provocation, neither of these cases can compare in atrocity with the Yankee war on the South. Though there is no objection with the Yankee government to the exercise of any amount of falsehood & duplicity, even policy does not conceal the Yankees' designs & objects. Their general emancipation acts, & general confiscation acts . . . are passed by the Northern Congress with no more hesitation or forbearance than if our subjugation & absolute submission had already been completed. Not only are the general & national benefits from the general & entire plunder of southern property counted upon to replenish the northern treasury, but the encouragement is further extended to operate on individual interests. Sundry letters to or from Yankee soldiers, captured on battlefields, & other testimony, have shown that it is a very common belief among the soldiers & people of the North, that each individual northerner, after the conquest, may "squat" upon & possess a farm in the conquered southern states. Some of these letter-writers have, in confidential correspondence, already indicated their preferences & selections of landed property. Probably every one of the invaders expects to become a southern [2030] landholder, & after the toils of war are over, to sit down in comfort, or in affluence, under the shade of his own southern "vine & fig-tree." Add to these objects of self-interest, both national & individual, the considerations of fanatical hatred of negro slavery, & also the general northern hatred, founded on envy, of the southern people, and it would be impossible to array or conceive stronger motives, as having impelled any people in invading & plundering & slaying a weaker nation. The starving condition of the first Gothic invaders of the Roman Empire, the thirst for plunder & blood of succeeding hordes of barbarians, invited & encouraged by previous successes, or the stern rage of Cromwell's army & government, executing what they deemed just retribution & punishment on Irish rebels & traitors, deserving no mercy—neither of these motives were so strong as the combined influences which impel the Yankee people & government to seek the profit of the universal plunder of the Southern people, through their universal ruin, destitution, & misery. And the hopes of gain are not all. In the eventual failure of success, the North will meet loss & ruin scarcely less than the South would find in subjugation by the North. Such are the powerful stimulants which have impelled the North to continue this most iniquitous & unjust of modern wars, & with increased efforts, even after the former declared objects, (the reconstruction of the union, by the conquest & submission of the whole South,) must have become hopeless to all thinking men, & are entertained seriously only by fools or fanatics.

June 15. Sunday. I rode to church, & arrived there half an hour before the time for commencing the services. I was surprised to see no person before the church, where the men usually assemble [2031] & talk until the service is begun—& some of them later. I was informed by a message through a young girl that all the men & boys present had gone to search for a "Yankee spy," & all later comers were desired to follow. Accordingly I galloped after—as did follow all others who arrived later. A man of suspicious appearance & movements had been observed, & who was supposed then to be concealed in a small body of thick woods not far from the church. Some men on horseback surrounded the woods, so as to see & pursue any one who should come out to escape, while 4 or 5 others, on foot & with guns, passed through & searched the close undergrowth. The fugitive, seeing that he could not remain concealed, surrendered himself, &, after being examined, was sent under guard & delivered to the nearest picket guard. The fellow had a pass, & leave of absence from the fortification opposite to Drewry's Bluff, but to go to Petersburg, & for 48 hours, which had expired. He was doubtless a deserter, & probably a northerner also, & aiming to get on to Suffolk (the way to which he had inquired,) & thence to Portsmouth or Norfolk, to join or be protected by the Yankee army.—In the afternoon, a remarkably heavy rain. Since about Christmas, or for 5½ months, rains have been so frequent & heavy that the earth has not once been as dry as ordinarily at the same time of the year. And never has a season been known so continuously wet, even for half the length of time. The land here was not dry enough for ploughing throughout the length of corn-rows yesterday, after an unusual number of rainless days. This rain will make it improper to plough any part of the field for some days more. Also, it will be renewed & increased cause for sickness in the armies—& of obstruction to the moving [2032] & use of field artillery, & to military movements in general. . . .

June 16. . . . The mail brought much of interesting news. The evacuation of Fort Pillow was effected without any loss, except of the heavy cannon, which could not be removed, & were partly destroyed, & the others spiked. The loss of this position compelled the retreat down the Mississippi of our flotilla of 8 armed steamers

& gunboats, to Memphis, where they gave battle to the pursuing & much stronger flotilla of the enemy, released by the evacuation of Fort Pillow—double in number & strength to our vessels. There was a sharp conflict, notwithstanding the great disparity of force, in which one of the Yankee vessels was sunk. But it ended in 7 of our vessels being either sunk, disabled, or otherwise compelled to surrender. One only escaped (for the present time,) by fleeing up Arkansas river.[31] The necessary & immediate consequence of this victory over our only remaining naval force, added to the evacuation of & falling back from Corinth by our army, was the occupation of Memphis by the Yankee forces, & without resistance, as there was no garrison, or means for defence. . . . The expedition designed by Gen. J. E. B. Stuart [2033], (of which he informed me confidentially, & for which he required the guidance & company of Mr. Sayre,) has been performed, with great success. There are different accounts in three of the Richmond papers of today—which though varying in particulars all agree as to the general operation. . . . There were 1400 men in the expedition—mostly cavalry, & the remainder artillery—with 3 field pieces. On Thursday (the day I left Richmond,) the corps moved no farther than near Ashland, where they encamped for the night. Early next morning they moved on rapidly & first came upon the Yankee out-posts near Hanover C.H. There, & thenceforward, at Old Church, & below to the Putney mill (Braxton Garlick's) on the Pamunkey, 6 miles above the rail-road at the White House, there was a succession of successful attacks on Yankee outposts, detached camps, wagon trains &c. all of which were routed or captured. There was no time to bring off anything except prisoners, & horses & mules. . . . Next they galloped to Tunstall's station on the York river railroad. The sound of the whistle announced a train approaching from the Pamunkey. Logs were thrown across the track. But there was so little time, that the obstructions were thrown off by the increased impetus of the train, the rapidity of motion [2034] being increased by the engineer as soon as he saw our troops. They fired one general volley on the

---

[31] This engagement, witnessed by hundreds of spectators from the heights overlooking the Mississippi at Memphis, occurred in the early morning of June 6, two days after the Confederates had completed their evacuation of Fort Pillow. Several hours after the defeat of the out-gunned Confederate flotilla, the mayor of Memphis surrendered that city to Federal authorities. Thus, Vicksburg became the last Confederate bastion on the Mississippi River.

passing train, doing much execution, including the killing the engineer. Eight flats, or platform cars were filled with soldiers, reinforcements for McClellan's army. How many were killed could not be known, as the train shot by so rapidly. There was no time to destroy the track—but the troops burnt the buildings at the station. They next moved on to cross the Chickahominy. The stream was there of considerable size, & swollen by rain. A destroyed bridge was found & repaired, to pass over the artillery train, of which all was saved except one caisson. The cavalry partly swam the river, before the bridge was made passable. Thence they came to Charles City C.H., & passed up the road near to James river (& at one time in sight of the Yankee gun-boats,) to Richmond, which the corps, with the prisoners (about 175) & the captured horses & mules, reached on Sunday afternoon, after having been for 48 hours together in the saddle. . . . We lost but one man killed, Capt. [William] Latané, commanding Essex cavalry, & had three wounded. The property of the enemy destroyed by this expedition, by rough estimate, was computed at $1,000,000. Why cannot 20,000 men from our lines near Richmond, follow in the brilliant track of Gen. Stuart, which he was obliged to pass & fight over, & leave so hastily, & seize & retain possession of the York river railroad, & the line of passage of the enemy's supplies & reinforcements?. . . . Rode to Ruthven in the afternoon.

June 17. Returned to Beechwood, in the expectation that Edmund would leave home, as he did, this afternoon, to go to N. Carolina. He began harvest today, with two scythemen only, & these from Evelynton. He could not have left home at a more inconvenient time. . . . Heavy & frequent reports of cannon from 8 to 10 this morning. But more or less cannonading is heard here now almost every day—& we have ceased to consider even the most frequent reports as evidences of a serious battle.—Last night 6 sheep & lambs were stolen out of Edmund's sheep-pen, & carried off. The pen had been placed, to be so guarded, in front of Old Jerry's & another house. Of course the [2036] *guards* must have known of the robbery when it was going on.

June 18. This morning one of the house servants came to my door to inform me that another gang of the negroes had gone off last night—21 in number, embracing three entire families, or all that remained of them, except two very old ones. This makes 47 of Edmund's separate loss, besides his undivided two-fifths of the whole number (about 60 I suppose) at Marlbourne. How these went last night is not yet known—but certainly by preconcert & regular arrangement, & probably by a Yankee boat & crew coming to take them away. One of the only two men, (from Evelynton,) one especially confided in, was one of the fugitives. The remainder were women & children—one old woman, & one or more infants. The delusion of the negroes is astonishing. From their statements made, it appears that they have been promised enormous wages, plenty to eat, & no work to do. It must be, from the present special efforts of the Yankees to induce the negroes to go to them, & their receiving even those who must be a burden & expense, that they have now a special object in view, in addition to the general design of injuring the proprietors, & the institution of negro slavery. And this special object I think is to cause the loss of the growing crops, & of the wheat now ready for reaping, by taking away the needed laborers. What the Yankees will do with all these negroes, & especially those incapable of labor, is difficult to conceive. It is said that Gen. Banks took 5000 across the Potomac, & who have gone to Pennsylvania. But the northern states will not submit to receive many more of this burdensome population (when free,) & still less the north-western states, most of [2037] which have already declared against their entrance. The men, if permitted to go to the North, may support themselves. But they will neither be able, nor willing if able, to support also the infirm members of their own families. These must be maintained by public or private charity, or perish for want. Though in their absconding, they have mostly gone in families when convenient to do so, there have been shown in every family some cases of utter disregard to family ties & affection. Husbands have left sick or pregnant wives—children have left parents, & parents children—between whom before subsisted, as supposed, as much affection as in any other cases. One woman here, who has been lying ill for a year, (& regularly attended by a physician, though she was an expensive burden otherwise, & her case deemed hopeless,) was left here alone, her husband, mother, & child & brother, all having gone off at different times. Why this property & Marlbourne should be especially losers of slaves, cannot be understood, for nowhere were they better cared for, or better managed & treated, according to their condition of slavery. One other plantation in this county, only so far, has been a large loser. This is Mrs. Willcox's, on the river, from which 35 slaves have been lost. Capt. H. H. Cocke has lost 17, & Mr. J. B. Cocke (off the river) 10. Very few other proprietors have yet lost any, on this side of the river. On the opposite side, I heard this morning that two proprietors have lost all their slaves, except a few very old—& two others nearly all. They there escape by land, to McClellan's camps in New Kent. No more have left Evelynton, since the first three. But their credulity & disposition to abscond are epidemic—& I think it not [2038] unlikely that every negro now remaining will follow, if the Yankee vessels & troops continue in possession of the adjacent water & land. . . . At night, my grandson George returned from Richmond, with repaired parts of the reaping machine, for which he had gone there yesterday.—2 hireling scythemen set to work today. I stayed with the work as long as other demands on my attention permitted.—The mail. A severe conflict has taken place on James Island between the Yankee forces previously established there, & our troops, principally from Charleston. The Yankee troops were much more numerous, & made the attack, & renewed it, & were driven back more than once, & finally. Our loss was large, for the number engaged. That of the enemy not known, but supposed to be much larger.[32] . . . The most thorough abolition papers of the north are loudly condemning McClellan for his slow progress in getting to Richmond. The government organs defend him by excuses which show that my view was correct, that he would not make an attack, for a general & decisive engagement, until he had received the reinforcements of two more armies & the fleet on James river. . . .

June 19. A fruitless attempt made to fix the reaping machine for working. The new parts will not fit to the old, & nothing can be done. Another hireling served to increase the reaping force to 4 scythes. 3 single ploughs only in the cornfield, driven by young boys who never ploughed until lately—& 3 weak hands at hoes. Even if no more of the negroes flee (& I expect more, or nearly all the remainder will,) both the crops of wheat & corn must be mostly lost, for want of labor to save them. The clover crop, which, because of the very wet season, was the finest ever known, has been already lost, for hay or mowing.—Corn is now selling in Petersburg at

---

[32] At Secessionville, South Carolina, on June 16, some 2,500 Confederate troops, commanded by Brigadier General Nathan G. Evans, routed a Federal force of 6,600, thus frustrating Union designs to gain control of the Charleston area. Union casualties numbered 683, while the Confederates lost only about 200.

$1.25, bacon (by retail) at 75 cents the pound & coffee at $2. The army horses are reduced in the allowance of food to half the usual rations. And at the same time, the Yankee army is supplied plentifully with our grain, forage, & meat & livestock, plundered from the farms, & without any cost to the plunderers. Such is the difference of the burdens of the war to the invaded & the invaders. We may not fail in resolution, constancy or courage—nor in soldiers, arms, or money. But I begin to lose hope of our Confederacy being able to carry on the war much longer, with such high prices & increasing scarcity of the necessaries of life, & supplies for the armies, & the enemy having the power, through their naval forces [2041], to take every thing produced or remaining on or near the borders of the navigable rivers (the most fertile lands,) or wherever, by aid of their naval supremacy, the enemy can advance armies, or spread out foraging & plundering expeditions. . . . If this state of things continues, the rich crops of wheat now to be reaped (by those who have slaves left to reap them,) the oats, also nearly ready to be harvested, & the crops of corn under cultivation, will but be made, & saved, & got ready, for the use of the enemy. And this may be in this manner of warfare, even though our armies, acting entirely in defence, may defeat the invaders in every battle. Would that this policy of our government, of keeping our armies on the defensive, & within our own territory, were abandoned! If Jackson's army were increased to 100,000 soldiers, & he permitted to invade Pennsylvania, & to subsist on the invaded country—to plunder, ravage, burn & destroy—we would make the northerners feel the evils of defensive war on their own territory. Moreover—the northern people who are so strong, & so superior to us in strength, as invaders, must be, as we are, weak & incapable of resistance at home. We may infer this from our own condition. Nearly all our able-bodied men, & nearly all our arms, are in our armies. Outside of our camps, & in the country generally, as well as along the navigable waters occupied by or accessible for the enemy, our people are powerless, & incapable of resisting, or of attempting opposition to [2042] any armed invaders, or even to marauding parties. Such must be the case with the northern states also. And probably an army of even 50,000, under Jackson, or Price, or half the number in guerrilla parties under such leaders as Morgan & Stuart, might lay waste to Philadelphia with fire & sword, or lay Cincinnati & even Chicago in ashes. . . . And when thus offered for free plunder, there would be found thousands of the destitute & vilest population of Philadelphia & Cincinnati, practical as well as theoretical agrarians, who would need nothing but our permission, & security from punishment, to sack & burn these richest cities, in aid of, or even in advance of the like designed action of our armies. It would be as rightful, & as feasible, for us to excite to such destructive action, & to our aid, the destitute population of the northern cities, as for the northern people & armies to excite our [2043] slaves to desertion or insurrection, as they have attempted & are attempting.—Through today, a schooner & two steamers were stationary, if not aground, on Harrison's bar, near to the Berkley shore. Just before dark, at high tide, the steamers & schooner moved up the river. . . .

June 20. After 11 A.M. stopped the reaping, & all the harvesting hands were employed until night in putting the bound wheat into shocks. All so secured, except less than an acre. With all the attention & care I can give to the harvest work—which is for the whole time that the late hours of breakfast & dinner permit—the work proceeds slowly & badly, even for the weak force engaged. . . . The mail. Nothing new, & certain, except that heavy skirmishing occurred on the lines near Richmond on the 18th. for several hours, in all which our forces had the advantage, though with a loss of 50 or 60 killed & wounded. . . . Different rumors of intervention by France in our war, but nothing reliable. England & Spain have both withdrawn their forces from the long threatened & delayed invasion of Mexico, leaving France only to persist in the slow operations. It is understood that France aims to convert Mexico to a monarchy, & that the king is to be an Austrian prince. In return, Austria is expected to yield her yet remaining dominion in Italy. The Lincoln papers express great indignation at the designs of the three powers on Mexico, & threaten signal vengeance of the U.S. as soon as they shall have crushed the southern rebellion, & have their forces free to act otherwise. . . . The great gains of the war, in the possession of the Mississippi, & of James & York rivers, & Norfolk, have fallen to the enemy. These (after the fall of New Orleans,) were the inevitable results of the enemy's naval supremacy. But every conflict that has occurred since & including the battle of Shiloh, has brought glory to our arms—& also success in each particular contest, except at Hanover C.H. & the recent naval fight on the Mississippi [at Memphis], in which success was impossible.

June 21. On my going out to the wheatfield after breakfast, I learned that two more of my son's negroes had gone off last night —a young man (the only one left here,) & a girl, his sister. Both were from Evelynton. Two hirelings, free negroes, only left reaping. . . . It is said that Gen. Beauregard's masterly retreat from Corinth was a defeat of Gen. Halleck's plans, & equivalent to a defeat in battle. It appears to me otherwise, & more like a defeat on our side. Halleck has no need to pursue our army to its new position, (which indeed would have been disastrous to him, at this season). He is no longer compelled to depend on the Tennessee river for supplies for his army, but holding Memphis, & commanding the Mississippi river, & the railroad to both, may be thence supplied. But by the retreat, we have lost all these. And if it was a necessity, I fear that the retreat indicates increasing inferiority of our army to Halleck's. . . .

June 22. Sunday. All, except myself, went to church. Soon after Edmund & Jane & their child arrived from Petersburg. . . . Soon after their arrival, Mr. Beegleston, the overseer at Evelynton, came across the river to report the additional loss of 21 negroes of that farm, who went off last night, in boats. Every man except one went. This makes 69 slaves lost by Edmund individually, which, with 23, his two-fifths proportion of the 58 at Marlbourne, makes his total loss so far, 89 [*sic*] slaves—including all of the most valuable, & indeed every able man & every boy above 12, except the one man remaining at Evelynton, & 12 before impressed & still employed as laborers for the government near Richmond. Mr. Beegleston heard that many, if not all the slaves who have absconded on this river, are employed by the Yankees on the Sandy Point estate in cultivating the corn, & harvesting the wheat & other matured crops. [2048] It also seems as if the conciliatory policy generally pursued heretofore along the banks of this river is about to be abandoned, as I was sure it would be, & then all will be subjected to like & general plunder & devastation. As an indication, (besides the report as to Sandy Point,) a party of Yankees landed at Westover, where Mrs. [John A.] Selden & her son Edward only remained. The latter has but one hand, & was also then confined to bed with rheumatism. They seized him as a prisoner, & had forced him into their boat . . . but yielding to Mrs. Selden's entreaties, they released him on parole, for a limited time. Because of these recent acts, Edmund now deems it unsafe for the females of his family to remain here longer. He will (if permitted) move all the remaining negroes & stock &c. from Evelynton to this place, preparatory to other & speedy removal. The crops at both places must be abandoned, & totally lost (unless any portion can be saved by hired labor)—as they have already been lost & laid waste at Marlbourne. This is reported by Mr. Sayre, who is at Ruthven. The fences were partly burned for fuel by the Yankee soldiers, their horses turned in the fields to graze, & even if the damage so caused were ever so little, all other stock of the neighborhood will have free access, & the destruction be made complete.—In the afternoon, all the ladies were sent to Ruthven, to remain. Edmund & his son George returned at 10.30 P.M. & also came Julian & Mr. Sayre. These 4, with other gentlemen of the neighborhood, patrolled this & other farms from 11 to 3, without discovering anything. I offered to join in the service—but it was not deemed necessary. And so I went to bed at 11. [2049]

June 23. Mr. Sayre was told in Richmond, by Mr. Newton, (who is informed by government officials,) that Gen. Jackson & a large part of his army had moved within 50 miles of Richmond, & into Hanover Co., by last Friday night (or was so expected,) to reinforce our army there, & to attack the enemy's right flank, in the general engagement expected then to occur as early as yesterday. . . . This forenoon, all the remaining slaves were brought from Evelynton, across the river, under charge of Mr. Beegleston, the overseer. To these, were added all then remaining at Beechwood, except a few, either old & infirm, or women confined by illness, or very recent child-birth. All were sent to the neighborhood of Petersburg, for greater present security against following their fore-runners to the Yankees—& except a few families, from which none had absconded, all others are designed to be sold. Though nearly all had shown, whether of those who had gone, or those who had remained, almost perfect disregard of their family ties, it was a painful necessity thus to sever more family ties, & also those before subsisting, (& supposed to be strong on both sides,) between the master & his family & the slaves. As I could render no [2050] aid to my son in this disagreeable business, I left at 10 A.M. for Ruthven. The wagons did not leave until 2 P.M., after which Julian returned home.—Edmund sold today 50 sheep, & will as soon as possible sell, to avoid their being stolen by the Yankees, all his remaining stock both at Beechwood & Evelynton. He has ceased to hope to save his crops at either place. And now, the farm which I first so enriched, & which my son has since still more improved, & which was so productive & valuable—with the mansion & adjacent grounds which are so beautiful, are left vacant & desolate, & probably will soon be laid waste by Yankee marauders, or their more authorized

& more effective plunderers & destroyers. As soon as the removal of the live-stock can be completed (or attempted in vain,) from Evelynton, the overseer & his wife, leaving that farm entirely vacant, will come to reside in the mansion at Beechwood. All Edmund's family, including his permanent inmates Mrs. Lorraine & myself, & Mr. Sayre his present visitor, & Julian's, will now crowd into the small dwelling of Ruthven. And though all of us are content to partake of the most humble accommodations, it cannot be otherwise than that so large an addition to the family, (which before had but one disposable bed-room,) must cause great inconvenience indoors, & also that the small laboring force of the farm must be much impeded, & loss thereby occur. But there could not be more earnest hospitality, kindness, & friendly & affectionate attention offered, without regard to their inconvenience or loss, than by both Julian & Lotty. How long their slaves may remain, or by a general absconding cause also the total income from their small property at Ruthven [to be lost], (in addition to the more valuable property already lost in Marlbourne,) is a doubtful question, of great interest to all of us. Unless a speedy & complete [2051] victory of our army shall drive off the invaders, we can expect nothing less than that all lower Virginia, within convenient access to marauders, from the rivers & the Yankee armies, will be stripped of slaves, crops, & stock, & everything laid waste or destroyed.

June 24. No sounds of cannon reached Ruthven this morning. Surely, in the present circumstances, of Jackson's arrival, & of McClellan's great reinforcements on the way,[33] our commander cannot much longer delay making an attack. And from the passes over the Chickahominy above Richmond, it seems to me easy for our forces to attack the out-posts & right wing of the Yankee army, & to beat & drive back that portion—& following somewhat in the route of Gen. Stuart's late expedition, cut off the rail-road communication, & attack McClellan's main body in the rear, while our right wing engaged him in front.[34] If our forces are ever to act, surely this is the golden opportunity. Julian went off early this afternoon to join other neighbors in a voluntary patrol on the Jor-

[33] It was thought in Richmond that the scattered Federal units in western Virginia would soon follow Jackson, and there was even a wild rumor that Halleck's army in north Mississippi would be sent eastward to join McClellan within two weeks' time.

[34] This was precisely the strategy devised by Lee during a conference with his principal subordinates on the preceding day and implemented on June 26.

dan's Point estate & beach, where it was whispered that absconding negroes were received by boats from the Yankee vessels. Rain caused the partial frustration of the plan, & Julian got back home by 10 P.M. On the nights of 21st & 22nd, he was out on patrol until very late. There have been more escapes of slaves very lately from four other farms in the neighborhood. Two proprietors besides Edmund, have sent off all their slaves deemed most at risk—involving, of course, the failure to save the crops. . . . [2052]

June 25. After 10 last night, Edmund returned here from Petersburg. He had been able to get through his disagreeable & painful undertaking better than was expected—though not with less pecuniary loss, & with risk of further escapes of the retained slaves. He sold to a single buyer, (who was buying for two southern plantations,) 29 slaves. These were the fragments of sundry families, of which the other members had gone off in the several previous elopements—& who were therein active participators, as all the adults who remained were passive, knowing well the intentions of the others, & keeping their secret. All these were sold in families, for as many of the members as remained. No family tie was broken, except what had been done before by the voluntary action of some members in eloping, & of others of their families in remaining. More than 30 others were retained, also in whole families, & including every family that had no members in the previous abscondings. These are placed on a farm above Petersburg, where they will be at expense, instead of their labor yielding any nett profit to the owner.—The present prices of negroes have fallen nominally about one-fourth only below the former highest rates. But allowing for the depreciation of the only circulating medium, C.S. paper money, the decrease of price must be fully one-half. Confederate States bonds had fallen to 92½ for the $100, when I left Richmond. But I was glad to learn that the market price has since gone up to 95. This is a gratifying indication of growing public confidence in the stability & responsibility of the C.S. government, at the very time when its capital is besieged, & threatened to be certainly captured, by the most powerful armament that the Yankee government has been able to bring together. . . . All of the Beechwood family, except myself, & assisted by Mr. Sayre, went this morning to their deserted home, & remained until near night, to pack up & bring away their clothing & other articles most necessary or important to remove. . . . The hearing of cannonading is almost of daily occurrence & has ceased to be deemed any indication of serious fighting. But this day, it was heard (near & loud at one time, but mostly distantly & too faint for my ear,) from early until late. [2054] This unusually long continuance, throughout the whole day, as inferred from the partial observation & reports of sundry persons, together with our previous expectation of the speedy joining of the great battle, induced the earnest & sanguine hope that our army was then engaged with McClellan's, & that we shall obtain a great & signal victory.[35] May God grant it!—When Capt. Farragut first had the U.S. flag raised in New Orleans, & before he had occupied the city, or any of the land, by a permanent force, as soon as his boat's crew left the shore, the flag was pulled down by a young man named [William B.] Mumford, & torn to pieces by the people. After his occupying the city, Butler had Mumford arrested, &, (whether tried or not,) deliberately sentenced him to be hung— which has been done, with all formality. For this atrocious outrage, our government ought immediately to retaliate, by selecting by lot, & hanging a Yankee officer. But that is not enough. An order ought also to be made & published to Yankeedom & the world, that if ever the brutal murderer Butler shall fall alive into the hands of any of our forces, that he also shall be hanged, for this & for other previous atrocities & violations of the laws of war, as soon as his person can be identified.

June 26. . . . No firing heard today to twilight. But very soon after frequent reports were heard, & most of them so loud, (so that they were plain to me,) that we thought they must be from gunboats near & below City Point. Many other reports were much more faint, & imperceptible to me. The sounds were heard, more slowly, until I went to bed, after 10 o'clock.

June 27. The house-servants reported that the firing continued [2055] all night—& Julian heard a few reports after he arose early this morning. One of the servants also observed a very bright light, as of a house burning, an hour before day-break. After breakfast, Mr. Sayre, who had gone to Petersburg yesterday morning, returned, & brought a paper, with the blessed news that our left wing had attacked the enemy's right yesterday afternoon, & that we had

---

[35] The cannonading heard this day at Beechwood and Ruthven heralded the beginning of the Seven Days' Battles (June 25–July 1). The Federals took the initiative on the first day but made little progress, as Huger repulsed attacks by General Samuel Heintzelman's Third Corps on the Confederate right east of Richmond.

driven them back until 9 P.M. when the engagement still continued. . . . My heart swells with joy & gratitude for this beginning.
Mr. Sayre heard of no cannonading near City Point, (which would
certainly have been distinguished in Petersburg,) & therefore the
reports we heard last night must have been from the battle above
Richmond. And strange as it seems, we must have also seen something of the flashing of the artillery. While I was standing in the
yard to listen for the reports, & to note the direction, I observed
many very faint flashes of light, like the faintest of sheet lightning,
all seeming to rise from the horizon, & in different points, but from
the same general direction. . . . From Mr. Sayre's information, I am
now sure that the flashes were of the artillery. He, & many others in
Petersburg, after dark, crossed the river & ascended the hill to the
high land opposite, & there they could distinctly see the flashes
accompanying the discharges of the cannon in the battle. No more
firing heard here since the few reports before sun-rise. We wait for
later reports, by the mail, or otherwise, in feverish anxiety. [2056]
. . . The loudest reports we heard last night were, as we then
supposed, from firing much nearer than the battlefield. It was an
artillery skirmish between part of the Yankee gunboat flotilla, & a
company of our artillery posted below Port Walthall on the Appomattox. Their shells were very destructive to the horses, among
which, where confined in the rear, the shells fell, & either killed or
wounded 10 of the number. A house also was burnt, the light of
which was what was seen here. Two only of our men were
wounded. They fired on the gunboats until the latter drew off.—A
neighbor who left Petersburg after 10 A.M. informed me that distant
cannonading had been heard, supposed from the great battle, to the
time of his leaving. . . .

June 28. Still & quiet as things appear here, the result of the great
battle must be by this time decided, & with it probably the war, &
the fate of Virginia. No mail will come to us for two days more. Mr.
Sayre set off for Petersburg, to learn the news—& prepared to
proceed to Marlbourne in the expected event of the Yankee forces
having been driven off from that neighborhood. I rode to the Post-
Office, in the hope of hearing later news from some private traveller
from Petersburg. I met with one, & heard of the statements of two
others, all from Richmond since 3 P.M. yesterday—& all concurring
in general in the same joyful reports, which to that time & later had
reached Richmond. These were, that the fighting had continued, &
our success & advance—that Jackson had reached & occupied the

York river R.R. cutting of[f] the rear of the Yankee army from their gunboats on York river—that Magruder had penetrated through their centre—that their right wing had been cut off & demolished—& that the complete defeat of the whole Yankee army was expected & deemed almost certain. From so many different informants, I trust that at least half of this good tiding may be true—& that will be enough to ensure to us a signal victory.[36] . . . Two or three days ago, Mr. Beegleston began the attempt to bring the livestock across the river. The first mule was drowned. 10 of the best & fattest hogs died with heat in being brought in a cart, & tied, to the landing. After this no further attempt was made. On [2058] being reported to my son, on the 26th, he ordered that the remaining stock & other moveables should be let alone, to await the issue of the then daily expected great battle—& in the event of our victory, to send all to Richmond, for sale.—At night, Mr. Sayre returned from Petersburg. The reports heard this morning were much too favorable. All that is certainly known is that our left wing had continued to advance upon & press back the enemy's right—taking batteries & intrenchments by hard fighting, & (as believed,) that we had occupied & partly destroyed the York River railroad in the rear of the army, cutting them off from their gunboats on York river. The enemy had defended their positions bravely & obstinately, & contested every inch of ground as they retreated in good order. From their most advanced fortifications (if not others,) they had carried off the artillery. Mr. Hopkins of Petersburg arrived there from Richmond in the train which left at 3 P.M. today. He saw on the bulletin board a dispatch from Gen. Lee to President Davis stating that our troops had obtained "a great victory, but at frightful cost of lives." With this, for the left wing & Jackson's forces, we must be content. No private reporters or other civilians not attached to our army are permitted to be in the camps, nor are reports from others there allowed to be sent back, except from or by authority of the commanders. Hence reports are few, & still fewer are authentic, or other than street rumors. It does not appear that McClellan's

---

[36] As the diarist suspected, these early reports were far too optimistic. In costly engagements at Mechanicsville on June 26 and at Gaines' Mill the following day, Lee had forced McClellan to begin shifting his base from the Pamunkey to the James River. Richmond was saved, for the time being, but faulty coordination and staff work had prevented the Confederates from registering a decisive victory. There was only minor action on the 28th as McClellan continued his withdrawal toward the James, slowed by the lengthy wagon trains which accompanied his huge army.

main force, (his left wing & centre) which had crossed the Chickahominy & entrenched there, had made any movement backward,
or otherwise—& our right wing, opposed, had continued there to
stand entirely on the defensive, in its position. But no doubt that
this, previously our main body, has been drawn upon, & much
weakened, to supply heavy reinforcements to the left wing for its
aggressive movement on the flank & rear of the enemy.—Upon
suspicion of some further movement of absconding slaves being
intended tonight, & of Yankee [2059] boats coming for them, a
voluntary patrol was hastily arranged. Edmund is to go, & I
determined to make another. Julian's recent & heavy service of this
kind required that he should remain at home.

June 29. Sunday. Last night at 10 P.M. Edmund & I set out from
Ruthven, & joined the others at the Beechwood grain landing. We
were 9 in number, armed, with double-barrelled guns mostly,
loaded with buck or goose-shot. Part remained at that landing, &
the others went to that at the extremity of the Point. At both landings, we kindled & kept lighted for some time, fires, such as we had
reason to believe had before been used to invite & to guide the
coming of boats to take off the runaways. We kept ourselves out of
the light, but close by, & in ambush, ready to fire upon any Yankees,
who might land in boats, & without notice, or to arrest any negro
fugitives. But nothing was seen of any persons except ourselves.
The sound of oars was supposed to be heard across the bay, & far
distant, at one time. We remained until near to dawn—& it was after
4 A.M. before we got back to Ruthven .... No sounds of cannon
heard either last night or today. But the great battle must be going
on in the rear of McClellan & near the Pamunkey. It was false that
our artillery company beat off the attacking gunboats near Port
Walthall—nor was it possible. They had only 6-pounders—& retreated very soon. The gunboats shelled nearly every building on
the lower Appomattox, damaging some greatly, & burnt some of the
before deserted buildings at City Point.

June 30. Last night, late, Julian went out on a solitary patrol, to
Beechwood & the landings thereof, but found nothing amiss.—
Very early this morning, Mr. Sayre & Edmund set off [2060] for Petersburg & Richmond, & the former also for Marlbourne, if he learns that
the Yankees have been driven entirely from that neighborhood. This
must have been the case last Saturday, when I think Mr. S. might
have proceeded safely.—After breakfast I rode ... to see Beech-

wood in its present deserted & desolate condition. I chose to be alone. I went into every apartment of the mansion, as well as into my own in the old house. The latter is as in my recent occupancy, except the removal of my trunk, some of the maps, & my writing materials. In the mansion, all the furniture as yet remains. But the removal of the curtains, pictures, & other ornaments, gives an appearance of desolation greater than would an entirely emptied house. Every apartment brought to my mind some tender recollections, & especially the death chamber of my daughter Jane. About the mansion, & elsewhere on all the farm, I saw no human being, except an old negro woman in the dairy, churning (at her discretion,) & a negro child sitting in the door of one of the few houses now occupied by the remaining old or infirm slaves. Afterwards I walked or rode through the lovely grounds near & below the house —the garden, the thinned & open woods, & the Wilderness. It was a melancholy gratification. I do not expect to see them again while existing circumstances continue, & the residents are exiles from their dearly loved & beautiful home. Next I went to the site of my old residence on Coggin's Point, now undistinguished from the remainder of the rich wheat-field of which it forms a part, except by the shade trees which ornamented the former yard, & most of which I planted. The wheat is already so much fallen, that even if there was labor for the harvest, half the value would be lost. There will be no such attempt—& less than one twenty-fifth part of the whole crop has been reaped. The oats will be a total loss—& as all cultivation of the corn [2061] crop has ceased, very little of the full product will be matured, if it can be hereafter saved. The few negroes left merely attend to the remaining live-stock, until all can be moved away. I next visited the burial ground, & read over the inscriptions of the head-stones, concisely & simply stating the names, & dates of birth & death, of the dear ones whose remains were beneath. And here I addressed to God my customary daily prayers, & added others for the welfare of my family & country, & the restoration of that prosperity & happiness recently enjoyed, or available, by both, and which have been so much reduced by the conduct of our vile public enemies.—

The mail. No news had been heard . . . since the day before yesterday. It is now so voluminous that I can merely here state great results—but so far as heard, all, in the general, is good, & bright for our cause, with the exception of the latest fact, that McClellan has eluded our army, & had gained 12 hours of advance in his retreat towards James river. In the succession of battles, separate combats, & skirmishes from 4 P.M. on the 26th. to the night of the 28th., our left wing, under Generals Longstreet, & the two Hills, had beaten & driven the enemy from their highest positions on the north & east (or left) side of the Chickahominy—to below Gaines' Mill, where we fought a severe battle, & achieved a splendid victory on the 27th., & to Cold Harbor in Hanover. Gen. Jackson (Stonewall) by an independent movement, in the meantime passed down in the rear of the enemy, & seized the York river railroad, & destroyed a portion, so as to entirely cut off McClellan's communication with Pamunkey river. On the 28th. there were sundry separate skirmishes or heavier combats, with results generally & on the whole in our favor. All McClellan's forces which had been north of the Chickahominy retreated to the south side. On Sunday morning, it was discovered [2062] that the whole army had retreated towards James river, & had gained 12 hours in advance of Gen. Huger, whose command had been set to watch for this movement. And thus it seems, that this imbecile, (if not worse,) who suffered by his neglect the disastrous loss of Roanoke Island, & the enormous sacrifices in the manner of evacuating Norfolk, has now been again trusted, & has permitted McClellan to elude him, & probably to reach James river, & the protection of his gun-boats.[37] These have been strongly reinforced lately—& we heard later that 13 more gunboats or other steamers had passed up today. . . . But whatever may be the final issue . . . it is certain that the great army & the great scheme of McClellan have both been signally defeated. Our army is in pursuit. But, as he had burnt all the lower bridges across the Chickahominy which he then occupied, I fear that he now holds our army divided, & that the portion south of that river is much inferior in numbers to his whole army now on that side—& that our forces on the north side will not be able to cross, & attack his rear, until too late. . . . Before we had read the newspaper accounts of the late battles, we observed, at 1 P.M., the loud reports of cannon, which [2063] were almost continuous, & which so continued until after 7 P.M. when the reports were more rare, & soon after ceased.

---

[37] Although Huger did not distinguish himself in this campaign, it was actually Magruder who failed to pursue McClellan's retreating army with sufficient energy on the 29th. Finally, about 4 P.M., Magruder launched a belated and uncoordinated assault on the Federal rear guard at Savage's Station. Federal losses were heavy (including 2,500 men left behind in a field hospital), but Magruder's ineptitude and Jackson's tardiness in arriving to support him had cost the Confederates an opportunity to strike a telling blow.

. . . The sounds of the cannonade, when heaviest, & when I could hear them plainest, seemed to me to be about from the direction of N.N.W. This might suit either for Drewry's Bluff, or the retreating route of McClellan's army.[38] At night, my grandson George returned from Beechwood, where, on the beach, he had met several gentlemen of the neighborhood, who had gone there to observe the cannonading more closely, & had made other unexpected & interesting observations. Numerous army wagons (Mr. [Edward A.] Marks supposed as many as 500,) were seen coming through the Berkley farm & in part proceeding towards Westover, as if to take shipping at the wharves of these two farms, which, unfortunately, have not been burnt, & now cannot be, to prevent their being put to this unlooked-for use. There were some steamers off the Berkley wharf, & they communicated by small boats with the shore. But there was no embarkation seen of persons or things. These wagons must be laden either with baggage or wounded men—& their being able to reach the shore shows, as they were sent in advance of the retreating army, that the way for the retreat was then open. The cannonading seemed to those on the shore (who could judge best,) to be a little west of north, & not more than 10 miles distant from the river. If the Yankee army was retreating by so low a route, it must have been that the nearer route to James river, above, was intercepted by our troops. I trust that this . . . battle on the later chosen & lower route indicates that they have been cut off there also. If not, & they can proceed, there must be either an embarkation of McClellan's army, at Berkley wharf, or a battle on the adjacent field, tomorrow. I will go early tomorrow morning to see—& the ladies here speak of going also, to witness so remarkable an occurrence as either would be. [2064] . . . Northern papers give articles from French papers, which indicate that the intervention of France in our war with Yankeedom was close at hand—even before any of the battles near Richmond had been heard of in Europe. We may count certainly upon the recognition of our independence, as soon as the series of battles, & of our victories, for the last five days shall have been known. . . . [2065]

---

[38] These sounds were from the battle of White Oak Swamp (or Frayser's Farm) which was fought on this day. Again the Confederates were plagued by poor coordination and execution, and thus lost their last opportunity to cripple McClellan before he reached the James.

July–September

∾

1862

SPYING ON MCCLELLAN'S CAMP ∾ DENUN-
CIATION OF SOLON· ROBINSON ∾ A NIGHT
ATTACK ON THE JAMES ∾ FLIGHT
FROM RUTHVEN ∾ THE YANKEES PLUN-
DER BEECHWOOD ∾ LEE AND BRAGG
MOVE NORTH ∾ SPECULATIONS ON
EUROPEAN INTERVENTION

July 1. This morning before sunrise, I was on horse-back on my way to the river, to view the remarkable scene presented last afternoon, & in expectation of seeing a battle fought on the Berkley farm. I took my position on the top & at the N.W. extremity of the high promontory of Coggin's Point, (Ruffin's Bluff,) which is within 1¼ miles of the Berkley wharf, & which offers a more commanding view of the broad inclined plane of Berkley farm, opposite, than could be had on any part of that farm. I found the numerous army wagons posted in a line parallel with the beach, but at some distance back. In the channel, off the wharf or landing, there were anchored 9 vessels—1 a large war steamer, another transport steamer, & the remainder sailing vessels. Before I reached my position, 3 more large transport steamers had just arrived from below, of which 2 were moored soon after at the wharf. Later, 2 large gun-boats arrived from above, & anchored farther out in the river. One transport steamer at first, & later two, only, kept up steam. The wagons continued to arrive, & they could be seen coming on the higher level of the public road, & also the arrival of every new number was indicated by a cloud of dust. Though every placed wagon was opposed to & exposed to my view, (except those behind scattered trees,) they stood too close to be counted. . . . They continued to arrive to 11 A.M., when I left, & without apparent abatement. All are alike, with white covers, & in such great numbers, present a novel & striking appearance. The line, not everywhere close, extended 1½ miles, parallel with the river. There was nothing seen to be embarked [2066] on the vessels, nor any indication of such intention.—All our ladies from Ruthven, except the seniors, Mrs. Lorraine & Mrs. Meade, arrived before 8 A.M. bringing also the three older of the young children. They brought provisions for dinner, & meant to stay through the day. They were delighted with the novel & unexpected scene offered to their view.—Except 3 or 4 reports of cannon, at long intervals, earlier in the morning, there was no firing heard until 10 A.M. Then it began, & continued, with considerable rapidity, though not comparable to that of yesterday afternoon—but was much more distant, & faint, & also from a more eastern direction.[1] . . . At 11, being wearied, & expecting no [2067] important change, I left for Ruthven—expecting to learn from those who remained, whatever might occur. The battle which I last night counted upon, to be fought today under my view, is evidently now removed to another locality. I am afraid of being too sanguine. But I cannot conceive how it is possible, now, for McClellan to escape from a disastrous defeat. And if his army can be kept from reaching either river,[2] & there getting under the protection of the heavy mortars of the gun-boats, it seems that the remnant of his army can only escape destruction, by entire and unconditional surrender. . . . Wrote a concise statement of the condition of the enemy at Berkley, & sent it to the Secretary of War—through the Officer of Videttes at Prince George C.H. & the military commander in Petersburg, if they shall deem the communication worth being sent by telegraph.—After dinner, Julian rode to Beechwood. About 7 P.M. we here (at Ruthven) heard the beginning of a brisk & loud cannonading, seeming to be in the direction of a little west of north—as frequent & nearly as loud as on yesterday. It became less frequent after 8, & ceased before 9 P.M.—It was not until after dark that our ladies returned—wild with excitement, & full of news of all that they had

---

[1] Unless the diarist is mistaken about the time, it is difficult to pinpoint this firing. The artillery duel which preceded Lee's assault on the formidable Union defenses at Malvern Hill did not commence until about 1 P.M. on this date. Yet neither Ruffin nor any other members of his household seem to have heard this heavy cannonade, which was closer to them than the firing at White Oak Swamp on the previous day. Perhaps a change in wind direction rendered the guns at Malvern Hill inaudible to those below the James.

[2] That is, either the York or the James.

seen.... They had left the Point at 12, & dined, & remained through the afternoon at the Beechwood mansion. During the time, there were sundry arrivals of other vessels at Berkley, & departures of some there before—&, on the whole, the number diminished. Before 6 P.M. there arrived an enormous passenger steamer, the "Vanderbilt," crowded with men. Julian, who saw it near, from the Point, supposed the passengers were not soldiers, (as he did not distinguish arms or uniforms,) but visitors from Baltimore, who had come to see the sights, & perhaps in confident expectation of the victory of their side. The vessel came near to the wharf, & then drew back farther from the shore, & anchored—none of the passengers were seen to land, or to leave the steamer.—This rapid cannonading, heard here tonight, from 7 to 9, & which was so loud that it must be within 15 miles, & seems in the direction of the upper part of Charles City, disorders my previous suppositions as to the situation of the armies. I had inferred that no part of McClellan's forces was left thereabout, or nearer to Richmond than at Berkley. I am entirely at a loss to conceive what is the true posture of things....

July 2. My intended return to the river was prevented by a steady easterly rain, which continued all day.—The mail. Much interesting matter as to the war in our neighborhood—but nothing of reliable details since the 30th.... Since then, the farther retreat of McClellan has carried the contest farther from Richmond, & obstructed the channels of information, & given us vague rumors instead of reliable reports. It seems [2070] only certain that we have continued to gain advantages, & to drive the enemy back from Richmond into Tuesday the 1st, but with much loss of blood & of lives on our side....

July 3. Heavy rain in last night, & even after daybreak. Overcast for remainder of the day.—After Breakfast, Julian & I rode to the end of the Point—& soon after followed all the young ladies, except Lotty. A great change since I was here before, on 1st. I counted 66 vessels, of all kinds, lying off Berkley landing & wharf—& must have passed over 10 or 15 of the smaller, (canal boats) which could not be distinguished in the crowd. Also there were 9 or 10 mostly large transport steamers at Westover Wharf. The army wagons were fully doubled in number, & there were also numerous tents interspersed, so that both together almost whitened the whole broad expanse of open ground on Berkley, & spread over a part of Westover. Great numbers of men also, & of horses, were seen on the land, & many men on the vessels, (some of which were within half a mile of our exposed position,) but we saw nothing of military array, arms, or distinguishable uniforms. Nearly all the vessels were anchored, & remained stationary. But a few steamers were generally moving, & some, at different times, went down the river, towing sailing vessels, or lighters. All such vessels had awnings over portions of their decks, which, in this cloudy & yet dry weather, could only have been required for wounded or sick passengers which I inferred that all these departing vessels [2072] were taking away. They seemed to be embarked at the sandy spit about a third of a mile above Berkley wharf, on which only wagons were seen to approach the water. But steamers were so clustered around, that we could not see what was embarked, nor which steamers left, until moving farther out in the river. There was cannonading north, which seemed not more than 6 miles from the river, from 9.40 to past 11 A.M., but not very rapid. The sounds of musketry also were heard, which discharges seemed to be (& must have been) much nearer—but not in sight. The explosion of bombs was frequently seen & known by the peculiar appearance of the smoke rising above the high woods, which bounded our view. Everything seen & also the sounds of battle heard, (in being so few,) were perfectly mysterious, & incomprehensible to me. Can this be Burnside's army & flotilla come to reinforce McClellan? The tents, & the stores on the transports, are enough for this supposition—& the wagons are far more than enough. Four deserters from the camp who got across the river last night, & were held as prisoners, said that all McClellan's army was there. But this seems to me incredible.[3]— From 11 to 12, three gunboats anchored off (& near to) Jordan's Point, kept up a slow firing of heavy artillery on the opposite land of Charles City. And afterwards, two other gun-boats did the like, from off the mouth of Herring creek below Westover, which continued until after I left, at 1.30 P.M. for Ruthven. . . . I have learned that the loudest reports of artillery, because nearest, are made by the gunboats, & are no indications of fighting going on. Yesterday was the only day lately during which not a single report of a cannon was

[3] Incredible or not, the diarist was indeed viewing McClellan's new base at Harrison's Landing on the James. The Union general would remain there for a month and a half before moving his Army of the Potomac northward to Aquia Creek on the Potomac.

heard. . . . [End of MS Volume 11—p. 2073] Mrs. Meade went to Petersburg this morning, & by the return of the carriage at night, we received today's papers, of Richmond & Petersburg, with gratifying reports of our continued successes in the long protracted conflict with the great army of McClellan. . . .

July 4. A clear day. Wind from N.E. After breakfast, I went to my place of observation, (Ruffin's Bluff,) & arrived 8.40. Most of the canal boats used as transports are gone. The vessels off Berkley landing, about 55. Off Westover wharf about 25. Full half of the wagons had disappeared from the encampment. A long train of them was seen on the public road which passes back of the open fields of Westover & Berkley, moving to the westward, which road leads either to Richmond, or the country back from the river. A smaller number of wagons were also seen coming towards the river, on the same road, meeting the greater number. . . .[4]

. . . Though I & others saw much of the general operations on the broad open ground of Berkley & Westover, from the high promontory opposite, yet misled by the newspaper reports, & having no private communication (either then or long after,) across the river, I was much mistaken as to even what I saw, until later times. Thus, it was not until Nov. 23rd. that I knew what were the facts of the firing of shells, as well as of musketry, that I heard back of Berkley on July 3rd. Mr. Beegleston, then overseer at Evelynton, & remaining there to that time, has informed me of that & other circumstances, which I will here state, as explanatory of facts which I (or others) then saw & heard, but misunderstood. The wagon train of which the foremost portion reached Berkley early in the afternoon of Monday the 30th of June, was in advance of McClellan's main army, which also reached Berkley in the course of the following night. The next morning, July 1st, when I was viewing the scene from Ruffin's Bluff, from 6 to past 11 o'clock A.M. I saw no troops, because they were hidden from my position by the covered wagons, which were in a line, as close as they could stand side by side, stretching for a mile & a half parallel with & far back from the river. And soon after, if not then, the troops were encamped among the

---

[4] The following note was inserted by the diarist on November 23, 1862, and serves to clarify his observations on this date and the several days preceding. The editor has deleted from this portion of the diary several extensive passages which were based upon erroneous newspaper reports concerning the events from June 30 to July 2.

trees of the woods back from the river, & covering the back parts of Westover & Berkley. It was not until the morning of the 3rd that any portion of our army reached (or perhaps found) the new position of the Yankee army. Then Gen. Stuart, with his command of artillery & cavalry, arrived at Evelynton farm, by the road coming from the direction of the Long Bridges. He first posted his artillery at the junction of that road with the road along the river, & from thence fired shells at & into the nearest part of the enemy's camp. Later, he changed his position to nearer the creek, & near to the Church in Evelynton. A portion of his men acted as sharpshooters also, & probably from positions as near to the enemy as permitted by the intervening creek & its low & wooded & swampy borders. The fire was returned by the enemy—though causing no damage. Probably our fire was not much more effectual—though it was reported that some loss of killed was suffered by the enemy, besides some prisoners (stragglers or pickets,) captured by Gen. Stuart. This was the firing which I heard, & the smoke from exploding shells which I saw, during the forenoon of July 3rd. And it was at Gen. Stuart's command, & its supposed positions, that the 3 gun-boats off Jordan's Point, & the 2 off the mouth of Herring creek, directed the discharges of their heavy artillery, making a cross-fire, the point of crossing being in the rear of the Yankee camps & forces. Sundry of these missiles (some of them shells,) struck or passed the houses & their closer vicinity at Evelynton, & near our troops, but hurt no person. Beegleston & his family took shelter in the ice-house. Stuart after this demonstration, & ascertaining the enemy's position, retired on the same route by which he had advanced. No notice of this movement of Stuart's command has been published in our newspapers, to this time. Immediately after this partial attack by Stuart, a part of McClellan's forces occupied & intrenched Evelynton h[e]ights. [end of note—resume diary, p. 2075]

. . . The scene on the water was still more striking, in the bright sunshine, & all the vessels displaying their flags, (which the strong breeze opened to advantage,) in honor of the day. At noon, salutes were fired successively, on sundry of the gun-boats. What striking inconsistency—what a farce, (if it were not so grave & bloody,) in the northerners thus glorifying the declaration & act of independence, which was the declaration of the [2076] *right* of every oppressed people to assert their independence & separate nationality, & their present action in making this murderous war on the southern states—which had not only all the reasons & provocations, & all the rights, to declare their separation, established in the Declaration of Independence—but also the different & perfect right founded upon their being separate & sovereign states, which had voluntarily entered into the Union, & had reserved the right to withdraw from it! . . . Before night, Julian & my grandson George, armed, rode off to act as a patrol on the beach nearest to the enemy's vessels, some of which (transports) are within speaking distance of our shore, & thus offering especial facilities for taking off absconding negroes. But they were prevented reaching their destination, by learning on the way that several troops of cavalry had been sent down from Petersburg, to guard the neighborhood, which rendered unnecessary any private & voluntary patrolling. The Prince George cavalry is one of these companies. Julian & George got back after 9 P.M. just after the return of Edmund. The latter brought us much interesting information, public and private, & we sat up conversing to a late hour. He went with Mr. Sayre to Marlbourne, on the 1st, & found there existing a remarkable condition of things. The Yankee forces had been taken completely by surprise, & were driven off at a moment's warning, on the approach of Jackson's division. The negroes, supposing that the condition of things all around them was general, & Yankee domination completely established throughout, were still more astonished at the sudden flight & disappearance of their Yankee friends & protectors. All the women & children, & the former foreman, Jem Sykes, & one other man, (besides one too infirm to leave,) still remained. The other men & boys, who had gone off (two within the last few days only,) had often returned frequently to Marlbourne, & gone again to the Yankee camps, at will. One young man, of these, was then sick at Marlbourne. The return of Mr. Sayre was evidently unexpected, & the reassumption [2077] of authority by the owners doubtless very unwelcome to all. But there was general & complete, if not willing acquiescence. All were called together immediately, & the views of the owners stated by Edmund, & an amnesty declared for the past insubordination, provided their future conduct should be good, as it had been generally previously. They were told that in consideration of their former good conduct up to their recent action, & to their having been deluded & imposed upon by the false statements & false promises of the Yankees, that all past conduct on this score would be overlooked & forgiven. They were told to communicate this promise to those who had absconded, & were authorised to extend it to all of them who should return soon to their duty. But at the same time they were told that this forgiveness of their very heavy offences was founded on their expected future good & obedient conduct—& that if any insubordination should be exhibited hereafter, the offenders would be at once sold. Further, they were notified that the heavy losses of the farm & its owners, caused in great measure by the misconduct of the negroes themselves, & all not by them, by the Yankees whom they had accepted & welcomed as friends & guides, would put it out of the power of the owners, for some time, to be as liberal in allowances to the slaves, as had been the regular usage heretofore—& that they would have to bear some part of the general loss [&] privations which they had aided to produce. They were then ordered to resume the labors of the farm—which all obeyed forthwith, before Edmund returned on the same day of his arrival. The extent of damage done by the Yankees was as follows: All the corn & wheat in the barns carried off—nearly all the fodder—all the mules & horses, except two, which Mrs. Lee was permitted to use to convey her to Richmond—all the carts & wagons. Some few sheep & hogs (as reported by Jem,) were taken—but none of the cattle. All the remaining livestock, doubtless they intended also to plunder, & it was only prevented by their unexpected & sudden expulsion by Stonewall's invasion. The doors of the barns & mansion were broken, for their forcible entrance, though the [2078] keys of all were at their service, if they had asked the negroes for them. My two cabinets of valuable collections of shells, fossil & recent, were broken into, & robbed of portions of their contents, & probably the most beautiful & precious. But not of a large proportion, as appeared to hasty observation.—Thus, this general rebellion of the slaves of Marlbourne, which was begun & established so quickly, & quietly, & yet so earnestly, was as quickly & quietly suppressed, by the first appearance of any of the owners, without arms, assistance, or violence of any kind. It seems probable that most of those who had gone off to the Yankees, will return voluntarily to their former home & condition. These are by far the more valuable portion, including nearly all the men, & all the boys above 10 years old.—Edmund had recovered all his 11 men still in the government service in Richmond, except one missing, who has probably absconded to the enemy. The others he hired for safety, & for the present, to the Danville Railroad Co. to work on the new extension of their road in N.C.

July 5. After breakfast, I rode as usual to the Bluff. Met on the way, or came afterwards, sundry of the troopers, & among them my grandson Thomas. . . . The number of vessels off Berkley & West-over about the same as on yesterday. But not one-tenth of the greatest number of wagons remain on Berkley. Some were seen on the public road returning towards Berkley. A large steamer came up, full of men, apparently in U.S. uniform (dark blue, appearing black). But they did not land at either wharf, & the steamer anchored in the channel. Past the nearest of the high woods outside of the open ground of Berkley, there was much smoke rising, & varying at different times, so that I . . . suspected that there was a large camp there . . . . Yesterday, I left the bluff a short time before the several salutes were fired, & did not see whence they proceeded, & inferred that they were [2079] made by different armed steamers. Julian remained longer, & saw distinctly that the salutes were fired from three land batteries—two in the open fields of Berkley & one in the woods beyond. This proves that troops are posted there . . . . No sound indicating that fighting was going on, or any reliable report thereof, has now been heard for three days. A strange cessation, when the opposed armies must be so near! . . .

July 6. Sunday. Went to church, earlier than usual, to see our acquaintances in the Prince George Cavalry & other companies encamped around the church. Major [Benjamin W.] Belsches[5] informed me that soon after I left the bluff yesterday (after 11 A.M.) the newly arrived troops were landed. There were some 13 cannon discharges heard last night, at 1 A.M., from the Yankee batteries. A balloon was sent up from their camp this morning, at 7A.M., & again at 10. Two deserters, who had crossed the river this morning, & surrendered to the first person whom they saw, were at the church under guard, & soon after were sent on to Petersburg as prisoners. These answered questions very readily. From their statement, confirmed by the Richmond Dispatch of yesterday, which I obtained soon after, it is now certain that McClellan's whole army occupies the camp back of Berkley. . . . Doubtless McClellan's army, strongly reinforced by the vessels, is already securely intrenched within two miles of the river, & under protection of the mortar & gun-boats—& he will strengthen his fortifications, & mount cannon on them, until they are impregnable to our force—&

---

[5] Major Belsches commanded the battalion of cavalry which had been dispatched from Petersburg on July 4 to patrol the south bank of the James opposite Harrison's Landing.

he can wait until his army is made as large & as powerful as he will desire—& I do not think he will be willing again to advance with less than 200,000 men, completely equipped & supplied. The deserters reported that our army was close to theirs, the respective pickets being in sight of each other. As the fatal error was committed of failing to attack McClellan before he had time to intrench his new position, it cannot be done now except at great disadvantage. Therefore I think that neither army will attack soon—& every day's further delay will increase our difficulties, & make the enemy relatively stronger, independent of their large reinforcements. I do not now expect another general engagement for two months. This is a great & mortifying disappointment of our sanguine expectation of capturing the whole of this grand army. Still, though that fate has been avoided by McClellan's skill, & generalship, his escape does not affect, (nor will even his future great success,) or lessen the sundry defeats & heavy losses his army has [2082] suffered since the commencement of the series of battles, & of his retreats, since the 26th of June. . . .

July 7. Made my usual early visit to the Bluff, & the shore nearest to Westover. No marked changes in the appearance of the fleet, except that it is more dispersed. There seem to be more tents & wagons scattered over the open ground of Berkley, & still more over Westover, than on the 5th. The picket guard has kept well concealed, & its being here must be unknown on the vessels. In evidence, two boats were brought ashore yesterday & this morning, with two Yankees in each, who were quietly taken prisoners.— Heavy firing heard down the river this morning, which afterwards I learned was the shelling of Flower de Hundred by gunboats. The taking off of slaves has begun again. Yesterday afternoon a Yankee boat took off 13 from Maycox, of which 12 belonged to the late proprietor of that estate, Dr. Cole, & now to his widow & children. Extremely hot. No doubt McClellan is busily constructing intrenchments—& for this he is desirous to obtain negro laborers to lessen the sufferings of his soldiers. Yesterday a large steamer full of negroes was seen to arrive from below.—The mail. Strange to say, nothing new of the armies so sure as I have seen or inferred by looking across the river. Our government has not made any publication of the events, since the very concise & general statement in the dispatch of Gen. Lee on the 27th.—My son Edmund & grandson George returned from Beechwood at night. The latter was present (or in sight) after I left the shore, at the capture of two [2083] more Yankees, who like the preceding 4, came in a boat & landed, on a pleasure excursion. Their approach was seen, & awaited by Dr. Dupuy, who was one of the two pickets on duty there, & as soon as they had landed he arrested them. These repeated visits of soldiers, without leave, indicates very lax discipline in the Yankee army. The last four of these 6 prisoners belonged to the Pennsylvania cavalry. The disappearance of these must raise suspicion of there being some military force here—& may induce the course usual in all such cases, of shelling all the suspected locality.—We are beginning to receive, from northern papers, the published accounts of the late battles, in the letters from persons in the Yankee army. Each one, taken alone, would seem to indicate their success in so much of the operations as described, or at least balanced advantages. But taken altogether, they cannot hide the great fact that McClellan's whole army has been driven back, from its being within 6 miles of Richmond to its present position 25 miles distant from the city.—A letter from Mr. Sayre. On the second morning, 4 of the absconding men had come in, & were at work reaping wheat. The following night, (as Mr. S. subsequently learned,) all the missing men were on the place, & debated the question whether to remain, & accept the offered amnesty, or not. They decided that they could not trust the promises—& expected that, if remaining, they would be sold—& the leaders declared that they then had it in their power get off & that they would do so. Under such guidance, all again went off, including the 4 men who had voluntarily returned the previous day—& leaving those only whom Mr. Sayre found there. He infers that the misconduct of most of the men, (in various respects, known to neighbors,) had been so great, that they were conscious that (independent of their insubordination & absconding,) they deserved heavy punishment, & they could not believe they could escape its being inflicted at a future time. [2084]

July 8. As usual went to the bluff & point landing. An armed steamer lying off the latter, at half-mile from the shore since yesterday noon. The pontoon wharf at the fishing point of Berkley extended by 5 or 6 masted vessels lying side to side at the outer end. Not much change in other respects as to the appearance of the fleet. Nothing doing at either of the Berkley wharves, & no vessels lying at or very near to either. I believe that most of the unloading of supplies has been at the Westover wharf. Much activity & movement on the open ground of Berkley. (That of Westover, now more thickly covered, is less visible from this side.) Many wagons were moving in different directions—single horsemen galloping as if conveying orders—& many more wagons on the public road, most of them moving westward. Still, no troops were seen arrayed, or embodied anywhere, though numerous persons scattered about, both on foot & on horseback. Smoke was rising from a broad extent of the woods beyond, showing a large camp—& more thickly from one central place. Signal flags, on poles, were raised on both chimneys of the Berkley mansion, & also on the middle of the roof between them. About 11 A.M. these flags were moved very actively, & for a considerable time, by being (with their poles,) lowered & raised & waved from side to side rapidly, as if to convey information or orders to a distance by previously concerted telegraphic signs. After waiting in expectation of seeing some consequent movement, in vain, until 12 M. I returned to Ruthven.[6]—This day, like yesterday, extremely hot. [2085]

July 9. Rode to the Point. By creeping to a cover on the beach, I was enabled to count the vessels lying off Westover, which cannot be seen from the Bluff. The whole number, as near as could be distinguished, lying off of Berkley & Westover, & including 5 gunboats lying above Jordan's Point & some miles below Westover, I made 103—exclusive of the canal boats & schooners placed side by side to make the foundation of the pontoon wharf at the fishing point, & which were 15 to 20 more. The tents, as well as wagons, in sight, were fewer than before. The extent of the camp beyond the first woods, & concealed by them, seemed to be enlarged westward, judging by the extent of the smoke rising therefrom. All the vessels at anchor, & quiet, except (as usual) a few of the smaller steamers, which were always moving up & down the space of the main anchorage, without any apparent purpose. No indication of the neighborhood of our army, (which we *suppose* to be close by,) & no movement seen or sounds heard from the Yankee army. I have, ever since I knew McClellan's army to be here, been anxiously expecting ours to renew the attack. But as every day's delay renders the enemy stronger, & an attack less feasible, I now almost despair of its being made. And if no attack is designed, no doubt our

---

[6] Had the diarist waited a few hours longer, he might have witnessed the arrival of President Lincoln, who was scheduled to reach Harrison's Landing at 5 P.M. to confer with McClellan and review the army. *Official Records*, Vol. XI, Pt. 3, p. 307.

army will not remain so far from its magazines & sources of supply, but will fall back upon them, & so much nearer to Richmond. The late operations are done. The Yankee army has been repeatedly defeated, & driven back from its positions 20 miles, & compelled to take shelter under the guns of the armed steamers. Now new operations will be begun by the enemy, & perhaps another elaborate plan for reaching Richmond, with an army increased to 200,000 men.—Another battalion of cavalry had marched to this neighborhood from Petersburg—in the major of which I was glad to recognise my former valued acquaintance, the Rev. Edgar Burroughs of Princess Anne. [2086] Also 3 other battalions have come, mostly infantry & some artillery, destined for Hoods. . . . At night, a startling telegram was received, from Mr. Sayre, sent this day from Richmond. It stated that "in six days the Yankees would be again in possession of Marlbourne"—& urged that my sons should go immediately [2087] to remove the slaves. At first this seemed to us utterly incredible that any such renewed advance can be soon made by McClellan—or that our commander, even if falling back, as we look for, will not hold the line of the York river rail-road, which would secure Marlbourne. But it was finally guessed that Mr. Sayre had learned in Richmond, & probably from Gen. Lee, that our army is soon to fall back, & farther than the rail-road, so as to leave Marlbourne again at the mercy of the Yankees. Accordingly Edmund & Julian arranged to set out early tomorrow morning for Marlbourne. . . . But I cannot yet believe, after all that we have suffered from the enemy having possession & use of the York river rail-road, that our authorities can mean voluntarily to surrender it again. For even if the whole iron track were torn up & removed, & the timbers burnt, McClellan, with his unlimited means could replace the track & bridges, & supply engines & cars, in two weeks after beginning the job. . . .

July 10. My sons Edmund & Julian set out early for Marlbourne.—After breakfast, I rode to Garysville, & saw Major Burroughs, whose very small command of cavalry is still there. He told me that very few slaves in his county, Princess Anne, & Norfolk Co. had voluntarily absconded, or gone to the enemy since their occupation—& of those who went early, a large proportion returned very soon to their masters. His own farm (on Back bay,) like many others, has only his slaves as residents—& he has not lost one of them. He ascribes these results [2089] to the bloody riot & butchery which occurred in Norfolk, & described in this diary, in which the Yankee soldiers killed outright 8 negroes, & wounded about 60 others, all of whom were not only innocent, but entirely ignorant of the offence which gave rise to these brutal & murderous acts, & which (the killing of an officer in self-defence,) was in fact committed by a northern negro who came with & was connected with the Yankee army.—From Garysville I saw the balloon of the Yankee army, for the first time. The elevation at which it stood did not appear (from that distance) to be more than 60 feet above the tops of the highest trees of the surrounding woods. It is sent up once or twice every day, for a short time.—The artillery was sent to Hoods (site of the old fort Powhatan) last night— & it was reported that this morning there was firing upon the passing vessels of the Yankee fleet. . . . Rain in the afternoon—after extremely hot weather for some days.

July 11. The affair of yesterday, at Hoods, was the firing of our field artillery on a Yankee steam transport, with injury, as supposed both to vessel & crew— & subsequently the shelling of our forces by gun-boats. Our troops drew off, out of range, without any damage. Like operations, & to better effect by our artillery, have been carried on at different points on the north side of the river, as stated by the papers of today.—The northern papers are full of lamentations, & of denunciations of different officials, for the admitted great disasters of the late six days' fighting. Although all their accounts lie as to particulars, & claim the advantage for nearly every actual defeat, none dare to claim victory on the whole result, except Gen. McClellan himself—who, in a proclamation to his army certainly entitles himself to be pronounced the greatest of liars. . . . Vicksburg still holds out bravely against the enemy's powerful bombarding fleet, although the bombs are knocking down the houses, & will probably destroy them all. A still heavier & more ruinous punishment is now threatened by the so far baffled foe. Vicksburg is on a high bluff, in a bend of the Mississippi, facing a low peninsula on the opposite shore. The Yankees are now cutting a canal through the neck of this peninsula, through which they design to bring their upper portion of their fleet to unite with the lower in the bombardment. Also, the shortened distance, & consequent increased velocity of the current through this new passage, it is expected will gradually cause the river to take that new channel, & so leave Vicksburg cut off from the river, & 4 or 5 miles distant. But though similar changes have often occurred, by the force of floods & natural means, on this great river, & though this canal may convert this peninsula to an island, & even divert more than half of the water, [2092] I have no faith in the present channel being rendered unfit or less fit for navigation. Gen. Van. Dorn, who commands our military forces & operations in that whole district, takes especial charge of the defence of Vicksburg. I trust that its site will not be surrendered, even though every building shall be laid in ruins, & all property be destroyed.—A new policy of the enemy has been just commenced wherever the enemy have supremacy in the cotton states. Whenever they visit the plantations in search of cotton, or other plunder, & find (as in almost every case,) that the cotton has been burnt, they inquire who burnt it. And if learning that it was done by the proprietor, or by his orders, he, if present, is taken off as a prisoner, & all the property plundered or destroyed. . . .

July 12. Julian returned to dinner. Edmund went to Beechwood. They did not go farther than Richmond, having met Mr. Sayre there. His was a false alarm, which had no foundation. Things remain as they were at Marlbourne when he wrote previous to his telegraphic dispatch. One of the absconding men had been captured, & ordered to be sold in Richmond. A boy, who had been left very sick, by the fleeing Yankees, & without aid, has been brought back to Marlbourne. 16 men still off. . . . Edmund heard in Richmond that a large portion of our army had already fallen back from the neighborhood of Berkley to the former lines near Richmond. This I expected would be, as soon as all intention of further attack on the Yankee army in its present camp was abandoned. It seems however, from recent military movements & operations, that our forces still command the rear of the enemy this side of the Chickahominy river, nearly as low as its mouth. . . .

July 13. Sunday. At Church. The two companies of cavalry encamped there give full congregations. There was yesterday more firing of our troops at Hoods on a passing transport steamer conveying troops to Berkley—but only with muskets, as the artillery had been withdrawn. The enemy's gunboats threw many shells in return. No damage to our men—& whether any inflicted by them, though supposed, is not known. Today all the infantry also moving up to Petersburg. . . . The fleeing of slaves from this neighborhood, which seemed to have ceased, has begun again. Mr. J. B. Bland lost 17 more a few nights ago, making his whole loss 27—though 5 were recaptured. More of Capt. H. H. Cocke's went off last night, making his losses 35 in all. A few other persons have lost a few only.

July 14. Major Burroughs called to see me, on his way to Drewry's Bluff, to which place his command of cavalry is ordered. He told me that the Yankee force now about Norfolk amounts to but 500 men, [2094] distributed in three sepa[ra]ted posts—500 in Portsmouth—& 5000 in Suffolk, of which 4 regiments are of drafted militia. It struck me that there could not be better conditions for another dash of Gen. Stuart's brigade. I recommended to Major B. to see & to offer his information to the Sec. of War & to Gen. Stuart—& also his intimate topographical acquaintance with the country—& I wrote a letter of introduction to both, for him to deliver, or to send.—The mail.—By statements from northern papers, it seems that the firing of our field artillery on the Yankee vessels lately, & from both sides of the river, was of damage both to the vessels & the passengers. Yet the artillery from this side is withdrawn, & will make a portion of 20,000 men just called to Petersburg. By the firing from Hoods, several Yankees were killed, & the steamer had afterwards to run aground, near shore, to prevent its sinking. The same day, after the shelling upon & retreat of our troops, (unhurt,) another steamer came up, (as reported,) bringing from Fortress Monroe to Berkley, Lincoln, Gen. Scott, & Stanton, the . . . Sec. of War.[7] What a pity that our artillery had not waited for them! . . . A long article copied from the N.Y. Tribune describes many of the James river localities, nearly enough to show that the writer has seen them. In the account of Beechwood, there is evidence that the writer is one of the sundry Yankees, who have enjoyed the hospitality & kind civilities of the proprietor & his family. I trust that there will be no more of such hospitality & kind attention extended to such privileged spies, & secret & malignant enemies. . . .

July 15. It occurred to me this morning, after long consideration, who is the writer of the letter to the Tribune. It is Solon Robinson[8]—& most manifestly by its contents, even if its signature was

---

[7] The newspapers apparently erred in reporting the date of Lincoln's visit to Berkley. That visit actually occurred on July 8, two days before the artillery duel at Hoods, and neither Stanton nor Scott accompanied the President.

[8] A pioneer in the development of northern Indiana, Robinson (1803–80) was best known for his agricultural articles and travel sketches which appeared in leading northern periodicals during the 1840's and 1850's. He was instrumental in organizing the United States Agricultural Society in 1852 and, the following year,

not his initials. He has some literary pretensions, & to agricultural information. Some 12 years ago, he travelled very extensively in the slave-holding states, under the pretence of collecting agricultural information, to be used in a future publication. At that time (unfortunately,) all the previous acts of northern malignity & treachery to the South, had not yet excited any general suspicion of or prejudice against northerners in the South. This man's real business was that of travelling agent for Allen, a N.Y. agricultural publisher, to sell his books, & to beg subscriptions for his periodical,[9] & to eke out his wages by letter writing to that publication, & to N.Y. newspapers, & by sponging his way through his whole progress, which occupied more than a year. His pretended object [2097] gained him even more ready access to the houses of farmers, & more welcome reception, than the ordinary & general habit of hospitality, which alone would have liberally, if not heartily, accorded entertainment gratuitously to every seemingly respectable stranger who asked for it. Robinson (according to his own later statement,) travelled 7000 miles, in the southern states, in his peddling carriage drawn by two horses. His success, & his meanness, may both be estimated by his boast (made to Mr. Sands of Baltimore,) that in all his journeys, he never paid for a meal for himself or for his horses. Among the hundreds of country gentlemen upon whose hospitality he thus thrust himself, & who entertained him & bore the infliction without complaint, there was probably not one who was not disgusted with him, in a few hours, as a low-bred, unmannered & impudent Yankee. I happened to hear the experience & opinions of three of the farmers whom he names in this letter, (Hill Carter, J. A. Selden, & E. Ruffin jr,)[10] who all concurred with me (who had his company at Marlbourne,) that for his total want of good manners, & his conduct unbecoming a gentleman, or a decent man, however humble & ignorant of the usages of good society, he deserved to have been

---

became agricultural editor of the New York *Tribune*. Following the war, he moved to Jacksonville, Florida, where he continued his writing activities until his death in 1880. His reputation in the North as an agricultural expert rivaled that of Ruffin in the South—which makes the latter's comments all the more interesting.

[9] Reference is to the *American Agriculturist*, founded in New York City in 1842 and coedited until 1856 by Anthony B. Allen (1802–92) and his brother, Richard L. Allen (1803–69). The two brothers also operated a farm machinery concern known as A. B. Allen & Company.

[10] Carter and Selden were the proprietors of the celebrated James River estates of Shirley and Westover, respectively.

ordered out of all our houses, & that he would not be allowed to enter either again. All the time he was travelling in the southern states, he professed to be a strong friend to the South, & was a noisy pro-slavery advocate. But as soon as he returned to the North, he dropped that disguise, & resumed his character of an abolitionist. This no doubt he had been throughout—and probably also was an abolition emissary, or voluntary agent, operating so far as he deemed it safe, & using the private facilities he enjoyed in every man's house whose hospitality & patience he abused, to whisper & instil discontent & insubordination into the ears of the servants who waited [2098] upon him, in his bed-chamber, or elsewhere.—After breakfast, I rode to the Bluff & walked thence to the Point landing. No important change in appearances seen, or heard of, since my last visit. There has been no firing of pickets, or otherwise, heard between the opposed armies—if indeed our army is still close to McClellan's, of which there is no indication visible to a viewer from this side.—Edmund set out this morning for a journey on the Danville R.R. in search of a temporary home for his family & remaining slaves—whether to be obtained by purchase, rent, or by paying for board & lodging.—When I came here, I brought some volumes of "Living Age," but had finished them some days past—& could not conveniently obtain more, until this evening. In the mean time, in default of more entertaining reading, I have read a child's book "Robinson in Paris," "Recantation" a foolish anti-papist novel, part of [Emmerich de] Vattel's "Laws of Nations," or the laws of war—& began this morning [Alexander F.] Tytler's Sketch of "Universal History"[11]—which I had not met with before, & which I find so attractive, so far as I have read, that I shall proceed with it.—Violent storm of thunder, lightning, & rain in the evening.

July 17. Another very hot day, & another thunderstorm late, & very heavy rain.—Indoors all day, & nearly all the time reading, though wearisome amusement when carried to such extent. My deafness shuts me out from the enjoyment of conversation, unless it is addressed especially to me, which is not usual, & not to be expected. And the more persons there are present, & the more cheerful & animated their conversation, the less do I distinguish, because of the confusion of sounds. Thus, while in company, I am

---

[11] This work was based upon Tytler's lectures at the University of Edinburgh during the 1780's. Tytler (1747–1813) was later judge-advocate of Scotland.

suffering the solitude & wearisomeness of solitary seclusion. It is better to be dead than to be deaf even to the partial extent that I am. . . .

July 18. More rain today.—The mail. . . . When Memphis was about to be surrendered, an unfinished iron-clad war steamer which was constructing there, was sent up the Yazoo river to escape capture, [2100] & since has been there completed & armed. This vessel, the "Arkansas," descended the Yazoo & Mississippi, & suddenly dashed into the portion of the Yankee fleet above Vicksburgh [*sic*], 17 or 18 armed steamers, including 4 iron-clad, & some 6 or 7 "rams"—attacked them, & fought its passage through to under the batteries of Vicksburg.[12] Two of the Yankee vessels struck their colors, & ran ashore to prevent sinking, & one of them burnt, & one other was blown up. The remaining vessels dispersed & fled. Subsequently, at night, 8 of this fleet passed down, firing into the Arkansas, or upon the batteries as passing. One ball then struck & went through the Arkansas, killing 2 men & wounding 3. In the previous engagement, our loss had been 10 killed & 15 wounded. This is encouragement to our government to build one or more such vessels on the upper waters of every river likely to be infested by the Yankee pirates—& especially in James river at Richmond, where the vessels would be perfectly safe so long as Fort Drewry & Richmond are not captured. There is one gun-boat of this kind building there, & the wood-work was nearly completed two months ago, & which still remains unfinished, to be destroyed (should our defeat possibly occur to require it,) as was the Virginia & others at Norfolk, & the Mississippi at New Orleans. . . . If, as represented, the "Arkansas" is so slightly damaged as to be soon repaired, & ready for action again, it ought to successfully defend Vicksburg, if not endanger the safety of the Yankee fleet, & of every Yankee steamer on the Mississippi. By Yankee reports, the canal through the neck of the low peninsula (¾ of a mile long,) is excavated, & the water will soon be turned through. This, though very inadequate to change the bed of the river, & to leave Vicksburg separated from navigable water, probably will enable vessels to pass without coming under the fire of the guns which defend Vicksburg—& would effect the great object of the enemy in giving to them the command of the whole length of the Mississippi—if the "Arkansas" does not prevent. . . . The Prince George troop, with

[12] This encounter took place on Tuesday, July 15.

several additional troops of cavalry, are today moved from Merchants Hope Church, & quartered a[t] the Methodist church, a mile above Garysville.

July 20. Sunday. . . . I finished reading Tytler's "Universal History." I have found much more to interest & instruct me in this work, than I had expected from so concise an abridgement. . . . It is singular that, while all other countries are considered, that had any history, or civilization, the author scarcely mentions the Jews, except to state as chronological epochs [2103] some of the remarkable events of Jewish history, as concurring in time with others of other nations. A historian can treat the political annals of the Jews but in one of two ways—as inspired & therefore unquestionable evidence, or as mere profane history, to be judged by the rules of human evidence. If the former, he can merely copy or abridge the narrative of the historical books of the bible—which even Josephus did not do, for the Roman public, without making some designed alterations: Or if the latter, no judicious historian could fail to reject as incredible & monstrous fables many of the incidents.

July 21. . . . Upon being offered the use of a house in Petersburg . . . this morning . . . [Edmund], with his wife & child & Sue & Mary, set out to begin this new residence, passing by Beechwood to gather up, & take in a wagon, articles necessary for house-keeping. Nanny remains here to attend to Thomas, (who is now admitted by Dr. Harrison to have typhoid fever—) & also will remain for a time, Mrs. Lorraine, George, & John. I would have designed to follow Edmund's family to almost any other place, as my home with theirs, except Petersburg—which for more reasons than one it is disagreeable for me to visit, & would be intolerable as a residence.[13] Until . . . Edmund's temporary residence there ceases, my home will continue at Ruthven, though there is scarcely room enough (without inconvenience) [2104] for any more than the usual family. . . . The mail. No new event of importance. . . . It is reported that the worthless general Huger has at last been removed from active command, but retained as Inspector of Ordnance. It is reported verbally, but not alluded to in the newspapers, that the inertness of Gen. Huger, & Gen. Magruder's being drunk, were the causes why these officers did not carry out Gen. Lee's orders, & of the consequent failure of his plan of operations, by which McClellan's army

---

[13] Because of the presence in Petersburg of the diarist's estranged daughter, Agnes Beckwith, and her family.

would have been prevented reaching James river, & the protection of the gunboats, without which his army must have been completely defeated, & probably compelled to surrender for want of provisions & other supplies. It is remarkable that the [2105] newspapers have said scarcely anything of our army near Richmond since the last battle on July 1st. I trust that this silence is not because there is nothing to tell, but for concealment of our leaders' designs from the enemy. I am hoping & expecting to hear of some startling & effective stroke, & looking for it especially in the Valley, & by Stonewall. It will not be against McClellan's main army at Berkley. For it is obvious that that was weakest immediately after the six days' battles, & our army then relatively at its greatest strength. . . . Believing there to be no hope of our aggressive action here, I anxiously hope that it may be somewhere else, & speedily—either by Stonewall sweeping down the valley of the Shenandoah into Maryland & Pennsylvania—or Morgan rushing across Kentucky & laying Cincinnati in ashes—or some other leader & army crossing into Illinois, & pushing across to burn & sack Chicago. I wish to put the cost & the sacrifices of war on the enemy's territory, & to make them feel the horrors of war, in our retaliating on them [for] their violations on our territory of the laws of war. . . .

July 22. Rode to the Bluff. While on the way, heard cannon which from the regularity of firing, & short continuance, I inferred was a salute—& found it was so, of 13 guns. Gen. [Gabriel J.] Raines [*sic*] C.S.A. was there, to whom I was introduced.[14] He told me that the salute was for a Major-General, & he inferred that Gen. Scott had arrived.[15] A large body of troops was drawn up, and remained stationary, as if waiting for a review. This is the first time that I have seen in the enemy's camp any troops in military array. Gen. Rains & his aid de camp, Mr. Tyler, went with me to Ruthven to dinner, & afterwards went on to Petersburg. Gen. R. had been sent to this

---

[14] A native of New Bern, North Carolina, graduate of West Point, and veteran of the Mexican War, Gabriel James Rains (1803–81) commanded a brigade under Daniel H. Hill on the Peninsula. Credited with being the first to utilize land mines and booby traps in warfare while covering the Confederate withdrawal up the Peninsula, Rains became a controversial figure. In 1864 he was appointed head of the Torpedo Bureau, and, despite much opposition in the Confederacy, he finally secured approval to mine the land approaches to Richmond, Charleston, and Mobile during the latter stages of the war.

[15] This inference was incorrect. It is more probable that the salute was in honor of Major General Ambrose E. Burnside, who assumed command of the United States Ninth Army Corps on this date.

neighborhood to examine different points on the margin of the river & their fitness for artillery to molest the enemy's shipping. He thinks Hoods . . . so eligible a position, that he thinks he could perfectly command the passage of the river, & prevent the passage of all but iron-clad gun-boats. He also thinks highly of Ruffin's Bluff as a position for a moveable battery, while the enemy's fleet are assembled opposite. If authorized to use such means as he could, he thinks he could clear the river above Hoods of all hostile steamers in a short time, by cutting off their supplies, & at the same time the supplies for the Yankee army, so as to make its present position untenable. He seems to be a man of action & energy, & I wish heartily that he may be entrusted with this duty. I showed him the different routes, available for artillery, for approaching & retreating from [2107] the Bluff. . . . In our later conversation, at Ruthven, I learned from him many things of interest in regard to military affairs. One was that we have no forces now near to McClellan's army, & that our main force is at and near Chapin's Bluff on James river, in Henrico, a short distance below Drewry's Bluff. Gen. Jackson & his army had moved about 8 days ago—& it was not known to the public where they had gone. . . . Gen. Rains told me that the losses of both armies were enormous in the late battles. Our loss was very heavy because attacking the enemy in their successively occupied strong intrenchments, & driving them out—& the enemy in turn lost heavily, because, after being dislodged, they fought retreating every day. He did not know, & did not pretend to estimate with any accuracy, but thought that our loss, in killed wounded & missing (including skulkers & deserters,) would reach 30,000, & the enemy's, 40,000.[16] He is of opinion that there were 40,000 of our army that never were brought into action in [2108] the whole six days of fighting, & who really did nothing, except serving as reserves, if called for. The non-use of this large proportion of our army was owing to the reprehensible custom which he says prevails in our battles, of sending out small portions of the army to bear the brunt, & to contend with greatly superior forces, until another portion is sent forward, & thus different corps in sucession. I heard afterwards from Mr. W. Sayre, who arrived at night, as what he learned in Richmond, that it was Magruder's & Huger's divisions,

---

[16] These estimates are a bit high for both sides. Officially, the Confederates suffered more that 20,000 casualties and the Federals nearly 16,000 during the Seven Days' Campaign.

amounting to 48,000 men, that made the body never engaged in action, (except a few); & that this was because their commanders did not obey orders, & allowed McClellan to escape them, & get to the river & the protection of the gun-boats. For this disobedience of orders, which saved McClellan's army from capture or complete rout, Magruder is arrested, & Huger has been merely transferred to the ordnance department, when he ought to have been cashiered, as he had also deserved previously. Our whole army is understood to have been 98,000—& therefore, deducting these divisions, only 50,000 fought the battles of six days in succession.—Learned from Mr. Sayre the particulars of some incidents of which the occurrence had been but generally & imperfectly stated in the papers, & which accounts will now be here combined. After the raid of Gen. Stuart, which so much damaged, & still more frightened & enraged the enemy, they took measures to avenge it, & to deter us from a recurrence of like acts. The commander pretended to believe that this strong & regular military action performed by a regularly arrayed force of 2500 [*sic*] cavalry & artillery . . . [was] the unauthorized action of irregular guerrillas. Previously, in the west, the Yankee authorities have threatened, & in some cases, executed reprisals or vengeance for guerrilla acts on the peaceable people of the locality. In this case, they not only falsely [2109] charged regular warfare to be private & unauthorised guerrilla action, but proceeded to punish for it the resident inhabitants, civilians, & who had been as ignorant of the intended or effected raid as the surprised Yankee forces. Under these pleas, of no validity if true, but which were entirely false, as soon as the raid had passed over, & the before occupying Yankees returned, they proceeded (of course by McClellan's order,) to capture & hold as prisoners all the resident civilians & non-combatants (as there were none others,) whom they could find suddenly, in lower Hanover & New Kent. There were no exceptions, except such as kept concealed, or the few who had gained previous favor by submission. Men of position were especially sought. But the captures embraced all classes of non-combatants, from the highest to the lowest of the white males, & the oldest & least capable for any military service. There were men above 70, & one man who had but one leg. The whole number so seized made above 240. They were conveyed as prisoners first to Fortress Monroe, & then to the artificial island, a heap of stones, on the Rip Raps. The subjection of such prisoners to even ordinary prison fare would have been a severe punishment, & hazardous to the health of the aged & most infirm. But here it was far worse. On a naked heap of stone, exposed to the broiling sun, & with water for drinking which lay in casks on the wharf in the sun, until it was heated to the average temperature of the open air & the heated stone floor. In addition, this water was brought from the creeks supplied by the Dismal Swamp, or "juniper water" stron[g]ly colored & impregnated with vegetable matter. . . . [2110] After thus detaining these men, so illegally captured, in this place of torture for some weeks, & until 4 had died from their sufferings, & 4 others were too ill to bear removal, the remainder were discharged upon the exacted condition of giving their parole, as if legal prisoners of war, but in a novel & unprecedented form, which would be illegal even if the persons were legal prisoners of war. The established form & obligation of a proper parole is that the discharged prisoner (one taken in arms of course,) shall not again serve in a military capacity against the enemy until exchanged. But the parole exacted from these illegally captured civilians went much further. To have given the usual military parole, however illegally required & therefore invalid, would not [have] affected our country as to the greater portion of the prisoners, because they were over the military age, or still more disqualified by infirmity from military service. But the terms of this parole require that the person accepting it shall give no information, aid or comfort to any forces or persons opposed to the Yankees. These terms are made so comprehensive, that some of the discharged parties, whether because of tender conscience, cowardice, or disaffection to our cause, have construed their engagement to forbid the giving directions to find a neighbor's residence, or a drink of water, when asked for by a soldier of our army, or supporter of our cause. It does not lessen the villany [*sic*] of this conduct of the Yankee authorities, that the parole, having been exacted not only illegally but under duress, is entirely invalid, & will probably be so considered by every one who does not expect to gain some selfish end by pretended regard for the sanctity of his obligation. For probably every one of the prisoners believed that his life would be sacrificed by much longer continuation of the sufferings [2111] to which he was subjected by the enemy. I do not excuse their submission, to make an illegal & false engagement, even on such ground of duress, unless it was to save from certain death, or intolerable torture. But whatever may have been the error of accepting the terms & entering into the form of engagement, there can be no validity in the illegal engagement, & it ought not to be respected by our government—which also ought to retaliate for this & all other outrages on the laws of war. If Jackson or Morgan shall invade the Yankee territory, in addition to laying it waste, there ought to [be] arrested two of the resident civilians (the more distinguished the better,) for every one of ours heretofore captured, & sent as prisoners to be treated with as much rigor as has been exercised towards our citizens illegally made prisoners.

July 23. The mail. . . . Gen. Johnston's official report of the battle of "Seven Pines," 31st of May & 1st of June, has at last appeared. . . . Gen. Huger's Division was one of four corps ordered & expected to be engaged—& waiting for its expected arrival & cooperation, Gen. Longstreet delayed some hours to begin the action, which he did at last without [Huger]. Gen. Huger did not appear at all, nor send his division [2113]—for which no reason is given. But Gen. Johnston remarks on this failure. "Had Major Gen. Huger's Division been in position & ready for action, when those of Smith, Longstreet & Hill moved, I am satisfied that Key[e]s' corps would have been destroyed, instead of being merely defeated. Had it gone into action even at 4 P.M., the victory would have been much more complete." So this hero of Roanoke Island was permitted to greatly impair the amount of our success at Seven Pines, as well as to frustrate, subsequently, the great object of our later battles of 6 days! And yet this general, so potent for producing disaster & loss, & so utterly worthless for good service & success, has obstinately been retained in his high & important commands through all these failures, & even now, instead of being arrested & tried, & cashiered or shot, is, though removed from active service, still retained at the head of a most important department![17]. . .

July 24. Today's paper obtained by private conveyance. At last, our military movements have made some small progress into a Yankee state. Some portion of our forces . . . occupied Henderson in Ky., & Newburg in Indiana. This town is not in my map. It is

---

[17] The diarist was too rough on poor Huger, although he was merely joining in the general condemnation to which the unfortunate South Carolinian was subjected, not only at this time but for years afterward. After a careful analysis of all relevant data, Douglas Southall Freeman concluded that Longstreet was primarily to blame for the delay in attacking at Seven Pines and that he deliberately (and successfully) contrived to make Huger the scapegoat. *Lee's Lieutenants*, I, 253–60.

probably a very small place, on the Ohio.[18] In it were taken prisoners 250 sick Yankee soldiers, & about as many muskets. Though this, of itself, may be a very small affair, I am rejoiced for its occurrence, by way of example. I am sure that our offensive operations will nowhere be so likely to meet but feeble or no resistance as on the border country of the enemy's old settled & rich territory. A war of invasion there, carried on according to the enemy's usage, & now declared rule, in our [2114] territory, would pay all its required support & expenses, & leave a large surplus of booty. Even if patriotism & public spirit were entirely wanting in such invaders, there would be enough inducement & reward in the pecuniary profits to be made. And if the invaders were mere brigands, killing & destroying for revenge, or in wanton cruelty, & capturing & robbing for private gain alone, so much the better would they effect their beneficial purpose of retaliating on the enemy's people & property the vandalism of their armies in our country, & also, by success & profit, increasing in numbers & in power, & striking terror through all the heretofore secure Yankee land & population. . . . A volume might be filled with accounts of such acts committed by Yankee soldiers, & mostly by authority of their commanders, as reported by the sufferers, or their friends. . . . At Shirley, Hill Carter's estate, many of the badly wounded Yankees were left, in their retreat. Mrs. Carter, with a rare exercise of humanity, & of what she deemed her Christian duty, attended to, nourished, & personally nursed & watched over these many wounded enemies, as carefully & tenderly, & with as much outlay of provision for their necessities & comforts, as if they had been our own soldiers, or friends, instead of invaders, plunderers, & incendiaries. Yet even after these acts of rare benevolence & charity, the property of Mr. Carter, under his eyes & in the presence of hearing of his angelic wife, (far too good for him or for this world,) was swept off as plunder for the army, & when not wanted, wantonly destroyed, as in other cases. Two days ago, a party of Yankees visited Eppes' Island, opposite City Point, & under McClellan's special orders, as they said, took off forcibly every slave on the farm, between 60 & 70 in number. The system of supplying their armies by plundering has been acted upon generally. But it is now openly declared as the uniform policy in a recent general order of Gen. Pope, & published

---

[18] The raid upon Newburg, a small town located just north of the Ohio River near Evansville, was conducted on July 18.

by him. He here proclaims that the country which his army marches through, or occupies, must furnish all supplies for its support, without payment. The only pretence of exception is of those furnishers of such forced contributions as are "loyal to the Union," & continue so to the end of the war—when their receipts *may* be paid, if they can then prove this merit. In other published orders, at the same time, Gen. Pope promises summary [2117] vengeance on guerrillas, & all residents who may try to obstruct the passage of the enemy, & the consequent devastation of the country, by destroying roads & bridges. And he declares accountable for such acts all residents within 5 miles of a road or bridge so destroyed. . . . Why our government does not severely retaliate for these & all other such outrages, is to me astonishing. And if doing so, one part of its notification of intention should be, in addition to other & immediate retaliation on prisoners now held, & on Yankee property when invaded . . . the sentencing to death & to be hung as felons whenever captured, the commanding officers who order, or authorise & permit these outrages—including [Ormsby M.] Mitchell,[19] Pope, Wool, Butler, & McClellan. . . .

July 25. The papers by today's mail bring no news, but are full of interesting reading, in extracts from northern & English papers. . . . The northern papers speak as if dispirited. They admit that the recruiting for the 300,000 new troops gets on slowly, though sundry cities have, out of their own funds, increased the bounty of $25 offered by the U.S. government, to $50, $75, & $100. It is counted on that a draft must be resorted to. . . . The bombarding Yankee fleet has withdrawn from the siege of Vicksburg. In the long bombardment, they have killed & wounded very few of our men in our batteries, & have not done very great damage to the buildings of the town. The determined attack, continued since sometime in May, has resulted in utter failure. Even the canal, which was expected to change the channel of the river, & leave Vicksburg inland, though completed, cannot convey any water because of the low state of the river—& will not, until high water shall again occur.—Gold in N.Y. had risen to 120. [2119] Cotton (middling upland) had sold at 50 cents. . . .

July 26. Rode to the river to see the Yankee fleet & camp, & also

[19] Major General Mitchell, commanding Federal troops in north Alabama, reportedly had just been summoned to Washington to answer charges of alleged brutality against civilians in the town of Athens.

visited Mrs. Cocke at Tarbay. There saw the army balloon elevated for observing, & then as kept suspended & inflated near the ground in the open field of Berkley. In passing by the cavalry camp on my way, heard of a daring & successful adventure. Last night, according to previous arrangement, 5 of the picket guards at the end of Coggin's Point, all members of the Prince George cavalry, took a very leaky boat (in which two Yankees had before come on shore & had been captured,) &, with two muffled oars, rowed out to take a large transport schooner. The vessel lay about midway of the river, & a little above Ruffin's Bluff. It was the vessel nearest to this shore, but sundry others were near to it beyond, & one of the nearest was an armed steamer, or gun-boat. They reached the vessel without being discovered, except by a small dog, whose violent barking aroused the captain, & brought him up from his cabin. The leader of our party was an Irishman, named Martin, who had been a sailor in both the English & the C.S. service. He was the first to climb upon the deck, immediately followed by the others—& there met the captain of the vessel, who was immediately seized & taken down into his cabin, as quietly as could be. A straw bed was emptied, & set on fire, by means of matches carried for the purpose. The party then hastened to their boat, with their prisoner. Besides the danger from the vessels anchored near, a small tug steamer was coming up the channel, & in the direction towards the schooner. One other man only had been seen, the cook, who slept in the captain's cabin. He also had been seized, but broke [2120] loose, & jumped over-board, & as supposed escaped. Five others (sailors,) were asleep below in the forecastle. There was no time to take them, or anything else, from the vessel. The party got to the shore & their post close by, as fast as their two awkward oarsmen could effect. Some time elapsed & the vessel they had left still remained shrouded in darkness, & they feared that the fire had been extinguished. But the dread was soon dispelled by the bursting up of a broad sheet of flame, showing that the saving of the vessel was impossible. By the light, men were seen on the deck, showing that the sleeping crew had been awakened & were safe. Boats from other vessels had before been seen rowing towards the burning vessel. There were 5 loaded muskets or rifles on board, but locked up, & which were heard as discharged when reached by the fire. The vessel was a large-sized New York schooner, laden with corn. The captured captain was sent a prisoner to Petersburg this morning. When I arrived at the river, a small part of the vessel remained unconsumed, & still throwing out dense smoke. I would have expected that this exploit would have caused a vigorous firing of bomb-shells from the gun-boats, at the woods in which the pickets might be supposed to be concealed, if not on all the nearest buildings. But there had been no movement of that or any kind, & the numerous vessels of the fleet were as quiet as usual. Before night, the war steamers were placed outside, & the outer transports moved within. —Heard from Dr. Dupuy that his brother, & my nephew, A. M. Dupuy was dead, of typhoid fever. A valuable man. His death will be a great affliction & loss to his wife & mother especially, & regretted by all who knew him. [2121]

July 28. The mail. The northern reports of the late naval engagement off Vicksburg, treat the matter as an "escape" effected by the Arkansas through or from their fleet. Very well! A vessel making its "escape" through a hostile fleet of nearly 20 war-steamers, (4 or more of which were iron-clad,) almost without damage, except of its smokestack, & fighting its way for some two hours through this fleet along a river not a mile wide, may well be deemed a victory for the single antagonist—to say nothing of the destruction or disabling of several of the fleet.—Gen. Pope's army, in & about Culpeper, is estimated at 30,000 at least, & by some as high (with forces in easy reach,) as 60,000. It is reported that McClellan has sent part of his force across the country to be embarked on York river—& it was supposed, by observers here, that steamers filled with troops had been sent down James river from his camp at Westover & Berkley. It is inferred that these are sent to the Rappahannock to unite with Pope, & thence to advance on Richmond, while McClellan will attack from his present position, & perhaps by a new route. . . . Gen. Halleck has been appointed commander in chief of the U.S. Armies—to reside at Washington. Thus, he supersedes McClellan —which would seem to indicate some dissatisfaction of the President with the latter. . . . The confiscation law of the U.S., recently enacted,[20] is now being put in force so far as can be at present. This law condemns to death every person thenceforward guilty of "trea-

---

[20] Signed with some reluctance by Lincoln on July 17, the controversial Second Confiscation Act was proclaimed to be in effect on July 25. Technically, it provided for the forfeiture of all property—including slaves—of those supporting the Confederacy, but this and other provisions proved to be virtually unenforceable in the courts.

son" against the U.S. government—that is, who shall not be a traitor to his state & to the Confederate States, & consistently until they shall be subjugated. Also, the property of all such offenders shall be confiscated, & their slaves emancipated. In accordance with the spirit of this act, Gen. Pope, by his declarations, & all other commanders in practice, are seizing all private property of the invaded country that can be used to aid their invasion, or the invaders. Further, by a new general order of Pope, & of other commanders, every male resident within their occupied military lines is required to take the oath of allegiance to the northern government, or forthwith to be sent out of the lines, & under penalty of death should he return. Thus every man, not a traitor to his state, or willing to become so under this coercion, no matter how old, sick, or infirm, who resides in any town, or any territory of country occupied by or under the military command of the Yankee government [2124], or its army officers, must immediately be banished from his home, business, & family—unless he can remove his family also into banishment, at a day's warning. The orders have already been published for putting this rule in force for Fredericksburg, & the country within Pope's lines, & some cities in the South-West. I am heartily rejoiced for the enactment or proclamation of these tyrannical & most oppressive rules. For, without being declared, they have been acted upon everywhere when profitable or expedient, & would be so still more hereafter. Now, as declared & made universal, all residents of the South will know that the occupation of their property by the enemy's forces will be equivalent to its total loss as to all moveables—& that their final success will sweep the land itself into the great fund of plunder. . . . There are many men in the South, who if free to choose, would be traitors to the South. There are doubtless many thousands, who under the stringent coercive tyranny of Yankee laws & generals, will take the oath of allegiance to the northern despotism. But the former class *cannot* act out such allegiance any longer than their homes & persons are protected by the presence & domination of the enemy's military forces—& the latter class *will not*—& could not even if willing. The noble example of Vicksburg will do much to induce other attacked cities to make a desperate defence. But still stronger will be the examples of the cities which have surrendered to the enemy, as warnings, in exhibiting the still more enormous losses thereby incurred, & of suffering & degradation endured.

July 29. This morning, before I was out of bed . . . I was summoned by a messenger from Capt. Marks, requesting me to go to the Point, to guide & inform another officer. I proceeded immediately after breakfast. I heard that Gen. D. H. Hill had been there yesterday, & viewed the ground. I regret much not having met with him. The officer whom I met was Major [S. F.] Pearson [*sic*], of the Engineer Corps.[21] I showed him everything I supposed important to be observed. But he examined things so superficially & carelessly, that I dismissed my previous belief that artillery was to be speedily sent to fire on the enemy from the Bluff & perhaps elsewhere. Before 12, Major P. left for Petersburg, & I for Ruthven.

July 30. The mail. No new incidents of importance. . . . The employment of negroes as soldiers is now legalized, & the policy openly acted upon in the Yankee army. A regiment of negroes, ("Zouaves d'Afrique") is being raised in Kansas, & recruits for it invited by published advertisement.—Heard this morning, by verbal report, that a force of artillery was coming on the route from Petersburg to Coggin's Point. At 4.30 P.M. I left Ruthven for the river, to fall in with the artillery or some of its superior officers. Passing by the mansion of Beechwood, to see Edmund, & there with him found 6 or 7 officers who had not long before arrived, & were beginning to look out for places on which to post some of their numerous cannon coming on—of which I heard there were at least 70 pieces. I was astonished to learn that it was proposed to place some in the Beechwood yard, where they would be more than [2127] a mile farther from the vessels, & the opposite shore, than at other & more eligible situations. We soon showed a far better place, on the high point west of Hamilton's Meadow. If firing from the yard, as first thought of, the destruction of the mansion would have been made certain, without any military benefit in compensation. Among the officers were Generals [William N.] Pendleton & [Samuel G.] French.[22] The latter now commands this military dis-

---

[21] Major Pierson was serving at this time as chief of artillery under General Daniel H. Hill. The latter, commanding Confederate forces south of James River, had been ordered by General Lee on July 28 to position some fifty pieces of artillery so as "to cut off General McClellan's communication by the river." *Official Records*, Vol. XI, Pt. 2, p. 936.

[22] A native of New Jersey, French (1818–1910) graduated from West Point in 1843 and saw service in the Mexican War. Resigning from the military in 1856, he moved to Mississippi and operated a plantation near Vicksburg until the outbreak of war. He commanded the Confederate batteries at Evansport on the Potomac during

trict, with his head-quarters at Petersburg. Gen. Pendleton, I was introduced to on the day of the battle of Manassas.[23] He was then but a captain of artillery, & a clergyman. I was glad to find so good an officer in command of this expedition, & he seemed well pleased to meet with me again. I offered my assistance as a guide, or to give any needed information as to the localities. Also, I made a request, & was promised its being complied with, that, if I could be present when the cannonading should begin, that I might be permitted to fire the first cannon. It was designed to place cannon not only at the two most advanced & best points, (Ruffin's Bluff, & the Point Landing,) but also at various other places along the edge of the high promontory, next [to] the river, for a mile in extent. Other cannon were to be sent to Maycox. It was designed to move the pieces to their positions after dark, so as not to be seen by the enemy, (& also to conceal the dust raised by the approach of the carriages, at some miles distance—) & when all were ready, to fire rapidly on the vessels, until the returned shelling from the gunboats, or any effort to land Yankee troops in the rear, should make it too dangerous for our artillery to remain longer—when there would be a general & hasty retreat to some miles from the river. The officers moved so slow, (or wasted so much time,) that they did not see the first suitable position for a cannon until nearly 6 P.M.—after [2128] which, I next guided them to the Bluff & Point landing, as the best positions for attacking. They did not reach there until within half an hour of sunset, when it was entirely too late to make proper observations, or even to go upon any other of the many suitable positions before darkness rendered the attempt useless. Still, the trains of artillery were ordered on, from the place of temporary halt, by Merchants' Hope Church. The sky was cloudy, & threatening rain, soon after dark. The moon, but two days old, soon disappeared. Not a star was visible for the clouds. The only light was from the almost continual flashing of very faint sheet lightning, which, though almost incessant, did not give enough light to enable the seeing the hands of a watch, to know the time. Still, we kept moving, either backwards or forwards, or halting & standing still, as if to proceed & commence the designed firing, & in the darkness, until near mid-

---

the winter of 1861–62 and at this time was head of the Department of Southern Virginia and North Carolina. Later, he served in the West under Joseph E. Johnston, participating in the Vicksburg and Atlanta campaigns.

[23] See above, page 80.

night—when Gen. Pendleton told me that he thought it improper to make the attempt this night, & that he would seek Gen. French, & consult with him as to what should be done. Finally, after our returning nearly to the Church, & again standing & waiting long, the undertaking was postponed, & we were so informed & were discharged half an hour past midnight. It had been slowly raining an hour or more previously, but it had then ceased. Some of the artillery had gone half-way into the farm (Beechwood,) when it was found to be the portion intended for some other place, & was sent back. Also there were ambulances & surgeons, that had gone as far, & also were sent back. Why the remainder of the artillery did not come on, was afterwards accounted for by reports that the conductors of part had mistaken their orders, & probably others had taken the wrong road. Altogether, the whole business exhibited astonishing inertness & carelessness, & bad management. Under the adverse circumstances, it was certainly proper to postpone operations—& [2129] it would have been wrong at any time to begin the attack, by artillery firing, in the night. But the great danger of this postponement is, that, having begun the operation & showed the intention, information will be conveyed to the enemy's gun-boats by some negro, or the artillery may be seen, next day, from the Yankee balloon, & so the whole scheme frustrated, by the gunboats taking the initiative, & shelling the shores before the cannon are posted, & the vessels also dispersing, so as to be in little danger of being struck. The artillery and other carriages returned to the neighborhood of the Church. I got back to Ruthven after 1 o'clock.

July 31. Immediately after breakfast, I rode again to the river, expecting to meet there the generals & some other officers of the artillery. But I waited until 11 A.M. & until the beginning of steady though slow drizzle, without seeing or hearing from any of them. Then I returned home, partly wet. Last evening there were 10 gunboats, forming an open line stretching from near Jordan's Point to the opposite side of the river. One gunboat only was seen among the other vessels lying off Berkley & Westover. This morning there were 13 gunboats in that line, off Jordan's Point. I attempted to count the remainder of the vessels (steamers & sailing transports,) & made out about 81 of the upper portion, when those below, off Westover, were found so close together that it was impossible to distinguish them, & so I guessed at this number, & supposed that all, including the gunboats off Jordan's, would make 145 to 150 vessels. This does not include the canal boats which make the pontoon wharf. The open ground of Berkley has fewer tents than formerly, & very few wagons. Probably both, with the great body of the army are in the camp in the woods, of which nothing is visible [2130] from this side except the smoke of the fires. A letter from the camp, published in a northern paper, states the number of wagons to amount to 3000! If so, I under-estimated them, when I saw probably nearly all at once, standing on the open ground of Berkley & Westover. There are yet many tents on the Westover part of the open ground, & near the river. Opposite, & still lower, the transports, partly steamers, but mostly sailing vessels, stretch in an almost unbroken line along the channel, for half a mile, besides many more scattering, above & below. Heard from the picket guards at the Point landing that their predecessors had fired on a boat last night, from which had been returned three musket shots. This is unfortunate, as it may cause increased watchfulness of the enemy, & make better safeguards be adopted, adverse to the concealment of our designed cannonading. The pickets on the bluff also told me that they had been fired at twice this morning by rifle shots from the vessels. And later, I heard that this firing at our pickets, without damage, was repeated at different times of the day.—At 4 P.M. the previous cloudiness changed to steady though slow drizzle—very bad for the designed operations, & for myself. This weather delayed my departure until past 7 P.M. when I set out for the river. It was dark before I entered the open fields of Beechwood, where I met with my nephew, Dr. Dupuy, acting with some others of the Prince George cavalry as pioneers, & he also as one of the guides for the artillery, which soon came on. My son Edmund acted as the principal guide, & was of most essential service. For, without his intimate acquaintance with the ground, it would have been impossible to move the artillery through such darkness. The farm road, which extended only about half the whole distance, was mostly avoided, because hard, & partly rough & stony, & on which the moving of the carriages would have been heard as far as the vessels. Softer & better ways were found over the fields, outside of the road, & beyond where the road extended. I have the infirmity of "night-blindness," (though I never found it out until last year, when on the night retreat from Centreville to Bull Run,)—that is, I am not able to see in the dark as nearly all other [2131] persons can. So, as well as I was acquainted with the localities, & had recently examined the route particularly with a view to the passage of the artillery, I could rarely see anything of what we were treading upon, or could have distinguished any obstruction of the track. When passing on the road through a part of the Grove, amidst large oaks, I could not see (except the sky above,) any more than if I had been totally blind. And here the after carriages of the train of artillery, though following close after, lost sight of the first, so that they were compelled to stop, & had to be sent for, & brought up, after they were missed. Strict silence was ordered, & so little sound reached my deaf ears, that, even though trying to keep close to my son, who was leading the train, I was several times separated from him & all others, & lost, for a short time. No sound of the carriages was heard by me until when getting near to the extremity of the high promontory—when, in passing over the several short & steep little hills along the edge of the bluff, or river bank, I heard enough noise of the wheels to alarm me for fear of the sounds reaching the nearest vessels, lying scarcely more than half a mile distant. Two of the lighter guns were posted at the old Point or Ferry landing— there being room for no more—8 on the small level at the extremity of the high Promontory, & just back of Ruffin's Bluff—4 farther back, near the edge of the continuation of the same line of bluff. Others were posted along the river bank (& low bluff) of George's Flat, half a mile to three-quarters above & farther back than the extremity of the Point—& 4 of the heaviest pieces on the high & narrow promontory west of Hamilton's Meadow, & about 400 yards distant from the Beechwood mansion. [Twelve] guns also were sent to Maycox, which position is nearer to the thickest lying of the shipping than anywhere on this side.[24] It was understood that the firing would be begun at midnight—giving time for all the batteries to be ready, & for the guns for Maycox to be carried there 8 miles, (heading Powell's creek,) over a very bad road. It was by accident that, on our route, I recognized Gen. Pendleton as being next to my side for a [2132] few minutes—& reminded him of his promise that I should fire the first cannon, to which he courteously assented, but which I afterwards found had not been provided for. After the artillery (near us) had been posted, I remained, together with my

---

[24] In all, forty-three guns, ranging from 12-pounder howitzers to long-range Parrott rifles, were installed by the Confederates on the south side of James River opposite Harrison's Landing between 6 P.M. and midnight on July 31. *Official Records*, Vol. XI, Pt. 2, pp. 941, 945.

[395]

son Edmund, & his young son George, & some other spectators, on horseback, on the farther bluff. The transports were mostly lighted by lanterns suspended in the rigging, which well indicated the positions of these vessels. The few campfires on the near land gradually went out. I had heard, & did not doubt, that the first gun (to serve as a signal for beginning at all the batteries,) was to be fired from the Point landing. When it was nearly 12, I went there, guided by my son & grandson, through the lower & shaded part, in what was to me utter darkness. I could not there see my horse, after dismounting, with my hand upon him, nor a man whose face almost touched mine. I was led to the cannon, near the shore, & where there was some light from the open water. I found the commander Capt. [Willis J.] Dance, & stated my object, & heard from him that the first gun was not to be fired from this place, but from the bluff, & from the battery of one of two officers. I thought it useless to attempt to pursue my object farther, through so much uncertainty of success, & the great difficulty of the darkness. . . . So with my son & grandson, & other spectators, I rode to the highest & most open spot on the line of bluff . . . & at about 200 or 250 yards distant from the nearest cannon posted on the border of the bluff. We remained there, on our horses, until nearly 1 A.M., when the firing began. With all my preparation, & eager expectation, the suddenness & violence of the first discharges startled & agitated me greatly, which was [2133] increased by the restiveness of my horse, & of others. However, in a few minutes they became & continued quiet. The flashing of the discharges was brilliant & beautiful, from the 12 cannon nearest to my position, & on the highest ground. I could see the flashes from no others, all being in places either too depressed, or concealed by intervening woods. But the reports from them were very loud, & almost incessant generally, & varying in tone & force from light field-pieces to 32-pounders, & one gun of 50 lbs. shell. At first, we had listened in disappointed expectation to hear the guns at Maycox, the most effective position, & nearest to the thickest crowd of Yankee vessels. But it was not long before the welcome reports began to be heard from that post also. Later, I learned that the guns there had not been quite ready at first, but were fixed in a short time & put in operation. On account of the great difficulty of conveying artillery to these posts near the enemy, & as much to withdraw under the (expected) heavy cross firing from the Yankee gun & mortar vessels, it had been determined that each battery should discharge but a limited & fixed number of rounds, which according to the distance of position, varied in certain allowances of from 20 to 30 discharges from each battery & gun. After these had been made, the guns were to be attached, & the carriages taken back to the assigned position some miles distant. There was no fire returned from the enemy, either on water or land, for perhaps 15 minutes or more—& afterwards, I saw but two flashes, indicating discharged cannon, from all the vessels exposed to our view, which was nearly all above the bluff, including all the gunboats opposite Jordan's Point. Of course these were too far off. But I expected them to come near very soon, (I had seen the steam kept up on three of them, in the forenoon,) & to begin to throw their large bomb-shells. I heard afterwards that some cannon were fired on us from the Yankee camp opposite, but that was not in my view. [2134] Our fire had begun to be much less frequent, as the ammunition of particular guns was exhausted, before the first loud response was heard from any gun-boat. And this, & all that followed, in number, after our firing ceased altogether, was not from the mortars of the vessels above our positions, but from others below, & lower than Maycox. I thought it much to be regretted, as the heavy firing in return was so slow to begin, that the caissons had not been brought, or much more ammunition. The whole number of balls & shells fired from our 40 cannon made about 800, & our firing was over in half an hour. I doubt whether the aim was not too inaccurate (because of the darkness,) to do much damage to the enemy's vessels or camp. If ever so much, we could not know, & will never be allowed to learn.[25] There was no change produced, visible to us, except that the lights which had been hung out on almost every transport vessel, soon began to disappear, & were all gradually extinguished. As soon as our ammunition was exhausted, & all reports ceased, Edmund returned to his assumed duty of guiding the trains on their return—not less difficult than the passage in, but conducted less carefully in guarding against noise from the moving carriages, & therefore effected more speedily. Expecting the return to be as slow, I did not wait for the coming on of the train, but, accompanied & guided by my young grandson, I rode on home-ward. The dis-

---

[25] In his official report of the incident, General McClellan asserted that "no damage of the slightest consequence was done to any of the vessels or depots," although the Federals did sustain minor casualties amounting to ten dead and twelve wounded. *Ibid.*, 935.

charges of shells from the heavy mortars of the gun-boats were now becoming more & more frequent, & they continued until we had gone two miles. The bombs, from the distant sound, & direction, must have been discharged at a distance of several miles below this farm. Yet some of the shells passed over our heads, & one seemed to fall (without exploding,) within 200 yards of us when we were passing by the barn, a mile & a half on our route. We stopped several times to look [2135] back, & observe the flashes of the discharges, which though not brilliant, because of intervening woods, rose high in the air, & seemed so much like faint sheet lightning, that I should have supposed it to be such, but for every flash being followed after a long & regular interval, by the loud though distant report. About an hour after the cessation of our firing, that from the enemy's mortars ceased also. Soon after, Edmund overtook us, he having previously led the artillery train out as far as the public road, on which the remainder of their route, towards Petersburg, was plain & safe. . . . We reached Ruthven after 3 A.M., when I went to bed, almost worn out by fatigue from the unusual exercise, & also exposure of the preceding two days & nights.—So far as we knew, & believed to be true of the batteries nearest to the enemy's vessels, not one of our men had been struck by any missile of the enemy. Musket or rifle shots were fired on our nearest posts, during part of our cannonading, from some of the vessels.

August 1. I felt so jaded & stiff, from my previous fatigue, & perhaps also wetting by rain, that, though anxious to learn the unknown incidents, I went out only as far as the cavalry camp, a mile on the way to the Post Office, & returned as soon as our mail was brought to me there. Julian had set out last night, as soon as the firing had begun, & rode to Beechwood House & landing to see the battle—but all the firing had ceased before he arrived. He heard that one of our men had been killed, & two or three wounded, by the explosion of a shell, at the battery of heaviest cannon, & most distant from the enemy, on the [2136] high knoll west of Hamilton's meadow, & at some 400 yards' distance from the Beechwood mansion. I heard at the camp, & afterwards, that all the artillery trains & troops, & also a large force of infantry (reported as two brigades,) which had come to Merchants' Hope Church, & encamped, two days ago, had all marched back, towards Petersburg & Richmond—without even sending any artillery to prevent, or dispute, the passage of the Yankee transports at Hoods! It seems to me that it is as ridiculous as useless to have made this whole movement—of so large a force not only of artillery, but of supporting infantry, & then marching all back after merely throwing 800 balls & shells, in half an hour, which I do not suppose served to kill 20 men, or sunk, or seriously damaged a single vessel. Yet the enemy must have been completely surprised, as there was no return of the fire (of any importance,) until our attack was nearly ended, by the designed limitation of discharges. The whole preparation & result, taken together, are so disproportioned, & seem to me so absurd, that I suspect that this show of great force was a feint, to draw the enemy's attention to this quarter, while the troops are sent rapidly to operate in some other quarter—perhaps under Jackson against Pope.[26] I hope it may be so.—Some news at last from Jackson, but coming first from northern papers. It seems that he occupies Gordonsville—& our papers expect an early battle between his army & Pope's. The latter has been lately & heavily reinforced, & is estimated at from 50 to 60,000. Pope is the present rising favorite commander with both the northern people & government. He is a Kentuckian by birth, of Va family—a capable officer, of great enterprise for bold & dashing operations, but wanting discretion & caution. I trust that Stonewall will manage properly, & humiliate & punish this base renegade southerner. . . . This afternoon we saw from Ruthven the light of a burning building—& soon after learned that it was the mansion at Maycox. Two gunboats had come in to near the landing, drove off our small picket guard, & put on shore a party to set fire to the house. This deliberate act of vandalism is, according to Yankee reasoning & usage, doubtless placed on the

---

[26] Ruffin's comments here are remarkably astute. Although the primary objective had been to interdict traffic on the James, thus dislodging McClellan from his position at Harrison's Landing, a secondary aim was to relieve pressure on Richmond so that sufficient reinforcements might be dispatched to Jackson to enable him "to drive, if not destroy, the miscreant Pope." *Ibid.*, 936.

It should be noted further that Lee was no more satisfied than the diarist with the relatively meager accomplishments of the recent bombardment from Coggin's Point. After acknowledging that "any positive damage inflicted upon their vessels, &c., was of course a positive gain to us," Lee reminded General Hill that "this does not satisfy the object I had in view. My desire was for you to cut off their communication by the river, if practicable, or should this be impossible, to render it so insecure and precarious as to oblige General McClellan to abandon his position, or at least to prevent any advance or attack on his part. This will require continuous and systematic effort and a well-digested plan." Like Ruffin, General Lee thought the most feasible site from which to arrest the passage of transports on the James was old Fort Powhatan (or Hoods). *Ibid.*, 938.

ground of *retaliation* for the attack made on them last night—8 pieces of our artillery having been placed in front of this house. But the villainous act, & violation of the law of civilized warfare, has less than usual color of excuse. This house belonged to Mrs. Cole, a widow & her young orphan daughters, who had not any near male relatives, & therefore had not any such one who was serving or could serve in our army.[27] Mrs. Cole had lost nearly all her useful slaves, who had lately gone across the river to McClellan's camp, & was herself a refugee from her home. Of course, under any circumstances, the occupation & use of her ground as a position for our artillery, was a matter in which she could exercise no choice, & which doubtless, if known to her in advance (as it was not,) would [2138] have been much against her will. Afterwards I heard that several transports had landed troops to perform this deed, the two gun-boats protecting them. All the offices, or neighboring houses were burnt, as well as the mansion. 300 of our cavalry were sent there soon after, but the enemy had then gone off, & after waiting some time, the cavalry returned to camp.

August 2. This afternoon I rode to the river, & viewed well the positions & surroundings of all the batteries on the Point, & at the Point landing. All of the guns on the high ground had to fire through more or less of bushes & trees. And from the marks of the balls or shells high on some trees, & the want of marks where they should have been made, I am still more of the opinion that the firing was mostly badly aimed, or without aim, & of little effect. Most of our missiles were shells. Yet, overlooking as I did through all the firing, all the broad expanse of water above the extreme bluff, I saw so few explosions of our shells, that I then supposed that but few shells were fired from our cannon, but balls generally. Of the explosions seen by me, sundry were either very high above the water, or very near the discharging guns—as otherwise they would not have been visible to me, when directed immediately across the river. I infer that most of them did not explode at all, or exploded too soon. The two flashes which I saw rising from near the water, & supposed to be from vessels off Berkley, I am now sure were from explosions of our shells. The more that I learn of the whole operation, & its accompaniments, the more does it appear badly managed, futile, & contemptible. But little change has been made in the positions of

---

[27] McClellan was under the mistaken impression that the mansion he ordered burned on this date was "the Ruffin house." *Ibid.*, 935.

the Yankee vessels. The authorities have not paid so much respect to our artillery attack as to place the vessels much more out of danger. However, they are stretched more down the river, & off & below Maycox. Also, a large gunboat lies off the Point landing, & apparently within 400 yards from the shore, & three others are within from 500 to 600 yards from the upper shore & bluff, & about 400 yards from each other. The pickets [2139] are ordered to keep well concealed behind the bushes near the shore, as they are within musket range of the nearest of these gunboats. I had heard in the forenoon, & now learned more particularly from the officer in command of the picket guard, that about 500 soldiers had been landed this morning from Yankee transports on Maycox, which is ¾ of a mile distant, & in full view from Coggin's Pt. landing, as before under the protection of gunboats; & that while two companies under arms served as a guard, the others, with axes, were cutting down all the trees & bushes which stood near the river, & mouth of the creek, which might have concealed the approach of troops, or the positions of pickets. This operation seemed to be nearly completed, as the whole ground, to a considerable distance from the water, was laid bare of every thing except the chimneys of the burnt buildings. As riding upon the promontory, I had not seen the troops except by the gleaming of their arms in the sun-light, which attracted my notice, & indicated the position of the troops. I infer that to make this clearing was the only object of this second landing, & that as soon as it is completed, all the troops will withdraw. Then, & probably tomorrow morning, or the next after, they will land on the extremity of Coggin's Point, to clear the land of trees & bushes in the same way, & for the like purpose of destroying the shelter for pickets, & all cover for approaching troops. But the job there would be much more difficult, & far less effective, than at Maycox, not only on account of the greater quantity of trees, but because of the intermixture of wooded swamp, low flat, & narrow ravines & steep hillsides. But if, as I expect, the attempt shall be made, an ambush of 50 brave men & good marksmen, with muskets or double-barrelled fowling pieces, loaded with buckshot, might make havoc among the men first landed, & with but little risk for our men. As I returned by the camp, I made known to Col. Phillips, the commander, what I had learned & seen, & also what I expected were the intentions of the enemy on this side of the river.

Aug. 3. Sunday. We set out to go to church. But in passing the cavalry camp, at Sycamore Grove Church, we were told that the enemy had [2140] landed on Coggin's Point. Julian & my grandson George immediately rode on, in the hope of being early enough to bring off the remaining negroes, & to drive off, to Ruthven, the mules & cows. I wished to have gone also, to reconnoitre at a safe distance from the Yankees—as I supposed they would not then advance far from the extremity of the Point. But Julian & the ladies so strongly opposed it, that I gave it up. It is the opinion, not only of my family, but of most or all others, that my capture would be especially desired by the Yankees, & would be certainly followed up by my close imprisonment, & very harsh treatment. I have been remonstrated with for my alleged imprudence in remaining at Beechwood, & since at Ruthven, where a party might have been sent on any night, & seized me in my bed. We had passed the camp half a mile, before turning back. When again passing the camp, I got out & stopped to learn the news as it would be brought there by videttes, the carriage with Lotty & Nanny going on to Ruthven. Rain was then begun, & soon increased to a heavy shower. I learned that Yankee troops, including cavalry, had been landed at Maycox, & were marching on. A portion of the cavalry had been sent on to meet them, & the remaining companies were getting ready. Soon after, the camp baggage was ordered to be put in the wagons, for removal & falling back towards Petersburg. In an hour, Julian, with George, returned, having met on this road the returning picket guards, before his reaching the open ground of Beechwood. These pickets told him that the Yankees had already passed the barn, & had advanced more than a mile through the open fields, which was past both the negroes' houses & the stock. Of course his objects were frustrated, & any farther advance was hazardous, & so Julian speedily returned, he [2141] & George both getting thoroughly wet. At the camp, we exchanged our news, which left to us, & to all others, no ground to doubt that the Yankees were fast approaching from two different landings. Julian determined to move off his family to Petersburg forthwith—& such was the wish, as well as the necessity, of all of us who were temporary sojourners. We pushed on to Ruthven (1½ miles from the camp,) & every one went to work to pack up the most valuable or essential clothing. There was no time or conveyance for anything more, except our arms. We had not been many minutes at the house, & thus engaged, when a frightened Sussex trooper galloped up in headlong flight from a skirmish, as he reported, with the advance of the enemy, on the main road, & within three miles of us. Soon after, we saw others, of the camp guards, who had been ordered to retreat with the baggage, & more reliable as evidence, who repeated different versions of the skirmish & state of affairs. All concurred on the facts that our party had been worsted, & had retreated before the advancing enemy, & that all the remaining cavalry were retreating, by order, towards Petersburg. Ruthven house is rather more than half a mile from the main road, & expected route of march of the enemy, & in view from it. Edmund's carriage was there, & that as well as Julian's were ordered—& also two wagons for the trunks & luggage. Edmund had driven away one of his carriage horses, so that the best team was a weak one, being two of Julian's mules. Thomas, still as weak & sick as at any previous time, was placed in one of the carriages, with a whole seat to himself, & a pillow, so that he could recline. Mrs. Lorraine & Nanny occupied the other seat. (John had gone to Petersburg with his father.) Lotty, her children, & nurse, filled the other carriage. I rode on horseback, & well armed—as was Thomas—& which we supposed possibly might be needed for coercion [2142] of the drivers, in the possible event of their wishing to abscond, & attempting to desert their charge. So, besides having a revolver, I rode with a double-barrelled gun for some miles, & until I had become very weary with the incumbrance. Before we set out, our cavalry were passing on in retreat, & the enemy had reached Garysville. We left at 1.30 P.M. It was then too dangerous to travel the usual & best road, as we might be overtaken by the enemy. So we took another road, a mile farther, to its junction with the mail road at the Court House. Julian & George remained to see to the loading, & then to accompany the two wagons. Before we reached the main road, we had seen sundry other fugitives, of the cavalry, aiming by this back way to join their companies, & some of our neighbors fleeing as we were to Petersburg for safety. From some of these overtaking us, & others meeting us, we were continually hearing new reports. Thus, we learned that we were ahead of our retreating cavalry, & therefore safe from being overtaken by the enemy, when we were entering the main road. This assurance was the more important, as our slow & weak team of mules took 4½ hours to travel the 15 miles.—From the time we learned that the Yankees were advancing far into Beechwood farm, I expected to see the smoke rising from the mansion, set on fire. But this did not occur up to the time of our departure, nor did we hear any such report afterwards. When more fully informed as to the actual occurrences, I learned that there were but 50 of our cavalry engaged—(none of the Prince George troop,) which were sent on in advance—& of these, one-half, stationed as a reserve, fled without firing a shot or striking a blow. One or two of the others were killed, & three or four wounded.—Edmund, since coming to Petersburg with part of his family, had been the tenant at will of his neighbor Mrs. Marks, who had rented a house for safe refuge, but afterwards declined using it. But now she also had fled [2143] with her family from the country (though 7 miles from the river,) & of course required her house. The adjoining tenement was vacant—& Edmund was permitted to occupy it until a more abiding tenant shall offer, or until he can determine upon whether to stay here, or where to go. He is greatly perplexed. . . . As I was riding into the town, I met Gen. French going out. I had already forgotten his face—but he accosted, & made himself known to me. I gave him all the information I had obtained as to the movements today. Then I inquired if any troops were marching down (as reported) to oppose the advance of the enemy. He said there were not, & that it was not intended at present—that it was desired first to see what were the enemy's intentions & destination.—Called with Edmund on Mrs. [Mildred] Campbell—& after supper we walked to Mr. Callender's where Mrs. Meade & her sick son & Lotty & her children are staying. Mr. & Mrs. Callender away at the Springs. I accepted the warm invitation to lodge there for this night, & may longer. We sat up talking of the exciting incidents of the day until 11. Julian did not come with George & the wagons, but remained at home (or hid himself elsewhere perhaps,) for the night, to send up two more loads tomorrow—for which the wagons will return, & George with them, early in the morning.

Aug. 4. Early in the morning, heard that the enemy had not advanced any farther than the cavalry camp, where they burnt most of the tents . . . . This loss a specimen of the usual carelessness and bad management. Also, the enemy had fallen back in the afternoon to the neighborhood & protection [2144] of their gunboats off Maycox. Nothing heard of the other body of the enemy at Beechwood. Edmund rode down to find out their position, & to see if possible to move away & save any of his remaining property. But he did not venture to approach nearer than the outer limit of the open land of Beechwood, having learned that pickets were stationed farther out than the barn, who of course would fire upon any one approaching from without their line. These pickets no doubt were the Yankees seen there yesterday forenoon. Our pickets before posted on the farm retreated too soon to see the landing of the troops. But the pickets at Beaver Castle, above the bay, could observe all, at the distance of some miles. They thought that about 3,000 troops landed, & were still encamped there. They landed wagons—& built a pontoon wharf. The probability seems to be that these forces will not advance—but will hold Coggin's Point & Maycox as out-posts, to guard the main army from future attacks from this side of the river.—The mail. . . . There have been no recent large operations. But since the battles near Richmond, as well as long before, the whole general indications of affairs seem to be in favor of our arms.—President Davis has proclaimed the rule of retaliation for the outrages intended & declared by Gen. Pope. But the measure of retaliation is to be confined to Pope & his officers,[28] which is partial & inefficient. Pope has only openly proclaimed as his role of conduct, what most other Yankee commanders have acted in practice, & which the recent confiscation law, & the policy of the Lincoln government fully sanction. [2145]

Aug. 5. . . . The same cavalry forces which had been stationed at Sycamore Grove, before being obliged to retreat hastily before the advancing enemy, have been sent back to occupy the same position. This was the farthest extent of [2146] the advance of the enemy's cavalry, before they returned . . . to Maycox. . . . The pickets of this cavalry force will serve to give notice of any future advance of the enemy from Maycox & Beechwood—but can do no other good. All of Edmund's remaining property at Beechwood is within the enemy's lines, & of course will all be lost or destroyed, including the growing crop of corn. Most of the remaining negroes were either old (& worthless, & would be rejected by the Yankees,) or young children, & two sick, & some left to nurse the sick. All will now be taken, except those so infirm as to be an incumbrance to any proprietor. . . . The late English papers speak of the affairs of

---

[28] According to General Order No. 54, promulgated on August 1, such officers were to be ineligible for parole, if captured, and liable to execution in retaliation for "the murder of any unarmed citizen or inhabitant of this Confederacy" carried out under any of the orders previously issued by Major General Pope.

the Yankee government & army, & the leaders, with bitter scorn & contempt of their veracity, & detestation of many of their acts. We in the south can see no English opinions, except such as Northern papers choose to publish, & through which channels only they reach us. But according to what we read, there is now scarcely a voice or public journal that remains favorable to the North, or believes in the possible final success of the northern arms. The general tone of their publications seem[s] to indicate that England & France will not much longer withhold the recognition of the independent nationality of the Confederate States, or continue to maintain their "neutral" position (so called,) which professed neutrality has operated entirely against us, & to the advantage of our enemy. . . . But I still believe that the greater our defensive successes—or the more equal the struggles of the opposed North & South—the more injury they are like to do each other, without either compelling the other to succumb—the better will the English government be pleased, & the more effectually will its selfish policy be promoted. While the parties in this wasting and costly war continue nearly equipoised in successes & losses, two darling objects of England will be more & more probable. These are, the bankruptcy of the North, & thereby the prostration of the great commercial rival of England—& the destruction of negro slavery in the South, the great object of English fanaticism. Instead of the victories & successes of the South inducing the friendly intervention of England, I think they put off any such action. Our greatest disasters, & probable complete overthrow would not only be more likely to bring about that result, but would be certain to do so. For England rejoices at the separation & weakening of this, her before most formidable rival & competitor, & will never permit any reconstruction of the Union, by northern victory & southern submission, or otherwise. We should cease to look to England for aid by intervention. We must fight for our independence, & can gain [2148] it only by the courage & victories of our armies. . . . Today, various rumors of the enemy below. It was generally believed that they were advancing. I wish they were, but do not believe in any such present intention. They draw back every night under cover of their gunboats. Our cavalry also have fallen back, to within 5 miles of Petersburg. I believe that it is the policy of our authorities not to oppose the enemy until after coaxing them as far as can be from their naval support. The worst effect of this delay is allowing the country within & near the Yankee lines to be plundered & wasted, & its supplies converted to their use. Every family that can remove from the neighborhood of the Yankee forces, has fled to avoid the outrages expected from their domination. Their losses are enormous in the property left behind, & in their business abandoned. In addition, the expenses of living abroad are enormous, & the privations very great, even for great expenses. [2149] The prices of all the comforts & necessaries of life are raised to rates that would previously have been deemed fabulous & incredible. Luxuries, & most ordinary comforts, may be dispensed with. But even when coming down to the mere requirements of necessity & decency, the expense of living will be enormous—& nearly all resources for paying cut off, with abandonment of the farms. And besides the expenses & physical privations of all refugees, I find for myself a miserable time in the (so far) total deprivation of books, & of all other sources of employment or amusement. Except my old friend Mrs. Campbell, (& Mrs. Callender, who is away,) there is not one resident in this town whose company I care for—or any others except the families of my two sons. . . .

Aug. 6. Edmund returned from Ruthven, bringing his bacon which had been placed there. From him I learned that the Yankees had not advanced permanently outside of the Beechwood farm. It was said that they were throwing up intrenchments there. The pickets of this part of the force had been extended across & joined with those thrown out from Maycox. Julian arrived late. He had been able to bring off his furniture, & stock of cattle, mules & horses, & also all of his few slaves.—Gen. Jackson is at Louisa C.H. with nearly half his command, & the remainder under Gen. Ewell is at Gordonsville—in all 50 to 60,000 men as reported. A collision, & decisive battle between this army & Gen. Pope's has been expected for some days, & cannot be long postponed. . . . It seems to me that there is now a good opportunity for a great military stroke, & success. Jackson's & Pope's armies are near together, & nearly matched in numbers. Gordonsville is within 5 hours of Richmond, & Louisa C.H. 4 hours. 30,000 men might be sent from the army near Rd. to reinforce Jackson, & enable him to demolish Pope's army, & the reinforcement return to Rd. probably before McClellan would know of their advance, or before he could . . . [mount] any new offensive movement thereupon. The destruction of Pope's army would permit Jackson to add 50,000 to the forces facing

McClellan, or otherwise to march to Washington, or to Philadelphia. But our policy, in regard to our great armies, is very different. It is to remain on the defensive—& to wait for the opposing commander to choose his own time & convenience, & usually the place also, for making the attack.

Aug. 7. Some of the enemy's forces lately attacked our outposts at Malvern Hills [*sic*], drove them back & occupied the position. [Commander David D.] Porter's heavy mortar flotilla has arrived at Fortress Monroe (& probably since in James river,) from the Mississippi. These two facts indicate a renewal of the movement of McClellan's army, & of the fleet on Richmond, in concert, [2151] with Pope's army to advance from its northern position. His nearest outpost is at Orange C.H. We have here, in Petersburg, every day, reports of the enemy advancing in Prince George. Yesterday it was said that their line of battle was formed, & also that of our forces some miles nearer to town. Neither was true. The enemy have not advanced farther than Merchants' Hope Church & Sycamore Church. . . . Our main forces, 3 brigades, are intrenching on Friend's farm 2 miles below Petersburg. . . . George returned from Ruthven with part of Edmund's furniture &c. & the latter arrived later with other loads of the portion he had before deposited at Mr. Edw. Marks'. These & another place, at which he had placed his furniture for safety, are now even more in [2152] danger of the Yankee plunderers & destroyers than was Beechwood until recently. We hear numerous reports of the outrages committed within & near the Yankee lines. But as we have no direct intercourse with the few still remaining residents, there is nothing certain in the details. Our minister, Mr. Hansburgh, with his very sick wife & other family, made their escape, in three different parties—after the Yankees having robbed, & insulted them by the most opprobrious language, & threatening to hang Mr. Hansburgh as a spy, which he thinks would have been done if he had been captured, after this charge being made. I will wait for reliable accounts before stating particulars of the general procedure of the Yankees where they have full control.—For want of all other books, I am reading the historical part of the bible, beginning with the Book of Joshua. This is returning to this reading for amusement, & for the same reason, the want of all other books, which I resorted to when between 8 & 9 years of age. I do not mean however that I have not also read the same portions at intermediate times. . . .

Aug. 8. . . . We have been in the troubles of "moving" ever since

[408]

our hasty flight from Ruthven. Yesterday the family left their temporary residence for one rented by the month on High Street—a very
old & ordinary house, but far back from the street, with a large yard
between set well in good grass & large shade trees—& with a
garden containing some growing vegetables. The house is very
plain, & the rooms mostly small, but in plenty. The out-houses
affording plenty of accommodation for the unusually large number
of servants, & especially of mothers & young children. Every day
Edmund has been bringing up some of his furniture . . . . Not near
all has yet been brought—or probably can be, before the Yankees
destroy it. Yet this house is lumbered up with what has been already
brought, & yet we are either without, or very deficient in other
things, the most necessary of themselves, or required to make
useful what we have. For example, the sitting room is so filled with
a pile of beds & mattresses that it can scarcely be entered—& yet
the bedsteads & bed clothes are mostly behind. . . . In addition to
all these discomforts, our table supplies are extremely deficient, &
very costly. Latterly we use no coffee, & would have no tea, except
that it was needed for the sick. On this account, there is used *black*
tea, which when best, none of us could endure, & which is very
mean though at $8 the pound. We have bacon from home, which if
to be bought would cost 50 cents the pound by wholesale, or 75 by
the piece. No one uses butter, except Thomas. We still have vegetables left of the supply before brought from Beechwood. When
they are gone, that will be the greatest want, & hardest to supply,
except at fabulous prices. I can live on as little & as humble food as
any one accustomed to plenty & to luxury—& I take care to do so. I
do not refer to these things because complaining, even in my
private thoughts—but to state the difficulties of the family, which
are cheerfully borne by all, & by none more so than myself. . . . I
slept last night, for the first time, at home, having before lodged at
Mr. Callender's, where Mrs. Meade & Julian's family are staying. I
fear that Mrs. Meade's son John is consumptive [2155], & scarcely a
hope for his life. His bad condition of health has been produced by
his exposure in serving in the army. To this cause will be owing the
early deaths of many thousands, & especially of the youngest &
most tenderly raised volunteers, & far more than will be killed in
battle. John Meade is a most worthy & excellent youth, son &
brother—& his death will be a most heavy affliction to his relatives
& friends. . . . The carriage driver of my son Edmund, William, who
was one of the first absconders, (& no doubt the instigator,) an

uncommonly intelligent negro, reappeared with the Yankees, as their guide. There could not be a better qualified guide for all that neighborhood, & for half the county. It is an unexampled state of things, of itself sufficiently indicating the understood villainy of the invaders, when every family within their reach flees in haste, & at enormous sacrifices. No family has remained except those too poor to move. We have heard of no individual accepting protection, & which would be obtained by taking the oath of allegiance to the northern power.

Aug. 9. Deplorable loss. The iron-clad steam ram "Arkansas," which had just lately commenced operations, & had performed such great & important feats, has been destroyed! It got near to Baton Rouge, when the machinery became deranged, & consequently its progress was stopped. [2156] While thus disabled as to movement, & endeavoring to repair the damage, the vessel was attacked by several of the enemy's war steamers, & after a gallant & ineffectual resistance, it was set fire to, evacuated, & blown up. This is the third powerful vessel of this kind we have had thus destroyed, to prevent falling into the hands of the enemy—& just after, as to two of them, they had acted better & had more success than our most sanguine anticipations would have indicated. . . . Northern reports, from correspondents in McClellan's camp, admit but the loss of 9 men killed, & some horses, by our ill managed night cannonade, & some vessels slightly damaged. The worst development is that very few of our shells exploded—which I fear is true—& nearly all the explosions that were within my view, were much too early, & too high, to do any damage. I fear, from this specimen, that our bomb-shells generally are worthless.—The Yankees have believed for some time that our iron-clad gun-boat at Richmond is completed, & northern papers even report that it is below Fort Drewry. I wish it may be ready in another month. Evidently it is a cause of serious alarm to the Yankees[29]—as [2157] was the Arkansas for the whole lower Mississippi. I fear that the fatality which seems to attend all our efforts to use iron-clad steamers will not change in this case. . . . Our military conduct in

---

[29] Union authorities were indeed worried about the C.S.S. *Richmond* (or *Merrimac* No. 2). For example, the Federal gunboats failed to respond promptly to the Confederate night bombardment of August 1 because most of them, as McClellan explained to Halleck, were "some 3 miles up the river, prepared to meet the Merrimac No. 2 and her consort, which had been reported to be on their way down from Richmond." *Ibid.*, 935.

Prince George shows great want of good direction by officers, & also of courage in the men engaged. Every day, a small troop of Yankee cavalry has advanced some miles from their camp, & beyond the posts of their pickets, & our pickets have regularly fled before these advances. If several parties of our men, 10 to 20 together, were placed in ambush in the margins of thick woods along the roads used, & would wait to fire on the passing troopers, with double barrelled guns loaded with buck-shot, they would kill half of the company, & easily escape from the still remaining superior force. Such defence would have also so alarmed the enemy that their marauding operations would have been much more limited.

Aug. 10. Sunday. The spell of extremely hot weather still continues.—Up to last night, the Yankee advances beyond their pickets had been confined to daytime. But last night a body of some 30 were out late, & drove off (as usual) without a shot being fired at them, our picket of 5 troopers posted a short distance above Garysville. Dr. Harrison, with the remainder of his family, with a wagon containing luggage &c. was then coming up, & the wagon captured, while the persons escaped with difficulty.... [2158]

Aug. 11. A previous discredited report is confirmed, that Lincoln has called out for service, in addition to the 300,000 men for the war, 300,000 more for 9 months—making 600,000 additional troops at once. As the half could not be obtained by volunteering, (& indeed very few volunteers had offered,) a draft of the militia must be enforced for the whole. I deem this astounding fact to be good news for us. It indicates the present weakness, the alarm, & the desperation of the Northern government. I believe that this unprecedented burden of such extent of military service will not be borne by some of the states. It will invigorate the so far dormant opposition to the government, of whose existence, though silent & ruled by terror, increasing evidences have been seen lately.... A partial engagement took place on the 9th between the armies of Jackson & Pope—in which the latter was driven back some miles. We know no other particulars, except that 300 prisoners, including Brig. Gen. [Henry] Prince & 29 other officers, had been sent to Richmond.[30] It was reported yesterday that heavy reinforcements had been sent

---

[30] At Cedar Mountain, on August 9, Banks's corps struck two of Jackson's divisions and drove them back until the timely arrival of A. P. Hill turned the tide in favor of the Confederates. Banks lost more than a fourth of his command—2,353 of 8,030—while Confederate casualties numbered 1,338 out of nearly 17,000 engaged.

from Richmond to Jackson on the evening of 8th. It was understood in Richmond that the greater part of McClellan's army had been sent to reinforce Pope. If this is true, if 50,000 men are sent to Jackson now it may not make him equal to Pope, when a reinforcement of 30,000 two weeks ago would have made him overwhelmingly superior in numbers. . . . Some 6 or 8 weeks ago there were serious & bloody riots in Cincinnati & other western cities between the negroes & low whites, mostly Irishmen & Germans, who were competitors for labor. The late increase of negroes in the north, by accession of deserters from the south, & their necessities, have induced them to hire themselves for very low wages, & by such competition to induce the discharge of the white laborers previously employed. These bitter & even bloody conflicts will naturally produce strong feelings of hostility between the two classes, which will extend to all negroes, & all whites of the lower class. And when this step is reached, the next consequence will be the massacre & extermination of the negroes in the localities where the greatest excitement has been raised. Like occurrences have lately taken place, & on a large scale, in Brooklyn, N.Y., & they are expected in Washington D.C. There a secret association & league exists among the negroes, to defend themselves from the attacks they expect.—It is stated that Lincoln has refused to accept the offered military service of two regiments of negroes.[31] This would indicate his opposition to the extreme policy urged by the abolition party. On the other hand, he lately was present, & was the chief speaker, in a [2160] popular meeting in Washington, in which Ex-Gov. [George S.] Boutwell of Mass. took the extreme abolition ground, including the employment of negro troops, & was loudly applauded, without any expression of dissent. Lincoln can have no scruples as to that or any other extreme measure of abolition policy. But he is afraid of taking either side boldly & consistently, & hence his vacilating [*sic*] course. By taking a decided stand against the measures demanded by them, he will offend & may lose the support of the extreme abolition party, now the most powerful. If he adopts them fully, he will increase & perhaps render potential the new conservative party, (embracing the democrats & all other opponents of the abolitionists,) which is now beginning to dare to speak. . . . Three of the oldest residents within 8 miles of Marl-

---

[31] The President suggested instead that the proffered Negroes from Indiana be employed as laborers. This incident occurred on August 4.

bourne, & two of them, Dr. Henry Curtis & Dr. William R. Nelson valued friends of mine, died within a few weeks after the occupancy of their farms by the Yankees, & their being driven off. Though all old men, their ages being from 71 to 87 years, I think it likely that their deaths, occurring so near together, were all hastened by the excitement & disturbance of mind caused by the actual & expected outrages of the Yankees.

Aug. 13. A short dispatch from Gen. Jackson claims having taken 400 prisoners & 1500 small arms. Other accounts state our killed & wounded at 800, & suppose (but can only guess) that the enemy's loss was very far greater. Gen. C[harles S.] Winder on our side was killed. . . . It is reported to the general (D. H. Hill) commanding here that McClellan is evacuating his positions at Berkley & Westover. If this is true, or even probable, it seems to me that this is the time, when his numbers are reduced (& if not by evacuation, certainly by sickness,) for our commander to attack his camp. It is certain that large reinforcements have been sent from McClellan's army to Pope—& if a complete evacuation should be designed, it probably will be to transfer the war to the north of Richmond. McClellan must have already despaired of advancing to Richmond from his late position. . . .

Aug. 14. The battle of the 9th. (of South-West Mountain, or Cedar Creek,) did not continue longer than that evening. The later accounts, though still imperfect, add more & more to the glory of our victory. . . . Northern as well as southern accounts report that our guerrillas are swarming & increasing daily in Missouri, & have command in northern Mo. Also in West Tennessee. . . . Guerrilla warfare is a most potent means for defence for a country like ours, invaded & ravaged by an enemy that disregards all laws of war, & obligations of justice or humanity. But in civil war, (as in Mo. & Ten.,) it is apt to become a contest of wide-spread robbery & murder. . . . And this system I would be glad to see established, if to [2164] be confined to men under arms. But as the invaded [*sic*— invad*ing*] party, the lawless enemy have the great advantage of their illegal captures & imprisonments of numerous civilians, & wherever in power they may extend such arrests to any desired number, & for killing, if that was the rule, as now for imprisonment, or parole release. Why our government has so far submitted to this outrageous policy of the Yankee authorities in taking or treating our civilian citizens as prisoners of war—& even in some cases exchanging for them lawful Yankee prisoners—is to me inconceivable. It is the well-grounded fear of such arrest, & imprisonment as the alternative of the prisoner refusing to swear allegiance to the Yankee government, that compels the flight of nearly all the population, wherever the Yankees have possession, or are expected, as now in our unfortunate neighborhood. . . .

Aug. 15. Reports continue, & seem credible, that McClellan's army, or the larger portion, is evacuating Berkley & the peninsula. All Burnside's command, which had come as reinforcement since the late battles, has since certainly gone to Fredericksburg—& probably many more of McClellan's grand army have also gone to reinforce Pope. . . . Together with Lincoln's order (through the War Dept.,) to arrest all persons trying to leave the country or otherwise evade the ordered draft, subjecting offenders to serve as if drafted, & also to pecuniary penalty, there has [been] issued another short order still more stringent, which, [2166] if submitted to, will make Lincoln as despotic, & unlimited in his exercise of power & punishment, as the rulers of Russia & Turkey. This order commands Provosts-Martial [*sic*] & other officers, military & civil, to arrest & imprison all persons who in any manner shall by speech, writing, publication or otherwise, discourage the volunteering or enlistment of soldiers for the U.S. service, or do any thing else to give aid or comfort to the enemy (the southern rebels). The writ of *habeas corpus* is already suspended. So that at the discretion of any subordinate officer, any person, for any word or act deemed unfriendly to the military action or policy of Lincoln's government, may be imprisoned, & detained under the worst treatment for an unlimited time, unless released by death. This order puts an end to all that before remained of the liberty of speech, of the press, or of voting or action, of any northern man opposed to the war or to the policy of the government. Degraded as are the Yankee people, & ignorant of constitutional restrictions & political rights, & accustomed to think every measure right & lawful that will operate to forward the views of the majority of the people, I cannot believe that they will quietly submit to this last & deadly blow to their rights & liberty, in conjunction with the drafting of 600,000 additional troops. . . . By proclamation of the Governor, in this day's papers [2167], all the militia between 35 & 45 years, & therefore exempt from present service under the C.S. conscript law, of 40 south-western counties of Va., are called into immediate service, to defend western Va. under Gen. Floyd. He was appointed to this service by the legislature of Va. & authorized to recruit 10,000 men then exempt from conscript service. But the voluntary enlistments have come in so slowly, that this compulsory measure is resorted to.

Aug. 16. . . . Two days ago I saw Judge Perkins here, on his way to Richmond to attend Congress. He asked & urged me to visit him there—& to suggest to him any of my views of public affairs. Though I expect no result from it, today I wrote to him a full sheet of hints & suggestions of public faults & abuses, & of measures which I think ought to be adopted or tried. I named as errors of the President the retaining in employment & trust proved incompetent officers, e.g. Gen. Huger, who had been retained to cause three great military disasters: the failure to punish deserters, spies & traitors: the employment of Yankee officers & agents, from which class nearly all deserters to the enemy, & traitors, had gone:—& as new measures recommended, the avoiding such errors: the withdrawal of further offers to England, & the offering special & exclusive (though only reciprocal) commercial favors to France for being the *first* to acknowledge our independence, & breaking the Yankee blockade: the enacting prohibitions on the future purchase, import, or use of all Yankee commodities, (after peace shall be made,) & the immigration & settlement of northern men, except under proper & valid restrictions, the use of northern vessels or agents &c.: the instituting negotiations, through secret agents, with the opposition party & its leaders in the north-western states, to bring about a separate peace with them, by offering not only the free navigation of the Mississippi, to which they would be entitled by the law of nations, but also of free [2168] trade with the Southern Confederacy, & every benefit & facility of trade & navigation, provided our municipal & police laws, & especially in reference to slaves, should be duly guarded & respected.—Afternoon, heard from Mr. [William] Pannill, the Provost-Marshal, that later evidences confirm the previous reports that McClellan's army is evacuating his post at & near Berkley, & going down the river. On reliable information Mr. P. had heard that 108 vessels, mostly transports full of men or of freight, had gone down the river within the last 24 hours. It is also said that very few vessels still remained off Berkley. The dependent posts at Beechwood & Maycox must also be evacuated with the principal post. This, at least, McClellan must admit to be defeat of his grand movement on Richmond. No doubt all these troops go to reinforce the armies under Pope & Burnside, extending from Culpeper to Fredericksburg. Large reinforcements have been going for some time also to Jackson, said to amount to near or quite 50,000 men. His prior force, including all, did not exceed 35,000. I fear that the opposed Yankee armies, now increased by all of McClellan's, must still be much more numerous than ours. Gen. Lee either had gone, or was about to go yesterday, to assume the chief command of our forces. A tremendous conflict must soon occur, with the most important consequences of a decisive victory to either side. We may be falsely confident—but there is not a doubt expressed by any on our side of our army being victorious. [2169]

Aug. 17. Sunday.—When the family returned from Church they were informed on unquestionable authority that the Yankees had evacuated Beechwood yesterday. As soon as hearing this, I determined to ride down there immediately after dinner. I wished to see the condition of things as soon as possible after it was safe to do so. Also I thought that some neighborhood pillagers would soon follow after the Yankees, if the place continued vacant. I rode to Mr. Callender's, & learned that Julian (before knowing this news,) had designed to go to Ruthven this afternoon, to carry on thrashing more of his wheat. I then rode on, & was soon overtaken by Edmund, who had not determined to go before I had left him. We rode on so briskly, as to cause to me much fatigue & soreness. Passing through Mrs. Cocke's (Tarbay) land, we saw the first marks of the Yankee picket posts, in their destruction of the growing corn on one side, & of the reaped wheat shocks on the other [side] of the road. However, it was not much more reckless than the usual like damages of our own soldiers, & previously exhibited on Beechwood. On entering the luxuriant corn growing on the field in which Beechwood mansion stands, as far as we could see on either side, & also much farther off, as seen later, every ear of the green corn seemed to have been gathered for "roasting ears." Such extent of use could not be supposed to be merely for this force, but rather, as I supposed, for all McClellan's army, or to be shipped with them for vegetable food. On approaching the deserted mansion, we saw evidences of the destruction. The yard was scattered over with rubbish—broken chairs & other furniture—broken dishes & plates & other crockery—feathers emptied from the ticks of feather beds, & the different other filling materials of mattresses. The doors of the houses

were all open, & many of the windows broken in glass or sashes.
The keys, which had been left together, & where easily to be seen
by the robbers, after the easy breaking into the house, had all been
[2170] thrown away or carried off, except the key of one closet,
which was found later. Most of the best furniture had been removed by the owner before the occupation by the Yankees. But
some of the best, & most of the inferior furniture had been left.
Among this, were all the mirrors—left because so liable to be
broken in being moved—& because the bombarding of the buildings was the injury looked for, & not the occupation by Yankee
forces, & the consequent pillaging by them, or by transient marauding parties. So the mirrors were placed in the basement, where
safest from bomb-shells, & were all stolen & carried off. The mansion is a new, & commodious & handsome building. The surrounding grounds, bounded by the firm & clear river sand beach, are the
most beautiful that I know—not so much for what art has done for
their improvement, as for their natural features.[32] The only credit to
be given to the villainous Yankees is that they did not burn the

---

[32] Apparently, the diarist did not exaggerate. In a letter dated August 11, 1862,
from Harrison's Landing, an unidentified Union soldier who had participated in the
occupation of Beechwood conveyed his impression of the estate to his brother and
sister in these words:

I wish I had the ability to describe the home of the Ruffins to you. It is the
only place I have yet seen that gave much evidence that the owner is anything
more than in name and pretension an F.F.V. The house itself is not very large
or pretentious, but it shows that it was the abode of wealth and taste. . . . The
grounds about this place are the most beautifully laid out of any I have ever
seen. It is the realization of the imaginary residences of the heroines we read
of in romance. Before the house is a beautiful clean-swept lawn, shaded by
magnificent oaks and tulip trees that look as though they have seen a century's
growth at least. And then, the winding walks and avenues, shady bowers and
summer houses covered with roses and drooping with graceful festoons of
flowers, whose names are unknown to me, but whose beauty and fragrance I
can appreciate—you must see them to know their beauty. The "servants'
quarters" are not the miserable log huts with mud floors like those at the White
House, but clean painted frame buildings, tastefully arranged in the shade of
those old trees. A little apart from the main building is a smaller one, where I
imagine the master spent most of his time. It was his library, study and office.
He is evidently a scholar and a writer of no mean ability. . . . His library was
very large and valuable, mostly of agricultural works, but containing a great
number of scientific and classical books. Thousands of books were carried off
by our men.

Typed copy in possession of Mr. and Mrs. Sterling P. Anderson, Jr., of Upper
Marlbourne, Virginia. For another description of Beechwood by a member of the
Union occupation force, see below, page 576, *n* 28.

buildings & did not materially injure the surrounding trees, of the yard & the open wood next to the river—or the wild & natural woods adjoining. Every apartment of the mansion, & also of the older cottage building of 4 rooms in the yard, (the earlier residence of the family,) were covered, still more thickly than the yard, with the rubbish & litter produced by the general breakage & destruction of everything that could not be conveniently stolen & carried off. It is needless to particularize the damages. Every article of furniture or crockery, showed not only material damage from breakage, when not totally destroyed, but in such manner as to be evident that it was not the result of accident, or neglect, but of wilful & malignant design. My own apartment, in the older Cottage, had been left just as I had used it, except that previously, or when I left with my son's family, I had sent to Ruthven a box containing my most valuable manuscripts & some scarce printed articles of my writing, & all my family letters—with a few of my best maps &c. My bed [2171] & other furniture, most of the contents of my drawers & desk, remained as they had been. Not a single book was sent off for greater safety either by myself or my son—& I suppose that our two libraries, together, amounted to some thousands of volumes & valuable pamphlets. My clothing, & some of my most precious smaller articles, all contained in my travelling trunk, were nearly all that were removed. . . . The mansion, though so greatly preferable as a house, was ill fitted for lodgers, because most of the beds &c. had been removed. Therefore, as I infer, it was abandoned to the private soldiers, or low officers. My room, being ready for use, with a new & excellent spring-buttressed mattress, & every chamber accommodation in a plain manner, was occupied & used by the commander of the force, whose name I have not yet learned. Hence the difference of action, generally, by the different occupants. The common soldiers had but small facilities for carrying away plunder—& therefore they mostly destroyed or damaged the moveables, & defaced & befouled the house. The commander, having at his will the requisite means for [2172] transportation, used them, either alone or in conjunction with other officers, to steal & send off, probably for sale in New York, & as a pecuniary speculation, all of our books, perhaps my other papers, & various other things of mine, & also the books, mirrors &c. belonging to my son. All my furniture, except the bed-stead, also was broken. Though all my drawers, three book-cases, & desk, were designedly left open, to prevent pillagers

breaking them open, every one was more or less broken. Open doors . . . were wrenched off the hinges, & every drawer was more or less damaged. My harmonicon, though lately unused, & valued mainly as a memento of past pleasures & incidents, had every glass removed. . . . A valuable magic lantern, with numerous glass slides of figures, was another of the stolen articles. Also some valued framed engravings. A terrestrial globe was broken. But what I most regret, though of no pecuniary value, & scarcely worth the stealing & removal, were all of my general correspondence, or letters written to me by all persons except the members of my own family . . . for more than the last twenty years. There were some rare fossil shells which I brought from Alabama—& a mass of silicified crystals formed on a calcareous core, or internal foundation, very beautiful & curious, which I obtained from the sand barrier of Florida.—The only exceptions to the universal plunder or breakage of all moveables, were in regard to some few articles of furniture that seemed to have been regularly used by the occupants of the houses—as my bedstead, my small writing table, some old mattresses & common chairs, used by the officers or soldiers. These were kept for their own use, so long as they stayed, & their final departure was evidently very hasty, so that there [2173] probably was not opportunity for the intended final destruction of these articles. . . . The hooks in the closets & other places in the mansion, for hanging articles upon, the screws, every bell of the establishment, & indeed almost every thing that could be detached from the walls, & of the least separate value, were taken off. All these stolen goods will furnish commodities for a curious auction sale in New York—of which, when it shall take place, I would like much to hear an account.—The walls ("hard-finished" with plaster of Paris) of the apartments of the mansion, were in some places defiled with being spit upon by tobacco-chewers, even when the operation cost some trouble. But this was nothing compared to the blacking & defacing the walls by the names of soldiers written with charcoal, & sometimes their opinions. Some of the latter show that malignity to myself, as well as to my son, for our zealous action in support of the independence of the South, was a main ingredient in the causes of destruction of the property. I will insert some of these examples of Yankee sentiment. I take the scurrilous abuse thrown upon myself very complacently—as being the only compliment or eulogism that a low-bred Yankee can bestow on me.
—"We pity but do not hate the rebels."

[419]

—(After the name of the writer—) "Soon coming again with the next 600,000."

—"This house belonged to a Ruffinly son of a bitch."

—"Old Ruffin don't you wish you had left the Southern Confederacy to go to Hell, (where it will go,) & had stayed at home?"

—"You did fire the first gun on Sumter, you traitor [2174] son of a bitch."

—"Miss Nannie

We had a very pleasant time last evening on board the (U.S. gunboat) 'Cayoga.' Very sorry that you were not there to preside at your Piano—Forte. We did in your place."

The writer of this, by similarity of hand-writing, seems to be the same who elsewhere wrote his name as "Prof. Thos. Lane, Co. B.—7th Pa. Cavalry." The scamp was mistaken in his supposition that the stolen instrument on which he performed, had been plundered from my granddaughter. It had been stolen from Mrs. Cocke's house.—Of 31 names which I copied, with their military positions, all belonged to one or the other of the 4th (?) 7th 9th 10th & 12th regiments of Pennsylvania Cavalry, (or P.R.V.C.) except one who signed himself of "12 Reg. Pa. Reserved Corps" & one other, who belonged to "16th Mich. Regt." Neither are these low blackguards of the "Pennsylvania Dutch." Of the 31 names, there are but six which are not genuine English or Yankee. Some of the charcoal writings were either indelicate or obscene—& had no other attraction. Yet an officer, (Lieut. H. B. Fox, 10th Reg. P.R.V.C.,) was one of these charcoal name-writers,[33] & doubtless other & high officers daily saw & did not discourage these writings, or the wanton destruction of furniture &c. In the four apartments of the cottage, there was but one name written, as if the offence there was promptly forbidden—& which goes further to prove that officers only were quartered therein, & performed the stealing, their peculiar operation, as that of privates was to damage, destroy or defile what they had no facilities for carrying off.—This occupation of this farm by the Yankees has caused to my son the further loss of almost every thing on it that was moveable or destructible [2175]. Among these latest losses of the farm, are 10 mules—all his remaining cattle except 3 . . . all his remaining hogs, except a few at large, & all the remaining sheep—nearly 200 bushels of corn then remain-

---

[33] Ironically, Lieutenant Henry B. Fox was killed in action two weeks later at Second Manassas. *Official Records*, Vol. XII, Pt. 2, p. 819.

ing—& all the slaves still here, 11 in number. Of these 5 were so old as, taken together, to be a heavy expense. Three of the five had been past labor for years, (or free from all regular labor,) yet receiving full allowances. Of course the loss of all these is a pecuniary gain to the owner. Also of another, a woman Pinkey, whom I mentioned before in respect to her husband, mother, & grown son, & brother, all going to the Yankees, leaving her on her dying bed. She had been for some 8 months confined to her room, & latterly to her bed, with a lingering but mortal disease—tenderly cared for & provided by her master & his family, including the regular attendance of the family physician, until he himself stated that he could do nothing for her—after which he only came rarely & when convenient to call, & merely to prevent the manifestation which his entire absence would cause to the doomed poor creature that there was no hope for her. When the successive heavy losses of slaves at last compelled Edmund to remove nearly all, & to sell a part of those remaining, of course this woman could not be moved—& could not be left without proper attendance, when the white family had removed. So her daughter of 18 years, & a younger one of 8, were left with her, merely as company, & to nurse & wait upon her. I then suggested to Edmund that the young woman would probably, on the first opportunity, desert her mother & abscond to the Yankees, following the example of others of the family. He answered that he thought it very probable. But if he was even sure of it, in his own mind, he still would leave the daughter to nurse the mother, as the most [2176] proper person. When the Yankees suddenly appeared here, & all others of the remaining slaves were either forced, or of their own will, crossed the river to McClellan's army (or worked in the trenches here,) this woman, & her two daughters, not only refused to go, but she left her home & made out to walk 1½ miles to a neighbor's house, where one old negro woman remained alone, because she pretended to be unable to walk, & therefore was left by the Yankee negro-stealers. . . . As soon as the retreat of the Yankees permitted any person to go to this place, Edmund came down this day, & brought tea & sugar & as necessary for her supposed condition, if alive. He went, & heard from the old woman that Pinkey & both her daughters had gone to the Yankees, notwithstanding her feeble condition. Mr. Botts' kitchen, where she was then lying, was near the daily passage of the Yankee scouting parties, & some of them called there almost every day. The inducement urged upon her, & to which she yielded, was the (doubtless false) pretence that her husband was at Berkley, & she would there join him. If he had been there, & desired to come to his wife, he might have done so by permission, any day since the occupation of Beechwood by the Yankees. Or, even if not desiring it, he would have been sent over with the others to work on the intrenchments. It is inconceivable to me why the Yankees should recently have departed from [2177] their first policy, of refusing to receive aged & useless negroes. Now, in this neighborhood, they have invited & forced off all, including the most aged & infirm, and also most unwilling, & such as must be altogether burdensome to their captors, unless abandoned to starve.—After having taken a late & hasty glance at the intrenchment, & heard from pickets that there were no Yankee vessels remaining off their late camp, we left for Ruthven—which I reached sometime after dark. . . .

Aug. 18. After breakfast, Edmund returned to Beechwood to meet his wagon & carts, & to gather what should be moved from the wreck of moveables—& I with him, to make more full observations of what I have already noted about the buildings, & to go to the Point. The intrenchment (still unfinished,) was dug along the margin of the highest ground near the site of my old residence, & extending to where the mansion stood, to defend the position against any approach or attack from outside of the peninsula. No cannon had been mounted, & probably none were designed to be used, as the work was more for deception than direct use. It now seems that the object of the occupation on this side of the river was only for the purpose of concealing the intended movements of McClellan's retreat, & to prevent attack on either his army or transports during the evacuation. The late advance of a strong force & their transient occupation of Malvern Hill had the same object of disguising his intentions, & effecting the evacuation before it would be suspected. The whole remainder of his army left the Berkley side, [2178] & passed down the river on Friday, the 15th, a day earlier than the removal of the force from this side. Besides the work of the intrenchment, the Yankees have cut down some 8 or 10 acres of the Grove, including many of the very large venerable old oaks, & the cluster of very large & beautiful hollies, preserved, with the remainder of this grove, for ornament, & especially for the many large & magnificent oak trees, ever since the farm was settled. Also they had cut down the thickets at the end of the Point, & the trees on some of the hillsides & ravines south of the peninsula, which might have concealed advancing troops. 8 or 10 acres of growing corn farther out, had been cut down for the same object. A very large & beautiful oak tree which stood on a high & open position in Middle Field, was killed by being cut around, for no use or object, except for wanton mischief.—Our cavalry pickets are again on the Point. Not a single vessel was near, except a line of gunboats, 9 in number, stretching from near Jordan's Point diagonally downward towards the Charles City side, with some 10 sailing transports in the close neighborhood. These gunboats have been here (or others) for nearly three weeks, no doubt expecting & watching for the arrival of our iron-clad steamer—which is still in preparation in Richmond, & I fear far from being ready. It is at least doing some service to keep from 9 to 12 Yankee gunboats (including the Monitor & Galena,) lying idle so long. In a bottom near the end of the Point I found a company of light artillery, with 4 brass guns, under command of Col. Thompson Brown.[34] They had arrived late yesterday evening. By incautious exposure of some of the men, the enemy had suspected the presence of increased force. A gun-boat had just before steamed down to just above opposite Ruffin's Bluff, & had fired 5 or 6 shells, & [2179] had already returned to its previous position above in the line. I had heard the first of these discharges soon after I had left the house to ride to the Point, & the others before I reached there. I saw from the smoke, through the trees which partially obscured my view all the way, whence the mortar-firing proceeded. Soon after I arrived, & heard from Col. Brown (who with other officers was looking out from the covered margin of the line of bluff,) that the shells had been aimed to this side. Very soon after, the same gunboat returned to its previous position— which as I afterwards found was such as to allow its shells to range along the stretch of straight road near the upper barn, & to have exposed to the same fire the barn, stable, overseer's house, & two other farm buildings nearly in the same line by side of the road. The

---

[34] The son of a prominent Petersburg lawyer, John Thompson Brown (1835–64) commanded the First Virginia Artillery at this time. His unit remained in the Richmond area until after Second Manassas, but he rendered distinguished service at Fredericksburg and Chancellorsville and was the senior battalion commander of the Second Corps artillery at Gettysburg. Colonel Thompson was killed in May, 1864, at the outset of the Wilderness campaign. Freeman characterized him as "an able and conscientious soldier, patient and diligent in administration but not brilliant." *Lee's Lieutenants,* II, 707.

first discharge of this renewed attack struck the upper branches of a tree on the edge of the bluff near where I was standing with the colonel, & fell about 200 yards farther on, in the open field. I suppose that a retreat was immediately ordered, as I saw it soon in progress, & in great haste. I had before mounted my horse, & was riding slowly homeward, but was very soon overtaken, & left far behind by the rapidly retreating artillery—which had not fired a gun, & could have done nothing if firing. Having stopped for a short time on the way, when I arose up the road to the highest ground, outside of the peninsula, the artillery company was half a mile ahead of me. Both by the noise made by the carriages, & the great dust raised, its course was easily distinguished by the gunboat, which continued to throw shells ranging very nearly with the direction of the road before & after it passes the barn. . . . When I was within 300 yards of the barn, where my route would diverge, a bomb-shell fell about 100 to 150 yards ahead of me, throwing up a thick cloud of dust, seemingly within 10 yards of the road. . . . The firing continued for more than an hour, regularly, & until 12 M. After reaching the house, I watched the discharges from the beach, where I could see the gunboat plainly. And though the aim continued to be (as I supposed,) still the same, & not ranging within a third of a mile of the mansion, the sounds of the shells seemed so unpleasantly near, that my son hurried off the wagon which had before been filled, & sent off the team & servants. I then proceeded to Ruthven, & Edmund also came later. The firing had been suspended. But when I was again approaching the road by the barn, & in full view, another shell was discharged, & struck the ground, (as shown by the heavy dust,) past the barn, & near the road. . . . The firing ceased then, but in the afternoon was renewed, & very rapidly for a short time only, as heard at Ruthven. . . .

Aug. 19. Edmund rode to Beechwood, to go thence to Petersburg. I also rode into the farm, to look more carefully for the marks or remains of bomb-shells of which I saw the striking, & knew nearly the places. From the first pickets met with, I heard that the gunboat, (which I saw anchored in the same place,) had been shelling the land early this morning, & that our pickets had then fallen back from the Point, & were now a mile out, & at the post below the barn. I therefore declined going then on the Point, for so unimportant an object [2182]. I then turned back to search for the first shell I had seen strike near the barn, & to my then position. I soon found two large hollows, gouged out of the earth, & within two yards of each other, & within 15 to 17 yards of the road. On the loose earth thrown out of each, I found a fragment of the exploded shell, one of iron, of about a pound in weight, & the other of lead of perhaps lbs. 3. . . . The firing (judging by the lead found,) was from a large rifled cannon—& the distance about 1¾ miles.—Returned by 11 A.M. I brought two fragments of the first seen shell, to add to my collection of such mementoes . . . . At night, by a servant sent by Edmund, we received newspapers of today. Congress met yesterday, & the President's Message is published. He recommends the organizing & preparing for service the reserve of the militia, including all from 35 to 45 years. Also, attention is called to the atrocities of the enemy, & some of the worst violations of the laws of war, & retaliation promised. I trust that these declarations will not be all.

Aug. 20. After breakfast, left Ruthven for Petersburg, where I found Edmund's family well, & Thomas continuing to strengthen slowly. [2183] . . . I had not seen all of the Yankee writings at Beechwood. There have been sent to us by Dr. Dupuy, an old book left there, on the blank leaves of which were written three several notes addressed either to my son or myself. Also, a letter left upon the mantel, more elaborate & pretentious in composition, in which the writer ironically offers thanks to the proprietor for the abundant supplies which the occupants had been luxuriating in, & boasts & claims thanks for the care they had taken of the property. One of the writings on the book was as follows:—"Owned by Old Ruffin, the basest old traitor rebel in the United States. You old cuss, it is a pity you go unhanged." . . . The letter left at Beechwood shows that the troops quartered there were part of the Third Brigade, Gen. [George A.] McCall's Division, of Pa.[35] There were among our stolen books my farm journals kept while I owned & resided on Coggin's Point. Another collection of writings (stitched together,) I also much regret the loss & probable exposure [of]. It contained nearly all of my earliest writings for the newspapers, &c. & also the letters of some distinguished [2184] correspondents, on agricultural subjects, written to me about 1821 & later. . . .

Aug. 22. The Express of this morning contains an editorial state-

---

[35] McCall himself was at this time incarcerated in Libby Prison in Richmond, having been captured in the engagement at White Oak Swamp on June 30.

ment, in contradiction to the previous acquittance of the Yankees, & which the editor obtained (as to the facts) from my information.[36] But neither my concise statement to him, nor my own in this journal, which was designed to be full, contain all of even important depredations. I omitted, by forgetfulness, the stealing & carrying off of two large & excellent farm wagons—& the breaking of the reaping & thrashing [2185] machines—the stealing of every valuable farm utensil & tool, even the most useless to them, including the supply bought in the Spring for this year's use, & which had not been used at all, because there remained none to labor with them. The two barns, overseer's house, & other of the farm buildings were seriously damaged in the tearing off the boarding, breaking of windows, doors &c. My son Edmund, the only wealthy member of my family, was therefore by far the heaviest loser by the plundering of the enemy—including 80 of his slaves from his two farms Beechwood & Evelynton, & 6 more being his proportion of those lost (finally) from Marlbourne, the joint property of himself & three others of my family. But all the direct losses, from plundering & destruction by the Yankee troops & vessels, & their taking off slaves, is less than the indirect losses of crops &[c]. . . . But this is not near the end. The season (& means) for ploughing for the next year's crop of wheat are already gone. And even if peace should be made in a month, two-thirds, at least, of what would otherwise have been the next year's crops of wheat must be lost. Besides, the business of the farms is broken up & suspended indefinitely, except at Marlbourne, where the weaker (or helpless) slaves remain, & are employed to little use—& where there is no remaining team force. What will be the total losses (already suffered & necessarily incurred) cannot be estimated with any approach to accuracy. But even if they should extend no farther than can now be clearly seen, I do not think that they would be covered by less than $150,000. . . . Wheat now sells at $2.40. If the three crops of wheat alone could have been saved, they would be worth $30,000 in market. The large crops of clover, of unprecedented luxuriance, would have been

---

[36] Reacting to an earlier article, printed on August 20, in which the writer had largely acquitted Federal forces of acts of wanton destruction upon the James River plantations in Prince George County, the diarist had immediately dispatched a letter to the editor of the Petersburg *Express*, detailing the damages inflicted upon Beechwood and Tarbay.

made into hay, & sold at $1.50 to 1.75 the hundred pounds, & would have yielded a larger amount than either the crop of wheat or corn, in ordinary times. The owners have already advertised the offer to sell Marlbourne, at private sale, but have had no bidder. [2187] It will be scarcely expedient, if possible, to re-stock & cultivate either of the three farms, while this region & our rivers are entirely open to the inroads & depredations of the enemy. . . . On a motion of thanks to our generals & armies engaged in the battles near Richmond, I am glad to see that an amendment was offered to except Gen. Huger. It was lost by 27 to 46 votes. But the discussion was full & free, & Gen. Huger gained but little by the vote. The minority embraced Speaker [Thomas S.] Bocock, & many of the most able & patriotic members. Of those who spoke in opposition to excepting Huger, there was but one who said any thing in his vindication. All the others disclaimed being his advocates or defenders, & opposed the amendment, as being contrary to all precedent, inexpedient, & improper in advance of full knowledge of the facts. One of these opponents of the amendment, Mr. [James] Lyons of Va, said that if what he had heard of Huger was true, he would be glad to vote for his being not only cashiered, but shot. Foote of Ten., who moved the amendment, among other severe remarks, said that Huger "had the reputation of being slow—very slow—slow all the time. He was slow in coming over to the South, when separation was determined on. He was slow at Norfolk; slow at Roanoke Island; slow at Seven Pines; slow [2189] in the battles of the Chickahominy. Who can vindicate him?" . . . Mr. Beegleston, lately overseer at Evelynton, today came to report the present condition of things. Nothing had before been heard since the ineffectual attempts to bring the livestock across the river, before the last battles near Richmond. I expected to hear, of course, that the farm had been stripped of everything moveable, including the grain, forage, mules, cattle & hogs—none of which had been even partly removed. But not only had all these been plundered, but every building on the farm had been completely torn down, & the timbers used, except a piece of the overseer's house, which only had been left standing. The barn & stable were valuable buildings, not long erected. To the additional injury of the farm, the enemy constructed through its length, along the high crest facing the river & Westover, a large intrenchment, which will require much cost of labor to level. Other farms within their lines were treated even worse. Even the brick chimneys of the demolished dwelling houses were pulled down, & used to construct ovens. . . .

Aug. 24. Sunday. . . . Wrote a plan for a war of retaliation & vengeance—which I afterwards enclosed to Judge Perkins. Considering that the outrages, in violation of the laws of war, practised by the Yankee forces, by orders of their commanders, & under authority of their government, can, for the greater part, be perpetrated only by invaders, *e.g.* the plundering & destruction of private property, the burning of houses & towns, the stealing our slaves, & consequent loss of crops, the imprisonment of non-combatants &c.—and that if we should (most justly) retaliate for these acts, by putting to death Yankee soldiers held as prisoners, the enemy, being in our country, cannot only capture as many military prisoners to retaliate upon, but can increase to any extent the acts of outrage on private property & non-combatants. The only mode of effective retaliation is to invade their territory, & visit upon the Yankees at home the like sufferings, tenfold increased. I would send three armies, each of 10 to 25,000 men, properly constituted & equipped for rapid movement & hard fighting, & led by such men as Jackson, Price, Stuart, Morgan & Forrest, to invade Pennsylvania, & (through [2191] Kentucky,) Ohio & Illinois or Indiana. I would proclaim in advance, "Peace to friends, & to the poor—war and ruin to enemies, & especially to the wealthy." The destitute & laboring classes should be invited to possess themselves of the property of the rich, in advance of the occupation by our army—or if not before, to join in sacking & burning every town occupied, unless ransomed from our forces (& not from their own desperadoes,) by paying heavy contributions. . . . Such incursions would strike terror into the great body of the Yankee people, who, at home, have been safe from & scarcely knowing the evils they have supported their government in inflicting on the South. After these successful & destructive inroads, I would proclaim that we had retaliated for & avenged the past enormities of our enemy, & were willing to return to our previous observance of the laws of war, if our enemy so chose, & would so act. If not, we were ready for [2192] warfare of extermination. . . . Began to read [Thomas B.] McCaulay's [*sic*] "History of England" for the third time, for the want of any thing newer. Was surprised to find how interesting it was to me still. When I first read it, it was as interesting as a good novel—& far more so than the far greater number of novels of reputation. The portion of the preliminary sketch of English history, which extends from the beginning of the reign of Charles I to the restoration of Charles II, is especially interesting in the portraiture of Cromwell, the greatest king, if not the greatest man that England has produced—the most virtuous of usurpers, & the most moderate, just, & benign of despots.

Aug. 25. In daily expectation of the great battle of the Rappahannock, which has for a week seemed imminent, & yet is still delayed. We have reports of several skirmishes between different portions of our advanced forces & the enemy's rear, in all of which we gained the advantage. But the accounts are so confused, & the details so conflicting, that they are not worth noting, until confirmed. . . .

Aug. 26. My feverish anxiety to hear of the great battle still disappointed. Indeed, the papers of today unusually barren of news from all quarters. It is only certain of our army & Pope's, that the latter has continued to retreat, & ours closely to pursue—with frequent skirmishes between the Yankee rear & our advanced forces. . . . However scant & contradictory the details of the [2194] many reports, the general effect has been to cause general rejoicing in Richmond, & sanguine expectations of great success to our army. . . . One significant fact, showing the confidence of our commander, I saw myself this morning. A regiment of infantry, which before had been sent to Richmond, was ordered back, & was marching through this town southward, as I supposed, to their previous camp near Petersburg. Of course our authorities must be sure that no more reinforcements are needed by Gen. Lee. . . . What can Gen. Bragg be waiting for? The Yankee force, the remains of Halleck's large army, is separated in five different & remote points, stretching along the whole northern border of Alabama. Their separation, & this season of low waters & malaria, seem to offer the strongest facilities for the assailing & separately defeating all these scattered bodies. . . . Julian came yesterday, & returned [2195] to Ruthven with his family, to resume their permanent residence—taking back two wagon loads of his most necessary furniture. This forenoon, driven by Edmund in his buggy, I went also to Ruthven, for my home while present circumstances continue.—I have not yet stated all the important losses, or least excusable depredations, at Beechwood. . . . My son's older (though still serviceable) carriage had been left in the carriage house. . . . The carriage had been taken out, & rolled down the almost precipitous hillside of the Dark Glen, adjoining the yard & the Wilderness, &, of course, smashed into worthless rubbish. The conduct of the robbers in the negroes' houses was as bad as in their owner's mansion—& their treatment of the negroes, in every case heard of from the few decrepit ones left in the neighborhood, was brutal. When most of those of Beechwood who had not previously absconded, had been sent [2196] to Petersburg, there was not time, nor means for conveyance, to take away but a small portion of their clothing, & none of their furniture. All the articles besides were left in their houses in charge of old Adam, the foreman, not one of whose family had then absconded, & in whom full confidence was placed to discharge this as well as other more important trusts. When the Yankees landed & first occupied the farm, as I have before stated, every negro remaining (except, for a few days, the bed-ridden sick woman, who escaped, but afterwards went off also with her two daughters,) was taken off so suddenly that they had to leave their bedding, & some of their best clothing—articles much valued by them, & which they certainly would not have left, unless forced off instantaneously. The feather beds & bolsters thus left by the negroes were ripped open & the feathers scattered, & the wooden furniture cut up & broken, & other things torn to pieces by the Yankee marauders, apparently with as much pleasure as they robbed & destroyed the moveables of the proprietor. Mr. Spain, a near neighbor, had a woman who was not only very old, but helpless, because of other infirmities. When the sudden approach of the Yankees forced him, like all others near, to flee, with such of their property as could be most speedily conveyed away, this old woman was necessarily left—& a young woman to wait upon her, with a sufficient supply of provisions for both. The Yankee robbers could not carry off the old woman—& wanted no such burden. But they carried off her attendant, & took all their provisions—though afterwards, upon the earnest entreaty of the old woman, representing that she would [2197] starve, they left with her a small part of what had been designed for her supply. These & other incidents rest upon the telling of negroes who were witnesses—but the circumstances seem to make them trustworthy. One of the men who were taken off from Maycox, against his will, made his escape from Westover, & returned to his mistress after a few days. He reported that the next day after the arrival of the negroes from Maycox, all the boys among

[430]

them, not fit for working in the trenches, were separated, put on board a vessel about to go down the river, & sent to some destination unknown to them, & to their parents & relatives left behind. This order for their separation & removal was effected so suddenly, that some of the boys, who had thrown aside their jackets, close at hand, were not allowed to get them before they embarked & the steamer moved off. Another man, captured & forced off across the river since the Yankees occupied Beechwood, was at Westover when the enemy began its retreat. He, with all the other negroes, (which other reports state as 2000,) he says were marched off in front, & with guards of Yankee soldiers on all sides of them, to prevent their escape. He stated that on the order & commencement of this movement of the negroes, there was great grief shown by many of them in screams & shedding tears, & altogether the scene was most sorrowful. Within a few miles, he managed to escape to a place of concealment, & after the passage of all the army, he shaped his course to Richmond, & thence to Petersburg, to his refugee owner.—9 or 10 & sometimes more Yankee gun-boats have continued at anchor, in line, across the river, stretching from Jordan's Point, [2198] for some 4 weeks, waiting for advent of the dreaded Richmond iron-clad war steamer & ram, which I fear will not be ready for many more weeks. . . .

Aug. 27. Except Mrs. Martha Cocke's & Julian's family none of the recent refugees from this neighborhood have returned to their residences, & some have no intention of returning to stay during the war. The neighborhood is deserted—& no labor will be performed except to thrash & remove the wheat, & the corn hereafter, by those who did not lose both. Our church will continue closed—& we have no post-office as yet. Our attempted arrangement to get out letters & papers through the mail-carrier, was to commence today, & we have received nothing. But George came (by Beechwood,) & brought the Petersburg paper, which is always behind the Richmond papers in news from farther north. This reports only the continued retreat of Pope's army, & the pressing on of ours. It is reported that a part of our advance is within 4 miles of Manassas Junction. . . . Mr. Foote has offered a resolution in the H. of R. that our government shall "guarantee to the North-Western states, in the most effectual manner, the free navigation of the Mississippi & Ohio rivers, to their mouths, provided that they shall at once desist from all further participation in this cruel & unnatural war." This is an excellent move. But it does not go far enough. We ought to offer much more for this great object—indeed every inducement of favor to the trade of the North-western states, in consideration of their making a separate peace with the C.S., provided that the favors so granted should be beneficial, or at least not detrimental, to the future interests of the C.S. .... I would give to them not only the full enjoyment of the right of navigation, but every proper & necessary facility for obtaining supplies, selling or transshipping cargoes: Added to these, should be unlimited & perfect free trade, in buying our products & selling their own, in our marts. These privileges of free navigation & trade should be reciprocal & mutual, & used for our vessels & products, if needed, in the upper navigable branches, & in their marts, as conferred in our waters & marts.—Let us see what must be the condition of the N.W. states, if remaining in their present ruinous connection with & submission to the N.Eastern [2202]—and contrasted with what would be their condition of prosperity, if accepting the terms proposed.—That the southern gulf states offer not only the best market for the products of the N.W. but almost the only valuable market, is sufficiently proved by the fact that corn in Illinois now cannot be sold for more than 10 cents the bushel. Yet the whole northeastern market is as much open, by both land & water, as ever it has been or can be—& the costs of transportation & agencies are the only deductions to be made from the final prices obtained in N.Y. or the northern Atlantic States. What is true of corn is generally the same with all the north-western products, being all agricultural, & all more or less of great weight & bulk in proportion to their market value. Wheat could pay for carriage much better than corn; but hay could not bear half the cost of freight. So much for the chances for selling N.W. products, without the southern market being available. The chance for buying foreign products or eastern (protected) manufactured fabrics would be no better. All imported articles would be to the consumer enchanced in price by 50 or 60 per cent, imposed by the Morrill tariff. By this protective policy, the people of the N.W. will be made to bear (as the larger purchasers) not only the greatest share of the burden of heavy taxation for support of their federal government, but also of the indirect bounties paid into the pockets, & for the exclusive benefit, of Eastern manufacturers & traders, the commercial & navigating interests. Such must be the wretched condition of the N.W.S., not only until peace shall be made with the C.S., but after such peace, unless it shall be between the [2203] contracting parties become entirely friendly—or otherwise, the South ready to enter into the most intimate & amicable relations with her northern most malignant enemies, & would-be subjugators & destroyers: a contingency most improbable, & to which, I trust, not the most distant approach will be permitted. Added to these crushing burdens, peculiar to the N.W., as being without manufactures, & having for sale only bulky & low-priced agricultural products, will be her very heavy though equal share of the direct war tax, & the interest of the enormous & unextinguished war debt. The only possible relief for the North-West, from all or any of these burdens, the submission of the South, & confiscation of all southern property for northern greed, deserves no consideration.—Let us next merely glance at the advantages to be secured to the N.W. by a separate & speedy treaty of peace with the C.S., on the general terms proposed. Their former market will be reopened & former prices & profits obtained for all their products: Every article produced in the C.S. to be bought free of all tax or obstruction: Articles imported in quantity from Europe, & transshipped in unbroken packages of large sizes, to be bought in N.O. with the benefit of draw-back of import duty: all other & minor imported commodities, bought at retail, enhanced in price no more than the amount of our moderate 15 or 20 percent duties on imports. Let any competent person estimate the values of these advantages, & they will show that their attainment will suffice to bring back to any of the N.W.S. their former highest condition of prosperity, besides the protection from heavy disadvantages & burdens, which have had no precedent in past times.—If these points, [2204] [which] have here been so cursorily sketched, were carried out, as the offer of conditions by a law of Congress, & accompanied by an argumentative report, to be published & circulated generally through the N.W., the measure could not fail in having good effect.—Heavy cannonading this morning, & sometimes also rapid, continued at intervals until 2 P.M. The sounds seemed to come from the direction of City Point. I suppose it proceeded from the Yankee gunboats. . . . Finished reading "The first year of the War," by Edward Pollard. Resumed Macaulay's History.

Aug. 29. Copied, with corrections & additions, the foregoing views on a separate peace with the north-western states—to be sent to the Enquirer. Received today, by private conveyance from the

C.H. our mail, and the Pet[ersburg] Express of today, but no Richmond paper except one of yesterday. As the Garysville P.O. is
suspended, by absence & resignation of the P[ost] M[aster], the
mail-carrier does not travel this road, & so does not bring our papers
outside of the mail. Nothing stated of our main force, or Jackson's
command, in the last two days. This is very strange—but I trust that
the silence indicates that our generals are occupied in important
movements, besides pursuing Pope in his continued flight. . . . The
heavy firing heard yesterday was from the Yankee gunboats, shelling the ground where our men were, or supposed to be stationed.
One shot only was fired from our side, from a light rifled field piece,
which struck one of the Yankee gunboats. From a trooper (of this
neighborhood) who was on duty in sight of the enemy, I learn that
the bombardment of the shore just above City Point seemed to be a
leave-taking salutation—as immediately every gunboat steamed
down the river, & with all the transports (altogether 27), passed by
Hoods & out of sight below, the same day. Not a Yankee vessel was
to be seen in this part of the river yesterday. . . . [2207]

Aug. 30. Our friend & kinsman Dr. J. J. Dupuy & Wm. B. Taylor,
who also was college class-mate & an old friend of Julian's, called
here yesterday on their way from camp to serve on picket guard at
Maycox. By hearty welcome, & needed refreshment, & earnest
invitation, they also called when returning to camp today. Two
other members of the Prince George troop also came here, on
business—& all took dinner & remained some hours. The unusual
enjoyment of ripe peaches, excellent water-melons in abundance,
& an excellent vegetable dinner, all doubtless combined to make
this a bright day in their ordinary dull life & coarse fare of meat &
bread rations. It is a general sentiment & disposition of our people
who are at home, to treat our soldiers with kind attentions &
hospitality—not only in such cases as just referred to, of friends &
acquaintances, & of strangers known to be gentlemen, but to all
volunteers bearing arms for our common cause. This favorable
disposition is not misplaced, for the greater number of cases, &
especially as to the volunteers who first offered their services in the
field. These, more especially, embraced the most patriotic & valuable of our citizens—men who sought no gain, or personal distinction, who entered as privates, & still are serving as private soldiers,
& undergoing all the hardships of their position, without a murmur.
Very many too were men of large property, accustomed always

before to comfort & luxury, & who could have easily provided substitutes, if they had not deemed that (as young & single men) it was required of them by patriotic duty & honor that they should oppose the invading foes in person, & in battle. Many companies may truly be said to have been composed entirely of gentlemen. For the few members who had been in lower rank, were at least decent & respec[t]able individuals, & they soon emulated the manners, & acquired the tone & sentiments of the greater number of educated & high-toned gentlemen [2208] with whom they served & messed as fellow soldiers. On the other hand, in many companies of the later raised troops, when volunteering was but nominal, & resorted to by thousands merely to avoid service by draft, & to obtain the bounty of $50, there were more scamps than either of gentlemen or others of decent character. And especially from the towns, companies were principally composed of low rascals, whose greater numbers in their companies made them bold & shameless. Wherever companies or regiments of this character have been stationed, the members have soon found every residence within some miles, & in all acted as either civil or sturdy & shameless beggars. And under the general good feeling felt by our people to our soldiers, these shameless beggars have rarely been refused gratuitous entertainment, even when the frequency of such applications, & the enormous prices of provisions, rendered such hospitality burdensome. Before all such soldiers (& even many of higher grades,) fruits, green as well as ripe, & roasting ears of corn, were used at will, without asking for. And where these troops had control, in neighborhoods that the proprietors had been compelled to flee from the invading Yankees, our troops of this sort showed themselves as unscrupulous robbers as the Yankees. In such cases, the locked mansions have been broken open, the inner locks on doors broken, & every article of food, or liquors, or anything else desirable to & easy to be removed by the plunderers, was swept off. It is still more deplorable that for the laxity of discipline, & want of firm control of volunteers by their officers, there never has been a case of punishment, or even investigation, of any of such numerous & atrocious acts.—In Sheffield, Lord Palmerston lately attended a public dinner, at which he delivered an anti-intervention speech. Mr. [John A.] Roebuck, the distinguished M.P. from Sheffield, was present, & replied to Lord P.'s remarks . . . . The opinions of Mr. R. favoring the intervention of England, may be considered [2109] as

[435]

the views of the large & enlightened minority which makes up the opposition party. Still, the government, supported by a majority, is against intervention, & will so continue under all circumstances of the war being still a maintained struggle between North & South. The only contingency in which England will interfere is (as I think) the impossible one of the North being about to completely conquer the South, & thereafter to reconstruct the former union. England will look on the war with complacency, so long as the opposed parties shall continue to weaken each other & carry ruin to both. . . . And even the French Emperor seems so bound with England in this question, that I have very little more expectation of his interference. Yet this submission to English policy is incomprehensible. For the Emperor & France are not influenced by anti-slavery fanaticism—they have no reason to fear war with the North, as they own no great amount of American bonds, & are in no danger of suffering worse in a maritime war. Further, if France would command the raising (or would break) the illegal & fictitious Yankee blockade, there would be little danger of its producing war—& if such would be the result, France could not be hurt by the power of the North. A commercial treaty, of reciprocal free trade between the South & France, or of duties of low limit, & granted exclusively to France as the consideration for putting down the [2210] blockade, would promote the commercial & manufacturing prosperity of that kingdom more than anything that has occurred in a century. . . .

Aug. 31. Sunday. No services at Church—nor like to be for a long time. Our late pastor, Mr. Hansburgh is in Petersburg, & his wife still as sick as when she had to [be] carried off on her bed, to escape from the marauders who had previously plundered the parsonage. It is not likely that Mr. H. can return—& if he could, Julian & Lotty are the only members of his congregation & of his few supporters, who are residing permanently at their former homes.—Ascertained today two more of my manuscript volumes having made part of our stolen libraries, which are great losses to me, but of but little value to any but my children, & scarcely worth the transportation to the robbers. One was the first volume of my carefully kept Farm Journal of Marlbourne—a thick folio, embracing my daily operations & observations for the early years of my labors, & all the great improvements made on that farm. The other was a small duodecimo, containing a compiled & abridged system of Geometry, taught upon a new & simple method, calculated to lessen the usual difficulties both of teachers & pupils. I used this method to begin the instruction in geometry of my oldest son Edmund, when he was but 11 years old, & the ease [with] which he overcame the difficulties which most learners of mature age find in their way, was evidence of the value of my method, if it was in general use. It was the only copy, & I suppose has already been destroyed.

September 1. After breakfast I rode to the C.H. (7 miles) for our mail. Our authorities still keep secret all the [2211] news from our army, & prevent all telegraphic reports to any other than the government. There have been daily & numerous & important verbal reports, of successes of our arms. But they are doubtless mostly exaggerated, or altogether false—& such as are true cannot be distinguished as such. . . . Our Congress, very foolishly, while we have scarcely an armed vessel afloat, & not a lieutenant's command in our whole navy, has established the rank of admiral in our naval service, & authorized the appointment of 4 admirals, & numerous port-captains & subordinate officers. This is but establishing, or extending greatly, our previous long list of pensioners & sinecurists in this service, who had nothing to do, and not even a distant prospect of general employment. . . . Afternoon, my grandchildren Nannie, Thomas, George & John Ruffin arrived, having passed by & stopped at Beechwood. They brought me Richmond papers. Dr. John Ruffin, (son of the Judge,) had reached Edmund's residence in Petersburg, from the army, very ill with a second attack of typhoid fever. Judge R. had been written for. Edmund had determined to shift his residence to Marlbourne, to my great gratification. His family will move there this week, unless the continued illness & stay of Dr. J. Ruffin shall prevent. . . . The first appointed admiral of the Confederate States & the only one as yet, has been worthily selected, in Capt. Franklin Buchanan, who, with the Virginia, achieved the marvellous victory over the Yankee squadron in Hampton Roads, sinking or destroying the frigates Cumberland & Congress.—In Congress there have been several fierce attacks on [Stephen R.] Mallory, Secretary of the Navy, on account of his inefficiency & incompetency. He ought never to have been appointed. He was a Connecticut Yankee settled in Florida.[37] In [2218] the U.S. Senate, where the chances of high promotion in a new state had placed him, he never exhibited talent. Our

---

[37] Mallory's father, Charles, a civil engineer, was indeed a Connecticut Yankee, but his mother was Irish, and Mallory himself was born on the island of Trinidad. The family settled in Key West, Florida, about 1820 when young Mallory was seven years of age.

President, when appointing him his first Secretary of the Navy, had not even the poor excuse of Mallory's popularity at home. For nearly all of the delegation from Florida were opposed to his being appointed. Mr. Davis has been very unfortunate in making many bad appointments to high places. But after he has made one, & the whole country cries out against the continued evidences of the unfitness of the officer, & of the detriment thereby caused to the public interests, the President clings the more obstinately to his support. Thus as to Benjamin, Sec. of War, whose total incompetency for that duty was believed by almost every man, & to whose incompetency many of our military disasters were ascribed, Mr. Davis retained him in office until he was at last removed by being promoted to the higher position of Secretary of State. If that dignified retreat had not . . . been accidentally vacant, I suppose we should be still saddled with Benjamin as Sec. of War, as we are with the very far inferior & common-place Mallory as Secretary of the Navy. . . .

Sept. 3. Our mail again failed to bring any but the Petersburg papers. These contain important & good news, though stated very generally [2219], & without any particulars. By a dispatch of Gen. Lee to the President, he announces that on the 28th & 29th, attacks were made by the enemy on the two wings of our army, commanded severally by Generals Jackson & Longstreet, & in both cases were effectively repulsed. On the 30th. he states "this army achieved this day a significant victory over the combined forces of Generals McClellan & Pope." He deplores the heavy loss which our army suffered as the price of victory. We may rely on Gen. Lee for these main facts. *Laus Deo!* (Pope, however, on 29th reported a victory over Jackson on 28th, & 1000 of our men captured. He does not usually content himself with publishing so small a lie, as of 1000 prisoners.) The Yankees had evacuated Fredericksburg, and burnt the R.R. bridge there. . . . Gen. Bragg has proclaimed the immediate commencement of his forward movement. Important military events imminent in Ten. & Ky. Movements of our guerrillas reported in various parts of both states. . . . A Lynchburg paper furnished to the Pet. Express some particulars of the late battle of the 30th. It was fought near Sudley Church, 6 miles west of Manassas Junction, & in part, the same ground of the former battle of Manassas. The battle stated to be more bloody than any fought previously. . . . In Washington great excitement & alarm prevail, in expectation of invasion. Papers of that city report that our forces occupied, or had reached Vienna, 12 miles distant—& other northern papers report that a large rebel force had reached the Potomac near Leesburg, & could cross into Md readily. The water at sundry fords not more than knee-deep. . . .

Sept. 4. Some days back a new body of cavalry was brought to this neighborhood, & encamped at Sycamore church. Many of the men soon found there [*sic*] way here, to sponge for food & to look for fruit, & finding the latter, were unusually troublesome. Julian, as always, was patient with & liberal to them, without a single exception. We had plenty of peaches for the family use, but not many to spare. In two days, the applicants, by leave asked & granted, came in such numbers that not a peach was left. And the nights following these two days, either some of the same (as is most probable,) or other soldiers came secretly to the neighboring water-melon patch, & of the good supply on the vines, stripped of[f] every one approaching maturity, & cut open & left as many quite green. So that after [2221] these two nights' pilfering, there are not water-melons left worth stealing or eating. . . . Such conduct permitted by the deplorably lax discipline of our volunteers & defenders, will render their presence or neighborhood a nuisance & a terror of the residents but little less than would be the Yankee invaders & licensed plunderers. The Prince George cavalry, lately serving here, & the members of which acted like gentlemen, have been sent away unfortunately for the residents. Their successors are cavalry from Norfolk & Princess Anne counties, & Currituck N.C.

Sept. 5. Late last night, Julian's wagon returned from Petersburg, bringing papers in advance of next mail. The uncertainties of the immediate & later results of the late great battle have scarcely been at all cleared away. It is supposed that our loss in killed & wounded amounted to 10,000—& the enemy's loss to twice as many, besides 4000 prisoners. Also that the enemy's force engaged was much larger than ours.[38] It is also reported (& so much seems on good authority,) that we took, & mostly destroyed, immense quantities of supplies—& also some 80 pieces of artillery. . . . Gen. Kirby Smith,

---

[38] These estimates were reasonably accurate. Of the 75,000 Federal troops engaged at Second Manassas, 1,724 were killed, 8,372 were wounded, and 5,958 were listed as missing. Confederate casualties numbered 9,197 out of a total of 48,527 effectives. Both tactically and strategically, it was a notable victory for Lee and his Army of Northern Virginia.

from Chattanooga, has sent a dispatch announcing our troops having beaten & routed the Yankee (or "Union") army under Gen. [William "Bull"] Nelson, near Richmond, Ky, routed it, & captured 3000 prisoners. . . . The mail brought us today's papers, but with nothing not before reported, & not much of additional or conclusive information of the late battle at Manassas. . . . The victory near Richmond, Ky. was achieved by Gen. Kirby Smith as commander of our force. Further particulars are, that he took 3000 prisoners including Gen. [Mahlon D.] Manson the Yankee commander. Gen. Bull Nelson, who came from Lexington with reinforcements in the midst of the fight, was wounded, but fled with the remainder of the force, closely pursued by our troops. . . . Our army marching on to Lexington, which was expected to be occupied. . . . May God grant that this movement into Ky. be successful & that both Lexington & Frankfort may remain in our possession, & the whole state soon follow. Besides the important public objects thus to be reached, I hope that I & my daughter Mildred may thus have our long suspended intercourse renewed. . . . A letter from Edmund informs me of the greater & extreme illness of Dr. John Ruffin. His father has come to him. This new & serious trouble will render it impossible for Edmund to move to Marlbourne as he [2223] had designed on next Monday—& will require his retaining the rented house for another month.—The Enquirer of today contained the article I sent to it, proposing the offer of conditions of a separate peace to the north-western states.

Sept. 6. This morning I wrote to Mildred, and resorted, for the conveyance of the letter, [to] the desperate chance of enclosing it in another directed to Gen. Kirby Smith "At his Head Quarters, Kentucky," requesting him to forward the letter for Mildred to Frankfort, should his occupancy, or our mail facilities, or other means for transmission extend so far.—My grandson Thomas Ruffin returned to Petersburg this forenoon. His late disease (typhoid fever) has ceased some time, but he has not yet got strong enough for exposure to camp hardships. When he was ill previous to this, he returned to duty too soon—& consequently soon was made ill again.

Sept. 8. . . . The papers. The Yankees have evacuated Winchester, burning their own stores & provisions, & also a square of the town. Winchester & Fredericksburg both occupied by our troops. By official dispatch from Gen. Lee, there was another fight on the second day following the bloody battle of 30th ult. at Manassas, at

[440]

Germantown, (on Sept. 1,) 2 miles east of Fairfax C.H. to which place our forces pursued the retreating Yankees, & again defeated them. . . . Great alarm prevails in Washington. Gen. McClellan commands there. It is reported that Jackson's division has crossed the Potomac (at Edward's ferry, & another ford above Georgetown,) into Md., & that Gen. Longstreet's & another of our Divisions were following. . . . The Yankee gunboats have been ordered up the Potomac, for the protection of Washington. For its defence, however, northern papers say that they have 70,000 men, under Gen. Wool, I suppose besides their armies retreating on Washington. . . .

Sept. 9. Julian & Thomas, with the two young boys, went to Beechwood for a whole day's shooting. They returned late with but little game (only 2 wild ducks saved out of 6 killed,) but with a valuable mule recovered—one left by (or escaped from) the Yankee robbers, who carried off all the others then left, 9 in number. Also I recovered what I had thought as much lost. In opening a box, packed & sent off by Julian, & since brought back, he found the large folio volume of my Marlbourne Farm Journal, which I had supposed to have been part of my private manuscripts stolen & carried off by the Yankees.—I spent this forenoon in writing the rough draft of a new will. The last written (in 1857) I had supposed & hoped would be the last required, & had been carefully & elaborately drawn.[39] But successive changes of circumstances required changes of its provisions—which were made in codicils added at different times, to alter, or to entirely substitute, or annul original portions of the will, until so much had been thus changed, that it became necessary to annul entirely the former writing, & to write anew to provide for the changed & existing circumstances. The changes of facts were such as these. The deaths of my daughter Elizabeth & soon after of her only child—& the consequent reversion of the property designed for either of them, if spared to live: The changes of investment, & of form, of some of the securities bequeathed: The new & present circumstances of my beloved daughter Mildred, caused by her marriage, & since residence in Kentucky, in what has so far been really the dominion of our northern enemies: the conduct of an unworthy son & legatee:[40] & also, the loss of several [2226] subjects of specific legacies, by the plundering or destruction committed by the Yankees at Beechwood

---

[39] See Volume I, 44–45, for the terms of this will.
[40] A reference to Charles, the diarist's youngest son.

& at Marlbourne. Another ground for changes of the former distribution of the future remainder of my estate, was that of my three now living & always worthy & beloved children, Mildred, in some compensation for our unhappy separation of country & political connections, (though not of opinions & sentiments,) at least is in good pecuniary circumstances, & has, as yet, with her husband, lost nothing by the depredations & destruction committed by the northern government & its invading armies—whereas, my sons Edmund & Julian have lost in this manner very largely, & Edmund, (besides his much greater other losses in his individual property at Beechwood & Evelynton,) in the Marlbourne estate, as the purchaser of Mildred's former share, had to bear what would otherwise have been her share of the losses, added to his own original share. These heavy losses I feel bound to take my part in—& to relieve my sons in part, by surrendering to them the larger portion of the residue of my estate at my death, as well [as] smaller portions to be assigned to them now or soon.

Sept. 10. . . . The mail. Numerous reports, but little certain information. It seems certain that our army, under the immediate command of Jackson, crossed the Potomac near Leesburg, into Maryland (75,000 men as said,) on the 5th . . . . Great excitement, &, among the Union men, panic in Fredericktown, & even in Philadelphia. . . . After the last battle, at Germantown, & the retreat of the Yankee army, they received reinforcements of two entire divisions, ([William B.] Franklin's & [Edwin V.] Sumner's,) but that did not induce the making another stand. The whole army has retreated to the Potomac—if not in part across—& the combined armies are under command of McClellan. So Pope has bragged & strutted, & lied for a few days only, & is played out & at an end. . . . Application was made this morning to Julian to extend his hospitality to a sick soldier in the neighboring camp, which he agreed to—& this afternoon he came. The company is from Currituck N.C. & seems altogether different from their thievish predecessors, who also were from that same region. This man . . . is suffering under rheumatism. In this small house, & with previous visitors, & more expected tomorrow, this addition of a sick stranger will be no light inconvenience.

Sept. 12. The mail—& a larger supply of papers soon after brought by my son Edmund, who came with Sue & Mary. Dr. Ruffin reported to be much better—& supposed out of danger. Not much news, for the sanguine expectation. Our army in Md. was at

Fredericktown, when last heard of. . . . Frankfort has been abandoned by the Ky government, & the seat of government moved to Louisville. . . . Though Yankee generals & the N.Y. Herald's report (published to send to Europe by the last mail-steamer) claim victories in the recent battles, the northern papers in general admit disastrous defeat.[41] . . . When prominent & influential journalists dare to speak thus boldly in condemnation of their government, & when there is both law (or government orders) & usage to put the publishers in jail for any length of time, & to suppress their papers, the facts indicate the beginning of a strong northern opposition to the war, which cannot now be suppressed by force. [2230]

Sept. 13. Edmund & his children went to Beechwood, to proceed thence to Petersburg. Thomas will go to his company, in service, next Monday. George has gone to enter the Va. Military Institute at Lexington.—Having before completed the alterations of my first rough draft, I made a fair copy of my new will, & completed it by my signature. Burnt the previous will. I have taken this trouble because I deem the continuance of my life very uncertain, & I am not willing to be even for a few days without a will, or with one drawn under very different from existing circumstances . . . . Finished the "Bride of Lammermoor" & began the "Legend of Montrose."[42]

Sept. 14. Sunday. By the kindness of a neighbor, I was supplied with the paper of yesterday. It has no news of events later than before heard of, but more extended accounts. And almost every statement is from northen papers, & yet mainly favorable to our arms. In such case northern reports may be believed. . . . The northern papers continue to publish doleful lamentations, & complaints about their government & military leaders, on account of the late disasters of their arms. . . . Pope has been removed from his command, & sent to command the Yankee forces in Arkansas.[43]

---

[41] Typical of the extracts from northern papers appended to the diary at this point is an editorial which had appeared in the New York *Times* on September 5, the day before Jackson's troops entered Frederick, Maryland, on their northward march. It began with this melancholy admission: "The Summer campaign which was to have given us the rebel capital, has come to a disastrous end. Richmond is relieved, and Washington is besieged. . . . Disguise it as we may, the Union arms have been repeatedly, disgracefully and decisively beaten. The whole campaign against Richmond has proved a failure."

[42] The diarist has returned to the works of Sir Walter Scott.

[43] Pope was actually sent to take command of the newly established Department of the Northwest, where he was immediately confronted with the task of subduing a major Sioux uprising in southwestern Minnesota which had erupted on August 17 and continued for more than a month.

Gen. McDowell, who was second in command in the late battles is removed, & not given any other place. So McClellan, so lately half-disgraced, & limited to the charge of the forces defending Washington, I suppose now has the chief command of the whole grand army.—Our guest, the sick soldier, being no longer sick, returned to his camp today, to our great relief. For he was not only ignorant, & occupied a whole bed-chamber, when there was no room to spare, but also he was ragged, dirty, & lousy—as he left living evidences on his bed. . . .

Sept. 15. I rode this morning to Beechwood, & to the Point & beach. Heard from the pickets that 5 Yankee transport steamers, under flags of truce, had passed down this morning. The same had gone up on Saturday. [2232] They carried away more than 3000 exchanged Yankee prisoners.—The mail. Very little news of military operations from our side, & none important—but the papers full of northern reports. These state (from Louisville Ky) that our troops had occupied not only Lexington but Frankfort—the C.S. flag was hoisted over the State House, amidst acclamations of resident spectators. From Cincinnati, accounts . . . report our army advancing, & . . . within 5 miles of Covington. Widely varying reports of the strength of our army in Md. (from 5000 only, to 120,000,) & of its progress. The most credible report is that the advance is already in Pa., towards Gettysburg. The Pa. papers show that the wildest excitement & panic prevail through that state, on account of the expected invasion. Yet the papers brag high of their means for defence. They say that numerous volunteers are already arrayed in arms, & that in a few days they will be increased to 50,000.—Gen. McClellan had marched an army from Washington to & beyond Pool[e]sville, on the route & in rear of our army, but *had not been able to find any enemy!* . . . [End of MS Volume 12—p. 2233] A Yankee transport steamer, having onboard two Dahlgren cannon, got aground in the Ten. river, & was captured by our riflemen from the shore. After saving the guns, they burnt the steamer. This & sundry other incidents prove, what I had said in advance, that the occupation of New Orleans, & even of sundry other of the most important cities, & even having a strong flotilla of armed vessels on the Mississippi river, will not give to the Yankees the command, or the navigation, of that river & its great tributaries. Every private vessel, or unarmed government steamer, attempting the navigation without armed convoy, will be in imminent peril of capture, in every day & night of its passage. . . .

Sept. 16. Mr. & Mrs. Hansburgh went to his late residence to gather up & remove his remaining furniture &c. Since the robberies committed before his family left, the Yankees have done him but little damage. Indeed, except in stealing negroes, they did but little any where in the neighborhood, except on the three river farms, Maycox, Beechwood, & Tarbay. No doubt that I & my son Edmund were the especial objects of their malignity. We learn from some of the neighbors whom the Yankees visited & conversed with, that [2235] on sundry occasions they expressed their strong desire to get hold of us. An additional cause for this anxiety as to my son, & perhaps the strongest, was their having learned, from the information of the sick negro woman Pinkey, that he had guided the trains of artillery to make the night attack on the Yankee vessels & camp, from Coggin's Point.

Sept. 17. A messenger from Edmund arrived late last night, with papers of yesterday, & a letter to me from Willoughby Newton.— The news good, though none of very important events. Our forces under Gen. [William W.] Loring advanced upon the Yankees in the Kanawha valley, attacked, defeated, & drove them in three successive combats. They were retreating towards Charleston. . . . Nothing from our army in Md (or Pa.?) except from northern reports. According to these, Gen. McClellan & his army from Washington had advanced to & passed through Rockville, & (as more loosely reported,) had reached Poolesville, designing to attack the rear of our army. . . . In the afternoon Edmund arrived, with Judge Ruffin, who had been with him in the forenoon to see Beechwood farm in its state of desolation. His son still improving, but too weak to be removed. More papers of today brought to us. . . . Gen. Jackson's army after reaching Hagerstown, Md. turned back to the Potomac, 6 miles distant, & suddenly fell upon the Yankee force of 8000 at Harper's Ferry & Martinsburg. That much is certain. But we have two reports of what followed. The northern report is that he was repulsed on the 14th. after a battle of some hours. The southern report is that he was, as usual, victorious, & captured all that he did not kill. The truth probably is between these two extremes. . . .[44]

Sept. 18. This is the day, appointed by the President's proclama-

[44] The truth was that Jackson had captured Harpers Ferry early on the morning of the 15th, taking 12,000 prisoners. The northern report apparently referred to the battle of Crampton's Gap on the preceding day, in which Major General William B. Franklin's Sixth Corps carried the pass against two Confederate divisions commanded by Lafayette McLaws but then delayed too long to relieve Harpers Ferry. Following his seizure of the latter town on the 15th, Jackson hastened to rejoin Lee,

tion, for a general public thanksgiving to God for the success of our arms. There never was more cause for a people's gratitude, nor a more suitable juncture for its expression. Judge Ruffin & Edmund set off immediately after breakfast for Petersburg, there to join in the public services of the occasion. As there was no church opened for such services in this [2238] still almost deserted neighborhood, Julian read the service directed by the bishop for his church, which were [*sic*] joined in by our family circle.

Sept. 19. The mail—& an extra supply of yesterday's papers brought by Mr. Hansburgh. None are published today. No official or certain account of recent affairs from Harper's Ferry—which is very strange—but continued & repeated reports all concurring in the main facts of a battle at Harper's Ferry on the 14th (Sunday,) & the subsequent surrender of the whole Yankee force of 8000 men to Stonewall Jackson. . . . At what was called a "War Meeting" in Troy, N.Y., the Hon. B. D. Noxon was chosen chairman. From his few remarks made on taking the chair, the following extract is taken: "———The object now was not so much to devise means to carry on the war, but to stop the war. Blood enough had been shed. Treasure enough had been expended. No man could desire the perpetuation of such a bloody remorseless struggle. It was not important who should be on the state ticket, except inasmuch that this war could never be ended except by the election of entirely different men to Congress than those composing the last Congress—" This is the most open declaration that I have yet seen. And as coming from a chairman, must be supposed to express the sentiments of many if not most of the meeting. Still that meeting, like almost every opponent of the administration, was still obliged to profess readiness to support the war. But if they can elect their candidates to Congress, there is little doubt that they will be strong enough to oppose the war. Whenever a minority in the North shall dare to take this step, that minority will soon become a majority. Three months ago, the speech of Mr. Noxon would have consigned him to imprisonment for an unlimited time—& any newspaper that published it approvingly would have been forthwith suppressed by the law-defying government. [2239]

Sept. 20. . . . By a Rd. paper of yesterday, & a private letter from Petersburg, we have received later news & still later reports of

---

who was gathering his sparse forces at Antietam Creek in preparation for the grisly climax of the campaign which came two days later.

important events. Nothing official—though it is brought by verbal information to Petersburg that Stonewall's official report of his victory at Harper's Ferry was in Rd.—& that he had taken 10,000 prisoners, 51 cannon, & large quantities of stores, & between 1 & 2000 stolen negroes. . . . On Sunday, the 14th, McClellan with his army of 80,000 passed through Fredericktown, Md., & attacked our rear, under Gen. D. H. Hill, near Boonsborough, Md, 18 miles from Fredericktown, & 15 north of Harper's Ferry, whose command was greatly inferior. The battle raged until stopped by night. Our army lost heavily, but held its ground. . . . By return of the carriage [from Petersburg], we received the papers of today, & in them the more full statements of the verbal reports sent to us last night. No official report yet—but from sundry others, including two to the Governor, there can be no question as to the great facts of the surrender of Harper's Ferry. These are that Jackson's attack (by cannonading from the surrounding heights,) began on the afternoon of Sunday 14th. (The smaller force at Martinsburg had been previously driven in to Harper's Ferry & partly captured). Next morning the enemy surrendered. Prisoners, by different reports, either 8000, or 10,000. Slaves retaken there, reduced to 600. An immense quantity of ammunition, many wagons, but small amount of provisions, as the army was nearly without supplies. Jackson's loss either very small, or *none*, as stated by the best authority. . . . Jackson's army speedily recrossed the Potomac, & was approaching the rear of McClellan's army, while D. H. Hill & Longstreet engaged it in front, & drove it back. In that battle, it is reported that the Yankees lost 5000 men. Our loss very heavy.[45] Another [2241] & still greater battle must have soon followed, when the army of Jackson came up with McClellan's previous rear . . . . I look with most eager & sanguine expectation for the results of this battle, as the most important & decisive of any yet fought in this war. . . . If Jackson was able to enclose McClellan on the south, & cut off his retreat, the latter must fight a decisive battle—& unless victorious, must have his army utterly destroyed. May God grant that I am not too sanguine, in expecting the last result!

---

[45] Fighting a desperate delaying action at South Mountain on the 14th, Hill's division lost 2,685 out of 17,852 effectives. Federal casualties numbered about 1,800 of more than 28,000 engaged. The report that the combined forces of D. H. Hill and Longstreet had driven back McClellan was false. It was the Confederates who withdrew from South Mountain, falling back to Sharpsburg on September 15.

Sept. 22. My anxiety to hear the news induced me to ride to the C.H. for our mail—but could not see or hear anything, except the Express of today. All the reports good—but not so good as I had hoped for. Jackson's official report. He not only performs more important work in less time than any other commander, but he tells of his performances in fewer words. He states, in a few lines, the surrender of Harper's Ferry & 11,000 Yankee troops & as many small arms, 73 pieces of artillery, & about 200 wagons—"with a large amount of camp & garrison equipage. Our loss was very small." . . . The battle in Md. on [2242] Sunday the 14th was between Middletown & Boonsborough, where the turnpike crosses the Blue Ridge. Gen. Lee had posted there Gens. D. H. Hill & Stuart, to hold the pass against McClellan, who was coming on with his large army to protect Harper's Ferry. . . . Gen. Longstreet was ordered to reinforce Hill, which he did by Sunday evening. Hill had been fighting & holding his ground against very superior numbers, but at last his right wing had been forced back. Longstreet's aid enabled this lost ground soon to be recovered, & maintained. The battle raged until in the night. The enemy's object, to reinforce Harper's Ferry, was frustrated. Gen. Lee learned, late that evening, that the enemy had occupied Crampton's Gap, on the direct road from Fredericktown to Sharpsburg, (which is near the Potomac, 8 miles west of Boonsborough, & 10 miles north of Harper's Ferry—) so that they might still endanger our forces there. Also, reinforcements had been received by McClellan's army. Therefore Gen. Lee ordered a concentration of our separated forces at Sharpsburg. The forces under D. H. Hill & Longstreet made the march unopposed, & occupied the new position in front of Sharpsburg by daybreak, 15th. McClellan's army moved up by 2 P.M. & both armies remained facing each other, inactive to the evening of the 16th. Our forces which had been engaged at Harper's Ferry had not then moved up. So far from the Enquirer, & of what is deemed certain. A later letter from the camp at Sharpsburg, to Warrenton, & telegraphed to Richmond, dated 18th, reports a "most terrific fight on 17th. The advantage on our side. Hosts killed & wounded. The whole strength of both armies engaged." . . . Nothing from Eastern Maryland. It is a very unexpected result, that, so far, there has been no rising there, & that everything remains quiet.

Sept. 23. Last night received by a servant from Edmund the Richmond papers of yesterday—which though of same date with that of Petersburg, contain accounts (as usual) a day later. The reports from our army in Md. & on the Potomac, & those from the northern papers, are so contradictory that it can scarcely be recognized that they speak of the same actions. And notwithstanding the undeviating course of northern papers (especially the most noted, the N.Y. Herald,) & not less of commanders of northern armies lying upon system, & for present effect, I cannot help feeling uneasiness lest there should be some truth in their details, omitted in accounts from our side. . . . Nothing is clear as yet, except Jackson's great success at Harper's Ferry. . . . [On the] night [of September 14] our force fell back to near Sharpsburg, where Jackson's army also came, & our whole forces were united under Lee. . . . McClellan's army did not move up to face ours in its new position before Sharpsburg, until the 16th, at 2 P.M. The fighting was renewed that evening at 6 o'clock—was suspended generally after 9, & resumed next morning (17th) & continued, with desperate efforts, & great slaughter on both sides, throughout the whole day. At dark the firing ceased. In the whole engagement our army had been on the defensive (being greatly inferior in numbers, but well posted,) & had repulsed every assault made by the enemy. On the morning of 18th, our army held its previous position, & stood ready to receive the enemy's expected attack. But none was attempted. During the day, we brought off our wounded, & were burying our dead, to which no interruption was offered by the enemy. Subsequently, Gen. Lee understanding that McClellan designed to make a flank movement by way of Harper's Ferry, anticipated it by moving our army across the Potomac, (fording it,) at Shepherdstown. To this movement, or retreat, also, the enemy made no opposition—which certainly would have been done, & with great damage to our army when fording the river, if the enemy had not been too much crippled in the previous engagement to make the attack. Our loss in the last bloody battle is estimated (probably on very [2245] uncertain grounds,) at 5000 killed, wounded & missing—& by the northern report, is put at 17,000. We had no means to estimate the enemy's loss.[46] . . . Thus, after all this severe fighting, & great loss of life, our army has again fallen back into Va. The object of invading Pennsylvania, if ever really entertained, has

---

[46] In perhaps the most costly single day of the war, Federal losses totaled about 12,500 out of 75,000 effectives, while Confederate casualties numbered nearly 14,000 in an army variously estimated at between 40,000 and 52,000 men.

been frustrated, & our aggressive movements changed to defensive. Still, so far as I can judge from my imperfect lights, & even if allowing both the principal engagements to have been "drawn fights," or equal in advantages & disadvantages to both sides, still the great balance of gain must be on our side. By our movement of invasion, we have at least struck terror throughout the assailable northern territory, & to its government—& have caused, & will make necessary, more new troops to be posted for defence, than the number of our army threatening invasion. Next, we have given strength to the rebellious feeling of Md. And the great success at Harper's Ferry is a clear advantage, even if all other things are balanced. . . . From an extract of an editorial article of the last Dispatch . . . it seems that some others are slowly coming to the opinion which I have held for a long time, viz: that England is best pleased to have this war to continue, & the parties engaged to damage each other as much as possible . . . & that she will be content to bear all her own heavy burden of suffering, growing out of our war, & especially the privation of cotton, for the benefits of having the commercial, manufacturing, & naval rivalship of the North destroyed, the negro-slavery of the South abolished, & by the consequent destruction of the export of cotton from this country, that England, in India, will become the greatest cotton-producing country of the world. . . . This extract from the Dispatch is the first evidence that any other person had come to a like conclusion.

Sept. 25. . . . Received the Richmond papers of 23rd & 24th . . . . It is very strange that to these latest accounts the northern & southern reports are still entirely contradictory [2248], as to the main facts. Each side claims for its army great victories both on the 14th & 17th, & having given disastrous defeats to the opposed army. It was not even known, on our side, to the latest reports, whether all of our army had recrossed the Potomac, or, if recrossing, whether all or any part had again gone into Md., or not. . . . Our highest authorities are inexcusably remiss in not giving to the public authentic accounts, when their publication can do no harm by giving information to the enemy. Except Jackson's very concise annunciations of his two separate victories, & Gen. Lee's of that at Manassas, we have not had an official & detailed account of a single fight since our army moved from Richmond, & indeed not since the official report of the battle of Seven Pines. We do not even know by what names our commanders will designate the most important (or any) of all these many later battles—& in referring to them, we have either to use the enemy's names, or to describe them by dates. Even the latter awkward mode does not answer, as more than one battle occurred on the same day. But though we cannot learn the truth, it is very certain that the Yankee reports, even the latest, are mostly made up of falsehood. Gen. McClellan, in his official reports, & the New York Herald seem to be contending for superiority in a contest of lying.—I have sometimes suspected that this most noted of all northern papers was really hostile & treacherous to the North, & was trying to urge on the northern government & people [2249] to the greatest excesses, for the purpose of their producing the greatest disasters to their arms, & the earliest defeat in this desperate war. Of such tendency are the threats uttered against France & England, of the vengeance to be inflicted on them, for past grievances, as soon as the North has finished the subjugation of the South. . . .

Sept. 26. The mail, including Richmond papers. But little news. The Rd. editors are at last informed that our army under Gen. Lee is on the Va. side of the Potomac—but decline to publish its more particular [2250] stations, for fear of informing the enemy. . . . We are still in the dark as to McClellan's movements or position, since the battle of Sharpsburg, as the enemy seems to be as to Gen. Lee's.—The following passage from a Northern (& as always, lying) account of the battle of Sharpsburg, conveys a very high, yet deserved compliment to the courage and conduct of our soldiers in battle.[47] Yet it is as strange as it is deplorable that in every battle, & every forward movement, the cowardly stragglers & skulkers, who fall back out of danger, are thousands in numbers. In letters from our army it is stated that there were supposed to be 5000 of such deserters from service in Winchester alone—& others estimate that in all the movements of our army from Gordonsville, that 30,000 of such stragglers have been lost to the various battles. It is strange that stringent measures, & bloody executions, are not put in operation to repress this evil. The mistaken lenity of the President has done great harm in this & many other cases—& I suppose is caused [2251] by his recent religious conversion, & his convictions run-

---

[47] "It is beyond all wonder," marveled the northern correspondent, "how men such as the rebel troops are can fight as they do. That those ragged and filthy wretches, sick, hungry, and in all ways miserable, should prove such heroes in fight, is past explanation. Men never fought better."

ning into fanaticism. One such result, (which I counted on from the first,) is the recent exchange, as prisoners of war, & sending off, all the captured officers of Pope's army, who, under the President's previous general order, & for retaliation, had been held as felons, to suffer for Pope's felonious outrages, in which these officers participated. There will be now a much broader field for the exercise of the President's mercy, at the greater expense of the interests of the country, & the claims of justice. . . .

Sept. 27. The entries in this diary are not always made on the day of their date, but, when of any length, more generally on the morning following. The cutting out extracts & pasting them herein, & writing the comments on the news, serve to occupy some hours of every day after receiving the newspapers, in addition to the time previously spent in reading them. Thus to kill two or three hours is to me a considerable gain. And I am very willing that both trifling employments shall be extended as much as my inclination may invite. Thus I spent more than two hours of this morning [2252] on the last pages under the date of yesterday.—The subject before Congress of inviting the North-western States to make a separate peace with the Confederate States, was referred to a Committee, of which the majority has made a favorable report, & the minority a report in opposition. I am glad that the proposition will thus go abroad, & pass under the consideration of the thinking people of the N.W. states.—The legislature of Va. was called together by the Governor to provide for the scarcity of salt—& has been in session since the 15th inst. Among its other business, one good measure, for which I have labored for more than 30 years, seems likely to be produced at last by the calamities inflicted by the Yankee invasion & occupation of a large portion of our country, & especially of the peninsula between York & James rivers. Nearly all the fences are destroyed, & in large spaces, also the growing timber. Where any crops still remain, it is utterly impossible for the owners to fence them in, & protect them from trespassing live-stock, which, under the existing general & unjust law, may range on any land not enclosed by a lawful fence. The proposition has been made in the legislature, & probably may be adopted under the present crying necessity, to compel the owners of live-stock to confine them to their own lands, instead of (as heretofore) requiring land-owners to fence out other people's stock, or to submit to their depredations. In this neighborhood, where I introduced the custom of such policy, first by voluntary agreement of neighboring proprietors, & later, by obtaining the sanction of a special law,[48] we have suffered no loss of this kind, either by the enemy destroying the enclosures, or our own troops, who are scarcely less destructive—because there were no fences to be destroyed. If such had been the established policy & usage in all the peninsula, the [2253] losses of the farmers would have been less by hundreds of thousands of dollars. . . .

Sept. 28. Sunday.—A neighbor brought a paper of yesterday. It gives a proclamation of Lincoln's, (in conformity with the acts of general confiscation & emancipation before passed by the Rump Congress of U.S.,) declaring the emancipation of all slaves of any states, or parts of states, which may be in rebellion against the U.S. government on Jan. 1, 1863. And all slaves, so offered their freedom, are indirectly invited to assert it by armed insurrection, by the assurance that the government will do no act to prevent or oppose any such effort. I am glad that this proclamation has been issued. It promises nothing more than what the Lincoln government & army have been trying to do beforehand, wherever they had the power—& this open declaration will serve only to strip off all disguise from the established policy. . . . Finished reading the two series of the "Chronicles of the Cannongate" [*sic*].[49]

Sept. 29. The mail. Nearly all the news from the Potomac & from Kentucky is from northern (or Union) papers, & of course deserving little confidence—& also very contradictory in most statements. But they agree, & are positive & particular, in asserting that the army of McClellan has partly crossed the Potomac, at Williamsport, & that his whole force is about to re-enter Va. A portion had previously reoccupied Harper's Ferry . . . which our forces did not continue to occupy, or defend. The prospects of the invading army are spoken of in very sanguine terms. The truth as to the results of the battles in Md. seems to be beginning to be suspected at the North. Even the [2254] Lincoln organ at Washington, the "W. Republican," admits that it was a drawn battle at Sharpsburg. . . . On the other hand . . . our subsequent retreat into Va., though so ably, leisurely, & safely conducted, as to be of itself sufficient evidence of previous victory, is also sufficient evidence of the defeat of our previous aggressive movement in general, & its object—whether

---

[48] See Volume I, 136, 150.

[49] The diarist continues to rely on the works of Sir Walter Scott for diversionary reading.

that had been to rouse Maryland to our aid, or to invade Pennsylvania. If, as it now appears, McClellan shall force his way into Va, in the face of our whole assembled army, it will prove his present superiority, whether obtained from his recent reinforcements, or otherwise. . . . In Ky., (& by northern accounts,) both Buell's & Bragg's army [*sic*] are in Northern Ky.—&, as I infer, the prospects of success to our arms are bright. The strongest indication is presented in the numerous Kentuckians joining our forces, [2255] & among them many of the organized "Home Guard," bringing with them their arms & equipments. . . . It is a significant fact, that notwithstanding the loud & general rejoicing of the northern press for their late great "victories," & professed confident anticipations of soon "crushing the rebellion," the price of gold in N.Y. has since risen to 119½ to 120—& exchange on England to 131. . . .

October–December

❧

1862

REACTION TO THE PRELIMINARY EMANCI-
PATION PROCLAMATION ❧ MOUNTING
HOPES OF EUROPEAN INTERVENTION ❧
RETAIL PRICES SOAR ❧ RETURN TO
MARLBOURNE ❧ CRIME IN THE CONFEDER-
ATE CAPITAL ❧ THOUGHTS ON THE PEACE
MOVEMENT AT THE NORTH ❧ GOOD NEWS
FROM FREDERICKSBURG

October 1. The mail. It is rare that we get any southern accounts from Kentucky—& whether early or late, nine-tenths of the
reports are northern, & from Union sources in Ky. or Ten. The
appended article from the Memphis (or Granada [*sic*]) Appeal is an
exception. This, & also northern letters, give very favorable accounts of our affairs in Ten. & Ky. . . . Our forces occupy (or have no
organized foes in) all the territory of Ky. except the S.W. corner
between the Tennessee & Ohio rivers—& all the towns except
Louisville, & a few others on the Ohio. . . . It seems probable that in
a few days [2256] Louisville, the head-quarters of southern abolition & Yankee sentiment, will be in our possession, with Covington
& Newport, & every other town along the Ohio, which the enemy's
gun-boats cannot command.—A bill has been offered in the C.S.
Congress, for a tax, or, more correctly, a forced loan of 20 percent on
the annual income of every resident—scrip bearing 6 percent interest to be issued for each man's loan or tax. I earnestly hope it may
pass. And for myself & all my family's interests, & for the C.S., I
would not object to the call being for 50 percent, if so much could be
obtained. . . . Probably the . . . emancipation proclamation of Lincoln may secure . . . much of the lost favor of the rabid abolition
party. But it will cause the loss of favor with all other northerners. In
the C.S., & still more in the states of Mo, Ten, Ky, & Md., I think this
proclamation will serve to do our cause good. It will convert

thousands of Unionists to Secessionists, & intensify the hatred & resolution of the previous true southerners. I think too that this measure will produce a shudder of horror throughout England & France, & doubled detestation of the Yankee government & people. For, in Europe, it will be believed that this general emancipation will produce what is certainly its desired & designed end, extensive or general insurrection of the slaves, & making another St. Domingo of the Southern States. As much as England may desire general emancipation, & France may be consenting to the end, neither can fail to view with horror this mode of bringing about the great object in view. [2257] For my part, (& I think that this opinion will be concurred in generally in the C.S.,) I heartily rejoice at the open declaration of this emancipation & bloody insurrection policy of the northern government & people. It is nothing more than what their officers & soldiers have already done wherever their arms had complete sway—& their operations can extend no farther. I do not under-rate their capacity to injure us deeply, &, in thousands of cases, ruinously, by seducing or forcing our slaves to leave their masters. But the recent open avowal of that policy, accompanied by the invitation for servile insurrection, will not in the least forward these malignant & villainous designs. All the previous arts, & stimulants, applied to the slaves, with more than 20 years' previous preparation through Yankee emissaries & agents, have not induced the slightest movement of negro insurrection. And I feel confident that such will continue to be the case, after this new & most powerful effort, made through the acts of the rump congress, & the proclamation of President Lincoln. . . . All the "stragglers" [2258] from our armies are not as condemnable as I thought, nor to be confounded with the cowards who skulk from the battlefields. On the contrary, very many, if not most of the "stragglers" separated from their corps during severe marches, are as brave & patriotic soldiers as any, but physically incapable of bearing up under the greatest labors required. As an example, during the late victorious career of Gen. Jackson, on one occasion, he marched his command 80 miles in three days, & fought twice in engagements of minor importance during that time. Of course, many of his soldiers could not keep up through that march, & who were left behind toiling to come up, & who did join their companies after different times of delay.

 Oct. 2. After breakfast Edmund returned to Petersburg, & I went with him, to visit his family. A small household now. Dr. Ruffin, having sufficiently recovered his strength, has gone home, with his family. Thomas has returned to his troop, (now at Culpeper C.H.). George is at the Military Institute, & Sue & Mary have gone to school in Richmond.—Gen. Lee's army is posted 10 miles north of Winchester, on the road by which McClellan's main force is approaching from Williamsport.—The armies of Gen. Bragg & Buell set out at the same time from their positions in Ten. by different roads. Buell & his army have reached Louisville. Bragg's army is close by. I fear that this strong reinforcement will render Louisville safe. . . .

Oct. 3. The two armies are confronting each other at 8 or 10 miles apart, between Winchester & Williamsport, but no conflict has been begun. It is supposed by some that Gen. McClellan's recent advance was made to recover *prestige*, & that he will not attack Gen. Lee, or do more than hold his army in check, & inoperative, unless our forces shall attack, & compel a battle. It is also conjectured, that while our main army is thus occupied, another attempt will be made to advance on & capture Richmond by other forces. . . . The Dispatch of today has several columns filled with extracts from the latest received English papers, (republished from N.Y. papers,). . . . The latest reports in England from this country, were of the retreat of Pope's army to Washington, & the advance of ours to that neighborhood. All the European commentators regarded the situation of the South as much triumphant, & the efforts of the North as desperate, as we here had estimated. The general inference to be drawn from all these comments is that there had been produced by our successes a great increase of the disposition to acknowledge, as a"fixed fact," the actual independence of the C.S., & to carry out this opinion to the extent of political recognition. The latter result, however, is not likely to be very speedy—or to come sooner than our practical triumph shall render foreign recognition of no value, or aid to our military success.

Oct. 4. Very little news. . . . 150 Yankee transports have lately gone up the Potomac, to Alexandria. This is another indication of a renewed attempt on Richmond. . . . After dinner, I returned to Ruthven. . . . Some days back, I released to Edmund & Julian $3000 . . . each, by giving credits for so much on their several bonds. In offering to them, & effecting this gift, I distribute during my life, so much of my estate which otherwise would take the same direc-

[457]

tion at my death, by my will. It is with the understanding that they will continue to pay to me as much as the interest amounted to as long as I may live. . . . The bill to extend the conscription, whenever the President deems it necessary, to a portion, or the whole, of the men between 35 & 45 years of age—omitted in the former law—has been enacted—& will soon be put in force. As it is impossible for *all* the men from 18 to 45 to be taken from their labors or business to serve in the army, it is probable that but a portion of those before omitted, say from 35 to 40 will be immediately called out—leaving those between 40 & 45 for a still greater emergency.—The Va. legislature has passed an act to authorize the governor to seize the salt-works, paying the assessed value, & to provide salt for the supply of all the people of Va. Salt has recently been sold regularly in Petersburg at 50 cents the pound, at retail.

Oct 5. Sunday. Mrs. Cocke has returned, for a time, to her home at Tarbay, & came this forenoon to visit Lotty.[1] Her house, like Beechwood, was stripped of every moveable by the Yankees, & either stolen & carried off, or broken & destroyed. Her losses have been much greater than ours, (in furniture &c. within doors,) as she had secured [2262] less by previous removal—& she will be reduced to great straits.

Oct. 7. Yesterday Lottie felt much better, & sat up most of the day. But today she is worse than before, & her fever higher. No physician is now in this neighborhood. Julian sent to Petersburg for Dr. Withers—& fearing that he could not come, he also described the symptoms particularly. Dr. W. could not come—but was confident that the disease was typhoid fever, & prescribed for it. The messenger brought us today's papers. The important news is of a battle, on the 3rd, near Corinth, between the Yankee forces of Grant & Rosecrans combined, & ours under Van Dorn, reinforced by Gens. Price & Lovell. Although the fighting had not then ceased, we may confide in the opinion & dispatch of Gen. Van Dorn, that we had secured a victory.[2] . . . The emancipation policy & proclamation

---

[1] Julian's wife, Lotty, had been indisposed for several days and was now confined to bed with a malady which had not yet been diagnosed.

[2] This claim was premature. Van Dorn renewed his attack the following day (October 4) but failed to carry the Union positions and withdrew in the early afternoon, having lost a fifth of his command in the two-day engagement. Although the Confederates had indirectly assisted Bragg in Kentucky by heading off reinforcements to Buell, they had failed to capture the key rail center of Corinth and thus could scarcely claim a victory.

have excited much indignation even in the North—& some of the papers express such sentiments in strong language, although, by the general suspension of the writ of *habeas corpus*, & the plain threats of the President, the utterers of such opinions are liable to be imprisoned without limit or redress—& many have been so imprisoned formerly, for less offences, & with less color of legal power. That such expressions are now published, & with impunity, seems to indicate that the Lincoln administration feels that it has lost popular support, & dares not exert its claimed power. This condition of things, if correctly inferred, indicates the beginning of a reaction at the North, & the arraying of a strong opposition & peace party—though no one yet dares to advocate peace, or to de[c]lare any opposition to the vigorous prosecution of the war, & crushing the southern "rebellion." . . .

Oct. 8. The mail. No continuation of the battle near Corinth on the 3rd., or confirmation of the then expected victory. On the other hand, a report that on the following day, (4th,) our army after having gained possession of the enemy's first position, was subsequently driven from it. . . . The worst is that Van Dorn, the commander, is said to be unfit for such a trust. On that ground only I feel discouraged. A decisive victory there would be of incalculable advantage to our cause. The enemy would not gain half as much in inflicting on our army as decisive a defeat. Still, it would be a great disaster, which would do away with all the recent discouragement of the North, & serve to prolong the war for a year longer than its termination will otherwise be reached. . . . The legislature of Va. has adjourned to Jan. 1, & Congress is expecting to adjourn in a few days more.—Finished looking through & partly reading 16 numbers of old British Quarterly Reviews & Blackwood's Magazine. [2265] Return to Scott—beginning again "Quentin Durward."

Oct. 9. In the first year of the war, & during the great reverses of our arms, President Davis was especially engaged in seeking to save his own soul, & was "confirmed," & became a member of the church. I do not mean to depreciate, or make light of this important duty. Yet I think that it would have been much better for his administration, & the public service, if he had effected, & completed, this individual & private duty before he began his presidency—or otherwise, had followed President Jackson's example, (which I would not advise in most other things,) & suspended his assuming his pious character, (which Jackson had begun before his election,) until he had ceased [2266] to direct the political & military affairs of the country. To the morbid tenderness of conscience of a "seeker of religion," & a new convert, I ascribe much of the imbecility of President Davis, in failing to punish military & political criminals—deserters, spies & traitors—& to carry out any measure of retaliation for the outrages of the enemy—which, however often threatened, & even lately ordered to be begun by the President himself, has not been done in even a single case. . . . . Butler has gone farther in New Orleans than has been done any where [2267] else, because, as I suppose, he deems the Yankee rule there impregnable. In addition to before levying a heavy contribution on the city, payable by the secessionists, he has recently required every resident to take the oath of allegiance to the Northern government, under penalty, for refusing, of confiscation of all property, & banishment from the city of all individuals refusing, & their families. It is obvious that the refusal is equivalent to poverty & exile to the rich, & absolute privation of the means of living to the poor, having no resources elsewhere. Under such circumstances of duress, it is not surprising that the greater number (Northern accounts state 12,000,) have taken the required oath, even when committing perjury. It is difficult to conceive what benefit can accrue to, or be expected by, the Yankee authorities, from such compulsory declarations of allegiance, when they are so numerous as [to] be considered merely formal, & when the compelled perjurers, by their numbers, keep each other in countenance. The next thing will be to require of all residents to pay the war taxes, & to render military service according to the U.S. laws. I am not sorry for these heavy requisitions. They will show clearly that no city will gain any alleviation of its worst fate, by surrendering to Yankee forces—& that the property-holders will lose no more by resisting to the last extremity, & their houses being destroyed by bombardment, or by voluntary general conflagration, than by submitting, without resistance, to the entrance & occupation by the enemy's troops.

Oct. 10. Finished "Quentin Durward." This is more of a romance than any of the Waverley novels, except Ivanhoe & The Talisman—& I think it is the most interesting, after the best, which I deem to be Waverley, Guy Mannering, The Antiquary, Old Mortality, & the Heart of Mid-Lothian. I have some doubt whether Waverley [2268] & the Antiquary ought to stand in the first rank, &

also whether they should be placed above Ivanhoe. Began Kenil-worth, without much inclination. I disliked this novel for its melancholy story, & the baseness of Leicester, & therefore it is one of but two or three that I have not before read at least twice, & mostly three times.

Oct. 11. Julian went to Petersburg yesterday, & brought back the papers, but late. As I had feared latterly, instead of the victory at Corinth, which Gen. Van Dorn too hastily announced for a then unfinished battle, our army has suffered a defeat—& the reverse I fear will be very disastrous to our military operations in Ten. & Ky. . . . Some skirmishing only between out-posts of our Potomac army & the Yankee forces opposed. . . . Its present position is in a country which has been ravaged & wasted by the enemy, & which can supply no provisions to our army. Of course, it is unfit for our army to remain [2269] in long, & much more so for its winter quarters. Under such circumstances, unless Gen. Lee designs another & a speedy aggressive movement, (which I deem very improbable,) I think he will soon fall back much nearer to Richmond, where he can obtain supplies for his army, & also more effectually prevent a new attack on the capital. . . .

Oct. 12. Sunday. Yesterday afternoon the weather became raw & drizzly, & continued so, & getting colder & more rainy through today. This is a bad change, & with a far worse prospect ahead, & through the winter, for our soldiers in the field, generally deficient in clothing, & many destitute of blankets & shoes. If our struggle was only in fighting our enemy, even with all their superiority in arms & munitions of war, & of naval means, I should not entertain a shadow of doubt of our triumphant success. But [2270] sanguine & confident as I am, some fears for the result darken my views of the future in reference to our great disadvantages in commercial & economical matters. All the articles of prime necessity—as sugar, coffee, cotton & woollen cloths of all kinds, & especially shoes, leather, & salt, & gunpowder—& latterly grain, forage, & all agricultural products—have risen to enormous & unprecedented prices. Much of this enhancement is fictitious, & the necessary consequence of the actual depreciation of the C.S. paper currency, our only circulating medium. But much the greater portion of the advance of prices is real, & over & above the depreciation of money. I cannot conceive how the government, under its financial difficulties, & the blockade of our ports, can supply our armies, or even keep them fit for good service. And thousands of individual proprietors, lately in either comfortable or affluent circumstances of property, have, by the invasion, been deprived of their incomes, if not of most of their moveables, & driven from their lands & homes, & when deprived of the means for buying the necessaries for support, are required to pay for them from three to ten times as much as former usual prices. To those proprietors, & especially farmers, who have not been plundered by the enemy, & forced to abandon their homes & crops, the rise of prices afford unusual & great profits, beyond what they may have to pay for the higher prices of necessary purchases. To very many, the war, with all its privations & taxes, has so far been greatly profitable. As many landowners will obtain a tripled income as there will be others impoverished by partial or total losses of crops, negroes, & stock, & devastation of lands & residences. And the strongest contrasts of these kinds are in many cases presented within the distance of a few miles. Besides those producers who have thus fairly profited by the necessary enhancement of the market prices of their [2271] regular & usual products, the whole country is overrun with speculators & extortioners, who bought up & monopolized every article on sale, of foreign supply, & obtained for them prices continually & rapidly increasing, & which seemed limited only by their forbearance, or by fear of too far trying the indignation & patience of the public. In these respects, we are in great trouble, & great danger. If the powers of Europe still continue to permit the blockade of our ports, (which is their grievance as well as ours,) & by their "neutrality," which is all on one side in its pressure, continue to exclude our privateers from all operation—& also if the Northern power does not soon break down under its financial burden, & the defeats of its armies—I do not see how our government can continue to find means to wage war, & our people will bear up under their heavy burdens. It is true that, even as a question of pecuniary self-interest, we had better give everything, & be reduced to universal & complete destitution, for defence, than to yield to the enemy. But I fear that not many of our countrymen will so reason. For my part, I wish the greatest & earliest possible general contributions & sacrifices to be made, & the strongest efforts, to enable us to conquer a peace speedily. It is delay, more than the arms of the enemy, that will do our cause most harm. . . . [2272]

Oct. 13. Another raw & cloudy day, misty & sometimes drizzly.—The mail. Nothing definite & certain as to the army movements. . . . The destruction of the entire year's product of sugar on the Mississippi, (where most is grown,) is threatened by the enemy. And while they can send armed gunboats anywhere with impunity, they can well & easily effect this great destruction of our wealth. Two armed steamers, with 500 troops, by passing up & down the river, & threatening every plantation, can effectually prevent any crop of sugar cane being worked up, & the sugar saved. It is a heavy & costly operation, requiring much expense, & the labors of many slaves. If commenced, its interruption only, would involve the loss of all previous expenses incurred, & future expenses prepared for. The destruction of the sugar house & steam engines would anywhere stop operations for a season—& to all other losses might be added the stealing & carrying off all the assembled slaves. Under the imminent probability of such injuries, no planter can dare to secure his crop of sugar, any more than a proprietor of one of the devastated farms on James river could re-stock it, & reassemble a force of laborers, to sow a crop of wheat—or earlier, to retain his slaves & stock to harvest his crops of wheat & oats, where the Yankee gunboats might call, & marauders ravage & plunder on any day. . . . Among the many villainies practised by the North on the South, none has been more extensive or successful than the counterfeiting of C.S. treasury notes, & also other paper money. This was the easier to do because of the much higher state of the art of engraving at the North—& also because Northern authorities, occupying southern territory, decided that such counterfeiting was not a crime. . . . The soldiers of the Yankee armies were well supplied with these fictitious bills, to circulate wherever their invasions extended. Other more adroit agents operated on much broader scales. The largest operation has recently been effected. Some men from Ky. went to Texas to b[u]y cattle, & actually bought 7000, with $200,000 [2275] of this counterfeit paper. They brought off their booty, & the cheat was not suspected until after their departure. When it was found out, the pretended government agents were pursued, & overtaken at Jacksonville, Mi., & all arrested, before they had disposed of many of the cattle. I trust they will meet with Texas justice, administered by Judge Lynch.

Oct. 14. No employment or amusement except in writing in this diary, & reading the "Pirate." This I think is one of the most unnatural & objectionable of Scott's novels. . . . At night, by messenger to town, came the paers of today. Yankee & northern papers (only) report what must have been a great battle at Perryville, Ky. between the armies of Bragg & Buell, on 8th & 9th, & still expected to be renewed on 10th. From the unusually moderate & subdued tone of the writers, I have no doubt that up to the latest writing, the Yankees had been well beaten. . . . On the 9th, at N.Y., the price of gold rose to 127, & exchange on London to 140—unprecedented heights. Gen. Bragg's report, & of the close of the battle, most anxiously looked for.—Northern papers are counting upon great benefits to their cause from the President's emancipation proclamation. It is to strike terror into the minds of the southern people—&, to save their slaves, & slavery, they will submit to the North before Jan. 1st., when otherwise the emancipation is to be consummated. . . . [However, I think] Lincoln's proclamation, in its operation on the southern people, & especially in the border states & on southern "Union men," will be worth to our cause as much as a reinforcement of 50,000 fighting men. . . .

Oct. 15. . . . The mail brought further telegrams (still all northern,) & information of the continuation of the battle at Perrysville [*sic*], & which (if credited,) go to overthrow my first inferences & expectations, & to declare a defeat of our army. . . . Afterwards, Edmund & Mr. W. Sayre arrived, from whom I learned still later news, (& still northern,) received by telegraph at Petersburg at 11 A.M., & read on the Bulletin board. This states that Bragg had indeed fallen back 6 miles—but in doing so, had so disposed portions of his forces as [to] mow down the enemy as advancing, & to cause great slaughter. I trust that this, though Yankee news, is to be believed—& thence infer that we have gained an important victory.[3]—Another daring & successful raid has been effected by Gen. J. E. B. Stuart, with a force reported at 3000 men; mostly cavalry, but with some artillery.[4] He crossed the Potomac at Hancock—passed around McClellan's army & its outposts, into Pennsylvania, & through the towns of Mercersburg, St. Thomas & Chambersburg (the last of 5000 inhabitants,) & thence returned by

---

[3] Although the Federals sustained heavy casualties—4,211 out of 36,940 effectives—in the battle of Perryville, Bragg's invasion of Kentucky was checked, and the Confederate commander was obliged to withdraw into east Tennessee.

[4] In his second ride around McClellan, conducted October 9–12, Stuart had with him a select force of 1,800 men, chosen from three cavalry brigades, and four guns of horse artillery commanded by Major John Pelham.

Emmittsburg [*sic*], Liberty, Newmarket, & Barn[e]sville, & re-crossed the Potomac at White's Ford, without losing a man. The details of this adventure not yet reported—nor the losses inflicted directly on the enemy. But whatever these may be, the indirect effects will be very costly & injurious, in striking Pa. with panic, & causing the militia & volunteers to be called [2278] out to oppose invasion. . . . In Richmond lately, Edmund met with Edward Selden, who was at Westover, his home, during the occupancy of the Yankees, & during our night cannonade. Of the latter, or its effects, he gave more particular information than was heard before, but agreeing in the main, as to the very little damage done. The shots were nearly all aimed too high, & passed over the vessels & the camp. Only two vessels were struck. On the land, 6 Yankee soldiers were killed, & a negro woman, & 7 soldiers wounded—& 12 horses killed. The attack was a complete surprise, & a perfect panic was produced. The results, poor as they were, prove that if daylight had been waited for, to direct the aim, enough damage might have been done the enemy to well repay the cost of the expedition, & to console the sufferers for the subsequent destruction brought upon their property by this foolishly managed & useless attack. Edmund also learned, from other sources, that the commander of the Yankee forces in Prince George was Gen. [Daniel] Butterfield[5]—& who no doubt stole our books & other moveables, & permitted the wanton destruction of everything else. His brigade was in the battle of Sharpsburg, & was there nearly cut to pieces. This is some comfort to me.—Edmund has bought a small farm in Amelia, adjoining Wm. H. Harrison's, & will soon send to it his negroes remaining on his hands (women & their children,) & some of his furniture. He will not get full possession of the dwelling house until the end of the year. Therefore he will still (as before designed,) move his own family to Marlbourne, for the intervening time. They will go in a few days, & I will [2279] accompany them, or follow after as soon as convenient. . . .

Oct. 16. Edmund went to Beechwood, & returning in the after-

---

[5] Son of John Butterfield, president of the Overland Mail Company, Brigadier General Daniel Butterfield (1831–1901) had rendered distinguished service during the Peninsular Campaign. Indeed, in 1892 he was awarded the Congressional Medal of Honor for gallantry in action at Gaines' Mill. He commanded the United States Fifth Corps at Fredericksburg and served as Chief of Staff, Army of the Potomac, during the Chancellorsville and Gettysburg campaigns. Transferred to the West, he saw service as General Hooker's Chief of Staff in Tennessee and Georgia. Following the war, Butterfield was a railroad and steamship executive.

noon, he & Mr. Sayre went back to Petersburg.—Two of the negro men who went to the Yankees from Marlbourne have been captured in that neighborhood, (the last within a few days,) & were forthwith sent to Richmond & sold, to be carried far south, & probably to Texas. Mr. Sayre supposes that a large proportion of the remaining absconders are still in the neighborhood, concealed fugitives. If so, they may yet be captured, & so lessen somewhat the amount of their loss, & the greater losses consequent thereon. It is surprising that the prices of slaves continue so high, notwithstanding their now precareous [*sic*] tenure wherever the Yankee forces can extend their occupancy, or even temporary marauding expeditions. After a slight decline through the earlier times of the war, because of the want of employment & profit of labor, more than the hazard of losing slaves, the demand in market, & the prices, have rallied, & latterly have been increasing. The *nominal* market prices now are higher than before the war, or at any previous time. But the depreciation of our paper currency makes a large deduction from nominal to real prices—how much I do not know, but perhaps 40 to 50 percent should be thus abated. Even with this abatement, the present ready prices for slaves are higher than any available employment can return a profit upon now. And however prices have been reduced by the general disorganization of agricultural labor by the war, & however much real decline of price may be disguised by the depreciation of our currency, it is certain that no sudden shock, or notable repression, was given to the current prices of slaves by either the general confiscation [2280] & emancipation acts of the Northern Congress, or the recent emancipation proclamation of Lincoln. And I do not believe that these measures (on paper, & of the threatened future,) have had the least effect on the market prices of slaves.—It is difficult to learn what has so far been done, & what will be done, by the northern government, with the great numbers of slaves already stolen by their armed forces in the C.S., & which, already taken from their owners, must be now largely above 100,000. We can hear of different dispositions made of a few hundreds—perhaps a few thousands—away from the regions whence they were stolen. But all thus designated as removed are nothing in numbers compared to the immense amount of all taken. Some have been taken to northern cities, & some to the rural portions of northern & western border states. But the out-cry raised in every case of such new immigration of negro settlers is enough to assure us that the settlers have not been very numerous—perhaps not 5000 in all. The people of these states are generally strongly opposed to receiving more of this very objectionable population & "citizens"—& still more the laboring class of whites, who dread & detest the freednegroes as rivals for employment, [& a]lways successful competitors, because reduced to labor for the meanest sustenance. Bloody riots have already occurred in the border states, & very lately in the city of N.Y., between low whites & negroes, because of discontent of the former increased by new arrivals & cheapened labor of the latter. While the Yankee invaders were busy throwing up intrenchments, as was so extensively done at first, they could employ great numbers of able-bodied negroes. And even the fugitive women could have some employment, & their special support be less a burden on the northern government. But that employment cannot be continuous, & indeed has nearly ceased at every occupied post. If the government supplies rations, (as [2281] has been done to great extent, if not as a general system,) then the burden on the northern treasury is enormous, & will increase with the extent of its emancipation operations. Even if so supplied, the helpless negroes must suffer greatly. And if not so fed, they must live by plunder or perish by privation of necessaries. It has been reported that many vessel loads of these fugitive negroes have been taken from Fortress Monroe & other receptacles for stolen slaves, & shipped to Cuba & Porto Rico [*sic*], & sold for slaves. But badly as I think of Yankees, I cannot believe this. For though they would not scruple at the deed of "man stealing," they would fear to be exposed—& such sales could not be made long before being found out & published to the world. . . . It has been computed by abolition authorities that the fugitive slaves cost for their support alone, (besides wages, if hired,) 40 cents each a day, which for 100,000 will make between 14 & 15 millions of dollars for a year. But the extreme abolitionists, both in & out of Congress, do not advocate or approve of any manner of removal of the stolen or emancipated slaves. Their plan & policy is that the freed slaves shall remain where they were, & occupy the country as the laboring class, if not as proprietors of the land, after the heretofore dominant whites are removed either by banishment or slaughter, caused by Yankee arms. If the locality is fit for the residence of Yankees, then they are to be the colonists & proprietary class of the wasted region, & the negroes, who before cultivated the lands as slaves, to cultivate them still, as hireling laborers for the new landowners. If the region is so subject to malaria as to be unfit for northern or white residents, (as are many of the low lands near the coast of the southern states,) then the negro "peasantry" may be made proprietors as well as laborers—& the whole population become Africanized. The fanatical fools who are working for these ends do not suspect, what every southerner knows, that the result of their plans of either phase, if they could be put in operation, would be to utterly destroy industry, production, wealth, refinement & civilization as far as the negro or mixed-blood population constituted the majority of inhabitants. But they *do* see, & do not object, that a result will be not only political [2283] equality, but the political superiority of the negroes, that the now slave-holding states, subjugated & so constituted, will be governed, wholly or in part, by negro legislators, governors & judges, represented in the congress of the reconstructed union by negro senators & representatives—& the negro military quotas furnished to the federal armies, to be commanded by negro officers. This consummation in prospect is delightful to the extreme abolitionists—such as [Horace] Greeley, [Henry Ward] Beecher, [Wendell] Phillips, [John P.] Hale, [Salmon P.] Chase &c. But it will be as much objectionable & disgusting to great numbers of northerners, who are theoretically opposed to negro slavery, & desire its abolition, but not if to be obtained at such costs as either men of sense & discretion deem inevitable, or extreme abolitionists would accept with readiness & welcome.

Oct. 20. Julian has bought Charles' share of the Marlbourne farm, & of the remaining slaves & other stock. I lend to Julian Charles' bonds still due to me for the purchase, (except a portion which I released,) to enable the former to make the purchase. As in my will, written but last month, I had especially recited & disposed of the largest of these bonds, this change of their form, & partial release, made it necessary to change so much of the late writing, that it was best to write a new copy. This I began yesterday evening, & finished today. In connection of the sale by Charles to Julian of all his interest in Marlbourne, I [2285] have executed in his favor, by deed or otherwise, full titles to the small tract of land bought for him in this county in 1856, & other property of which likewise he had enjoyed the possession & profits, but of which I deemed it prudent for me to retain the legal title. Now there is no longer any connection of my affairs with his, nor any necessity for my having anything to do with his affairs or with himself.—The Confederate Congress adjourned (to January,) a week ago. I do not know that it has done anything, in regard to all the important measures before it, except to pass the second conscription act . . . & the act declaring who shall be exempt from military service. I cannot follow up the progress & changes of bills, & their being sent from one to the other house—& even when the final passage is announced, it is not intelligible what shape was finally given to the bill after it was first published. Both our Senate & House of Representatives are weak bodies, & much more talkers than workers, even for the little they are fit for action or counsel.

Oct. 21. Received our mail last night. Not yet any official or other authentic accounts of the battles of Perryville. . . . We have one vessel [2286] of war at sea, which is doing good service. It is the steamer, & also fast sailer, Alabama, Capt. [Raphael] Semmes, known before as the "290." Capt. Semmes bought this vessel for our government in England, where it was built by order, for its designed purpose. Capt. Semmes brought her into Mobile under the fire of the blockading squadron, without being able to return a shot—has since gone out to sea, and (as northern papers say,) has already captured & burnt 14 northern ships with rich cargoes. Unfortunately he has to destroy all his prizes, as they are not permitted to enter European ports,& could not often pass the blockading squadrons into our ports. . . . Great excitement at the North, & especially in N.Y. in regard to the [congressional] elections now in progress! Ohio & Indiana have gone for the Democratic (or "Conservative") ticket, against the Lincoln & Abolition ticket. In other states, the abolition ticket was elected by reduced majorities. . . .

Oct. 22. The mail. The latest news dissipated my previous belief in our great victory [at Perryville], as moderate as had been that belief compared to what all our lying telegraphic reports, however conflicting in details, agreed in asserting in the main. Gen. Bragg's official report . . . indeed claims a victory, & I still believe truly—as our force took cannon & prisoners, drove the enemy two miles, & held its advanced position—& with smaller numbers, produced more [2287] loss to the enemy than was suffered on our side, as supposed. But if a victory, & however honorable & glorious to our troops engaged, as usual we gained no solid fruits of victory. It was barren of all advantages, except glory. And because of the reinforcements received by the Yankee army after the battle, making its superiority of numbers overwhelming, Gen. Bragg had to retreat, & was retreating out of Ky, towards the Cumberland Gap, pursued by Gen. Buell's army. Gen. Bragg is a first-rate officer to discipline & train soldiers, to put an army into the best fighting condition, to hold & defend a position, or to command in advancing movements subordinate to a commander of greater promptitude & ability. But he is too cautious, & too slow to command in chief in invasion—& his slow movements have lost nearly all that he was so near to gaining. In their respective marches from Mississippi, he allowed Buell to get ahead of him, though marching a longer distance. And instead of seizing Louisville when it was weak, he waited (no doubt to put everything in the best order,) until reinforcements made Buell's army stronger than his. The whole campaign in the west from Ala. & Miss. to Ky., has been lost to us, & almost nothing done by our armies (except some bloody & barren victories,) while the western rivers were so low, that the enemy's gun-boats could not navigate them. Now they will soon be again high, & continue so for 6 or 8 months, & the borders of every western river will be at the mercy of even a single iron-clad gun & mortar steamer.—Julian set out yesterday afternoon for Danville, to attend to his negro men there, hired to work on the rail-road (to remove them from the neighborhood of the Yankees). . . . By appointment, Edmund sent for me, Mr. Sayre driving the buggy, & after dinner I went with him to Petersburg . . . . Found all of Edmund's still remaining furniture ready for removal, & his family prepared to go to Marlbourne tomorrow. . . .

Oct. 23. Edmund could not leave today, as a canal boat which had been engaged to carry his furniture, & a portion of his negro women & children to his new place in Amelia, had not arrived. His family, that is Jane & her infant (& nurse) with Nanny & Mrs. Lorraine & John, under Mr. Sayre's charge, set out in the carriage & buggy for Marlbourne. I set out for Richmond in the train at 8.45 A.M. & . . . after staying in Rd until after 12, I walked on slowly until the carriage overtook me about 2 P.M., when I took my seat, & we reached Marlbourne after sunset. . . . I approached & reached Marlbourne with painful feelings, for more than one cause. My last visit was on the occasion of the dying of my daughter Elizabeth.[6] Since then great misfortunes have occurred. The general [2289]

---

[6] See Volume I, 508.

rebellion of the slaves, though passively obeying the Yankees' orders in that respect, by those now here, was without exception other than two of the house servants belonging to Mr. Sayre. And though all remaining home, since the retreat of the Yankees, & the resumption of the owners' authority, have been obedient & orderly, it is to me very painful to meet my former slaves, to whom I was attached by ties of affection on their part (as I believed) as well as on mine, under such changed circumstances. It will also be difficult for me to preserve towards them the same manner as if they had not offended—& which I, & all others, must try to do, as forgiveness of the past was promised to all who remained to return to their duty, or others then absconding, who might return. Not one of these has returned.—The Whig of today . . . contains later news of Bragg's retreat. The movement is treated as being necessary, not so much for Buell's superior forces, as to save the immense quantity of supplies obtained in Kentucky. These made a wagon train of 40 miles in length—& all this baggage, as well as the army, is now deemed safe . . . . According to a letter from the Yankee army . . . our whole force in Ky did not exceed 40,000 men—& according to that authority, & our own accounts, our forces & also the portions engaged in battle, fell greatly short of the opposed Yankee forces in numbers.[7] And so it has been in almost every battle, & every series of military operations throughout the war, that the enemy's forces were more numerous than ours. This inferiority on our part truly serves to augment the honor & glory of our soldiers, & the reputation for bravery of our people. But it is a great error, & evidence of defective military conduct in our commanders, & the government, that our engagements should almost always be made with our forces out-numbered by the enemy's. . . . [2291]

Oct. 24. . . . I was closely employed from early this morning to past 2 P.M. in bringing up my reading of newspapers, & filling the last pages of this diary, & afterwards in moving my remaining shells which were exposed to further depredations, into other parts of the two cabinets & lower locked cases, so that more glasses must be broken or locks again forced, before any one can get to them. When Mr. Sayre returned after the retreat of the Yankees, he found the

---

[7] At Perryville the Confederates were outnumbered by better than two to one in effective troop strength. Because of an atmospheric phenomenon known as acoustic shadow, Buell was not aware until late in the day that a major battle was in progress and consequently did not utilize his superior forces effectively.

locks had been forced, or wooden doors broken, & sundry glasses of the glass doors to the cabinet of recent shells broken, to pick out the desired articles. . . . How much the Yankees stole & how much the negroes afterwards, I cannot tell. But many articles have been removed from both cabinets, & especially of the most beautiful of the recent shells, & sundry of the most . . . valuable specimens among the fossil shells. . . . When I can get boxes, I will pack away the [remaining] shells, for greater safety. Independent of the taking away, the value of hundreds of very small specimens is destroyed by being separated from the labels. These were mostly of fossils from various European localities, which were sent to me by Sir Charles Lyell, & which I would not know how to identify, & to name, even though all the labels were left, as many were, though separated from the shells.—[2292]

After dinner I walked out on the farm. The crop of wheat left, & its remains of prostrate straw, with the rank weeds everywhere, make an almost impassable cover over the fields, through which no one would attempt to walk. And even the formerly regularly used farm paths, I found so grown over by disuse, that it was difficult to walk along, or even to see them throughout. A melancholy scene of waste & loss—yet nothing compared to Beechwood—& even that is still far better preserved than Evelynton. . . . Not only the European papers, & their writers, but the northern correspondents residing in Europe, intimate more & more strongly that some of the powers of Europe will interven[e] in our war, in some way, before long. The N.Y. Tribune declares (on such information,) that European intervention will certainly occur by January, unless the North shall previously gain great & unprecedented victories. [John W.] Forney's Phila. "Press" declares that it will be better to make peace with the South than for the army to go into winter quarters before gaining overwhelming success. These are two of the leading & extreme abolition papers, & most violent for the war of subjugation.—

On our drive from Richmond, on 22nd [*sic*], we passed through part of the battleground of the Mechanicsville engagement, the first of the series of daily conflicts near Richmond. Mr. Sayre's previous acquaintance & information of the circumstances, enabled him to know what was under our view. I saw the marks of the passage of cannon balls through houses at Mechanicsville, of limbs & trunks of trees cut down, & the graves of sundry of our killed, & the bones of [2293] horses killed near the road, & which had been suffered to rot, & all the flesh to disappear. After the first battle of Manassas, it was noticed by many of our men from the lower country, where buzzards are so plenty that any dead body left exposed for a few hours will bring them in numbers sufficient to soon devour it, that not one of these birds was visible, though thousands of carcas[s]es of men & horses were exposed over miles, & for days together, & many for weeks, contaminating the air with the odor of putrefaction which is so grateful & attractive to these obscene birds. The same remarkable absence of buzzards followed the bloody battles in this neighborhood. Not one of them was to be seen throughout all the broad space in which probably 20,000 dead bodies of men & horses were scattered—& from all which space, in other times, all the buzzards would have been drawn to a single exposed carcase. The strange fact can only be accounted for by supposing that all the buzzards within reach of the sound were frightened & driven far off by the noise of the artillery, & did not venture back for some weeks. This explanation would be incredible, but for the certain fact that not a buzzard was seen, though many bodies, either left unburied, or not entirely covered by the slight burying, were exposed to both the senses of sight & smell, for weeks, or until nothing was left except the bones.

Oct. 25. . . . Edmund, by previous arrangement, was sent for at Richmond, & arrived in the afternoon. He brought the papers of today . . . . English papers to 7th received. Nearly all denouncing Lincoln's proclamation, as I expected—but, as I did not expect, they mostly take our view of it, that it will be powerless for its designed effects of either intimidating & humbling the South, or of exciting negro insurrections.—The northern papers are urging a new advance of McClellan's army, so strongly, that Lincoln will probably be again constrained to such action, by this out-side pressure. The effect of Stuart's late raid into Pa. has caused great apprehensions of an advance there of our army—& a northern paper declares that the next great battle of Lee's army will be fought in Pa. Stuart's instructions, & his official report of his raid have been published . . . . Both these papers, & also the northern accounts (of residents,) show that our troops paid marked respect to private property—& did not enter a private dwelling even to ask for a drink of water, or to warm by the fire, (when out all the night in rain,) without politely asking & obtaining leave. The only private property touched was horses, all of which were taken that were come upon in Pa. (Nothing was taken in Md.) If the troops had taken or destroyed all private property, including every town & every house & stock on the route in Pa., it would have been, in my opinion the proper course, & but partial retaliation for the outrages, in violation of the laws of war, & usages of civilized nations at war, practised by the Yankee armies, soldiers, & authorized by the commanders, in all the southern territory where they have had sway. . . .

Oct. 28. The mail. . . . The N.Y. Herald & other northern papers are vehemently urging that McClellan should advance. I hope that their clamor may be effective. . . . Under authority of a late law of Congress, Pres. Davis has appointed 7 (or 8?) Lieutenant Generals. It seems that he has done this in furtherance of his usual policy of appointing incompetent favorites. Of the whole list, there are only two, T. J. Jackson & Longstreet, of military renown, gained in well-fought battles. Kirby Smith has done well what was before him to do & probably is indeed an able officer. But he has never commanded in regular battle, & scarcely been in battle, except at Manassas, where he was immediately disabled by a shot. Gen. [John C.] Pemberton, another of the Lt. Generals, (now sent to supersede Van Dorn,) is said to be an excellent training officer—but has not been in battle during this war. The others I forget.[8] But they were without either experience or reputation on fields of battle. . . . There is a growing belief both in Europe [2297] & Yankeedom, of the probability of European intervention in our war, & its approaching cessation, owing to that cause, aided by others. I cannot help myself placing some faith in this belief—& deeming the occurrence of peace within a few months more probable than the longer continuance of the war. If the powers of Europe, or any one of them alone, shall recognize the independence of the C.S., disregard the Yankee blockade of our ports, & offer equal & sufficient advantages to our privateers & their prizes in their ports, the Yankee government would not therefore dare to make war on the intervening power, but would truckle, & take back all previous threats & boasts, as it did in the affair of the Trent. The occurrence of European intervention, the financial difficulties of the Yankee govt., & the continued discouragement of the hope of subjugating the South, all or either may dispose them to make peace. But in my

---

[8] The others, appointed October 11–13, 1862, were Leonidas Polk, William J. Hardee, and Theophilus H. Holmes.

opinion a still stronger cause than any of these (except armed intervention,) will be found in the political divisions of the Yankee people. Already the party opposed to Lincoln, as shown in the recent elections of three great states,[9] has become so strong as to defy & oppose the illegal despotism of Lincoln. Men already are thus emboldened to utter in public speeches, & to print & publish, expressions of opinions & facts, which if six months earlier, would in every case have caused the immediate arrest of the offender, & his unlimited imprisonment in Fort Warren, or some other prison. No such case of punishment or arrest has recently been ventured, while the provocations for them have increased 100 fold. Thus with practical freedom of speech & of publication restored, & with a very large minority (at least) to use them, the Yankee people will be enabled to hear the truth, from which they have been entirely shut out previously, as to the conduct of their rulers, since the beginning of the war. It is true that, in politic subservience to the still blind fanaticism of the majority of the Yankee people, the opposition speakers & writers all profess to favor a strenuous prosecution [2298] of the war, & the coercion of the C.S. & reconstruction of the former Union. But this must be designed only to blind the ignorant & fanatical multitude. For every argument of these professing advocates for more effective war, goes to prove the hopelessness & folly of all war on the South. I infer that as soon as the leaders of the opposition have sufficiently enlightened the profound ignorance of the mass of the Yankee people, & feel strong enough, they will throw of[f] this present disguise, & advocate peace with the C.S. And when this is done by a party which embraces in its numbers even a large minority of the Yankee people, with the majority in three or four large states, it will have power to arrest the mad progress & war policy of the heretofore ruling party. . . . Commander M. F. Maury is on his way to Europe, sent by the President on a diplomatic mission. This is a good selection, which ought to have been made at first. Maury has a world-wide reputation—&, at the beginning of this war, his name & talents were probably better known in Europe, & more highly appreciated, than those of any other citizen of the Southern Confederacy. . . .

Oct. 29. The condition of this farm, in the entire deficiency of able men slaves, of live-stock &c., & the great hazard, as well as great expense of re-supplying the needs, caused the owners to offer

[9] Ohio, Indiana, and Pennsylvania.

to sell the farm, at private sale. All chance for a crop of wheat had before been lost, by the inability to plough the clover-hay, or even the little & foul spots of corn land, for seeding. Nearly all yesterday & today, two persons have been here to see & bargain for the land—Talbot & Williams of Richmond. They have the option until next Tuesday, to buy the land at $75,000, & the remaining slaves at $700 average. As it is necessary to sell the land, its sale will involve the necessity of selling the negroes. And the most humane disposition of them that can be made, will be to sell them altogether to the purchaser of the farm, with the understanding that they will be retained here. Of course no obligation that they shall be retained can be required, or expected. The owner of slaves must be free to dispose of them as future circumstances may require. And though the present owners have earnestly sought to effect this best disposition of the slaves here, & will be willing to make some sacrifices to do so, little do these slaves, formerly mine, deserve such care to keep them together at their long-used home, & to prevent further [2300] separations of their families. Their conduct in connection with their siding with the Yankee marauders was worse than suspected at first. The amnesty offered to them by Edmund & Mr. Sayre, when resuming possession, has been carried out so fully, that no difference of treatment has been made, of course no punishment for the past offences inflicted—& as far as could be, there has been no difference of manner used towards them. This course required that no investigations should be made as to the pardoned offences. Therefore, it has been only by accidental information, & voluntary & proffered confessions of one of the captured runaways, (since sold,) that more of the misconduct was learned. As to the general quiet rebellion, & the assuming the supposed freedom offered to them by the Yankees, all who remained might be excused, because of their ignorance, & their temptation. But in addition, they aided & participated in the maraudings of the Yankees, to great extent. The negroes (those who went off, as well as they who remained,) sold wheat from the barn to all buyers, at 75 cents the bushel, & some of the poor neighbors were mean enough to buy of them. About 40 of the hogs were killed by them, (though they were supplied with bacon for 5 months ahead,) & a regular business carried on in cooking the pork, & selling it to the Yankee soldiers in the neighboring camps. From recent facts & appearances, they do not deserve the care designed to prevent separation

[476]

of families, as they have shown no such care or consideration themselves. Every man & boy that went off (20 at first,) left here, or elsewhere in the neighborhood, all his female & nearly all other near relatives—all except such as were their companions of their flight. Every family or individual left here was thus separated, by voluntary action on one side & ready consent on the other, from some father, husband, brother, or son. Yet these separations [2301] (in this & all other such cases,) have not seemed to produce sorrow, or trouble, or even transient uneasiness, evinced in words or manner. Under such circumstances, however my feelings are concerned in reference to this unfortunate close of the service of my patrimonial slaves, I do not deem that there will be anything more required of my successors, to prevent further separation, than the present earnest effort to sell them altogether, & to the buyer of the farm. If this cannot be done, it will be superfluous to attempt other indulgence of this kind, than to sell together, to one buyer all the remaining members of each family.—Took a long walk, with Edmund, over part of the farm. The labors of the farm, since direction of it was resumed by the owners, have been worth very little—indeed not so much as the cost of food. For if the farm shall be sold, the labors will not add a dollar to the price—& will do little for preparation for future crops, if no sale shall be made.

Oct. 31. Edmund & Nanny having to go to Richmond, I took a seat in the carriage to attend to some business of my own. Sue & Mary returned with us, to stay from this Friday to next Monday morning. We set off too soon to have got our mail. But on the road to Richmond, we heard the exciting news that there was strong probability of an early proposal by England & France, of a long armistice—which, if declined by Lincoln's government, would be followed by intervention more effectively.... I found that the report was not relied upon in Rd. If not unfounded, (as have proved many less positive & particular reports,) I suppose that this is *premature.* But I am persuaded that some equivalent measures will be adopted before long, & that this war will be ended in a few months. For the causes of peace, I look more to disappointment [2302] of the Yankee people, their growing discontent, & future despair of success in their war of aggression, than to anything else. ... At latest accounts received direct from our army, there had been no important changes of position of main bodies, either of our forces, on this side of the Potomac, or of McClellan's on the Maryland side.[10] This continued inactivity on his part, & the holding of our positions so long, would be enough to prove that the Yankee "victories" in Md. had been barren of results. . . . Gen. Jackson has effectually destroyed the superstructure of the B. & O. R.R. from within 3 miles of Harper's Ferry for 25 or 30 miles towards Martinsburg. . . .

November 4. This is the important election day for New York. Several regiments of U.S. troops have been sent to the city of N.Y. doubtless to overawe the electors opposed to the Lincoln administration. Increased & stronger evidences have been afforded of British sympathy with the Confederates, in recent speeches of Mr. Gladstone, a leading member of the ministry, & other members of parliament—& in the approving comments thereon of British newspapers. . . . Gen. Bragg was called from his command to report himself in Richmond. This was understood as showing the displeasure of the government. But if so, he has removed that ill-opinion, & has been sent back to resume his command. It is a singular position of public opinion as to the late battle in Ky, & the subsequent retreat of the Confederates, & in strong opposition to what is usual, that both sides, instead of claiming victory, admit defeat in the general operations, & while we have denounced Bragg for retreating, & evacuating Ky., Buell is even more loudly denounced in Yankee papers, for having (by his misconduct) suffered a repulse at Perryville, & afterwards, to allow Bragg to retreat without loss, & to secure all the enormous waggon [*sic*] train loaded with valuable supplies.[11] . . . Yesterday, bacon was bought in Richmond, for the negroes here, at 70 cents the pound. If giving the usual allowance heretofore on this farm, of 3 lb. a week to men, & in proportion to women, young hands, & children, the cost of meat alone would not be reimbursed by the value of the labor of the laboring hands—to say nothing of the slaves who do not labor. All other articles of necessary consumption are also very high—& all will have to be bought for this farm. The negotiation for its sale is ended, by the intending purchasers withdrawing, by notice this day.—A body of

---

[10] Unknown to the diarist, McClellan's army, after much prodding from the impatient Lincoln, had begun crossing the Potomac on Sunday, October 26.

[11] Ruffin is not aware that Buell had already been removed from command of Federal forces in Kentucky and Tennessee. On October 30 his successor, Major General William S. Rosecrans, assumed command of the newly created Department of the Cumberland.

500 cavalry was sent to Jamestown island to destroy the negro banditti that occupied it . . . . The approach of the Confederates was made known to the negroes in time for them to escape to the Yankee forces in Williamsburg. And these having been strongly reinforced, as was understood, were too strong to be assailed by our cavalry. On their return, they captured & brought back 150 of the runaway slaves, who occupy, or roam over & plunder & lay waste all of the peninsula below New Kent, & are masters of all outside of the Yankee encampments. No portion of our country has been so much damaged, or the owners left in such miserable condition. All who have not fled, leaving at the mercy of the Yankees nearly or quite all of their property, have lost everything & are exposed to all privations, as well as to [2306] the continued insults of Yankee soldiers, & pilferings of runaway or lawless negroes. My sister Mrs. Dorsey, whose farm & residence is on James river, a few miles above Jamestown, & 7 miles from Williamsburg, has lost every one of her slaves—& we hear that she & her son's wife have to cook & wash for their family.—There seems so much stillness on the Potomac border, (notwithstanding the Yankee accounts of the advancing movements of their army,) that it may be inferred that the campaign is ended, (as to grand operations,) & that both the Yankee & Confederate armies will soon go into winter quarters. I cannot help believing that the last of our great & bloody battles has been fought—& that negotiations for peace will be on foot before the winter is over. A sensible writer in the Enquirer, who has lately been in the North, & had there opportunities of hearing opinions from many well-informed men, predicts a long war, on the ground that all the people, interests, & localities of Yankeedom are making great profits by the war. I can well believe this as to New England, & the Atlantic states. But it is not so as to the North-western states, whose people lose in every way by the war, & who are being exhausted & ruined for the gain of New England. The manufacturers, & all others of the industrial interests, are indeed reaping a rich harvest of gain & riches, derived from government contracts & the high protection of all northern manufactures. The enormous sums lavished by the government for all supplies for & munitions of war—the building & hiring of hundreds of steamers—give not only to the contractors profits & wealth in unprecedented floods, but compel them to demand & employ labor, at high rates, from every laborer in the country. The present income of both the rich &

the poor is so great that they scarcely consider as any counterpoise the debt of $1,200,000,000 they have already contracted, & which two years more of war would double. They have not yet felt the weight of taxes necessary to [2307] pay the mere interest of this debt—& if they had, the burden would not equal half of the excess of their present enormous profits, whether on capital or wages. The heavy protective tariff, however prospectively injurious to the community, for the present is the more profitable for New England—& the depreciation of northern currency aids the operation, by causing the rates of protecting duties to be actually higher.— Gen. Jackson burnt the extensive stationhouses &c. at Martinsburg, which, together with all the other destruction of the B. & O. R.R., is computed by some newspapers (no doubt most extravagantly,) at $5,000,000 of loss to the company & to the U.S. government. The existence of this railroad has been productive of the worst evils of the war to Va. especially, & to the C.S. in general. All along the route through Va. the numerous northern employés, the northern interests, & the northern feelings & opinions introduced, long before the war began, served to Yankeeize all that line through the State. Hence it followed, that when the secession of Va was declared by its Convention, all the agents of this company, & all connected with its business & interests, amounting to some thousands along the route & including almost every man of influence, were Yankees in sentiment & interest, & inimical to their country of residence or birth, & to the South in the great question of secession. This influence enabled & aided the north-western portion of Va successfully to revolt. And, protected as a northern work by the adjacent population, this road has been of incalculable aid to the Yankees, by transporting men & supplies, & of injury to the Confederates & their war operations. Even after peace shall be made, unless Maryland is made part of the C.S., this road through Va should not be allowed to exist.—Formerly, & until Richmond became the capital of the C.S., & therefore the sojourning place of thousands of soldiers & office seekers, & of hundreds of desperate adventurers [2308] & villains, it was one of the most orderly towns in the world. Since the access of this floating population it has become as remarkable for disorder & crime. . . . Street robbery, effected by violence & sometimes murder, burglary, & bloody assaults & homicides, besides smaller felonies, are of nightly occurrence. Formerly, no one, however weak & defenceless, thought

[480]

of any danger in walking anywhere in the city in the darkest night. Now it is very unsafe for any man, alone, to venture abroad, even in the most frequented streets, & much more so in the out-skirts, or parts of the city of least respectable population. The foreign & almost unknown crime of "garroting" has become common—& has in one case been committed in daytime, & in sight of witnesses, who were too timid or too weak to interfere before the criminals had effected their robbery, & escaped. The manner is for two or more persons to throw a cord, or some substitute, around the neck of the victim, choke him to incapacity to cry out, empty his pockets, & then let him loose, in a state of insensibility usually, & escape unrecognized by the sufferer, & usually unseen by others. Drunken men, & strangers from the country, are especially in danger of these attacks. Prudent & sober residents, who are aware of the danger, can very easily & surely guard against it.

Nov. 5. Two companies of cavalry passed by our gate today, from New Kent, where they have been stationed lately, on their way to Fredericksburg.

Nov. 6. . . . [2309] The subject matter & the plan of this diary, without any intention, have been almost entirely changed since the war has been well in progress. From being, as at first, a mere record of personal acts, incidents, & opinions, my diary has become, since I began to note all the important events of the war, almost exclusively a record of public events, or of their coloring, true or false, as they are stated, & seem to be credible, in the newspapers, or by other experience, & private or public reports deemed credible. More lately, this labor, undertaken to amuse myself & to kill a part of my wearisome time, has been much extended, by my adding to it the extracting articles from the newspapers, & appending them, as more full documents & illustrations of my concise statements & comments. This addition has increased the interest (to myself,) of my labor and I regret that I had not adopted the same plan from the beginning of the war. But however interesting it may be thus to note, & preserve for future reference, the reported incidents as their occurrence is first known, with the impressions on the public mind & my own, the attempt shows in the plainest & fullest lights, the little trust & credence that contemporary events deserve to receive, & the extreme difficulty, if not impossibility, of the writing of truthful contemporaneous history. . . . If any one, having good judgment to discriminate, impartiality, & good memory, would write, day by day, the military & political events of these or any other exciting & important times, such a record, though it would necessarily be full of mistakes, & undesigned falsehood, would, nevertheless, be most interesting to readers in later times, when the true version of the facts might be understood. Such writings, even if by the ablest hands, would not deserve the name of history—but would serve as admirable materials for history to be written a century, or more, later. Such would be the case as to all contemporaneous political events. But it seems to me that the difficulties of ignorance, & false information, are especially great as to present & recent events of this war—owing to the general & successful silence & concealment as to past battles & war operations, practised by the Confederate government, & the general system of deception by the most unlimited & shameless lying of the Yankee government. I suppose that in the records of the War Departments of both governments, the true facts are noted, & will be preserved, of the actual & exact strength of each army in service, the state of its equipment, supplies, military condition &c.—& of the loss in killed, wounded & missing, arms, supplies &c., suffered in each battle & campaign. But such facts have not been yet made known, on either side, as to very few armaments, or battles, during this war—& in no case have such true statements been published for months after the occurrences. Thus, even as to hardly-fought & bloody battles, fought by large opposing armies, we have remained for weeks, if not for months, misinformed & ignorant [2311] as to which side really gained the victory, or the fruits of victory. This uncertainty is not entirely caused by the designed concealment, or misrepresentation, of the facts, by either or both governments. Another cause has been in the indecisive characters & results of some of our greatest & well-fought battles. In this war, though the ranks have been filled mostly with raw volunteers, (entirely so in the Confederate armies,) there have been opposed armies remarkable for their great numbers, bravery, hard fighting, & also for the amount of blood-shed suffered. Yet if our generals (or some of them) can fight well, & beat the enemy, or withstand very superior forces, they do not seem to know how to improve their successes, or to reap the fruits of victory. Except the rout of the Yankee attacking force at Bethel (our first battle, & an undoubted victory,) & the great route of the Yankee army at the first battle of Manassas, & a few later battles in the west, there has been

[482]

no crushing victory in any of our great & bloody battles in the open field. At Manassas, though there never was a more complete rout, & disorganization, of a beaten army, we did not follow up the victory—& gained nothing by it except reputation, & the stopping the enemy's progress for some eight months. The two days' bloody battles at Shiloh left both armies nearly in their previous positions. The battle of Seven Pines did no more. And [in] the other succeeding great battles near Richmond, continuing for 6 or 7 successive days of hard fighting & great slaughter, it is true that our great object was effected of driving the Yankee army backward, & saving Richmond from its attack. But had not Richmond been there, the only visible fruit of our victories would have been that Gen. McClellan retreated some 20 to 25 miles, to occupy a stronger position for defence, from which he [2312] still threatened Richmond by the river route—& which position he continued to occupy, undisturbed by our victorious army, as long as he found it convenient to remain, & then retired without any annoyance. In the late great battle of Sharpsburg, or Antietam, the Confederates claimed the victory, & as it seems to me justly, because they held their ground, & next morning offered to renew the battle, in vain. The Yankees claim the victory, because in afternoon of that morning, the Confederate army, without opposition, retreated across the Potomac. But whichever army was victorious, neither has gained any later fruits of victory. Both armies, to this time, remain within a day's march of the other, & neither is strong enough to attack the other in its position.—But little as our government allows us to know of battles & their results, we are still less informed of the positions & condition of our armies between one great battle & the next great movement for attack or retreat. We do not yet know where Bragg's great army has been at any time in the last two weeks, or more—& if it were possible, might well suppose that the army was no longer existing. Such concealment of preparatory operations is proper & commendable—& it is wonderful that our authorities can so effectually effect such concealment.—Whenever time shall have developed the facts which now are hidden, I think . . . that the full truth will add to the glory of the Confederate soldiers, for brave deeds & endurance, & will detract still more from the reputation of some of their officers high in command—to whose incompetency or misconduct most of our disasters have been due. I think it will appear, when the facts are laid bare, that in almost every pitched or considerable battle . . . the Confederates were inferior to the Yankees in numbers, in arms, equipments & supplies, & that we had no countervailing superiority, except in the better moral [2313] character, (high principle & resolution founded thereon,) & in the higher capacity of some of our commanding officers to most of those of the enemy. Passing by small affairs—in which surprise & accident frequently determine the results—& naval attacks by the Yankee war steamers, in which they have every advantage, & we possess almost no power—in all the many great & bloody land battles, I think it will be found that the Confederate armies were greatly inferior in numbers & equipment in every case of their defeat, & also in most cases in which they were victorious. The northern soldiers have generally fought with a degree of bravery that was not looked for by us, & not before exampled in raw troops & volunteers. But in these respects they have not equaled the Confederate volunteers, who, as men, ar[e] far superior to the Yankee soldiers in position, worth of private character, principle, & intelligence.

Nov. 7. . . . In the morning, the ground was covered with snow, & the snow still falling fast, with strong N.W. wind.—The mail. A letter from my grandson Thomas, dated 2nd, to his sister Nanny was especially interesting to us. He was engaged in the late affair in which a Yankee train was burnt & 93 prisoners captured. . . . His company (F.) Prince George cavalry, with others of 12th Regt., have latterly been employed in the severe duty, both to men & horses, of scouting between their outposts & those of the enemy, as far as Bull Run. . . . [End of MS Volume 13—p. 2315] A large force of the Yankee army has entered Loudoun [County], & has passed along the eastern base of the Blue Ridge, & seems pressing on to Front Royal in Warren. It seems to be the advanced movement of McClellan's main army. Our forces, west of the Blue Ridge, are said to be falling back up the valley. . . . On the suggestion of Gen. Beauregard, the Mayor of Charleston has advised all the non-combatants residing or sojourning in that city, to leave it, with their families—so as [to] enable more effective defence, or more speedy evacuation, if the city is attacked. This seems to imply the expectation of impending attack, & also desperate resistance. The vast naval preparations of the enemy, & also many intimations in northern papers, indicate speedy & vigorous attempts on sundry parts of the southern sea & gulf coasts. Besides Charleston, long threatened, & the especial object of Yankee vengeance & hatred, & Savannah, it seems probable that Mobile is among the chief & first aims for conquest. Its possession by [2316] [the] enemy would necessarily convey also the command of the great rivers Alabama & Tombigby [*sic*], & by them the command of the greater part of the territory of Alabama. Galveston is already occupied—& if the northern papers are to be believed as to intentions, the whole coast of Texas, & the Mississippi river will soon be the objects of great aggressive movements of the enemy's naval & land forces. The beginning of winter removes the great previous danger of malarial diseases in these regions—and this with the mildness of the winter in the south, invite the early & most vigorous efforts of the enemy in that region. In our almost entire want of naval force, I fear that we shall suffer greatly in this respect. It is not improbable, with their very superior & great means for naval warfare, & attacking fortifications for defence of ports & rivers by gun & mortar steamers, in many cases iron-clad, & bearing the heaviest & most powerful artillery, that in this winter & the season of high waters, the enemy may occupy every southern sea-port, & every great southern & western river to their respective heads of steam navigation. . . . Yankee naval forces have destroyed extensive & valuable salt works on the [2317] coast of Florida. All such works on the sea coast & salt rivers are exposed to such danger that we can hope little from this otherwise cheapest mode of supplying salt. The great salt works on the Kanawha have again been occupied, with the Kanawha valley, by the Yankee forces . . . . The legislature of Va. passed a law under authority of which the Governor of Va. had taken possession of the great salt works in South-western Va, the owners to be fairly remunerated, & this to supply salt to the people of the state, at a moderate price compared to those extorted by extortioners & speculators. The retail price in Petersburg lately was 50 cents the pound—& later it was 70 cents at Atlanta. . . . The warmth of the earth caused the snow to melt fast. Yet it was 5 or 6 inches deep before it ceased falling fast at 3 P.M.

Nov. 8. Though the air is still very cold, for the time, the snow had nearly disappeared in the afternoon.—A Richmond paper of today, which was obtained by accident, brought the important news of the success of the democratic (or combined opposition) party in the N.York elections, by astonishing majorities. The change of votes in the city, in one year, was nearly 49,000. The democratic candidate for Governor, [Horatio] Seymour, & other officers elected by the votes of the whole state, are unquestionably elected, & by large majorities, though all the districts had not been heard from. Of 28 members of congress whose election was known, 25 are democrats, & 3 only abolitionists, or "republicans," as they call themselves.[12] In New Jersey, the democratic [2318] ticket is elected by overwhelming majorities. From these changes, the N.Y. Herald pretends to expect new vigor in the prosecution of the war & the speedy crushing of the rebellion. It also asserts that McClellan is moving on upon Richmond, & is nearer to it by 50 miles than the Confederate army, &, in all probability, will soon be in possession of that city. Illinois has either gone for the democratic ticket, or (like Pa.) is about equally divided.[13] The New England states & the extreme north-western, only, so far as heard from, maintain the abolition representation. Now it is true that every democratic candidate, & every advocate for them, professed to be in favor of a vigorous prosecution of the war. And if I believed this profession, I should regret their success, inasmuch as I think that if the war is to be zealously carried on against us, it is better for the Confederates, & for their best prospect of success, that the leaders of the Yankee people shall be the fanatical & demented, violent & villainous abolitionists, than men more moderate, judicious, & conciliatory like their opponents, but pursuing the same end of conquering the C.S. But I do not believe their professions—which are necessary to be made to muzzle & deceive the ignorant multitude. If the two parties agree in this end, of conquering the South, they disagree completely as to every mean for the end, & on every question as to men or measures. The strong opposition will thwart & obstruct the measures & policy of the administration, so that the operations of the war will be paralysed, & finally its objects shown clearly to be unattainable. When secure of popular support, then the leaders will throw off their present disguise, & the democratic party will demand peace. The members of [2319] congress elected this autumn, will not act as such until December 1863—& until then the actual

---

[12] The Democratic sweep in New York was not quite this extensive. The final count was seventeen congressional seats for the Democrats to fourteen for their Republican adversaries. Seymour's majority in the gubernatorial context was approximately 11,000.

[13] The Democrats carried Illinois by a margin of 16,500 votes, winning nine of the fourteen House seats in the process.

majority in Congress may not be diminished. But as soon as it is manifest that a majority of the States, & northern people, are in opposition to the administration, the administration will not dare to carry out measures condemned by a majority of the people. Already, in advance of the elections, the U.S. government, before so despotic, has ceased to use its power to imprison its opponents. . . . Policy might have directed this moderation on the eve of the elections. But now they are over, there will be no reason why the government shall not fully resume its previous tyrannical rule, & arbitrary punishment of all opposers, unless fearing the numbers & strength of the opposition. This will soon be seen. If Lincoln does not resume his system of severe despotism, it will only be because he dares not do so—& I will construe the omission to indicate the speedy breaking down of the power of the abolition & war party of the North. . . .

Nov. 9. Sunday. Finished the 4th vol. of Macaulay's History of England. I have read the first two volumes three times, & the last two twice—& even the latest reading, deprived of much of the great charm of novelty, was to me more interesting than any other historical or political work. It would be to me a great blessing, & offering one of the greatest resources of intellectual pleasure, if I could forget the contents of this fascinating history, after each reading, as completely as if it had not been read by me before. . . .

Nov. 10. Having nothing left for amusing reading, I looked, for reference, into [Adam] Clarke's Commentary on the Bible,[14] & read Ecclesiastes & the Song of Solomon. I had never before read the former—nor the latter for many years. Both are literary curiosities, of remote antiquity. But I cannot conceive any claim of either to have been deemed inspired by Almighty God, or even to be deemed religious works, fit to be recognized in the canonical scriptures. The commentator, who was more learned, & candid, & not less pious than his popular brethren of that craft, in his introductory remarks, truly pronounces the Song of Solomon to be a mere amatory poem—he might have said in plain words a licentious & libidinous poem. There is nothing in the comments & teachings of divines in regard to the letter & purport of the canonical scriptures, more shameful than the efforts made by nearly all of them (to whom

---

[14] Originally published in eight volumes during the period 1810–26, this was the principal work of the distinguished Wesleyan theologian, Adam Clarke (1762?–1832).

the learned & honest Adam Clarke is a bright exception,) to invest this production with a highly religious character, & to interpret the sensual raptures of the male & female personages into the reciprocal devotion & action of Christ & the Christian church.

Nov. 11. The mail. Our papers state that the hostile armies lately on the Potomac are getting near together, & that a general engagement seems impending. Gen. Jackson's command is facing the enemy in the Shenandoah valley, & Gen. Lee in Culpeper. . . . The wonderful changes in Yankee sentiment shown in the great success of the opposition in the late elections, have not less alarmed than surprised the Lincolnites. The triumph of the winners is strongly & boldly expressed in many speeches & newspaper articles . . . . The declarations of the triumphant opponents of Lincoln still mostly are in favor of the vigorous prosecution of the war. But some desires for peace also cautiously are indicated. These, I am confident, will become more generally & strongly expressed. And before two months will pass, I predict that this opposition war party, now forming a great minority of Yankeedom, will become a peace party, & be fast growing from a minority to a majority of the northern people. . . . Salt is higher than ever. 85 sacks were lately sold at auction in Petersburg, at prices ranging from 55 to 64½ cents the pound.—Yesterday morning Edmund set off for Prince George, to attend to his business at Beechwood.—There are very few books here, & none that I wish to read. The only means I have had to obtain any was from the Library & Reading Room Association in Rd., of which I am a member. From this, I can have two volumes at a time, & keep any one not more than two weeks. The frequent opportunities since our arrival here [2324] have enabled me to obtain & return books within the limits required. But such accidental conveyances cannot be expected to be regular. Yesterday thus procured [Ephraim G.] Squier's "Nicaragua."[15] . . .

Nov. 12. Mr. Sayre saw a gentleman of the neighborhood, from

---

[15] Published in two volumes in 1852, this work has been characterized by the noted Latin American scholar, Hubert Herring, as "invaluable" even today for its coverage of the early history of Central America. A native of New York, Squier (1821–88) had served as United States chargé d'affaires to Central America in 1849–50 and was a leading proponent of an interoceanic canal through Nicaragua. At the outbreak of the war he was chief editor in the New York publishing house of Frank Leslie, in which capacity he inaugurated *Frank Leslie's Pictorial History of the American Civil War.* Appointed United States commissioner to Peru in 1863, he remained in that post for the balance of the war.

Richmond this forenoon, & heard from him as the report there that [Major General Franz] Sigel was pressing upon Jackson, in the Valley, & McClellan on Lee in Culpeper, or wherever his army is. It was understood that our armies were much inferior in numbers to those opposing them, & in wretched condition for want of clothing, shoes, & other needed supplies. Even if our affairs are as bad as this, I do not distrust the result of battle. I have abiding confidence in the superior courage & endurance of our soldiers, & the greater talent of most of their leaders, including Lee & Jackson.

Nov. 14. Mail. A large, if not the main part of our army, is at Culpeper C.H., & has been there for some time. It is thought by some that our armies will remain on the defensive, ready to fight if attacked—& that the enemy will not attack—so there will be no great battle in that direction. . . . Northern reports, coming through Fredericksburg, state positively that McClellan has been superseded in his command by Burnside.[16] This will be good news, if true, not only for the loss to the Yankee army of its best commanding officer, but still more as likely to exasperate the opposition in the North, now the majority, & with whom McClellan is the especial favorite, & appreciated much above his real merits. . . . Finished Squier's "Nicaragua"—passing very hastily over the Appendix, relating to the interoceanic canal, the ancient inhabitants, & the recent revolutions & anarchy of the people & states of Central America. The author is a genuine Yankee, an abolitionist, & apparently not opposed to amalgamation of the races. In his statements of the universal neglect of industry, he intimates no conception of the great cause being the absence of slavery of the inferior races, & consequently of compulsory labor. In the causes of political anarchy, he does not perceive that a sufficient cause, if no other cause existed, in such a population, for the destruction of free government & all valuable political rights, would be political equality of all men, & universal suffrage. In a thinly-settled, fertile, tropical country, where the few necessaries of life may be bought for very small prices, & men can live almost without labor, there will be no steady continuous labor, unless it is compulsory, or that of slaves. When the most destitute class is wholly or considerably composed of negroes, this disinclination to labor will be much increased; if of

---

[16] These reports were accurate. His patience exhausted, Lincoln relieved McClellan from command of the Army of the Potomac by orders dated November 5, and five days later McClellan bade his troops an emotional farewell.

whites, the physical inability, in the tropics, will be so much the greater. And whether in the torrid or the temperate zone—among an ignorant & mongrel population as in Central America, or the most enlightened of the United States, or the [2326] Confederate States—no people will retain long the blessings of free government, where the class owning no property, & paying no taxes, have equal voices & power in raising & disbursing the taxes with those citizens who own the property & who furnish the taxes. . . .

Nov. 15. Gen. McClellan has certainly been removed from command of the army, & without any ceremony. The supposed causes are his failure to obey, first a recommendation, &, secondly, a peremptory order from the government (through Gen. Halleck,) to advance on the Confederate army—& also because McClellan was censured by the Court of Inquiry for the loss of Harper's Ferry. As I expected, it seems from northern reports (in today's paper,) that his dismissal has excited the indignation of the opponents of Lincoln, & even is strongly disapproved by some of the abolitionists, who pronounce it wrong to change the commander of the army in the face of the enemy, & when battle is imminent. When thus placed in command, Gen. Burnside must feel himself bound to advance & attack—& therefore I change my previous view of the case, under McClellan, & now expect an immediate renewal of the movement "on to Richmond." I hope it may be so, & in the present direction.—Every person, farmer, manufacturer, or merchant, who now has products or commodities for sale, is making money, beyond all precedent, from the enormous prices for every necessary of life, & for every article of ordinary consumption. Even if allowing for the depreciation of our paper money as much as 100 percent of the advance [2327] on former & usual prices, there will still have to be added 100 or 200, & in many articles more than 300 percent more, to reach the rates of current prices—& which seem to be every day rising higher. Every producer, who has his ordinary products for sale, is reaping profits beyond all previous example, or conception. All persons deriving income from industry & capital, of any kind, (except in fixed amounts of interest, or money,) find, in the high prices, great profit in the war, after paying all of its proper & legal burdens. But these high prices double or quadruple the sufferings, and difficulties of support, of all whose property & homes have been over-run & plundered or laid waste by the enemy; & who have thus lost, & perhaps driven away from every thing that they expected to sell for support, or to which they might again resort, if permitted by the recurrence of peace. These thousands of unfortunates, in addition to having thus lost all their sources of income, & much, if not all, of all their moveable capital, have now to buy all that they need, (if able to buy at all,) & if farmers, the grain & meat &c. which before they sold, at prices from four to eight times greater than ordinary.—The Governor of Georgia has been denouncing the military laws (or "conscript acts") of the Confederate government as unconstitutional—& that opinion has now been sustained by the unanimous opinion of the Supreme Court of that state.[17] This is an unfortunate occurrence. What trouble it may bring I cannot understand, or conceive the end of. Many other persons, public & private, have held the like opinion. But all others waived their difficulties on account of the great military necessities of the Confederacy. There are like difficulties, & others more operative, opposing the latest military law of the rump Congress. The constitutionality of the law ordering the draft is opposed in Pennsylvania to the verge of mutiny & rebellion [2328]—& the draft itself, has been resisted, without regard to law, not only in Pa. but in several other states. . . . There is evidently great unwillingness of the people, everywhere, to meet the requisition, & a disinclination of the authorities to resort to the rigor necessary for compulsion of the people. . . .

Nov. 18. The mail brought little news. The papers avoid stating any recent position or movements of our armies—& thus all such are usually a week or more old before known to the public, & most commonly then learned through republication from northern papers. . . . Our Secretary of War, G[eorge] W. Randolph, has resigned. Gen. Gus[tavus W.] Smith succeeds [2330] him *pro tem*.[18] This resignation was unlooked-for. Gen. Randolph had so managed the department as to satisfy the public.—We were rejoiced today to get a letter from Mildred, to Julian, of Oct. 14th., the first for more than 13 months. It stated little as to herself except that she & family were well—& the painful position of having heard nothing from her family here since a chance-received letter of last spring. All

---

[17] In reality, the unanimous decision of the Georgia supreme court was just the reverse—much to the consternation of Governor Joseph E. Brown.

[18] Smith served only three days in this temporary capacity. On November 21 President Davis named James A. Seddon to the position, which he retained until the closing months of the war.

others have miscarried, & she knows nothing, but only fears, our latter losses caused by the known invasion & occupation of our residences & farms by the enemy. Her letter was short, & in general & guarded terms, as if written in expectation of its being intercepted & read by the Yankees. . . . Some fears or expectations are entertained that the expedition of 12,000 Yankees that lately moved to take Goldsborough, & re-embarked from Greenville,[19] in conjunction with the stronger force at Suffolk, will move upon Weldon, or otherwise on Petersburg, & therefrom to Richmond, to meet the northern army. We are at a loss where to expect the enemy's first attack—whether in this mode, or from the Potomac army on Richmond, or on the southern [coastal] cities. And little as we know of the positions of Lee's army, we know still less of the army lately in Ky. & that which was defeated at Corinth—or of the Yankee armies confronting both.

Nov. 21. The mail.—Gen. Foster's naval expedition with 12,000 land troops, retreated after its advance had reached within 5 miles of Tarborough, on hearing that a large force was embodied to resist his attack. . . . It seems that the bulk of the Yankee army now under Burnside has advanced upon the Rappahannock, & mainly upon the bank opposite Fredericksburg. They are within musket range of that town, but had not (on 20th) crossed the river to enter it. All the cotton & tobacco in Fredericksburg had been burnt or destroyed. It mostly belonged to speculators, & was sent there to be smuggled into Yankeedom. . . . Except skirmishing of outposts, nothing heard of our main army under Lee's immediate command, at or near Gordonsville, or of Jackson's army in the Valley.—A Yankee correspondent states the wretched & suffering condition of the numerous negro fugitives at Cairo, [Ill.,] & especially because of exposure to cold. If so before the beginning of winter, what will not be the suffering before its end? One of the loudest complaints of Yankee abolitionists against southern slavery, was the separation of families, by sale. In truth, all such separations were less frequent, numerous, & general than occurred in the families of all northern people of the poorer & even the middle class. For with them, it was almost universal for the young men to leave their families to earn a living more easily in the far remote west or south. And few of

---

[19] This reference is to a Federal expedition from New Bern, North Carolina, under command of Major General John G. Foster, which was stopped short of Goldsborough in mid-December after a number of minor skirmishes.

the daughters failed to do the like, if having any offered employment abroad, promising more ease & profit. Every family looked forward, & contentedly, for such separation of most of the members from those remaining at home, & for such separations to be in most cases final & complete, or to be scarcely better, in the [2334] very rare & uncertain chances for meeting of the separated relatives. If anything was wanting to display the falsehood & hypocricy [*sic*] of this Yankee charge of inhumanity on southern slave-holders, it is furnished in the systematic separation of the slaves stolen by, or absconding to, their armed forces in this war. They are separated into the two classes of able-bodied men, & of weak or burdensome slaves, whether women, boys & girls & younger children, & the aged & infirm, & sent apart with no more compunction than if ordering the sending off of horses & cattle to a separate position from the men of the army. I have before stated that of the slaves taken from Maycox, to McClellan's camp at Westover, all the boys were speedily shipped away—where to, neither they nor their parents left behind, had any information. In the papers of today appears a much more general military order (as stated, without remark, in northern papers,) by which all the able negro men at Fortress Monroe, & that vicinity, were to be sent to Washington, where they were wanted, & all the women, children & infirm, to be sent to Crany Island—there, I suppose, to suffer even worse than those at Cairo. . . . The prices of necessaries of life continue to rise . . . . The Richmond paper of today says that salt sold there yesterday, by retail, at more than $1.50 per pound! The Yankees have recently broken up various salt-works on the sea-coast of Fla, La, & elsewhere—& it seems that none can be safe from their attacks. . . . The President has appointed James A. Seddon Secretary of War. I have a very high opinion of Mr. Seddon, as a patriot, a [2335] statesman, & a man of high intellect & ability. But he has had no experience of military matters, & I fear that he may want the peculiar qualifications for this office. I think that Seddon would be better placed as Secretary of State. I am glad of his highest advancement to positions he is qualified to fill—for he has shown for me more esteem & regard, & seemed to assume towards me more the position of a private friend, than any man of his present high station, now living, in our country. And more than any one deserving of as high station, except Willoughby Newton. . . . I have inserted an extract from Ex-Gov. [Charles S.] Morehead's speech at a public meeting in England, in which he describes a conversation of President Lincoln's with some of the southern members of the "Peace Congress." Even from this short sketch, what a clown & mountebank must the public of England infer (& correctly) to be the last President of the United States![20]—For the last he will be, though he may have many successors to preside over the remaining fragment, or "rump."

Nov. 22. John Van Buren has been the most frequent, copious, & popular speaker of the opposition party in New York, in the late canvass, & since.[21] While the general purport of all his speeches seems to recommend peace, & to promise, (if his party is in power,) speedy peace, still, like all other orators & papers of that party, he professes to be in favor of a vigorous prosecution of the war. I have thought, & so said before, that the leaders of that party must know that the North cannot reconstruct the Union by conquering the South, & that they can have peace only by recognizing the separate nationality & independence of the Confederate States—& that the profession of prosecuting the war was a false pretence . . . . Very lately, Van Buren has delivered one of his characteristic speeches, to the Democratic Association of New York city, the published sketch of which I will append, as well as the more open remarks, following, of Fernando Wood, also a very prominent democrat, formerly Mayor of the city, & recently elected one of its members of Congress. In these speeches, it seems to me, glimpses of the ulterior objects are displayed more clearly than before. Van Buren also seems to hint something of his preferred plan of operations, to bring about the reconstruction of the Union. He repeats that peace may be attained by Jan. 1st., that President Lincoln & his Congress should declare an armistice, to enable elections to be held, & invite

---

[20] Among other things, Lincoln was alleged to have illustrated one point by recounting an anecdote from Aesop's fables. Apparently, such earthy humor did not strike a responsive chord among Southerners at the Peace Congress.

[21] Son of the former president, Van Buren (1810–66) had assumed a radical posture during the 1840's, helping to organize the Barnburners and playing an active role in the Free Soil movement. However, he returned to the Democratic fold in 1849, supported the Compromise of 1850, and was a peace activist ten years later. During the war he was a vociferous critic of the Lincoln administration, denouncing its treatment of General McClellan, its policy of arbitrary arrests, and its use of Negro troops. After campaigning for Seymour in the New York gubernatorial election of 1862, Van Buren supported McClellan for the presidency two years later.

the southern states to elect & send members to the (northern) Congress—which Mr. V. thinks they would certainly do: that this general Congress shall call a Convention of all the States, & that this Convention shall amend the Constitution, secure the rights of the South, & also elect a new President, & for the term of six years as a constitutional amendment, & such as is made in the constitution of the C.S. Now if we consider that the speaker's recommendations of carrying on the war, & electing McClellan as the new President, are (as I suppose,) intended merely to deceive the mob, his scheme for reunion will amount to what I have before seen intimated by some northern writers viz: that if the South will not join with the North . . . the North shall join with the South, under the amended constitution of the Confederate States, & any additional guaranties required for securing the maintenance of southern rights. But, if this is meant—& if every northern state & man should concur—if severally & jointly, the northern states were to adopt the C.S. constitution, & ask admission into the confederacy—further, if every guaranty should be given, & made part of the constitution that the most jealous defenders of southern rights [2337] could frame & write—still, Mr. Van Buren & his party will have to learn, that neither on these terms, nor on any terms, would the south consent again to be united under one general government with the northern states or people. Even if the war debt & consequent necessary taxation, (which alone would be a sufficient objection,) did not exist, there would be an insuperable barrier to reconstruction in this: it has been fully proved by large experience, that no constitutional restrictions, obligations, or guaranties to a minority, have had, or will have, the least force to withhold the northern people from violating them, when they have the power of a strong majority of votes, & the control of all the three great branches of the administration. The Northern States are, & must be, sectional in interest, in fanaticism, & in opinion—& having twice the numbers & political strength, will always, (under a common general government,) be able to control the weaker South, & will do so, with no limit but its will, & despite of all conceivable constitutional defences & safeguards of the weaker section of the Union. The former constitution of the C.S. is still that of the North, & professed to be reverenced by every northern man. Though very defective for our defence, the South never would have complained, still less seceded, if this constitution had been respected by the

North, in spirit & in letter. But long continued violations, & much worse in prospect, of the constitutional defences of the South, caused the disruption of the Union, & the construction of the Southern Confederacy. And since then, & [now] that there are no longer southern statesmen in the rump Congress, to watch & defend state & popular rights from the tyranny of a majority in power, not only have the constitutional rights of the [2338] southern, but of the northern states & people been trampled under foot by an unlimited despotism. What would all the constitutional defences of liberty, that could be devized [*sic*] by the wisdom of man, amount to, in opposition to the single illegal & general suspension by the President of the writ of *habeas corpus*, & the consequent free exercise of the power to imprison for unlimited times, & under unlimited hardships, every man (or woman) who offered the slightest opposition to the administration, in writing or speech, or indeed without either? Yet this power of supreme dictatorship Lincoln has seized, & has used both on private citizens, & on the representatives of the people & of states, as far as he (or his leaders) had sense to direct, or courage to perform. This all-absorbing power of control Lincoln still holds, & by his solemn proclamation he has declared that he would exercise it on all offenders. That he has not done so latterly, is to be imputed to his fears, founded on the manifest changes of opinion in his before universally submitting & silent subjects.—The remarks of Wood are more clear & significant than Van Buren's. He declares his confident expectation that the "Governor elect will stand up for his state against any legal usurpation"—will "assert the rights of New York" & "protect its citizens from arbitrary arrests" &c. Now to do this would place New York in opposition & "rebellion" to the U.S. government, if the President shall dare to continue to exercise his proclaimed power of arbitrary imprisonment. Further—the law of the U.S. Congress, for drafting soldiers, has already been opposed as unconstitutional. If this plea is made in N.Y. & supported by a triumphant & violent majority of the people, the Supreme Court of that very corrupt state will readily confirm the popular construction, & so make it the duty of the Governor to prevent the draft. And if [2339] the powerful state of New York is placed in full opposition to the Federal Government, the latter will not be able to bear up under such an addition to its previous difficulties.

Nov. 23. Sunday. A Richmond paper of yesterday contains much interesting & important matter . . . but no decisive event. Burnside's army (reported 100,000) is threatening Fredericksburg from the opposite hills of Stafford, & has summoned the town to surrender, & on refusal, has bombarded it to slight extent. Still, this attack is supposed a feint, that the main Yankee army was embarking on the Potomac, on which there were numerous transports, & designed to attack Richmond by another route. Even when this doubtful point is settled affirmatively, it will still be uncertain whether the attack will be by way of York, or James river, or partly or wholly by Suffolk & Petersburg. . . . Evening—Mr. Sayre heard, by verbal information from Richmond, that Fredericksburg was to be defended, & that Lt. Gen. Longstreet's command had arrived for that purpose. The women & children had been ordered to leave Fredericksburg, to escape the bombardment, & two trains filled with them had reached Richmond yesterday [2340] evening. If Burnside's intention is, as I suppose, to embark his army on the Potomac, I hope that Gen. Lee's whole force may get there when but half the embarkation is effected. If we could now give the enemy an overwhelming defeat, it would so strengthen the opposition party at the North, that it would be quickly converted from a (professedly) war party to an avowed peace-seeking party—& the war would be ended in two months—& that without European intervention.

Nov. 24. Edmund set out this morning to visit his negroes in Amelia, & those hired on the new railroad near Danville. . . . Received more books (2 vols) from the library in Richmond—& the Nos. of Literary Messenger which I had not called for since last Spring. . . .

Nov. 25. The mail. No renewal of the bombardment of Fredericksburg to yesterday afternoon. On the contrary, though the surrender of the town has been demanded & refused, there has been an agreement between the opposed authorities that acts of hostility from the town will not be permitted, & that our forces will not occupy it, while hostilities, or the attempt to occupy, are suspended from the enemy. So it seems that a partial truce exists, for the present. In the mean time, Baltimore & other Yankee papers are publishing full & particular statements of the plan of Burnside to march on Richmond by the land route from Fredericksburg. This, with his delay to attack Fredericksburg, serves the more to strengthen my previous belief that he has no intention of going by that route, but after feigning it as long as useful, will embark his army on the Potomac—& probably has done so already. . . . Gen. Jos. E. Johnston, who until lately continued disabled by his wounds received at the battle of Seven Pines, has been ordered to take command of the South-western army, lately under Bragg, who will be second in command. . . . The Yankee papers boast, & I think they have more ground than usual for boasting, that their military affairs in general are very promising. It is certain that they are reinforcing heavily, & advancing, in Tennessee & in western Virginia. In the latter they now occupy from the Ohio to Highland county, next to Augusta. We have done nothing in Tennessee & the south-west generally during the season of low water, when the Yankees could not use their most powerful & unrivaled means for naval warfare. And now the time has begun, & will continue for 5 or 6 months, when all the long western rivers may be navigated, & their borders commanded, by their heavy gunboats. . . . The last arrival from Europe brings another report of speedy intervention. This time it is that France has called on Russia to unite with France in inviting England to demand an armistice, & if refused by the North, to recognize the Southern Confederacy. No doubt that some such report will be true at some future time. But I shall no more pay any respect to any such, until it is an authentic declaration by one or more of the European governments. . . . Mr. Sayre went to Court today, & there heard that Gen. Lee & his army had reached Fredericksburg. The [2344] truce covers only the town of Fredericksburg, which both parties agree not to occupy, or use for military purposes—for which it is not necessary. It covers but little space. All offensive operations can as well be carried on, by either army, without making the town a battle-field, or subjecting it to bombardment. Thus, the Yankees began to construct a pontoon bridge across the river, (either above or below the town,) & their work was stopped, & the party driven off, by firing from our troops. The agreement to exempt the town, on conditions, was not made by the Yankee commander upon considerations of humanity, but (as I believe,) to consume time, & the better to aid Burnside's feint of moving thence direct to Richmond, & to conceal his real intention of embarking his army on the Potomac. I suppose that the embarkation was well advanced before Gen. Lee's army arrived. If not, its arrival, & opposition, will compel Burnside to take a different route, whether he designed it before or not.

Nov. 27. Wrote letters to Newton & to N. F. Cabell. My correspondence has dwindled almost to nothing of late. I now receive so few letters, & write so few in answer or otherwise, that my writing one requires an effort—& if I do not force myself to make such efforts, my (formerly large) labors of letter-writing will soon entirely cease.—Resumed & finished reading the latter part of Vol 1 of Barth's Travels, of which I had read the preceding part last winter when in Rd., & have now obtained the volume again from the library.

Nov. 28. Began De Quinc[e]y's "Confessions of an Opium Eater"—second reading.—The mail. . . . A long letter from Dr. Bachman of Charleston, in answer to my last. . . . He is sanguine of the defence of Charleston against any attack by the enemy.—The papers silent as to the situation of our army near Fredericksburg, & they know little or nothing as to the Yankee forces. Burnside, so far, has done nothing in advancing towards Richmond. Certainly not by land—& if so by embarking on the Potomac, it is to be presumed that the movement down the river would have been seen from the bank, & reported to our authorities. Every day's additional delay, at this time of year, makes the chance worse for aggressive operations by land. . . .

Nov. 29. Heard yesterday evening that W. Newton had come to Summer Hill, his son's place in this neighborhood. I rode this morning to see him. He had fled from the enemy's foraging parties, & had made a narrow escape. I found him alone, the ladies of the family being out, & spent more than two hours in conversing with him, & exchanging our views as to the war, & the political condition of the northern states, & the prospects of the Confederate States. In our general political views [2347] we rarely, if ever, have differed in latter years. He & I entertain the same opinion of the newly raised & strong opposition, conservative, or democratic party in the northern states—that it is really, in disguise even to most of its members, a *peace party*—& will be so avowed as soon as the leaders can indoctrinate the mass of ignorant followers, & the party is beyond question the majority of the people, as it seems already to be. Mr. Newton had heard that the Yankees had occupied Tappahannock, which is on the direct (& mail) route from his residence to Old Church & Richmond. Burnside has sent foraging parties into the Northern Neck, & no doubt they will plunder or destroy very extensively. That narrow peninsula, lying between the Potomac &

Rappahannock rivers, both of which are commanded completely by the Yankee armed vessels, is entirely undefended, & incapable of being defended by the Confederates, & therefore lies at the mercy, or will, of the enemy. It has been to me a matter for wonder, that they had not plundered it & wasted it, generally, long ago. It is unusually full of grain, because since the war the farmers have been cut off from their accustomed, & latterly of all transportation to market. All the surplus products of this year, & most of those of the preceding year, probably are still on the farms. Returned to dinner.—Mr. Sayre went to Richmond & Edmund returned with him. Before their arrival, one of the young men who had absconded (with 17 other men & boys,) to the Yankee camps, returned & sent for me to the door, & delivered himself. I had not much to say to him, & dismissed him to go to the quarters of the negroes, & come again after the arrival of the two owners—which he did. He was allowed to come under the former offer of amnesty to all who soon should voluntarily return to their duty—though his long delay would debar him from a right to it. He is the only one who has returned—though two others are here who came (or were brought) back, because of their extreme illness, & who both would have died, if left in the Yankee camp, or absconding elsewhere. Two others were captured, & sold.—There is no apprehension [2348] that Burnside can advance to Richmond, or even across the Rappanhannock. His long delay opposite to & threatening Fredericksburg, shows that (contrary to my first opinion,) he had certainly designed that movement—& already may despair of this last & new effort to reach & capture Richmond. . . .

December 1. . . . The French Emperor has formally proposed to the governments of England & Russia, that the three powers shall intervene in the American war, & ask of the contending powers an armistice, & complete cessation of hostilities both on water & land, for six months. England & Russia both express great solicitude for the object, peace, but decline to interfere, lest the effort shall do harm, & postpone its object.—Finished reading Vol 1 of De Quincey's collected writings—containing his "Confessions of an Opium Eater," & Appendix, & . . . Sequel—the appendix & sequel being longer than the main work—the tail more bulky than the head & body. The end of the "Confessions," as originally published alone, which sets forth the reformation of the opium-eater, left me more than doubtful whe[ther] the writer had not still continued his dreadful habit & vice. The Appendix shows that he had not then abandoned it—& the "Sequel," which has very little direct bearing on its professed subject, seems as if composed throughout under the inspiration or influence of opium. The book is far from being a dissuader from the use of opium—but the reverse. . . . If I could believe that the author's sensations & experience would be mine—& I looked merely to my own feelings & present interest—without regard to the opinions of my family or the world, or to the shame & sin of the habit—I would at once commence the practice of opium-eating. . . . But putting all this aside, I do not know any writer whose *manner* of writing is so unrestrained by rule, & yet is so fascinating. . . . He permits his pen to run anywhere, & to any thing, without regard to or connection with his proposed subject. If any other author were [to] pay so little respect to his readers, his extraneous matter would be deemed impertinent & inexcusable, & the writer both offensive & insolent. But De Quincey may speak of the most trite & humble subjects, & the most remote from that which he professed to treat, & yet he is almost always interesting. . . . [2352]

Dec. 2. The mail. The Confederate forces in Ten. are concentrating at Murfreesborough & Tullahoma. At the latter place it is supposed the battle between the two armies will soon take place. Its natural features will enable our inferior numbers to meet the enemy on equal terms. The Yankees in Nashville have been largely reinforced. The railroad from Nashville to Louisville has been repaired, & opened for transportation.—No late changes near Fredericksburg made known. . . . The late heavy rains had rendered the condition of the earth & roads too bad for wagons or artillery. This is the excuse given for Burnside's not crossing the river, & the slow progress of the "On to Richmond!" advance, which was promised to be completed in 10 days. It now seems that the previous plan had been to move upon Richmond by way of Culpeper C.H., which was foiled by the opposing front exhibited by Gen. Lee. It was the second choice to move by Fredericksburg, by which Burnside expected, & northern papers boasted, that he would be at least two days in advance of Lee's army. But when his army reached the opposite bank of the river, he found Longstreet's corps facing him, & soon after all Lee's army was also there. If, after all this delay, Burnside shall draw off, to attempt some other route, or to go into winter quarters, it will clearly indicate that he did not design a feint, but a settled purpose, which was completely [2353] defeated by Gen. Lee. If, on the other hand, he shall attempt to force a passage across the river & on to Richmond, I do not question that he will be defeated in battle. . . . The public mind, both north & south, is now exercised with the question whether the Emperor of France will withdraw from his proposition to intervene in the war, or to persevere in it alone. If he does persevere, & to the extent of recognizing the C.S. & requiring & enforcing the raising of the blockade of our ports, (which is all that we need desire,) he would have nothing to fear from the hostility of Yankeedom, which England so much dreads. France cannot be damaged greatly, as England may, by Yankee confiscation of English property in American stocks, or by privateering—& not at all by Yankee inroads on colonial possessions. On the other hand, France has fewer merchant ships exposed to privateering than the U.S.—has as strong & well armed a steam navy, & that now unoccupied—& if involved in the war, with our aid, France might cause far greater injury to the U.S. than could be returned. If desired, a strong French squadron, conveying an army, could either conquer & hold the Pacific states, or at any rate detach them from subjection to or connection with the Northern U.S. And besides the spoils of war, & the glory of naval success, so long strange to France—the C.S. could well afford, & would doubtless be glad to offer for such cooperation, peculiar commercial advantages which would be of incalculable benefit to the commerce & manufactures of France. In view of these prospective advantages, I [2354] have been surprised that the wise & unprincipled despot of France has not long ago obtained for his country the great available advantages in view. Now that he has displayed his views, & invited England & Russia to act with him, & they having declined, I see no reason why he should not proceed alone to require an armistice, & on its refusal, to break the blockade. . . .

Dec. 3. This evening Mr. Sayre saw a neighbor who had just returned from our camp, & who told him that all of our late Potomac army was near Fredericksburg—Jackson's army being on the railroad route, 8 or 10 miles from the town. Both the opposed armies are constructing fortifications on the heights & mounting cannon on them.—There have been many statements published, in northern papers, & from northern writers & witnesses . . . showing the heartlessness & cruelty with which the Yankees have treated the runaway slaves, after having deluded them by unmeasured deception, & such gross lies as none but ignorant negroes could believe, to leave their masters, & their before happy homes—happier & better supplied with the [2355] comforts suitable to their condition than the homes of the poor whites in New England, or in the city of New York. Their first discontent (in the general) was produced by the false teachings & seductive deceptions practised on them by Yankee abolitionists; & their greatest suffering & unhappiness have been caused by the poisoning of their minds in this respect, & the false promises of the Yankee military officers, & by every common soldier, being consummated in their deserting their homes & masters, & fleeing to the Yankee camps or gun-boats. There they received just so much aid & support as to keep up their deception long enough to draw on other slaves. The deluded victims had been told that they would be *free*—which a negro understands to mean being free from all obligations to labor—& that every one would find plenty of employment, & light service, at high wages. Instead, as a general rule, & after they were secured, they were worked harder than ever before as slaves, with uncertain employment for able men—still less for the women, & soon were in extreme suffering for food, shelter & fire. Every one who was extremely sick must have died for want of attention & necessary comforts. Before this winter will end, it is probable that one half of the women & children, & other infirm & helpless of these fugitives, will die of want, or of diseases caused by hunger, cold, & exposure. While such tendencies were clearly stated by previous northern writers & eye-witnesses in their camps, they also deplored the results. But a late number of the N.Y. Evening Post, (whose chief editor is [William Cullen] Bryant, eminent as a literary man, & in social position—) rejoices in the approaching extinction of life of all the slaves that shall be emancipated, & of the whole negro race in the South, & of course must approve the actual & necessary means, the subjection to want & misery, the necessary consequences of emancipation. This editor, one of the leaders in the abolition school & movement, says: "As the Indians were crowded westward, & out of our bounds, by the irresistable [*sic*] advance of the white man, so will the blacks be, whenever that powerful [2356] *protective system with which the slave-holders have guarded them* is removed. It is the destiny of the free white working men of this country to possess it; the efforts of the slaveholders have hitherto robbed them of one-half of it—the richest & fairest half—*& devoted it to the* *blacks.* It is the slave-holders who have *preserved the negro race* from decline among us; it is the slave-holders who have increased the blacks from 700,000 in 1790 to four millions in 1860." All this (as to the negroes, & their future in a state of abolition freedom,) is perfectly true. It is not at all strange that a well-informed Yankee should see it, as clearly as do all intelligent southerners. But it is strange, & surprising, that a leading abolition organ should openly & broadly proclaim these truths, as early as in the second year of this war for freeing the slaves, & before more than 100,000 of the 4,000,000 of slaves have been seduced to accept their freedom, & to begin the process of their extinction by want & suffering. . . .

Dec. 4. Finished the 1st vol. of [De Quincey's] Literary Reminiscences, & began Vol. 2nd.—At dark, Mr. Newton arrived, having (for want of a horse,) walked from Summer Hill. With him I (& my family) had much pleasant conversation to late bed-time.

Dec. 5. Drizzle increasing to steady soaking rain. According to the northern reports, Burnside's army had been delayed & greatly embarrassed by the previous heavy rain having made the earth & roads miry. This rain will double the previous disadvantage.—The mail brought no news of important movements or changes. Nothing mentioned to account for slow cannonading heard yesterday afternoon, from a direction seemingly lower than Fredericksburg. . . . Mr. G. W. Bentinck, M.P., has made a public speech . . . taking strong ground for & eulogizing the C.S. & as strongly denouncing the Yankees, & advocating the recognition of the former.[22] It is a striking & remarkable fact, that the tone of English speakers & writers has completely changed as to the people of these southern states. It has not been many years, if not up to the beginning of this war, that the people of the former U.S., & more especially those of the southern states, were generally spoken or written of in England in degrading terms. Even the eulogists of our government, of our policy & institutions (excepting negro slavery,) & admirers of our wonderful progress, qualified their compliments with sneers of civil contempt. Especially in military virtues & capability was the southern people held to be inferior to those of the North, & still more to those of Europe. Wonderful indeed has been the change in this respect—as seen in Mr. Bentinck's . . . speech, & in most

---

[22] An outspoken Confederate sympathizer, Bentinck had earlier supported an abortive resolution introduced in the House of Commons in March, 1862, which sought to have the blockade declared ineffective.

comments on the military conduct of the C.S. Among such now frequent compliments, the London Dispatch offers the highest eulogism in the fewest words, [2358] as follows: "Never, we assert, with the utmost confidence, was there known a people so heroic, so brave, so prudent, so devoted." . . . After reading the newspapers, we spent the remainder of the day in conversation. The rain became [2359] more heavy about 2 P.M. & continued slowly into the night. Mr. Newton was detained by the weather, & consented very willingly to stay.

Dec. 6. Mr. Newton left us at noon—my son sending him to Summer Hill in his buggy, with a servant to drive it back.

Dec. 7. Sunday, Severe cold. The thermometer was not looked at early—but between 9 & 10 A.M. it stood at 23°.—Late last night, the day's paper arrived from Richmond. The cannonading heard here on the 4th. was near Port Royal. Some of the Yankee gun-boats showed themselves there & were fired upon by some of our artillery. They returned the fire, & the contest continued for nearly two hours, when the gunboats drew off. The only damage to our side was that a few of the enemy's shot struck houses in Port Royal. . . . The Yankee congress met last Monday. The paper contains Lincoln's message. It is long, yet contains very little that is notable. He recommends an amendment of the U.S. constitution to carry out, in detail [2360], the policy which he formerly proposed, of general (& now of gradual) emancipation of slaves, with compensation to the owners. But this is not to "stay" the more prompt & general emancipation of the slaves of rebels, proclaimed in Sept. & to be consummated on Jan. 1st. I think that this part of his message will displease all parties. The northern opposition party will denounce the emancipation scheme *in toto*. The abolition party will object to it because its completion is delayed so long.[23] And the whole north will object, & will never consent, to paying for the emancipated slaves. The rebels, of course, will be opposed, & the unionists among them also, because of the very small prospect of their ever receiving any of the promised compensation for their emancipated or stolen slaves. One article of Lincoln's proposed amendment of the constitution provides that all slaves who shall acquire their freedom by the "chances of war" or otherwise during the present rebellion, shall remain free. . . .

---

[23] Under the Lincoln proposal, compensation would be extended to owners in each state which voted to abolish slavery before 1900.

Dec. 8. At 7.50 A.M., Temp. 16°. Terrible & distressing cold for our soldiers, none of whom have yet gone into, or (as I suppose) are even provided with houses for winter-quarters—& but few are provided with tents, & many are without shoes, or blankets, or warm clothing. The continued threatened advance of the enemy's armies, both in Va. & Ten. for a month & more, must have made it impossible for our commanders to know where they would winter, or to fix upon localities & prepare for winter-quarters. This early occurrence of severe cold must also serve to disconcert Burnside's intended operations, if he had not previously abandoned advancing. Luckily for him, the deep water has not yet been winter-chilled—for if so, 48 hours of this weather would freeze the Potomac, & prevent navigation by ordinary transports. In that case, unless the roads should be frozen & remain perfectly hard, his transportation of provisions would be cut off, & his army in danger of starvation. But whatever can be done by industry, unconquerable perseverance, & with the aid of all necessary means & applyances [*sic*] previously prepared, no doubt had been done, or will soon be done, for the best mechanical aid to the Yankee army. The Yankee military authorities deserve all praise on this score—& continually their armies excel ours in labors of construction, as much as they are beaten by the Confederates in fighting. Burnside had had the rail-road from Fredericksburg to Aquia creek, & the wharf, reconstructed, in three days, [2362] of mostly rainy weather. It seems almost useless for our armies to destroy rail-roads & bridges, & even their materials, so rapidly are they replaced when occupied, or reached, by the Yankee armies. This severe freeze will so obstruct military operations, (whether with or without a speedy thaw,) that it will probably close the campaign, leaving both the opposing armies under great disadvantages as to arrangments for winter-quarters, or for other movements. And besides such disadvantages for Burnside, if he goes into winter-quarters anywhere, without effecting anything, or trying the hazard of a battle, it will be clearly a defeat of his great effort, & utter disappointment to the sanguine expectations of the Yankee people. But may not the Yankee army, if mainly holding its present position, inactive, enable its great object to be effected by other forces? Edmund & I have been discussing this question, & we concur in thinking that by another procedure, Richmond might be much more endangered than if Burnside could have advanced on it, as designed. It is understood that there are 30,000 Yankees at Suffolk, who were supposed to threaten Weldon & the railroads mainly—& the forces at Norfolk, Fortress Monroe & its outposts must be 10,000, making a total of 40,000. While Burnside's whole army is facing the Rappahannock, Lee's whole army must be required there to oppose its advance. Before the movement could be made known to Gen. Lee, nearly the whole Yankee force now near James river, (excepting say 3000 men as garrisons for but a few days for Norfolk & Ft. Monroe,) might be suddenly embarked on transports, & either landed in Henrico [County] below Fort Drewry, & march upon Richmond, only 10 miles distant, direct—or otherwise to land on the opposite side, & attack Fort Drewry in the rear, or land side, capture it, & then proceed to Richmond. 37,000 men thus attacking the fort on the side where no attack has been looked for, & the defences certainly must be very weak, there can be no question of their success. The mortar boats could then move up to Rocketts, & shell the city, aided by the land forces. Exclusive of the garrison & support of the fort, there are probably [2363] not 10,000 troops about Richmond. Those protecting Petersburg are looking to Suffolk as the only probable source of attack, & might still continue under that delusion after the Yankee troops had reached Fort Drewry. Thus Richmond would have but its present small garrison to meet the onset of 37,000 land forces, either with or without the aid of a bombardment by the gunboats. It would seem, if the movement could be but concealed until in progress for 24 hours, its complete success would be far more probable than any of the sundry other plans & attempts to take Richmond. Still, I do not believe that this course will be attempted, because the enemy will be afraid to venture the attempt. . . . Wind changed to be southerly, & of course the weather warmer. At 5 P.M. temperature 29°. This freeze will make the roads still worse after thawing than from the heavy rain preceding.—While we were at tea, two more of the men who went off to the Yankees came back voluntarily, & delivered themselves to Edmund. They professed great penitence & sorrow for their past conduct—& were admitted under the former promise of forgiveness of the past. These also pretend to know nothing of the other absconding slaves, or recently of the Yankees.

Dec. 9. Thermometer showed 22½° at 7 A.M. . . . Last night, the day's paper brought from Richmond. Besides the number of Yankee merchant vessels captured & destroyed by our only war vessel at sea, the Alabama, & the great additional loss in causing the raising of insurance on Yankee ships, there is another important loss inflicted in the expenses of the vessels [2364] of war sent to cruise for & to capture the Alabama. These are mentioned generally in the late report of the Yankee Sec. of Navy as "quite a fleet" on the ocean in pursuit of the Alabama. It was reported in northern papers that another such Confederate steam war vessel was on the ocean, to operate in like manner. I fear that this report is false. But even the false report will increase the terror & loss of the Yankees. Great as have been the services of the Alabama, & the losses inflicted by it on the enemy, it seems to me that they might be much increased by an extension of the plan of operations, thus: Let any such war steamer, fitted out in England, take out, in addition to its own armament, as many cannon & their carriages, as would not be too heavy freight. With these guns, a suitable fast prize vessel might be armed, & enough men to man it enlisted from the prize crews—so as to make another cruiser. The needed supplies of coal might be maintained by supplies from the captured vessels—& thus our single war steamer might be increased to many. . . . The C.S. war steamer Sumter, which was so operative on the ocean early in the war, is still in the port of Gibraltar, watched by a Yankee war steamer [2365] in the neighboring harbor of Algesiras [*sic*]. The Nashville C.S. war steamer, in like manner, is blockaded in the English port of Southampton. Nevertheless, these vessels are doing good service, as they keep inactive two much stronger & more expensive Yankee steamers to watch them, & prevent their departure from their anchorages. . . . Report came by passengers from Fredericksburg last evening that a large portion of Burnside's army had moved (or was moving) down the north side of the Rappahannock, as supposed, to cross at Port Royal, where the gun-boats could operate to protect the construction of a pontoon bridge, & the passage of the army. . . . Today, the hands & very poor team force engaged in putting up ice—which is 1½ inches thick. Last winter had so little of hard freezing weather, that there was scarcely any ice saved in lower & middle Va. . . .

Dec. 10. Still milder.—At 3.20 P.M. cannonading was heard here in the direction of Fredericksburg. Mr. Sayre came from Richmond. He brought no paper—but had read the official report of Gen. Bragg to the War Dept. which states an important victory gained by Gen. [John H.] Morgan not far from Nashville, over a body of the enemy's forces—taking 1800 prisoners. . . .

Dec. 11. Soon after sunrise, Edmund & I set out, in his buggy, for Richmond. After 1 P.M., he continued to Petersburg, while I remained for the night in Richmond.—The telegram from Gen. Bragg states that Gen. John H. Morgan on 7th inst. surprised & attacked a body of the enemy at Hartsville, (on the Cumberland,) killed & wounded 200, captured 1800 prisoners & 2 pieces of artillery, 2000 small arms, & all the stores at that position. Our loss, about 125, killed & wounded. . . . Richmond is today in feverish anxiety as to the contest on the Rappahannock, but no one seeming to doubt of the result being victory to our arms, if the enemy dare to join in battle, as seems now indicated. Telegrams state that this morning, at 5, the enemy attempted to cross the river, & renewed the attempt afterwards at two other points. All three [2368] movements were repulsed, &, as reported, with heavy slaughter to the foiled Yankee troops. At night, another telegram, to the War Department, stated that in a fourth attempt, at 6 P.M., the enemy had succeeded in constructing a pontoon bridge across, 3 miles below Fredericksburg, & in passing over a portion of their army. The passage was protected by their cannon, & by the position of the high land on our side, covering the enemy from our fire. The place of landing is a low flat, on which there was room only for some 10,000 men. To advance farther, they must ascend the higher table land, where they will be exposed to the fire of our batteries. The moon will rise 2 hours after dark—& it is supposed here that the battle will be renewed either by the bright moonlight, or become general early tomorrow morning. All of us earnestly desire that Burnside may make a general attack, & bring on a general engagement as soon as possible. For though none fear the trial there, and few even doubt our victory, I find that many persons now entertain the fears that I have before stated for myself—& the Examiner of this morning has an editorial article to this purport, viz: that while Burnside will occupy the attention of all Lee's army 60 miles from Richmond . . . a Yankee flotilla, with another army, may suddenly, & without warning, run up James river & land within 10 miles of Richmond. . . . President Davis' lenity to Yankee spies &c. is past comprehension. Two, who came from Washington to Rd., a year ago, were detected, tried & convicted, on the clearest testimony, to which was afterwards added their own full confessions. They were sentenced to be hung—but were respited, & after long confinement, have been pardoned & are to be sent North—no doubt much improved, by their residence & long stay in Rd., to serve the Yankee government as spies, & who will doubtless soon return to the C.S. to renew that service.—While our arms have well maintained the honor & glory of the C.S. in eastern Va, & while we fear no reverse of our great army under Lee, almost everything, on a large scale, has gone against us in the west. Yet most of all the great battles fought there have given victory & glory to the Confederates—& likewise a still larger proportion of the numerous smaller but yet important conflicts of our partisan corps, under Morgan, Forrest, [Albert G.] Jenkins (in Va.,) & many others. The general result is, that in all Missouri & Ky, & in N.W. Va, we have no longer any military post, or troops in the field. In Missouri, for [a] long time, there has been no armed opposition to the Yankee domination, except by self-supporting guerrillas, acting in their own neighborhoods—& these seem to have been latterly entirely suppressed. In Arkansas, a slow contest is feebly carried on against the Yankee army & supremacy. In Ten. & Miss. the Yankee armies seem to have general control. And if the tide of success has been against us during all the dry season, when the rivers were too low for the Yankee war steamers—when we have made no use of that season to construct fortifications on the western rivers, or to obstruct [2370] their narrow channels—what chance for greater success can we have when soon, & for 6 months to come, the enemy's flotillas can ascend all the western rivers to the highest points accessible by steam navigation? I confess that I look with most gloomy anticipations to the winter & spring campaign in the western states. As to western Va, it is already again occupied by the enemy from the Ohio to the Allegheny (& farther east in the north,) & to south of the Kanawha. . . . After supper, reading newspapers &c. at the Reading Room until bed-time. Slept at the American Hotel.

Dec. 12. At 3.30 A.M. I was called up, & soon after went to the R.R. station. Set off at 4.15, & reached Petersburg at 6, before daybreak. . . . As Edmund had intended going on to Ruthven, I went [2371] with him, in his buggy, at 11, & found Julian alone. . . . Nothing had been heard in Richmond, or Petersburg, of the battle supposed to be going on, when I left those places. So I shall probably remain uninformed until our next mail day, the 15th.—If the enemy should attempt, as certainly would be the procedure most promising of success, to send another army up James river, or in part by York & Pamunkey, Julian's family here, & Edmund's at Marlbourne, may again have to flee at very short warning. If the forces of the enemy should again occupy Marlbourne, we think [it] is most probable that nearly all the negroes there will abscond again, & effectively. They could not be removed to any other place of more security, if against their will, at a moment's warning.—In Petersburg, in the street, I met Maj. Gen. [Samuel G.] French & had some conversation with him. I spoke of my fear of the enemy sending another army up the river, & inquired as to our means for repelling it. I learned nothing satisfactory—but only that every such contingency had been prepared for, so far as our (I fear very scant) means admitted. . . .

Dec. 13. Edmund visited Beechwood. He found, as on every previous late visit, that the house had been again broken open, & some more articles stolen. This pillaging is probably committed by the negroes of some of the neighbors.—I was nearly all day engaged in writing the entries of yesterday, & inserting the printed extracts. A great waste of time, if mine was worth anything—but as it is, I am glad if I can waste or kill as much time on every mail-day.—No news heard irregularly today, to relieve our great anxiety.—Edmund heard 9 heavy guns, at Beechw[oo]d.

Dec. 14. Sunday. I walked to the camp, about a mile off, to inquire for news, & Capt. [D.] Bell lent me some of yesterday's papers. . . . Fredericksburg has been shelled, [2373] & a large force of the enemy has crossed the river. Heavy skirmishing on Friday, but no important battle. So much, in general terms, seems reliable. . . . It was expected in Rd. that a general engagement would be begun yesterday, or today. An officer at the cavalry camp told me today that he there heard numerous reports of cannon yesterday afternoon. . . . The cavalry company here, (Capt. Bell, from Currituck, N.C.) have put up good log huts, & are comfortably lodged, as if for winter-quarters. . . .

Dec. 15. Monday. Edmund left us for Marlbourne. He is now, as he has been ever since the first ascent of the Yankee gunboats up James river, in great difficulty as to what course to take, or what he may suddenly be driven to, to best secure his family & his yet remaining property from the incursions & depredations of the Yankee forces. His desolated property & former residence Beechwood is altogether unsafe as either a residence, or for renewing cultivation. Evelynton is worse, every building being destroyed, & the land a waste. At Marlbourne, his latest place of temporary refuge, the now probable ascent of the York & Pamunkey by an invading flotilla, would compel the abandonment at an hour's warning, probably leaving & losing all the heavy moveables, & most of the slaves, now retained by a very doubtful tenure. Also, if Burnside should be able to advance & besiege Richmond as McClellan did, even if ultimately defeated & driven back, Marlbourne might be again for weeks in the power of the marauding Yankees, & all retreat for the remaining residents then cut off. . . . The mail. Thank God! We have had a victory, (on 13th,) though not a decisive result. On Thursday 11th, (as we heard very incorrectly reported in telegrams to Richmond, on that day,) the Yankees began very early to construct a pontoon bridge to the town of Fredericksburg. The men were fired upon by our pickets & stronger bodies of sharpshooters, & driven off with loss. The attempts were renewed, & to protect the operations, the town was shelled from the Yankee batteries, & especially the position of the Confederate troops. Nearly every good house in the town was more or less damaged. Some of the residents were killed by the enemy's shells. Many had remained to occupy their houses, & others who had before left them, had returned, supposing, on the faith of the late agreement, that the town would [2375] not be shelled without due notice. All had now to flee. . . . In the course of the day, the enemy were driven back from three several attempts to complete the pontoon bridge, by the destructive firing of the small Confederate force engaged, [William] Barksdale's brigade. At last however, about dark, they succeeded in landing, & occupying the town. Our troops made no further resistance, & retired. . . . The next day (Friday 12th,) there was heavy skirmishing along the lines of the opposed armies, & artillery firing of opposite & distant batteries, but no important conflict. I forgot to say that another pontoon bridge had also been constructed three miles lower down the river—& by both, a large force, & probably the main army, reported to be 110,000, had been crossed. On Saturday, 13th, the main armies were engaged—or at least, on our side, Jackson's & Longstreet's corps. After severe fighting, the enemy were driven back 1½ miles, into Fredericksburg & under the protection of their batteries. Our loss in killed & wounded was heavy, but that of the enemy was supposed to be very much greater. Gen. Lee telegraphs that the battle continued from 9 A.M. to 6 P.M. when the enemy were "repulsed at all points." The battle was not renewed, as expected, the following day (yesterday). . . . Three great armies of the enemy are in Ten. & Miss., & threatening further invasion as soon as the rivers rise. . . . The Yankee papers boast of their certain triumph in the south-west—& so far as they may count on their superior force, I fear they have good grounds to be sanguine of victory, & a series of successes.

Dec. 16. Tuesday. Walked to the camp, & exchanged newspapers. In the Enquirer or Whig of 15th saw some additional particulars. . . . The Yankees continued to construct more pontoon bridges, until they have 5 in all. This looks like making abundant provision for hasty retreat. Some suspect that Burnside will be content to establish secure winter-quarters, & to live upon the abundant supplies of the Northern Neck, which narrow peninsula he can effectually command by gunboats on the two rivers which enclose it. . . . A Rd. newspaper of today, obtained from Petersburg, states that the later accounts show our [2377] advantage in the battle of 13th. greater than at first supposed. It was expected that Burnside would renew the engagement next morning—but there was no such apparent movement—& no fighting since, except some distant & harmless cannonading, mostly from the enemy's batteries. Among our killed, were Generals Maxcy Gregg of S.C. & T[homas] R.R. Cobb of Mi. [*sic*—Ga.]—both good officers & valuable men. Gen. Gregg was my acquaintance. Gen. Cobb was the author of the very instructive "History of Slavery," one of the best works of the many written on the different branches of that copious general subject. . . .

Dec. 17. Wednesday. The mail. While all had been anxiously expecting every day, & desiring, to hear of the renewal of Burnside's advance & attack on our lines, the surprising news has come (by dispatch from Gen. Lee,) that the Yankee army had recrossed the river, & moved off from its late position—in what direction not then known. Whatever may be the cause, or the new object, this result is full proof of the complete defeat of his army in its late great object, of moving on upon Richmond. Gen. Lee's official report of the battle of Fredericksburg, [2378] (a rare exception permitted by our government to the usual procedure,) has been allowed to be published already . . . . It is worded so modestly, & with so little assumption of the great advantages & glory certainly achieved, that it presents a remarkable contrast to the official reports of the Yankee commanders. I expect that Burnside will claim more honor for this defeat, than Lee does for . . . inflicting it. If I had seen any official report of a Yankee commander, claiming &

describing a victory precisely in the words used by Gen. Lee, I should have thence inferred that he had really suffered an awful defeat. . . . Good writing (letter) paper, such as formerly was sold by the single ream for $3, is now at $40. Envelopes are as dear in proportion. Very poor ones, roughly made of coarse brown paper (for wrapping,) sell at 50 cents for 25. Julian had some quires of much better paper, formerly used for covers for the numbers of Farmers' Register, & left with other rubbish of my printing establishment 20 years ago. I tried to make envelopes of this, & succeeded in making them as neatly as those usually sold, as well as of better material. In my first trial, & in less than half of yesterday & today, I made more than 100.

Dec. 19. Friday. As some messenger goes from the cavalry camp to Petersburg almost every day, & always buys newspapers, I have arranged to purchase one for myself, to be obtained by the same conveyance. It is true that it will arrive at the camp too late for me to see it the same day. But it will add to the supply for the officers & others, & the next morning (as I did this morning,) by walking there, which exercise is needed for my health, I will obtain my paper, & also a sight of theirs. . . . The mail. Letter from Marlbourne. Another one of the negro men who had gone off to the Yankees returned—John. This is the fourth voluntary return.—Nothing certain yet as to the destination of Burnside's army. As seen from our lines, the first direction was towards Aquia creek. The retreat was begun early Monday night (15th) & the army finished crossing next morning—fired at by our batteries, but to little purpose. The pontoon bridges at the town were only cast loose on the south side of the river, & so floated to along the north side. The enemy's guns still remained on the intrenchments on the Stafford hills, bearing upon the town & protecting the river & bridges. . . . More captures by the Alabama. The vessels burnt numbered 22 when last reported. If I correctly construe a northern paragraph which enumerates the Yankee war steamers which have been sent to cruise for the Alabama, those sent, & those getting ready & about to go, amount to 14 in all. This is indeed "quite a fleet," kept occupied by our now only active cruiser. A year of such service of the Alabama will cost Yankeedom, in loss of vessels & cargoes, loss of foreign freights, & expenses incurred for its capture . . . many millions of dollars. . . .

Dec. 20. Saturday. Nearly half the day making envelopes. Much

improved in skill. I made 100, complete, in less than 5 hours. . . .
The Yankees completely sacked Fredericksburg, before they retreated across the river. But a few houses escaped, either because
overlooked, or for want of time. In all the others the procedure was
alike. Everything was stolen & carried off that the robbers could put
to use. Everything else was broken or destroyed. The buildings,
including the churches, were defaced & defiled. Nothing of destruction & malignant mischief was left undone, except that the
buildings were not generally burnt. According to the published
reports . . . in every mansion & on every property in Fredericksburg, there was repeated the same operations which were carried
out on the Beechwood house & farm, & which were perhaps the
first to be so thoroughly executed. Previously, & generally, wherever the Yankee troops had access & sway, there was wide-spread
robbery & no little of wanton destruction of private property. But
recently, judging by effects, it would seem as if the Yankee government & military commanders had expressly authorized & ordered
that the country shall be plundered & laid waste, & every moveable
either carried off or destroyed. Such has been the procedure in
North Carolina & in Mississippi, under recent Yankee army movements, as well as at Fredericksburg, & sundry other places in
Va—indeed nearly wherever they have occupied long enough for
such work. We who had heard from our fathers, besides what
history had recorded, of the acts of marauding & destruction committed by British soldiers in lower Va & in S.C. during the revolutionary war, had supposed that humanity could not be more
outraged by any civilized people, professing to carry on war in
accordance with its laws & usages. But the Yankees have as far
excelled the plundering & destroying bands of Tarl[e]ton & the
traitor Arnold, as these did any hostile forces observing every law &
courtesy of honorable warfare. . . .

Dec. 21. Sunday. The Rump Congress has just enacted the construction of "Western Virginia" as a new state, & admitted it into the
United States. This is another as flagrant as foolish & useless violation of the Federal Constitution, according to its plain letter & to
Yankee views of the Union. If the northern government had previously declared Virginia to be independent, & rightfully or actually
disconnected from the former U.S., then, while carrying on war
with Va, the North might declare this portion to be conquered

territory, & annex it as a new state. Even then, during a war, & the secure possession still undetermined, such annexation would be in utter violation of the usage & courtesy of countries engaged in war—& also in violation of sound policy, & common decency. Still, as exercised against an independent power, there would be no objection as to the right, if the annexing power could maintain possession of the conquered territory. But the Yankee government loudly declares that Virginia, altogether, is still one of the United States, under the Federal constitution & of course must be held & treated as a state, in rebellion or in any other condition, & in all respects. The constitution expressly declares that no state shall be divided, or a new state made out of a portion of its territory, without its consent. This provision is flagrantly violated by this recent act of the Rump government, making a new state of some 48 of the north-western & some south-western counties. This, like every other mad & foolish infraction of the constitution, & of right, will serve our cause, & I am heartily glad of it. The measure must cause difficulty & trouble to its authors. "Western Virginia" of course will be fully represented in the Rump Congress, because there are enough traitors in every district to hold elections, nominal or real, under the protection of Yankee soldiery. Orders from the military commander have already been issued also to hold elections for the two southeastern districts of lower Va—at which, under the bayonets [2385] of the Yankee garrisons of the Eastern Shore, Fortress Monroe, Norfolk, & Suffolk, a few traitors only will vote, & return Joseph Segar & another traitor of his stamp.[24] These will (I suppose) represent all "Eastern" Va in the rump Congress. Thus there will be representation for two states, in place of one, & every representative an abject tool of Lincoln, who has permitted him to usurp his seat, & to draw its pay. The new opposition of the northern states is already beginning to exclaim against this mode of increasing the abolition votes in Congress, & the political power of Lincoln's administration. The election of members to Congress, in like manner has been ordered for the portions of N.Ca. & La occupied by the Yankees; & in like manner there may be admitted,

---

[24] Denied admission earlier to the Thirty-seventh Congress, Joseph Eggleston Segar (1804–80) was successful on his second try and served in the United States House of Representatives from March 15, 1862, to March 3, 1863. He failed in three subsequent attempts to have his credentials as member-elect or senator-elect validated by Civil War and Reconstruction congresses.

to swell the abolition votes in Congress, one or more "Union" members from every southern state in which there is a Yankee military occupation, & a dozen native traitors, or imported Yankees, to officiate as voters. I trust that the game will be played boldly—& that the northern opposition party will clearly see that thus their majority will be effectually neutralized & over-balanced—or that they must use their undoubted superior physical force to maintain their political rights. I trust that the madness of the administration, & its radical abolition supporters, will steadily drive towards, & reach, the crisis of physical collision between the two great parties in which the North is being arrayed. The first blow that is struck between these will both give peace to & avenge the South.—Whatever may be the grounds, the opinion is becoming more & more prevalent, in France & in Yankeedom, that the French Emperor will persevere in his plan of intervention in our war, & intervene singly, if he cannot jointly by aid of the other great powers. It is so clearly to the interest of France, in my view of the case, that I cannot but believe he will do so. Further, it is beginning to be seen in Paris that England's peculiar [2386] interests, (to say nothing of her fanaticism,) will be favored by the utter destruction of cotton production in the Confederate States, by the now expected extinction of slavery. That idea was not until lately expressed by any one, if entertained by any, except myself. But when it is once considered, it seems to me so obvious that few correct thinkers will deny its force. If the opinion should be presented to Louis Napoleon's far-seeing mind, he is not likely to continue to second England in this policy of making her East Indian territory the great & almost only cotton-exporting country of the world, & thus acquiring the monopoly of supplying cotton to the manufacturers & consumers of all Europe. I trust that our Commissioner Mr. Slidell sees the force of this position, & will use it with skill in his diplomacy. If France would, by intervention, establish a right to exclusive commercial benefits from the Confederate States, it would be perfectly safe (from all danger of Yankeedom making war,) as well as in the highest degree profitable. Yankeedom would no more dare to make war on France, for her refusing longer to recognize the validity of the blockade, than the Yankee government dared to stand up to its boasts & threats in the case of the Trent, & under the apprehension of war with England. And if, contrary to this expectation, the resentment of Yankeedom should surpass her discretion,

& war should be made on France, there would be no more safe & profitable war to the latter country. . . . The French people are ready to sustain their government in a war in which glory is the only available prize. In a war with the U.S. at this time, there would not only be offered the glory of successful achievements, & naval & territorial conquest, but also substantial & important gains.—The weather had been growing colder for some days back, & this morning the thermometer stood at 13°. But, under a bright sun & with a southerly wind, the temperature soon became mild.

Dec. 22. Monday. The Yankee forces maintained their position & their batteries on the Stafford hills, commanding the river at Fredericksburg until the 18th, when (as reported) the last were withdrawn. Since, a reconnaissance by a body of our cavalry, under Gen. Hampton, has been made, & large bodies of the enemy were found in & near Dumfries & on Bull Run. Gen. Hampton inferred that the enemy was retreating towards Washington. He captured one of their wagon trains, & some prisoners. Reports from our men captured, & carried to Aquia creek, & since paroled & returned, repeat what had been stated before by Yankee prisoners, as to the demoralization & insubordination in Burnside's army after the battle. This seems the probable cause of his not renewing the attack, which intention he stated in his dispatch to Lincoln as late as 4 A.M. on 14th., & to take place that morning.—Reports of northern papers do not pretend to claim a victory, & admit their heavy loss, & much greater than ours, in the battle of Fredericksburg. This subdued tone is a remarkable exception to the almost universal course of claiming a victory for every defeat. . . .

Dec. 24. Wednesday.—The mail. . . . At latest accounts, the Yankee cannon had not all been dismounted from their batteries commanding the river at Fredericksburg—though the main body of the army was supposed to be far on the march towards Washington, there to go into winter-quarters. The northern [2389] papers continue to rise in the estimates of Burnside's loss in the late battle. From the first (Burnside's) report, of 5000, it is raised by one paper to 10,000, by another to over 13,000—& by others, later, to 15,000 & more.[25] Their comments, instead of being (as usual,) boasting, are in the tone of lamentation & gloom. But the most remarkable effects, & manifest acknowledgment of this disastrous defeat have

---

[25] Actual Federal losses in the carnage at Fredericksburg totaled 12,653. Confederate casualties were estimated at 5,300.

been displayed at Washington. A private meeting (or caucus) of the members of the Senate was held, which requested the President to dismiss Seward, & to reconstruct his whole cabinet. On this Seward has resigned his post of Secretary of State—& it is understood that all the other heads of departments will speedily follow—& Halleck, the Commander in Chief of the Armies, also. But it is said that Lincoln protests against this informal assumption of dictatorship by the Senate, & will not obey—& especially clings to his incompetent Secretary of War, Stanton.[26] I am sorry to lose Seward, *per se*, from Lincoln's cabinet—& indeed all the other Secretaries. Seward is the only member of the administration who is really an able man. Yet he for his great & fully exposed baseness & villainy, & the other ministers for their blind fanaticism or incompetency, are the best to injure their own cause, & to benefit that of the South. But we may well afford to lose this benefit, in the far greater injury which this breaking up of the cabinet will inflict on the Rump government, in affording evidence of the discord there reigning, & of the government estimate of the magnitude of the late defeat of its army, & of its plans. . . . President Davis has issued a proclamation announcing his intended retaliation, & the causes requiring it—of which I only hope the performance may bear some proportion in vigor, to the present promise. . . . After reciting the case of the murder of [William B.] Mumford in New Orleans,[27] & the long & vain efforts to obtain information or any satisfaction thereupon from Lincoln's government, he orders that Gen. Butler, the murderer, if taken prisoner, shall forthwith be executed as a murderer. Any & all officers of his army who may be taken prisoners are to be confined as felons, & held subject to punishment as such. Then the other & general & flagitious violations of the laws of war by Yankee troops are recited, & general measures preparatory to retaliation are stated. But [2391] there is nothing definitive, & beyond change,

---

[26] These reports were essentially correct. Following a caucus of thirty-two Republican senators on Tuesday, December 16, in which Seward was severely castigated by supporters of Salmon P. Chase, the secretary of state submitted his resignation. In the ensuing confrontation between Lincoln and his senatorial critics, the former held his ground and on December 20 ended the crisis by declining to accept the resignations of either Seward or Chase, who had tendered his own letter of resignation on that date.

[27] Charged with tearing down the United States flag at the New Orleans mint immediately after the Federal occupation of that city, Mumford was executed on June 7, 1862, by order of Major General Benjamin F. Butler.

ordered in any case except as to Butler—who will take good care never, as a prisoner, to incur the risk. In all other cases, the prisoners being confined as felons, I fear, will merely be the preparatory step to their having the benefit of the President's tender mercy, pardon, & exchange or parole. . . .

Dec. 26. Friday. The mail, with papers of yesterday only, none being published last night for today. At the request of Lincoln, Seward & Chase have withdrawn their previous resignations, & so the begun breaking up [2392] of Lincoln's cabinet is suspended. But the rupture & causes which produced the difficulty remain, & the discontent of the Senate & abolition party will be increased by being disappointed of their expected vengeance. Burnside has taken upon himself the responsibility of the attack at Fredericksburg, & therefore of his defeat—& so will probably screen Halleck, & so save himself from dismissal. . . .

Dec. 29. Nearly all day pasting envelopes.—Julian went to Petersburg, & brought the mail on his return at night.—A case of small-pox has occurred in the neighboring camp. There is much of this disease in the country, & especially in Richmond, Petersburg, & other towns. Besides this, there are other severe diseases very general in Richmond, & among them, scarlet fever of peculiarly malignant & dangerous [2393] character.—Banks' expedition has at last turned up, at New Orleans. Only 8000 land forces arrived with him. He supersedes the Brute Butler—which I am sorry for, as I wished his rule to continue.[28] Milder measures are expected under Banks. It is understood that latterly the Yankees have got much cotton in the parts of the South-West occupied by them, or within their reach—by purchase, if from Unionists, & by plunder from all secessionists. All of the latter class, (or nearly all the proprietors,) would much prefer to burn their cotton, as was the general course at first of all in imminent peril. But that procedure has mostly ceased, because every planter who has voluntarily burnt his cotton, has had all the remainder of his moveable & destructible property plundered or destroyed, whenever the Yankees could visit his plantation. By this potent means of punishment, they have repressed such self-sacrificing & patriotic action of every man who

---

[28] For weeks there had been much speculation in the Confederacy regarding the ultimate destination of Banks's naval expedition. The latter officially relieved Butler as commander of the Federal Department of the Gulf on December 16—much to the delight of New Orleans residents, if not of the diarist.

could not incur, or risk, the loss of everything he possessed. By the like infamous but potent means, the Yankee authorities discourage or repress guerrilla defence, & even all partizan action by small bodies of regular military. For whenever Yankee plunderers are fired upon, or a Yankee steamer is captured, or any other punishment inflicted on their forces or property, by small or unknown bodies, whether of regular or irregular troops, they inflict, in return, heavy exactions, or destruction of property, & imprisonment of resident civilians, on all the vicinity of the places of such actions by Confederates. Such conduct is by no means confined to the Brute's command—but is practised wherever Yankee forces have access & control. Yet this outrageous & potent system of violation of the laws of war has not been mentioned in the long list of Yankee outrages arrayed in President Davis' proclamation, & threatened with retaliation. [2394]

Dec. 30. Tuesday.... Among several articles appended, as evidences of northern sentiment, is a strong & bold letter from W. B. Reed of Phila.,[29] in which he says—"It is my firm belief that the paramount wish of the masses of the North is for peace—though timidity, or considerations (mistaken, in my opinion,) of expediency prevent them from saying so."—The remarkable change of the Yankee administration, from all-daring despotism & defiance of all legal & constitutional restraints, to the late & present meek submission to whatever men & newspapers may choose to utter in denunciation & vituperation of Lincoln, his subordinates, & his policy, sufficiently indicates the sense of weakness of the administration. One tenth-part of what now is uttered in every issue of the New York World, & even the Herald, would, six months ago, have consigned the authors & editors to speedy imprisonment, at the unlimited discretion of the government. There was another powerful mode of controlling the press, & preventing truth reaching the people, which also has recently been given up. This was, that when newspaper editors did not venture to publish anything strong enough to allow their imprisonment, & the forcible suppression of

---

[29] A prominent Philadelphia lawyer, William Bradford Reed (1806–76) had switched to the Democratic Party in 1856 and was rewarded with an appointment as United States minister to China under the Buchanan administration. In that capacity he negotiated the Treaty of Tientsin (1858), which conferred upon the United States sweeping most-favored-nation privileges within the crumbling Chinese empire. However, his bitter opposition to the Civil War adversely affected his professional reputation and ultimately made him a virtual social outcast in his native city.

their publications & business, but yet were deemed unfriendly to the administration, their papers were refused conveyance in the mails. This refusal was as illegal as the more summary & violent measures—& scarcely less effective to break down any paper of widely extended circulation. For this prohibition of mail carriage must cut off nearly all circulation, except in the city in which the paper was printed. . . . Finished my laid-off job of making envelopes—[2396] amounting to more than 1200 in all. The labor has served to occupy pleasantly my spare & otherwise wearisome time. . . .

Dec. 31. Wednesday.—The mail. A letter from Edmund, who has gone to Amelia.—Rosecrans' army, or a large force, posted at Stewart's creek, 10 miles from Murfreesborough. Skirmishing going on, & our advance had fallen back some miles, but had been reinforced, & ordered to recover the lost ground. A general battle expected there. . . . Rosecrans' army (whose headquarters is Nashville,) is supposed to have 35 to 50,000 in the field, threatening ours near Murfreesborough. Grant & his force, driven from Holly Spring[s],[30] & cut off from communication with Rosecrans, is probably in communication, & within supporting distance, of Gen. Sherman's army on the Yazoo, assailing the outpost defences of Vicksburg. Several attacks have been already attempted on Vicksburg, but all repulsed, with little loss on our side. As reported, our loss, 36 killed & wounded, & the Yankee loss 350. They had landed on the Yazoo 25,000 men. . . . In [2397] the now progressing attack on Vicksburg, by land & water, & by enormous forces, brought because of the enemy's previous signal failure, there is much to fear. And if judging by the enemy's general success wherever their mortar boats have operated, or even threatened, there would be little to hope for the defence. But Vicksburg has already bravely withstood, & successfully repulsed, a bombardment of great severity & duration—& was thus the first town to prove that mortar boats were not such dreadful & invincible assailants as supposed. I trust that that noble example will be repeated—& that, if the

---

[30] On December 20 Major General Earl Van Dorn, with a contingent of 3,500 cavalry, had struck Grant's secondary supply depot at Holly Springs, Mississippi, taking 1,500 prisoners and destroying more than $1,500,000 worth of supplies. This raid, together with Forrest's simultaneous attacks on railroads to the north, forced Grant to withdraw from Oxford, Mississippi, to La Grange, Tennessee, and lessened the chances for success of Sherman's Chickasaw Bluffs operation against Vicksburg.

defences of Vicksburg shall have at last to be abandoned, it will not be until every fort is taken, & every building in the town demolished or burnt. Of the also impending (& probably progressing) battle between Nashville & Murfreesborough, I have better hopes. Yet no doubt that our forces there, as well as at Vicksburg, are inferior in numbers. Gen. Johnston also has very lately assumed the command, & scarcely can be as competent for the charge as he would be at a later time. Still, with all our present disadvantages, I prefer that the great battle with Rosecrans' army shall come of[f] now, before the rivers rise, & give the Yankee war steamers full access through the country by the now low rivers. If our heretofore general ill-success in the west can now be reversed by an overwhelming defeat of the Yankees in a great battle, it would go far to satisfy Yankeedom that the war had been prosecuted far enough.—An express messenger to Julian arrived late in the evening with the telegraphic information of the death of John Meade[31]—which occurred this morning, at Augusta, Ga. Julian immediately made hasty preparations, & at 7.30 P.M. set off for Petersburg, to proceed to Augusta early tomorrow morning. This most lamentable loss had long been counted upon as certain—& therefore the mother & sisters of the deceased were very fully prepared for the consummation. The fatal disease (consumption,) of this most worthy & estimable [2398] young man, was certainly caused by exposure during his military service, & therefore his death, as much as if he had been killed on the battle field. . . .

---

[31] Brother of Julian's wife, Lotty.

January–March

❧

1863

A PROPHET CRAVES HONOR IN HIS OWN
COUNTRY ❧ SPECULATIONS ON A SEPARATE
PEACE WITH THE NORTHWESTERN STATES
❧ REVELATIONS CONCERNING THE VIR-
GINIA SECESSION CONSPIRACY ❧ THE
FRENCH EMPEROR PONDERS INTERVENTION
❧ MOUNTING CONFEDERATE ECONOMIC
WOES

January 1. Thursday.—The lately published official Army Register of U.S. shows the Yankee army now to be more than a million of
men—besides 30,000 seamen on board armed vessels. No doubt
there are so many soldiers on paper, & on pay. But I doubt whether
there are as many as 800,000 in the field. If so, where can they
be? . . . The year which is just closed has been almost everywhere
glorious to our arms, & the military operations & results were such
as to increase the reputation of the C.S. & add to their favor &
prestige in Europe, & to discourage the hopes of our enemies, &
enfeeble their future attempts of subjugation. But still, the balance
of accruing advantages have been decidedly in favor of the Yankee
military & naval arms in the west. We have completely lost all
[2399] occupation in Missouri & Kentucky, Louisiana, & in
North-western Va. And the enemy's armies occupy at will large
portions of, & domineer in, Ten. Ark. & Miss. In every region &
military district, not only in the west, but in the east, & in almost
every pitched battle, the Yankee armies have been greatly superior
to ours there opposed to them. Their full military numbers, of all
kinds, probably are nearly thrice as many as ours—supposing theirs
to be 1,030,000, & ours 350,000. Yet, it is evident that no despondency, or the slightest disposition to yield the contest, has been
produced to us, by all our losses & disasters. And on the other hand,
the northern publications offer abundant evidence that a very large

number, which soon will include the whole conservative or opposition party, (which is already a majority of the northern people,) are heartily discouraged with the cost & ill-success of the war. The loudest of the complainers so far only advocate seeking peace through a general convention of all the states, (including the seceded,) to amend the U.S. constitution, by securing all rights to the South, & so reconstructing the former union. I can scarcely believe that any intelligent northerner, at this late day, can believe in the possibility of the seceded states being willing, under any circumstances, to reconstruct the former union, or to meet the North in convention to confer on any such object. I infer that this view is merely presented by the leaders, to blind their ignorant followers, until they can be prepared to admit the independence of the C.S. as an inevitable necessity. Gov. Seymour this day assumes the chief magistracy of the great state of New York. Though, unfortunately, the lately elected opposition legislatures of that & sundry other states will not supersede the present abolition bodies for nearly a year to come, yet the governor of N.Y. alone, backed by a known majority of the people, & of the legislators [2400] elected, can do much in opposing the lawless despotism of Lincoln—& I trust that he will have the boldness & ability to adopt that course. . . . In another respect, this first day of 1863 must be viewed in Yankeedom & in Europe as most important to the fate of the Confederate States & the southern people. But no such importance is attached to it, or to measures it was to inaugurate, by any southern community, and by no one individual whose opinion I have heard. This is the day on which, by Lincoln's proclamation of September, general emancipation of slaves in every still "rebellious" state was to begin—&, as a condition to that end, certainly counted upon, & even acknowledged, insurrections of the slaves, to achieve by slaughter of their masters, the freedom thus offered to them. [2401] It is true that another proclamation was promised, to be issued this day, to declare, (if such was the fact,) the non-acceptance of Lincoln's offered mercy by the submission of any of the seceded states, & their thereby refusing to escape the penalties of bloody insurrection & general emancipation of their slaves. But this subsequent proclamation would be merely formal, & declaratory of the continuation of the "rebellion" which everybody knew would have no relaxation because of these threatened penalties. I fear that Lincoln will not now dare to issue his consummating proclamation. But I desire its being issued merely for its effect on weak minds abroad. For in effect, & for every practical purpose, the measure & policy of general emancipation & insurrection of southern slaves was *completed* on the day in which it was proclaimed as intended, & its execution on this day to be contingent on the continuation of the resistance of the C.S. which was certain to be continued. This policy, of encouraging insubordination & insurrection of our slaves, & effecting their abduction, & their pretended enfranchisement, has been practised throughout the war, wherever Yankee forces occupied our territory, & had access to & controlled the residents. No farther could they operate. Just so far they can & will act after the one, or the two proclamations . . . . But, if all the slaves had had the will & the power to avail themselves of the invitation held out to them in Lincoln's September proclamation, to be consummated on Jan. 1st. thereafter, they would do so just as fully without a subsequent proclamation, as with it. Therefore, I maintain that so far as it was possible to carry out the policy indicated, it was consummated, & the act made complete, when it was promised by the proclamation of Sept. And, if no subsequent proclamation, declaring the consummation, shall appear—or even if the former proclamation should be withdrawn, [2402] & declared null & void, the intended policy of insurrection & enfranchisement would not be thereby impaired—but would be as effectually carried out in practice, as could have been done by the promised second proclamation, & by the most earnest efforts of the Yankee administration. . . .

Jan. 2. Friday.—Obtained (from the camp,) papers of 1st. Nothing more of the fighting near Vicksburg. Rosecrans' army had advanced to within 3 miles of Murfreesborough, where our army was drawn up to receive his attack, which was momently expected. The outposts of the two armies were within half a mile of each other. . . . Wendell Phillips, the great anti-slavery orator & lecturer of Mass., predicts that if this war is protracted to the next presidential canvass . . . there will be a ticket in the North-West for the secession of those states from the North-East (or remainder of U.S.,) & their reunion with their natural allies the Confederate States. The N.Y. Mercury, commenting on this, predicts the exclusion of the New England States, from any combination of the U.S. Also [2403] it is reported that Gen. Fremont is in St. Louis, & that he is holding levees, & publickly in conversation advocates the secession of the North-western States, & their union with the Southern. I think that the latter report is premature. But I have no doubt, whether in war or peace, that this separation will take place, & that the union of the north-western states with the C.S. will be desired & sought by the former—but in vain. Fremont perhaps is enough a fool to move first in this matter, to gratify both his spite & his ambition. But he has not ability to carry it out. If, however, he or any one can encourage those who now secretly approve, to dare openly to advocate the one or both of these great means for saving the interests & prosperity of the north-western states, the doctrine will soon spread, & its supporters rapidly increase. The continuance of the war, or even peace, with the C.S. left independent, & hostile in feeling to the North-Western states, will be to their destruction. Nothing but timely separation from the remainder of the U.S., & friendly commercial relations with the C.S. can prevent the utter ruin of the states & territory on the upper waters of the Mississippi & Missouri. . . . By the neglect or misconduct of either mail-carrier or the postmaster, the mail today passed without being opened at the C.H., & our messenger obtained nothing for going 7 miles to the P.O. This disappointment especially vexatious, when I am so anxious to hear from the engaged armies at Vicksburg & Murfreesborough.

Jan. 3. The papers of yesterday bring important & good news. An [2404] official dispatch from Gen. Bragg announces a battle near Murfreesborough, of our army under his command, & that under Gen. Rosecrans. It is to this purport:[1]—Thank God! But this is not the end. The enemy's extreme left, which still held its position, had to be routed—or otherwise it may afford a rallying point for the Yankee army to reestablish its strength, & inflict a reverse of fortune on our forces. I think that our continued & increased success is much the more probable. . . . Another assault, & attempt to storm our fortifications near Vicksburg was made by the besiegers, &, as before, repulsed. . . . In Richmond, on Jan. 1, brown sugar sold by the barrel at 95 cents the pound, & molasses, wholesale, at $6.10 to

---

[1] Attached to the diary at this point is a clipping containing the following dispatch from General Bragg, dated December 31, 1862: "We assailed the enemy this morning at 7 o'clock, and after ten hours' hard fighting have driven him from every position, except his extreme left, where he has successfully resisted us. We captured Four Thousand Prisoners, including two Brigadier-Generals, Thirty-One Pieces of Artillery, and some two hundred wagons and teams. Our loss is heavy, but that of the enemy much greater." See also *Official Records*, Vol. XX, Pt. 1, p. 662.

$6.25 the gallon. Retail prices, respectively, $1 to 1.10, & $7.50 to $8. The current price of the meanest whisky, (formerly 20 to 25 cents,) sells at $25 to $30 a gallon—& French brandy at $40 to $50. Yet still, many people get drunk, & at the private & illegal drinking shops, at higher prices. [2405] . . . Last accounts from Europe continue to repeat, & with increased confidence, the probability of intervention by France, & also by England, consequent on the expected change of the ministry. The inferences of the principal northern editors are that intervention by France is imminent.— There are new examples of the illegal & outrageous policy, systematically adopted & carried out in practice, & openly [2406] proclaimed by Yankee commanders. Gen. Sherman, whose headquarters are at Memphis, has ordered that in every case in which a Yankee vessel is fired upon, or molested, no matter when or where within his (nominal) command & military jurisdiction, he will drive out of Memphis 10 resident families, selecting in preference those of which the male members are in the Confederate army. Three steamers were recently fired at from the shore, &, in consequence, 30 families have been driven from their homes in Memphis, & from all means for support. These families necessarily consist of women & children, or in part of old men, as the able bodied males (being secessionists,) are of course either soldiers in service, or earlier exiles & refugees abroad. So the sentence of exile, in alleged retaliation for acts of legal warfare, committed by others, & men in arms, is certainly a consignment of the victims to destitution & severe suffering, if not in many cases to death, by starvation & exposure. Gen. [Robert H.] Milroy, also, commanding the Yankee forces in north-western Va, & posted at Moorefield, Hardy Co., is emulating Butler, on his smaller theatre of action. By his recent proclamation . . . he requires every man & woman residing in his lines, or within his control, to take not only the oath of allegiance to Lincoln's but also to [Francis H.] Pierpont's government of "Western Virginia." What makes this coerced oath as ridiculous & absurd as it is unjust & oppressive, is that the law creating this new state, though enacted by both houses of the Rump congress has not received Lincoln's signature—& may not. The law has been pronounced unconstitutional by the U.S. Attorney General, (as everybody knows it is,) & though Lincoln does not regard violating the U.S. constitution, & his oath to observe it, yet he may for policy's sake pretend to respect it in this case. Every resident, male or female, of "Western Virginia," who shall refuse to take the oath of treason to their state, & of allegiance to the Northern Federal government, & a pretended state government which does not exist even by illegal legislation . . . are [*sic*] denied all protection [2407] of the U.S. military, which means that they may be plundered & maltreated, & outraged by Yankees or tories, without any hope of redress. Further, they are subjected to oppressive restraints, of their persons, & their property subjected to confiscation for Yankee benefit, either in the lump, or from time to time in special contributions levied on particular portions of territory. While Yankee commanders, by authority of their government, are thus executing what they call retaliatory punishments, on innocent & helpless civilians, non combatants, & especially (for the much larger number of the victims,) on women & children, our president refuses to retaliate on the armed brigands [for] their unprecedented outrages, & violations of all the rules of civilized warfare. For, even his proclamation, & all previous threats to retaliate, amount to nothing certain, but ordering the *confinement* of Yankee prisoners, as felons, who will be subsequently, as heretofore . . . released, & paroled as prisoners of war. The only exception is ordering the hanging of Butler, in the very improbable case of his ever permitting himself to be taken prisoner. It is undoubtedly legal & customary warfare for our troops to fire upon, & capture & destroy, any of the enemy's vessels, armed or merely commercial, on the rivers of our or of their territory, as much as if on the ocean. Our right & our ability for such attacks & captures constitute our potent & effective means for debarring our enemies from the control, or the safe use, of the western rivers & their navigation. If we are to be prevented making use of this powerful means for defending our territory by endangering or destroying the enemy's vessels, by the threatened or executed barbarous cruelties inflicted on distant women & children, then we may be also driven to renounce other & the most common means for warfare. The instant discharge of all Yankee prisoners, captured in open battle, may [2408] be required, or the future capture of all others prohibited, by the Yankee commanders condemning to be bayonetted two or ten of our women & children, for every such prisoner held. They may extend the like retaliatory punishments, varied or increased by general burnings, & laying waste of certain spaces of our territory, for every Yankee killed or wounded in battle. And if we are to submit to what they have already so required—i.e. to avoid molesting their vessels, defending our property from marauders, obstructing our roads & rivers against invaders, burning our own cotton, to prevent its being their booty—then they can as well compel us to avoid every means of warfare & of defence. For nearly all of the illegal outrages committed by the Yankee armed forces, retaliation of the like kind is impossible, because . . . it is by an invading army only, & upon the invaded population & property, that can be committed the outrages of robbing, burning & laying waste private property—maltreating, imprisoning, or slaying non-combatants—ravishing & otherwise abusing women—stealing slaves, & inviting them to insubordination or insurrection. For all the innumerable acts of illegal outrage of these kinds, we have no means for retaliating but in one mode—& that is the putting to death the captured soldiers of the enemy. And this ought to have been done, & continued, if it had required for due retaliation, the execution of every Yankee soldier captured in the last year. . . . Our soldiers & our people would indeed incur an awful responsibility—but which is necessary to be incurred for defence, & to prevent their continued submission to outrage inviting our enemies to increase it ten-fold. But the alternatives for our enemies would be very different. It would be to have every one of their captured soldiers executed, or otherwise to carry on hostilities according to the rules of civilized warfare, & to refrain from crimes which, however productive of suffering to the victims, & shocking to humanity, have not operated in the least to aid the Yankee arms, or cause, but the reverse. Every partial & limited measure of retaliation yet put in force on our part, has had immediate effect in correcting the particular offence it was designed for. And I do not doubt that a general policy of retaliation, even if reaching to the execution of every Yankee prisoner, would be as effective in putting an end to the brigandage of the Yankee armies.

Jan. 4. Sunday. . . . The news as good as anticipated. Gen. Bragg's official dispatches of 1st. announce that "The enemy has yielded his strong point, (held by the left wing through & after the battle,) & is falling back. We now occupy the whole field, & shall follow." . . . In another dispatch, also of 1st., Gen. Bragg said, "The expedition under Forrest has fully accomplished its object. The railroads in West Ten. are broken in many places, large amounts of stores destroyed, many arms captured, & 1200 prisoners paroled. Morgan has done his work, but the full effect is not known. The enemy in

Ten. & Mis. are without railroad & telegraphic communications with their rear." These conditions give good hopes that Gen. Bragg will be able to inflict still heavier blows on the beaten & retreating enemy. . . .

Jan. 5. Monday. I have reached another anniversary of my birth, & this day enter upon the 70th year of my life. This is six years more than the age attained by any of my progenitors, male or female, since my great-grandfather Edmund Ruffin, the carpenter, who was a man of herculean frame & strength, & iron constitution, & after an industrious & temperate life, died at the age of seventy-seven. My always feeble body & constitution, & my continued bad health for 15 years of the earlier [2411] part of my manhood, afforded no prospect of my living to near my present age, or being the oldest of three generations of my family. But though the end has been so long & unexpectedly postponed, there are many indications that it must now be near, independent of my life having been already protracted so much beyond all reasonable & actual calculations. Within the last year, or a little more, my infirmities have all increased.[2] . . . All these things assure me that my death cannot be now far off. That conviction is not distressing to me, or even painful. My infirmities have deprived me of nearly all the pleasures I formerly enjoyed, mental as well as physical. Especially do I suffer for the want of society, which I have [2412] lost the capacity to enjoy, & am unfit to mix with. Except for the deep interest I feel in the present war, & all its incidents, & my wish to witness its termination, with success, glory, & the sure prospect of prosperity to my country, I have no inducement to desire the extension of my life. With this one exception, I should not care how soon the last summons may come to me. I only & earnestly desire that when it comes, it shall be unexpected, & immediately obeyed in sudden & painless death.

The mail. A letter from Nanny—with the information of the death of my daughter Mildred. This entirely unexpected & most deplorable intelligence has come indirectly, & through a circuitous channel, but cannot be doubted. She is reported to have died of paralysis, about the first of November—which was but three weeks after her writing the only letter (to Julian) which any of her family had received from her (& rarely any other report,) since Sept 7th

---

[2] There follows a recital of various infirmities ranging from thinning hair to a failing memory.

1861. My present calmness & apparent insensibility very soon after my learning, so unexpectedly, [of] the death of [my] daughter, are scarcely less surprising & shocking to my understanding, than her death so announced. Has her absence, & our far & complete personal separation for two & a half years, with 17 months cessation of all correspondence by letter, so weaned me from her society & love that I have become comparatively regardless of both? Or have age and decrepitude so impaired my faculties, paralysed my affections, & dried up the sources of parental love & of all deep feeling, that I scarcely grieve for the death of her [who] was my best beloved remaining child? [2413]

Jan. 7. Wednesday.... I have to note the news received in the papers of the last two days.—The confident expect[at]ions of continued success of Gen. Bragg have been wofully disappointed. The accounts are very meager, & obscure; but it is certain that the movements of both armies had been reversed, that ours had retreated, & the enemy had advanced, & occupied Murfreesborough. Gen. Bragg had pursued the retreating enemy on the 1st., & a bloody conflict had taken place either that afternoon or later—& on the 2nd., he had fallen back, & the enemy had again advanced, & held Murfreesborough, while our army retiring before them, was on the retreat southward.[3] But our previous spoil of the victory of 31st ult. was secured, at least to the extent of 4000 prisoners, 24 cannon, & 5000 stands of small arms &c. I hope that the mail of today may afford later & more satisfactory explanations. But so far, this victory seems to be like those of the first days at Fort Donelson, at Shiloh & at Perryville, a bloody & truly glorious success leading to disappointment, reverse, & disastrous defeat or loss. Even our greatest victories, & undeniable great defeats of the enemy's armies, leave no fruits to repay the bloody costs. Such was

---

[3] This early report was somewhat confused. After the bitter day-long contest on December 31, in which the Confederates won a decided victory, the two armies remained on the field. The battle was renewed on the afternoon of January 2 when Bragg ordered John C. Breckinridge's division to take some high ground on the Federal left. Though initially successful, Breckinridge was soon halted by a massive artillery barrage and compelled to retire to his original position after losing 1,700 men. On the night of January 3–4, Bragg withdrew toward Shelbyville, Tennessee, but Rosecrans elected not to pursue. Although the South could claim a tactical victory in the battle of Murfreesboro, or Stone's River—Confederate losses were 11,739 out of almost 35,000, as compared to nearly 13,000 Union casualties out of 41,400 effectives—strategically the campaign was a failure for the Confederates.

the first battle of Manassas, & such, as it seems from late developments, was our great victory at Fredericksburg. There has been an investigation of the causes of the defeat of Burnside's army, by a committee of the Yankee congress, before which most of the generals engaged, & highest in rank, have testified on oath. By means of this investigation an unusual amount of facts has been made known. Among them, it appears that for two days after Burnside's disastrous defeat, on 13th, his army was huddled & crowded mostly in the then ruined town of Fredericksburg, exposed to our artillery on the heights, & confessedly unable & afraid to renew the attack, & unable to retreat, if under the [2414] fire from our artillery, without incalculable loss. The retreat over the pontoon bridges was at last effected, & with safety, in the darkness of night, & during a storm of rain. Now why during this time, our artillery (secure from the possibility of attack,) did not pour balls & bombshells on the army crowded in the town, & sheltered only by the buildings, I cannot conceive. It is difficult to conceive that Gen. Lee should have been unacquainted with the general facts of the enemy's position & condition. . . . Other news is nearly all good, though none to counterbalance the ill news from Murfreesborough. The Yankee forces made another (the third) assault on the defences of Vicksburg, & were again beaten back. Then they re-embarked, & their fleet steamed down the Yazoo. It was inferred that they would either abandon the siege, as desperate, or wait for heavy reinforcements to renew the attempt. . . . Lincoln's promised proclamation has appeared, to my surprise as well as gratification. I had feared that he would shrink from this formal consummation of his general negro emancipation & insurrection policy & plan. In this proclamation [2416] . . . he declares immediate enfranchisement to all the slaves of the 11 states which have formally (by action of their state governments) seceded, with the following exceptions: Tennessee wholly—the portion of Louisiana occupied by Yankee forces, the 48 counties of western Virginia, designated as the new state, together with the counties of Berk[e]ley, Accomac, Northampton, Elizabeth City, Warwick, York, Princess Anne & Norfolk—all which excepted territory is considered as brought back under Northern rule. Lincoln has done another benefit to the C.S. in signing the bill making a new & separate state of western Va.—The mail. A telegraphic dispatch from Gen. Bragg, of Jan. 5th at Tullahoma, says—"Unable to dislodge the enemy from his intrenchments, & hearing of reinforcements to him, I withdrew from his front night before last. He has not followed me. My cavalry are close on his front."—So it is certain that Gen. Bragg, after beating & driving back Rosecrans on the 31st ult., pursuing him on the 1st inst. & fighting another bloody battle on the 2nd, had to retreat, leaving the enemy [in] possession of his own former ground, as well as of the fields of battle.... The Northern letters & papers, though having claimed the victory first as well as last, do not boast much of it. They admit heavy losses & unprecedented bloodshed....

Jan. 9. Friday.—The mail.... The Yankee papers, & their correspondents in Europe, seem certain that the French emperor will soon intervene in our war. It is believed that he will first address another note, inviting their co-operation, to the courts of England & Russia—& then, if still refused, will act alone. In what manner is not understood, beyond the advising an armistice, & a conference for peace. If he limits his action to advice, or even if he should follow its rejection by the North by a naked recognition of the independence of the C.S., his intervention will do us no good. But if he will break up the blockade, we can then maintain our contest without recognition. Or, if he will add thereto the admittance of our vessels of war & prizes into French ports, [2421] we can soon conquer a peace on the ocean. Or, if Yankeedom should so resent the intervention of France as to make war, France & the Confederate States, together, could soon destroy the Yankee power.... The legislature of Va met on the 7th. I am glad that the Governor has begun retaliation, which the president has merely threatened. Of the 118 prisoners captured by Gen. Floyd's command, the Va State troops, in Ky, & sent to Rd., the Governor has had the two highest officers put to hard labor in the Penitentiary, for two Va officers long imprisoned as traitors & rebels in the Penitentiary at Washington—& 5 other officers & privates are put into solitary imprisonment, in retaliation for Col. [Richard] Thomas, or Zarvona, kept in a dungeon, & under most cruel privations, for the last 18 months.[4]

---

[4] Richard Thomas, alias Zarvona, was a prominent Marylander who received a commission as colonel in the Virginia Volunteers and achieved notoriety early in the war by engineering the seizure of the steamer *St. Nicholas* on the Potomac River (see above, page 54). Arrested in July, 1861, he was charged with piracy and incarcerated as a political prisoner, first at Fort McHenry and later at Fort Lafayette. Governor Letcher's retaliatory action apparently had the desired effect, for Thomas—known popularly as "the French lady"—was exchanged for seven Union hostages in the spring of 1863. For the extensive correspondence concerning the Thomas case, see *Official Records*, Ser. II, Vol. II, 379–415.

Jan. 10. Saturday. Julian sent to Petersburg for his family. Lotty & children, & Mrs. Meade, got home at dark, through a heavy rain.—The papers of today. Northern (& also official) reports of their late great victory (so claimed) near Murfreesborough. It appears that Rosecrans had drawn back his advanced line, at the very time that Bragg's retreat was beginning—& that Rosecrans did [2423] not re-occupy his abandoned positions, or again advance, until nearly a day after Bragg's retreat, & then far removal, had been fully ascertained. Taking together the whole of the several days of fighting, including the undenied & great victory of our army on the 31st, & its subsequent reverse & retreat, the results may be deemed as about equal to both sides. The enemy in recovering the battlefields, & advancing beyond, & in following after (however slowly & cautiously,) our army which had before retreated, may claim the victory according to military understanding. But Gen. Bragg has gained the greater fruits of success, in his captured prisoners, cannon, wagon trains, small arms &c. . . . I have just learned, through Mrs. Meade, that Capt. Cuthbert, commander of the Palmetto Guard, under whom I served at Morris Island & Bull Run, was killed in the battle of Fredericksburg—as were two or three of the lieutenants of that company, at the same battle.[5] . . . I greatly regret Capt. Cuthbert's death especially. He was a rich planter in Port Royal, S.C. who has been in constant service from the time that S.C. first called for volunteers. His plantation was laid waste, & about 100 slaves taken by the invaders. So little thought had I of his death, that I wrote to him a few days later.—This morning, read my own pamphlet "Political Economy of Slavery," which was enough forgotten to be interesting, & Byron's "Two Foscari."

Jan. 12. Monday.—The mail. Letters from Edmund & from Dr. J. J. Dupuy. The latter has been appointed an Assistant Surgeon —which will be much relief, compared to his heretofore service as a private trooper.—The western rivers rising fast.—Vicksburg so far is safe—& the Yankee army has been repulsed with heavy loss in every attempted assault. . . . The Rump House of Representatives, by a vote of 83 to 28, has honored Brute Butler with [2426] the thanks of that body. This is another benefit to our cause rendered by the Rump. . . . From Dr. Dupuy's letter I learned more of Gen.

---

[5] This report was erroneous. Neither Captain George B. Cuthbert nor any other officer attached to the Second South Carolina Regiment was killed at Fredericksburg. *Official Records*, Vol. XXI, 583.

Lee's army than all stated in the newspapers. He has been intrenching all the line (or crest) of the heights from Fredericksburg to Bowling Green, 15 miles, & all the batteries so constructed are masked, by thick hedge-rows of cedars, which are on the side of the road. . . . The position is much the same, & as favorable for defence, as the ground near Fredericksburg, which was occupied by our intrenchments & artillery in the late battle, & found impregnable by the enemy. The preparing these extensive defences seems to indicate either that Gen. Lee expects another attack from the Yankee army, by the same route, or that he means to withdraw a large part of the Confederate army for other operations, & leave the remainder to man these masked batteries, as sufficient to repel any new attack. . . .

Jan. 15. Thursday. . . . The legislature of Va. is engaged in the election of a C.S. Senator, in place of Ballard Preston decd. There are four candidates—Judge [John J.] Allen, [Charles W.] Russell of Wheeling, Wm. C. Rives, & Gen. Floyd. I know but little of Russell & nothing of Allen, who has not been engaged in political life.[6] Therefore perhaps I prefer him. I have objections to Russell, but would greatly prefer him to either Floyd or Rives. Floyd I believe to be destitute of honesty in pecuniary trusts. Rives is respectable in his private life—but a traitor in sentiment to the South up to the secession of Va, & I would not trust him for anything better since. . . .

Jan. 16. Friday. The mail. . . . The message of President Davis to Congress, in the last papers, is an admirable state paper. In it, he declares the intention, if not disapproved by congress, of holding every Yankee officer hereafter captured as responsible for being accessory to the insurrection policy of Lincoln, & of transferring such prisoners to the state governments to be treated by them as aiders of insurrection, according to the laws of the several states. This measure, so far as refusing to exchange captured officers, is already begun. And the Yankee military authorities have refused to receive their captured privates without the officers. This is like to put an end to the whole existing arrangement for exchange of

---

[6] Russell, at this time a member of the Confederate House of Representatives, had acted as chairman of the Virginia delegations to the Democratic national conventions in Charleston and Baltimore in 1860. A former single-term Whig congressman, John James Allen (1797–1871) had been a member of the Virginia supreme court of appeals for more than two decades and the presiding justice of that body since 1852.

prisoners, if not to inaugurate antagonistic retaliatory measures. This retaliatory policy begun by President Davis is excellent in theory & intention, but I fear there will be insuperable difficulties in the practical execution through the instrumentality of the state governments, [2430] acting by their statute laws & courts.—The aggregate debt of the Confederate States, on Jan. 1st., amounted to $556,000,000.—The Governor of Va. has called out the militia between 40 & 45 years of age (those only not being already in service,) of 15 counties & towns south of James river, & between the Blue Ridge & tide-water, to rendezvous at Petersburg. The object is to guard this state against any advance of the enemy from N.C. The call includes Petersburg, but does not reach to this county.—Foote, of Ten., has offered in the H. of R. a series of resolutions . . . which are now under discussion. Their general spirit is good, & it is well to have the views thus presented to the notice of the people of the North. But I should very much object to the adoption of some of the resolutions. One of these is that which offers, under any condition whatever, however favorable to the C.S., after a separate peace, to make an alliance, offensive & defensive, with any portion of the present U.S., except New England, thus separately acknowledging the independence, & making a separate treaty of peace with the C.S. Another objectionable resolution is that which declares against the acceptance of any armistice, until the Yankee government shall have acknowledged the independence of the C.S. This requisition as a preliminary to negotiation for peace, that one party shall yield the main, & substantially the sole matter in contest, would be absurd. It would be enough for us to require, as a preliminary to an armistice, (& which certainly should be insisted upon,) the withdrawal of the enemy's armies from all the territory of the C.S. & their vessels of war from our waters. On these terms, an armistice for 6 months would enable us to make ready for carrying on the war for any extension of time thereafter, if our enemy still refused to make peace on our terms. Indeed, I would greatly prefer a naked armistice, & complete cessation of hostilities, & then to negot[i]ate for the conditions of peace, & take the risk of renewal of war, than to have from the Yankee government a full recognition of the independence of the C.S. in advance of the entire cessation of hostilities, & the continued occupation of any of our forts & harbors.—Read parts of Introduction &c. to Webster's Dictionary.

Jan. 17. Saturday.—Reading (second time,) "Doctor Antonio," by my Italian name-sake, [Giovanni] Ruffin.

Jan. 18. Sunday. . . . The election for C.S. Senator still going on, & a heated contest. Rives' first vote was 42, & largest of the four. On the 6th ballot, he had sunk to 12. I trust that the turn-coat & traitor to the South is now politically dead—& it is still better that by thus being a candidate, he has made unquestionable the extinction of his former influence. It is yet uncertain who will be elected. It seems only certain that it will not be either of the four candidates first brought forward. . . . The Balt. & Ohio R.R. has been again repaired by the Yankees, & is in operation throughout. In all mechanical operations our enemy displays a degree of energy which is admirable & wonderful.—Mr. Russell of Va. has introduced to Congress a very short bill in furtherance of the President's declaration, which is an improvement thereon, & which I hope may be enacted. This bill makes the mere service of any officer in the Yankee army, within any of the Confederate States, after Lincoln's last proclamation, equivalent to inciting insurrection of slaves, & orders that, if captured, he shall be punished by death. But instead of being turned over to the state authorities, & the civil judicatures, [2432] the guilt is to be ascertained, & the punishment decreed by courts martial, of the Confederate States armies, & by summary process. I still fear, though, even if this bill should be enacted, that the morbidly tender conscience of Pres. Davis will, by respites & pardons, defeat its object, & his own proposition. If this law shall be passed, & executed, it must produce one of two results: either the Yankee authorities will draw back, & hereafter refrain from all the customary violations of the laws of war by their forces—or, if persisting in them, there will soon be no prisoner spared on either side, & the war will be carried on thereafter as if under the black flag. If it is to be the latter alternative, I should still approve the course now proposed. A war of extermination of all soldiers, & even of all male adults captured, would not double the sufferings inflicted on our people by the illegal outrages of the Yankee forces. While the like measure, though limited to captured combatants, would increase a hundred-fold the dangers and punishment of the invaders, who have not yet suffered anything, except what was justified by the laws & usages of honorable warfare. . . . Therefore I infer, that if the bloody alternative of giving no quarter is accepted, & acted upon, the change will strengthen our arms, & intimidate &

weaken those of the enemy. But the stronger probability is, that our new policy will teach a lesson of necessary [2433] moderation to the Yankee government & armies. The great horror of the enforcement of the bloody alternative also must have much effect in strengthening the opposition party of the North, & quicken its conversion to a peace party. That conversion seems to me more probable & imminent. The legislature of New Jersey, which in both branches is democratic, has already adopted resolutions conforming in general to those proposed & recommended by a public meeting in New York . . . but still more strongly indicating a peace policy & movement. If there was the same sentiment & concurrence in the three branches of government of the powerful state of N.Y. as in N.J., the peace policy would soon be established. But, there, while the Governor is all that could be wished, & he is supported by the city of N.Y. & by a great majority of the State, the present or old House of Representatives is equally divided between the two parties, & the Senate remains decidedly abolition. Yet the Governor, alone, sustained by the people, may do much to check the wheels of Lincoln's government, if he is bold enough to lead in a civil revolution. There are other indications of change, or of weakness of Lincoln's administration, worth notice. So far during this war, the States of California & Oregon, & the other territory of the Pacific slope, have done nothing to aid the general government, except in the accustomed payment of duties on importations from foreign countries—& there has been no demand made on them for soldiers. Otherwise, except for such individuals as chose to enlist as volunteers in the Yankee army, these Pacific states & territories have been neutral—& the Lincoln government is evidently afraid to require their equal contributions of men & money. These states can revolt from Yankee rule whenever they may wish, without danger of coercion—& they will revolt whenever it will be more profitable to them than continued submission. Such a contingency will occur, should a war appear imminent between Yankeedom & France or England. For either of those [2434] powers could speedily subdue the Pacific coast, if it remained dependent on & connected with Yankeedom.

Jan. 19. Monday.—The mail brought no news of new & important military operations. Reported that there are indications of the Yankee army again crossing the Rappahannock for attack, both above & below Fredericksburg. I rather suppose these to be feints, to prevent any of Lee's army being sent to N.Ca. or Ten. . . . After 20 ballotings in the Va. legislature, Allen T. Caperton of Monroe, was elected C.S. Senator. He is a man of moderate abilities, & highly respectable as a man, & deemed true in support of the South. But he *was* a unionist nearly to the latest moment, & a whig, as well as belonging to western Va. The two last, if not also the first of these three qualifications served to secure his election. . . . Further evidences appear in northern papers, & expressions of opinion of public bodies & popular meetings in the North, of opposition to & denunciation of Lincoln's policy, & in favor of making peace. . . . In addition [2435] . . . there are increasing indications of conflict of interests, & fast-growing antagonism & hostility between the New England & the other northern states. There are many opinions published against the great & unjust preponderance of representation in the U.S. Senate, enjoyed by New England, under the Constitution. Each state having equal representation, the six New England States, having in all but 3,000,000 of population, have 12 Senators, while the state of N.Y., with 4,000,000 of inhabitants, has but 2 senators. Enough can & will be made of this to cut down this superiority of N.E. But there are other publications going farther, & urging that New England shall be excluded from the federal union entirely. A public meeting of the people of Huntingdon [*sic*— Huntington] county, in northern Indiana, adopted & published some of the strongest expressions of this general character . . . & which, also, indicate a disposition to be connected, in any event, with the possessors of the lower Mississippi. These results, or the most important of them, I predicted long ago, as the inevitable consequences of the independence of the South. They seem already only to await the undoubted establishment & permanency of that independence. Probably the offers of a separate peace to any of the North-western states, with the free use of the waters & ports of the lower Mississippi, informally held out by the Confederate Congress, may have had good effect. At any rate, every well-informed & intelligent man must know that when our independence is established, & peace is made, the mere naked right, under the laws of nations, of the vessels of the states on the upper waters of the Mississippi, to pass through the lower, to sea & to & from foreign ports, will be worth nothing, without the friendship of, & further privileges accorded [2436] by the Confederate States; & that without both the free navigation, & the markets, of the lower

Mississippi, the states on the upper waters will be ruined. To conquer these advantages would be the shortest & best mode of possession, if that mode was as feasible as at first believed in Yankeedom. But that belief has ceased to be held by many, & soon will be by the great majority of the North-western states—& then they must act according to their corrected views, of what is essential for their salvation. . . . [2437]

Jan. 20. Tuesday.—In my latter years, & more especially in the latest, my faculties & powers of mind, as well as of body, have been greatly impaired by age. But while, by such increasing infirmities, my mind has lost most of its former ability to retain recent impressions, or to receive new ones—or, at least, much of the capacity to acquire new knowledge by reading & study—it seems to me as if, in another respect, new lights had opened to my understanding, & that, by the lifting of a heretofore obscuring veil, I am now enabled to see, clearly & correctly, occurrences & circumstances of nearly or quite half a century past. These newly exposed views are of my own acts of folly, or weakness, or violations of moral duties. I am thankful that I have not to reproach myself for any guilt of deep dye—or of any act, or omission, deemed by me criminal at the time of its occurrence. But many lighter moral offences—& many more acts of folly, especially results of my vanity & love of notoriety, my simple credulity, & confidence falsely & foolishly placed—& which were obscured from my view for many, many years—have lately been brought clearly & vividly to my perception, to be regretted & ashamed of, or to be more deeply deplored & repented. . . . It has been my singular fortune, throughout my life, to have my real & worst transgressions from the path of rectitude to pass uncensured—and to be severely judged, & condemned, in public opinion, for minor & venial offences against propriety—&, further, to be visited by misconstruction & calumny, censure & hostility, for acts of stern devotion to duty, & of self-sacrifice, for which entire commendation, & applause, were my just due.—My temper is neither quick nor violent. I am slow to suspect enmity, or to take offence at doubtful affronts. But when justly aroused suspicion has once disturbed my credulous confidence, it is not to be allayed. And when my slow anger has been raised to the point of hostility & vindictiveness, my resentment is implacable. Many times I have overlooked, & soon forgot, unpremeditated affronts or injuries, which other persons, even better though quicker tempered than myself, would have met with angry resentment. But a real deliberate & malicious aspersion, or act of hostility or hatred without just cause, I have rarely forgiven. Subsequent lapse of time, absence of or separation from the offender, or even his death, & the passage of many years thereafter, have not operated to alter my opinion of the guilt of my enemy, or sensibly to abate my feelings of hatred & vindictiveness.—It is my natural disposition, & incurable propensity, when in friendly or ordinary conversation with other persons, to be unreserved, frank, & free in my expressions. This would be an admirable trait of character, if combined with the discretion & caution of avoiding so to speak except before those friends who would hold such expressions as confidential. But, unfortunately, this was rarely my case. With my usual freedom from all suspicion, I foolishly treated & trusted to every auditor as if worthy of my confidence—& moreover as if more careful to protect me by a safeguard of discretion than I was myself. Hence, with the indulgence of such a habit of speaking [2440] freely, & with as much sarcasm or censure as the subject deserved, exercised without caution, it is not strange that my free remarks were often repeated, & often with exaggeration & distortion. . . . But my indiscreet & free remarks & censures were not always so innocent. I never could tolerate base conduct—& it was apt to be made the blacker in my opinion by my prejudice against the guilty party. Still more were my scorn & contempt increased, in proportion to the elevation of the offender in fortune, family, social or political position, & the favor of sycophants & of the public, acquired by any of these advantages. Nor were my grounds for censure or strong denunciation limited to vices universally deemed serious or infamous. Of the class of offences of which the world is too tolerant, I especially abhorred & denounced demagoguism [*sic*], as the most dangerous evil under a free government. A thorough demagogue is, under a popular government, & among a people as yet free, the same base & despicable creature with the flatterer & sycophant of the monarch of a dispotic [*sic*] government. The flatterer & the demogague, for like selfish objects, offer their unlimited adulation to the sources whence flow all promotion, office, & political benefits. And the popular demagogue is worse than the flatterer, even of a Caligula, inasmuch as the successful pursuit of the latter, in benefiting himself, can do no more harm to his country. But the demagogue, to promote his own selfish gains, is undermining the (as yet) remaining public virtue & political liberties of his country, & cannot achieve any success in the one respect, without being more or less effective in the other. Further—demagogues can only have full sway in governments where the popular power is supreme, & made so by universal suffrage. This condition is equivalent to the political power of the country being wielded, under the [2441] prompting & direction of the demagogues, & solely for their benefit, by the majority of the people—of the most destitute, ignorant & degraded class, feeling little interest in the welfare of the commonwealth or preservation of its liberty. This "swinish multitude" is necessarily less respectable than is a single despot, who if as vicious, is obliged to be better educated & more refined than the sovereign mob. . . . All successful office holders, & representatives of the people, are not demagogues. A very few, by their exalted virtues & abilities, have reached & retained high stations, as did Aristides & Calhoun, & others whom I could name, not less patriotic & virtuous, but comparatively unknown to fame. Neither are all others thorough demagogues—or willing to use all the corrupt arts of demagogism. But there are not many who are in public life, in these times & places of universal suffrage, who have not been more or less aided by the dishonorable arts of the demagogue. It was with me a favorite & frequent theme, in conversation & in print, to delineate & denounce demagogues, their arts, their designs, & the consequences to the commonwealth. I did not hesitate to call names, when the occasion required. But that was not necessary to point my general censures, & to draw to me the hatred of those who were conscious they deserved the censures. And when I pointed out the corrupting influence (under the former union with the North,) on political leaders in the South of their being candidates for the Presidency of the United States, & tempted to betray the rightful interests of the South to buy northern support—I might be overlooked by the high dignitaries in question, but their partisans & supporters (for expected benefits to themselves,) applied my just remarks to their respective leaders, & took care that my offence should be remembered to my disadvantage. [2442]—Further—I had some talent (always unfortunate for the possessor,) for sharp & biting satire—& my delineations of my subjects, sketched in a few striking words, though meant as ludicrous caricatures, were sometimes so striking as likenesses, or amusing for their oddity, that they were repeated by auditors who had no wish to harm either myself or the subjects of my remarks. With such a propensity & habits, indulged with little discretion or restraint, it is no wonder that I made many enemies, & became unpopular with a large portion of the little public around me, & even of the great & more remote public. I confess this class of my offences freely, & without excuse or extenuation. I have very long been sensible of my misconduct in this respect, & have made hundreds of resolves & efforts to avoid the recurrence—but in vain. . . . This evil & invincible propensity, this "besetting sin" of mine, has been so often the cause of regret & penitence, (too soon forgotten,) that it affords another reason, (added to my want of hearing, & of memory for faces,) for me to avoid company, & personal intercourse with the public, as much as possible. It is surprising to me that these offences, & their exaggerations, have not been attended with more disagreeable personal consequences than the forfeiture of popularity. But of the five or six personal quarrels in which I have been involved, not one, nor any complaint of any one offended, was founded on my evil-speaking of individuals.—Thus while my heavier sins have been ignored by those persons best acquainted with them & with me, my responsibility & punishment were misplaced, or the weight doubled on minor & comparatively trivial violations of propriety. [2443] But this punishment has been light, compared [to] that which has been visited upon me for what I may proudly claim as acts of virtue, & of rare self-sacrifice to a high sense of moral duty.—A small portion of my life only has been public, in the ordinary sense. The only occasion was my being elected (in 1824,) to represent my district in the Senate of Virginia, for the term of four years. I reached this position almost without seeking either public favor or any of its rewards—& certainly without my using any electioneering arts, which I always despised, & had not the tact to exercise, even if willing to be so aided. My chief & perhaps only merit, as a legislator & representative, was in zealously & diligently attending to the duties of the office, & aiming to decide correctly & vote honestly on all questions. But I soon found that my views of duty were very different from those usually acted upon by other representatives—& that for conforming to mine, I should be like to have no reward, save the approbation of my own conscience. In all matters for private legislation, or appointments to office, or to places of emolument, every legislator is expected to promote the personal & private interests of his friend, his constituent, or his political supporter, even at more or less sacrifice of the public interest. When such favors were expected of me, I was not always firm enough to withstand all such personal influences. But it was very rare that I became so entangled—& never to gain any selfish object. In nearly all cases, I firmly adhered to my rule of serving the best interests of my country, & of my constituents, according to right & justice, & to decide on the claims of individuals according to their merits—& of candidates for offices by the measures of their fitness for the posts sought. To the uninitiated, this may seem a very simple duty, & easily performed. But it is very different in practice—& most legislators vote on these, & even on much more important public questions, with a single eye to their own private interests, & mainly to their own political interest & advancement. [2444] My constituents found no fault with my votes on the most important public questions, in which the public interests only were involved. But whenever my sense of public duty made me oppose, or refuse to advocate, some private & selfish interest, there I certainly made an enemy of the disappointed seeker. For these & other causes, I became tired & disgusted with being "a servant of the people," & resigned my place a year before the expiration of my term. I left the position of a representative & legislator under the conviction that I had not discharged the duties with perfect honesty—& yet that I was much too honest to long retain the popular favor which had withdrawn me from my previously secluded private life.—But though this early & short legislative career made up the whole of my public service, either by election by the people, or appointment of government, it bore a very small proportion, even in time, to my much more useful labors for the public good. Indeed, with the exception of three separate intervals, during which I withdrew, in some disappointment, & disgust, from all such connection with the public, through all the remainder of my adult life, I have zealously & diligently labored to promote the good of my country. In various modes, & for different particular objects, I have labored as a reformer—& in almost every case I have received the usual reward of every reformer—neglect, ingratitude, villification [*sic*] & persecution, from those whom I sought to benefit. As an agriculturist, I have made discoveries, & have introduced in Virginia improvements of the most important value—which have already added many millions to the intrinsic value of this region, & have enabled thousands of individual farmers to triple & quadruple the productive value of

their property. As founder & sole conductor of the "Farmers' Register," during ten years I still more, & widely, extended agricultural
knowledge & improvement, & profit. As a writer & publisher in
that, & also in political or other journals, I strove to defend the
general [2445] interests from being cheated & plundered by the
predaceous minor interests sustained by protecting duties, the
fraudulent paper money system, &c. But the public loves to be
cheated better than to be undeceived—& in this latter course, as
well as in other efforts, I met with no thanks for my attempts to
defend, & bitter enmity from the plunderers & all their connections, & also from many belonging to the plundered classes. In a
faithful & laborious service of six years as one of the Visitors of
William & Mary College, I moved & carried important reforms, &
especially in putting down gross abuses, which not one of my
fellow visitors, though approving, dared to propose, because their
existence fattened some private interests at the expense of the
College. For this, as in all such cases, I incurred odium & gained no
thanks. Long after, as President of the State Agricultural Society of
Virginia, I set myself to put down the many abuses, of extravagant
charges & expenditure, & peculation, which had grown up under a
long course of previous neglect or indulgence. I was partially
successful, in thus preventing frauds, & so saved to the Society
some $1500 a year—& cut off a system of lavish expenditure,
serving base private ends only, which if continuing as before unchecked, would have been doubled every year, until the Society's
whole income would have been wasted. For these services, I
gained neither applause nor thanks from the public, nor even from
the Society, but the hearty dislike of every former extortioner &
plunderer, & of all their friends & numerous connections. And
when my constitutional limit of service arrived, & I left that position, I had, by the faithful discharge of my duties, gained more
enemies, than all my other & previous services to the Society & to
agriculture had before made for me favor & approvers. And thus has
it been through my life—& in some private duties, as well as in
most of my efforts to serve public interests. Many as have been my
acknowledged sins & errors—& however numerous may have
been others less apparent to myself—all have caused me to suffer
less in public opinion & favor, & of those I especially aimed to
protect & serve, than my most commendable & disinterested acts,
having no object but the greatest benefit to [2446] the interests,

whether public or private, which I aimed & professed to serve. . . .
Among my efforts & labors for the public good, I have not enumer-
ated the latest & the greatest, & also the most striking example of
the usual rewards of my services, as presented at home, & by my
countrymen. I was the first, & for some years, the only man in
Virginia, who was both bold & disinterested enough to advocate,
openly & loudly, the dissolution of the union between the Northern & the slave-holding states. From 1850, I zealously labored for
this object—in travelling to agitate the discussion, in urging my
views in talking, writing, & publishing. My efforts became more
energetic & continued, & I trust were not inoperative, as the consummation sought seemed more hopeful & near at hand. Until
then, I had effected nothing in Virginia, (at least nothing that was
manifest,) except to draw upon my efforts & myself the hatred of
many, & the disapprobation of nearly all. My few approvers were
earnest, but mostly still silent. When finally, the majority of the
people of Virginia had been so enlightened on this great question,
as to be ready to follow the noble examples of South Carolina & six
other southern states in throwing of[f] the Northern yoke—the
submissionist Convention of Va. was coerced by the pressure of
popular opinion to vote for the secession of the state. Then, when
my opinions had become triumphant, I, who had so long maintained them under reproach & vilification, might have been expected to rise high in general favor. But not so. Jealousy, envy, &
malice were not to be so appeased. With some exceptions, those
who had before disliked or hated me for my advocacy of disunion,
proclaimed & urged vehemently for eleven years of their time of
willing submission to Yankee oppression, [2447] continued to dislike or hate me after they had come over to my before objectionable
opinions. If I had been a candidate for office, or a seeker for the
favor of either people or government in Virginia, the most abject
prior submissionist who had professed conversion from his errors at
the latest moment, or a man of bad morals & habits as well as of
recent unsound political views, would have been preferred to me,
by either the legislature or the people—& especially by the people
of my own county, in which I was born, & mostly lived & labored,
& to which I had rendered more benefit than any other individual
of Virginia, whether acting in a private or public capacity.—Yet,
from other sources I have had bestowed on me much praise &
eulogy—perhaps more than I deserved. But, except so much as

[547]

came from my many old & highly valued personal friends, of long & intimate acquaintance, the praises, like most of the censures on me were misplaced—on acts in which I had but little merit, while my most important services & sacrifices for the public good, & especially in behalf of the outraged rights & endangered liberty of the Southern States, were either unknown, or very lightly appreciated. Further—& in part it is to my own shame for the confession to be made—most of the complimentary honors which have been bestowed upon me, I owed to strangers, or received in places remote from the country of my birth, residence & my most useful labors. . . . I have found myself, when travelling in crowded public conveyances, the object of general notice & attention, & of flattering homage from those who sought to converse with me. My unexpected appearance has called forth cheers of welcome, & applause by acclamation, from crowds of civilians, or of companies on military [2448] service. In my travels to agitate & urge disunion, though as a private & obscure individual, I have been honored & even embarrassed, by compliments unexpectedly offered me by legislatures, & Conventions. But nearly all such popular or other honors so bestowed on me were in other lands than my own, & when on the soil of Virginia, were offered by military companies from other States of the Confederacy. Almost universally in Virginia—(& even with most of the individuals who have most praised & honored me,) my long continued literary labors in behalf of the southern cause have been received with mortifying neglect—& the great benefits conferred by me on the agricultural improvement & wealth of my country, have not gained for me enough gratitude & good-will to counterbalance the envy & malice of my enemies & maligners. Yet, I have been elevated by fame to the character & position of a hero, & among the most lauded of the defenders of the Confederate States & their holy cause, merely for the accident of my having fired the first gun against Fort Sumter. My action in that case entitled me to no applause, beyond the merit of all my military companions—& my having enjoyed that distinction I owed entirely to the complimentary selection, & request, of the Palmetto Guard, in which I was then serving, & to which company had been awarded the complimentary duty of firing the first gun, for which I was chosen as the instrument. My whole service, on this occasion, was indeed in evidence & in earnest (as I had designed it should be,) of my readily embarking in the "rebellion" which I had so long advocated in

[548]

words, & of my readiness to encounter all the consequent risks to life & property. But I had done, & had risked, & sacrificed, far more, & during long time, & these services had been slighted or ignored. It seems to me, that, but for the accident of Fort Sumter, my patriotic labors & efforts would [have] been unknown—& my name almost forgotten in my own country, & by the generation which I have so zealously & effectively labored to serve. I appeal to future generations for the due appreciation of my efforts, & their effects. [2449]—"A prophet is not without honor, but in his own country, and among his own kin, and in his own house."—St. Mark, vi, 4.—

Jan. 21. Wednesday.—When before referring to the lately aroused northern opposition to Lincoln's administration & policy, I omitted some evidences which will now be noticed. The legislature of Pa. has elected as U.S. Senator, [Charles R.] Buckelew [*sic*—Buckalew], a democrat, in place of David Wilmot, & in opposition to Simon Cameron. The legislature of Illinois, by 66 to 34 votes, elected to the U.S. Senate [William A.] Richardson, a democrat,[7] who had very recently exhibited his strong opposition to Lincoln in a long speech in the H. of Rep. The democratic members of the Il[1]. legislature, when in caucus selecting Richardson as their candidate, passed a series of resolutions . . . . The Washington "Chronicle" (Lincoln organ,) accepts these resolutions as indicating the course of the new senator—& of course they must indicate the sentiments of the majority of the legislature & people of Lincoln's own state. The resolutions, in calling for "peace, fraternal relations, & political fellowship" to be restored "in the speediest & most effective manner"—& in recommending (forthwith) a "cessation of hostilities," which can only be done by action of the northern government—manifest the willingness to make peace *with* separation, if they cannot obtain by peaceable means, the reconstruction of the former union.—The mail. The military & naval news nearly all from northern sources—& therefore to be doubted, or believed exaggerated, when in favor of their arms. The most important item, & very disastrous for us, if true, is the capture of Arkansas Post, a fort mounted with [2450] 5 heavy cannon, & 4 others, about 70 miles up the Arkansas river. It was attacked on

---

[7] A veteran of five terms in the United States House of Representatives, Richardson (1811–75) was elected to fill the senatorial vacancy created by the death of Stephen A. Douglas.

the 10th. & surrendered the 11th. to the combined forces of [David D.] Porter's gunboat fleet & [John A.] McClernand's army. The Yankee loss reported 200. Confederate loss, 550 killed & wounded, & 5000 to 7000 prisoners[8] —& an immense amount of munitions of war. . . .

Jan. 22. Thursday.—At a public dinner on the 8th, in New Jersey, sundry prominent men made speeches strongly indicating disaffection to Lincoln, & the strong desire for peace. Some of the sentiments would seem to extend to a violent disruption of the rump U.S., if no other remedy for misrule is available. Ex-Gov. [Rodman M.] Price[9] "held that the Union was broken—that the central government had no power to control the rebellion—& this being so, he contended that *the states fell back into the original elements, the same as before the Constitution was adopted.*" . . . "Subjugation, coercion, was repugnant to the feelings of American citizens, & it cannot be effected." Mr. G[eorge] P. Androus said that "the States had now taken back their original sovereignty, & New Jersey could take her stand *in any Union* that may be formed. Now that emancipation was proclaimed, *our army should be called back at once* . . . . This war must cease, & the rights of the South must be respected; or, in the last resort, we must perforce *turn our artillery upon those Africanized guerrillas*, who have garroted the Constitution & every popular right. (Applause.)" The Hon. T[homas] Dunn [English] (presiding, & a state Senator of N.J. elect,)[10] said, "*If this war on the South continued much longer, we would have war at the North, at our own hearth-stones.* . . . The people would seek a

---

[8] As might be expected, these casualty figures from northern sources were too favorable to the Union side. In reality, the Federals lost more than 1,000 men (most of whom were wounded) in the assault on Arkansas Post, or Fort Hindman, while Confederate casualties numbered 28 dead, 81 wounded, and nearly 4,800 captured. Although it was a successful operation, McClernand's unauthorized expedition up the Arkansas River did little to advance the primary Union objective in this area—the capture of Vicksburg.

[9] Price (1816–94), considered the father of the public school system in New Jersey, served as governor from 1854 to 1857 and, in 1861, was a delegate to the ill-fated Washington peace conference. He made the remarks attributed to him by the diarist at a festival sponsored by Bergen County Democrats to commemorate Andrew Jackson's victory in the battle of New Orleans.

[10] A native of Philadelphia, Thomas Dunn English (1819–1902) was admitted to the bar in 1842 but devoted most of his time to various literary pursuits. His sympathy for the South was doubtless stimulated by a residence of five years in Virginia during the 1850's. Long after the war, English served two terms (1891–95) in the United States House of Representatives.

remedy in the Constitution; *but if that should fail, they would turn on them* (the Lincoln Administration) the *mouths of their cannon & points of their sabres.* (Loud & prolonged applause.)"[11] This spirit, having a mouth-piece in the [2452] legislature & whole government of N.J., & stimulated & supported by the majority of the 4,000,000 of the people of N.Y., to say nothing of sundry other concurring states, must have sure & speedy effect. It is true that even now there are but few who openly advocate peace, *with separation.* (Very lately, there was not one.) All these zealous advocates for peace profess to expect it, *with reunion* with the South, by declaring an armistice, calling a general convention of representatives of *all* the states, southern as well as northern, & therein enacting, & making as amendments of the federal constitution, any guaranties for the maintenance of southern rights that the representatives of the southern states may require. All these, the great opposition party, as its leaders avow, would readily concur in. Such guaranties, if established three years ago, would have saved the former union, & rendered hopeless the objects of all those who, like myself, would not have been willing to remain in union with the North under any possible conditions. But these concessions would be accepted now by no southern men who have joined in defence of the South in this war. The democrats of the North, & all of this newly raised opposition party, seem as if ignoring the facts, that they, unanimously, at first supported Lincoln in his war measures, & the invasion of the South, & with as much apparent zeal as the abolitionists. No doubt, very many would have opposed, but were frightened into apparent zealous approval by terror of Lincoln's tyranny. Even if this party (as a then minority,) had, as honest & brave patriots, advocated their present sentiments in our favor throughout, it would not have gained a southern state to desire reunion, & but few individuals, who had ever been for disunion. But as it is—while we may & do wish well to the present efforts of this new party organization, & while we ought, for policy, to be willing to exchange reciprocal benefits with any particular north-western states, to detach them from their present union, & to make a separate peace with the [2453] C.S.—we owe to this party neither thanks nor good-will, for their lately professed sense of justice &

[11] The above remarks were quoted by Ruffin from an appended newspaper clipping. All italics and ellipses were inserted by the diarist.

sentiments of amity for the South. . . . Gold has risen as high [2454] as 148, in N.Y., but on the news of the victory in Ark., it declined to 147. But the recent rapid rise was not so much owing to military occurrences & prospects, as to the enormous new issue of paper currency proposed by the Lincoln administration, which will amount to about 1500 millions of dollars increase of the already greatly bloated currency, to be issued within a few months. This expectation has already caused a considerable depreciation of all paper currency, & the advance of gold. The like causes have operated with the C.S. causing great depreciation of all paper money & securities, but especially of those of the C.S. . . .

Jan. 23. Friday. The mail brought us two long letters from Edmund & Jane—with the important family news that Edmund, for Julian & himself, had bought out Mr. Sayre's share (one-fifth,) of the whole Marlbourne estate. The sale was made on the following evaluations:

The land about 1400 acres, (including 300 poor & waste . . . added to the Marlbourne tract proper, of 1100 acres,) $75,000
43 slaves, at $700 average   30,100
Farm stock, utensils, &c. (perishable property)   4,500

Total, $109,600

And which is put, in round numbers, at $110,000. Of this sum, the fifth part, Mr. Sayre will be paid $22,000, in cash, or bonds bearing interest at once. In addition, if any more of the absconded slaves return, he is to have for each one the fifth part of $700, the average valuation. And if any are captured, he is to have one-fifth of the net amount of sales. Thus, at last—& much too late—has been got rid of this great evil of a foreign partner in this property—but at a very heavy cost to the purchasers. My former distribution of this estate among 5 of my children . . . & more especially the admission of Mr. Sayre as one of the joint owners, was the worst blunder of my life, & the participation & superintendence of Mr. Sayre, have been attended by the most disastrous pecuniary losses. Still I do not blame myself for doing what [2456] I then deemed best for all parties. I thought that I could not do better for my children than to give up to them all my property, except that reserved for my own support. Yet the most judicious of my children remonstrated against my thus divesting myself of property & employment, as likely to be detrimental to my own happiness. Being determined on this general course, & the land not admitting of division, except at great loss, I left it in joint ownership. Neither of my two older sons, who only could have done justice to the trust, was willing to leave his own home, & individual property, to take personal charge of, & reside on this more valuable joint estate. Mr. Sayre, the husband of my daughter Elizabeth, had recently sold his market farm near Norfolk, & had bought a large tract of unimproved land in Westmoreland, to which he designed to move. His wife was in bad health, & not likely to get well. It was an important object with me, & with her brothers & sisters, to save Elizabeth from this distant exile among strangers, & at the same time to fix her at the home, & in the neighborhood & society, to which she was most attached, & which Marlbourne offered. Therefore, Mr. Sayre, in his own right (& not as representing his wife,) was, with the consent & approval of all parties, permitted to become a joint shareholder, by purchase on the same indulgent terms with my own children. Further—this part of the arrangement was made with the understanding that Mr. Sayre would reside on & superintend the farm, at the liberal salary of $1000 a year, & important perquisites. At that time, & long after, I & my sons had a very high opinion of Mr. Sayre's qualifications & habits, as a man of tried energy & industry, & turn for good management, which would more than compensate, as we thought, for his having had no experience in large farming, & on a grain farm. Incidental benefits expected from this arrangement were that my daughter Mildred would continue to reside at her beloved home of Marlbourne, & in company [2457] with her beloved sister, greatly to the increased comfort & gratification of both. In their society, I was also to continue to make Marlbourne my home, though I expected to be mostly abroad, & travelling, for some length of time, & certainly until the new government was in full operation, & until the slaves had learned (a difficult lesson it was,) that *I* was no longer their owner, & the real director of the farm government. All things worked badly. The negroes could never understand their belonging to a co-partnership—& the acting owner & director being to them a stranger, [was] viewed with unjust suspicion & growing dislike. The strong disposition for loyalty, which is natural to the negro race, had no place for growth. The negro needs to look up to, for protection & control, one individual master or mistress—which here had no existence. The negroes could not feel great attachment to a co-partnership of owners, though they would have gladly belonged to either of my children alone—& still less, when all the authority of the copartnership was exercised by a stranger whom they first disliked, & subsequently hated heartily. This I did not learn until in my late visit to Marlbourne. I then learned that this strong hostile feeling had existed for years—& I now am convinced that its existence has been the motive & cause of most of the disastrous losses suffered on this estate. For years after the two fires, which, with their incidental & consequent losses, cost the owners not less than $16,000, I would not believe them to have been made by any of our own slaves.[12] But since, for a long time now, I have changed my opinion, & have concurred fully in the general belief that the incendiaries were some of our own slaves, & prompted by dislike of their new & singular condition as to ownership, & to dislike to be governed by Mr. Sayre. They doubtless expected that such great destruction of property by fire would induce a breaking up of the [2458] existing arrangement, & the division of the slaves among owners in severalty. But this did not occur. Mildred's subsequent marriage & removal from Marlbourne, & also the soon succeeding difficulties produced by the wish, & absurd claim or expectation, of the brothers Sayre, who were husbands to my daughters Elizabeth & Mildred, to buy out the shares of my sons—& the offensive conduct to me, of Mr. Wm. Sayre, in reference to this absurd plan, rendered Marlbourne so disagreeable to me, that I did not visit it again, except on two occasions, & for short times. The last of these was on account of my daughter Elizabeth's death—& not again until recently, when Edmund's family went there, as a place of refuge. My two sons also were so attached to their own homes, or so engaged otherwise of late, that their visits to Marlbourne were very few & short. Thus the negroes scarcely ever saw any one of those, either of whom they would gladly have had as a sole master—& were left entirely to the government of one whom (however injustly,) they hated. Under these conditions, the Yankee army arrived, & proclaimed freedom to every slave, & further that the slaves had the best right to possess their masters' farms & moveables. All the Marlbourne slaves at once accepted these offered boons, & stopped work—& then or later, every able-bodied man, & every boy above 12 years old, went off to the enemy's camp. Perhaps they might have done the same if circumstances had

---

[12] See Volume I, 111–12, 169–70, 249–50, for accounts of the mysterious fires which struck Marlbourne in October, 1857, and March, 1858.

been reversed. For, my son Edmund, always a humane & judicious master (as also was Mr. Sayre,) lost a much larger proportion of slaves from his residence & individual property, than in his share at Marlbourne. However, whatever were the causes, all the most valuable slaves absconded, (18 at first,) & for want of their labor, the standing crops of wheat & oats & clover, & nearly all the crop of corn, was lost. In addition to all these losses, Mr. Sayre seems to have lost, for some time back, all his former devotion to his business, if not utterly disliking it. And since the first coming of the Yankee forces, if not earlier, he seems not [2459] to have given even very slight personal attention to the labors of the farm, & to have felt no interest or duty in its direction. This became very apparent to me when I lately was there for some weeks. But previously, I had not suspected or supposed the possibility of such neglect.—The newspapers. A bearer of dispatches from the C.S. government, to our commissioners in Europe, was captured some time ago, & the letters have been published in the Yankee papers. There is nothing in them that will damage our interests, & it is well that they have been published, as the instructions will thus reach those for whom they were intended. And there are two things which I am glad to be so exposed. One is a severe & well deserved censure of Earl Russell for his supercilious & insulting treatment of our commissioner. The other is the exposure of intrigues conducted by two French consular agents, in Galveston, with the design of inducing the separation of Texas from the C.S., & having it made a separate state, nominally independent, but really under the protection of France, & serving to give to that power a valuable cotton-growing dependency. It does not appear whether these agents were instructed by their government, or acted in advance, & in confident expectation of support. They were both driven out of the C.S. as soon as their operations were known. It is not unlikely that the wily French ruler postponed his intervention, waiting for the development of his plot.—The Alabama has performed another & more important work—this time, in the fighting line. We have only the northern report, & that very meager, but which, so far as it goes, may be believed when telling of a Yankee defeat. The New Orleans Picayune contains the official report of an engagement between the Alabama & the U.S. gunboat Hatteras, 20 miles from Galveston. The Hatteras was sunk, & all her crew perished, except five, who

[555]

were picked up by the Brooklyn.[13] The Hatteras was an iron-clad, carrying 3 rifled 32 [2460] pounders. (The Alabama is a wooden vessel.) The Brooklyn was in pursuit of the Alabama. . . . The recent & sundry captures of armed steamers, & even of strong gunboats, in the western rivers, by Confederate cavalry,[14] present a remarkable contrast to the general condition of things a year ago. Then, such terror had been produced by mortar vessels, & the prospect of bombardment, that the presence of one or two gunboats was sufficient to cause the retreat of an army, or the surrender of a town as soon as surrounded. But heroic Vicksburg has removed the popular & military delusion of gunboats being irresistible, & a bombardment as intolerable, & certainly destructive to the [2461] attacked post or army. In addition, Forrest, Wheeler, & others have shown that these heretofore dreaded & terrible gunboats may be successfully fought, & sometimes captured by land forces of the kind seemingly the least suitable for naval warfare. . . . Northern papers contain more full statements, & more alarming for Yankee-dom, of growing opposition to the government in northern states, & especially in the great states of Illinois & Indiana, whose geographical position is even more important than their great political & military power. These reports . . . indicate that in these two states resistance to the war, & the policy of Lincoln, will be made by physical force, & revolt from the rump, if legal & milder measures will not serve. If these (northern) reports are to be relied on, as to the state & violence of popular opinion in these two states, they cannot stop short of revolution. I think that the informal offer, or suggestion, by the C.S. congress, in merely considering the proposal, of making a separate peace with any of the north-western states, has already had some effect. And when that subject, & its connections, are studied by thinking men of [2462] the North-West,

---

[13] Northern sources apparently were unaware that the *Alabama* had picked up all members of the *Hatteras* crew who had not been mortally wounded in the actual firing. The *Hatteras*, a converted iron paddle-steamer, took a shot in her boiler and sank in thirteen minutes on the night of January 11.

[14] The most recent such Confederate success was the capture, on January 13, of the United States gunboat *Sidell* and three transports by cavalry troops under command of Brigadier General Joseph Wheeler. This incident occurred just below Harpeth Shoals on the Cumberland River in Tennessee. Earlier in the month, other Confederates had seized a Mississippi River steamer and the U.S.S. *Grampus No. 2* in separate incidents near Memphis.

already opposed to the war, it is difficult to see how they can reject the incalculable benefits of a separate peace, giving to their states the free use of our navigable rivers, & of our markets. If, acting on such views, & preferring such advantages to being burdened & starved in the union with New England, these two states were to secede from the Union, it would be a crushing blow to the remaining states. The secession of Illinois & Indiana, & their either occupying a separate & independent political position, with military aid & concert of the C.S., or with the closer connection which these states would desire, (but which I trust we will never consent to, unless they become slave-holding,) in either case, they would be as unconquerable by Yankeedom, as now are the C.S. Their independence, even though subject to be invaded & harassed, would ensure the resuscitation & success of the Confederate cause in Ky. & Mo.—& later, bring Ohio, as then standing alone, to join Il. & Ia. But if Ohio did not soon follow—the secession of these two would cut in two the present rump confederacy, & separate the parts by a broad & impassable hostile territory on an inland sea. The separation would necessarily grow to be final, as to all the north-western states, & the immense western territory. But Ohio must go with Il. & Ia. & then the separation of the other states would be more complete, & made at Lake Erie, where British territory lies just across. In my neglected "Anticipations of the Future," I predicted as a certain consequence of a dissolution of the union of the North & South, a later dissolution of that of the North-eastern & the North-western states. That inevitable result seems now to be much nearer at hand than I had recently supposed. . . .

Jan. 26. Monday. . . . The mail. The N.Y. Tribune gives statements of its army correspondent, dated 20th., in minute detail, of the then readiness & intention of Burnside to make another & immediate advance across the Rappahannock, on Gen. Lee's army. Gen. Burnside's address to his army was there published, which announced the renewal of a forward movement to be imminent. Also, the Washington Chronicle of 22nd. stated as probable that the advanced portion of Burnside's army had already crossed the river on the 21st. If these statements alone had been seen on the 22nd, I should have supposed it almost certain that a great battle had already been begun. But, up to late last night, nothing was known to, or at least published from, our army of the enemy's new advance.

Perhaps the heavy rain which fell during the night of 20th. may have delayed the movement.[15] But it is very strange that these intended movements should be published, & should thus be made known to our authorities, by northern papers brought by Yankee steamers, (coming for exchanged prisoners,) earlier than we could get information direct from Fredericksburg. It looks to me very much like a feint, intended to deceive Gen. Lee. But if the information is [2465] correct, certainly Gen. Lee & our government must have had full notice to prepare for the threatened attack. I hope it is true. For after the recent disastrous defeat, Burnside & his troops must begin another attack with but faint hope of victory. . . . There is a good article republished from Blackwood's Magazine, which strongly denounces Lincoln & his policy . . . lauds the C.S., [&] predicts the certain success of the latter. Though written in Sept., before the late elections & political movements, this article pronounces as a necessity, the separation of the N.W. from the N.E. states, & the connection of the former (if they can effect it,) with the southern states. Also it ridicules the opinion of Sir G[eorge] C. Lewis, one of the Ministry,[16] that it was contrary to national law, & usage, for the British government to acknowledge the independence of any new state before it had made peace with the former ruling power. The writer shows, by all examples which have occurred for a century—the South American States, Greece & Belgium —that the law of nations & the practice of the British government are exactly the reverse. He asserts the perfect right of that government to now acknowledge the independence of the C.S.—but doubts the expediency, unless the recognition were followed by armed intervention, if needed, which the writer seems to recommend. . . . According to a more full abstract . . . of the Annual Report of the Sec. of Treasury, the debt of the C.S. to end of Dec. in the aggregate, was $556,105,162. The expenditures of the government from 18th of Feb. 1862 to 31st of Dec. amounted to $416,971,735, or at the rate of $480,115,525 a year, or $1,315,385 a day.

[15] The diarist's supposition was correct. On January 19 Burnside had set his army in motion, intending to cross the Rappahannock at United States Ford, some ten miles above Fredericksburg. Heavy winter rains struck the next day, and, after battling the hostile elements for two days, Burnside's "mud march" ground to a halt. Following the failure of this campaign, the unfortunate Burnside was superseded by Major General Joseph Hooker as commander of the Army of the Potomac.

[16] Secretary for war in the Palmerston cabinet.

Jan. 27. This day I gave to my sons Edmund & Julian, by release of their bonds to me, the additional amounts of $5800 to each. Some months earlier, I had in like manner given them $3000 each—& in 1861, about $4000 to each, in other funds, which had reverted to me as part of the life-estate property of my deceased daughter Elizabeth & her infant. In all, these three recent gifts make about $13,000 to each. The understanding is that so much as I may require of the interest of my reserved capital (held before in the hands of Edmund & Julian, now released,) will still continue to be paid to me so long as I may live. It is most probable that I shall not need half so much—& the surplus they will retain.—Gen. [Frank L.] Woolford [*sic*], in command of Ky. troops (probably Home Guard, or militia,)[17] in Yankee service at Lebanon Ky, in a speech delivered on 13th inst. before a public assemblage of 3000 persons, discharged his men for 20 days, telling them to go home—& that if at the end of that time, Lincoln should not have modified his emancipation proclamation, he would not recall the troops to fight for the North, but that he himself would take the field on the side of the South. This is well for the spirit & effect. But how foolish to talk about "modifying" or even revoking the proclamation. That measure was consummated, not only when declared [2468] final on Jan. 1st, but when merely threatened conditionally in the previous September. No revoking now could be of the least effect to undo any of whatever mischief the proclamation has produced, or can produce. Fortunately, that mischief, though designed & expected to be wide-spread & overwhelming to the C.S., has been very partial & slight, & is overbalanced 100 fold by the indirect benefit that the proclamation will bring.—Opened the box of my most valued papers, which only were saved from the Yankee theives [*sic*]. Began to read the volume of my diary beginning in August 1860, & found it so interesting to me that I continued it regularly.

Jan. 30. Friday. In my reading of my diary, passed through the incidents connected with the first battle of Manassas. Soon after this portion had been written in my diary, I copied it, with large additions & extensions, & sent that writing, together with a similar one of the siege of Fort Sumter, to my daughter Mildred, for whom I

---

[17] Presumably, this reference is to Colonel Frank Lane Wolford (1817–95), who commanded the First Kentucky Volunteer Cavalry from 1861 to 1864. A Democratic presidential elector in 1864 and again in 1868, Wolford later served two terms (1883–87) in the United States House of Representatives.

had prepared both the papers. . . . Since the death of my daughter, & the removal of the deep interest which she must have felt for the safe preservation of these papers, I fear that they will be, if they have not already been, destroyed. This I should much regret—as my only other records of these incidents, as at first written in my diary, are less full & correct. I will endeavor to supply the defects of the portion of the battle of Manassas, by the insertion of addenda, in the form of notes.[18] This task I began today. . . .

. *Jan. 31.* . . . No advance yet of the Yankee army near Fredericksburg. Northern reports state that it was attempted, & persevered in for four days, & then abandoned for the present time, because of the [2470] wet & soft condition of the earth, the roads being of deep mire, & the impossibility of transporting thereon wagons & artillery. The accounts . . . represent difficulties of this kind almost incredible, & quite insuperable. . . . However great these obstacles were, it is supposed that there was another of still greater importance. This was, that Burnside's soldiers, depressed, "cowed," & demoralized by their late disastrous defeat, & subsequent hardships, were so unwilling to renew offensive operations, & to assail our army, that the commander feared to enforce the order to march, lest the army should become more insubordinate. . . . Some citizens of Indiana & Illinois have arrived in Richmond, & it was conjectured & soon currently reported, that they were deputies from those states, empowered to negotiate with [2471] the government of the C.S. for terms of separate peace. This is not credible. But these refugees, (as they must be thenceforward, while their states are under Lincoln's rule,) if they are influential persons at home, are doubtless acting for the peace party—& through them, secret negotiations may be begun, & advances made to the great object of a separate peace with these two states. When this end is reached, I hope that there will be further made, & to continue only until a general treaty of peace shall be made, an alliance, offensive & defensive, with these & any other like-acting North-Western States. But never their admission to the Southern Confederacy—unless they shall admit by their state constitutions, & protect effectually by their laws, the institution of negro slavery within their boundaries. This should be the indispensable condition for the admission of new states—& especially for those now

---

[18] See above, page 69.

making part of Yankeedom. But if their laws were so altered, I would not require the actual presence of slaves, or their possession by any of the citizens. That consequence would soon enough follow the legal permission & security of the possession. Such changes of the laws would indicate that the popular fanaticism on this subject, at least of a majority of the citizens, was extinguished. And if the laws sanctioned & protected the holding of slaves, & popular prejudices or fanaticism did not forbid, slaves would be desired, & rapidly bought & imported into these two states. In the southern parts of both, negro slaves would be valuable for field labor. But even in the far northern states of Michigan & Minnesota, though not profitable for field labor, negro slaves would be very desirable for domestic servants, & would be eagerly sought for by thousands, if their being held was not forbidden by the laws, & by public opinion.—The Yankee government seems to be acting under the conviction that its military power must soon be on the decrease, & that the days of its political power are already numbered, & the number known. Therefore, whatever it can do, in wielding [2472] this enormous power, must be done speedily, or not at all. Hence, when the approaching death of this great abolition power is obvious[ly] in prospect, the most gigantic efforts, beyond all precedent, are made for the destruction of the C.S. We are threatened at the same time with attacks by four enormous armies bearing on different & remote points, & also sundry other smaller armaments, but yet designing important aggressions. The great operations are a renewed attack on General Lee, the threatened assault in N.C., & those by the armies in Ten. & in Miss. Their success in either of these cases would do us much injury, & would protract the war to some extent. But their success in all would not ruin us—while one signal victory gained by us, (not a fruitless victory, but one properly followed up,) would put an end to the war, by putting an end to our enemy's resources for attacking us. The Northern power apparently is already doomed. Nothing can bring a reprieve, but a series of great victories. And even if obtaining such victories, nothing can save the North from utter ruin, except the complete subjugation of the South, & the confiscation of all southern property to pay the debt, & compensate the losses of the North. But the diminution of the armies, & military strength, by the expiration of the terms of service of 300,000 men before June—& the failure of funds, which may occur not much later—are not the only nor the earliest agencies, as it seems to me, for breaking down Lincoln, his party, & their policy, & compelling their defeat by the new opposition, which is just now beginning to permit its true objects to be named as those of a *peace party*. . . . The term of service of the present Congress will end on March 4th—within 33 days. And unless Lincoln should call an extra session of the new Congress, it cannot meet, or act, until in next December. He certainly will not so allow the new congress to advance its regular & stated session, if he can avoid it. For the first day's session of that body will be the political death [2474] [of] the power & policy of Lincoln & his party. If he can be brave & firm enough to refuse to call the new congress, he, still executing the laws & measures of the present congress, may continue until next December to urge on the war measures & policy, despite of the opposed wishes & remonstrances of a large majority of the people, & of their already elected representatives in Congress & the different state legislatures. But is Lincoln the man to play this bold game? For the chief magistrate of an elective & popular government thus deliberately to put himself & the government in opposition to the ascertained majority of the people, & of their elected representatives, upon questions of the highest importance & vital interest to the country, would require a man of not only great moral & physical courage, but of unsurpassed political wisdom, discretion, & knowledge of mankind. If placed in such circumstances, Cromwell, one of the greatest of men & of kings, would have deemed it good policy to yield his preferred measures to the wishes of the commonwealth. The iron & despotic will of Andrew Jackson would have yielded to such opposing influences, with pretended willingness, when he knew that at most he could control for but nine months longer, when the popular will would defeat his, by due course of law. More timid rulers, more feeble in judgment, than these, or others more patriotic or conscientious, would not offer to resist the known will of the community & the Congress & state legislatures elect. How then can it be supposed that the opposite course can be firmly pursued by the despicable wretch who is the chief magistrate of Yankeedom? It seems to me utterly impossible. Yet, I have seen no intimation of that opinion in any newspaper, or heard of its being uttered or entertained by anyone. Yet I deem it certain, that as soon as can be after the 4th of March, Lincoln will be *forced* to call together the new congress,

& thus to aid in the overthrow of his own policy & power. Such a result could not be avoided even in a law-abiding community. [2475] Indeed, under such circumstances, the forcing of a free people to their ruin, by a defeated & extinct Congress & a stupid minority-elected President, the most law-abiding people would be justified in resorting to revolutionary measures to oppose such a temporary tyranny. But the people of the Northern States are not scrupulous in obeying laws which they dislike, or deem oppressive. It will be sufficient reason for their resisting odious laws that they have the power to resist effectually. I do not know in what manner it will be effected—but I am confident that by coercion of some kind applied to Lincoln he will be compelled to call together the new congress within a month of the commencement of its term of service. . . . 5000 hands are enlarging the canal dug last spring through the swamp peninsula opposite Vicksburg, to open safe passage for the Yankee gunboats out of range of our cannon at Vicksburg. Then their upper & lower fleets, heretofore kept separate, can unite, & cooperate. I fear that the Yankees will succeed in this scheme. But as to its leaving Vicksburg without navigable water, the expectation is an absurdity.

February 2. Monday. The mail brought much news—none bad, & some that is glorious. A signal naval victory has been gained by our little flotilla prepared in Charleston, over the Yankee squadron blockading that port. On the 31st. the C.S. gunboats, Palmetto State, Capt. [John] Rutledge, & Chicora, Capt. [John R.] Tucker, with two small steamers, the Etiwan & Chesterfield, all commanded by Com. [Duncan N.] Ingraham,[19] made an attack on the blockaders before day-break, & sunk two, crippled a third, & drove off all the others . . . to sea, & out of sight. Late in the evening, as our vessels were returning to Charleston, 4 Yankee steamers hove in sight in the distance. The whole blockading force, at the time of our attack, amounted to 13, with two first-class frigates, the Susquehanna &

---

[19] A native of Charleston, Duncan Nathaniel Ingraham (1802–91) was a veteran of fifty years in the naval service. Appointed midshipman in the United States Navy at the age of nine, Ingraham served in both the War of 1812 and the Mexican War. From 1856 to 1860 he was chief of the Bureau of Ordnance in Washington, D.C. Following the outbreak of war he transferred his allegiance to the Confederacy and was appointed chief of the Ordnance Department in Richmond, occupying that post until November, 1861, when he assumed command of Confederate naval forces on the South Carolina coast.

Canandaigua. The Palmetto State (iron-clad,) sunk the Mercedita, of 11 guns & 158 men.[20] . . . Four of the Yankee steamers were set on fire by our guns, but the flames soon extinguished. The Quaker City was so damaged that its flag was struck—but afterwards it escaped. The fight began at 4 A.M. Not a man hurt, or a boat struck by shot, on our side. Gen. Beauregard & Com. Ingraham have issued a proclamation, that the blockade was raised, by the blockading squadron being defeated & driven off, & that (by the law of nations,) the Port of Charleston is therefore open to foreign traders, until a sufficient time after due notice shall be given of a renewal of the blockade. . . . Gen. Burnside has at last been superseded, by Gen. Hooker, known as "Fighting Joe." Generals [William B.] Franklin & [Edwin V.] Sumner, his previous superiors in rank, refused to serve under Hooker, & yielded their commands, & tendered their resignations. It is reported that they are arrested, & will be tried, for this & other charges. (Gen. Fitz-John Porter has already been tried & cashiered.) "Fighting Joe" now *must* advance & attack Gen. Lee, in spite of mud or mutiny. The ground for Burnside's removal, the orders of the government, the expectations of all abolition Yankeedom, & his own pet name, all will combine to force "Fighting Joe" to advance & attack very soon. The sooner the better. . . . Mr. [Willard] Saulsbury, of Delaware, in the U.S. Senate, lately made a violent opposition speech, in which he called Lincoln an "imbecile." After being called to order, he was ordered by the chairman to be taken in custody by the Sergeant at Arms. Also the editor of a Philadelphia newspaper, the Evening Journal, has been imprisoned for publishing articles indicating sympathy with the South, or as so charged. These arrests seem like the beginning of an attempt to renew the "reign of terror." If the attempt is made, it will show that the strength of the administration has departed, & that it can no more exercise vigor beyond the law. . . . Gen. Hooker, in assuming the chief command of the Yankee army of the Potomac, made an address to the troops, in which is this sentence: "In equipment, intelligence & valor, the enemy is our inferior. Let us never hesitate to give him battle wherever we can find him." He did

---

[20] Although she surrendered after being rammed by the *Palmetto State*, the *Mercedita* later got under way and escaped. The *Keystone State* and *Quaker City* were also damaged heavily during the engagement, but, contrary to initial Confederate reports, none of the vessels in the blockading squadron was sunk. *Official Records*, Vol. XIV, 207–208.

not mention *numbers*, in which our opposing army is doubtless inferior, as we have been in every great battle that has yet been fought. So "Fighting Joe" will have no excuse for delaying to attack, or pursue, Gen. Lee.

Feb. 4. Wednesday. The mail not received until 1 P.M. It brought a letter from Edmund, requesting Julian to meet him in Richmond tomorrow, to return with him (from his trip to Amelia,) to Marlbourne. I had before arranged to go with him. Set about getting ready immediately. . . . We set out in the carriage at 4 P.M. & so bad was the road that it was 8.45 before I reached [2480] Petersburg. Extremely cold today—& then snow fell this morning. . . . Lodged at the [Bollingbrook] Hotel.

Feb. 5. Thursday. Fine snow falling very slowly, which after some hours changed to drizzle, which continued into the night. Also turning warm. The train set off at 8.45 A.M. As soon as reaching Richmond, & getting our passports, I called on Mr. [Robert R.] Howison to leave my Diary & Notes on my Manassas incidents, & conversed with him on the subject of his History of the War, for half an hour. I told him that I selected that portion as only suiting his wishes—but that I do not think that my records, of my personal experience only, can be suitable materials for a general history.— Called first at the H. of D. to see Newton for a few minutes. Later, in the Ballard House, saw Boulware who had just arrived from his farm on James river. Julian & I had found that there was no carriage or buggy of Edmund's waiting. . . . So we took a room at the Ballard House. Edmund arrived at 8, having been detained 3 hours longer on the R.R. by the snow. Saw Mrs. President Tyler in the ladies' parlor, at night, & conversed with her some time, on the subject of her late visit to N.Y. to visit her mother & other near relatives. She was, as heretofore, very pleasant in conversation, & cheerful in manner. She certainly is not playing the part of a disconsolate widow. Spent the remainder of the evening, to 10 o'clock, in Newton's room, with my two sons.—I shall postpone any statements of late news, (of which there is [2481] none very striking or important,) until I can have time & quiet, at Marlbourne.—On the train this morning I met with Capt. [Robert B.] Pegram, who commands the iron-clad steamer lately built at Richmond.[21] He introduced me to a General, who was sitting by him, & whose name I did not hear.

---

[21] See above, pages 274, 275.

When I had an opportunity to ask it of Capt. P., I heard it was General Huger, who ought to have been cashiered, or shot, for either of the three disasters which he caused by his misconduct—Roanoke Island, his own failure at Seven Pines, & at Malvern Hill.

Feb. 6. The rain continued falling slowly until after morning. The earth must be made too wet again for Gen. Hooker's advance.—Edmund & Julian set off, in Mr. Sayre's buggy, after early breakfast. I waited for Mr. Boulware to finish his business, & after 12, in his carriage we set out together for Marlbourne, where we arrived after 4 P.M. All well. . . . At night came Henry T. Cocke, on his way from the camp in Essex, on furlough, going home. The ragged condition of his pantaloons showed that he needed repairing damages. . . .

Feb. 7. Saturday. . . . Of the news received since the 3rd, I will now note the most interesting items. . . . There is a strong & bold article . . . in the Boston Post,[22] which far exceeds anything that I could have expected in New England. It maintains that the certain result of Lincoln's emancipation [2483] & war policy will be to cause the north-western states to join the South—& not only these, but that the middle states will join in the movement, & that New England will only be excluded from the new construction. I believe with the editor as to the coming willingness of the North-western states to join with us—either in & through the war, or permanently, if permitted. And if that would be done, that N.J., Pa., & N.Y. will be glad to follow. But he is entirely mistaken in supposing that the South would receive any of these accessions, unless they offer to come in as sharers & protectors, by constitution & laws, of the institution of negro slavery.—A Yankee gun-boat (iron-clad,)[23] has passed down by Vicksburg, despite of the fire from our batteries, by which it was struck with three balls only. . . . This shows that iron-clad steamers can safely pass by our batteries, to reinforce the fleet below. The river was then high enough for water to be passing through the new canal, from 2 to 4 feet deep. 5000 men widening it. No doubt, if the labors are not obstructed, the passage will soon wash deep enough for the gun-boats as well as transports to pass up & down. Then there will be no use in our holding Vicksburg, so far as respects controlling the passage of vessels. The enemy are assembling an immense naval & land force for another attack on

---

[22] A clipping appended to the diary indicates that this article actually appeared in the Providence (R.I.) *Post.*

[23] *Queen of the West.*

Vicksburg, & next on Port Hudson (in La.) below. The defences of
both these ports are said to be impregnable. But that has been said
of so many other fortifications that were afterwards easily taken,
that I am suspicious of all such statements in advance of trial.
Vicksburg, however, has been tried, & severely, & the people of
Vicksburg have bravely & nobly borne, & the defending troops
have repulsed & driven off, two several and long continued attacks,
or sieges & attempts to assult, of gigantic armaments.—Northern
[2484] newspaper reports, & also naval indications, threaten a
speedy & tremendous attack of naval & land forces on Charleston. I
wish it may be so directed. But I much fear that these doings &
showings of the enemy are but a strong feint on Charleston—& that
after they have drawn to its defence the greatest amount of our
forces . . . they will suddenly turn to assail Savannah or Wilmington.—The imprisonment of [A. D.] Boileau, editor of the Phila.
Evening Journal, for publishing an article condemning the policy
& conduct of Lincoln, excited a violent state of public feeling in Pa.
The judge charged the Grand Jury thereupon, & the Grand Jury,
though declining to condemn in plain terms, made a long statement
of the facts of the illegal outrage, with telling effect against the
government. The legislature took up the case, and were about to
take very strong ground. If Boileau had been a man of courage &
firmness, & had merely refused to yield anything, he would have
been made a hero of, & the popular movement in his favor, &
against the government, would have been tremendous. But he must
be a timid & mean-spirited wretch. He signed a general declaration
of his "loyalty" to the government, (which every man professes,)
upon which the government discharged him from prison, & no
doubt were glad of an excuse to get rid of him so easily. Of course,
after his release, there was nothing remaining to keep up the excitement, & things soon became cool & quiet. . . . There never was
a finer chance lost than in this case, by the cowardly submission of
the prisoner, & the eager acceptance of it. [2485] . . . The correspondent of the Examiner writes from Fredericksburg, Feby 2nd.,
that the melting of the snow (which had been 6 inches deep) by
soaking rain, had so wetted & softened the clay soil of Stafford, that
no military movements of the enemy could be made for a long
time. . . . I have not until today seen or heard the locality of Port
Hudson. It is on the east bank of the Mississippi, about 25 miles
above Baton Rouge. All the long distance thence to Vicksburg,

between the two posts, was secured from Yankee vessels. But now that the iron-clad "Queen of the West" has passed down, by Vicksburg, to Vidalia, near Natchez, even if no more shall pass, this whole distance is exposed to being robbed & ravaged, by this one gun-boat alone. . . .

I was able when in Richmond to obtain full information in regard to a part of the secret history of this revolution, of which I knew very little before. Before the attack & capture of Fort Sumter, which precipitated the action of both sections of the former U.S. & forced all in the South who before hesitated to take their position, for or against the secession movement, the occurrences which I shall narrate were commenced. My then & later absence from Va, [&] the very slight notice given in the newspapers, prevented my then knowing any thing of the facts. And when I returned to Va, immediately after learning that the state had seceded, & my sojourning for a few days in Richmond, the later & more impressive events occupied every mind, & prevented my hearing anything of these important facts, which then were overshadowed by the later engrossing events of the secession of the State, the capture of Harper's Ferry & the Navy Yard at Portsmouth, & the war preparations of both South & North. It was not until long after that I had some intimations of these matters, which induced me to seek for full information from the best authority, & on the earliest opportunity. This information I have just obtained from Willoughby Newton, as to general facts, & also from David Chalmers of Halifax, as to persons & particulars.

Before the attack on Sumter, the chances for the secession of Va, by the action of its submissionist State Convention, seemed desperate. In that body, at first, the submissionists (or Union men, as they called themselves,) had outnumbered the secessionists in the proportion of full three to one—& there had not been any changes made in opinions, & not many by instructions from constituents. There had been a great change in the popular sentiment, & fast growing, in favor of immediate secession, [2487] even before the capture of Fort Sumter, which event afterwards operated in that direction instantaneously, & with a power ten-fold greater than all other recent causes. It was when there was no hope from the patriotic action of the Convention, & no faith given to the Governor, that some of the ardent & active secessionists then in Richmond consulted together, & began a private movement. Some of the movers were members of the Convention—who, as such, could only consult & advise, & could not give their names to the invitation, nor their presence in subsequent formal deliberations. A circular letter, approved by all the prime movers, & signed by some 10 or 12 of their number, known to the public as true men, was secretly printed, & copies directed to some hundreds of individuals throughout the state, & to someone in each county of the state, who were known to be true to the South, & believed to be patriotic & brave, & ready to aid in the scheme. These persons were invited to meet at Richmond on a named day, to confer on the then state of affairs, & to take such action as was necessary. As the general fact of such an invitation could not be concealed, it was also put in the newspaper that a convention of private citizens was invited to meet, the members to be either designated by election in their counties, or by voluntary action, to confer & exchange information as to the then state of popular opinion. Of course, everyone would infer that it was designed to try to influence the State Convention by the pressure of popular opinion. Any ulterior views, of resort to physical force, were carefully concealed. Still, the "Whig," then edited & directed by [Robert] Ridgway, a rank submissionist, denounced the designed assemblage as an effort to over-awe & intimidate the State Convention, & as ridiculous for the feebleness of power, as it was abominable for the evil intention. It was this denunciation which I saw abroad that gave me the [2488] then only information on the subject.—These invitations brought some 200, of those invited, to Richmond at the appointed time. This had been set as early as would give time to the distant localities. Still it was after the capture of Fort Sumter, wh[ich] had already produced many changes to the support of secession, in the State Convention, in the state at large, & especially in the population of Richmond, which but lately [had] been submissionist by an overwhelming majority. The *private* convention was brought together quietly & secretly by notes of invitation addressed to individuals by a self-appointed & secret committee, care being taken that no one was invited, or admitted, who was not a true & reliable supporter of the South, & of immediate secession. About 200 members met. All were men in private life—& even as a class, were so much the better & more able on that account. For since our present universal suffrage constitution has been in operation, & consequent demagogue rule established, the "post of honor has been in private station." With but few exceptions, the representative bodies have been since becoming more & more weak & base—& but few able men have continued representatives of the people, unless they also were accomplished & unprincipled demagogues. This body was organized, & elected David Chalmers President, & Willoughby Newton, Th[omas] J. Randolph, & some others Vice-Presidents. Some general resolutions, indicative merely of general opinions, were passed, & several loose committees appointed, to confer more conveniently, & to prepare the business. Then the meeting adjourned, with a recess of one or two days. During this recess, the members were actively & efficiently operating in the committees, or as individuals in talking & agitating secession in private or in public. Nothing of overt action had been adopted or proposed in the general meeting. And it was not necessary when the body met again. So [2489] that strictly speaking the convention, as such, did nothing—& merely passed resolutions on abstract propositions, & heard sundry vehement speeches in favor of immediate secession. But the general plan of action, though arranged & fixed in private conversations, or in committees, was not the less determined, & certain to be attempted, if subsequent & speedy occurrences, in the action of the State Convention, had not rendered all private or revolutionary action superfluous & improper. The plan of designed action was as follows: After waiting a sufficient time, (& the limit was once fixed at only 30 hours ahead,) to see whether the State Convention would continue to give way to the popular sentiment, so that a majority would vote for the secession of Va., it was designed to resort, as quietly as could be, to . . . physical force. Capt. O. J. Wise, who had been one of the first, most zealous, & efficient movers, commanded the "Blues," a volunteer company which could be relied on for support, & one or two other companies of volunteers of the city. Gov. Letcher was to be arrested or kidnapped, carried off, & confined in secret, for the time necessary. The Lieut. Governor, [Robert L.] Montague, a true man, would then be acting governor, in the absence of Letcher, & could be relied upon to take measures boldly & discreetly, for the best interests of Virginia, & for her effective secession & resistance. The leaders of the traitors in the State Convention, [George W.] Summers, [John S.] Carlisle [*sic*], [Waitman T.] Willey[24] &c. were to be seized

---

[24] A native of Monongalia County, Virginia, Willey (1811–1900) had attended the Constitutional Union national convention of 1860, which nominated John Bell of

& imprisoned. And if, in that time, the Convention had not passed the act of secession by a majority, that body, or the portion still for submission, would be arrested, & taken out by an armed force, & the secession of the State declared by the revolutionary party. Suspicions of such general intentions were entertained by the submissionists in the Convention, who were still the decided majority. And the reality was known to some of the most zealous secessionists in [2490] that body. These members urged their friends in the private convention to postpone action somewhat longer, as there were strong indications that so many of the submissionists in that body would soon yield to the various influences operating from without, & render all illegal or revolutionary action unnecessary. These remonstrances had effect in extending postponement. And in a very short time, the act of secession was passed by a majority of the State Convention. Though this was done in secret, & the secret was tried (in vain) to be kept for some days longer, so as to allow Harper's Ferry, the Navy Yard, & perhaps other important posts to be seized by the State, information of the important enactment was immediately sent to the private Convention, then in session. Of course, its object was then completely effected, & its designed work done. The body remained in session long enough to hear sundry rejoicing speeches, & then adjourned.

Feb. 8. Sunday.... Edmund lately visited his ruined farm of Evelynton, to see its condition—& also saw Berkley & Westover. He describes the destruction generally as exceeding all his anticipations, & especially as to Evelynton. We had before heard that all the buildings had been pulled down, except a part of the overseer's house, & the materials removed for use of the camp. There was not anything moveable, or capable of destruction left, of even the least value. In addition, the farm is greatly damaged by the extensive intrenchments made through a large portion. At Berkley, the buildings only had not been destroyed. At Westover, the mansion & other buildings near, the garden &c. had been protected, & seemed but little damaged. My son heard what induced the belief, that our cannonade in the dark, from the other side of the river, foolishly as it

---

Tennessee for president. In July, 1861, he was elected to the United States Senate to fill the seat vacated by James M. Mason, who had resigned following the secession of Virginia. After serving as a delegate to the West Virginia constitutional convention, Willey was again elected to the Senate—this time from West Virginia—and remained in that body from August, 1863, until March, 1871.

was conducted, must have damaged the enemy much more than they admitted, or we had supposed. He stopped at Col. [2491] James Willcox's. During the occupation by McClellan's army, some of the officers & soldiers were there every day—& Mrs. Willcox especially heard much said by them. The officers were very reticent as to the effects of the cannonade on their camp. But she heard from an officer that 40 horses belonging to his regiment had been killed. Another officer said that his company had had 9 horses & 15 men killed.[25] Privates admitted, in general terms, that their forces suffered considerably. Gen. McClellan's tent, in which he was lodging, was not far from the Berkley buildings—& he fled from it very quickly, to a safer place.—Mrs. Willcox said that the Yankees were anxious to know which farm was *my* property, & some believed Evelynton to be mine. Considering their ample means for information, from the negroes of my son then in their camp, they had very confused ideas of our persons as well as our property. Both of my son's farms, Evelynton & Beechwood, seem to have been supposed to be mine, if not Marlbourne also, by some of the occupying robbers & destroyers. Others, judging by their writings left at Beechwood, confounded me with my son, the proprietor. Again, he was confounded with Dr. Cole, the deceased proprietor of Maycox. For when the burning of the Maycox buildings was reported in a Yankee newspaper, the property was stated as belonging to the "celebrated Dr. Ruffin."[26] So it is probable that Maycox suffered the more because of my son's bad character with the Yankees—& that he also suffered more severely than for his own political & military offences, because of his being my son, or for his identity & mine being confounded. I have heard from so many different sources, & in various localities, of the wishes expressed by the Yankees to capture me, & of their threats to hang me, that I cannot doubt their having so complimented me—as I did doubt it, when first hearing such [2492] reports. This reminds me of another compliment of somewhat similar character, though not indicating such danger to my person. On one side of Ruthven is a neighborhood, called the Holly Bush, of which all the residents are poor & ignorant, & many

---

[25] In his official report of this incident, which occurred on the night of August 1, 1862, General McClellan admitted only trifling losses: "We lost 10 men killed and 12 wounded. Some half a dozen horses were killed and one wagon smashed." *Official Records*, Vol. XI, Pt. 2, p. 935.

[26] This error apparently originated with McClellan. See above, page 400 and *n* 27.

both lazy and vicious. Such people cannot have any exalted sentiments of patriotism, & must regard the war almost exclusively in reference to the sufferings it has caused to them, in taking the men to serve as soldiers, leaving their families at home in greater want, & enhancing enormously the prices of everything they need to buy. One of the residents, who, owing to peculiar circumstances, is very superior to the others in education & character, lately told Mrs. Meade that it was the settled & unquestioned opinion of all these our ignorant neighbors, that *I* was the whole & sole cause of the war. As this must be but a different mode of stating the proposition that I was the cause of the dissolution of the Union with the North, of which the war was the consequence, I am willing to lie under the imputation, though it is made in anything but an approving or complimentary spirit—& the charge is doubtless as malicious in intention as it is beyond the truth & my merits. If it were fully true, & established in public opinion, I would desire no more glory & fame, than to be truly believed to have been the chief cause of effecting the separation of the Southern from the Northern states, even at all the general expense of blood & property, & ruin to individuals, which it will cost. All that I can justly claim in this respect, is that I have exerted all my feeble powers to start & afterwards to forward the separation—&, as part of the necessary price for the great benefit, I do not grudge the heavy sacrifices & losses caused to myself, & to some of my children. . . .

Feb. 9. Monday. My sons completed their business with Mr. Sayre, of perfecting the purchase of the Marlbourne estate.—I took a walk on the farm with Edmund, the first that I had had time for—but could not go far, on account of the wetness of the ground.

Feb. 10. Tuesday. After breakfast, Julian & I, with Nanny & John, left in the carriage for Richmond. Set out thence on the R.R. at 2.30 P.M. for Petersburg. There, Nanny stopped at Mr. Graves', to spend some week or more with his wife, before proceeding to Ruthven. Julian went to spend the night at Mr. [2494] Callender's, & I to the Bollingbrook Hotel, to pass a lonesome & disagreeable time. . . . The papers for yesterday & today contain no striking events. Preparations are in rapid progress for very important events. More than 70 Yankee vessels are now assembled in Port Royal harbor, of which 15 are gun-boats, 4 or 5 iron-clad steamers, & the residue transports. Everything, including all Yankee publications, indicate[s] that a powerful attack is designed on Charleston—except (in my opinion,) the openness of the avowals of this design, which make me suspect it is a feint . . . . The great armada on the Mississippi, from above, has approached near to Vicksburg, & landed the troops on the La. side, out of reach of our batteries. Northern papers tell of the enormous efforts about to be made to take Vicksburg—& some of them speak despondingly of the prospect. . . . The canal does not promise to answer its purpose. The "Queen of the West" armed steamer, which passed down by our batteries, (protected by cotton bulwarks,) has already done great damage. It ascended Red River, & captured 3 of our transport steamers, on which there were large & very valuable cargoes of provisions &c. for our army.—The facts of our late naval victory in Charleston harbor were greatly exaggerated. The darkness of the night & also fog, prevented anything being seen beyond very short distances. This doubtless caused the mistakes. It now appears from northern accounts, that neither the Mercedita, nor [2495] any other of the Yankee squadron was sunk, & lost, by our fire, though several were greatly damaged, & escaped . . . in crippled condition. The Mercedita was supposed to be fast & certainly sinking, by its own officer & boat's crew who came on board the Palmetto State, & begged for aid. But though the victory & damages were so much overestimated, Northern accounts admit great damages, & that their fleet was "dispersed"—& that their defeat was a most humiliating affair.—More reports of demoralization, & even disaffection, & numerous desertions from the Yankee army near Fredericksburg especially—& next of Banks' force. It is thought that the bad condition of his army in these respects has prevented his threatened attack on Port Hudson. . . .

February 11. Wednesday.—My bill for supper, lodging & breakfast, was $5. The regular board is $6 a day. I lodged in a room without a fire, & the table fare very mean. At the Ballard House in Richmond, prices were the same—but the fare better, though far from good.—Julian had some matters to attend to, so we did not set off, in his carriage, until 11.30, & were 5 hours getting to Ruthven. My niece Juliana & my granddaughter Jane Dupuy were here. John Ruffin came with us. It will be a joyful [2496] meeting for the two boys, as it has been for the two Janes.[27] Each of the four has so far been secluded from the companionship of any play-mate of their

---

[27] The permanent residents of Ruthven referred to here were Julian's two eldest children—Meade, aged ten, and Jane, aged six.

own sex, age & condition, which privation is now removed from all. The two boys are nearly of the same age, & so are the two girls to each other. I am much gratified in having them together. But for Juliana having come, & at my request, bringing my granddaughter, I should have remained at Marlbourne.—The mail brought no important news. The expectation of tremendous attacks from the four different great armaments of Yankees grows stronger every day. Awful & bloody battles must soon be fought in three if not four places.—I never heard an intimation of the scheme of a separate peace with the North-western states, before I suggested & urged the attempt by our government, in a letter I wrote to Judge Perkins, about Sept. 1st. Soon after, the policy was proposed in Congress, in resolutions offered by Mr. Foote, which were not put to a vote. I followed these forthwith by my anonymous argument in favor of a separate peace, published in the Rd. Enquirer. Latterly, the scheme has grown rapidly in public favor in the C.S.—& also in Illinois & Indiana, though there there is no mention of a separate peace, *eo nomine*, but of other things which would amount to the same thing. Thus, the leading opposition men argue for peace in general terms—or insist on being united with the South, & cutting loose from New England—& there are strong intimations of a "North-Western Confederacy." The wife of ex-Senator [Jesse D.] Bright of I[ndian]a is in Richmond, & is understood to be there acting as agent (whether authorized or not,) for the disaffected in that state. The subject of the secession of some of the north-western states is openly sopken of in northern papers the most hostile to the measure, & devoted to the policy of Lincoln & of New England. Bitter hostility is fast growing up between these north-western & the north-eastern states, which must come to a [2497] very serious issue before very long. This condition of things is an additional & powerful cause for the closing of the war, because of the inability of Lincoln's administration & party to continue to carry it on. If one-half of the reports are true of the disaffection & numerous desertions in the Yankee army, these effects must increase more & more—until the soldiers of the disaffected states will march off to their homes by [the] thousands. The news of today gave another notable indication. A bill for paying arrears of pay (in part due 12 months) to troops in Missouri, was prevented being passed in the Rump Senate, by two opposition members only, Saulsbury & Richardson, leaving the hall, & leaving no quorum. If *two only* can do this, at a favorable time, *all* the opposition members so acting can defeat all legislation in aid of the war, for the short remainder of the term of this abolition congress. . . . But few of the important war bills, if any, have yet been acted upon finally in the Senate. And if the opposition members of that body could prevent any such measures being enacted, before the end of this Congress, it would cripple the war policy, & also compel Lincoln to call the new Congress, or otherwise have the wheels of government stopped.

Feb. 12. Thursday. . . . My niece brought to me a portion of a letter from a Yankee soldier, or officer, who was one of the gang of robbers who were posted at Beechwood. The letter was found in the pocket of the writer (as inferred, & as I trust it was,) lying killed on the second battlefield of Manassas . . . . The letter was shown to Mr. Charles Dupuy, of the La. Washington Artillery—who being acquainted with my family, & having visited at Beechwood, obtained possession of the letter, to deliver to us. . . . The writer was ashamed to tell, even to his sister, the general system of robbery, & of breakage & destruction of everything which could not be carried off, both in the houses & on the farm. Perhaps all these acts were implied in the general term of "confiscation."[28] This one of the robbers, (who from his obvious education, & his being quartered with officers, & his writing paper, I infer to have been an officer,) supposing Beechwood to be my property, strengthens the opinion I lately stated, that this error prevailed to considerable extent—& caused the more injury to my son Edmund, the owner of the property here & elsewhere. The latter part of this fragment is interesting testimony, & may be trusted, although from a Yankee, of the heavy losses suffered by McClellan's army in his campaign [2499] in the peninsula—if the company & corps to which the writer belonged is to be taken as a sample & indication of the whole army.[29]

---

[28] The letter, dated August 22, 1862, and addressed to "sister Mollie" by a member of Company I, Sixteenth Michigan Regiment, contained this reference to the occupation of Beechwood: "Confiscated the estate of the Hon. Edmund Ruffin, the man who fired the first gun at Ft. Sumpter [*sic*]. His house was a palace almost. He left the largest library I ever saw. Also all his furniture, but the best of all was a sacred harp, Piano & two melodeons. Lt. Swan Brown, the Adjt. and myself lived on music all that week, with a spricling [*sic*] now and then of a small quantity of green corn, peaches, pears, apples, figs, onions and potatoes, to say nothing of a young porker we bayoneted every morning."

[29] According to the unknown writer, his company was then fifty-eight men short of its complement at the beginning of the Peninsular campaign.

Feb. 16. Monday. The mail brought no news of important & final events, but, from Yankee papers, very important indications of things impending. The latest European steamer arrived at Halifax on 9th. Its papers & passengers not arrived at N.Y., but telegraphic reports. One of these, fully believed in N.Y., is that the Emperor has offered his friendly mediation to the belligerent powers here, & has sent to invite them to depute commissioners, to meet in Mexico or Montreal, to settle terms of peace.—The Alabama . . . has gone into Kingston, Jamaica, where it landed more than 100 prisoners saved from the Hatteras, & to have repaired the [2501] damages received in the action—4 or 5 shot-holes, of which one only was serious, & all of which could be repaired in a few days. Six Yankee war steamers were immediately sent to lie off the port of Kingston, to watch or blockade the Alabama. This will be almost as serviceable employment for the Alabama as cruising—to keep idle, & always ready for action, 6 war steamers, while the guarded Alabama may have its fires down, & even its crew dismissed, if the vessel cannot escape. . . . There [are] still increasing reports, & from northern as well as southern sources, of numerous desertions, disaffection & demoralization in the Yankee armies. A correspondent of a Yankee paper, from Hooker's grand army states that more than 200 soldiers are under trial for military offences so serious as to demand the punishment of death for all convicted. . . . Nothing for attack, yet attempted by Hooker, nor by the forces at Port Royal—nor near Vicksburg, except the diligent widening of the canal. The dilatory movements of all these great armaments, & also of [2502] Rosecrans' great army in Ten., & Banks' at Baton Rouge, all seem to indicate that the commanders are doubtful of their soldiers.—Evidences of opposition to the government, & of determination to have peace by separate action of some of the states, continue to increase. Yankee Lincoln papers at last notice & denounce the movement in the opposition state legislatures, & no longer, by silence, affect to ignore the danger of disruption of the now U.S. Sundry strong resolutions, in favor of armistice & peace, & against the policy of Lincoln, are before the legislatures of New Jersey, Indiana & Illinois. Report adds Ohio to the malcontent states that will join in separate action for peace—& the N.Y. Herald supposes that the States of New York & Pa. will send delegates to the proposed Convention of States. To this proposed convention, all the states, South & North, will be invited. But it is certain that none of the C.S.

[577]

will be represented, & not likely that any of the thorough abolition states will. Then it will be a convention of the malcontent northern states, & principally of the North-western states, which will together discuss their prospective condition, and whose deliberations, as I think, will result in a rupture of the present northern confederacy, or consolidation. . . . Will these states, with their present views, & their vital interests involved, decide to continue to bear their part in a hopeless war, with their utter ruin the only visible result—or will they put an end to the war by *their* secession from New England & its continuing allies, & at once obtain peace, good markets, commercial prosperity, & safety, with avoidance of all further Yankee tribute & debt, & with possession of most of the vacant public lands, by making a separate peace & alliance with the C.S.? To my mind there is no doubt of the latter course being chosen . . . . New England will be left alone to starve—unless New York, New Jersey & Pennsylvania will remain in connection with, & help to support these always begging & predaceous states— which heretofore have had the South to exact tribute from, & must now obtain it from whichever of the northern states shall continue in union with & under the political domination of New England. . . . [2506] Another Yankee iron-clad gunboat[30] has passed down by our batteries at Vicksburg. . . . This accession will increase the previous great exposure of all the river plantations between Vicksburg & Port Hudson. It is a strange neglect by our authorities that all the piled fuel along the banks has not been burnt, to prevent its supplying the enemy's steamers who have got into this before secured portion of the river.

Feb. 17. Tuesday. Heavy rain last night, & drizzle today. This will further postpone Hooker's advance, if (as probable,) it had not been before abandoned as hopeless. After a warm spell, turning cold. Strong wind from N.E. at night. I hope that the 4 additional iron-clads expected from the North, may now be off Cape Hatteras. . . .

Feb. 18. Wednesday. Drizzle. Wind N.E. but not strong.—The mail. Gen. Beauregard has issued a proclamation to the people of S.C. & Ga. declaring that the attack on both Charleston & Savannah is imminent—urging all non-combatants to leave these cities, & inviting all able citizens to come & aid to defend them, & to bring their best arms, if these should be no better than pikes & scythe-

---

[30] U.S.S. *Indianola.*

blades. . . . The enemy's armies near Murfreesborough, Vicksburg, & the land & naval forces under Banks, below Port Hudson, as well as the great armada in Port Royal harbor, still have kept quiet, & made no attack or hostile movement. The delays of each & all are very strange, after such long notice of their intentions of attack. Though fighting, with victory to us, [2507] would be still better, all these delays are much more to the damage of the Yankee armies, & cause, than to ours. Important & also early victories are absolutely necessary for them, & every week of doing nothing is operating to weaken their means & darken their prospects of success. . . . The French emperor has already offered his friendly mediation, or advice to make peace, to the Northern government. He cannot do so to the C.S., because their political existence as a separate nationality is ignored, & he cannot address anything directly to their government, without, by that very action, recognizing our independence. By a dispatch through the French minister at Washington, the French emperor respectfully invites & advises the U.S. government to confer, through commissioners appointed by both parties, with the C.S. on terms of reconstruction or of peace—the commissioners to meet in neutral territory, or the place of meeting to be declared neutral for the time it is so used—& the operations of war not to be suspended during the conference of the commissioners. To this letter, dated Jan. 9th, Seward replies on Feby 5th, through the Yankee minister at Paris, & respectfully but positively declines any such arrangement. And this refusal may be deemed final, so long as the Yankee government retains any hope of success. Seward has the best of the argument on the general question & on such of his premises as are, or might be, true. But some of his premises are either absurdly false, or foolish. He maintains that the U.S. government could not consent to discuss the claims of the rebel states, by appointed commissioners, without thereby recognizing the right & the power of these states to treat as equals. It certainly would weaken the moral power of the U.S. both at home & abroad. So far Seward [2508] had good ground for his argument, & he maintained it well. But as he seems to consider that lying is an essential, if not the most effective, part of every state paper, he adds that favorite feature of his logic. To show the great success of the northern arms, he gives a general & glowing description of their territorial conquests & present occupation of territory in the C.S., claiming the larger portion, in extent, value, & strength of position,

[579]

as already conquered. But even if this statement of boundaries of conquests were true, he omits the important statement that all these conquests had been made nearly a year ago—& that since, their armies have been defeated in almost every battle, & have had their previous extent of occupation rather lessened than increased. Again—as a reason for the inutility of a board of commissioners to discuss & settle terms of adjustment between the North & South, he says that the Congress of the U.S. is now such a body, & the best for that purpose: that already portions of the rebel states are therein represented by their elected members, & that every other district & state may be so represented, if so choosing. So, the Confederate States are to be represented by the [Andrew] Johnsons, Carliles & Segars, despicable traitors, fraudulently deputed by small minorities of traitors like themselves, to represent the rights of the great majorities, which these traitors are as much opposed to as Seward himself. Even in Maryland, Delaware, & Missouri, where only there was the semblance of general election, the polls were controlled by Yankee troops, & secessionist candidates, or those who would have voted for them, would have forfeited their liberty, & risked their lives, by appearing in these characters. . . . But putting aside all this . . . no [2509] plan could be more absurd, deceptious, & suicidal for the southern states, even if the elections were fairly made, every state & district fully represented, & that all the seceded states, & Md, Del, Ky & Mo. added thereto, all sent only members who were secessionists & true & faithful to the south. All this array would still be but a minority, in both houses, reduced still lower than existed before the beginning of secession. Of course, the same northern majority, & brute force of numbers, would still, as formerly, control the southern minority. It would be as hopeless, & absurd an expectation, of southern rights & claims being respected & secured in the Congress so composed, as by the joint votes of a board of Commissioners authorized to decide upon terms of peace, to which board the Yankee government deputed two members, & had therein two votes, & the C.S. but one.—I infer that this by-gone correspondence is the only ground for the late report of a proposal of French mediation having been brought by the last steamer from Europe. . . . But this second attempt, already made by the French emperor, gives stronger indication that he will persevere. And this positive rejection, & also final, under existing conditions, of his invitation made only to the U.S. government, I think will induce his own separate action, which can only be begun by recognizing the political existence of the C.S. And as that bare recognition, alone, would be of very little service to the C.S., & none whatever to France, I infer that, if made, it will be followed up by other steps which will essentially promote the welfare of both countries. . . . The Yankees have cut the *levee* of the Mississippi, at Yazoo Pass, Greenville, & opposite Lake Providence, to inundate the country before protected by the levee.

Feb. 19. Thursday. Another rainy & gloomy day. In the afternoon, the first sunlight for three days.—Our congress is discussing the subject of finance, with closed doors. It is of vital importance that something effective shall be done to guard & preserve public credit, & to properly direct the actual means of our people for the defence of the country. But little has yet been done by this weak body, which does not approach what is needed for this crisis, & does not truly represent either the spirit, the intellect, or the self-sacrificing patriotism of the people of the C.S. By relying almost exclusively on emissions of treasury notes, serving as the only currency, & now amounting in the public expenditure to $50,000,000 monthly, as a necessary consequence, this currency has depreciated to less than half its nominal value, & is fast descending lower. The proper remedy—heavy taxation—which the people would bear, & all patriotic & well-informed men have earnestly called for—has not been applied, & I fear will be too long delayed. In the meantime, [2511] all persons are subjected to the disadvantages of a greatly depreciated currency. All having fixed incomes, in nominal amount, are actually deprived of half or more of their means for support. Still worse for all of the thousands, who, deprived of most or all their revenues by the enemy's ravages, are required to pay for every necessary bought, prices increased in rate from three to ten-fold their former rates. But worst of all for the government now, & perhaps the public creditors hereafter. The government, in borrowing, or emitting its obligations as money, incurs, in the depreciated currency a debt which will hereafter have to be repaid in specie, of twice or thrice the real value. And in making purchases, (the principal expenditure for the war,) prices at the least three-fold the true or specie value, have to be paid for all supplies. The evil is growing with frightful rapidity. It is the only evil which our people could not bear up under, in carrying on the war—& which, & which only, *may* compel us to yield to our enemies, unless they still earlier are overwhelmed by similar financial evils, which threaten them as much. If our downward progress in this respect is not soon & effectually checked, the credit of the C.S. will be utterly blighted—or the loans & issues will be so greatly depreciated, that national bankruptcy, & repudiation of the whole public debt will inevitably be the future result. The people will scarcely be able to pay the enormous debt, at its nominal value—& if they *can*, they *will not*. . . .

Feb. 20. Friday. The mail. Many extracts from European publications, brought by the last steamer. My opinion of the French emperor's next step, which was written yesterday . . . seems already [2512] to be confirmed by the general opinion expressed by both the French & English newspapers, commenting on the Emperor's proposal to Lincoln. It seems that nobody expected the acquiescence of Lincoln's government—neither of the French or English press—nor Mr. Slidell, who had not been consulted. The French papers, (including the "Nation" understood to be the Emperor's special organ,) & the English, all infer that his advice in favor of a peace conference, by Commissioners of the North & South, being sure of rejection, was but a preliminary step, to be followed up by some other more effective, & by France alone, if other powers still decline so acting in concurrence. Any further action by the Emperor cannot fall short of recognition of the C.S.—& can scarcely stop there. With recognition, if it is to be made of any use to either the C.S. or to France, must come the breaking of the blockade. That will be all that we need for our successfully conquering peace & our independence. . . . Whenever the French Emperor shall have determined to interfere in our war, it would be a capital & successful move for him previously & secretly to send a squadron of 6 or 8 ships of war to the Pacific. As the Yankee government cannot have any respectable naval force there, these few ships could blockade San Francisco, & either bombard the city (if required,) or compel its submission—or more easily still, negotiate for & obtain the declaration of independence of California, & a commercial treaty giving great advantages, if not absolute free trade to France. There are existing already several subjects of difficulty between Yankeedom & France. These are, the French invasion of Mexico—the alleged robbing of French subjects by Butler in New Orleans—the recently exposed intrigues of France to acquire possession of Texas—the charge by Seward of falsehood on the French minister

Mercier—& the late refusal of Seward to accept the friendly invitation of the emperor, to confer with the C.S. on terms for peace. And last of all, Lincoln has complained to his Senate that the emperor has obtained some hundreds of negro soldiers, from the Pacha of Egypt, to serve in his army in Mexico, to garrison Vera Cruz, or other sickly posts. This would be good ground for complaint by our government. But it is ludicrous, & must be especially offensive, from Lincoln, when made at the very time that his commanders are endeavoring to enlist negroes by thousands, & a bill has just past [*sic*] the H. of R. of the Rump, to recruit an army of 150,000 negroes! All these subjects will furnish to France as many & as good grounds for a quarrel as could be desired.—The French invasion of Mexico has been very languidly prosecuted, though it has met with very little resistance by the Mexicans. It will serve admirably to cover the sending naval & military forces into the Gulf of Mexico, ready [2514] to be moved farther northward, if required. . . . Every one is now awaiting, with intense anxiety, the commencement of the attack on Charleston threatened by the great armada now at Port Royal. I still fear that Charleston will not be its first destination, but Savannah, or some other weaker point. Charleston, because of its low & flat ground, is naturally much exposed to attack, & little capable of defence. But its artificial defences are as strong as the natural features admit—& I have great confidence that the defenders will do all that courage & even desperation will direct. In addition to all ordinary incentives to the assailants & defenders, there are others operating to render this conflict especially determined, sanguinary, & urged to desperation. The Yankee people & government hate Charleston most intensely, as the first & main cause of secession, & the scene of the first armed assault upon, & signal humiliation of the Yankee power, in the conquest of Fort Sumter. Charleston, in common with all South Carolina, returns this hatred of Yankeedom, with interest, & rather than to yield the city to the enemy, would prefer [2515] that it shall be made an utter ruin under the bomb-shells & conflagration of the assailants. The pecuniary, commercial, & military values of the position, to be gained or lost by the conquest, great as they are, will be probably less operative considerations with the assailants & the defenders of the city, than the intense hatred, & desire of vengeance acting on both. The conflict will [be] memorable, throughout all future ages. . . . Our cause is like to be benefitted by another act of madness by the enemy, which, within its sphere of operation, I trust will serve us as well as Lincoln's emancipation policy. Gen. Hunter, who had first attempted to embody negro troops, by voluntary enlistment, & probably had found that mode ineffectual, has ordered the forcible enrollment of all the able-bodied male negroes on the lands within his lines, or under his military rule in S.Ca. This measure is expected to add 3 or 4,000 men to his army. The more the better. If he can have these recruits *caught* & embodied, half of the number will run away before getting into battle, & the remainder at the first shot received into their ranks. . . . The cutting of the levee had another object besides the injury to the properties to be thus submerged. The cutting of the left bank, at 6 miles below Helena, is expected to overflow the adjacent country for 50 miles in width, & spread 10 feet depth of the flood to the neighboring upper portion of the Tallihatchie [*sic*], a tributary of the Yazoo, if not into the Yazoo directly, whose upper channel is not much farther from the Mississippi river. Thus the enemy expect to float small armed steamers on the flood into the Yazoo, & to capture all our vessels in that river, & to get in the rear of Vicksburg, above its defences on the Yazoo.—There have been strong "peace resolutions" offered in the legislatures of 5 states—Illinois, Indiana, Ohio, Kentucky, & New Jersey—those for Ky especially strong in denouncing Lincoln & his measures. But I have not seen that such resolutions have been finally acted upon in either state. . . . One report, however, is that the legislature of Illinois had appointed delegates to a convention of states to meet at Louisville, & then had adjourned to June, to await the action of the convention. Let the convention but meet, & the military condition of the U.S. be no better, or worse, than now, & I do not doubt the effective revolt & resistance of the malcontent states. But, if the Yankee forces could take Charleston, & Vicksburg, or gain one or two great victories in Tennessee or Virginia, the North-western states would become quiet, in their renewed hope of conquering the navigation of the Mississippi, & as eager as at first for the bloody subjugation of the C.S. I wish to use their present discontent & disaffection, for our own benefit. But I have no more love for the malcontent north-western states than for New England.

Feb. 22. Sunday. Snow 4 inches deep—followed by slow rain, & then a change of wind, & turning severely cold.—My reading of printed rubbish literature varied by reading over some of my own old & private manuscripts—which probably will also be rubbish to any other eyes than mine. Among these, the "Incidents of my life."[31] [2518]

Feb. 23. Monday. The mail. The Yankee iron-clad war steamer "Queen of the West," which first passed our batteries at Vicksburg, has been captured in Red River. . . . This iron-clad gun-boat, which though struck by 15 balls when passing Vicksburg, was not hurt, & has since done us so much mischief, may be of incalculable benefit to our forces. It has been secured under our batteries—& if its damages can soon be repaired, it may enable us to capture all the Yankee vessels between Vicksburg & Port Hudson. Most of these were recently captured from us by this vessel. . . . Reports increase of the disaffection of, & numerous desertions from the Yankee armies—& recently, also, of many & daily desertions from the Yankee gun-boats on the Mississippi. The numbers of deserters actually coming in to surrender themselves as prisoners, to be paroled, would go far to sustain these reports. But these deserters further report that the general disaffection is very great, & that thousands will desert on the first opportunity. Another indication of these reports being true to important extent, is the late inactivity of all their great armies. The Yankee army now in S.C. is the only one of which I have heard no report of disaffection, & great disposition to desert. But this one alone cannot be sound & reliable, if all other Yankee armies are otherwise. . . . The Illinois legislature has had its further action frustrated, & its session broken up, by the abolition members all withdrawing, & so leaving no quorum. This unusual & desperate measure tells well for the strength & objects of the majority. I have before expressed my surprise that the democratic minority in the U.S. Senate did not play a like game, & prevent all [2520] further legislation through the short remainder of time that this U.S. Congress will exist. It also surprises me that I have met with no remark in any paper, northern or southern, as to the very few days, (8 only,) now left to finish the necessary enactments of this Congress, & the great probability of some of the important

---

[31] This was Ruffin's three-volume autobiography, written in the early 1850's. The last two volumes, covering the period 1823 to 1853, are included in the Edmund Ruffin Papers and Books now deposited with the Virginia Historical Society, Richmond (microfilm copies in the Southern Historical Collection, University of North Carolina, Chapel Hill). Unfortunately, the first volume apparently has been lost.

measures being lost for want of time. . . . A speech has been lately delivered in the Rump H. of R. by Mr. [Martin F.] Conway, of Kansas, an ultra abolitionist,[32] & said one of the ablest members of that party, which offers strange & remarkable indications, from such a source. He boldly opposes the continuance of the war, & also the reconstruction of the former union of the now severed states. He pronounces the President's emanicpation proclamation to be a failure, & worse—& that the army will, as voters, strengthen the opposition party. . . . Still, Mr. Conway shows that he is not actuated by any good feeling for the South, but by the abiding abolition hatred, & determination to effectively destroy negro slavery —& by the Northern zeal to make & keep the South tributary. For if peace was made & our independence acknowledged, upon such treaty conditions as proposed in the second resolution,[33] the Confederate states would be as much as ever tributary to the North, & their institutions & safety as much in danger from northern emissaries & agents, until the time should arrive for crushing the Confederate States by armed force. But there is not the least danger of any [2521] of Mr. Conway's proposed conditions being accepted by the C.S., even if serving unquestionably as the price of peace & of recognized separate nationality. But I wish him success in his proposition, so far as it can be effected by the Yankee government. Even if this bold speech has not the support (as alleged,) of the most prominent leaders of the abolition party, still as the unsupported declaration of one prominent & able member, it must have effect, in strengthening the advocates for peace, & weakening the moral force of the administration & war party. The speech is mysterious to me, considering it as opposed to the policy of the speaker's party. The nearest I can arrive at its interpretation, is that its tenor is the combined result of two different influences—viz: the long avowed hatred of the most rabid abolitionists to union with slave-holders,

---

[32] Born in Harford County, Maryland, Conway (1827–82) moved to Kansas in 1853 and soon became a prominent member of the free-soil faction. Following statehood, he was elected to the United States House of Representatives and served until March 3, 1863. Although he was a Republican, Conway had attended the peace convention held in Washington during the secession crisis.

[33] According to Conway's proposal, the United States would recognize the independence of the Confederacy provided the latter agreed to the following propositions: a uniform system of tariff rates for both countries, free trade between the United States and the Confederate States, free navigation of the Mississippi River, and mutual support of the Monroe Doctrine.

unless as *rulers*, able to abolish slavery—& the interest of Kansas, in common with all the North-West, to have opened the waters & markets of the lower Mississippi.

Feb. 24. I have been carefully examining the Coast Survey Chart of Charleston harbor & the surrounding water & land, & especially the main ship channel by which (as affording the deepest water,) the Yankee fleet must approach to attack the forts & city. The shallowest part of the channel (over the bar, below the harbor,) has but 10½ feet water at mean low tide. With the rise of 6 feet of tide, this would be 16½ feet at mean high water. It would scarcely be safe for a hostile squadron to bring any vessel drawing more than 14 feet—& therefore none of the larger vessels could come. If (as I infer, because most reasonable,) the Yankees sunk their stone fleet in the shallowest & narrowest part of the best & deepest channel, it must have been on the bar—& thereby, if of any effect, additional difficulties will be presented to the entrance of the Yankee fleet. The earthworks which were at Morris Island when I was [2522] there, were soon after levelled, when the garrisons were removed—& I do not know where others have since been constructed. But the nearest land (Lawford's Point) is within two & a half miles of the channel across the bar, & less than two miles of the further course of vessels. I should suppose that some heavy rifled cannon mounted there, could greatly annoy a squadron creeping as slowly as care would require over the bar. Above, for more than a mile of the shore below Fort Sumter, batteries would be within a mile & a half, or less, of the track of any invading fleet. There are other, but still shallower channels. And the best of these (Maffitt's,) runs much nearer to Sullivan's Island, & the guns of Fort Moultrie. This examination of the chart strengthens my previous confidence in the defeat of any attack by water. Nor do I see how a land attack can be made directly on Charleston, with the numerous topographical obstructions of passages of water, which even if narrow & shallow, have miry bottoms, & swampy & boggy margins, & are mostly through extensive marshes. The only chance for a land attack that I see is on the lower end of Morris Island, to take all the batteries thereon in the rear—& after successively reducing them, turning their cannon (& others) on Fort Sumter—& if compelling its surrender, then for the fleet to come in to aid Sumter in reducing Fort Moultrie. Thus, perhaps, step by step, the enemy may be able to subdue the water defences of Charleston, & so leave the city . . .

incapable of further defence or resistance. But this will require a long course of uninterrupted & successive successes, & the conversion of our fortifications for defence, to theirs for attacking us. But the more I consider the matter, the more confident I am that our defence will be successful & glorious. . . .

Feb. 25. Wednesday. Our messenger returned from the Post Office without any mail, or news—the carrier not having returned from his downward trip, delayed probably by the snow. A great disappointment to us all.—Besides reading much of my own old & private manuscripts, I have lately finished "The Diamond & the Pearl" by Mrs. [Catherine G. F.] Gore,[34] & the attractive articles of two old Nos. of [2524] the "Museum of Foreign Literature."

Feb. 26. Another gloomy day, & some drizzle. Afternoon, Edmund arrived, but not bringing Nanny from Petersburg, as arranged, that being prevented by the wet & threatening weather, added to the previously very bad roads. Papers of today brought by Edmund. No news of any important event—though indications of some approaching. But as I still am without the papers of two preceding days, I will wait for the mail, to refer to events in their order—& here will note only some of verbal information, which will not be in the newspapers. These are, that, in consequence of the withdrawal of the main body of the Yankee army from the Rappahannock,[35] Stonewall & his command only have been left in the late position of our army, & the other & much larger portion of Lee's army has been sent to other points. Gen. Longstreet (before erroneously reported as having gone to Ten.,) is in command from Richmond to N.C., & his command mostly has approached Suffolk. D. H. Hill & his command already in N.C. which department he is to command. Other forces have marched, or are moving to other positions, as yet unknown to the public.

Feb. 27. Friday. The mail—but not one daily paper of today.— The "Queen of the West" was soon repaired, & put to service. The

---

[34] This novel by the prolific English writer Catherine Grace Frances Gore (1799–1861) was first published in 1848.

[35] Rumors to this effect, though mostly false, had been circulating for weeks in the Confederate capital. To be sure, the Federal Ninth Corps had recently moved down the Potomac to Hampton Roads. In response to this threat, General Lee, on February 18, had ordered two of Longstreet's divisions to take up positions east of Richmond, and on this date, February 26, Longstreet himself assumed command of the Department of Virginia and North Carolina. However, the bulk of Hooker's Army of the Potomac remained in winter quarters above the Rappahannock.

Yankee iron-clad gun-boat Indianola passed down by our batteries at Vicksburg on the night of 14th, & on the 24th, was engaged with & sunk by *our prize*, the Queen of the West, & all the crew captured. The Indianola is in shallow water, & partly above the surface, on the eastern side of the Mississippi, & may be saved to us, if not prevented soon. . . . A military bill has passed the U.S. Senate, & will doubtless pass the H. of Rep., placing the whole male population, between 20 & 45 years of age, subject to conscription, at the will of the President. This will enable him to retain in service (*if they will stay,*) the 300,000 men whose terms of service will expire in May—& to add immediately, or hereafter, any number of others within three millions—which number the conscript bill is estimated to include. Also, a financial bill has passed both houses, making all necessary appropriations for the war, for 18 months, & putting at the disposition of the President all the revenue & credit of the government for that time. Nothing of means, in men & money, will be wanting, if the soldiers & the people will submit to such unheard of requisitions, and a majority of the people being in opposition to the administration. I do not believe in such submission. . . . The base Kentucky legislature, having adopted peace resolutions, & inviting a Convention of States to meet at Louisville, repealed them the next day. A private convention, called by individual action, & for Ky alone, met at Frankfort, on the 18th—but was dispersed by the Yankee military force, before being organized. . . . It seems to me that the French emperor's late movements indicate his settled purpose to intervene in this war—& as I deem him too wise to stop at a mere empty recognition of the C.S., which would amount to nothing, the only alternative & sensible course will be to raise the blockade. And as his main, if not only, object will be to obtain a full supply, for the future, of cotton, that measure must be effected very soon, to induce the planting of cotton for this year, & a full crop — or perhaps half a crop. Add to this strong inducement of national interest, the several existing grounds for dissatisfaction or quarrel between the governments of France & of the U.S.—& the superiority of [2527] France, with aid of the C.S., in war with the U.S.—all these reasons combined serve to bring my mind to the conclusion that there will be French intervention in this war within the next month, & of efficient character—& war with the U.S., unless the latter power shall yield (as I believe it will,) to whatever France shall insist upon, & whose demands *must* include the cessation of the blockade of the ports of the C.S. Let us have this, & the use (as a recognized power) of French ports for our prizes, & we need nothing else for enabling us to make a successful defence against our enemy, & soon to conquer a peace. But if the blockade continues, & the prices of the necessaries of life continue to rise above the present enormous rates, I confess that I cannot see how the people or the government of the C.S. are to support the burden.—Yankee gun-boats have entered the lately opened "Yazoo Pass," & a strong force is at work to clear out the obstructions of fallen trees &c., & not without resistance. Some small skirmishes have occurred between this force, & some of our troops, endeavoring to impede the Yankee progress. Formerly, before the extension of the levee so high up the Mississippi, this pass was open, & used by boats & small vessels—but has been obstructed since the floods were dyked out, & the country laid dry for tillage. The passage, even if made as good as formerly, must still be narrow, shallow, & crooked—& the Yankee vessels which will attempt the navigation will be in great danger of being captured or wrecked.—The Cleveland (O.) Plain dealer publishes two letters from a soldier (1st Massachusetts) in the Potomac army (near Fredericksburg,) to "a gentleman, his brother," who gave them to the editor. I infer that they are genuine, & may be relied on, at least as the opinions truly stated of the writer, who is evidently an educated & intelligent man. He gives a bad account of the condition of the Yankee army, its prospects, & [2528] especially of its new commander, Hooker, (as a drunkard,) & of the officers generally. In regard to disaffection & desertions, there is (dated Jan. 27th) the following passage: "The men in the army of the Potomac are deserting every day. A good many have left us, & many more say they are going if we have to cross the river. The fact is, the men have no confidence in the generals, nor in their officers. Things are in a bad shape in this army, & I should not be surprised to see a rebellion in the army. The men talk it right out, & say they will lay down their arms before they will fight under such generals as we have to command this army. I hope there will be no trouble, but I fear it, if there is not a change for the better soon. Gen. McClellan is the only man who (is competent to) command this army." In another part of these letters, this Massachusetts soldier, who doubtless was at home a thorough abolitionist, says—"I would not turn my hand over to free all the niggers of the South, for they are better off where they are than they could be if they were free." I expect many thousands of abolitionists will be cured of their fanaticism, & opposition to negro slavery, by their seeing the negroes in the South—& that under instruction of these numerous military converts . . . much of the ignorance of abolitionists at home will be enlightened, when this war is ended.

Feb. 28. More light rain. The earth lately & now very wet. . . . As Edmund has to buy almost everything needed for the consumption of his family, & for the Marlbourne farm, he is necessarily well informed as to the current prices of such commodities. From his recent inquiries, [2529] or purchases in Richmond, I note most of the following prices. And for others, which he did not know, I add on other authority. The prices are for cash, & for quantities as large as suitable for large families. Bacon, 110 cents the pound—Brown sugar, 100—salt (by retail,) 25 cents, lately, since the time for curing meat has passed—before it had been as high as 125 cents the pound. Turkeys—cocks $11, hens 6—corn $4.50 the bushel—wheat $3.50—ship-stuff, $1.50—bran, 60 cents—sweet potatoes, $12 the bushel—Irish potatoes, $8—Hay (timothy & herds grass,) $6 the 100 lbs.—Shucks, $3. Fresh pork 70 cents the lb. Fowls (grown chickens,) $2. Fresh beef $1. Cotton oznaburgs, 75 cents the yard. (The former price was 10 to 12½ cents.) . . . Edmund went yesterday & today to Beechwood. As [2530] after every previous interval of absence, he found the house had been broken open, & more pillaging of the remaining damaged articles. He has placed there to reside one of his house-servants, Abby, with her children, to serve in some measure as guardian of the mansion.

March 1. Sunday. Mrs. Cocke, being at her house for a few days, came here to dine. It is arranged that I will not wait for Nanny's visit here, & its conclusion, to go with her & my niece to Marlbourne—but will set out for Petersburg with Mrs. Cocke, in her carriage, when she returns on the 4th, & thence proceed to Marlbourne. . . . Though my stay here has been very agreeable to me, it has already extended much longer than I had expected at first, & I am anxious to get back to Marlbourne, which while being my son Edmund's residence, will be my other home. I do not expect to visit any other house, unless some much valued friend's, except these two, during the remainder of my life—nor to be abroad, except in passing from one of these residences to the other. And such passing will be rare, in the present difficulties of the journey. Some months ago, I had wished, & confidently expected, to visit, before this time, some distant friends—Wm. H. Harrison of Amelia, Judge Ruffin's family, & especially to go to Charleston. But the sundry impediments—& above all my increased deafness—have finally caused me to abandon all such intentions. . . .

March 2. Monday. The mail. . . . The Richmond Examiner of today states as advanced prices—Gold $260—butter, $2.75—fresh beef $1 to 1.25 the pound—corn meal, $5 the bushel. . . . It is still doubtful (according to the Examiner,) whether more than 15,000 men have been removed from the Yankee camp near Fredericksburg, the great body of the great army remaining in its position near Fredericksburg. I cannot believe this. For Gen. Lee must know—& he has sent off the great body of his army.—It is now two months since there has been any important battle, or important success of any kind, of the Yankee armies. And these two months were of the highest water in the western rivers, when their naval forces have every facility, [2532] of movement, to exert their almost unopposed supremacy. Yet in this time, nearly all the naval successes have been ours—& on the land, the Yankees have done nothing, & their immense armies & fleets, & preparations for action, lying idle, at the Rappahannock, at Vicksburg, in the lower Mississippi, at Murfreesborough, & at Port Royal. The long delay & inaction of all these forces, is equivalent to a great defeat in battle, which would not be more than counter-balanced by one future great victory, by some one of these five threatening armies. On the other hand, if their first attack should be effectively & disastrously defeated, it will be a calamity that all the other armies cannot compensate by any probable amount of success.—Finished reading Madame De Stael's Corinne—which I read before more than 50 years ago. I do not like it—& as a work of fiction, deem it very objectionable as to plot, incidents, & characters—& especially as to the character of its hero. Began "Harry Lorrequer."

March 4. Wednesday. Left Ruthven early & rode to Tarbay, whence with Mrs. Cocke went in her carriage to Petersburg. . . . Set off on the R.R. after 4 P.M. & reached Richmond after 7. Went to the Exchange, where I could not obtain even a single mattress & bed-clothes on the floor, & so had to share W. Newton's bed as well as his apartment, as I had designed if [not] getting a bed. Spent the evening with him, until 11, in very pleasant conversation. Mr. Forbes of Fauquier & of H. of D. & M. R. H. Garnett of H. of R.

came in, & joined us for [End of MS Volume 15—p. 2533] some time. I was glad to learn that a heavy tax bill was nearly prepared in Congress, & that an efficient one would certainly be enacted. Newton told me that a body of foraging & marauding Yankees, from Hooker's army, had lately visited Westmoreland, & committed extensive robberies of private property. From his family (at their home,) had been taken 5 valuable horses, & some 45 hams from his store of bacon. But he got of[f] cheaply compared to many of his countymen, who were stripped of almost all stores of food, horses, & even their stock of bacon burnt, when not carried off. That peninsula is especially well stocked with grain & other products, because of the want of means for two years to get to markets. Many farmers had sold no crop for two years. I suppose now that all will go to the plundering & destroying enemy, as there is no possibility of our defending that region, almost surrounded by broad waters, from the enemy commanding the water, & having every naval facility, of which we are totally destitute. . . . Several laws have been enacted in the Rump Congress which operate effectually to subvert the U.S. constitution, & all free government, & state rights & powers throughout Yankeedom, & to make Lincoln an unlimited dictator & despot. The financial bills give to him the command of the whole money & credit power of the government, & for 18 months. The military bill enables him to call into active service (& without any intermediate action of state authorities) any part or the whole of the male population between the ages of 20 & 45. He is further invested with the power of suspending the act of *habeas corpus*, when & where he may choose, & of course to imprison, without limit, & to any extent of torture, any & all opposers, without even a charge of violation of law. Of course, with these powers, the ruler is as much the master of the government, country, & people, as is the czar of Russia. And if Lincoln had one tenth-part of the intellect & talent for command of a Cromwell or a Bonaparte, he would be despotic monarch of the northern states (at least) not only for his term of service as President, but for his life, & perhaps leave the power to his son. But Lincoln is a low minded & narrow minded man, & deficient in courage as well as in intellect & education. He is utterly incompetent to exercise the enormous powers with which he has been so lavishly endowed. He must be strongly urged by his trusted ministers & leaders, to dare to attempt what he has legislative authority for. And if so daring, will the people of the North, &

especially the opposition party, (now nearly or quite a majority,) submit to this unconstitutional & crushing despotism? That is the question on which the issue will depend. Base & abject in submission to the former despotism of Lincoln, unauthorized by Congress, as were the northern people, I cannot believe that, since opposition has been aroused, & its strength estimated . . . they will submit to these regulated & formal and unconstitutional enactments & measures for the complete subversion of all freedom, individual rights, & [2535] state powers. If they do submit, the power of Lincoln, or rather of his leaders, is supreme throughout Yankeedom—& by the immense strength thus obtained, & all directed to crush the South, we may be ruined utterly, if not subjugated. But if there is enough of the spirit of freedom existing in the North to actuate the opposition party, & to increase its strength, the despotism will soon be prostrated, by revolutionary force. A first step has already been taken to exercise the new powers, & an indication of the government's intending to watch for & prevent popular insurrection, in the following: Gen. Wool has ordered & begun a strict search for all private arms & ammunition in the city of New York. This must be preliminary to their seizure by Lincoln's authority—& indicates the like disarming of all populations who are not entirely submissive to the despot & all his measures. . . .

March 5. Thursday. . . . After attending to various matters for myself, Julian, & Edmund, I left Richmond in the buggy (which had been sent for me,) before 3 P.M. & reached Marlbourne at 6. The family now reduced to Edmund & his wife & their child, Mrs. Lorraine & Mary—the last still detained from school by an obstinate tetter, & the care required for its cure. Since the purchase of Mr. Sayre's share of the property, he no longer resides here.

March 7. Saturday. . . . After the late overthrow of the U.S. constitution by the Congress, gold rose in N.Y. to 174, but settled at 172½. The "World" says that the price will be 200 by April. Cotton has latterly been 86 cents. At one time, some weeks past, it was 95. It is stranger that at New Orleans, ordinary cotton is at 60, & at Memphis, nearly as high as in New York. Flour at Mobile is $73 the barrel.—In the "Panhandle," the most traitorous part of N.W. Virginia, there seems to be a strong reaction against Yankee rule. Opinions are publicly uttered by leading men, & heretofore unionists & even traitors, which are surprising as being entertained by their authors, & expressed in that region, & still more so that they are ventured under the Yankee rulers, & military power. The report is from the Wheeling Intelligencer, a thorough Yankee abolition paper, & therefore of undoubted authority in this case. A public meeting in Wheeling was addressed by Sherrard Clemens, the former representative of that district in the U.S. Congress, & in the late State Convention—& who as soon as the act of secession had passed, adhered to the North, & has (with the North-West in general,) since remained a subject of Yankeedom.[36] . . . Such public declarations, in Wheeling, are more remarkable, as indications of reaction, than if the locality had been in Illinois or New Jersey. The boldness of the disaffected in Wheeling stands in strong contrast [2538] with the easy & speedy manner in which the Kentucky Convention in Frankfort was lately silenced & dispersed by the Yankee military force. . . .

March 8. Sunday. [Took a] . . . walk to see the farm, & especially the condition of its drainage, which is very bad, having been much neglected of late. So far as I can see, there was no clearing out of the open ditches last spring, which is a necessary & heavy job—& but few repairs of the failing covered drains. With the few men here, it will be impossible to put the drains in order this spring.—Found here Dante, translated into English verse—a work of which I have often read, but had not before seen. Began to read it—but so far, I find nothing attractive.

March 9. Monday. Another heavy rain last night—though clear this morning. The wetness of the earth & my only pair of shoes, though new, being thin-soled & very mean, have prevented my walking much. Walked before dinner, & from dinner to nearly dark I was with the [2539] men cleaning out the smaller open ditches in South Field. As yet the weather & water being too cold to stand in the water, this work has been executed imperfectly & slowly, & only of the shallower open ditches by broad hoes, the laborers standing on the dry margins. The ability to do this is an advantage of my plan of lowered ditch margins—though that plan has been yet but very partially & imperfectly carried out. I trust that I shall soon come to take as much interest in this, if not other farm-work, as I did formerly—& that I will thus be enabled to "kill time" more agree-

---

[36] A native of Wheeling, Clemens (1820–81) had been elected to Congress three times as a Democrat during the 1850's. In his public address, the former representative delivered what the Wheeling paper characterized as a "vindictive tirade" against the proposed new state of West Virginia and its leaders.

ably for myself, & also beneficially for the farm. That the property is my sons', & that I have no personal interest in its profits, will not in the least lessen the other interest that I may feel.

March 10. Tuesday. Snow, hail & rain.—The mail—& not half of our due supply of newspapers. . . . The armada of Banks & Farragut (19 war vessels & 30,000 land troops,) is moving up to attack Port Hudson.—Rosecrans' army is very cautiously advancing towards Johnston's & Bragg's at Tullahoma. . . . Board at the Ballard House, Rd., had latterly been at $6 the day, for transient persons—but was raised yesterday to $8. The prices at other houses were probably not much lower—& the food, at the best, & everywhere, very inferior. Yet 14 boarding houses in Rd. have lately been closed by the proprietors, because not remunerating the costs of keeping. Butter yesterday at $3.25 the pound. . . . Finished *looking through*, & very partially reading, Dante's "Divina Comedia." I soon wearied of reading regularly, & then read only such parts as, (directed by the headings of the Cantos,) I supposed would be interesting. . . . It is curious that Dante, who, a Florentine of the year 1300, I suppose must have been a lover of liberty, placed in the lowest abyss of hell, Brutus & Cassius, together with Judas Iscariot, the only three of the occupants he mentions.—A writer in a London paper has addressed a letter to Lord Palmerston, stating & denouncing the number of war steamers now building in Britain for the C.S., in violation of law, & the declaration of neutrality. I hope that the report is true. But if, as this writer charges, the British government has, illegally, & in violation of its professed neutrality, favored the Confederates on the ocean, & indeed enabled us to do all that our few cruisers have done, it is no contradiction, but the reverse, to what I have before charged, that the British government wishes the two parties to this war to do all possible damage to each other. Without an armed vessel for ocean service, [2541] without seamen, with all our ports blockaded, & European ports closed against our prizes, & our obtaining naval & military supplies, the C.S. could have done nothing on the ocean, & the Yankee mercantile marine, in safety, would still have successfully rivalled British ships. Therefore the government connives at the evasion of its neutrality, & permits a few armed cruisers to sail & make captures under the Confederate flag—not to send them into port, & save them in existence, as future competitors with British ships—but to destroy them, & so extinguish so many future competitors, whether as northern or southern property. To aid the C.S. so far, & in this manner only, is to enable them to fight for the benefit of England, & as much in promotion of its interests as their own. On the other hand, by denying to the C.S. the free supply of arms, ammunition & military equipments, (by recognizing as legal the blockade of our ports,) while the Yankees are supplied to any extent, & by the excluding from us, in like manner, all necessary supplies of clothing, &c., the C.S. are practically prevented from exerting half of their military power on land against their enemy, who is under none of these disadvantages, & thus is enabled to inflict a double amount of damage on the unprotected southern states. Thus, by pretending to observe neutrality, & by violating it in different modes against both parties, England enables the C.S. to greatly injure Yankeedom on the ocean, & Yankeedom to injure the C.S. on the land, & in general—&, in both cases, to forward to the greatest extent the desire & policy of England, of the North & South destroying each other, & neither gaining any power from the losses it inflicts on the other.

March 11. Raining slowly all day yesterday & last night. Snowing this morning, but cleared off by 9 A.M. The earth saturated with water, & the streams greatly swollen. Very bad for the farm, & especially [2542] as to its much needed & very backward ploughing & draining—both now stopped for some days to come. This will add another fortnight to the delay of the advance of Gen. Hooker's army—even if, as northern reports state, its demoralization did not prohibit its advance. . . .

March 12. Very cold. Strong west wind. . . . A messenger from Mr. Boulware (passing on to Richmond,) brought a letter with a present of 6 ducks, & a loan of a few books. Both the present & the loan very acceptable. One of the books, "A Strange Story," by [Edward George] Bulwer[-Lytton], is the only publication, other than a few Yankee newspapers, which I have seen, brought from the North or from Europe, since the beginning of the war.[37] Though all other commodities are obtained (at enormous prices,) either by smuggling from Maryland, or from Europe, by running the blockade, all books & periodicals have been completely shut out. Even the extracts from European newspapers which are republished in ours, are received only through Yankee reprints. Began at night to read the "Strange Story."

---

[37] This novel was published in 1862.

March 13. Friday. Very raw & cold.—The mail. Almost no new events of war. It seems confirmed, by repetition & lapse of time, that the Yankee army of the Potomac still holds its former position near the Rappahannock, and threatening to advance by way of Fredericksburg, when the state of earth will permit. This long suspension of nearly all military operations by the enemy, & every delay now, is to their great disadvantage, & indirectly for our benefit. But whenever they shall begin to advance, I hope it will be with this army, & upon Charleston. [2543] . . . A heavy loss by fire has occurred in Richmond, in the burning of the public (State) tobacco Warehouse. The tobacco burnt, (for which the State is responsible,) & the building, estimated at from 2 to 500,000$. And military stores belonging to the C.S. in the same building, & lost, from 1 to 200,000$. The whole loss, to both public & private owners, nearly $1,000,000.—The Yankee authorities have determined to have the farms near Hampton, which have been wasted & abandoned, planted in cotton. A ton of seed has been sent (from N.Y.,) & of course the slaves who have deserted or have been stolen from their owners, are to be the cultivators. This farming will prove as unprofitable as the like attempt in S.C. last year—of which, it was declared in a speech in the Yankee congress, & not contradicted, that every pound of cotton so produced cost the government $20.—At Norfolk, as in every other place within the lines of the Yankee armies, & entirely submitted to their domination, (& as it was here last May,) the slaves are free from their [2544] obligations & usage of service to their owners. With few exceptions, they render no service or obedience, & do no work. They occupy the houses of their refugee owners, or others, use their furniture, & live upon or sell the provisions or other moveables. When not at compulsory labor for the Yankee armies, the male slaves perform little steady work for their own support. Many find easy living as waiters to the Yankee officers & soldiers. Many females get good wages as washerwomen. And all can pick up something to eat in or about a camp. But where these facilities have ceased to be available, as in Washington, the condition of the numerous absconded & stolen slaves is wretched in the extreme. Thousands will have perished with cold, hunger, & neglect in sickness, before the end of cold weather. It was reported lately that in Washington alone, the negroes were dying of small-pox at the rate of 15 a day.—It is a mystery what has become of all the numerous slaves which have been in possession of the Yankee armies & fleets, after making every allowance for those gaining support by employment or by pillage, & all removed by emigration & death. A few shipments were made to Hayti. But that soon stopped. Some (say even a few thousands,) have gone to the northern cities, & to the north-western states. But all these could scarcely amount to 5000. For such clamor was produced in the North whenever any negroes were brought there to settle, by the laboring poor who deemed that injurious competition was thus forced on them, that we should have heard of more discontent, & popular outbreaks about immigrant negroes, had their numbers been very great, or the supply continuous. It has been charged that vessels full of negroes have gone from Fortress Monroe to the South-east, & supposed to Cuba, for sale. But allowing for all removals & deaths, there must be full nine-tenths of all the stolen slaves, now living, still in the C.S., under protection of the Yankee forces. These will be much lessened by disease & death, if the war lasts much longer. But when [2545] peace comes, with the established nationality of the C.S., what will become of the one or two hundred thousands of still remaining abducted slaves? The Yankee people, east or north-west, will certainly not receive them in their territory— & even if willing to have them as residents, would not pay the necessary expense for their removal, & support of the helpless. They will not pay either to remove them to Liberia— & if willing to pay the expense, the negroes would reject the boon, & prefer the alternative of their return to slavery. Thus, I think that most of the living absconded slaves will remain in the country, & fall back to their former condition & owners. But hereafter, especially as to these recaptured slaves, but also as to all others, a more strict police & government or discipline will have to be enforced, than had prevailed before the war. . . .

March 14. Saturday. Still very cold. Walked out to the work, (in nearest field,) morning & afternoon—but did not remain long. . . . The insurrectionary movement in Russian Poland is gaining strength, & assuming formidable proportions.[38] Prussia, Austria, & France, in different ways, as their peculiar interests are like to be affected, are indicating their concern or fears. I fear that this prospect of more extended difficulties between European powers may

---

[38] This revolution erupted in January, 1863, and was not fully suppressed for more than a year. Efforts toward diplomatic intervention by France, England, and Austria were frustrated by Prussia's firm stand in support of Russia.

indispose the French Emperor to bully Yankeedom, lest he might have more wars on his hands at once than he could well manage. Otherwise, & if he knows the true interest of France & of himself, as may be supposed of so sagacious a ruler, he will use the offered opportunity to break the Yankee blockade, regardless whether war with Yankeedom is to follow or not—& as the price of that service, obtain from [2546] the C.S. a commercial treaty of reciprocal free trade & navigation (or a near approach to both,) which will more promote the commercial interests of France than any & all such advantages acquired in the last century. While for such benefit to us, I would be glad to make such a treaty exclusively with France, for a long but limited time, I would also be glad of it because it would inflict a heavy blow on both English & Yankee commerce, which England deserves for its cold-blooded enmity to us, & desire for our greatest injury from our enemy, short of absolute destruction. As to Yankeedom, I trust that its future peaceful trade with us will always be burdened by imposts far heavier than on those of the "most favored" & friendly nations. Within 15 days I expect to hear important news from France. Or if not, my hopes of indirect aid to the C.S. from that quarter will be at an end.

March 16. Monday. . . . The continued rise of prices, much of which (at least as to provisions,) must be owing to the depreciation of our paper currency, & the financial credit of the C.S.—the difficulty of the purchase of necessaries by individuals, & not only the difficulty & high cost, but the impossibility of the government supplying our armies—all cause to me gloomy for[e]bodings of our future. In a general & gradual depreciation of the currency, the ignorant see only a general enhancement of prices. And even to the better informed who understand the general fact of depreciation, it is difficult to estimate its full measure, & to allow for as much as is admitted, generally, in every particular purchase. Thus, even though admitting that our currency may already [2547] [have] depreciated 50 percent, or that the current dollar is worth but 50 cents, I & most others cannot always bear in mind that full one half of the high price of every article is nominal, & that the real cost, or price, is but half of the nominal amount. This error may, & probably does, produce some economical benefits. For, under the general mistake that all commodities are sold at double the true cost, every buyer & consumer is prompted & even compelled, to buy & consume as little as possible—& every producer, by the same mistake, is stimulated to produce, by increased industry & economy, as much as possible for sale, of the products of his business, while they are commanding prices supposed to be double of what the scarcity of the commodities would alone require.—Gen. Banks, commanding the Yankee forces in Louisiana, is trying to carry out in practice, & in detail, the Yankee theories of emancipation. He has established rules for a general system in all of La. under his military domination. In these regulations, the planters (yet remaining there,) have concurred, doubtless under coercion, to avoid the alternative of losing everything. Their apparent concurrence is no evidence that they do not deem the scheme as absurd & impracticable as I do, & as ruinous, if the trial should be continued long. The slaves of La, as all others within the long-continued military occupancy of the Yankee forces, were practically freed, long before Lincoln's proclamation of emancipation. According to Gen. Banks' later orders, & prescribed system, the planters are to hire the labor by the year, of their own slaves, and to furnish them food (& perhaps allowances of other necessaries of life,) at certain general rates ordered by Gen. Banks. In return, the negro hirelings are required & to be compelled to perform fair work, & obey their employer's proper commands. . . . Every abolitionist of New [2548] England believes that by thus merely changing slave labor to hireling labor . . . everything will work well. Every man raised among negro slaves knows that the scheme, with any variations of particular features, is sure of utter failure, & probably before the first diminished crops will be partially secured. As the planters have acceded to this scheme, to prevent their lands lying waste, & their yet remaining slaves being dispersed & lost, so, for the same reasons, & for a few months, they may continue to pay high hires, & to comply fully with their heavy obligations to their former slaves. But even if so, the negro laborers will presume on their new rights of freedom, & of protection against their master by a higher & despotic authority, to be more or less wanting in due respect to the employer, to be careless of strict obedience, to be indolent, if not still more insubordinate. Such conduct will demand punishment, (if to be proved,) & may receive it, under Gen. Banks' rules, & by sentence of his subordinate authorities. It is easy to foresee that these effects will be causes of still greater effects of like kind. The laborer's violations of duty, when slight, will rarely be capable of being proved if charged before the Yankee tribunal. The employer's tyranny, & failures to supply the engaged allowances, in many cases will be as difficult to be proved—& whether true or not, such offences will continually be suspected by the negro, & often brought as charges against the master. From these causes alone, there would be general & growing irritation, faults on both sides, & probably, even by the judgment & sentence of the Yankee judicial protectors of the negro laborers, there would be much more of punishment inflicted for each plantation, than had ever occurred when every laborer was the slave of a master exercising almost unlimited authority. So far as to the laborers & hirelings. But these will not be half the difficulties. Each laborer is free—& therefore is bound to support his wife & children incapable of labor. The sons, [2549] of mature age & strength, must support their infirm & helpless parents. In all such cases, these burdens will be grudgingly borne, by husbands, fathers, & children—because they have been accustomed to have them borne by their former masters, & also because the ties of family affection among negroes are generally too feeble to induce the heavy sacrifices required for such duties. If the support of infirm wives, young children, & aged & helpless parents, is to be a voluntary duty, one half of such burdens would be speedily thrown off—& the helpless will be left to starve, unless saved by some other aid than that of their able-bodied husbands, fathers, or sons. Such results, & illustrations, might be greatly extended. But it is unnecessary. It is safe to predict the entire failure of this, & also of any other variations of the experiment of the great abolition problem of converting negro slaves to profitable free laborers, by merely giving them freedom, & offering to them fair wages for fair labor. Even if this change can ever be produced, in general, as to negroes, (which I do not believe,) it can only be done, & to a limited extent, by the emancipated slaves passing through an intermediate condition—which would be that of hunger & general privation & suffering, next to starving. But few white laborers, of the lowest classes, will labor continuously unless under the compulsion of hunger & suffering of themselves & their familys [*sic*]. Still fewer free negroes will labor without this compulsion . . . . Now I readily admit that by this way of impending starvation, & by this only, the negro, like the white laborer, may be compelled to work, & even to work effectively, & for low wages—lower than would be the cost of his maintenance as a slave. But for this, certain conditions are required, & these do not now exist in Louisiana. They are presented in the north-eastern states of Yankeedom. [2550] There, the land is fully occupied, & put to use. Most pursuits of industry are also filled, & new competitors for employment have difficulty in obtaining it. The long & severe winters greatly increase the necessity & costs for shelter, clothing & fuel. If the southern fugitive slave is removed to where these conditions exist, his natural indolence & improvidence must yield to hunger. He *must* labor, & continuously—for the day on which he suspends labor will precede one without bread. . . .

March 17. Tuesday. Mail day—&, as is not unusual, out of three different Richmond papers which we take, we got not one of to-day—& only one, of Petersburg, as late as the 14th. But by going to the Post Office, I saw a paper of today.—The light Yankee flotilla had descended the Yazoo Pass to near the mouth of the Tallahatchie river, where it empties into the Yazoo river. Our Fort Pemberton stands there—which the flotilla attacked & bombarded, on the 13th, to little purpose, & then retreated. It is strange that this fleet has been permitted to go so far, with so little opposition. But I trust that the return of the vessels will be intercepted by the falling of trees across the many narrow passages on this route, & that they will be captured. Another & more important repulse, or defeat, of another Yankee fleet occurred on the 15th inst. Farragut's whole naval force assailed our batteries at Port Hudson, & bombarded them for a considerable time, doing little damage. Two of the armed vessels only succeeded in passing up by the batteries, but both (as supposed) much damaged by our cannon. One large steamer, the Mississippi, [2551] carrying 11 cannon, was set on fire by our batteries, & burnt to the water. Some others supposed to be damaged—& all the remaining vessels retreated from the contest.—A terrible accident has occurred in Richmond. An explosion of gunpowder in a government cartridge factory killed 10 or 12 of the operatives, & burnt or wounded, more or less severely, from 20 to 30 others.[39] Most of the sufferers were young women. . . . I fear that the finances of the C.S. are in great danger, & mainly from the inefficiency of our despicable Congress. This body has been now for months discussing a tax bill, in secret session, & has yet completed nothing to sustain the public credit. I fear that the end will be repudiation of the public debt, which will be worse because

---

[39] Actually, sixty-nine persons, sixty-two of them women, were killed or injured in the explosion at the Confederate Ordnance Laboratory on March 13.

more disgraceful than bankruptcy, or absolute inability to repay the public debt, or provide for the punctual discharge of its interest. Prices of all commodities continue to rise, & more rapidly of late. Some of those of farming products, for yesterday, as obtained from the best authority, were as follows: Wheat, $5 to 5.50 the bushel—Corn, $5 to 5.25—Oats, $5 to 5.50—Wheat, oat, or rye-straw, packed in bales, $3 the 100 lbs—Bacon, $1.25 the lb.—Irish potatoes, $9 to 10 the bushel. Gold in Rd. is $4 premium, & the brokers asking $4.25. State bank bills (which have long disappeared from circulation,) are 75 to 90 cents premium on C.S. Treasury notes, which make the whole currency. Yet, I have made all of my small investments in C.S. bonds—& with any surplus funds should still do the same, not knowing what better to do, for both private & public interests.—For want of anything else to read, began on the plays of Shakespeare. All these I read before I was 11 years old, & sundry of them not later. . . .

March 19. Thursday. This morning we were surprised to find that my grandson Thomas was here. He had arrived from his camp about 1 or 2 o'clock in the night—& rather than disturb any of the family by knocking for entrance, he lay down on his blankets in the porch, & slept there the remainder of the night. He came to exchange his horse, & will go on to join his company tomorrow morning. His brigade set off yesterday from the camp in Essex, for Culpeper, to meet the advance of the Yankee army. Part of the cavalry & light artillery of Hooker's army had crossed the Rappahannock into Culpeper, having driven back our out-posts on that route.—I was out from immediately after breakfast to nearly 2 P.M. superintending & directing work, & with much interest. It was the clearing out of fallen trees, & other obstructions, in the stream which is the dividing line between this farm & Spring Garden, & into which our main ditch discharges at its north outlet. There is much more fall in this boundary stream than I had suspected. If it was straightened & deepened, it would be a great improvement to the main ditch, by drawing off much of the sand & mud which the caving [2553] of the sides puts therein, & which mostly remains there until thrown out. . . . At 5 P.M. fine snow began to fall fast, with a strong N.E. wind.

March 20. Friday. Snowing still fast though fine, & wind N.W. Sent for the due mail both morning & evening, but it had not been brought to the Post-Office—& now, probably will not be, until the next semi-weekly time. The disappointment was doubly great in this very dull time, with nothing to employ or amuse me, & sanguine expectations of there being important news in the papers which are thus withheld from us. The snow ceased falling after 3 P.M. when its depth was about 6 inches, as judged from the windows—as I did not go out of the house. Wretched weather, & a wretchedly dull time.

March 21. Saturday. Again snowing this morning, next fine hail, & then very slow drizzle, or thick mist, through the day. Warmer, & snow melting fast.—In afternoon, I rode to the Post Office in hopes of seeing some paper, or hearing some news. A paper of yesterday had been seen by Mr. Lipscomb, the tavern-keeper & Post Master. It stated of the fight of which we had before heard the first rumor, that the enemy, 12,000 strong, crossed the Rappahannock into Culpeper, & were opposed by Gen. Fitzhugh Lee's brigade of cavalry, posted there, & only 2000 in number. There was fighting on the 18th & 19th—which ended in the enemy being completely repulsed, & driven back across the river. Our loss of men was heavy, said to be 250. The enemy's loss not then known—but it must have been much heavier, if their numbers & their defeat were truly stated.[40] They left most or all of their dead where they fell. [2554]

March 24. Tuesday. The mail, & sundry newspapers, at last, but not half as many as were due. No full particulars yet of the late attacks & repulses of the enemy at Port Hudson & Fort Pemberton—nor of our later victory in Culpeper. Our advantages in the latter were not over-stated at first. The Yankee gunboat flotilla made two attempts on Fort Pemberton, & were repulsed effectively in each. . . . By private letter, we learn that a brigade is now at work again constructing fortifications on James river, at old Fort Powhatan. If this had been done, & in proper manner, early in last year, it might have prevented the Yankees passing higher up the river, & all the pillage & devastation they have committed above—laying the river farms waste—& even have cut off the supplies from

---

[40] This second-hand report of the sharp action at Kelly's Ford on March 17 was inaccurate with respect to numbers and casualties of the opposing units. The Federal force, Brigadier General William W. Averell's Second Cavalry Division, numbered only 2,100 and suffered but 78 casualties. Confederate losses numbered 133, including Major John Pelham—"the gallant Pelham"—who was mortally wounded by a shell fragment while leading a charge at the height of the engagement.

McClellan's army, after its retreat to James river. It might have made a difference to my son Edmund, alone, between $100,000 of value lost on his two farms Beechwood & Evelynton, & perhaps 40,000 made thereon, if the property had been saved, & the crops secured, & sold at the later enormous prices.—Our Congress has at last passed [2557] a currency bill, & is about to pass a heavy tax bill. These long delayed measures will now, I trust, do much to stay the depreciation of our currency, & sustain the credit of the C.S. Of the tax-bill, the particular features are not yet known. Of the efficiency of the currency act I am not qualified to judge. Its designed operation is to induce & coerce the funding of the treasury notes, which make up nearly the whole of the currency of the C.S., in bonds, to make part of the public debt of the C.S. The continued issue of treasury notes, to the limit of $50,000,000 a month is authorized. I fear that this issue will exceed all the absorbtion of that currency by new investments in the bonds of the C.S.—It is reported, in European papers, that a loan of considerable amount (but particulars not stated,) for the C.S. had been negotiated on the continent.[41] In this loan, English capitalists had no share, which they seem to regret. This, if true, will be good aid for our cause—not only in the direct benefit of the money borrowed, but in exhibiting the confidence of European capitalists in the success & pecuniary responsibility of the C.S.—Port Hudson is described as a very strong position. The fortifications are on an elevated bluff—& the channel & current of the river compel all passing vessels to come in very near to the bluff, & so exposed to the fire of our artillery, that no vessels can pass without injury, or attempt it without great risk of being destroyed. A land attack from the rear, in sufficient force, only can take the place. Such attacks, by land forces combined with the gunboats, are the great threatened dangers of both Port Hudson & Vicksburg.—Slow rain began again before sunset—increased to bed-time.

March 25. Wednesday.—Rain all night, & until after sunrise this morning. The earth again soaked with water, & much standing on the surface on the ploughed land. All early prospect of work on the

---

[41] This was the celebrated Erlanger loan, opened on March 18 by an influential French banking house. The loan was based upon seven percent bonds secured by southern cotton and payable after twenty years. The scheme proved to be highly lucrative for Erlanger and Company but not to the Confederacy, which ultimately received but $2,600,000 from bonds backed by cotton valued at $45,000,000. Still, this was better than the gain realized by the bondholders, whose investments became a total loss following the collapse of the Confederacy.

farm, in the two greatly needed operations of ploughing & draining, again postponed. . . . The last published prices current of provisions in Richmond . . . show the enormous & still increasing expenses of living, & of the bare necessaries of life, to those who like us have everything to buy, & nothing to sell. The premium on gold [which] had risen as high as $4.25, (or the price, $5.25 in C.S. treasury notes,) fell 50 cents, or to $3.75 premium in one day. . . .

March 26. Thursday.—The arranged beginning of regular ditching was attempted this morning, but prevented by the threatening of stormy weather. There was, however, no more than slow drizzle, with some fine hail, & a change of temperature to colder. I was much disappointed. I shall, it being with consent, & wish of my son, direct the draining labors in general, & superintend them so far as may suit my ability & convenience. It will not only be a profitable means of killing much of my tedious time, but a great pleasure, to renew & continue to carry out & perfect my general plans of drainage. These have been but little advanced or improved, by any labors performed, since I ceased to direct the drainage of the farm. Yet my previous labors, as then expected, have grown in their draining effect. Parts of the formerly very wet low ground, with no addition to my former labors, are now much freer from injurious under-water than six years ago, though this winter & spring so far have been the most rainy ever known. On other parts, where the covered drains, of later as well as early construction, have failed, or have been unable to carry the unusual supply of water, the land is as wet & miry as if no draining had ever been performed. The drizzle ceased by 10 A.M., & I took another long walk, examining the operation & failures of drains.

March 27. Friday. The mail—but as most usual, no paper of today. . . . A letter from Thomas. After proceeding a day's journey towards Culpeper, in pursuit of his brigade of cavalry, he learned that its attempted march was made impracticable by the bad condition of the roads, & that all had been ordered back to their former quarters in Essex, where he had followed & joined his company. For some time back, the men have had but little more than half rations of bacon—& the horses no food but corn. Under such privation of long forage, the horses must sink rapidly, & die before long. I fear that such want of food is very general in our army in eastern Va. . . . Before sunset, our friend Mr. Boulware arrived, from Richmond, on his way homeward. Of course, we had with him very agreeable conversation, though to me much lessened by my difficulty of hearing when four or five persons are engaged in conversation. . . . Our conversation (as always,) mostly on the present political & military condition of the country, & the recent events. Mr. B. brought us a paper of today, with later news than I had seen. According to the official dispatch of Gen. Pemberton, another attempt, on 25th, was made by two of the Yankee gun-boats to pass down the river by our batteries at Vicksburg. (Of course they must have been strong iron-clad steamers, as none others could have any chance to escape.) They were fired upon from our batteries, with great accuracy & effect. One was sunk by the fire, & went down opposite the batteries, with all on board. The other was lying at the "mouth of the canal" . . . & apparently had been severely crippled.[42] . . . Mr. Boulware brought some interesting statements which have not been published. He had seen a manuscript article written in & sent from England lately, by our distinguished countryman Capt. M. Maury, C.S.N., on our political affairs, & English opinions in regard to them. The writing was without his name, & without any direction as to its use, but sent to a near friend & relative, & must have been designed to be published, as I trust it will be. The writer says that the mass of the people of England are opposed to the C.S. & their success, & favorable to the cause of the North. (This opinion receives confirmation, as to the laboring classes, in the resolutions, favoring the North, of several public meetings, in districts suffering greatly by the war, & especially by the privation of cotton.) He further says that many capitalists, holding some 400,000 bales of cotton at the existing enormous prices, are opposed to the success of the C.S. & to peace, as either would bring down the price of cotton, to their great loss. Our only friends in England are among the aristocracy. But these are mostly abolitionists, who [2563] earnestly desire the independence of the C.S., but under the opinion that that result, by removing the (supposed) heretofore existing *support* of slavery by the North, will most effectually cause the downfall of the institution of slavery in the South. An important cause & element of the hostility of the common people of England to the South, & to its institution of negro-slavery, is, that a million & a half of emigrants from Britain & Ireland are residents of the

---

[42] This report was essentially correct. The Federal ram *Lancaster* was sunk, though most of the crew escaped, while *Switzerland* was disabled in this attempt to run the Vicksburg batteries from north to south.

northern states. These naturally assume the abolition creed, & strong hostility to the South, of the Yankees among whom they are settled, & from whom they learn all that they know of slavery. These emigrants keep up correspondence with their friends in Britain, &, on them, operate as propagandists & missionaries of abolition doctrines. These views of Capt. Maury seem to me to have much force. But our friends in England, who are so because hoping for the destruction of our institution of slavery through our separation from the North, will be completely disappointed in that expectation. Thousands of slaveholders will be robbed of their slaves by the Yankees during the war, & thereby empoverished [*sic*] or ruined. But even if we should thus lose 300,000 slaves, it will scarcely affect the general condition & value of slave property. And after peace, the institution of slavery in the C.S. will be more firmly established, better secured, & more profitable to the owners & to the community, than ever before. This greater value & security will be owing to our separation from the North, & thereby cutting off (& partly extinguishing,) the anti-slavery propagandism & hostility of Yankee missionaries. When separated from the North, they will have no political ends to serve in warring against slavery in the South—& they will become as quiet on that subject in regard to the C.S., as they have always been as to Brazil & Cuba. But independent of this operation, the people of the North will be greatly changed in opinions as to slavery by the opportunities afforded by the war to see slavery & [2564] the slaves at home, & both in something like their true colors, instead of through the false medium of ignorant prejudice. Most Yankee soldiers who have served in the South, will return to their homes either better informed of, & therefore less inimical to the institution of slavery—or otherwise with strong feelings of hatred or contempt of the negroes, in place of their previous theoretical favor to them, & of hatred to their owners. . . .

March 29. Sunday. Strong & cold north wind. More rain fell yesterday [2565] . . . & the earth is again very wet. The water in the two wells has been gradually rising through the winter & spring, & now stands higher than known before. In the well near to east side of North Field, by rough measurement, I found the water today within 30 inches of the surface of the ground—& in the well by the farm road, the water at 15 inches.—The number of the wounded & badly burnt, by the late explosion of the cartridge factory in Richmond, who have since died, increased the killed from the first named 12, to 34.

March 30. Monday. Edmund set out for Amelia—to return next Thursday, & by appointment to bring home Nanny, & Juliana [Dupuy] &c, from Richmond.—Still cold—a strong N.E. wind. I was with the work (cleaning out northern end, & out-let, of main ditch, with broad hoes,) nearly all day.—Edmund sent back by his servant newspapers of today.—The Yankee account of the late fight at Kelly's Ford, states their whole number of casualties as within 40 men. Our reports of our total losses began with 250, & reduced them to 100. However much the Yankee reporters may have lied, I believe that ours beat them in that respect on this occasion—& that our much boasted & great victory, as represented by *all* reports on our side, was really more a defeat than a success, in the fight. I infer this from the latter silence of our authorities, as to all details, & from my sifting the particulars of the full private statements published on our side, as well as from the enemy's opposite report. Whatever was the object & intention of their advance was doubtless frustrated, or cut short, by the resistance of our troops. But in the fighting, I am forced to believe that our side was more damaged than the enemy. It is a pity & a shame, that our first reporters of battles, & even some of official character in the first concise dispatches, seem to emulate Yankee commanders in their monstrous falsehoods, in exaggeration or perversion of facts. . . . Northern papers have more false news of the excellent condition of their armies & prospective successes. Their Secretary of War has been assured that we were preparing to abandon Richmond, & that our authorities & defending forces would retire farther south for safety. Lincoln is said to be more sanguine than since the war was in full progress. They report various successful operations which we know to be entirely false, but which serve to keep up the spirits of the northern people—& such reports are not contradicted, except by facts in the lapse of time. Among these reports are these—that *all* of Admiral Farragut's fleet (instead of two vessels only,) passed by Port Hudson, with the exception of the Mississippi, admitted to be burnt & destroyed by our fire—& that their light flotilla had got through the interior waters into the Yazoo, & in rear of Vicksburg. . . . The N.Y. Herald expected the attack on Charleston to be made at the equinoctial & also new moon high tides. As it was not then ventured, it may be about the 2nd of April, with the full moon high tides. An early attempt is the more probable, as the armada at Port Royal has lately been increased by 25 vessels, & when last reported from Charleston, the whole number of war vessels & transports amounted to 150. . . . The London Quarterly Review, referring to the American policy of the Palmerston ministry, says—"Whatever may have been the merits of its American policy, we have obtained in that quarter simply the hatred of the North, the contempt of the South, & the ruin of the staple industry of England."

March 31. Tuesday. Heavy rain last night, & still continuing slowly today. It has been raining half of the past month, which is usually so drying, added to the wettest preceding two months ever known. Raining until noon.—The mail brought but few of our due papers, & in these, no later news. [2569] . . . It is to be feared that the insurrection in Poland, & the probability of its extending war to other continental powers, will prevent any chance for the intervention of France in the American war, which otherwise there was such good grounds to expect. . . . Sunshine after 3 P.M. &, I trust, the weather becoming mild. The earth again soaked, & full of water—& the streams much swollen.

1863

THE RICHMOND "BREAD RIOT" ☙ UNION
IRONCLADS REPULSED AT CHARLESTON ☙
"CONSULTING AGRICULTURIST" AT MARL-
BOURNE ☙ STONEMAN'S CAVALRY RAID
MARLBOURNE ☙ A EULOGY TO STONEWALL
JACKSON ☙ DENUNCIATION OF JEFFER-
SONIAN DEMOCRACY ☙ GRANT BESIEGES
VICKSBURG ☙ LEE PREPARES TO MOVE
NORTH

April 1. Thin ice. Still strong wind, first North & then West,
until night. This wind will serve to counterbalance much of the
effect of the full moon, in making high tides, & so far will operate
against the threatened entrance of the Yankee fleet into Charleston
harbor, which was understood, since the last postponement, to be
fixed for tomorrow or next day.—Two walks & reading Shakespeare
(very dull,) occupied my time through the day.

April 2. Thursday. Violent wind from S.W. all day, & at night still
strong, from South. Turning warm fast. . . . This morning, very
early, the carriage & a wagon, & a saddle horse sent to Richmond to
meet & bring home Edmund &c. They arrived early in the afternoon—Nanny, my niece Juliana Dupuy & my granddaughter Jane
R. Dupuy, John & Meade Ruffin, & also Sue to spend at home her
holidays for Easter. A paper of today contained no news—but my
son brought verbal report of more awful portent than the loss of a
bloody battle. Provisions especially, & every necessary of living,
have continued to rise in price still more rapidly of late. Corn was
sold yesterday at $11 the bushel. One consequence was a "bread
riot," a thing without precedent in this state before. A mob of low
men & women (the latter mostly Irish,) openly broke into stores
containing bacon & other provisions, plundered & carried off the
stolen articles to their homes, & almost without resistance—though

finally the plunderers were dispersed, & some of the men arrested. Edmund did not see the mob except at a distance—but saw low Irish women hurrying from the scene of operations, with their arms full of bacon or other plunder. At the time, he was getting from the R.R. Depot a hogshead of bacon, which he had bought some weeks before in Petersburg, & which narrowly escaped being seen & of course plundered by the mob. He had to send his wagon & bacon by a remote circuit to again reach the hotel, there to take in the ladies' trunks, & thence by a back street homeward. As was to be expected, the plunderers did not confine their pillage to articles of food, but seized & carried of[f] everything else they could find, & of any value to them whether for use or sale. And these crimes were openly committed in the principal business streets of Richmond, the capital of Virginia & of the Confederate States, & almost without opposition from the police, or danger to the criminals! The first example of such a [2571] "bread riot" occurred lately in Salisbury N.C. There, the actors were all women, mostly soldiers' wives, & doubtless in great want. Their demands were quieted by a few barrels of flour &c. from each of the largest holders of provisions in store. In consideration of who were the plunderers, & the subjects of plunder, this ominous beginning was passed over without any attempt at punishment, & indeed was regarded by the public more as subject for amusement, & indulgence, than for legal punishment. Next, the example, with increased vigor no doubt, was attempted in Petersburg, on yesterday. But there was forewarning of the design, & the rioters were quickly suppressed. The next attempt, & successful to considerable extent, as I have stated, was this in Richmond. And if the police & the government are so shamefully inert, we may expect that portable property of every kind will soon be at the mercy of the necessitous & vile, & not only in towns but throughout the country, & on every private farm & residence. On the abandoned & vacant farms it had been so before—except that the general pillage had been effected in secret, & not openly & boldly. All the stores & mansions in Richmond were closed as soon as this riot was known to be in progress.—But setting aside these worst consequences, which the inertness of governmental authority only will invite & permit, what can be done by the people who have to buy food at these monstrous & rapidly growing prices? A still more important & awful question, is, how can the government

support armies with corn at $11 the bushel, and all other neces-
saries at prices not much less enormous? This state of things causes
to me the first & only feelings, & presents the only grounds, for
despondence for our final military success, & triumph over our
enemy. The Yankee authorities are fully aware of this being our
greatest danger. And for nearly a year back, their always villainous
outrages on private property, have been especially & systematically directed to [2572] destroying every where, (when they could
not carry it off,) the food of the country, & destroying all the means
for tilling & making later crops. With this view, they have stolen or
enfranchised the slaves, carried off the beasts for labor or food,
broken the farming utensils, &, where they had power, forbade all
cultivation, unless under their control & for their benefit. And on
vast spaces of the most fertile & productive lands, along the rivers
open to the passage of their vessels, though they could not occupy
these lands, the Yankees have made or threatened hasty raids, for
plunder & destruction, the mere liability to which would prevent
any proprietor attempting to cultivate a crop. Thus now lie waste all
the farms on James river which were abandoned because of the
former close vicinity of the enemy—& [on] all other farms thereon,
which will be cultivated, it will be done under the conviction that a
single transient visit of a single gunboat may destroy all the prospects, or fruits, of the labors of the year, & also all the moveable &
destructible property of the farm. Under such circumstances, there
will be but little cultivation on thousands of farms which perhaps
may never be occupied by the enemy, or visited by their plundering parties. Where cultivation is attempted, in the exposed
localities, as on this farm, it is under great disadvantages, for want of
sufficient & proper laborers, teams, & other stock & facilities,
which cannot be at once replaced, when there is risk of losing all by
another sudden invasion of the plunderers & destroyers.

April 3. Friday.—Wind N.E. & pretty strong. Continued the . . .
ditching work, & attended to it with much interest through the day.
At night, its suspension was ordered, because the weather had
become so cold. All others of the family went to church.—The mail.
As usual, not half our papers. In the only one for today, no allusion is
made to the mob & riot of yesterday, silence being dictated by
policy. . . . The N.Y. "World," an opposition paper, pronounces that
the Yazoo pass scheme, & the other west of the Mississippi, are
hopeless failures—& that the canal by Vicksburg only has not

already failed of any success.[1] . . . As it seems that our fortification Fort Pemberton is impregnable to the Yankees' arms, they are trying, & expect confidently to overflow it, by the water of the Mississippi. They are cutting away the levee for a mile or more in length, & will, to that extent, turn in the flood, which is now 8 feet higher than the waters of the Yazoo &c. The ground on which our fortification stands, though the highest, is but 4 feet above the previous height of water. Thus, they expect, by overflowing the site, to render our fortification useless & untenable, & also, by the general & high overflow of all the neighboring country, to prevent the approach & ambuscades of our infantry, by which the invaders have been much annoyed & impeded. Also the like plan of destroying a long stretch of the levee is to be carried out on the western side, greatly raising the height & violence of the flood which had already been so turned into Lake Providence, & the head waters of the Wachita [*sic*—Ouachita], Black, & Tensas rivers. This emptying of the high water of the Mississippi on the before dyked lowland, will cover thousands of the most fertile plantations, & lay utterly waste an extensive region of before productive country. This flooding on the West side can aid no military or naval operation, & is therefore entirely for the destruction of private property, & the ruin & destitution of all the inhabitants. [2574] So barbarous & extensive an act of general devastation has not been executed by any power in modern times, since Louis 14th. laid waste the Palatinate. . . . The Va. legislature adjourned finally on 31st. ult. A heavy state tax bill was passed. . . . A long & able paper, by W. B. Reed of Phila, & also an able speech of [Clement L.] Valandingham [*sic*], delivered in N.Y. to the Democratic Association, have lately been published. Both advocate the immediate cessation of the war, unconditionally, & the making of peace with recognition of the C.S. Vallandigham treats with due severity & scorn the democrats who, while professing to desire peace, advocate the vigorous prosecution of the war, & reconstruction of the former Union as a condition

---

[1] Following the failure of the Yazoo Pass expedition in mid-March, a cooperative venture involving the gunboats of Admiral David D. Porter and infantry commanded by General Sherman was initiated against Vicksburg by way of Steele's Bayou. This too failed, as did other projects west of the Mississippi. Finally, on March 29, Grant began to open a road for his army from Milliken's Bend, Louisiana, to a point south of Vicksburg on the west side of the river. Inaugurated after five fruitless attempts to capture Vicksburg, this operation was destined to be successful after three months of bold and imaginative campaigning.

of peace. It is true that he also looks forward to re-construction, as likely to be the wish of the independent C.S. after time shall have smoothed the asperities & abated the animosities produced by the war & its outrages. If Mr. V. & the northern peace party can "lay this flattering unction to their souls," be it so—& we need not trouble ourselves, or say a word, to dispel their illusion. On the contrary, I wish it may extend as far as possible, & have the greatest effect, on northern minds. Their error will bind us to nothing for the future. And if, without compromising our independence, or any political principles or rights by surrender, I am willing to make peace almost without conditions, & leave it to the future, & our then established strength & abundant means for war, to assert & maintain any rights ignored & passed over at first. But if peace is made, & the boundaries of the recognized C.S. merely include the slave-holding states which by their free & formal votes choose to make parts of the C.S., though many of our just & important rights of property may remain unsatisfied, we will have peaceable & more operative means than war to obtain justice. While we should be ready to make a treaty of peace upon the mere cessation & withdrawal of the [2576] invasion & occupation of our territory & waters, we should never consent to yield, or to reciprocate, any commercial advantages, or to permit any trade or commercial operations of the Yankee people in our territory, or in our waters, unless under heavy burdens compared to the facilities of friendly & favored nations, until such measure of justice had been rendered to us as we would be content with as an acquittance for all claims. Such postponed yet to be enforced claims should certainly include the payment for the just share of the former U.S. navy for the C.S.—their just share of the value of the public lands—the surrender of the island fortresses on Key West & Tortugas—& payment for the slaves abducted from & lost to their owners. Individually, I would go farther, & even make demands for amounts that will be impossible to be repaid. These would be our expenses & losses of every kind produced by this unjust, predatory, & iniquitous war, & all the outrages contrary to the laws of war perpetrated by the Yankee government & their armed forces. Until all these claims were satisfied—or, in other words, forever—I would not accord a commercial privilege to the Yankee people, nor permit one of them to enter & sojourn on our territory, except under special licence, & safe bonds for his good conduct. Our mere refusal to buy of the Yankees, or to employ their vessels, or subjecting their commodities & their vessels, & any artizans employed under licence, to heavy discriminating taxes, would control the Yankee government & people more effectually than the exercise of our whole military & naval means, in warlike operations. . . . [2577]

April 4. Saturday. I was told this morning that the wind rose in the night, & blew furiously for a time. Today it continues very strong, first N.E. as yesterday, & changing to North—very cold & piercing. After a hurried walk, I was glad to return & remain in the house. Unless counteracted by the opposite tendency of the strong south-west wind of the 2nd, I fear that the easting of this long & violent wind, combined with the full moon, may give the Yankees very high tides to attack Charleston. On the other hand it may be doubted whether the violence of the wind, when easterly, would not have rendered the sea near the coast dangerous to a fleet.—Having obtained the 2nd vol. of Barth's Travels from the library in Rd., I returned to that work today. I have been so much interested & engaged in the ditching for the two last days, that I read nothing, except the newspapers.—About sunset, the wind N.W. & increased in violence—& the beginning of very fine & thin snow.

April 5. Sunday. Snowing continued to past 9 A.M. though thawing. It seemed to be 4 or 5 inches deep. Milder—though wind still from N.W. No sunshine. At night, the snow had disappeared on many places, & scarcely anywhere remained more than an inch thick.

April 6. Easter Monday, & no work. Wind S.W. & much warmer. —Finished 2nd. vol. of Barth . . . . Read part of an odd number of Russell's Magazine. It contained an interesting article comparing Hamilton & Burr, & showing a remarkable resemblance of these distinguished men & rivals & antagonists in numerous points of their lives, acts & talents, up to the time of Hamilton's death by the hand of Burr.[2] There was another resemblance of intentions & action, though not of consequences, which the writer did not advert to. At one time, when Hamilton had ceased to hold public station, he planned, & designed to lead, a private military & naval expedition to South America, (Caraccas [*sic*], I think,) for conquest & to establish himself as ruler of the conquered territory. For [2578] this unquestionable intention, which failed, but not for want of his zeal & efforts, Hamilton did not suffer in reputation &

---

[2] "Burr and Hamilton," *Russell's Magazine*, III (September, 1858), 548–58.

position, either with his contemporaries or their successors. But Burr, for a similar intention, & partial attempt against another Spanish province, Mexico, was denounced not only as a lawless offender against a peaceful power, & his country's neutrality, but was persecuted as a traitor, & pursued by all parties to ruin, destitution of fortune & of character, & misery. . . .

April 7. Tuesday. Wind north, & very cold.—The mail. But one of our four papers of today, & little news of importance. . . . Northern accounts of their operations on the Mississippi river are confused & unintelligible. But though there are claims of the good progress, & confidently expected success of the Yankee arms, at Vicksburg and [2579] on both the newly attempted routes, to the Yazoo & to Red river, it seems, by many other statements & indications, that they have had to encounter great obstacles & dangers in all the attempted routes departing from the main river—& that there is really but very slight ground to expect success. . . . Nothing has lately been done either against Vicksburg or Port Hudson—nor by Adm. Farragut, with his three gunboats, which got by our batteries of Port Hudson & Vicksburg, to the water between those two posts. . . . Our last report from Charleston to Apr. 5th, states only that important movements were in progress, which could not be published. By verbal report from Rd., it is stated that all communication with Charleston has been forbidden by order of our authorities. It was inferred that the attack was imminent, if not already commenced. . . . [2580] The N.Y. Herald estimates the actual destruction of northern property, in ships & their cargoes, by our few C.S. cruisers, at from 10 to 15 millions of dollars. But this must be much less than the consequent general enhancement of the cost of insurance on all northern vessels, & the loss of the carrying trade. The capture, by our Alabama, of the Ariel, a California line steamer, at once put an end to the before general shipment of gold from Cal. to N. York, & directed all the gold to England, & on English ships. Later, the capture & destruction of the Jacob Bell from China, (ship & cargo estimated by the Herald at from 1 to 1,500,000$,) involved the transfer from Yankee to English ships of all the rich freights from China to the U.S. . . .

April 8. Wednesday. Still north wind & very cold. Therm. 31½° after sunrise.—Edmund went to Richmond, & carried Sue to return to school, & brought back the newspaper of today, & a later published telegraphic dispatch from Charleston, with important &

good news. On the 7th. a dispatch to our war office stated that the Yankee fleet had previously arrived off the harbor, & a portion of the steamers had passed over the bar, & anchored within. This day, later dispatches reported that the squadron attacked our forts, at 2.30 P.M. on yesterday . . . concentrating the fire mostly on Fort Sumter. The attacking force consisted of the iron-clad ocean steamer frigate "[New] Ironsides," & 9 iron-clad "Monitors" on the plan of the first & original steamer so called, which fought our iron-clad Virginia, & which afterwards sunk at sea. Vessels of this peculiar construction are designated by the general name of "Monitors," & are almost invulnerable to balls or shells from the heaviest artillery. They lie so flat & low on the water, that very little of the vessel is exposed to be struck, except the [2581] "turret"—& that & every other part are so thickly covered with iron plates, as to be impenetrable to any missiles. The firing from the enemy's vessels soon became rapid, & was replied to from our batteries on Morris & Sullivan's islands, & Forts Moultrie & Sumter. The Ironsides & Keokuk (Monitor,) at 4.30 P.M. withdrew from the action, both, apparently, badly injured, & retreated out of the range of our guns. At 5 P.M. the fire from the assailants slackened, & soon after ceased—&, I infer, (though it is not expressly stated,) that all fell back out of range, as all firing had ceased, except that occasional guns were heard. The early renewal of the attack was confidently expected—but it had not been made to 11 A.M. of this day. Intense excitement in Charleston among the crowd on the promenade Battery viewing the fight—& everybody sanguine & confident of our success in defeating the assailants. Besides the heavier damage to the Ironsides & Keokuk, all the Monitors were frequently struck by our shot—but with what effect was not known to our side.[3] Our known casualties were these: One killed & 5 men badly wounded at Fort Sumter—& one gun dismounted & one man wounded at Moultrie. . . . For these results, so far, we may well rejoice, & be thankful to God—& feel increased confidence as to the final issue. It is cause for much gratification that the enemy attempted the

---

[3] Five of the eight *Monitor*-type ironclads were "wholly or partially disabled," and the *Keokuk*, struck ninety times, sank the next morning. Following the unsuccessful attack, Rear Admiral Samuel F. Du Pont, who commanded the Federal squadron, pronounced the monitors "miserable failures where forts are concerned" and concluded that Charleston "cannot be taken by a purely naval attack, and I am admonished by the condition of the iron-clads that a persistence in our efforts would end in disaster." *Official Records*, Vol. XIV, 437, 442.

direct passage to Charleston, instead of aiming to avoid our defences of the harbor, & approaching the city in the rear. I had another fear, which so far seems unfounded. This was, that the enemy's iron-clads, relying on their impenetrability, would pass as rapidly as they could steam, by the fortifications & under their heaviest fire, & go to or above the city, & destroy it, & defeat our weaker rear defences & their defending forces, by bombardment, & the assailants out of range of our main batteries, & comparatively safe from danger. But as this [2582] mode of attack was not ventured upon in the beginning, when there was most probability of its success, I think that it will scarcely be now attempted.—Other good news, & also some bad. From northern report, the Yazoo Pass expedition has proved a failure & has been entirely abandoned. . . . European papers confirm the report that a loan for $15,000,000, for the C.S., had readily been made in Europe—& offers were to the extent of 18 millions. The day after the subscription for the required sum had closed, a premium of 3¾ to 4¼ percent was offered by purchasers for the bonds. The payment of these bonds, when required, is to be made in cotton, at a stated price, to be placed by the C.S. at any of our sea-ports to be designated by purchasers, & at their risk for export. This will make an additional inducement to European powers to put down the Yankee blockade. . . . On Friday, the mob again assembled for renewing pillage [in Richmond], but was soon dispersed by the police. A number of the offenders, on both days, were arrested, & examined before the mayor. 10 men & 15 women (mostly low Irish & other foreigners,) were retained in custody, to be tried either for felony or misdemeanor.

April 10. Friday. At last a south wind, &, by noon, the first warm or seasonable weather, except one previous day.—The mail. No report of later offensive operations of the Yankee fleet in Charleston harbor. A dispatch from Gen. Beauregard, & also others, state that the double-turreted Monitor, which was crippled in the engagement, has since sunk, about 1000 yards from Morris Island, where its smoke-stacks above the water, are visible. The failure to renew the attack, so long, indicates heavy damage or great discouragement to the enemy. . . . The defeat of the insurgent Poles is expected, in Europe, to put an end to their struggle. . . . The quelling this insurrection, & cessation of the previous prospect of continued, or perhaps, general war in Europe, will leave the Emperor of France free to quarrel with Yankeedom, if he wishes it, as I had before supposed—& in that respect, the defeat of the Poles may be of great advantage to us. [2586] Nevertheless, I much regret the failure of this renewed effort of this noble people to regain & re-establish their freedom & independent nationality, after having been subjugated, & under a crushing despotism for some 70 years, & after having made several strong efforts, by insurrection, which were suppressed in blood.—The Richmond papers did not all fail, as I thought, to notice what was so improperly termed the "bread riot".... The riot was not to obtain bread—nor were the actors persons in destitute condition. The intention & the actual operation were to plunder valuables of all kinds. Stores were broken open & plundered, which, as was well known before, contained no article for food. The actors were mostly women, prostitutes & low foreigners, set on & encouraged by men of bad character. It is probable that most of the criminals will be punished. But it is to be deeply regretted that the mobs were not fired upon by the military, & 50 or more shot.

April 11. Saturday. The first warm morning. The cleaning out of the main ditch was begun, regularly, the men in the ditch, & working with spades & shovels.... The day's work, by 4 men, finished 223 yards of cleaning & deepening the ditch .... I spent the whole day, from immediately after breakfast to nearly sunset, (excepting returning to eat dinner,) attending to & directing this work, with unwearied interest. In no day has my time been so agreeably occupied, with mere amusement, for [2587] a long time back. The chief source of my pleasure is in my thus prosecuting & extending the operation of my former general plan for draining this farm, by deepening, & sloping the margins, of the main ditch gradually—& towards which object nothing has been done ... since I gave up the management, 6 or 7 years ago.... In my personally directing particular operations, in which I may take especial pleasure, & also in offering my opinions & advice on others, & on the general management of the farm, I take care to avoid attempting to exercise any improper authority, which might impair discipline, or in the slightest degree operate to counteract the supreme & complete authority & direction of the resident proprietor & manager. Our understanding, upon my own proposition, is, that I will act as *consulting agriculturist*—will give my advice freely, & suggest any measures of improvement (according to my views,) but that my son will not accept for adoption any of my recommendations, unless with his own hearty approval. . . . We hear, from verbal reports, that the Yankee troops occupying & fortified at Gloucester Point are robbing every farm & proprietor of almost every kind of portable plunder in that county—& that they declare that no crops shall be raised. There is another evil, less extensive in operation, but still worse & more fearful so far as it has gone, from plunderers of our own armies, near their encampments, & to their lines of marching. I have before spoken of the great nuisance of our soldiers, of low & bad habits, acting as sturdy beggars or concealed pilferers. But much worse offences have lately been committed in Chesterfield & Prince George. Unprincipled soldiers, straggling from their line of march, or from their camps, in parties, by force & openly, have, like banditti free from all control, plundered farms & houses, shot down fowls & hogs, & carried off their booty by force of arms & terror. In such action, they usually have no persons present to see, except negroes, who could not (as probably no other persons could,) identify the plunderers, and if they could, the testimony of negroes is of no validity. In Chesterfield, a party of soldiers, showing a forged order to search for spirit, entered & pillaged a store, & then slaughtered [2589] & carried off from their stye [*sic*], 5 valuable hogs belonging to the proprietor of the store. If some of these robbers are not soon convicted & severely punished, (the penalty should be nothing less than hanging,) there is no estimating the extent [of] such enormities of armed banditti.

April 14. Tuesday.—The mail. The Yankee fleet of iron clad Monitors & the frigate Ironsides, after drawing off from the battle, did not make any movement to renew the attack. The Monitor deemed the most formidable, the Keokuk, with two turrets, was so damaged that it could not be kept afloat, & sunk, about 1000 yards from Morris Island. It has since been visited, & it was seen that a shot from our artillery had forced its passage through the plating of the turret, which was supposed to be impenetrable. [2591] This missile is supposed to be that of the Brooks [*sic*] rifle cannon, a late improvement, & manufactured in Richmond.[4] Another of the

---

[4] Invented by John M. Brooke (1826–1904), chief of Naval Ordnance and Hydrography for the Confederacy, the Brooke gun was manufactured at the Tredegar Iron Works in Richmond. The Brooke rifled cannon which proved so effective against the Federal monitors at Charleston were of seven-inch caliber, loaded with armor-piercing wrought iron bolts. See Charles B. Dew, *Ironmaker to the Confederacy: Joseph R. Anderson and the Tredegar Iron Works* (New Haven: Yale University Press, 1966), 278.

Monitors had disappeared earlier, &, as supposed had been taken off for repairs, soon after the battle. The remaining 8 iron-clads, after lying within the bar, & about 2½ miles from our forts, for some 30 hours, all went out to sea. And thus, after a fight of two hours, & the certain destruction by our fire of one vessel, & the probable severe injury of others, has ended this expedition of a powerful armada—which has been preparing & collecting at Port Royal for some months, & which has been deemed ready for some weeks— which at last amounted to 150 vessels, & a strong army. About 30 vessels only of this great armada arrived off the bar of Charleston harbor. Where the others were, & where the land forces were, has not yet appeared. Reported, but not believed, that the whole force is coming to James river, to aid the attack by Hooker on Richmond. Accounts from the Yankee fleet & army before the attack on Charleston, & comments in N.Y. papers, show that the greatest confidence was entertained of easy success. Certainly never did any such great military & naval undertaking, with such great force & means, & so much vaunted, & after such long preparation & the best possible equipment, come, & in so short a time & after such feeble efforts, to such a "lame & impotent conclusion." All the combined force of Yankee effrontery & mendacity cannot disguise this defeat, or claim it was a victory & gain to their arms. Putting aside the loss & disgrace of the battle & defeat, the mere failure of this immense armada to effect any important object, will be a loss to Yankeedom not less than the battle of Fredericksburg. . . . Reports of important movements supposed to be impending where the several great armies are in face of each other. The Yankee armies, in every position, have now been inactive for from 3 to 4 months. And those in the west have as long been losing the great benefit of high waters for their making advances into the interior. If they do not effect very important objects in the next 8 weeks in the west, before the rivers fall—or in 12 weeks on the Atlantic, before malaria becomes dangerous, the [2594] year 1863 will be lost for great military operations & successes. . . . [2595]

April 17. Finished 3rd vol. of Barth's Travels in Central Africa. . . . The mail. . . . The Yankee forces in Suffolk, by report from our side, amount to 20,000 men, mostly new levies. Gen. Longstreet, (with 4 divisions, as the Yankee accounts report,) had nearly invested & surrounded Suffolk and the Yankee army. His artillery commanded the passage of the narrow Nansemond river, & there was on the 14th. heavy cannonading, & other firing be-

tween the battery & Yankee gunboats which came up the river &
attacked, but were defeated & driven back, & with heavy damage,
as reported otherwise. The two railroads offer the only other passages for reinforcements from Norfolk. Of these, our troops had
occupied the Petersburg & Norfolk R.R., & were marching to
occupy the Seaboard R.R. These three communications being held
by our forces, the Yankees in & near Suffolk will be separated from
Norfolk, & the only routes for speedy reinforcements or supplies,
by the whole breadth of the great Dismal Swamp, an impassable
morass of peat bog. If the reports of the situation are correct, most
important results must follow, & perhaps the defeat & capture of
the whole Yankee garrison. . . . A portion of Hooker's forces lately
crossed the Rappahannock into Culpeper, where they were met by
Gen. Stuart's command, & driven back after a severe fight. . . .
General engagements continually expected between the armies on
the Rappahannock, & in Tennessee—& frequent skirmishes, or
bloody conflicts between out-posts of the armies in Tennessee. But
the long delay & inactivity of the enemy, the invading & aggressive
party, seem to render their [2598] speedy attack very doubtful. . . .
A few days ago, our nearest neighbor was offered, & refused, $10
the hundred pounds for corn fodder. Today, Edmund heard in
Richmond that the price for good hay had risen to $25 the hundred!
It seems to me that our country & cause are now, for the first time
during the war, in great peril of defeat—& not from the enemy's
arms, but for the scarcity & high prices of provisions, & the impossibility of the government feeding the horses of the army, which is
even much more difficult than to feed & support the men. In the
cavalry brigade to which my grandson belongs, the horses have
rarely had any food but corn for some months—& are generally
without any hay or other long provender, & for weeks together.
Horses cannot live on grain alone, even if plentifully supplied with
it. As might be expected, the horses are reduced very low in flesh &
strength, & many are dying, & more failing entirely. I do not know,
but infer that this brigade is not worse supplied than all other of our
cavalry in eastern Virginia. And if so, the cavalry & the wagon &
artillery teams cannot be capable of performing hard or even moderate service.—A letter from Julian states the increase, & general
extension near the public road, of brigandage by armed bands of
soldiers belonging to Gen. Longstreet's corps, which, successively,
are marched by brigades, from Petersburg to work at Fort Powha-

tan, & back, when relieved. Our army contains, & perhaps for its larger number, the most patriotic, worthy, & estimable men of every state. But also it contains a full proportion of the worst class of every community. And a few scoundrels in each regiment, banded together, & permitted by slack discipline to straggle from their camp, or route of march, may be enough to make all the neighboring farms subject to plunder, & indeed render all property [2600] in provisions insecure, & the outrages of the robbers intolerable. Some of these armed bands have visited many residences or farms in Prince George. If their demands as sturdy beggars are complied with, they are content. But when the repetition of such demands have rendered them intolerable, & they are refused, they openly declare they will take by force what they ask for . . . . Julian has been so visited, & some of his turkeys seized in the presence of his family, & without the least concealment. It can rarely happen that any person thus robbed can know the persons of the stranger robbers, who are seen for but a few minutes, or could identify them afterwards. Therefore, it is almost hopeless for any sufferer to complain to the commander of the corps to which the soldiers are supposed to belong. He would be required to prove everything, & could prove nothing. It is clear that they should be prevented from occurring, by proper discipline & strict regulation.—More arrests continue of males, & more females, for participation in the late riot. It is to be hoped that all the criminals will be tried, & severely punished. In the examinations & subsequent proceedings, it has been made evident that not one of these rioters was impelled to their criminal conduct by hunger or destitution. Of all who have been permitted to give bail for their appearance for future trial, all except one only had sufficient property to obtain & secure their bail sureties—& all ordered for trial have engaged legal counsel, & at high fees. During the riot, some morbidly charitable people, supposing that the rioters were realy [*sic*] suffering for want of food, offered, & began to make, a distribution of flour & rice. But the benevolence was soon put an end to, by the bounty being contemptuously [2601] thrown down in the street by those who had received it, they declaring that if *that* was all to be given them, the givers might "go to hell."

April 18. Saturday. This the sixth day in which more or less of force has been clearing out the main ditch, & in all equal to the labor of 19½ days of one laborer.

April 19. Sunday. Walked in both forenoon & afternoon, observing the ditches, & their operation since the late deepening. . . . At church Edmund heard of a dispatch, received in Richmond yesterday, stating that 8 of the Yankee iron-clad gun-boats, from above Vicksburg, had attempted to pass down by our batteries—& that though 3 of them had been forced to return, the other 5 got by, under our fire.[5] This is a serious misfortune to us. Farragut's naval force will now be increased from his previous 3 iron-clad steamers to 8. He will now be able to overwhelm our small naval force in Red River unless those vessels (3 prizes) can be protected by our earth-fortification on that river. And, at any rate, all of that & other navigable tributaries & the Mississippi between the guns of Vicksburg & Port Hudson, will be at the will of Farragut's squadron, acting as plunderers & incendiaries.

April 21. Tuesday. Last night strong wind from N.East & continued, though less violent, through the day. Cloudy & cold.—The mail. As heard & stated generally before, on the night of 16th., 8 of the Yankee steamers from the fleet above Vicksburg attempted to pass down by our batteries. They were fired upon, & returned the fire. 5 of the vessels, (4 ironclads, & 1 transport,) succeeded in passing. Of the others, one was [2602] set on fire, & burnt to the water's edge. Prisoners from the wreck reported that this was the transport Henry Clay, & that the ram Lafayette was sunk by our batteries.[6] Another gunboat said to be disabled—but whether it passed, or not, does not appear. Two heavy guns from a battery of the enemy opened on 17th on the city, & fired for 6 or 8 hours, but with no effect. The Yankee canal, as extended, is 8 miles long, from Milliken's Bend, above, & will reach the Mississippi near New Carthage below. 64 steamers had left Memphis, for the Yankee fleet & camp near Vicksburg, with many troops, both white & black. The "Yazoo fleet" had gone to the same place. If this means, as I infer, the vessels that failed to reach the Yazoo by the Yazoo Pass & the Sunflower river, their escape is an unexpected loss to us. Another

---

[5] Actually, all eight of the gunboats, commanded by Rear Admiral David D. Porter, succeeded in running the Vicksburg batteries on the night of April 16. However, three transports, loaded with commissary stores and towing barges, suffered extensive damage. One, the *Henry Clay*, was set afire and totally destroyed; a second, the *Forest Queen*, was disabled and had to be towed to safety by the gunboat *Tuscumbia*. *Official Records*, Vol. XXIV, Pt. 1, p. 517. This operation was designed to facilitate Grant's crossing of the Mississippi River below Vicksbrug.

[6] The latter report was erroneous.

[626]

direct attack on Vicksburg expected soon, from the recent & great increase of the Yankee forces. The Mississippi was falling rapidly—in one day, as much as 26 inches. . . . Another attempt to cross the Rappahannock into Culpeper has been made by a portion of Hooker's army, & severely repulsed by our cavalry & other force there posted. From private information brought from within the enemy's lines, it is reported, & some of the informed believe, (though not all,) that Hooker is about to "change his base of operations," & to attempt to approach Richmond by the former route of York river & the White House, on which McClellan failed. This report is somewhat strengthened by the fact that two Yankee gunboats, full of troops, came up York river on 16th. . . . No definite accounts from either Hill or Longstreet, which is strange & discouraging. We have northern reports of the early operations of both, & they show that the enemy were in much alarm for the safety of both Washington N.C. & Suffolk. . . . Some doubts are expressed whether Gen. Longstreet really intended to attack Suffolk. The presence of his army has enabled him to reach, & to purchase at low rates, large supplies of provisions, from the country before controlled by the enemy.—Both houses of our Congress have at last passed a heavy tax bill, & I trust that it may be in its details, as certainly is the general measure & policy, good for our cause & its success. . . . It is said that the Yankees are about to try another inland passage by Vicksburg. This is by Walnut bayou . . . . But I do not believe that they will try another interior passage, after failing in four previous trials. Their best chance, judging by their recent success, is to run their vessels by our batteries, taking the risk of their damage.—[2605] Earl Russell, the British Minister for Foreign Affairs, has, in their correspondence, treated our Commissioner Mr. Mason, with so much slight & disrespect, & also the C.S. government with so much unfairness & injustice, & even using falsehood & fraudulent construction to favor the Yankee illegal & invalid blockade, that the general wish of the people is in favor of recalling our commissioner from England, & ceasing all attempts at diplomatic intercourse with that government. Why our President has not done so, long ago, is to me surprising & incomprehensible. But while our enemy has been so greatly favored by England, professing neutrality, at our expense . . . still its government is greatly dissatisfied with that of England. The building [of] war vessels in England to be sold to the C.S., (though not armed or equipped before being delivered to our agents,) has been complained of by the U.S. minister, loudly & in offensive terms. And to such complaints, & charges of illegal & partial action, Earl Russell has replied as curtly & almost as insultingly as to our Commissioner. Hence, with all the care of England to conciliate Yankeedom, the relations of the two governments are in an uneasy state, & may, by any act of imprudence, or of vigor, on either side, at any moment . . . become hostile. At the North it is manifest from the tone of the principal papers that war with England is deemed not improbable. And the offensive language of these papers, & the threats against England, & boasts of what can be effected in war, are calculated to deeply offend the proud English nation, & compel its government to cease its forbearance, & submission to Yankee insults to England, as well as its injustice in sustaining the illegal blockade in violation of the just rights of the C.S., of the law of nations, & the interests of England.—[2606] . . . Prices have fallen in Richmond, though still enormous—& the decline has been greater everywhere else than in Richmond. It is reported that provisions are abundant, & the prices low (compared to Virginia,) in the southern & western states. . . .

April 23. Thursday. Raining nearly all last night, & continued to near night. The long continued wet weather is very bad for all clay or lowland farmers—& especially for this farm, because of the bad condition & operation of the main drains. And late as it is, even if the land had been & was now dry enough, it is too cold to plant corn. . . .

April 24. Friday. Cold, cloudy, & showery. Finished cleaning out the main ditch throughout its length—but most of it will need going over again slightly, because of the many slippings of sides since the passage of the laborers. Equal to 32 days' work of a single man. . . . The present depth of the ditch I think will average 7 feet below the original surface. . . . The mail. The news hoped for has not come, & now seems hopeless. Gen. Hill has not been able to prevent the Yankee gunboats passing his batteries, & so they have reinforced Washington. It is understood that Gen. Hill has withdrawn from the siege, & it will no longer be attempted to take the town & its garrison.[7] As to Suffolk, Gen. Longstreet, if he designed it, has not

---

[7] The Confederate siege of Washington, North Carolina, which began on March 30, was abandoned on April 15 after two Federal vessels slipped in with supplies for the beleaguered garrison.

been able to cross the Nansemond river, of which the Yankees command the passage by their gunboats. There has been heavy firing between them & our shore batteries, & one gunboat completely disabled (by northern report,) for the time, & as believed, one or two others much damaged. Still some gunboats [2608] forced their passage, & now lie off the town, ready to burn it if required by our success. The Yankee commander has had every male secessionist arrested, & confined in the jail. They destroyed the bridge over the river. Of course our forces do not command either of the two railroads leading from Suffolk to Norfolk. It does not seem likely that our troops will be able to cross the river in force. . . . Another Yankee gunboat & 5 transports, in the night after 22nd, attempted to run by the Vicksburg batteries, & succeeded—though two of the vessels were so damaged by our batteries, that they floated down, unmanageable.[8] If a floating boom, or chain, such as protected Charleston, had been placed across the Mississippi, no such passage could be effected. As it is, even the wrecked & sunken vessels are carried down by the force of the current, & freight vessels without crews, & reach the enemy below. . . . By last northern accounts, the monitors had all gone from Charleston to Port Royal, & most of them for necessary repairs. Gen. Hunter's land forces, which had been brought to cooperate in the capture of Charleston, if the vessels had been successful, still remained where disembarked, on Folly & Seabrook's islands.

April 27. Monday. Clear—&, after a cold night & morning also a warm day—& the first, save one, in all this spring. The planting of corn was begun. The ditchers began to clean out the smaller stream ditches—which will be continued, with such force as may be spared for that purpose (& now 4 men) until that portion of the much needed repairs of drainage is completed. . . . Looking over, & reading here & there, the satirical poems of Thomas Moore[9]— which, for some time back, have in this manner been interspersed with the reading of Shakespeare's [2611] plays, when nothing more amusing than either was at command—& when I had not the interesting employment of attending to the ditching & draining

---

[8] The Federal flotilla on this occasion actually included six transports and twelve barges. One transport and half the barges were sunk, but the remainder effected the passage safely.

[9] A noted nineteenth-century Irish poet, Moore (1779–1852) also wrote a biography of Lord Byron and edited the latter's works.

labors. Of this, I have scarce[ly] lost an hour in any day, from after breakfast, when weather did not forbid.

April 28. Tuesday. Cloudy, & some scuds of light drizzle.—The mail brought but little intelligence, & none of importance. . . . The smoke-stack & upper works of a Yankee transport steamer, which was riddled by our artillery in the last passage by, are visible above the water where the vessel lies sunk, 5 miles below Vicksburg. The Yankee fortification, which only, from its heavy artillery, can throw shot to reach the city or our defences, has continued to fire more or less every day latterly—but without doing any damage worth notice.—A portion of Hooker's army has entered Fauquier—& there, as well as in King George especially, the Yankees are plundering & laying waste. A number of the most respectable residents of King George, non-combatants & above the military age, have lately been arrested & sent to Washington to be imprisoned.

April 30. Heavy rain last night, & continued slowly to 11 A.M. The earth was very wet before, considering the drying winds [2612] since the previous rain. It will now be in terrible condition—& long before fit for plowing or planting. . . . The ditching resumed after 12 M. & was again with it from after dinner.—From about 4 P.M. to sunset, frequent reports of cannon were heard here, from the direction of Fredericksburg as supposed. Even I could hear some of the reports, after my attention had been called to the occurrence. They were not heard so frequently for the time, as here during the battle of Fredericksburg. The wind favorable for bringing the sounds, being north-east.

May 1. Friday. The mail. A very important movement of Hooker's army, even before the cannonading of yesterday afternoon, of which nothing more has been brought by the papers, except that other persons also had heard the sounds. In the morning of 29th. (Wednesday,) as early as 3 A.M., a large body of Yankee troops, in boats rowed by muffled oars, very quietly crossed the river, about two miles below Fredericksburg, at a place called Deep Run, & there surprised our pickets, & the Ga. regiment stationed there. Another regiment (of La) came later as a reinforcement—but both had to retreat. . . . Pontoon bridges were soon laid down to the same point, & before 5 A.M. the Yankees were crossing in strong force, & continued to cross to 2 P.M. They threw shells in advance & around, for their own security, & some artillery shots were fired on their position, or the bridges. But there was no serious resistance to their movement, or taking their position, by pickets, as far as Hamilton's Crossing, on the adjacent railroad. At about 5 P.M., there as [2613] here, slow rain began, & the tents of the invaders were pitched. If the rain of the following night & next day was as heavy there as here, it must have seriously disconcerted Hooker's advance, if intended, with artillery. But whoever made the advance & attack, there must have been an engagement between the armies on the afternoon of the 30th, when the sounds were heard here. The number of troops that had crossed the river was unknown. But doubtless as many as Hooker designed to meet our force there. It is also understood that a large portion of his army had previously attempted, & to more or less extent with success, to cross the Rappahannock at Kelly's ford, into Culpeper. There Gen. Stuart's cavalry was hang[ing] on their skirts, skirmishing with out-posts, & had taken prisoners belonging to three different army corps, indicating the presence & cooperation of at least as many corps, & a strong army. From both of these movements in advance, & at both localities, we must soon hear of very severe fighting, & important results. . . . A tug steamer, having barges on each side for bulwarks (& probably the bulwarks built of cotton bales,) passed down the river by Vicksburg the night preceding the 27th ult. Indeed it now seems that three-fourths of all the passing vessels can get by, if there is no objection to risk the loss of vessels, & of the crews, by the dangerous fire of our artillery. . . . The whole naval & land forces now threatening Vicksburg from the vicinity are expected soon to make another direct attack on that city & its defences, & to be aided by the movement on the flank, or in the rear, of the army now advancing [2614] southward from the northern border of Mississippi.[10] Both these armies, & Rosecrans' in Ten., have been largely reinforced lately, & both he & Grant are expected to advance & engage soon.—Gen. Pemberton has sent a dispatch stating that 6 gunboats, averaging 10 guns each, had opened a terrific fire on our batteries at Grand Gulf, on Apr. 29th, & kept it up from 7 A.M. for 6½ hours, when they withdrew. Several of the gunboats seemed to be damaged—& one was disabled. . . . The renewal of attack ex-

---

[10] A reference to Grierson's Raid. On April 17, Colonel Benjamin H. Grierson had led 1,700 cavalry southward from La Grange, Tennessee, in a daring raid designed to divert attention from Grant's major operation against Vicksburg. Grierson's indefatigable band finally turned up in Baton Rouge on May 2, having traveled six hundred miles in sixteen days in successfully completing its mission.

pected. Transports laden with troops were in sight, but inactive. I am glad thus to learn that we have a battery at Grand Gulf, (between Vicksburg & Port Hudson, & near the mouth of the Big Black river,) which is so formidable to the enemy's armed steamers.—The Yankee forces are making successful & extensive progress in the interior of La., &, as elsewhere, are laying waste the country they occupy. It seems that the Yankee government has been strongly impressed with the supposed indications afforded by what were falsely designated as our "bread riots"—& by the more truthful accounts of scarcity of provisions in some localities, & for our army in Va., & of high prices more generally. It is a general Yankee belief that the people & armies of the C.S. are on the borders of starvation, & that they can damage us most effectually by destroying our means & preparations for subsistence. To this end, they are now aiming all their efforts, & their war policy. They, by destruction even more than plunder, waste our existing provisions wherever it is in their power to do so—& also destroy the means for the cultivating & harvesting other crops. This atrocious policy the Yankee government, through the invasions & predatory raids of its armies & gunboats, have it in their power to carry out to great & terrible extent. The enfranchising & arming & embodying the negro slaves, which is now moving with new vigor, is now cherished by Yankeedom even less as offering military aid, & favoring [2615] abolition fanaticism, than because it is a potent means for preventing the cultivation of the soil & reaping its products. It was clear enough, even before Lincoln's proclamation, that this was, or would be, the practical policy of the Yankee government. Before, to great extent, but systematically & generally since that proclamation, Yankee military & naval commanders have been encouraging the stealing of slaves by their subordinate officers & soldiers, compelling or inducing the slaves to abandon labor, or to assert their freedom, enrolling them as soldiers, & in all these modes, indirectly, if not directly & openly, endeavoring to incite the negro class to general & bloody insurrection & rebellion. But while this whole policy was obvious enough, it has not been so plainly & explicitly expressed as in a recent speech of Gen. [Lorenzo] Thomas, U.S.A., delivered at Lake Providence, La., & where he could have had only Yankees & negroes for auditors. The writing & publishing his speech . . . is the exposition of Lincoln's negro policy. For Gen. Thomas declares himself the authorized exponent of Lincoln's views & intentions, &

fully empowered to embody negro troops & to select & commission their officers.[11] . . .

May 2. Saturday. A verbal report, as stated from a newspaper of today, that Hooker's movement in advance below Fredericksburg was only a feint, & that his forces had re-crossed the river—& that his real advance was at Chancellor's, some 20 miles higher up the river.[12] But no reliance can be placed on such rumors now, as all communication from our army had been interdicted by Gen. Lee. As nothing of explanation has been received of the cannonading we heard on Thursday afternoon, probably the fight was indecisive & of but little importance.

May 3. Sunday. At church, some further rumors were heard, from those who [had] seen other papers of yesterday, or had been to Richmond. These were that the enemy had advanced in force by the upper route—& that a portion had repulsed our cavalry, & reached the Central Railroad in Louisa county, & destroyed a part of it. These particulars not believed. Of course all are excited & eager about this movement & effort of the enemy's great army—but not as if being personally & individually concerned in the result, & our capital & all eastern Virginia threatened with desolation by the success of a fast & near approaching army of 150,000 men. On the contrary, the people in Richmond, & no doubt all of the vicinity, are as quiet as if they had no special interest in the attack, & only excited & anxious as they would be for the progress of such a movement on Vicksburg or Charleston. We may be foolishly & falsely confident. But such is the fact that almost all of our residents seem to expect with certainty the defeat of this sixth great attempt [2617] to reach & capture Richmond.

May 4. Monday. Soon after writing, early this morning, the foregoing entries for yesterday, a sudden & most unexpected change has occurred, by a Yankee raid, & its plunderers even

---

[11] Brigadier General Thomas, who was assigned responsibility for the enrollment of colored troops on March 23, 1863, had come to Lake Providence for the specific purpose of raising "as many regiments of blacks as I can" for rear guard service in occupied portions of Louisiana.

[12] This report was correct. Hooker's initial strategy in the developing Chancellorsville campaign was to outflank the Confederate left by crossing the Rappahannock at Kelly's Ford with approximately one-third of his massive 134,000-man army. The movement across the river below Fredericksburg by units of Major General John Sedgwick's Sixth Corps was only a diversion, designed to keep Lee in place and to mask the enveloping movement.

visiting this house. By previous arrangement, my niece Juliana Dupuy, & her little niece & ward & my granddaughter, Jane, set off after breakfast, in the carriage, for Richmond, & for Nottoway, & Nanny with them, to go as far as Richmond. Edmund & I had waited until their departure, & then he rode to his distant work, & I walked to the ditchers, close by & in open view from the rear of the house. I had not been there 15 minutes before the boy carriage-driver was seen riding down the hill towards me, mounted on one of the carriage horses, still in the harness. He told me that the carriage had turned back from Lewis Johnson's gate, where the ladies were informed that a large body of Yankee cavalry had this morning been plundering Spring Garden, our next neighbor's farm above, on the river, & were close by us. Though incredulous of the strange report, the ladies returned. The boy had scarcely made his hasty statement, & I had sent him on to find his master, & I was walking to the house, when my grandsons, John & Meade, running, met me with further news, & Jane's urgent request that I would not come to the house, but would hide myself, as two Yankee troopers were already at the stable & mansion, & were inquiring for me & my son, & that one had taken the other carriage horse. We afterwards learned (as stated by this Yankee to the ladies,) that they had, from the mail road by Old Church, seen the carriage turn about, & that these two had pursued it, to take the horses. One of the horses was saved by the accident of being sent to me & my son. The Yankee trooper soon found & seized the other carriage horse, & carried him off, committing no other depredation, & not entering the house. He stated to the negro servants that he belonged to a very large body of cavalry.[13] His first [2618] inquiry made here was "Where were the damned Ruffin men?" & when told by the servants that we had both gone away, he said he knew we were here this morning, & that they "were bound to have our heads."[14] We afterwards heard that six,

[13] The troopers were from a detachment of Major General George Stoneman's newly organized cavalry corps, which had been harassing Lee's lines of communication since the beginning of the Chancellorsville campaign. On this date units from Stoneman's command raided in Hanover County and fought minor skirmishes at Shannon's Crossroads, Tunstall's Station, and Ashland Church.

[14] Julian Meade Ruffin II, whose father was one of the youngsters who ran into the field to warn their grandfather of the approach of the Federal troopers, gives this version of the incident, as recounted to him by his father:

There was a free Negro in the edge of the yard when the troops came up . . . and they leveled a revolver at the Negro's head and said, "Where's that

including these two, had before come to the Old Church tavern, where they had inquired for me, & made like threats. Of course when I heard of these Yankees being then at the house & stable, I got quickly into the adjacent bushes, but on an eminence where I could see over the flats, & farm road, & partially the rear of the house & yard. After remaining half an hour, & neither hearing nor seeing anything, I moved cautiously to the garden paling, whence I could have a limited view across the front yard. After a while, I saw the house servants, & also my ditchers, attended by my grand-daughter Mary, moving the bacon from the meat house. As this was manifestly not under Yankee direction, I inferred that the robbers had gone off, & I returned to the house—but was met in the back yard by a servant to urge my absence & concealment as (so was the belief & report to me,) . . . the whole body, or a large portion of the Yankee force, was then posted on the public road just outside of our gate, whence they could see our front yard & door. I then again retreated—but, keeping under cover, crept to the fence alongside of the road where the Yankees were said to be, & could see none, nor any signs of them. I then went to the house, (at 10 A.M.,) to report my news & to learn that from the family. Very soon after Edmund came back—the messenger having reached him almost as soon as he had reached his ploughing near the river. He had seen, as crossing the public road (Newcastle lane,) through the farm, the recent tracks of a numerous body of cavalry, going down. But, however strange, in this direction at this time, he did not doubt that these were our own troops. His head ploughman told him that he & the other ploughmen & teams had been kept waiting by the passage of the cavalry, before they could cross the road to the work. He

---

damned Ruffin?" and he says: "I don't know where he is. He was here at breakfast time but I don't know where he is." And he didn't mention where he was or anything. He could have told them. My father said that he and his cousin were so winded when they got down there they could hardly tell grandfather what the trouble was. They ran and ran down there to tell him . . . where he was working, but they finally managed to tell him that the Yankees were in the yard up there and he hid down there somewhere. . . . Father said on one occasion, it could have been the same time, some Yankees rode up in the yard and one of his aunts, I suppose, had a revolver hid[den] in her dress, and he was so scared that something might happen and she would kill one of the Yankees. But nothing happened. The Yankee asked her some questions. I don't think he came in the house. [But he] had them all rather scared.

Interview with Julian Meade Ruffin II at Upper Marlbourne, Virginia, August 19, 1974.

added that he believed they were Yankee troops. This Edmund [2619] at once pronounced impossible. Just then the messenger arrived to inform him of what had been commenced at his house. I had sent an intelligent negro, through the back way, to Old Church, to inquire the true state of things. Mr. Lipscomb, the P.M. & tavern proprietor, sent word that the cavalry force was then (before 11 A.M.) stopping to feed opposite Ingleside gate (a mile below Old Church,) & that 6 only of the troopers had before come to his house, of which two came on to Marlbourne. He understood that the "army was below." This large body must have passed down the road this morning through the low grounds, & plundered Spring Garden on the way—& then turned up the mail road to near Ingleside, where they stopped to refresh, as we heard. It is a mystery whence they came, & where they are going, by this crooked route. I suspect it is a raid directed for the York river Rail Road. But my son thought, & I fear correctly, that the presence of this body here truly indicates that Gen. Lee's army has been too weak to fight the invaders, & has fallen back toward Richmond. If so, the Yankees may be upon us here for some time. One of our negro men came this morning from his wife's house, between Richmond & Mechanicsville, & arrived here after our sending to Old Church. He reports that our pickets had been sent from Rd., & had reached Mechanicsville before he passed—& that it was said there that the Yankees had possession of Hanover C.H.—In the evening Edmund rode to Ingleside to learn the news, & heard reports there, & also of other neighbors on the road. It seems that this is a most bold & daring raid, by a large corps of cavalry only, which first reached the Central R.R. in Louisa, (as before heard,) & thence came on to Hanover C.H. There they burnt the station buildings. Next the force divided, & the larger portion went by Gaines' Mill, & the smaller through our farm—both, as I had guessed, aiming for the York [2620] River Rail Road. It had been heard that they had reached Tunstall's Station, & had there a fight with some of our troops, & were repulsed, with the loss of 6 killed. Since, it was understood that the Yankees were stretched along the right bank of the Pamunkey, from Piping Tree ferry, 7 miles below this, to much farther below. If we have any force in Richmond, I should think these Yankees could scarcely get back without heavy loss. They destroyed part of the Central R.R. & burnt a bridge across the Chickahominy, & probably committed much more mischief than is yet known. They actually reached within three miles of Richmond. Also a report had been brought by two strange C.S. officers who came down the road from Richmond today, that a dispatch had been received in last night from Gen. Lee, announcing his having gained a signal victory over the main Yankee army, & driven it back across the Rapidan, but at great cost of blood-shed. I fear that this good news is not certain. It is not in the paper of today—though that omission would follow if the dispatch arrived after 11 last night. It was also heard that all the militia, or present residents, of Richmond, because of the alarm of this raid, were under arms through last night. If so, there must be all the notice required for our authorities to oppose this invading force, whose objects & action still seem as mysterious, as the main act is remarkable for daring.

May 5. Tuesday. No mail came, greatly to our disappointment. But my son rode out as far as Piping Tree, to learn the present condition of things, & also he saw an extra slip printed yesterday in Richmond containing Gen. Lee's dispatch, heard of yesterday. It reports a severe battle (on Sunday,) & a signal defeat of the enemy. Gen. Jackson, (Stonewall,) had attacked the enemy in the rear, & Gen. Longstreet in front.[15] They had been driven from all their positions, & were retreating across [2621] the river.... Gen. Jackson was severely wounded, & Gen. A. P. Hill & Gen. [Henry] Heth slightly. Gen. [Elisha F.] Paxton killed. Our loss heavy. Gen. Lee expected a renewal of the fighting. Another (private) dispatch, from Gordonsville, stated that 5000 Yankee prisoners had been then brought in, & that these were not all. Thank God for this.—Of our own invaders the following information was heard: On their route, the Yankees captured a number of the residents, (civilians & non-combatants,) and on their approach to Tunstall's Station, where we have a military post of infantry, they placed these prisoners in the front of their advancing column. Our men fired on the column, killed a few Yankees (6 reported,) but luckily none of our citizens thus illegally arrested, & so infamously exposed to protect the Yankees. These prisoners were afterwards turned loose. On being thus fired upon, the Yankees did not even return a shot, but hastily retreated, & returned to Piping Tree ferry, & began to cross the narrow Pamunkey in the large flat boat. They were crossing all the

---

[15] The reference is to Longstreet's First Corps. Longstreet himself, with the divisions of Pickett and Hood, was still engaged in operations near Suffolk and was not present at Chancellorsville.

afternoon, & then took the road towards King William C.H. Two of the Yankees who had lost their horses, (one of them being killed at Tunstall's Station,) were made prisoners by the two C.S. officers who came down yesterday from Rd. on a scout, to obtain information of this raid. These men were found asleep in a barn, exhausted by fatigue. One of the two was the very scoundrel who came here yesterday & stole the carriage horse—& who soon after stole another horse from a near neighbor, on the road. Last evening, early, a battalion (250) of cavalry, Major [John F.] Wrenn's [*sic*—Wren] command, arrived at Old Church, from Rd., sent after the Yankees. The commander was satisfied to hear that the enemy had crossed the river, & did not pursue the 5 or 6 miles to the ferry. Or, if these troopers had crossed at the higher Newcastle ferry, close by, they could soon have overtaken these exhausted & dispirited Yankee thieves. It seems that they have been five days on their expedition, & both the men & their horses [2622] are worn down by fatigue. But our battalion of fresh cavalry, after a march of 15 miles, halted & delayed nearly as many hours, & then this morning after breakfast, moved back to Richmond. The object of this raid was to pass rapidly through an undefended route & region of country, & to destroy as much public & other property as possible in as short a time, especially on railroads. The amount of their damages probably is not half known to us as yet. But it is understood, that besides operating on, or attempting to injure several railraods, they reached the James river canal at Columbia, & cut the dam there. I trust that some capable & energetic commander of brave soldiers will yet cut off the retreat of this body of marauders. Their passage through this farm, & the other connected incidents, have interrupted & disordered our work, & its usual regular procedure. Still, there was no cessation of labors—& I resumed my attendance on the ditching yesterday after dinner. Immediately after the visit here of the Yankee troopers, the members of my family here urged my departure, as deeming me to be in especial danger of being searched for & arrested by the Yankees, so many of whom, & on various occasions, have proclaimed their malignity, & their anxiety to capture me—& the certainty, if captured, that I would be made to suffer a very severe imprisonment, through which I could scarcely live long. . . . I had not before thought of getting out of the way, & removal would be very disagreeable now. But under such general urging, & then being entirely in the dark as to the future movements of these marauders—& then even fearful of the worst as to Gen. Lee's army—I consented, & prepared for a start this morning to Richmond, to proceed thence to Ruthven. But the rumors heard yesterday [2623] evening, of Lee's victory, & the certain repulse & supposed scattering of this corps of Yankee marauders, made me delay my removal for another day. And the confirmation of both reports today, has induced me to postpone my flight indefinitely. So I will continue to enjoy my greatest pleasure, in attending to the ditching & draining operations of the farm. . . .[16] It was a strange fact—& more strange that we heard nothing of it throughout this day (5th) or before—that another detachment of the Yankee cavalry remained idle at the site of old Hanover Town (near Dabney's ferry,) & within less than 4 miles of our house, & on a public road, nearly all of yesterday (Monday 4th.) & to 6 P.M. Then they met 30 C.S. wagons at the ferry, laden with provisions for our troops, all of which they burnt. On the 5th. this detachment proceeded to Aylett's, & there burnt a store-house of government bacon, & other property. I saw the dense smoke this morning, about 9 A.M. (10 miles distant,) without then suspecting that the enemy were still so near us—or that they had been within 4 miles nearly all of yester-day.—In afternoon, about 6, a thunder storm & very heavy rain. The earth before had been barely dry enough to permit ploughing on the dryest parts of the fields designed for corn—& nowhere through the rows. This speedy renewal of soaking condition will add much to the delay of planting, already so much too late. Never was so much rain known, & at short intervals, from in January to this time. Having wet land to cultivate, the draining out of order, & the teams very mean & weak, & but little corn for them, these con-tinued spells of wet weather seem to make it almost hopeless to make a crop of corn—& never was a large crop so necessary.

May 6. Rain in last night more slowly, & drizzle this fore-noon.—Borrowed from Mr. Lipscomb a Rd. paper of yesterday, containing Gen. Lee's dispatch, referred to before, dated Milford, 3rd. The battle was fought on 2nd & renewed on 3rd. The enemy had been dislodged from all his positions, from Wilderness, above, to & around Chancellorsville, & was then retreating across the Rappahannock by Ely's ford. Afterwards received a note from Mr. Newton (at Summer Hill,) begging for papers & news, & reporting

---

[16] The following passage was inserted at this point in the diary on May 6.

to me later & still better news, if it can be relied on. He saw an officer yesterday, from the Junction (of Fred. & Central RRoads,) who stated that he had yesterday morning seen a telegram to Gen. [James Johnston] Pettigrew[17] informing him that on the 4th. the enemy had captured & occupied Marye's Hill, (near Fredericksburg,) & that our forces had recaptured the position [2624] the night following, & made prisoners of 20,000 Yankees! I am afraid to believe it.[18] From the servants who have come here as messengers, we have heard much of the movements & depredations of the Yankee force in this neighborhood. . . . The newspaper gave a northern report, stating that the whole cavalry force, commanded by Gen. Stoneman, amounted to 10,000 men, when it set out, & first entered Louisa—after which it separated in sundry detachments directed to different objects for destruction & plunder.—Information was sent to Edmund this morning that his stolen horse had been left in New Kent—& he had to go off immediately in pursuit. His trip was in vain—the information being incorrect. He heard a new report, sent through the neighborhood & believed, that another detachment of the Yankee cavalry force was coming down by the river road. We shall keep a look-out for any such new visitors, but I do not believe there is any foundation for the report. Edmund saw Mr. Boyd, who was one of the prisoners of this neighborhood, which the detachment which passed here had captured, & carried to Tunstall's station, & all of whom they subsequently turned loose. He heard much of their conversation—& inferred from what they said & other indications, that they were worn down with fatigue, & only anxious to make their escape. Their first aim was to get to Williamsburg—but being turned back, at Tunstall's, & then crossing the Pamunkey, Boyd supposed that they then aimed for the Yankee post at Gloucester Point. . . . I trust that yet these invaders [2625] & depredators may be defeated & captured.— Heavy rain.

May 7. This morning I rode to Old Church, & saw P. H. Aylett, just from Richmond. On his verbal information I can rely, & he also

---

[17] Serving at this time as a brigade commander under General D. H. Hill in North Carolina, Pettigrew rejoined the Army of Northern Virginia in time for the Gettysburg campaign.

[18] Although the report of prisoners was greatly exaggerated, the Confederates did retake Fredericksburg on May 4, driving Major General John Sedgwick's Sixth Corps back across the Rappahannock.

gave me a newspaper of this morning. . . . First—the report of the capture of 20,000 prisoners on the 4th, at Marye's Hill, is false. The following are some of the incidents of the recent battles on the Rappahannock. The Yankees' line of battle extended from Wilderness to Chancellorsville, in Spottsylvania [*sic*]. They threw up intrenchments on Friday night, & protected the works by abattis [*sic*]. On Saturday, these defences were attacked by our troops, & carried—the enemy falling back in the direction of the United States ford, where they collected their scattered forces, & proceeded to fortify that position, while Gen. Lee had to suspend the operations on Hooker's main army, to go to the assistance of our small force left near Fredericksburg, on Marye's Heights. The fighting began at this point on Sunday. The enemy, making a flank movement as to Gen. Lee's main army & its then position, threw a very large force against our troops at Marye's Heights, which consisted of Gen. [William] Barksdale's Brigade. The enemy carried the position, capturing 6 pieces of the La. Washington Artillery, & some 500 or 600 of the infantry. The next morning, Monday, Gen. Early (the commander left in charge,) was reinforced, & the Yankees were driven in haste from their newly captured position, & over their pontoons to the Stafford side of the river. The guns of the Washington Artillery were recovered, & 5 others were captured from the fugitive foe. The number of prisoners captured, (in all the several days' fighting I infer,) will amount to from 6 to 7000. Our losses in killed & wounded very heavy—probably above 7000.[19] Gen. Jackson's arm required to be amputated. But we thank God that he is doing well.—The Yankee cavalry that passed through this neighborhood into King William, (two detachments, crossing respectively at Dabney's & at Piping Tree [2626] ferries,) next crossed the Mattaponi [*sic*—Mattapony], & have escaped to their post at Gloucester Point. It must have been wretchedly managed on our side, that, with a few exceptions of stragglers captured, all these marauders have escaped, after having done much damage, & inflicted heavy losses on both public & private property. . . . We have an official dispatch from Gen. Bragg, stating the incidents of another strong & at first successful Yankee raid, but with a very different result. On 18th ult. 5 regiments of Yankee cavalry & 2 of

---

[19] Total Confederate losses in the Chancellorsville campaign amounted to 12,764, while Hooker, who had more than twice as many effectives as Lee, lost a total of 17,287, nearly 6,000 of whom were captured by the Confederates.

infantry, & 10 pieces of artillery, moved from Corinth towards Tuscumbia, Al. . . . The enemy advanced to & entered Tuscumbia on 25th. Nothing more occurred to 28th. On that day Gen. Forrest arrived with his brigade, & fought the enemy, (but as it seems without much effect,) & Forrest fell back. On that day, he discovered a heavy force of cavalry, under Col. [Abel D.] Strait [*sic*—Streight], marching on Moulton & Blountsville. He pursued this force with two regiments, fighting them all [2627] day, at . . . Sand Mountain, suffering a loss of 5 killed & 50 wounded—& the enemy left on the field 50 killed, 150 wounded—& [our] troops burnt 50 of the Yankee wagons, turned loose 250 mules & 150 negroes. On May 3rd, after 5 days of marching & fighting between Gadsden & Rome (Ga.?) Gen. Forrest captured Col. Streight & his whole command, then amounting to 1600 men, with as many horses & Enfield rifles &c.[20] If *we* had had a Gen. Forrest in command here, as good an account would have been given of our Yankee raid. . . . The rain last evening, & again in the last night, very heavy—& the land as wet as possible this morning. Some drizzle, & cloudy & damp & cold throughout.—Digging two new ditches to substitute parts of old covered drains which had become obstructed, & so had failed. . . . [2628]

May 8. Friday. More rain last night, & to 8 this morning, & a lowering sky after.—I had not been half an hour at the ditching, when a messenger recalled me to the house. Mrs. Braxton wrote a note [conveying] . . . the report of a party of our soldiers who had been posted at West Point, & who had fled (or "cut their way" as they termed it,) from that place yesterday, after Yankee gunboats had arrived & landed troops there. I suspect that they fled on the first report of the gunboats being near. This force was supposed to be advancing towards Rd., & through our neighborhood; & . . . induced to my son, & still more to his wife & daughters, the belief that we should probably, & speedily, be subjected to more visits of Yankee troops, & the infliction of their plunderings & other outrages. They all united in urging my immediate escape from the danger—& all of the family proposed themselves to move off, except my son, who will alone remain. I did not believe in the

---

[20] The pursuit and capture of Streight's command, effected through characteristic bluster and deception by a force of barely five hundred men, was one of the spectacular exploits that was to make Nathan B. Forrest a legendary figure in the western theater of operations.

supposed danger—& advised that all the ladies should stay. But as *my* remaining was not required for any important use, & as all urged my departure—& as possibly the special hatred & malignity which the Yankees seem to entertain for me, might (with my presence,) the more endanger my son's property & family—I had no ground for objecting. So I agreed to set off—& only delayed my departure until a portion of the household & luggage could be ready to go to Rd. under my charge. At 1.15 P.M. we set out, with the carriage & wagon. The persons who accompanied me were my grandsons John & Meade, who will accompany me to Ruthven—& my niece Juliana & granddaughter Jane Dupuy, & Mrs. Lorraine. My niece & grandaughter thus resume their before frustrated return to Nottoway. And Mrs. Lorraine [2629] will accompany them so far on her way to her son's house & residence near Lynchburg. The carriages returned to Marlbourne tonight—& tomorrow, if the continuance of the alarm should continue the necessity, Jane & Edmund's two daughters will also leave. But where to go had not been determined—though most probably to Judge Ruffin's in N.C. I hope however that their removal may be deemed unnecessary, & be postponed entirely. I was more hopeful of this after my calling on Mr. Seddon, the Secretary of War, (to report to him the recent events & rumors in our neighborhood,) & hearing his opinion that there was no danger of any invasion of the enemy from any of the points below. I omitted saying before that I had heard, on my way, that some 500 Yankee cavalry had yesterday come from Williamsburg to New Kent C.H. (15 miles from Marlbourne,) & returned. I saw on the road, a few miles below Rd, Gen. Wise's command, posted for defence. I informed Mr. Seddon of the shameful conduct of the Wren batallion of cavalry, which was sent to Old Church so fruitlessly.—I have scarcely had opportunity yet to read the papers of today—& will not attempt to note the news generally until I shall have time tomorrow. I will now only state the main facts, that Hooker, availing himself of the opportunity offered by one of the late heavy storms of rain, recrossed the Rappahannock, & escaped from Gen. Lee's intended assault. I suspend my writing at 10.30, in my chamber, at the American Hotel, Rd. . . . [2630]

May 9. Saturday. At 6 A.M., with my two grandsons, I left in the train for Petersburg. This & all other trains now travel very slow. At 8.30, reached Petersburg. We met another train conveying a strong force of artillery, men & guns, to Rd., from near Suffolk. At 9 A.M. we set off on the Norfolk train for Disputanta. There I could not hire, or find, any conveyance for Ruthven. When about to leave our luggage, & walk, a cart passed by, with meal brought from mill. I hired in it a passage for us & our luggage. We had to go out of the way 1½ miles by the owner's house, to leave his meal—& then lost two more miles by mistake of the road—& reached Ruthven after 4¼ hours. . . . Found Mrs. Meade at home, & the two younger children.—Return to the newspapers. . . . It is believed that the late raid, commenced by so large a force as 10,000 cavalry, under Gen. Stoneman, was designed to cooperate, as a diversion, or otherwise, with Hooker's main attack on Lee. Several of the detachments, by taking undefended routes, have penetrated very far, have caused much surprise & alarm, & have effected much destruction of public & private property—have inflicted an insult on our government—& have escaped with but little loss. Still, the results [2631] have been very small compared to the opportunities—& do not compensate for the cost & the risk of the expedition, & still less for the abstraction of so much strength from Hooker's army during his recent severe trials & defeats. . . . I had stated before that the two detachments of the Yankee cavalry which passed through & near Marlbourne, had, through King William, escaped to the Yankee post at Gloucester Point. But what has become of the great body seems still doubtful. It is most probable that they have returned northward, & got across the Rappahannock—though the direct information is wanting. Yet in a Rd. newspaper of yesterday, it was supposed that a large portion of Stoneman's command had not yet left Louisa, or got within their own lines. This seems to me incredible.[21] . . . The gun-boats which lately came up to West Point & the Pamunkey, have returned. These caused the false alarm of an invasion from that quarter which on yesterday so excited all our neighborhood, & caused the beginning of another general flight of our family, from Marlbourne. I earnestly hope that later & better information has prevented the movement being completed as to the remainder of the family. . . . Since the passing of so many gunboats by our batteries at Vicksburg & Port Hudson has given to the Yankees the complete control of the waters included between

---

[21] The last units of Stoneman's cavalry corps returned to Federal-held territory on May 8. In ten days of operations the entire body had suffered fewer than one hundred casualties.

these two posts, they are attempting in another direction to get in the rear of Vicksburg, by way of the Big Black river, which empties from above & back of Vicksburg into the Mississippi below. They have already made some advances on that route, both by naval & land forces, & there [2633] have been some skirmishes of no decisive result. Our post at Grand Gulf, (from which the Yankee gunboats were lately repulsed,) had been evacuated, under the pressure of overwhelming superiority of threatening forces, & one of our regiments was captured.[22] . . . Julian returned from Disputanta. We had abundant subjects for interesting conversation.— This the first day of sunshine of late.

May 10. Sunday. A clear & cloudless as well as bright sun & atmosphere. Besides the strong artillery force which I met yesterday on the railroad, Julian heard yesterday, at Disputanta, that great numbers of soldiers have been passing for some days from below (near Suffolk). As these cannot be needed, since the last battle, on the Rappahannock for our defence, I hope that it may be designed by Gen. Lee to make an aggressive movement on Hooker's army, & possibly farther north.—In this region, we have now such slow & irregular communication with the eastern border & all west of the Mississippi, that Yankee reports, through N.Y., of every event reach us before any accounts from our side. Therefore we have plenty of reports of bad news for us—most of which will probably prove [2637] to be false, but some of which may be true. . . . I fear . . . that it is true that Gen. Banks has extended Yankee success & domination through most of western Louisiana. . . . It seems, too, that the fortune of war has latterly been going against us in Mississippi, everywhere there was [a] contest except at Vicksburg. And the long, heroic, & so far successful defence of this position may be rendered vain, if the enemy command the river above & below, & also cut off the communication between Vicksburg & the country, & sources of supplies, in the rear. . . . There is a general & remarkable perversion of ideas of right & wrong exhibited in the expressions of northern people in regard to the war, & their procedure, & its motives, in carrying on the contest. But, considering the source,

---

[22] News of Grant's decisive campaign against Vicksburg was slow reaching the East. After moving his forces across the Mississippi at Bruinsburg on April 29–30, Grant captured Port Gibson on May 1, forced the evacuation of Grand Gulf two days later, and began marching in a northeasterly direction toward Jackson.

no such expression has been so extraordinary & monstrous, as the following passage,[23] extracted from a late public speech delivered by the distinguished historian [George] Bancroft—& who, like his compeer [Edward] Everett, was formerly a minister of the gospel—& no doubt is still a professing Christian. Who, if otherwise uninformed of the speaker's views, could ever conceive that these fine & soft phrases, [2638] which at first glance seem as if inspired by philanthropy & benevolence, & by affectionate interest for Virginia, even when reproving her errors—were really meant to advocate & urge the fullest prosecution of an unjust war whose whole object is plunder & bloodshed, & ruin to the whole of the invaded people, & to be conducted to the extent of general plunder & confiscation & destruction of the property, & expelling in destitution, if not exterminating the people, by acts of war of unexampled wrongfulness, cruelty, & atrocity—& then seizing & occupying the wasted desert, which had been Virginia, by the Yankee conquerors, spoilers, & robbers, incendiaries, & murderers on the most extended scale of operations ever known in civilized regions, or attempted by a people claiming to be Christian!!!

May 11. Monday.... Since last at Marlbourne, I had (when having nothing at hand more attractive,) read again all Shakespeare's tragedies, except three read not long before—& most of his comedies. Three or four only had not been then re-read, when I left Marlbourne. This morning began to read "Dream Life."—The mail. A great calamity has fallen upon the Confederate States in the death of Gen. Th. J. Jackson. He died [2639] on the 10th. from pneumonia combined with the effects of his wounds. Our country & its cause could not have lost near so much in the death of any other one citizen, soldier, or statesman, unless of Gen. Lee. And neither the death of Lee, nor of any other citizen, no matter how

---

[23] The passage to which the diarist alludes read as follows:

Take Virginia, for an example. Her soil is fertile, her air salubrious; her springs renovate health; her mountains glisten with precious ores. There, in her many chambers, where nature has heaped up stores of gold and silver, of gypsum and iron, of salt and copper, an evil spirit has cast over her its spell, and she sleeps in almost hopeless lethargy.—Who will mourn if the time has come when her long and deep slumber shall be broken?—Who will grieve if the procession of the Star-spangled Banner, borne onward to the songs of liberty, shall wake her from her trance of centuries? Then let her clothe her beautiful limbs in the robes of freedom and open her hundred halls to the hands of self-directed enterprise and skill.

much deserving & possessing the esteem & gratitude of our people, would be half so much regretted & deplored as the death of Jackson. Perhaps no other man, in this or any other country, was so universally admired & venerated. Neither his defects or his virtues & merits were of the character to produce enmity or ill-will in others—& he had the good fortune, which rarely attends the most distinguished worth & valuable public services, of having acquired no enemies. Jackson, as a military commander, had the qualities & the success most suited to earn general approval & admiration. He had led & fought in numerous bloody conflicts, & always conquered. In all of his numerous battles, & in all his other military operations, he has never once been defeated, or failed, or was successfully opposed by the enemy's force against which he operated. Yet with all this unexampled success, throughout his brilliant career, & with all the praise heaped upon him from every quarter—with applauses [*sic*] in which the highest civil & military authorities concurred with the most obscure private soldier & citizen—Jackson never seemed to be the least excited or uplifted, or to exhibit any indications that he was not insensible or ignorant of his own great merits. He seemed to have but one object—to perform his duty in the best possible manner. Prominent as were his military actions, & continually as his services placed him conspicuously before the public view, & brought to him new evidences of public & universal favor, he never did or said anything to direct attention to any act or opinion of his own, or to any of the numerous brave & glorious services of the troops which he had trained & so often led in battle. He did everything that was required to obey the orders of his superiors—strictly & fully, & without hesitation or question—& to perform all his duties when commanding on his own discretion—& he neither did nor said anything more. [2640] High as was his military rank, & exalted as the respect paid to him even by his superiors in command, he seemed never to think of himself but as a subordinate, whose inflexible duty it was to respect & obey his superior officer. And whether thus under immediate command of another, or on separate service & in independent command, he not only thus performed his duty, special or in general, but it was done as silently & quietly as the nature of the circumstances permitted. Few men have lived of whom so much can be truly reported as in regard to what he has done, with so little of what he has said, or offered his opinions to the public. If he

had lived to continue his military service to the end of this war—with unabated success & still increased glory—he would then have retired to private life, (if his countrymen did not prevent,) & have been content to act the part, for the remainder of his days, of an unobtrusive & obscure citizen—claiming no distinction for past services, & no reward for the exceeding great measure of his duties performed.—Another quality of Jackson's which I may not be competent to properly understand or appreciate—but which, at least, I can, & do, hold in honor & veneration. He was earnestly & zealously religious—a sincere & devoted Christian.—Gen. Burnside has had Mr. Vallandigham arrested, (for expressions in a public speech,) by a military company, & the breaking down the doors of his house. He has been tried by a Court Martial, (whose authority he refused to acknowledge, & would not defend himself before—) & the sentence had been agreed upon, but not then made known. The arrest was made in Dayton, Ohio, Mr. V.'s residence, & in the congressional district which he lately represented. His illegal arrest, & imprisonment, caused a riot by some of the people on his side, & the burning of some houses, & destruction of property to considerable amount. But the outbreak was quelled by the military, acting under Burnside's orders, & some 15 of the rioters were arrested for trial. These results seem to indicate the impotence, for resistance, of the people opposed to Lincoln, & the full supremacy of the military power. . . . This afternoon, Julian was written for, by our friend & neighbor, Edw. A. Marks, with the melancholy information that he had received the unexpected news of the death of his son Henry, in an army hospital—& that the body would be brought home & buried this evening. Julian, & I with him, went to pay respect & offer our aid. The body arrived too late to make some new & necessary arrangements for the interment—which therefore was postponed to tomorrow at 9 A.M.

May 12. Tuesday. Before the appointed hour Julian & I again walked to Mr. Marks', & with most of the now few resident neighbors, attended the burial services of the deceased.—The Mississippi had fallen 16 feet. It was expected that the low land above Vicksburg would soon be left bare of water—& then that the Yankee forces would land there, & make another attack on the city & its defences, in combination with the fleet, & perhaps also another attack from the rear. Great expectations have been enter-

tained by Yankeedom of starving the C.S. into submission. One part
of the system of measures, devised & in progress to bring about this
result, will, I suppose, be effectually executed, & mostly has been
already. This is to cut all the embankments on the borders of the
Mississippi, which guarded against inundation the immense region
of the most [2643] valuable & productive lands in the world. No
doubt this vast fertile region will be laid waste. But when all of the
broad border lands of the lower Mississippi have been converted to
a "howling wilderness," the river will not thereby be placed under
Yankee control, & made safe for use & navigation. Our people will
then have nothing there left to lose. Our guerrilla forces will incur
no risk except from the artillery of the Yankee armed steamers.
Every mile of the embankments, though cut through, will offer to
them a safe breast-work for concealment, or for safe attack—no
unarmed vessel will be able to pass 500 miles without being captured or destroyed—& even armed or iron-clad steamers will pass
only at great risk from concealed sharp-shooters, or masked batteries.—Wearied of skimming over "Dream Life," & began to read
(for second time,) [Joseph G.] Baldwin's "Party Leaders."

May 13. The mail. Yesterday & the previous afternoon Richmond
was occupied with receiving, & paying respect to, the remains of
Gen. Jackson. In obedience to his wish, the body will be buried in
Lexington, Va.... According to Yankee accounts, all the canal
cutting near Vicksburg has failed to effect the object of enabling the
vessels to pass through. Many of the Yankee land forces had moved
down the river, as supposed to attack Vicksburg in the rear, or cut
of[f] its supplies from the interior. I greatly fear, now that the enemy
command the waters between Vicksburg & Port Hudson, & can
ascend the Big Black river in the rear, that Vicksburg will not be
much longer tenable. The Yankee land forces [2644] seem to have
almost no opposition—& ... our brave & effective defensive battles have been fought only by the batteries of Vicksburg, Port
Hudson & Grand Gulf, & against naval or land forces attacking from
the front, or river side. To oppose such attacks only our defences
were planned & constructed.... 30 of the persons concerned in the
riot at Dayton have been arrested for trial, by Yankee military force,
& without delay or difficulty. It must now soon come to an issue,
whether the democrats & malcontents of Ohio & the North-West
will resist the usurpation & most oppresive as well as unconstitu-

tional & illegal [2645] despotism of Lincoln—or, (as I fear,) will submit to all its oppression like the crouching & cowardly slaves of an Asiatic despot. . . .

May 14. Thursday. Finished reading "Party Leaders." A good & interesting book—& remarkable for the impartial views of the writer. Indeed his most exalted panegyric seems to be offered to those whom he opposed in party contests. For it is clear enough that the author sided with the old federal party, & was one of the modern Clay-Whig party, the lineal but unworthy descendant of the former. As such, I am not surprised at his unmixed admiration & too general approval of the high-minded & highly gifted Hamilton. But [it] is strange that a Whig, or even a discriminating & just writer of opposite politics, should so laud as one of the greatest men, the selfish, ignorant & vulgar despot Andrew Jackson. With all my abhorrence for him, I do not deny that Jackson was a great man. But his greatness was not founded on either virtue, magnanimity, (whether springing from natural impulse or acted for artful policy—) intellect, or wisdom. His first claim to popularity was his courage, daring, & ferocity, fully displayed in his frontier life. And founded partly on this quality, & its evidences, was his power to influence & control men—which is the most valuable of all aids to ambition, & to constitute a leader & governor of men, & of a state. Jackson was not less insensible to shame than to fear—& by both he was aided in his election to, & firm position in, political eminence & power, exceeding that of Washington, or any other President of the United States. [2646] Had Jackson possessed more purity & virtue, or had he been vulnerable to shame or contempt, he would either never have perpetrated many of his actions, or would have cowered under the censure deserved for them from all virtuous men. As instances of such acts, (& without referring to his private life, or to his highest deeds of regal power,) I will adduce the following: The introducing (or permitting the introduction,) into the treaty of peace with the Creek Indians, (he acting as Commissioner for the U.S. government,) an article giving to himself 60,000 acres of the valuable lands surrendered by the Indians. This monstrous grasp of peculation could not be permitted, & was struck out by the Senate from the ratified treaty: The mean & false attempt to incriminate (by silence) [Walter] Lowrie, the U.S. Senator from Pa. (in which President Monroe meanly participated,) & who would have been crushed under the charge of having falsely calumniated

Jackson, but for the accidental discovery of the letter of Jackson to Monroe, in which the charge was substantially sustained:[24] His appointments to high offices of his creatures, Henry Lee & [John H.] Eaton—of the latter of whom, in reference to his acts & character, Randolph said "he stunk"—& Lee's moral character stood so low that in the Senate his nomination to office did not receive a single favorable vote:[25] His thorough support of Eaton's wife, a woman of no character for virtue, & to force whom into society, Jackson even broke up his cabinet, & retained no ministers, or friends, except those persons who like Van Buren would second all these acts & pay adulation to Mrs. Eaton, or the supple W. C. Rives, who sent his wife to visit her, to forward his obtaining the mission to France. These, & many other base acts—including that which corrupted & revolutionized the government, the general proscription of all office-holders of the adverse party, & conferring every office, & emolument, as reward to personal devotion to the President, Jackson would have shrunk from, or, if committing, would have sunk under the confessed turpitude & odium, if he had not been encased in armor of proof against the shafts of shame, & the contempt of the virtuous. [2647]—The portraitures of Jefferson & [John] Randolph in "Party Leaders" are very interesting, & have much truth. But that of Jefferson touches but very slightly his worst political acts & offences—& Randolph's evil disposition & private vices, & the infirmities of his great mind, are glossed over, or treated too tenderly. The reading of [Henry S.] Randall's Life of Jefferson gave me a more favorable impression of his disposition, & private character, than I had before entertained. With all the coun-

---

[24] The reference is to an incident in the presidential campaign of 1824. Seeking to broaden the appeal of their candidate, supporters of Jackson privately circulated copies of three letters written by Jackson to Monroe in the winter of 1816–17, in which the former had urged the incoming president to ignore party passions and ties in making appointments to political offices. When partisans of William H. Crawford—among them Senator Lowrie—sought to utilize the letters to discredit Jackson among strict Republicans, the Tennessean denied the veracity of published reports concerning the correspondence. Incensed by this imputation against his integrity, Senator Lowrie fought back and finally forced publication of the letters in May, 1824.

[25] Son of "Light-Horse Harry" Lee and half-brother of Robert E. Lee, Henry Lee (1787–1837) was active as a pamphleteer and speech-writer in Jackson's presidential campaign of 1828. As a reward for his services, he received a recess appointment as consul general to Algiers. However, the Senate, in March, 1830, unanimously declined to confirm his appointment, basing the rejection largely on alleged acts of personal immorality.

terbalance of his vices, I should infer that Jefferson was a man of kindly & benevolent feelings, amiable disposition, & whose private virtues greatly preponderated over his vices. But, so far as his good qualities & acts served to built up that unlimited political sway which he acquired over the minds of his partisans, it may be truly declared of him, "Curse on his virtues, for they've undone his country!" By means of his marvellous & unaccountable political influence & power over the minds of his followers, He has succeeded in impressing them with his political theories of democratic perfection. Thus he has been enabled to infuse a corrupting & poisonous principle into every constitution of government of these states, & of the U.S., & he has caused more evil, and done more to destroy free & sound institutions, & to upset all that was stable & valuable in our government, than all that the real & avowed opposers of popular rights could have effected, if their power had equalled their wishes—or than all that demagogues could have effected in practice, if they had not been given strength & power by constitutions founded on universal suffrage, & equality of the people in theory, but truly the supremacy of the lowest & basest class, led & directed by baser & mercenary demagogues, seeking exclusively their own selfish benefit. Jefferson was, *par excellence*, the apostle of the most extreme democratic doctrines. He advocated universal suffrage, & all elections, [2648] of public functionaries, to be made by the popular vote. At any rate, this last & worst result is the necessary consequence of universal popular suffrage. By his teaching & influence, these principles of destruction have been fixed, never to be removed, fully in every state constitution, & in great degree in the federal constitution. Virginia in its old constitution, founded on freehold suffrage, (imperfect as was that first written & hastily constructed constitution of free government—) enjoyed the best form of free government in the world—under which the rights of all citizens were best secured, & there were the best chances for bringing into the public service, the most competent & honest men. All this has been lost. The last & now existing constitution of Virginia, more than the preceding, & first changes, was the work of demagogues, & constructed in obedience to Jefferson's dogmas of the perfect equality & virtue of all men, but also especially designed, & so the constitution has worked in practice, for the benefit & gain of demagogues. The theory of popular equality, & of popular virtue, independence & patriotism, (which would impel every citizen to vote for the most worthy public functionaries,) is very plausible & seducing to youthful minds, or inexperienced students of political affairs. To believe in & to zealously advocate such notions is pardonable in boys at school, & in mere closet students of the science of government. But it is inconceivable how a man of Jefferson's political knowledge & wisdom, his knowledge of mankind, & his long political experience, should have zealously advocated these doctrines of extreme democracy, not only in his time of ardent & confident youth, but in his mature age. There is no greater fallacy than the supposition (the foundation of this theory of government,) that men will generally be directed in their choice of representatives, & all elective functionaries, by considerations of the superior [2649] competency & trust-worthiness of the persons voted for. On the contrary, these considerations (even if not entirely misunderstood, or unknown,) have no influence on the great mass of voters under universal suffrage—& are rarely the most operative even on the better & select class that properly restricted suffrage would only admit. Most voters, & all of the most ignorant & baser sort, vote, not for the most capable & honest representatives, (even in their incompetent judgment,) but for those whom they have most personal liking for, if the voter is honest—or, if mercenary, for those from whom they expect most to gain by thus favoring. Therefore the selections so made by this class, so far from being the best, will more often be among the worst offered for choice. With properly restricted suffrage, the electors having all property to guard, & much more of education, ability, & virtue, than the general mass, a much more discriminating & better choice of public functionaries would necessarily be made. But putting this aside, & allowing nothing for greater virtue or wisdom directing the voters, they (as all others,) will certainly be directed in their selections by considerations of self-interest. They will especially require that their individual rights & interests of property shall be guarded & preserved. And if their representatives are judiciously chosen even in reference to this selfish object alone, they must be men who are competent in intellect & education, honest & trustworthy—better representatives & functionaries than could possibly be expected from the exercise of the utmost virtue & wisdom under unlimited suffrage. But in truth, when the mob bears the sway in elections, it knows little, & cares not at all, for the superior fitness or honesty of candidates. Each of the lowest voters gives his vote, or the direction of his vote, to some one the nearest in qualities to himself, or by whose [2650] favor the voter expects to gain something for himself. As it is impossible for the ignorant, the obscure, & the secluded, to judge of the claims (according to any standard,) of candidates out of their own narrow sphere, & personally unknown to them, such voters necessarily must trust to artful & often vulgar demagogues to guide them. Thus the increased powers which the letter of a constitution ostensibly confers on popular suffrage, the people hasten to transfer to the hands of demagogues, who will always wield the popular favor & power for their own personal selfish, & base purposes. If each influential demagogue (or base flatterer of the lowest people,) cannot procure himself to be elected for the office in question, he lends his influence & votes to some stronger demagogue, under a bargain, implied if not expressed in words, to be repaid in wages of corruption. So far my remarks apply to elections of legislative representatives—the only public functionaries which ought ever to be elected by a popular vote, whether limited or universal. But many fold greater are the solid objections to the extending, (as has been done by our present constitution,) popular election, &, still worse, by unlimited suffrage, to the appointment of judges, of the highest as well as lowest courts, of governor, & of other functionaries executive, judicial, or adminstrative, whose constituencies embrace the people of either the whole state, or a large section of the state. Of course, it is impossible that such widely spread constituencies, (even if suffrage were restricted,) could correctly judge of the qualifications of unknown & remote candidates—& especially for judicial or legal appointments. Therefore, even if the voters be generally honest, patriotic, & well-informed . . . & the election be fairly & honestly conducted, (that is, not directed by demagogues, or their political machinery for nominating [2651] candidates,) the probability is, that the candidate who has most personal friends will obtain the plurality of votes, & be elected, though his supporters did not amount to one fourth of the votes given, or one-tenth of all in the electoral district. Still worse will it be, for the concentration & exercise of the popular voice, whether that would be discreet or foolish, when the whole state has to vote, as for the governor, lieutenant governor, & Attorney General. In these cases, (& in somewhat less degree for any large judicial district,) it is *impossible* for the popular vote to elect, without its being *directed*, & so concentrated. This the dema-

gogues of the Convention well knew, & designed, & for the especial purpose that they should direct the popular vote. To this end
voluntary & self-appointed "conventions" or caucuses, mainly
filled with office-seeking demagogues, have assembled, & nominated candidates for such offices. While the state was divided into
the two political parties of Whig & Democratic, (which I rejoice
now are nearly extinct, & powerless as such,) each party had its
convention, & nominated opposing candidates. But this was all the
choice permitted to any voter. If throwing off the shackles of party
rule, a democrat might indeed vote for the candidate nominated by
the convention of whig demagogues & wire-pullers—or, *vice
versa*, a whig might vote for the democratic candidate. Such exceptions rarely if ever occurred. And otherwise, the voters had no
choice except to vote for the only candidate of his [*sic*] own party
indicated by the managing demagogues. Thus, the constitution,
when professing to extend popular power to the election of state
officers, really restricted it. For the influence of each individual
voter was greater, as exercised on his representatives in the legislature, when the legislature elected these state officers, than now,
when they are virtually elected by a self-apppointed & irresponsi-
ble convention of interested office-seekers, who may commit any
act of baseness & corruption with impunity. To Mr. Jefferson's
[2652] influence, we are indebted mainly, if not entirely, for the
engrafting on our government the practically corrupting & destructive principles to which he was so wedded in theory. And this evil
work of his far outweighs all the benefits which our country, & the
cause of free government, owe to his republican principles &
conduct, his undoubted public services, his patriotism, & his commanding intellect.—The foregoing objections apply mainly to the
incompetency of the people directly to elect executive & judicial
functionaries—& of the more ignorant & poorest class to select
judiciously any functionaries of government. But there is even a
stronger objection to universal suffrage, or the extension of suffrage
to the classes who own no property, & pay little or nothing of the
taxes. Individuals of this class are not only, as the general rule, too
ignorant to vote judiciously, but, having no interest in the preservation of the public revenue, they care nothing for its disbursement &
waste. Further—while they have no interest in taking care of the
public funds, in numerous cases they have, or think they have,
individual interests to be aided by the most profuse waste of the

public funds. As laborers to be employed, or their wages raised—or as pensioners on the treasury—or as employees of or dependents on rich & influential contractors—the greater number of the most destitute & ignorant voters will learn to favor the high amount & waste of the taxes as more conducive to their private interests, than the most wise & faithful economy. Then, when in the progress of time, these poorest voters make the majority in any community, their interest, always opposed to that of the tax-paying class & property holders, will, from being more & more detrimental to the latter . . . be predominant. Then comes the awful consumation [*sic*] to which universal suffrage always tends & approaches, that is, when one class of the people owns the property & pays the taxes—& another class, grown to be a majority, having equally the right to vote in all public matters, fixes the amount & directs [2653] the expenditure of the taxes & of all government funds. Such has already become the condition of things in the great northern cities, & is fast growing to be in the old northern states. And unless the institution of slavery prevents, such may hereafter be the case in the southern states. And whatever may be the letter of the written constitution of government—no matter how free in theory, & just & wise to preserve the equal rights of all citizens, (at least according to Jefferson's doctrines,) whenever one class of citizens pay the taxes, & has [*sic*] no power to assess or disburse them, & another class has these powers, & contributes nothing to the taxes, that country will be governed by a grinding despotism—more unscrupulous, shameless, & oppressive, than would be the unlimited rule of a single master.—The Polish insurrection was not quelled with the defeat of the army, & the capture of the commander & dictator. The struggle is still in progress, & the insurgents presenting a strong front. Thus, the apprehended ill bearing upon our war is continued.—Read Edmund Burke's sketch of his speech in the celebrated debate in parliament on the Army Estimates, in 1790. Began to read for the third time (the first was fifty years ago,) his "Reflections on the French Revolution."

May 15. The mail. Two letters from Edmund. No others of his family had (on 13th) left Marlbourne. The alarm which was in that neighborhood the day I left, was not so baseless as I thought then, & since, until receiving this report. My son writes that the alarm & uneasiness in the neighborhood still continued—& more so in King William county, across the river, whence many families had already fled. He writes, "there seems to be good evidence that the enemy has landed in considerable numbers, & is entrenching at West Point. Thence we will certainly be subjected to Yankee raids, or the fear of them. The night before you left us, the Yankees landed at the White House, & attempted to destroy the railroad bridge, (across the Pamunkey). They had some 2 or 3 gunboats or transports within sight. They were driven back that night, without their effecting their object; & next morning, neither the land forces nor the vessels were to be seen. The same day, (Friday, 8th.) a body of Yankee cavalry advanced, from Williamsburg, as high as New Kent C.H., but retired." If our government [2654] cannot, or does not, drive off the Yankees from West Point, or place troops to securely prevent their higher incursions, by land or by the Pamunkey, the whole property at Marlbourne will remain in great peril, if not to be generally sacrificed. All the lands on our side of the narrow Pamunkey were overrun & laid waste last year. But King William county, though so near, was not then touched, & now offers a rich & tempting prize to the foraging & plundering expeditions of the Yankees.—After our defences at Grand Gulf (at mouth of Big Black river,) were evacuated, (& also those at Bayou Pierre close by,) our troops, under Gen. [John S.] Bowen, about 6000 strong, withdrew to near Port Gibson, all in the county of Claiborne [Miss.]. There they were attacked by five times their number of Grant's army, on the 1st inst., & the battle continued from early in the morning to after sunset, when our army was withdrawn to prevent a flank movement by the enemy, who had been lately reinforced. . . . Gen. Bowen retreated to the other side of the Big Black river, & there took a position which it was expected could be maintained against Grant's advancing army, which was estimated at 50 to 60,000 men. He was 10 miles north of Port Gibson, on the route towards Gen. Bowen's army & Vicksburg. A Yankee letter from their army speaks confidently of their success, & the certain capture of Vicksburg. From our side, statements are as confident of the enemy's repulse & failure. . . . On the 11th. the enemy advanced a column 10,000 strong upon Raymond (Hinds Co.) where Gen. [John] Gregg was posted with 4100 men, of which a few were cavalry, but no artillery. He opened battle, with musketry alone. [2655] But learning that the enemy had been reinforced, Gen. Gregg retired & made a stand at Mississippi Springs, where he was subsequently reinforced by cavalry & artillery.—The Yankees are still threatening to renew the attack on Charleston. Their iron-clad monitors lie in North Edisto—& their land forces have intrenched on Seabrook's & Folly islands. On the latter, they have extended their posts to Light House Inlet, which separates it from the south end of Morris island. The pickets, on the opposite sides of the inlet, are near enough to converse. Latterly, the Yankee authorities seem to have been trying to console Yankeedom (for a time,) for Hooker's defeat, by excelling themselves in lying reports of successes, & good prospects. Besides Sec. Stanton's official proclamation that Hooker would soon resume offensive operations, & the like threats against Charleston, late northern accounts affirm positively that Hooker's army had again crossed the Rappahannock, & found no opposing forces, Gen. Lee having retreated towards Richmond. Another report is that Gen. [Erasmus D.] Keyes had advanced from West Point, & actually surprised Richmond, & occupied, & still held the city! . . .

May 16. In compliance with Edmund's request, this morning I rode to Beechwood, to look over the land, & especially the condition of the clover, & reported to him by letter. A refugee from Hampton, a pilot named Topping, & his family, have been placed by Julian to live in the old house, to try to take care of the house & land, & to keep off thieves & trespassers. In both respects, there has been much improvement since Capt. Topping's sojourn there. It is painful for me to visit the place, formerly so flourishing & beautiful, & now a waste & a ruin.—My time passes heavily except for the time when I have newspapers to read. . . . In having to leave Marlbourne, & my diligent attention to the ditching, my loss of pleasure has been very great. It is in vain for me to attempt, as I have here made some faint & daily efforts, to create, through habit, feelings alike interested in any other farming operations. [2657]

May 17. Sunday.—The Yankee public has been making merry, with the accounts of their newspapers of the panic in Richmond, & the imminent danger of its capture by Stoneman's cavalry raid, when his force approached within a few miles—though not so little as two miles, as they assert. Though these accounts consist chiefly of falsehoods, & of gross exaggerations of truth, it seems true that Richmond was almost without any previously organized defensive force—unless of a few hundreds of such undisciplined, ill-commanded, & therefore worthless troops as the Wren battalion of Henrico cavalry. If, on or before the first alarm, Stoneman had thrown 2000 cavalry into the city, I do not doubt that he might have captured & held it for a time—long enough to destroy millions worth of public & private industrial works, put the officers of government to flight, & to have burnt a large portion of the city. But the enemy had not the boldness necessary for attempting to put such a loss & disgrace on our government. . . . Finished Burke's "Reflections on the Revolution in France." I had supposed that my last reading of Scott's Novels had been too recent for me to begin them again. But, having nothing else left more attractive, I was reading some of the Introductions, & thus, by accident, dipped into the Antiquary, & found it so much forgotten, & therefore so interesting, that I began to read it again regularly—I suppose for the fifth or [2658] sixth time since its first appearance. . . .

May 18. Monday. On last Friday, the Crenshaw woolen factory in Rd. took fire by accident, & was burnt. The fire extended to the outer workshops of the Tredegar Iron Works, some of which also were burnt. The loss supposed to be not less than $250,000. And though both establishments were private property, the loss to the government will be more than the pecuniary value burnt. The woolen factory, the most extensive & effective in the C.S., supplied most of the cloth for the army—& the Iron Works most of the cannon, shells & balls, & was almost wholly employed in their production. The operations of the latter will not be materially obstructed, nor for more than a few weeks.[26]—The army of Grant has advanced, & towards the rear of Vicksburg. By reports from C.S. sources, it was stated that Raymond had been occupied by the Yankees—& subsequently Jackson, which is the capital of Miss., but not otherwise a town of much importance. . . . I fear the worst for Vicksburg & our forces in Mississippi. As the land [2659] forces of Grant have passed below, & to the rear of Vicksburg, & as many of the Yankee fleet as desired have passed down by our batteries, I do not understand what important use there can be in our continuing to hold & defend Vicksburg—the safety of the position, & of the large garrison & powerful armament being now greatly endangered by the enemy being in the rear, & communication & all supplies like to be cut off. But it may be, contrary to my supposition,

---

[26] Damage to the ironworks was more serious than Tredegar officials admitted publicly. The machine shops were virtually gutted, and the Confederacy lacked the tooling facilities necessary to replace the items destroyed. For a full account of the damages inflicted upon the Tredegar Works by the May 15 fire, see Dew, *Ironmaker to the Confederacy*, 194.

that our positions can be kept supplied, & also well defended—& if so, I do not doubt they will be. Our defences stretch 10 miles or more along the river. If the change of attack, by the land forces, from front to rear, can be prepared for & vigorously opposed, the assault of the Yankee army & fleet will be a bloody affair. If they should not gain a signal victory, they will probably meet with a heavy & disastrous defeat. The close approach of the sickly season—doubly to be dreaded by the Yankees because of their having laid all the low country under water which will soon be stagnant—will hurry Grant's offensive operations. Whatever can be done by him must be done within a few weeks, or disease will probably so weaken his army as to frustrate his plans, & render all the gigantic preparations useless. The same danger threatens the Yankee army on Seabrook's & Folly islands. Except immediately on the sea shore, this region is dangerously unhealthy before June. It is true, & strange, that the Yankee forces remained on the S.C. sea coast, & also in New Orleans, through last summer, & without suffering greatly by disease.—In northern papers, there continue strong intimations & threats of the early renewal of attack on Charleston, & also by Hooker's army, which is represented as strong as ever, & already advancing. But I think that these threats are uttered by order, & to deceive our authorities, & prevent the sending off reinforcements from Charleston & Lee's army to the west. . . .

May 19. Tuesday. Finished "The Antiquary," & began to read the second volume of the "Memoirs of the Margravine of Bareith."[27] The first volume of this very curious & remarkable book has been lost, not by the plundering of the Yankees, but by the borrowing of some one of the reading young ladies of our neighbors of Marlbourne, who are fond of borrowing books & rarely think of returning them. I valued this book very highly. It [2661] is the only copy that I ever met with, & obtained after long seeking. I think that it presents the most accurate picture of private royal life, & the meanness & baseness thereof, that ever was written—& especially of the obscure petty sovereign princes & courts of Germany. Though the royal authoress designed to present herself in a most favorable light, & though exaggeration, falsehood & calumny of all

---

[27] An English dramatist of some note, the authoress married Charles Alexander, margrave of the Hohenzollern principalities of Anspach and Bareith, following the death of her estranged first husband, the earl of Craven, in 1791. Her memoirs were published in 1826, two years before her death.

her friends & intimates are obvious in the general tone, yet, as false witnesses sometimes indirectly best establish the truth of facts, so the Margravine unintentionally exhibits true pictures, even when she designs to overpraise herself, or to make other characters blacker than they deserved. . . . If a person whose pursuits had necessarily made him intimately acquainted with the lowest & most vicious classes of European society, including paupers, beggars, thieves & murderers, were to write his memoirs, & describe all the characters, good & bad, with whom he had been associated, there would not be such general absence of virtuous or commendable characters, & of worthy & amiable traits, as in the whole catalogue of the Margravine's imperial, royal, & noble associates.

May 20. Finished the "Memoirs."—Tried to attend a little to, & to take some interest in Julian's work, which I did, to small extent.— The mail. Grant's army, supposed 50,000 strong, occupied Jackson on the 15th, our troops, (a weak force,) having previously evacuated the town, without fighting there.[28] The Yankees remained but two days, in which they burnt, destroyed (or carried off to such extent as could be,) immense amounts of public & private property. The destruction estimated [2662] at above $5,000,000. . . . Grant evacuated Jackson on the 17th,[29] & moved on in the direction of the Mississippi & of Vicksburg. 3000 negroes in the county of Hinds alone, had joined Grant's army, or accepted their offered emancipation otherwise. . . . Grant's army, if it has not already (as before reported,) fallen back to the Mississippi, may be so far separated from its supplies as to have its communications endangered, or cut off. I have great reliance on Gen. Johnston's judgment & ability. If he can defeat Grant's objects, or defeat his army in battle, it will be for us a great success & a glorious triumph. But if Johnston should be compelled to lose Vicksburg, & retreat—or, worse, be defeated

---

[28] Actually, Federal forces entered Jackson about 4 P.M. on May 14, after routing two Confederate brigades numbering 6,000 men.

[29] These early reports of Grant's movements following the capture of Jackson were distorted and inaccurate. On May 16 the major portion of Grant's army, having already departed Jackson, encountered near Edward's Station a Confederate army of 22,000 under the command of General John C. Pemberton, who was belatedly attempting to unite his forces with those of General Joseph E. Johnston. In the ensuing contest, known as the battle of Champion's Hill, Pemberton was repulsed and forced to retire toward Vicksburg. Initial telegraphic reports of this engagement, the most severe in the Vicksburg campaign, had already reached the East, but they were so distorted that Ruffin's references to them have been deleted from this portion of the diary.

in battle, it will be one of the heaviest blows that could fall upon the Confederate States. . . . Though the sentence of Vallandigham, by Court Martial, has not been officially announced, it is reported in Washington that it was to two years' confinement, & hard labor (with other condemned criminals,) on the fortifications of Dry Tortugas. But that Lincoln had commuted the punishment to exile to the seceded states. If true,[30] I trust that this will not be permitted by our authorities. If permitted, it would be a capital stroke of policy for Lincoln, to identify Vallandigham with secessionists & their cause, & so render him suspected by his countrymen, & destroy his popularity & influence. It would more certainly defeat his election as Governor of Ohio, (for which he is a candidate,) than his being confined & treated as a felon at Tortugas. . . .

May 21. Thursday. Heard, from the military post close by, that information had been received from the Signal Corps now stationed at Sandy Point that some Yankee gun boats yesterday ascended James river & turned off up the Chickahominy, & proceeded out of sight. This movement, & all such, will increase the uneasiness & sense of insecurity of the residents of Marlbourne & the region between these incursions & Richmond. Though I do not expect any serious invasion so high, & still less another early movement "On to Richmond," it seems very probable that the actual successes, (exaggerated four-fold in Yankee belief by their lying reports,) of late Yankee raids, will encourage others to be attempted, both by land & water. And in the Chickahominy & the Pamunkey & Mattapony rivers, they have offered available & undefended channels for their gunboats, & on the two peninsulas included undefended land routes to pass over, & a defenceless country to plunder. And they have, in their military stations at Williamsburg, Gloucester Point, & West Point, & their naval stations below, points from which they can send off expeditions, whose arrival would bring the first intimation of the movement having been begun. It places my son, at Marlbourne, & thousands of other proprietors & residents, in a most uneasy & perilous position. For on any day, without an hour's notice, either by land or water, a raid might destroy all the farming means & values of the farm for the year at least, sweep off the negroes & stock, plunder the provisions, which could not be replaced, even if stopping short of

---

[30] The report was accurate. Vallandigham was turned over to Confederate authorities in Tennessee on May 25.

burning the houses, & maltreating the family. . . . I await, with great anxiety, the next mail—though the fate of Vicksburg can scarcely be decided so soon. . . . As Gen. Johnston's . . . general command extends over Tennessee & Alabama, as well as Mississippi, he has had at his disposal all the means that the general defence of that whole region left available—& I will trust that he has neglected no available means to strengthen his immediate command & charge at Vicksburg. In addition to all other motives of duty to call forth Johnston's utmost efforts for success, his emulation & ambition must have been stimulated to the highest pitch, by the recent glorious victories achieved by Beauregard at Charleston, & Lee on the Rappahannock. Johnston has already & deservedly acquired high distinction as a commander. If he should now be defeated, it would be to him doubly a defeat, in contrast with the recent victories of his noble compeers. Gloomy as are our present prospects (so far as known,) on the Mississippi, & many & heavy as have been our past disasters, I am encouraged to look hopefully for the impending results.

May 22. Friday. The mail. . . . No new events near Vicksburg, or of the opposed armies—but some explanations of what have already been noted as first heard. . . . It is good news for us that nothing more had been done. Every day's postponement of operations will be in our favor—notwithstanding that large reinforcements are coming on to Grant. It is reported that Vicksburg has provisions for 4 months—& that the force *now* in the field under Gen. Pemberton (doubtless since joined by Gen. Johnston,) was 50,000 men, besides those left in Vicksburg. . . . In the mean time, Grant's lines of communication with his sources of supplies are very long, the transportation difficult & hazardous, & great probability of his supplies being cut off. If Gen. Johnston can successfully stand a siege in Vicksburg for two months, the ultimate defeat of the enemy will be scarcely doubtful. And our success may be otherwise effected much sooner, either by a crushing defeat of Grant's army in open field, or, by cutting off its supplies, compelling its disastrous retreat. There are two long northern articles in the papers today, presenting opposite views of the probable result. One, a letter from a correspondent of the N.Y. Times, with Grant's army, gives in advance a despondent picture of the great difficulties of Grant in thus attacking Vicksburg from the rear, & from so far in the interior—& especially on account of the great obstacles &

dangers to the passage of his supplies, on every available route, by land or by water. The other article, editorial of the N.Y. Times, is of later date, &, like most other northern opinions, treats the capture of Vicksburg as now being both imminent & certain. At great length the writer descants upon the incalculable value of the expected capture to the North, & of loss to the South. . . . Without admitting the extent of any of this writer's estimates & consequences of our loss of Vicksburg, it would be a disaster under which the C.S. would stagger with difficulty. May God defend us from it! And from the tenor of the reports today, I am much encouraged in my hopes for our successful resistance, & the complete defeat of our villainous foes. . . . A very large public meeting, called by formal notice, of the democratic party, has been held in the city of New York, in which speeches were made, & opinions uttered, of the most violent character in denunciation of the administration & its violations of the constitution. All the utterers of these sentiments are as guilty, & as amenable to punishment as felons, as Vallandigham. It is reported that many thousands of men in the north-western states have leagued together, & bound themselves by secret oaths, not to submit to the conscription law, & to resist its being enforced, even by arms & bloodshed. But I have ceased to attach much importance to any such indications. If the malcontents truly designed to resist illegal & unconstitutional oppression & tyranny, they have had enough of better grounds than the conscription law. The arrest & sentence of Vallandigham alone would be enough to drive to armed resistance & insurrection every true defender of his political rights. I think that the federal administration has measured the extent & value of the threatened resistance, & correctly estimates it at nothing. In New York, with a malcontent governor & an equally divided legislature, & in New Jersey, with both governor & legislature malcontent, the case may be different. And if those think so who think for [2669] & direct Lincoln, no illegal or unconstitutional punishments will be attempted to be enforced against citizens of these states. . . .

May 23. Saturday. . . . The late reports from Mississippi & La. have brought nothing but a continued succession of misfortunes. And especially as to the struggle for Vicksburg, the enemy have gained & we have lost in every late operation. But though not an item of better fortune, or of good news, has reached us, reflection on the situation of the opposed armies makes me more & more sanguine of the final & signal defeat of Grant's army. My increased hopefulness, & confidence, are founded on the belief that Vicksburg is provided to stand a siege of some length—my high opinion of Gen. Johnston & his soldiers—the long extended routes, difficulties & perils of the transportation of all supplies for the Yankee army—& the sickliness of its position, & the close approach of the hottest & most sickly season.

May 24. Sunday. By accident looked into the Introduction of Webster's Dictionary, & was attracted to read through several of the different divisions, including those under the heads of "Orthography" & "Pronunciation." My hearty dislike to the most of Yankee peculiarities, caused me to take up a strong prejudice against this dictionary. Ignorantly, I supposed it to be the embodiment of Yankee language, & the authority for Yankee deviations from standard English. I would not look into it—& was entirely unacquainted with its true general character, until the loss of my library, & Edmund's, & the removal (for safety,) of the greater part of Julian's left but one English dictionary [2670] accessible to me, & this was Webster's, belonging to Mrs. Meade. My slight examination of the changes he has adopted in the spelling of some classes of words, & his general reasoning in support of his changes, & his differences in other respects from preceding lexicographers, compel me to confess my previous error, & to approve of most (though not of all) the changes for which Webster is the authority. . . .

May 25. Monday. . . . The mail. The papers of the 23rd published telegraphic reports (from Jackson) very unfavorable to us, if true, but not trustworthy. These were, that in the battle of 17th. near Edward's Station (in which Gen. Pemberton had been compelled to retreat to Big Black river,) our retreating army had abandoned & spiked 30 pieces of artillery: that our batteries at Snyder's Bluff, (above Vicksburg,) & Yazoo city had been captured: that another battle had occurred on Big Black river on the 18th.[31] (the Yankee army having crossed some miles above the bridge, & attacked in our rear,) in which we were defeated, with heavy loss, burnt the bridge, & retreated to Vicksburg. . . . Probably something may be

---

[31] Once again the date is incorrect. Pemberton, seeking to impede Grant's crossing of the river, was defeated in a one-hour engagement at Big Black River Bridge on May 17, losing 1,700 men and eighteen guns to the advancing Federals. He then retired to the defenses of Vicksburg, where he was besieged by Grant on the following day.

true, as certainly the outposts will be evacuated, & may be captured, & the strength of the army concentrated near Vicksburg. Later telegraphic dispatches received yesterday report that Grant had made several attacks on Vicksburg, & had been beaten back in all, & had suffered heavy loss . . . . An official dispatch from Gen. Johnston, dated 23rd, says "An officer who left [2672] Vicksburg on Tuesday (19th) reports that an assault near the Yazoo road on Pemberton's intrenchments had been repelled." If indeed the enemy's assaults have been made repeatedly, & so successfully repulsed, there is little ground to fear the capture of Vicksburg soon. And unless effected soon, its capture will be impossible by the present invading force. It is said that Grant's army has received & will receive heavy reinforcements. But this will in proportion increase the difficulty of his obtaining supplies of provisions. If these are cut off, before he can conquer our army & capture Vicksburg & its defences, Grant will not be the stronger, or the less in danger of ultimate & utter defeat, & perhaps surrender, by having 20,000 or more men added to his first force. . . . Though every movement & every conflict, up to the defences of Vicksburg, has been a success to the enemy—& even if these late discredited reports of further & great losses to us were true—I still feel sanguine, & almost confident, of our final & signal success. And if this great Yankee army should be defeated, & at the same time its supplies be cut off, there will be good ground for the further hope that the whole army of the invaders may be compelled to surrender. . . .

May 26. Tuesday. This morning Julian received from a neighbor an Enquirer of yesterday, which though of no later date than ours, contains additional & also authentic dispatches from Gen. Pemberton, & Vicksburg. These dispatches are of earlier dates (20th & 21st,) than those before received [2675] but that delay was owing to their having to be sent to Jackson. The fact that such communication was open from Vicksburg to Jackson, is in itself good news. . . . We are assured that to 3 o'clock P.M., on 21st, & after three days of attack & fighting, Grant's army of 60,000 men,[32] aided by gun-boats, had effected no material damage to our works or men, & had been repulsed with heavy loss.

May 27. Wednesday. Lotty returned home. . . . Jane & her child,

---

[32] This figure is slightly inflated. At the outset of siege operations Grant's forces numbered 45,000; this total was swelled by reinforcements to more than 70,000 by the time Vicksburg capitulated on July 4, 1863.

with Nanny & Mary came to Petersburg on Monday, on their way to Ruthven. But as . . . they wished to remain longer in Petersburg, they will come next mail-train day, Friday, to Disputanta, & thence here.—The mail, & several extra papers. Nothing decisive yet at Vicksburg, & no important changes since the previous & last accounts. . . . Firing of cannon had been heard from Vicksburg up to 9 A.M. on Sunday 24th—& not later, to the sending of the last dispatch from Jackson on that day.—Vallandigham's destination to Fort Warren had been changed by Lincoln's commuting his punishment to exile to the Confederate States. He was brought, under flag of truce, & turned loose near Shelbyville, Ten., where he was received. I hope that neither he nor our authorities will consent to the continuation of this arrangement. He ought not to remain, nor our authorities to permit his remaining. If he does remain, it will be giving effect to a capital stroke of policy by Lincoln, or by those who lead him. There has been another popular meeting in New York, by which still more violent resolutions were adopted than by the previous meeting—& by which peace is called for unconditionally. This is a step far ahead of any before taken by any northern malcontents.—In pursuance of a general system of policy of the Yankees in regard to the towns occupied for a long time by their forces, they have lately expelled from New Orleans, & sent outside of their lines, more than 5000 of the "disloyal" residents—by which term they designate all who are not traitors to their country & government, & who are favorable to the southern cause. Most of these exiles are either old & infirm men (not subject to military service,) or women with their young children—& all sent forth nearly destitute, after being robbed of nearly all their property. The same cruel policy has been pursued at Newbern, St. Louis, & other cities. The objects are, by the fear of this terrible punishment, first to compel as many as possible of the more timid, or less scrupulous, secessionists to abjure their previous professions, & to take the oath [2677] of allegiance to Yankeedom, & to assume all the consequent obligations: and next, by forcing so many destitute persons into our lines, to subject the country to the cost of their support, & so much the more increase the scarcity of provisions. Such a barbarous course is unexampled in the warfare of civilized nations.—I had for some length of time believed the report that Capt. George B. Cuthbert had been killed at the first battle of Fredericksburg.[33]

---

[33] See above, page 535.

Afterwards, that report was denied, & I remained doubtful, & without any reliable information until today. His obituary notice, just (correctly) published, states that his death did not occur until at the late battle near Chancellorsville, where he was killed. He was a devoted & noble patriot, & excellent officer—though he remained to the last without promotion, & closed his military career as he began it, with the first investment of Fort Sumter, as Captain of the Palmetto guard, of Charleston. . . .

May 28. Thursday. The general election day. With Julian . . . drove in the carriage to the Court House. I voted for Wm. Smith of Culpeper for Governor—& for Congress, Judge Th[omas] Gholson, & for the House of Delegates, Capt. Taylor of Surry. In the two latter votes, I was not so much impelled by favor for these candidates as my hearty dislike to their opponents, & the previous incumbents, & my desire to get rid of them as representatives, & in public trusts. . . . The Northern papers continue to publish that Hooker's lately defeated army is again & soon to make another advance to Richmond, & that the defeated Yankee fleet is again to attack [2678] Charleston. I have no idea . . . [that] either of these forces, so lately & signally repulsed, will soon return to again attack the forces that repelled & defeated the previous attacks. If there was any truth of such intentions, the Yankee authorities & Yankee newspapers would not be so open in announcing & continuing to repeat the threatened movements. I believe that, in addition to the usual disposition of Yankees to boast & threaten, there is an object in these published threats, to prevent any of our troops, from Lee's army, or from Charleston, being sent to reinforce Vicksburg.

May 29. Friday. . . . The mail. The last dispatch from Vicksburg is official, from Gen. Johnston to the government, & dated 27th. This states that Gen. [Carter L.] Stevenson, in Vicksburg reported to Gen. Johnston, that "hard fighting had been going on there since the 14th, with continued success (of the besieged garrison,) & that our men are confident & in high spirits." . . . This dispatch, & others to like effect & more in detail, but which are of no authority, are published as "Cheering News." So it is, that to the 27th Vicksburg remained ours, & safe & confident. The first I believe. The second part I fear was stated too favorably to Gen. Johnston, who being outside, could not himself know particulars. But when even the most favorable report is compared with, & its *anticipations* are tested by, the official & other Yankee reports of the *previous* repeated & rapid successes of Grant's army & the Yankee fleet, I am compelled to believe that the besiegers have so encircled Vicksburg, & pressed in so near to the town, & had previously given Pemberton's forces such damaging defeats [End of MS Volume 16—p. 2679] in the field, & had captured & occupied so many of our outer batteries, that Vicksburg must also be compelled to yield before many days. The only chance for its being saved, as it seems to me, depends (not on its own yet remaining means for defence,) but upon Gen. Johnston's army being so reinforced as to be able to engage Grant's in the rear, & to defeat it, & so to relieve Vicksburg. Of this, I fear there is now little probability—unless Vicksburg can still hold out longer than now seems possible. I will append Adm. Porter's official report of his occupation (on the 18th,) of our strong fortification at Haynes' Bluff, which guarded the Yazoo river, as well as Vicksburg on that side—& other official, & also private reports of the previous successes of Grant's army, & the losses of ours. Allowing even so much for the regular exaggeration & positive lying of all Yankee reports, official included, there cannot be doubted the main facts, as follows: That Grant defeated Pemberton (as before stated,) in the successive engagements at Baker's creek or Edward's Station, & Big Black river—drove him, with heavy loss, into Vicksburg—has since captured, or occupied after their evacuation, most of the exterior batteries—& that his right wing has reached the Mississippi above Vicksburg, & is there in communication with Porter's fleet, & supplied by it with provisions: Further— that a heavy mortar battery, of six mortars, established by Porter at Haynes' Bluff, was firing continually on Vicksburg & its remaining defences—while his gunboats had ascended the then opened Yazoo, to destroy everything on that river. The gunboats also were joined in the attack, & were shelling Vicksburg from the Mississippi. . . . A very ugly suspicion is raised even as to our own published official dispatches, that our government [2680] has stooped to deceive the public by concealment. Gen. Johnston, if able to receive reports from Vicksburg as late as 27th, must have known of our loss of Haynes' Bluff, & the command of the Yazoo, which occurred on the 18th. And these important losses must have been communicated to our government. Yet not a word of them has been published—& we only know the facts from northern reports, recieved [*sic*] by the circuiotous [*sic*] way of New York. I have never before, at any juncture felt so despondent, as now in regard to

Vicksburg. May God grant that my fears may be misplaced! . . . The Yankees posted at West Point, Va., are plundering & ravaging the neighboring country—& no military repression yet attempted. It is thought by some that the next invasion to attack Richmond, & perhaps speedily, will be made from this point. Further & extensive plundering operations & other outrages have been lately committed in Gloucester. A Yankee steamer on York river was fired upon by some of the artillery belonging to Wise's command, from the New Kent shore. In consequence, some gunboats landed a force, & burnt the houses & c. of three neighboring proprietors. This is the manner in which the Yankees, on system, practice what they call "retaliation" for our operations of legitimate warfare, & in defence of our invaded homes, on residents who had no participation in, and usually were [2681] entirely ignorant [of those operations] . . . . [34] I will append three Yankee documents (with a Kentucky commentary thereon,) [35] which will exhibit clearly the Yankee system of freedom & hired & voluntary labor, offered to & to be enjoyed by the slaves in Louisiana, where the domination of the invaders has been extended & established. 500 large sugar estates being vacant of resident owners, (they having been despoiled of all, & compelled to flee from the conquerors & robbers,) are offered for rent to Yankee or loyal capitalists, on terms stated, & of which I will here only repeat the main items, in reference to the employment, hires &c. of the "freed" negroes, & their "voluntary labor." The negroes are *compelled* by military orders & the alternative of severe punishment (to be inflicted by arbitrary power & functionaries acting at their discretion,) to return to & remain on the plantations on which they had worked before as slaves. They are to labor under the direction & control of the Yankee occupants, or tenants, [2683] (& strictly & severely even according to the published rules & requisitions,)—each negro to remain in his or her cabin from "the last tap of the bell" at night, to the first next morning—& at no other time go more than a mile from home without a pass. Lost time & lazy work to be compensated by deduc-

---

[34] Water damage at this point in the diary renders much of this page illegible. From what can be deciphered, it is apparent that Ruffin is once again advocating Confederate reprisals for these alleged outrages perpetrated against southern civilians.

[35] An attached clipping indicates that the following account was printed in the Louisville *Democrat*.

tions from the wages. The wages are fixed at $1 for the month, for women & boys, $2 for men, & $3 for mechanics, or $12, $24, & $36 a year, for these respective classes, for full work! with the usual food & clothing. And by an estimate of expenses, these & all expenses ("hire & supplies") of a laborer (I suppose a *man*) for a year, to the employer, is stated at $125. Of course these maximum amounts would be paid only for the full labor (as estimated by & satisfactory to a Yankee employer & task-master) for every working day of a year. Every deficiency (for even 10 minutes delay after the morning "tap of the bell,") every day's sickness, & every other deficiency of full labor, would be deducted from the hire. Every necessary outlay for the laborer, or for his family unable to labor from infirmity or tender age, would have to be paid for by himself. (What is to become of the helpless who have no father, husband, or son, able & willing to support them, is not intimated.) It is obvious to every man who knows anything of negro character & negro labor, that under such regulations, & more especially under the exactions of Yankee masters . . . *no surplus* of clear wages would come to even the most obedient & industrious negro laborer—and that all of them, the most obedient or the most lazy, the able-bodied, & the infirm or the sick, would be reduced to a condition of grinding & murderous slavery, compared to which their former & all ordinary personal negro slavery was freedom, with ease & comfort. Then as to the *voluntary* feature, which is essential to true freedom, & loudly demanded by Yankee philanthropists. The negroes (that is, all able to labor—perhaps those unable may starve anywhere—) are forced to remain on specified plantations [2684] never to leave them, even on Sundays, a mile, without a pass from the employer—nor their cabins through the night at any time—under penalty of being worked on the fortifications, or other military public works *without pay*. Besides these, & all other means for coercion & punishment, a negro who would (or could) refuse to hire himself to the particular Yankee occupant of the plantation, could not seek any other employer, nor obtain a mouthful of bread from any other source. Necessarily, therefore, he must submit to serve for even $2 a month, even though he may find the payment of that pittance reduced in fact to nothing, & himself made a debtor for more. Every slaveowner would be greatly profited in immediate income, if he could have exchanged his slaves for "free" hirelings on these terms, & even by the preliminary measure of emancipating all his slaves

[671]

gratuitously. We all know that the whole wages promised by this Yankee scheme, to the "freed"negroes, would not pay for one half the expense of the average & usual indulgences (beyond the allowances of food & clothing,) medical attendance, nursing of the sick &c. to say nothing of the great & main charge of supporting the infants, aged, & infirm—which makes no part of this Yankee system of free & hired labor. The slaves in Louisiana (as in Va. & elsewhere) have gladly accepted the Yankee offered boon of freedom, deeming that it meant the privilege of doing no work, & still getting full support. After being made free upon this latest Yankee plan, there will be more danger of these negroes, so freed, rebelling against their Yankee emancipators, than of those who still remain in their former condition of slavery to individual native masters, being induced to seek their emancipation by insurrection. I infer that one of the alternative punishments of the new freedmen for failing to thus hire themselves for "voluntary" wages, will be to impress them into military service—and that thus to aid the enlistment of negro troops was one of the objects of the Yankee government. But this alternative, however palatable to the laziness & the vanity of [2685] negroes, at first, hereafter will be more dreaded than hard labor. So much reluctance has already been shown by the negroes to enrol themselves in the Yankee military service, that forcible draft or general impressment has been adopted in place of voluntary enlistment. Gen. Banks, by published proclamation, is endeavoring to raise a negro army in La. under his designation of the "Corps d'Afrique." So far as may be from the many thousands of abducted & absconding slaves. I hope that Banks will be able to stock & cultivate the abandoned (or wasted) plantations with "free" hireling laborers, & also to enlist & embody the 18,000 negro soldiers. The first will be nearly all in the swamps, as runaways & banditti, before crop time is over—& the first encounter on the battlefield will send the negro soldiers as fugitives after the laborers, to conceal themselves in the swamps.—The report stated last week of gun-boats having gone up the Chickahominy has not been confirmed, & therefore must have been false, & without the asserted authority of the Signal Corps.

May 31. Sunday. This & the last preceding day have been especially dull & wearisome. I have had no employment or amusement, except to read, & that mostly by dipping into & skipping, or merely glancing over articles in old Reviews—which were used in the same manner as late as last autumn. . . . The only other occupation of my mind, since reading the papers of the mail of 29th, was the anxious desire to hear later accounts from Vicksburg, & to await the coming of the next news, with impatience, yet with dread & gloomy anticipations. Throwing aside the remaining Reviews, before night I resorted to Waverley, [2686] though this had been last read still later than the Reviews. . . .

June 1. Monday. The carriage was . . . sent to Disputanta for the Marlbourne family, & returned at 1 P.M. with Jane, her child, Nanny, & Mary.—The mail. The papers full of war events near & at Vicksburg, & especially northern reports. But nothing of later date (certainly,) than the last previous advices from Gen. Johnston, which were of the 27th. But silence is good news for us. Three more days have passed, & Vicksburg is still defended, & seems in less danger than before. The last received telegraphic dispatch is from Jackson, via Mobile, & dated 29th ult. But when its contents left Vicksburg, or our army, does not appear. That reports that Grant's army had fallen back from its farthest advance, & was fortifying its position by intrenchments & rifle pits. . . . The Yankee reports continue to predict the capture of the city & all that it contains, with all Pemberton's army, as certain & imminent. . . . Important movements are intimated of both Hooker's & Lee's armies, but nothing definite known. Hooker's movements however, so far, have not indicated another advance across the Rappahannock, towards Richmond. . . .

June 2. Tuesday. Finished Waverley. Returned to the dull & wearisome reading of the old Reviews. Most of my time of late, indeed nearly all except a few hours succeeding the arrival of each mail, has been wretchedly tedious & heavy. In addition, for some days past, & especially the two last, I have been indisposed & troubled with [2688] disordered bowels. The recurrences of this disorder have been less frequent than in the early part of 1862, when I was sojourning in Richmond, (when the habit seemed fixed,) but still are enough to indicate a marked change of my constitution. I had before (when at the worst) believed, & now again suspect, that this change is the indication of the breaking down of my constitution, & bodily powers, & the precursor of death not far off. Not on account of my frequent disease, (which indeed has not been known fully except to myself,) but because of my age & weakness, my children at whose houses I have latterly remained,

& especially their wives, have urged me to abandon my general habit of abstinence from all intoxicating liquors, & to drink a glass of toddy every day. . . . These members of my family have been impressed with the propriety of my using spirit moderately by the opinion & practice of Judge Ruffin, who maintains that it is necessary for aged persons. I do not believe it. And if true, it would apply to females as much as to males—an application which would be repelled in disgust by persons of both sexes, of well ordered minds. . . . I have not been under any pledge or rule to abstain from intoxicating liquors. But I have entirely avoided the habit, & have very rarely permitted to myself rare & transient departures from my usual entire abstinence, for the last 16 or 18 years, upon considerations of expediency & bodily comfort. Entire abstinence, from any greatly relished indulgence, is to me not very difficult—& far less difficult than moderate & limited indulgence. . . . In my earlier time of manhood, falling in [2689] with the then bad & universal usage of our country, I began, without love for it, the daily use of spirit. The long continued use induced the love for spirit, & the daily consumption (though always small in measure,) of more than my feeble constitution & health could bear regularly without detriment—to say nothing of the tendency to other conditions far more worth consideration than bodily health. It was easier for me to resort to entire abstinence, (which indeed I never found difficult beyond the first few days—) than to the limited & harmless use. With such views, & reasons, I have at three different times abandoned all intoxicating drinks, & for each time abstained for years together. I had other reasons for banishing such liquors from my table & as a common beverage for guests. . . . Thus I avoided what I think is the greatest danger of the habitual exhibition & even most moderate use of liquors in a family, the indirectly inviting the young & the previously abstinent, to begin the use & extend it in future time to the abuse. . . . I thought it better, & a good . . . which I was willing to purchase by some restriction on my personal pleasure, to remove all such temptation from my young children & grandchildren, by permitting no habit of drinking, nor habitual exhibition [2690] of intoxicating drinks. Never seeing it at home, & being duly instructed as to the danger, they never wanted or thought of the use. Well! in despite of all these considerations, I have this day given my consent to drink a glass of toddy every day—& have directed the buying for my use a gallon of whiskey which will now cost $32, & which is of no better quality than could have been bought for 50 cents, at most, previous to the war. I foresee the difficulties in my way, even if my prudence & firmness of will shall prevent all dangers of excess. The drink will be very palatable, & for some time, the single glass will be as much as my appetite may require. But after a time, I shall be inclined to extend the quantity. If extended, perhaps two glasses in a day might not do my health or manners any harm—& would again suffice for appetite. But again the appetite would grow—& would more strongly demand a third drink than previously the second, & still more strongly than the desire for the first—which, indeed, was nothing, when no indulgence had been renewed.

June 3. Wednesday.... The mail. Telegraphic dispatches (private) from Jackson to June 1st. The little they contain in relation to Vicksburg ... is of good purport.... Though I distrust the particulars, I fully confide in the great main fact ... that up to June 1st. Vicksburg was still ours. Even if there had been a total absence of late reports, in the existing condition of things, no news is, for us, equivalent to good news. Every day that the relative positions of the opposed forces continue unchanged, will increase the chances for our successful resistance, & the defeat of the enemy. And my hopes for these results, merely, have again risen nearly to my former confidence, & on the ground that the besiegers have gained nothing in the last 6 days. But as we had previously lost the command of the Yazoo river, & Grant's army had reached the Mississippi both above & below Vicksburg, was in communication with the Yankee fleet, & obtaining supplies from the vessels, there is no longer ground for my previous expectation that our forces would cut off Grant's supplies, & thereby force his whole army to surrender.... Gen. Banks has invested Port Hudson.... Reports continue to come to us of Hooker's giving indications of movement, but nothing definite as to the direction. Northern accounts show that the Yankees are also expecting an aggressive movement of Lee, & there is great fear of his moving to attack Washington. Perhaps Hooker's movement is to ward off that expected from Lee. It would confirm this view, if it is true, as reported, that Hooker is fortifying, on the south side, two of the principal fords across the upper Rappahannock, to prevent the crossing of our army.... In the late Yankee raid in Matthews & part of Gloucester [counties, Va.], in addition to the usual plundering & devastation being carried to extremes, as the marauders there had full time, & no fear of resistance . . . they destroyed the agricultural implements generally, so as to put it out of the power of the proprietors to cultivate & save their growing crops, even when not otherwise prevented by the stealing of their slaves & working teams. I fear that this most diabolical & effective policy will be repeated, & especially just before or during wheat harvest, & to greater extent & in various places. Yet no defence or safeguard seems thought of by the government for all the exposed country near to tide-water, which, like all the unconquered & loyal parts of Va, has abroad in the army every man from 18 to 40 years of age, who is not exempt from military duty because of physical infirmity. A general loss of the crops through eastern Va. this year, as occurred last year in the parts occupied by the invading forces, would starve or banish the proprietors, & render it impossible to longer hold the country from the enemy. . . . Of the various reports from Vicksburg, which I have stated in short, the latest have always been from Confederate sources—& the most important of the facts, & especially in regard to our losses, have been afterwards confirmed & amplified by the northern papers. For minute particulars we are indebted almost [2693] exclusively to northern writers & papers. And these, while claiming, & no doubt greatly exaggerating, almost continued successes of their forces, in gaining battles, capturing artillery & fortified positions, &c., also admit some heavy repulses, & great slaughter of their troops in their various attempted assaults. These confessions, so unusual from Yankees, more than the general assertions of the unknown & unreliable reporters on our side, are enough to prove that Grant's army has already suffered severely. . . . If Johnston can cut off the lately established communications between the Yankee army & the Mississippi & the fleet, we may well hope, not only to finally & effectually repel the invaders, but with a measure of loss far exceeding that following any of their previous defeats. For it has been our remarkable misfortune throughout this war, that while we have defeated the enemy's forces in numerous great battles, & have rarely been defeated in open field or pitched battle, all our victories have been barren of benefit or gain, except in obstructing & postponing the enemy's then aggressive movement. In no case have we been enabled by even a great & undisputed victory to roll back the wave of previous territorial conquest & occupancy permanently—& but twice for a short time, & limited space, soon to be again yielded to the increased & returning hosts of the invading enemy. This misfortune of gaining nothing, or but negative benefits from great & even repeated victories, has in great measure been owing to the inferiority of our numbers. After every victory gained, & with the great losses inflicted, the enemy, after the defeat & the loss, was still more numerous, & better provided than the victors, [2694] & physically able to renew or to meet the renewal of the contest, with good hope of success, if the troops had been as brave & determined, & had been as well commanded, as ours. Still this reason cannot have been always operative, or sufficient for every such result. There must be a great & general defect of our commanders in this respect, that after fighting well, & beating the foe, they do not understand how to make proper use of the victory, & the advantages it offered.—There has been another remarkable feature of this war, & in regard to both the opposed forces, which is quite different from what I anticipated, & from all the previous military experience of the world. I had expected our raw troops to be subject to timidity in battle, to panic, &, until disciplined & somewhat used to be under fire, to be far from exhibiting courage in general, or being otherwise than very poor & unreliable soldiers in battle. But the case has been very different, & almost without exception, as to our raw troops—&, I must admit, generally also as to the Yankee soldiers, though as to them, with some large & notable exceptions. Our men, with few exceptions, went into service & into severe fighting usually soon after, without any previous acquaintance with war, or military discipline. Yet, so far as I have heard, in open field & expected battle, or in any pitched & great battle, there has not occurred a case of want of courage, & its effective exercise, being shown by any of our armies, or by any part thereof, division, brigade, or even by so many as a regiment. I speak of those arrayed in battle. For certainly, there were many individual exceptions in cowardly skulkers & stragglers from every army about to engage, or after engaging in battle. I myself saw hundreds of such skulkers from the field of Manassas, & later, many more from that of Seven Pines—& they were thousands in number whose aid to their braver comrades was withheld at later & more bloody & well contested battles, as those of Shiloh & Antietam. But however shameful & numerous were these individual acts of cowardice, & however injurious to the army & the cause, on such occasions, they did not prevent the conflict being maintained with courage [2695] never before equaled, throughout by raw troops, & which would have been honorable to well-disciplined veterans. Now it is no contradiction to this statement, that there have been shameful surprises of sundry small commands, & consequent panic flights of our surprised soldiers. Such disasters have almost always been caused by the negligence or incapacity of the commanding officer. . . . Such I consider was the failure of Gen. Lovell to defend New Orleans, & its surrender necessarily following his retreat. In all such cases, the fault, or deficiency, whether of courage or of conduct, was not in the surprised & therefore panic-stricken company or out-post—or of the army ordered to retreat or surrender—but in the respective commanders.

Index

∽

Adams, Nehemiah, 21 and *n*

Alabama, C.S.S.: exploits of, 469; effect of, 508, 514; duel with U.S.S. *Hatteras*, 555–56; puts in at Kingston, 577; disrupts shipment of gold from California, 618

Aldrich, Alfred P., 10

Alexandria, Va.: Federals occupy, 33, 36; Federals retreat to, 98

Allen, John J., 536 and *n*

American Revolution: compared with Civil War, 45, 515

Anderson, Joseph R., 12, 16, 31, 222

Androus, George P., 550

Anticipations of the Future: Boulware praises, 12; predictions in, 122, 557; sales of, 232

Antietam, battle of, 448, 449

Ariel, steamer, 618

Arkansas, C.S.S., 379, 389, 410

Arkansas Post, 549, 550 and *n*

Arms (Confederate): deficiencies of, 63, 283, 410; furnished by Va., 190; shortage of, 233, 237; at Naval Ordnance Laboratory, 273; effectiveness of Brooke rifled cannon, 622 and *n*

Arms (Union): superior quality of, 204

Ashe, William S., 130

Atkinson, John, 94

Atlanta, Ga.: price of salt in, 485

Austria: and Polish revolution, 599

Averell, William W. (U.S. general), 605*n*

Aylett, Patrick H., 640

Bachman, John, 499

Bachman, William K., 130

Badges: as means of identification in C.S. army, 75, 328

Baillie, Joanna, 151 and *n*, 231, 235

Baker, Edward D., 152*n*

Baldwin, John B., 47

Baldwin, Joseph G., 153, 649, 650, 651

Ball's Bluff, Va., battle of, 152 and *n*, 153 and *n*

Baltimore, Md.: secessionists disarmed in, 24; occupied by Federals, 28; refugees from, in Richmond, 28, 29, 31, 32; political arrests in, 133–34

Baltimore and Ohio Railroad: Jackson destroys portion of, 478; northern sympathies of employees, 480; repaired by Federals, 538

Bancroft, George, 646

Banks, Nathaniel P. (U.S. general): opposes J.E. Johnston near Harpers Ferry, 113; in Valley campaign, 253, 257, 262 and *n*, 287, 307, 313, 316*n*, 323, 333, 334; receives contrabands, 346; at Cedar Mountain, 411*n*; relieves Butler in New Orleans, 520 and *n*; disaffection in army of, 574; and Port Hudson campaign, 596, 645, 675; prescribes rules for Negro hirelings, 601; enlists Negro troops, 672

Barbour, James, 217

Barksdale, William (C.S. general), 84*n*, 512, 641

Barnwell, Robert W., 229 and *n*

Barnwell, Robert W., Jr., 64 and *n*

Barron, Samuel, 128

Barth, Heinrich, 239 and *n*, 499

Baynard, Ephraim, 165 and *n*

Beauregard, Pierre G. T.: commends ER for Sumter role, 27; arrives in Richmond, 40; in Manassas campaign, 55, 58, 67, 70, 71, 74 and *n*, 77–78, 80 and *n*, 81*n*, 91*n*, 98, 100, 124; army of, after First Manassas, 112–13, 120, 140–41; transferred to West, 224, 233; ER expresses confidence in, 257; in Shiloh campaign, 261, 276, 279–80; appeals for plantation bells, 276; retreats from Corinth, 299, 333, 350; and S.C. command, 484, 564, 578, 620

Index

Beckwith, Julian R. (grandson of ER), 330, 331

Beckwith, Thomas S. (son-in-law of ER), 330

Beebe, Gilbert J., 201

Beecher, Henry Ward, 211, 468

Beechwood plantation: ER supervises farm work on, 43, 47–48, 51, 282, 349; wartime difficulties on, 48; impressment of slaves from, 134, 140, 285, 287; ER seeks overseer for, 279, 282; thievery on, 284; impressment of livestock from, 299; defensive measures on, 301; Federal gunboats sighted from, 302; preparations to evacuate, 304, 351–52; slaves flee, 323, 337–38, 345–46; theft of sheep from, 345; sale of slaves from, 351; evacuation of, 353; ER takes leave of, 358; Confederate artillery posted at, 391–93, 395; Federal occupation of, 402–407 passim; Federal depredations on, 416–22, 425, 426, 429–30; Union soldiers describe beauty of, 417n, 576n; pillaged by civilians, 511, 591; caretaker appointed for, 658

Beegleston, Mr. (Evelynton overseer), 350, 351, 356, 365, 366, 427

Belmont, August, 286

Belmont, Mo., battle of, 163

Belsches, Benjamin W. (C.S. major), 369 and n

Benjamin, Judah P., 259, 438

Bentinck, G. W., 504 and n

Berkley plantation: McClellan encamps at, 360, 361; ER views McClellan's camp on, 363–72 passim, 388, 393–94; McClellan evacuates, 413, 414, 415; Federal depredations on, 571

Bermuda, English blockade-runner, 149, 154

Berret, James G., 132 and n

Bethune, Thomas Greene (Blind Tom), 226 and n, 227–29

Big Bethel, Va., battle of, 43–47 passim, 127n, 169

Bland, J. B., 375

Bledsoe, Albert T., 144

Blind Tom. *See* Bethune, Thomas Greene

Blockade: proclaimed by North, 7; effec-

tiveness of, 17, 210, 233, 237; European attitude toward, 40, 137; C.S. Congress seeks to counter, 122; relation of *Trent* affair to, 172, 205; use of "stone fleet" in, 191–92, 200, 210; impact on Northwest of, 216–17; threatens Confederate cause, 276, 462, 590; declared raised at Charleston, 564

Blockade runners: from Savannah, 149, 154, 159; profits of, 154; from Charleston, 158, 216; from New Orleans, 237; from New Smyrna, Fla., 259–60

Bocock, Thomas S., 240, 427

Boileau, A. D. (editor of Philadelphia *Evening Journal*), 567

Bonham, Milledge L. (C.S. general): arrives in Richmond, 9; addresses crowd, 10; supports F. J. Thomas' request for arms, 12; slovenly dress of, 60; in Manassas campaign, 64, 66, 69, 70, 71, 80, 81n; occupies Centreville, 97; mentioned, 156, 333

Boteler, Alexander R., 178 and n, 179, 306–307, 308

Botts, John Minor, 8, 246

Boulware, William: name misspelled in Vol. I, 11n; biographical sketch of, 12n; lauds *Anticipations of the Future*, 12; reports on Norfolk defenses, 31; on *Trent* affair, 168; contributes to Keelan fund, 169; criticizes conduct of war, 313, 320; describes Seven Pines battlefield, 327; visits Marlbourne, 607, 608; mentioned, 11, 52, 96, 113, 152, 174, 193, 237, 321, 322, 331, 565, 566, 597

Bounties, 387, 435

Boutwell, George S., 412

Bowen, John S. (C.S. general), 657

Boyce, William W., 59, 230

Boykin, Alexander H., 52

Bragg, Braxton: evaluated by ER, 257, 429, 470; and Kentucky campaign, 438, 454, 457, 464, 470, 471; criticism of, 478; superseded by J. E. Johnston, 498; in battle of Murfreesborough, 527 and n, 530, 532 and n 534, 535; mentioned, 596, 641

Branch, Lawrence O. (C.S. general), 222, 322, 323

Index

als, 308, 656–57, 662; R. E. Lee's family takes refuge at, 315 and *n*, 318, 319; slaves assume control of, 317–18, 320; reportedly searched by Federals, 334; Federal depredations on, 337, 351, 368, 472; owners resume control of, 367–68; runaways decline amnesty offer, 371; owners seek to sell, 427, 476, 478; sale of runaways from, 466, 500; Julian purchases Charles' share in, 468; change in master-slave relations on, 471; misconduct by slaves on, 476, 554; provisions allowance for slaves on, 478; runaways return to, 500, 507, 514; valuation of, 552; ER criticizes W. Sayre's management of, 552–55; ER supervises farm work on, 595, 604, 607, 621, 628; raided by Stoneman's cavalry, 634–35; family flees, 642–43, 644

Marshall, C. K., 244 and *n*

Marshall, Humphrey, 152 and *n*, 156, 158, 206

Maryland: prospects for secession of, 7, 14–15, 16–17, 24, 137; legislature considers bill to establish Committee of Public Safety, 21, 24; occupied by Federals, 26–27, 28; ER urges invasion of, 98, 101, 105, 112, 141; political arrests in, 118, 133–37 *passim*; Confederates invade, 441, 442

Mason, James M.: on secession prospects in Md., 15, 16–17; departs Charleston, 154, 159; and *Trent* affair, 167–68, 172, 192, 193, 195, 201, 204, 206; departs for England, 210; G. B. Cheever demands execution of, 211; slighted by Earl Russell, 627; mentioned, 178

Maury, Matthew F.: appointed counselor to Va. governor, 8–9; on Union military strategy, 178; proposes construction of gunboats, 186; appointed to diplomatic mission, 475; analyzes English views on Civil War, 608–609; mentioned, 148, 161, 162, 182

May, Henry, 133 and *n*

Maycox plantation: flight of slaves from, 370; Confederate artillery posted at, 392, 395, 396; mansion burned by

Federals, 399–400; Federals land at, 401, 402, 405; Federals separate slave families on, 430–31, 493; confused with Ruffin properties, 572

Meade, John (brother-in-law of Julian), 263, 409, 523

Mechanicsville, Va.: ER views battlefield of, 472–73

Memminger, Christopher G., 142, 144, 154*n*, 173

Memphis, Tenn.: falls to Federals, 344; C.S.S. *Arkansas* escapes from, 379; Sherman orders retaliation against civilians in, 528

Mercedita, U.S.S., 564 and *n*, 574

Mercier, Henri, 583

Merrimac: scuttled at Norfolk, 6; reported ready for service, 234, 239; F. Buchanan reports on condition of, 240. *See also Virginia*, C.S.S.

Merrimac No. 2. *See Richmond*, C.S.S.

Mexico, 182, 349, 583

Meynardie, E. J., 57

Mikell, J. Jenkins, 176

Miles, William Porcher, 174 and *n*

Militia: called out in Va., 65, 253, 254, 262, 414; ER criticizes training of, 268; ER criticizes mass call-up of, 271, 295, 296; Davis recommends organization of, 425

Mill Springs, Ky. *See* Logan's Cross Roads, Ky., battle of

Milroy, Robert H. (U.S. general), 334, 528

Minnesota, U.S.S., 155*n*, 249–50, 252, 256

Minor, Franklin, 178, 182, 186

Mississippi, U.S.S., 603, 610

Mississippi River: fall of New Orleans and control of, 289; naval action on, 379, 389; Union gunboats on, 568, 669; Federals cut levees on, 581, 584, 615, 649

Missouri: prospects for secession of, 16; political conditions in, 106–107, 111; Fremont's policies in, 125, 131; admitted into Confederacy, 186; Federal depredations in, 189; Confederates reinforced in, 234; Confederate guerrillas active in, 413

Index

glish, 183, 286; advocate breaking levees on lower Mississippi, 211; on Union military strategy, 213; on European intervention, 229–30, 234–35, 534; seek to thwart European intervention, 246; on Shiloh, 283; on Seven Pines, 335, 336; censorship of, 341; on McClellan, 347, 473; on Seven Days' Battles, 374; on Second Manassas, 443 and n; praise valor of Confederate troops, 451 and n; reaction to Emancipation Proclamation in, 459, 464; denounce Buell, 478; boast of successes, 498, 610; sanguine of victory in West, 513; on Fredericksburg, 518; on anti-Lincoln sentiment in North, 556, 577; threaten offensive movements, 660, 668; on Vicksburg campaign, 676

Newspapers (Confederate): inaccurate reporting in, 33, 43, 157; complain of inaction after First Manassas, 112; censorship of, 280, 450, 451, 669

Newton, Willoughby: nominated for Va. legislature, 22; ER discusses legislative topics with, 179; on disaffection of nonslaveholders in Va., 187–88; eulogizes Tyler, 217; ER complains about militia call-up to, 295; fears capture by enemy, 299, 314; flees Federal scouting parties, 308, 499; estimates numbers in opposing armies, 312–13; defends Davis Administration, 313, 314, 320; reports anti-Davis plot, 331; ER expresses esteem for, 493; visits Marlbourne, 504, 505; and Va. secession conspiracy, 568, 570; loses property to Federals, 593; mentioned, 178, 182, 186, 226, 229, 306, 307, 315, 321, 322, 326, 327, 338, 351, 445, 565, 592, 639

New York: peace movement in, 446, 494–96, 539, 551, 577; 1862 elections in, 478, 485–86; opposition to draft in, 496

New York City: suppression of newspapers in, 117; effect of Trent affair on, 195; banks suspend specie payments in, 212; race riot in, 467; Federal troops dispatched to, 478; Wool orders search for arms in, 594; peace meetings in, 664, 667

New York Evening Post, 503

New York Herald: sanguine of northern victory, 33 and n; promises vindictive war, 36 and n; predicts movement on Richmond, 39; exaggerated reports in, 124, 286, 443, 449, 451; predicts capture of cotton, 245–46; threatens vengeance against England and France, 451; urges McClellan to advance, 474; on 1862 elections, 486; anti-administration posture of, 521; on peace movement in North, 577; predicts attack on Charleston, 610; on damages inflicted by Confederate cruisers, 618

New York Journal of Commerce, 117

New York Mercury, 526

New York Times, 443n, 663–64

New York Tribune: urges confiscation of southern land, 13; recounts excesses of Federal troops in Washington, 24n; predicts movement on Richmond, 39; on conditions at Fort Hatteras, 174; denounces McClellan, 284; threatens to hang ER, 297; admits reverse at Seven Pines, 336; letter of Solon Robinson in, 376; predicts European intervention, 472; on Burnside's intentions, 557

New York World, 521, 614

Nolte, Vincent, 213 and n

Norfolk, Va.: destruction at Navy Yard, 6; defensive capability of, 31; civilians flee, 234; martial law proclaimed in, 246; ER visits Navy Yard in, 263–64, 273–74; ER inspects fortifications at, 269, 270; Federals threaten, 294, 296, 298; evacuated by Confederates, 300, 301; Wool's coercive policies in, 332, 336–37; riot in, 336, 340–41, 374; Federals reduce garrison at, 339, 376; suppression of newspapers in, 341; life of contrabands in, 598

North Carolina: secession movement in, 5, 8n, 32; ER's agricultural writings on, 14, 174, 190; rail travel in, 116, 126, 129–30; disaffection in eastern counties of, 188

Northern attitudes: toward South, 12–13, 14, 18, 23, 30, 184; toward constitutional government, 50, 119, 414,

[693]

HEADQUARTERS

Ruffin   H-296330
Ruffin
Diary of Edmund Ruffin, v2

Ruffin   H-296330
Ruffin
Diary of Edmund Ruffin, v2

WEST GEORGIA REGIONAL LIBRARY SYSTEM
HEADQUARTERS

DEMCO .